CW00504885

The Indomitable
Marie-Antoinette

SIMONE BERTIÈRE

The Indomitable
Marie-Antoinette

Translated from the French
by MARY HUDSON

Éditions de Fallois

PARIS

French Title: *Marie-Antoinette l'insoumise*
© Éditions de Fallois, 2002

© Éditions de Fallois, English Translation 2014
22, rue La Boétie, 75008 Paris, France

ISBN 978-2-87706-846-8

CONTENTS

PART II. THE QUEEN

TRANSLATOR'S NOTE

The Indomitable Marie-Antoinette *is the last in a series of six biographies of the queens, regents and royal mistresses of the French monarchy since the 16th century by the esteemed French historian Simone Bertière. The author describes them as "a sort of family history" of the modern French monarchy. Having read all six of them, among other works by Madame Bertière, I wanted very much to translate them. I was and remain convinced that they are a priceless contribution not only to women's history, but to history plain and simple. Having read Stefan Zweig's* Marie-Antoinette *among other fine biographies of the ill-fated queen, I was overwhelmed with admiration for the author's ability to bring her and her world to life in a way that no other author had. Madame Bertière's prose is elegant and stylish, her research is of the highest quality, and her psychological insights into the historical figures she writes about are of astonishing depth and complexity. Remaining aloof from ideological arguments about the protagonists' actions, Madame Bertière succeeds in making us understand what it must have been like to be those people. For they were simply people – living in exceptional circumstances and positions of great power and privilege, but human beings all the same – with their flaws and virtues like everyone else. If the task of a translator is to reproduce in the new language the same effect upon the reader that the original work achieved, then I hope that the reader will find in these pages the immense pleasure I felt in reading this extraordinary story.*

I wish to heartily thank Madame Bertière for taking the time out from her writings and scholarly work to answer the questions I had about the manuscript, and for generally guiding me throughout. Any errors that might be lurking in the text nonetheless are entirely of my manufacture. My sincere thanks and admiration also go to Madame Bertière's publisher, Monsieur Bernard de Fallois, for venturing into the uncharted territory of publishing one of his books in the English language.

Finally, taking a page from Madame Bertière's book so to speak, I would like to dedicate this translation to the memory of my late husband, Jack Holland.

MARY HUDSON
1 August 2013

To André,
in memoriam

PROLOGUE

May I begin by revealing something about myself? I did not undertake writing a book about Marie-Antoinette without some apprehension. First of all because of the number of those who preceded me: yet another biography of that unfortunate woman! Yet another, after so many others – some of which of such excellent quality! What else is there to say about a story so often examined, dissected, repeated over and over again, a life about which everyone assumes all is known? Added to this handicap was my predilection for writing books about multiple characters, where many women, queens or favorites, square off against each other, or balance each other out and reveal each other, in what has become a sort of family history of the French monarchy. Alas, Marie-Antoinette took up the entire stage. Her sisters-in-law were uninteresting, her husband modest, taciturn and secretive, without even a hint of a mistress. In the absence of a rival who could challenge her preeminence after Louis XV's death and Madame du Barry's banishment, she overshadows her entourage and captures the limelight.

However, just because I had to aim the lens squarely on her, I could not pass up a gift history offered me: a romantic and tragic heroine. Her story brought to a dramatic close a series on the modern queens of France whose lives I had undertaken to recount. It is a fitting end to the series, answering better than any others did questions fundamental to my guiding principles: What fate awaited a young woman when she married the king of France? How did each of France's queens adapt to her condition? As the age of French monarchy was coming to a close, Marie-Antoinette provided a good example of how the model that had prevailed until then was decaying. Devoured by revolutionary turmoil, the accepted notion of a queen's function disappeared with her and the Ancien Régime, which the following century would not be able to resuscitate. As if to compensate me for my audacity and my persistence, my long acquaintance with her predecessors offered me some different perspectives and invited comparisons that, I hope, will shed new light on her personality and her fate.

★

Let's say it straight off: it cannot be denied that her marriage to Louis XVI was a disaster, a disaster for him and, to a lesser extent, for France. It was a disaster for her too. This disaster was not limited to their private life; it was just as much political as personal. The grafting of this child of the Hapsburgs of Vienna onto the stalk of the French Bourbons did not take. The failure was not an accident or a result of happenstance. It was inscribed from the beginning in her very situation, which her personality only aggravated. We sometimes contrast the happy years – when she did not know what lay in store for her – and the terrible years, those of her descent into hell. But there were no happy years; there were frivolous years, which is not the same. Yet her life had begun so well, fairly bursting with promise. How did the dream become a nightmare?

All the fairy godmothers seemed to have gathered at the cradle of the baby girl: they gave her an illustrious name, very close and loving parents, powerful kin, a family tree so thickly adorned that it lacked none of the great names of the European ruling elite. If they didn't give her a perfect face, they gave her the gift of grace, more beautiful still than beauty, and the knack for pleasing and winning hearts. They only forgot one thing: wisdom. But there would be time for the little girl to acquire that with age. Even though she was the last of a whole squad of archduchesses to marry off, they promised her the most ostentatious and prestigious prize of all: she would be Queen of France. No one saw the wicked fairy cast a twofold evil spell on her future marriage: she would be the pawn between her homeland and her country of adoption at a time when their alliance was tearing at the seams, and when the absolute monarchy, brought to its point of perfection by Louis XIV, was threatened with ruin.

At the age of fourteen she was married. Much too soon, merely in order to fulfill political imperatives. Not having the time to prepare her for it, her mother sent her off blindfolded into a universe whose laws were a mystery. At Versailles there was no one to take her in hand. Louis XV's wife Marie Leszczynska was dead, as was her daughter-in-law Marie-Josèphe of Saxony. All the women who ordinarily ensured the family's continuity from one reign to the next were gone. No one was there to welcome the newcomer, to protect her, to show her the way. Of the preceding generation, there remained only four aging maiden aunts (one of whom was a Carmelite nun) unbending in their distaste for Madame du Barry, the sparkling creature the king had chosen to show off at his side, in defiance of all decorum. The dauphin, the future Louis XVI, both of whose parents had died, was an unattractive adolescent, cripplingly shy. Marie-Antoinette was thrown into the first rank of the hierarchy, alone and defenseless in one of the most malicious courts in the world.

We know just about everything there is to know about the ten years from her arrival in Versailles in 1770 to her mother's death in 1780. As a counterpoint to her own letters, those from the faithful ambassador the empress sent along to chaperon her spare us nothing of the ins and outs of her daily life. And if we want more details, there is no lack of testimony from the French side outlining her days and hours. Even so, we get the impression that we don't know her. Right from the start, she inspired powerful, contradictory reactions. She drew attention to herself; whether for good or ill depends on one's point of view. She was talked about; she was either admired or detested. She managed to irritate even the most well disposed. She provoked and stoked conflict. She reacted like an element thrown into an unfamiliar chemical environment. From one observer to another, or even – like the ambassador Mercy-Argenteau – from the same observer from one moment to another, we get an image of her that breaks up and becomes incoherent, whose pieces do not fit back together again. By turns she appeared unassuming or arrogant, compassionate or merciless, candid or dissimulating; and her taste for pleasure was mixed with a tenacious, fundamental melancholy. She was never just one thing, as we are led to believe. She slips through our fingers, our words. She cannot be grasped.

It would remain so for her entire life, because the ambiguity was within her. This cannot be put down to any depth of character – she had none whatsoever – but to an extreme degree of volatility, as if, unable to stay put, she were endlessly trying to find herself, to define herself, to find her place in a world that was not her own. She gives the impression of being elsewhere, of being a stranger to her own life. To quote François Furet, "Her personality harbors something irreparably closed, a lack of attention to advice and realities that makes her behavior difficult to decipher." Her trajectory seems just as inexplicable. Once she became queen, the exquisite dauphine adored by the French seemed to delight in flouting them. Sucked into a suicidal spiral, deaf to all warnings, she became increasingly imprudent and wound up triggering a torrent of calumnies that would eventually be her undoing. The "air head" intoxicated with extravagance, would eventually gain some wisdom, but she would not succeed in repairing the damage. We cannot help seeing it all as an absurd waste. Then, suddenly, as she faced the ultimate ordeal, it was another woman who emerged who was firm, dignified, and intelligent – yes, just look at her trial! – to climb the scaffold as a heroine.

★

Of what use is it then to pile up more information, accumulate evidence, pore over contemporary records and archives in search of as yet undiscovered anecdotes or details that might have escaped the vigilant eyes of the ferreting researchers? It is better to try to get beyond the contradictions and to understand a bit more clearly the young woman's personality and what François Furet freely calls her "secret." Are there two distinct women in Marie-Antoinette, who when struck by calamity, went from weakness to strength and from culpable frivolity to real greatness? The only way to answer this question is to closely reread the basic texts.

And these texts offer us many surprises.

The first concerns Marie-Antoinette's marital life. We know that for the first seven years, her marriage remained infertile, with major political implications. Although at the time all of Europe talked about these secrets of the marital bed, historians of the 19th and early 20th centuries thought it proper to throw a sort of Noah's cloak over them, omitting in their writings any passages deemed too intimate. Stefan Zweig was the first to propose an explanation for them, based on the originals of the letters between the young woman and her mother, an explanation that gained great authority. The presumed impotence of Louis XVI and his longstanding dread of an operation to remedy a slight physical malformation, have since taken on the mantle of truth. They were supposed to explain Marie-Antoinette's nervous instability. But Zweig didn't compare these letters to those between the empress and her ambassador. And the censored passages slumbering in the Vienna Archives leave absolutely no room for doubt: despite the gossip, Louis XVI suffered no malformation and he finally consummated his marriage without ever undergoing surgery. This leads us to reconsider the entire history of the strained relations between the royal couple, and to question the image of the young dissatisfied wife hoping each evening that her husband would finally acquaint her with love.

Another surprise awaits those who, struck by Marie-Antoinette's frivolity and her extreme intellectual laziness, see her as an indolent, insipid, lifeless soul, devoid of all but the most mediocre desires and passions, aspiring to a queenly life like that of her predecessors. For the empress Maria Theresa tells us the exact opposite. Complaints about her daughter's intractability and her great feats of ingenuity in order to get her way return like a leitmotif in her correspondence. "She's very headstrong." "Once her mind's made up she never gives in." "She follows her own whims and knows how to dodge and weave to get her way." Echoing these reproaches, the ambassador denounced her "taste for independence, her abhorrence of being governed," her "extreme cleverness at using any ruse to deflect criticism." The young woman herself confirmed very proudly to a friend, "You know, when I get an idea into my head, I do not let go." This stubbornness showed two opposite but symmetrical sides. The relentlessness she deployed to get what she wanted was only equaled by the resistance she mustered to thwart what she didn't want. To this was added the pride in her lineage and her rank that bridled against all obstacles.

Much of her energy was invested in futile pursuits because she remained a child for a long time, reduced to a state of irresponsibility by people fearful of what she might do. Her intelligence stagnated while her resolve strengthened. She would learn, and mature, but very slowly. And what she devoted her energy to would change over time. But there was no metamorphosis: it was the same Marie-Antoinette who would address not a single word to Madame du Barry and who haughtily squashed the revolutionary tribunal's accusations. The immature adolescent became *in extremis* an adult woman, with the same personality traits, the same faults, the same vehemence, the same aversion to compromise, the same denial of reality. But her stubbornness became courage, and her taste for gratuitous provocation was transformed into heroic defiance.

A further point must not be left out: we cannot understand Marie-Antoinette without reference to her mother. To Maria Theresa she owed her headstrong character, her impatience, and her strength. She also learned from her the model of a matriarchy where the male-female relationship was turned upside down, where the queen held full authority over states that owed allegiance to her personally. In the eyes of the little girl who had no idea that power entailed responsibilities, only one thing counted: her mother obeyed no one; everyone obeyed her. Attempts to prepare her for a very different destiny would be to no avail. Her mother's stamp would mark her for life. Upon arriving in France she discovered the confining obligations expected of her. She must make haste to provide heirs for the dynasty, and play her part in the grand spectacle of the royal family's daily life offered for the benefit of her subjects. Her rejection of this minutely regulated and highly restrictive program was immediate, vehement and complete. She refused to be sacrificed to her role. Throughout her life she was put in an untenable position because she was forced to hide this refusal, but it inevitably broke through in her behavior. Throughout her life she felt like a prisoner, before actually becoming one during her last three years. Throughout her life she struggled to escape from this prison.

The title I have chosen, *The Indomitable*, will undoubtedly surprise some readers, because it diverges so sharply from our usual notion of her. I employ it in all of its meanings. It implies first of all a refusal to obey. But someone indomitable is not only in revolt; she or he is also a deserter. When Marie-Antoinette judged her obligations intolerable, she fled from them. After she acceded to the throne, as soon as she felt herself hemmed in, she escaped. She would be seen to reject her wifely and queenly duties, to leave her husband's bedside for the opera or a ball. She would then abandon the court in the great chateau in order to lead her own private life at the Trianon. Rather than give in, she evaded and dodged. Only when cornered would she confront an issue. Faced with the Revolution, her reaction was also a rejection, very quickly radicalized, all the more violent as the hostility toward her increased. Her desire to escape became an *idée fixe*. All her attempts to do so would only lead to harsher prisons. Indomitable, she would face the scaffold, finally finding deliverance in death.

*

A few words about how I conceived of this book and the difficulties encountered. It is rare to have such a plethora of documentation about an historical figure. But never has any documentation been so unreliable, because it lends itself so readily to affirming everything and its opposite. Certainly no one today still sees in Marie-Antoinette the she-devil dragged through the mud by the revolutionary pamphleteers, or the angelic martyr celebrated by royalist hagiographers. But on the line that goes from one of these extremes to the other her image never stops oscillating, and judgments of her, which range from harsh to indulgent, from sympathetic to censorious, say more about their authors than about their subject. For her fate, sealed by the French Revolution, was tied to the very fundaments of French national culture. It is a touchstone of the feelings and opinions of every one of us. I tried as much as possible to avoid cut-and-dry judgments, because as a general rule I believe it is not easy to distinguish between good and bad people. In her tragedy, which was the tragedy that all of France was going through, responsibility was widely shared, and those who were the most questionable characters were often motivated by the best intentions.

In addition to the queen, I've given a large place to her mother, her brother and especially her husband who is too often belittled as a weakling, and who deserves infinitely better. Of course I have portrayed her idyll with Fersen, highlighting his secret role of adviser to the royal couple, which is less well known. Politics, in which Marie-Antoinette awkwardly tried to play a part and of which she was most assuredly the victim, have carved out the lion's share of this book, especially in the last section when with the Revolution, her fate was played out alongside that of France. Five bloody years where history went at it, where events collided with each other at a fierce rate in a space of time hardly long enough to contain them all. I have tried to strike a balance and say enough for the readers to follow easily while avoiding overburdening them with information. I hope to be forgiven for the inevitable omissions.

Regarding the flood of anecdotes conveyed in the memoirs that flourished during the Restoration I had to be selective. Let's face it; they're all suspect. But if we discard them all we are left with nothing that can give back to the past its living substance. I chose to keep those anecdotes that had the ring of truth and that convey in a considered and balanced way the ideas and feelings that accord with the facts. My choices do not necessarily discredit those that I didn't use. They are so plentiful that it was impossible to include them all.

In order for my narrative not to dissolve into a dust storm of details and in the interest of continuity, I used the same technique as in my previous volumes of not following a strict chronology. Within distinct, succeeding periods of time, I grouped certain chapters around a particular theme. Taking slight detours when doing so in time and space, I sometimes went forward, sometimes back, and ushered the reader back and forth between Vienna and Versailles. I hope the latter will forgive me for imposing these light intellectual gymnastics.

Lastly, I would like to acknowledge my debt to all of those whose research and publications brought to light the documents that I in turn was able to use; to all those whose studies of these historical figures and their epoch nourished my own reflections and sharpened my curiosity; to all those who suggested to me different points of view or new avenues to explore. To Zweig, in particular, whom I only contradicted with reluctance, because his work was decisive. He set off the spark that gave life back to Marie-Antoinette. All of us since have found warmth at his fire.

Part I

The Dauphine

CHAPTER 1

THE NUPTIAL MARCH

Germany, April 1770. On country roads, muddied and rutted by persistent rains, proceeds a peculiar cortege made up of supply wagons piled high with the necessary staff and stuff of a fortnight's journey. At the heart of the cortege at a ponderous pace roll two enormous coaches, dripping with gold trimmings and crowned with bouquets of golden flowers. The interiors are plushily lined and upholstered in embroidered velvet. In one of them the four seasons are depicted against a scarlet background, in the other the four elements against a background of blue. These luxurious, oversized jewelry boxes were manufactured in Versailles expressly for this journey – in duplicate, just in case. In one is ensconced a young girl being sent off to her husband. Along the route people gather to greet her. She smiles, deploying all her grace. She loves being loved; she seems to be the center of the universe. And if a few tears mingle with her smiles, the good people cheering her will not distinguish them from the trails of raindrops streaking the windowpanes. Her head is spinning from the ceremonies, the speeches, the festivities; but she is soothed by the rocking of her carriage as she is shunted from one rest station to another, and numbed by the constant change of scenery and faces. So she sometimes forgets that she has just left her childhood home forever and that she will never again see her "dear mamma." She had been told so often how happy she should be, that she ends up believing it. Is she not going off to marry the heir to the greatest king in Europe? True, she herself is the daughter of the empress-queen Maria Theresa, who has reigned for thirty years over Austria, Bohemia, Hungary and the Low Countries as well as a few less notable domains. Is she happy? For the moment she is compliant, acquiescing to the wishes of the prince of Starhemberg, who is responsible for delivering her in good condition – excuse me – of "handing her over" in the proper parlance, to her future family, and her future country, France.

Marie-Antoinette is proceeding toward her destiny.

The wedding of the century

Strictly ruled by tradition, princely weddings through the ages did not differ greatly from each other. But some were more loaded with political messages than others. This one would unite the two most prestigious families in Europe and sanctify their very recent reconciliation after decades of fratricidal wars. Only Louis XIV's marriage to the infanta of Spain had excited this much interest. An Austrian archduchess on the French throne had not been seen since Élisabeth, the retiring and short-lived wife of Charles IX. Two fiancés with more illustrious ancestors than the newly betrothed couple could not be found. In their interlaced family trees were arrayed – if we deign to consider the distaff side – Saint Louis, Charles V, Louis XIII and Philip II, as well as most of the German emperors, not to mention lesser shoots from Lorraine, Savoy, Tuscany, Bavaria, Saxony, Poland and so on. They personified the finest flowering of Catholic Europe. By causing them to be born within a year of each other, he the elder, she the younger, providence seemed to have decreed them destined for each other. People were inclined to see in their marriage a match made in heaven.

The two courts, despite their chronic financial distress, very much wanted the event to be marked by unforgettable pomp – in Vienna especially, for reasons we'll come back to. And each one was prepared to make any sacrifice to show itself worthy of its glorious past, and to try to outdo its counterpart in splendor. They agreed without too much difficulty, in private, to the terms of the contract. Louis XV and Maria Theresa acted in good faith; neither tried to finesse the other. Marie-Antoinette would give up her family's successorial rights, and bring a dowry of 400,000 florins, half in coin, half in jewelry. The French countered with 100,000 écus, and guaranteed her if she were widowed an annual income of 20,000 écus. But they haggled hard over appearances. They would not budge on matters of precedence. Neither party should outshine the other in the many events where they would officiate together. Luckily there were guidelines to help resolve the thorny issues that would inevitably arise: feverishly consulted archives provided a good number of solutions. As for dealing with the unexpected, each side left it up to the savoir-faire of their diplomats.

It was out of the question for the bride to leave her native country without being joined in holy matrimony to her distant spouse. According to custom, two nuptials were in order, one by proxy in Vienna and the other at Versailles in the actual presence of the two spouses. This way of doing things, aside from putting a stop to any second thoughts on the groom's side, avoided favoring either side over the other. Each one would have its exact quota of ceremonies and could offer its people the required festivities.

The young girl would enter France in Strasburg, as had the previous princesses of German descent. The "handing over" would take place on neutral territory, in a structure specially outfitted for the occasion on an island in the Rhine. Nothing impressive here about the organizers' ingenuity; they willingly followed an example that had a long history. It was noted already in 1530 when Éléonore of Austria crossed the Bidassoa. At the time they merely used a pontoon anchored by chains in the middle of the river. By 1615 for "the exchange of the princesses" on Pheasant Island – Élisabeth of France was going off to marry Philip IV while Anne of Austria was going to join Louis XIII – the technique had improved. It attained perfection in 1660 with the marriage of Louis XIV. The Germans had merely to adopt the formula. Very recently it had been practiced with a slight variation* when Marie-Josèphe of Saxony married the dauphin, son of Louis XV.

Having abruptly and simultaneously changed her country and family, the young girl would see her Austrian entourage replaced by members of "the dauphine's household" in France. It would still be a few more days before she'd meet her husband. The king and his grandson would set forth to meet her – just a few miles, to honor her. But they mustn't overdo it, not so much as to abase themselves. There too, precedents made the law. Tradition set the rendez-vous at a forest crossroads – in Fontainebleau for those coming from the south, and in Compiègne for those from the east, which was the case here. Despite its pretense at charming spontaneity, the encounter was timed and codified down to the slightest word and deed. The new arrival would leave her coach for that of the king, who would bring her to a chateau for a night or two, enough time to introduce her to the most minute details of etiquette. For early on the day set for her arrival in Versailles, she would be immediately taken in hand by the women responsible for dressing, coiffing and bedecking her with

---

* It was January and the violence of the river was such that the ceremony could not be held. Outside Strasburg's walls, therefore, a house was found as close to the border as possible and was fixed up according to the model required by tradition.

jewels. She would then be whisked off to the chapel to be married again.

At this point there would be two weeks of uninterrupted receptions, banquets, performances, balls, illuminations and fireworks, all of which were breathlessly anticipated. Everyone would give their considered opinion as to whether the celebrations, if they did not surpass, at least lived up to all the previous ones immortalized by written records and engravings. These were so widely distributed that many have come down to us today.

Such was the program in store for the little archduchess. Six weeks would go by from the time the marquis de Durfort, France's ambassador, arrived in Vienna on April 15th bearing the marriage proposal and May 30th when the last Parisian fireworks were spent; six long weeks jam-packed with official duties. The people had to get enough gorging and pageantry to last a long time; it was not every day that the heir to the throne of France was married, and each little town promoted to the ranks of the chosen few that would host the future queen knew that it would never again enjoy such an event within its walls. Would the young girl have the staying power to survive this trial that could overwhelm a much hardier adult? Yes, she would, proving that behind her apparent fragility lay uncommon energy.

Goodbye to Germany

As soon as it was clear that the marriage would take place, the little fiancée was removed from the children's suite, which had become less jolly anyway as one by one her older siblings left it. The runway lights, now squarely on her, flattered her youthful pride. She gracefully received the homage of the noble Austrian and Hungarian guards, and learned by heart a few Latin words to answer the Academy's pompous discourses. From her balcony she admired the French ambassador and the beribboned cavalcade he led, prelude to the official presentation of the marriage proposal. She was not present at that ceremony, but was summoned at the end of it to receive the letter the marquis de Durfort delivered from her future bridegroom and a medallion containing his portrait, which was solemnly secured around her neck. She had already received five images of him; three engravings representing "the dauphin in the fields" that were supposed perhaps to show his interest in a flourishing agriculture, and two other portraits in royal dress, more likely to rouse the interest of a bride-to-be. This latest one was a piece of jewelry, mostly of symbolic value. That evening was devoted to a show of Francophilia. The court's theatre gave a presentation of Marivaux's *Mother Confidante* – was it a role Maria Theresa was ready to play towards her daughter? – and a pastorally themed ballet *The Shepherds of Tempé*, choreographed by the famous ballet master Noverre. On April 17th, Marie-Antoinette swore on the bible that she renounced her Austrian inheritance. The party given the same night by her brother the emperor at the Belvedere matched in brilliance the one given by Durfort at the Lichtenstein palace. The ambassador had to rush so that the archduchess could attend before becoming dauphine, as afterwards etiquette forbade him from receiving her under his roof.

The wedding took place at six o'clock in the evening of April 19th in the Augustinian church. The star attraction wore a long dress of silver cloth. The part of the dauphin was played by an adolescent of his same age, Archduke Ferdinand, the bride's brother. A quarrel over precedence deprived the cardinal-archbishop of officiating: the ambassador refused to cede place to him. The papal nuncio was therefore pressed into service, but as he wasn't a cardinal, he had to give way to France's representative. The sacrament was no less valid, as Versailles was immediately informed. To Maria Theresa's official letter to Louis XV she added another where the young girl told her "dearest grandfather" of her contentment and desire to please him – in phrases too well turned to be her own.

In a more private vein – two preventive measures being better than one – Maria Theresa entrusted to the young traveler one of those sentimental letters in which in her halting French she excelled:

> Good sir my brother, it is my daughter, but rather more Your Majesty's, who will have the good fortune of conveying this letter to you. In losing such a cherished child, my entire consolation is entrusting her to the best and most tender of fathers. If it please His Majesty, guide and command her; she is of the greatest good will, but I dare pray Him to prove indulgent toward any thoughtless blunders proper to her age. She greatly desires to merit His kindness by all of her actions. I commend her to Him once more as the most tender pledge of happiness between our States and Houses.

Clearly, the empress harbored a few doubts about her daughter's judgment. But reading her, one would never suspect that she was even less sure of Louis XV's aptness for guiding the young person on the right road. We'll see a bit later what she really thought of him.

Then it was time for the goodbyes. They were awash in torrents of tears, as was always the case in such circumstances. The journey from Vienna to Strasburg was a carefully orchestrated political maneuver. It resembled a triumphal march. Unlike her Bavarian and Saxon predecessors, Marie-Antoinette was a foreigner nowhere along the route because even outside of Austria, she was in German territory, where everyone – the grand Electors, the holders of the tiniest principalities, monasteries and free cities – was a vassal, at least in name, of the emperor. The journey was designed to honor one or another of them, and to display for all to see, friends and above all potential foes, the might of the Hapsburg family and the solidity of its ties with France.

In setting up the itinerary they had to take into account each one's ability to host the royal visitors, which was often greater in abbeys or isolated chateaux than in large towns. They needed to figure out where the 376 horses could be changed five times a day. And the young traveler must not be overtaxed; she could not be expected to undergo more than eight or nine hours on the road a day. Even in a royal coach equipped with good suspension and made draft-proof to protect her from the colds to which she was prone, it was enough to grind her down in less than a week. True, every night she had her own cozy bed with all its frills set up and dismantled at every stage. There were two of everything in her luggage so that the supplies office could send one set ahead in time for the next night. To give her some breathing room, two rest days were set aside with accommodating hosts, but when she was spared the bumpy roads, she had to deal with visiting the local sights and grace the tiresome performances held in her honor.

On departure day, the 21st of April, she was not overly homesick. Her eldest brother Joseph II accompanied her to Melk where the Benedictines of the famous abbey offered her the staterooms reserved for sovereigns. There was even "the emperor's chamber" which had often welcomed Maria Theresa and her spouse. Before being able to retire in peace, our travelers were treated to an opera performed by the good monks' students, which snatched a few yawns from the young girl. The next day they traveled along the Danube to Enns, where they left it to turn south. Near Linz when she saw the good old familiar river disappear, she was overcome with sorrow, and suddenly pleaded to be brought back to Vienna. It was out of the question of course to give in to such childish behavior! As planned, she was brought to spend the night in Lambach, then on to Altheim and Altötting. And so she arrived in Bavaria for a day's rest. In his summer residence of Nymphenburg, the prince elector lavished a warm reception on her – all the warmer as he had some delicate issues with the Viennese cabinet. How she would love to run around in the vast French-style garden with its "water steps" as smooth as mirrors. She couldn't, unfortunately; she was hauling behind her a host of courtiers in a hurry.

The rains didn't let up. She caught a cold in Bavaria, but she wasn't coughing too much and her mood remained good, her mother was assured in a letter from Starhemberg. On to Augsburg and Günsberg – another rest stop. The prince complained that she had ordered them to expedite to France the gifts given her by the towns she'd traveled through instead of redistributing them on the spot. On to Reutlingen and Stockach. They took a southern route around the Black Forest. A stop at Donaueschingen, at the home of the prince of Fürstenberg, margrave of Baden, brought back a hint of home. Here are the headwaters of the beloved river, a mere slender stream that eventually becomes the mighty Danube. The next day found her in Brisgau, which the Hapsburgs had owned since the 14th century. Once again, she was at home: Freiburg welcomed its sovereign. But she would soon be torn away. In order for her to arrive at her destination fresh and well disposed, the stages were shortened. In a few miles she was at Schüttern Abbey, where she would spend her last day on German soil, Sunday the 6th of May 1770. The count de Noailles had already arrived to greet her and work out with his Austrian counterpart the final details of the transfer of powers. The little archduchess had only to cross the Rhine for her universe to be transformed.

The official hand-over

On the Île des Épis, in the middle of the Rhine, carpenters had been busily putting up a wooden pavilion worthy of the performance about to take place. The term pavilion can be misleading. Spread out from east to west, the structure had a certain allure with its 19 windows and terraced roof enclosed by a balustrade. Both sides were rigorously symmetrical, as they would house both the French and Austrian cast members waiting in the wings. In the middle of the large reception room between them was an imaginary line representing the border. Straddling this central line was a table draped in rich red velvet. Along one wall a canopied armchair, two of its legs in Austria and two in France, awaited Marie-Antoinette. There wasn't enough time to decorate properly so the furniture left something to be desired, and the archbishop's attics had to be rifled to dress the walls with the requisite tapestries.

In Strasburg the preparations were the talk of the town, and crowds of curious onlookers greased the palm of a watchman to get a peek inside the famous pavilion. Admiring murmurs did not drown out the protests of a young student more cultivated than the rest, however. He recognized in the tapestry framing the royal armchair the legend of Jason and Medea. On one side the hero's new bride Creusa is writhing in pain in the poisoned robe given to her by her forsaken rival; on the other Medea is fleeing in a fiery chariot as Jason looks down in horror at the corpses of their children whose throats she has just slit. The young Goethe – he had just turned twenty-one – was disgusted. Images, he said, are powerful; their meaning is imprinted on the margins of consciousness and there excite presentiments. "Is there nothing else to offer to the first impressions of the beautiful and kindly queen than these appalling specters?" As he was addressing his indignation to the crowd, his friends, fearing a scandal, quickly bundled him out of the room.

At Schüttern Abbey Marie-Antoinette was not visited by such somber images, but she was weeping. This was the point of no return: she must accept the fact that she would never again see her mother, nor would she ever again see the places where she had spent her childhood. The next day, May 7th, in late morning, she crossed the bridge at Kehl amidst the cheers of the dense crowds that had come in spite of the rain and gusty winds. She stepped inside the pavilion on the Austrian side.

In the Middle Ages, the "handing over" of the fiancée included an examination of her entire body to confirm that she was hiding no physical deformities. Eventually the custom became more humane. It was enough to strip her of everything she'd brought from her native country and dress her in clothing and jewels offered by her country of adoption, a sort of symbolic naturalization. This ritual too would become less burdensome. If the new arrival's attire was changed, it was so that it would not clash with the fashions of the new country*. What was fashionable in Austria or Spain might look odd in France. In Marie-Antoinette's case, this was not an issue. The Viennese couturiers were up on Parisian styles. Her trousseau contained a ceremonial robe cut from golden cloth as well as her

---

* Madame Campan, who would only later become her lady of the bedchamber and whose account dates from later still, has often been quoted to the effect that she was subjected to the ancient ritual. But all the contemporary accounts affirm the contrary.

traveling apparel. She did not have to give up her childhood jewelry; she could substitute or add to it as she wished from the new gifts of jewelry she would receive.

The prince of Starhemberg conducted her to the armchair where she listened distractedly to the count de Noailles' grandiose welcoming address, followed by the reading of the marriage contract. Done: she was now French. Protocol would have it that her entire Austrian suite depart before her new "household" arrived. But overcome by curiosity, the French rushed into the room before their Austrian counterparts had turned their heels. Suddenly presented with the countess de Noailles, the panic-stricken girl ran into her arms and burst into tears: a grave breech of etiquette that the unyielding lady-in-waiting firmly rebuffed and would later try to cover up. The child was obviously overwhelmed, and with good reason. But here too, tradition had mellowed in her favor. Her Austrian ladies were allowed to accompany her to Saverne. And contrary to custom, her tutor, the abbé de Vermond, whom she loved, would follow her to Versailles. True, the abbé was French, but we'll get back to that.

Her warm welcome in Strasburg was reassuring. The city had not forgotten that before being conquered by Louis XIV, it was for a long time part of the Austrian Empire. The first magistrate began his speech in German. But she interrupted him, crying "Speak no German, sir, from this day forth I will hear nothing but French." Words right for the occasion, but they had already been spoken in identical circumstances by Louis XIV's daughter-in-law Marie-Anne of Bavaria. Marie-Antoinette had been primed, of course, but really, she was playing her role well, and that's already quite a lot. For fatigue was setting in, and was aggravated by anxiety. And there was the state dinner[*], then public appearances, fireworks, the ball, and presentation of the Alsatian nobility. The old cardinal-archbishop was ailing and just about mustered the strength to greet her, so his nephew and assistant bishop would say mass the following day. Under the vaults of the rose-colored cathedral, the prince Louis de Rohan, well turned out in his pontifical robes, waxed eloquent:

> Amongst us you shall be, Madame, the living image of that cherished Empress who has long been admired by all of Europe, as she will be for all of posterity. It will be Maria Theresa's soul that will be united with the soul of the Bourbons. From such a beautiful union can only be born days of the golden age…

---

[*] "Dîners à grand couvert," or official state dinners, were solemn affairs, where members of the royal family dined before the assembled court.

Back on the road! She had still to cross a jubilant Lorraine, home of her father's family. In Lunéville, Nancy and Commercy no one had forgotten her grandmother, Louis XIII's grand-daughter Élisabeth-Charlotte. The latter had been inconsolable when her duchy was taken over by France[*], and she had been determined to end her days there. Intense feeling was the order of the day. The cumbersome cortege wound its way through Bar-le-Duc and Saint-Dizier. The next-to-the-last stop was at Châlons. The lady of the hour found it hard to follow the play on offer, Collé's *Henry IV's Hunting Party*, despite having the script in front of her, which she pretended to be engrossed in. Distressed, Starhemberg wrote to her mother that "all the while she made faces, she bit her lips, held her fingers and her handkerchief in her nose, scratched her head constantly, leaned back on her chair, in sum, did not conduct herself as fittingly as I would have desired." The closer they got to their destination, the more nervous she became, which is understandable. Sunday the 13th, at Soissons, she could rest. The decisive encounter would take place the next day.

The first meeting

On the edge of the Compiègne forest, the crowds who had gathered since dawn near the Berne bridge crossroads wiled away the hours admiring the French guards, the musketeers and the gendarmes at their military spiffiest. Even the heavens were cooperating; it was a lovely day. The king and the dauphin arrived, flanked by courtiers. Finally, they would get a look at the future queen. What was she really like? For they knew that in such circumstances, descriptions and portraits were highly flattering. France's ambassador to Vienna the marquis de Durfort, aware that his dispatch would doubtless be opened by the Austrian secret service, prudently restricted himself to eulogistic generalities:

> She is an accomplished princess both in the beautiful quali-
> ties of her soul and in the grace of her person. She has fine
> judgment, goodness in her character and gaiety in her spirit.
> She likes to please, greets everyone with pleasant remarks, and
> possesses to a supreme degree all the qualities that can insure
> the happiness of a husband.

---

[*]   More precisely given to Stanislas Leszczynski, for as long as he lived. At his death in 1766 it became French.

About the latter point the empress went even further in an epistle to the dauphin dripping with moralizing sentimentality:

> Your spouse, my dear dauphin, has just left me; just as she brought me delight, I hope that she will make you happy... Therefore, love your duties to God, I tell you, my dear dauphin, as I have also told my daughter. Love the good of your people over whom you will reign all too soon. Love the king your forebear, inspire and nourish his attachment to my daughter; be good like him! Make yourself available to the unfortunate; you cannot, if you conduct yourself thusly, but share their happiness. My daughter will love you, I am sure, because I know her; but the more I answer for her love and her care, the more I ask you to devote to her your most tender affection. Farewell, my dear dauphin, be happy, make her happy! I am awash in tears!

And she signed, "Your loving mother."

We don't know what effect these mawkish effusions had on the recipient. But we do know that Louis XV was wondering about more trivial things. The painter Ducreux, sent to Vienna especially for the purpose, had enormous difficulty finishing the portrait of the young archduchess, harassed as he was by an empress never satisfied with it. Of course Louis XV said he was enchanted with the one he received. "I like it much," he wrote to his grandson the infante of Parma. But a few days later he expressed some doubts: "I fear that Antoinette is too hefty for her age." So there's nothing like the eyewitness account of an independent witness. Upon his return from Strasburg, the secretary sent to read the contract was questioned by the monarch. "How did you find Madame la dauphine? Is she well endowed?" Embarrassed, the secretary replied that she had a charming face, and very beautiful eyes. "I didn't ask you that, I'm asking whether or not she has a bosom." "Sire, I did not take the liberty of casting my regard in that direction." "You ninny," the king laughed, "that's the first thing one looks at in a woman."

What were the dreams and desires of her intended? He confided in no one. He was happy enough just to follow his fiancée's itinerary on a map, as was the practice at the time. We can't say whether this showed his interest in her or in geography, about which he was particularly fond. As the big day approached, his impatience, already pronounced in the preceding months, had grown. Can we conclude therefore that he was entirely delighted at the idea of getting married? "The groom is counting the days and the places she's been," the king wrote on May 7th, "and I think he's impatient to see her, and for it all to be over with." In the adolescent, the pride of entering once and for all into the ranks of manhood seemed mixed with a strong dose of worry. He would like for the whole ordeal to be over with.

The solemn event was about to happen. The cortege was in sight; it was moving forward, greeted by martial music and the acclamations of the people. The king and dauphin were standing in wait. Hardly had her coach come to a halt when the dauphine hastened out of it, and with a light step, threw herself at the sovereign's feet to kiss his hand. But he did not let her complete her genuflection. He embraced her and presented his grandson, who in turn embraced her. Make no mistake about it; all of these gestures that offered the appearance of charming spontaneity were drawn from ancient models. They had been studied, calculated and timed, as the correspondence between Starhemberg and the empress shows. And we can be sure that Marie-Antoinette rehearsed her role over and over again. But no matter, she played it well, and that's what counts. She seemed to have a gift for "presentation" – an essential ingredient in the profession of queen. Louis XV declared himself satisfied.

All the more so as she was quite charming. Was she pretty? Undoubtedly not according to the canons of the day. She was blond, evenly so, tending toward strawberry blond. Once powdered her hair would take on a rosy hue. Her light eyelashes and brows accentuated her blondness. Her pale blue eyes were a bit too prominent, her face with its bulging forehead was of an oval shape, but too long. Her nose, which promised to be aquiline one day, lacked grace, and her somewhat heavy, almost pouting lower lip was a Hapsburg trademark. But she radiated a grace that erased all of these imperfections. On her translucent, pearly complexion, heightened to a delicate pink by emotion, there were a few slight reminders of smallpox, as if to reassure us that she no longer had anything to fear from this redoubtable disease that killed and disfigured. But her defining characteristic was an extreme nimbleness of movement. She walked as if on air. She already held her long neck and head like a queen. Her facial expressions never stopped changing. Her seductive smiles threatened to molt into bursts of laughter. From all of this a quivering life bubbled up, explaining why painters found it so difficult to capture her. She existed in movement only.

Had she a bosom? No, decidedly not. At fourteen and a half, an age when some girls already look like fully-grown women, she was still a child. Louis XV must have been aware of this, because he knew that she only recently had her first period – at 5:15 in the evening of February 7th to be exact, as the empress informed him via special courier. Of course no one bothered to tell him that there had been no reoccurrence. His fears were groundless; she was not hefty. But her silhouette was that of a girl as yet lacking in curves. The duchess of Northumberland, who happened to see her one day, remarked how very short and slim she was. To her the child looked no older than twelve. She was far from having grown to her full height; all contemporary witnesses agreed, those who called her tall wrote long afterwards. But this delay served her well. Her freshness and fragility added to her appeal; they inspired indulgence and protective feelings for her.

Before her stood a scrawny, gangly fifteen-year-old boy, who had just had a growth spurt. He was already tall. With his regular features, his linen-hued hair, his eyes like clear water, so dreamy that he seemed nearsighted, he would not lack charm if he were not so terribly awkward in a body that he was not yet quite used to. Ill at ease in the freshly minted frame of a man not yet fully grown, he stepped on his own feet and did not know what to do with his hands. As usual, he said not a word, half out of shyness, half out of respect for his grandfather. Marie-Antoinette hardly looked at him, and for the moment had no opinion of him. Her only thought was to follow her mother's advice. Seated between them in the coach on the way to Compiègne, she had eyes and ears only for the king, whose heart she had been told to capture. Mission accomplished. He conducted the conversation with ease, proof that he was satisfied. He liked the youngster. He would declare that he was "enchanted" with her.

Introductions

It would take no less than a day and a half to acquaint her with everything that mattered in Versailles.

France's minister of foreign affairs and the principal crafter of the marriage, the duke de Choiseul, did not want to get lost in the crowd, so he sought and got permission to meet her a bit ahead of the others, and conversed with her in the sole company of Austria's ambassador to Paris, the count de Mercy-Argenteau. She knew perfectly well how much she was indebted to Choiseul. "I will never forget, sir, that you have brought me this happiness." "And that of France," he rejoined weightily.

Next came the royal family, in the order imposed by protocol. Despite being ill-disposed to the newcomer, the king's three daughters, Adélaïde, Victoire and Sophie, would not have given up their precedence for anything in the world. Always ready to uphold their rank, they were there to meet their future niece and give her the requisite kiss. At the Compiègne chateau, the princes and princesses of the blood were standing at attention to greet her. Following them the titled lords and ladies came forward. The more taxing festivities were fortunately reserved for the days to follow. After supper she had only to try on different rings to find one that suited her, and she was left to her bedchamber, while the dauphin, who could not sleep under the same roof, went off to lodge with the count de Saint-Florentin, the minister who headed the king's household.

In the little notebook the dauphin used to jot down a summary account of his days, he wrote simply *"Interview with Madame la Dauphine,"* thus causing to rain down on him accusations of crude indifference. But this notebook, or rather these notebooks, as there would be others, had nothing of the intimate diary, as they sometimes have been carelessly named. They were more like daily planners written after the fact. In them he wrote down as dryly as one would in a daily planner, not his upcoming obligations, but an indication of his daily activities – an account above all of his hunting, which explains the large number of negative entries: *"Nothing,"* he wrote on days when he hadn't hunted. He methodically mapped out the passing of his time, in the same way that elsewhere he recorded, day after day, the exact state of his personal finances. But never would he dream of confiding any intimacies to these notebooks, especially not his sorrows. *"Death of my mother at eight o'clock this evening,"* he noted simply on Friday the 13th of March 1767, even though he was deeply affected. The only exceptions to this reserve would come later during moments of intense joy, at the birth of his children, as we shall see. We therefore can conclude nothing from his notebooks' silence about his relations with Marie-Antoinette.

The next day brought the last stop before Versailles. A visit was made to the Carmelite convent in Saint-Denis. The king's youngest daughter, Madame Louise, had just begun her novitiate there, but felt herself no less a member of the family for all that, and wished to meet her new niece. The latter, smiling but collected, made an excellent impression on the community. One nun wrote, "Her features have an air of grandeur, of modesty and of gentleness all at once. The king, Mesdames and especially Monsieur le Dauphin seem delighted with her. They never tire of saying 'She's incomparable.'" The rest of the journey was made between crowds of onlookers lining the roads, which got denser as they neared the capital.

In the evening they arrived at the chateau de la Muette, just outside the Boulogne wood. On her night table she found – it was part of the ritual – a superb set of diamonds. She had already been informed that the bracelet bore a portrait of the king. She hastened to attach it to her wrist, replacing her own, in imitation of her late mother-in-law Marie-Josèphe. "She gets along marvelously with the king, she greets him with the customary courtesies," the marquise de Durfort pointed out, "... She seeks always to please him." More introductions: she met the dauphin's two younger brothers, the counts de Provence and d'Artois.

When it came time for supper, if she sensed uncommon excitement all around, she could be forgiven for assuming she was the cause of it. She would figure it out later on. For the time being, she replied amiably to the praises of a breathtakingly beautiful young woman in white wearing just enough diamonds to avoid appearing vulgar. If she was told her name she did not retain it. When the mysterious individual sat down at the end of the table, admittedly, far enough from the king – but all the same! – the room fell into icy silence. He dared to do it! He took advantage of the naïve dauphine's presence to stifle any reaction and impose the company of his new favorite. Seeing the young girl's glance fall on the smiling countenance of the new acquaintance, the king leaned over and asked her, "How do you find this lady?" "Charming," came her innocent reply. Soon overcome with curiosity, she in turn leaned over toward Madame de Noailles to ask what place this beautiful lady occupied in the court. For a moment disconcerted, the lady recovered her wits and replied, "Her functions? Why, the king enjoys her company!" "Well," came her boastful reply, "in that case, I shall be her rival." She spoke loudly enough to be heard by her neighbors, who lost no time in peddling the phrase at court and in town, much to the mortification of the upstart when she found out about it. Those dictating the dauphine's conduct could not after all have thought of everything, especially not the unthinkable! They'd felt it morally incumbent upon them to hide from her the moral failings of the grandfather they had portrayed as being blessed with every virtue. "How *tharming*, this little one!" lisped in turn the radiant du Barry.

The anecdote was certainly doctored, if not entirely cut from whole cloth, but it conveys accurately an impression everyone had: the dauphine quite made up her mind that no one would dispute her preeminence at court. For the time being, however, the king, delighted to have thus enthroned his beloved, was grateful to his new granddaughter for having provided the opportunity. His letters to the empress brimmed with satisfaction.

Pomp and circumstance

The actual wedding was scheduled for the next day, May 16th. The weather was superb as Marie-Antoinette first passed through the gates of Versailles about ten o'clock in the morning. On the second floor, the great bedchamber of the queen destined for her use was not yet ready. Royal finances were not what they should be. The craftsmen working on it had not been paid and didn't rush. For now she would inhabit the apartments of the previous dauphine Marie-Josèphe of Saxony on the ground floor right next to those her future spouse would occupy until he became king, the very same his own late father had occupied. She was delivered into the hands of the ladies in charge of her wardrobe. Two hours later she emerged, her torso enclosed in a stunning white brocade dress whose immense panniers made her look even more slender. She glided seemingly on air to the king's cabinet amidst murmurs of admiration. She greeted him and kissed his hand "with great good grace and ease" noted the duke de Croÿ, who knew a beautiful woman when he saw one. The dauphin was there, outfitted in a diamond-studded gold suit crossed by the blue Sash of the Holy Spirit.

A royal wedding is a spectacle offered by the king to his beloved subjects. Onlookers thickly lined the corridors leading to the chapel, taxing the safety officials. All one needed for admittance was to be dressed to the nines. Persons of quality furnished with invitations gained entry to the galleries and grandstands. The rest were sorted according to how dashingly they were decked out. The most dazzlingly dressed ladies were pushed to the front row, just behind the crowd-containing barriers. There they would make up part of the decor. At the very top of the social ladder a few privileged individuals were admitted to the religious ceremony. At the very bottom – well not exactly, as they did have to be decently dressed – the good people were invited to a fireworks display in the park.

Slowly the cortege made its way to the chapel, where the sunlight serendipitously streaming in heightened the colors on display and sparkled off all the gold, to the tumultuous strains of the great organ. The newlyweds proceeded to the foot of the altar where the archbishop of Reims welcomed them. They knelt down on the crimson gold-tasseled velvet cushions. As soon as the homily was over, the king and the princes moved forward and stood together behind them, as required by immutable ritual. The prelate blessed the young woman's wedding ring and the traditional thirteen gold coins*. When the time came to slip the ring on her finger, the dauphin, very moved, turned as per custom to his grandfather, who nodded his assent. Then came the solemn blessing, followed by the mass. Once arrived at the *Pater Noster*, a silver brocade cloth was held aloft over the couple's heads. Before leaving the chapel they had to sign the documents for the registry office of the parish of Notre-Dame, which included the chateau. According to protocol, the dauphine signed after the king and the dauphin. She took the quill into her trembling hand and – touchingly, as it reminds us just how young she was – she adorned her four Christian names with an inkblot.

She withdrew to her suite where all the servants attached to her service would swear their oath of allegiance, one after another, from the highest-ranking officials of her household and ladies-in-waiting to the lowliest scullery maid who scoured her pots. Soon she was brought her wedding gifts in a beautiful coffer that cabinetmakers and goldsmiths had outdone themselves to produce. Aside from a blue enamel pendant on a diamond chain and a few other jewels from the king, she found in it a whole assortment of gifts she was to distribute to her entourage. And in order to avoid any embarrassing blunders as had occurred in the past, each gift bore the name of its recipient. Next she must attend the reception in the great hall whose mirrors cast an infinity of candlelight glowing from the crystal chandeliers. There the public could behold the king and his grandchildren at a gaming table enjoying an innocent game of *cavagnole***. The privileged few were seated on little benches, the rest were cordoned off in the narrow passageways behind the barriers, obliged to file past at a regular pace, permitted neither to turn back nor stop, as if being ushered past some sort of icon. Outside the weather had turned awful. The rain was pouring down, and everyone knew there would be no fireworks; they were all sodden. The dejected onlookers turned to go home; their kind were barred entry to the ballrooms.

Louis XV managed to bring to fruition a project that Louis XIV kept having to postpone for lack of funds: he had the architect Jacques Ange Gabriel build at Versailles a sumptuous theatre

---

*   According to a custom dating back to the late 16th century, the thirteen coins – simple farthings for the poorest – were distributed in two parts. Ten were for the priest who kept the marriage contract. The groom took the rest and having placed the ring on the bride's finger telling her "*With this ring I you wed*," he slipped them into her hand and added, "*And with my wealth I you endow.*" This second element of the ritual had been lost, but the thirteen coins offered to the church survived.

*   A game for small stakes similar to our lotto much enjoyed by Marie Leszczynska.

equipped with highly sophisticated stage machinery. It could put on all the delights of the lyrical theatre with divinities descending from the heavens or emerging out of hell; but it could also be transformed at will into a large dining hall or a ballroom, thanks to a movable floor that could extend out from the stage to cover the theatre seats. Gone were the days when they had to hasten to turn the riding school into a ballroom. Marie-Antoinette's wedding saw the inauguration of what remains to this day the chateau's opera house. And for her wedding there was of course a music-filled dinner "*au grand couvert,*" that is to say open to the public.

Flanked on his right by the dauphin and on his left by the dauphine, Louis XV presided over the long table of princes and princesses of the blood – twenty-one guests in all. Various courses were served. Marie-Antoinette hardly touched a thing, even though she seemed not to have had a bite to eat all day. Perhaps she had something in the middle of the day that no one cared to mention, no doubt because it wasn't on the program. Regarding the dauphin's appetite, the accounts differ. One detail has caught the attention of nearly all historians. As the young man demonstrated a hearty appetite, the king apparently teased him with a winking admonition not to overdo it. "You mustn't get too full now, think of tonight." To which came the naïve reply, "But why not? I always sleep better after a good supper." The anecdote is said to come from Marie-Antoinette's lifelong friend Madame de Lamballe via the memoirs of Catherine Hyde, at one time in her service. Very different were the observations of an English visitor, the countess of Northumberland, present for the occasion. She found that he ate little, and seemed lost in his thoughts while staring down at his plate and toying with his knife. It is possible of course that his appetite waned during the course of the dinner. But let's not kid ourselves. The fact is that, as with Marie-Antoinette squaring off against Madame du Barry, we see at work here the reconstruction of events or simply selective memory based on what happened subsequently. Legend seeps into history and truth is impossible to pin down.

The supper over, they were conducted to the nuptial chamber, the young woman's bedchamber, for the bedding ritual, also public. The archbishop blessed the bed. The king must hand his grandson the nightshirt that protocol required the duke d'Orléans to hand the king. Together, they brought him to his own bedchamber for the purpose – a mercifully modest innovation – while the highest-ranking married woman, in this case the duchess de Chartres, handed the dauphine hers. The king led the dauphin back, conducted him to the bed, closed the curtains momentarily while he got in, then opened them wide so that the princesses and courtiers fortunate enough to have the right of "entry to the bedchamber" saw the newlyweds lying side by side and could testify to the validity of the marriage. The king whispered a few bawdy encouragements into his grandson's ear – that too was required by tradition. After the last curtsies and bows, the two children were left to their own devices in the bed finally closed to the world.

They looked fresh the next morning when the court elite, devoured by curiosity, came to greet them upon wakening. But no triumphant communiqué graced with military metaphors was forthcoming after this wedding night. On May 16th, the young man noted in his diary *My marriage. Reception in the Hall. Royal feast in the opera house.* The next day he would write *Nothing*, which simply meant he didn't go hunting. Would he have entrusted to his diary any nuptial exploits? Nothing is less sure. But in any case, it is clear that the marriage was not consummated. This is hardly strange, given their age. But for the moment it was not a pressing matter. It would become more pressing as the months turned into years, to the point of preoccupying French public opinion and the chancelleries all over Europe.

Dazzling festivities that end badly

Marie-Antoinette was duly wed, but her task was not over yet. On the program were still two weeks of festivities. On Thursday the 17th of May, the stage works were inaugurated as the floor was removed to reveal the new opera house. Tradition dictated the choice of Lully's *Perseus*, which the vigorous albeit middle-aged Louis XIV had delighted in when the court transferred to Versailles in 1682. But a lot of hard work had been put into adapting it to current tastes, recounts Pierre de Nolhac. It was reduced from five to four acts; recitatives were cut out and vocals added. A new ballet was added ending with an allegory in honor of the dauphine: the imperial eagle descends from on high to light the flame on the altar of Hymen. Alas, Lully's music suffered from the butchering; the as-yet untested machines worked badly, and the dauphine failed to hide her boredom. The only time she enjoyed it was when Perseus tripped and tumbled to Andromeda's feet as he tried to save her from the monster's clutches. It was wrongly concluded therefore that she wasn't fond of music.

A day of rest followed. The dauphin went hunting. She dined alone, but in public. The next day she had to undergo a fearful ordeal: the official grand ball. The atmosphere was a bit tense as quarrels over precedence raged. The house of Lorraine argued that their status as foreign guests and their family ties to the dauphine gave them the right to pass in front of the non-hereditary dukes and duchesses who, furious, decided to snub the event. Upon the explicit order of Louis XV they finally dragged their feet to the ball. The same blue and gold space was again metamorphosed and symbolically adorned with chubby-cheeked cupids cavorting amid dolphins and eagles to represent Psyche. The entire court was arranged in a circle around the dance floor to fix their unforgiving eyes on the couples, who had to follow each other onto the dance floor in the order imposed by the king. The newlyweds had the perilous honor of opening the ball. A minuet facilitated the task. The general consensus was that the dauphine acquitted herself well. Perhaps she danced slightly out of step, as the prince of Starhemberg had noted back in Saverne. But she was so lithe, and light, and graceful, that this was forgotten and some were even tempted to say, as would Horace Walpole later on, that it was the music that was off tempo. Besides, compared to her husband she looked good. Charitably, the king avoided assigning her the more intricate dances. Accompanied by the young duke de Chartres, she only stepped out onto the dance floor again for a familiar German number.

The postponed fireworks took place that night. The pyrotechnicians produced an amazing show, outdoing anything before seen in the number and ingenuity of the displays. Whirling suns carried aloft France's coat of arms and the couple's interlaced initials. The grand finale apparently contained no fewer than 20,000 rockets, something previously unheard of. No sooner did the last spent squibs fall to the ground than the buildings and gardens burst into light. Along the rooftops, the flowerbeds, the pergolas and the hornbeam groves, along the water basins and the fountain edges, glass-encased candles traced shimmering lines, outlining the contours of the chateau and the park. The Temple of the Sun stood majestic at the end of the Grand Canal. Joyful music by the French Guards burst forth from boats whose lanterns flickered to the rhythm of the oars. Hidden among the groves were bands, dance floors and makeshift stages for street performers, acrobats and tightrope walkers; there were even theatres where impromptu shows were put on in honor of the newlyweds. The jubilant populace would celebrate until dawn.

Fascinated, Marie-Antoinette watched the fireworks from the central balcony. Then, startled as the lights burst forth, she jumped. She had itchy feet, and was keen to go see all of these marvels for herself, to rub shoulders with the crowds, to be engulfed in the universal joy. Alas, the king held her back; dauphines do not do such things. There she remained, fighting back the tears before the forbidden fruit, discovering all of a sudden the servitude of her position. Did the king take pity on her and authorize a brief carriage jaunt among the crowds? Here again accounts differ, so the question must be left unanswered.

Everyone took a rest on Sunday May 20th in anticipation of the masked ball on Monday. Marie-Antoinette was not in disguise. A simple hooded cape known as a domino, however, prevented her being recognized in the Salon of Hercules where she ventured a turn on the dance floor. She was allowed to enter the rooms where the masked figures were all awhirl, and the great hall where they were feasting at the buffet tables. She had hardly savored this semi-freedom for an hour when she was sent to bed. But she had gotten a foretaste of the enchanting pleasures that her new life could offer.

The plays chosen later to introduce her to French theatre were not all to her liking. Among the tragedies the first pick was a monumental work, admirable to be sure, but austere, Racine's *Athalie.* The dauphin loved it – he knew it by heart – but his little bride found it boring, weighed down by its high-flown rhetoric. Wasn't there anything more modern? Voltaire, the *philosophe* of Ferney, was too contentious a figure to be acceptable to the court, but his plays were a must. So his *Tancrède* and *Sémiramis* were put on. Next up were a remake of *Perseus* – better this time – Rameau's *Castor and Pollux,* then a ballet by Madame de Villeroy, *The Enchanted Tower,* the story of a princely wedding that ends with a tournament in which carts are drawn by real horses.

As the days passed there were fewer entertainments, the schedule was less grueling. But tradition demanded that the people of Paris get their share of the festivities. So on Wednesday, May 30th, there were more fireworks and dense crowds in the Place Louis XV (now Place de la Concorde) and along the boulevards* lined with

---

* The whole area was under construction. Place Louis XV, today the Place de la Concorde, would not be finished for another two years, but already at its northern edge the two pavilions by Gabriel could be seen. It was surrounded by a wide drainage ditch spanned by bridges. The Rue Royale connected it to the boulevards, which had just been built over the remains of the ancient ramparts, starting from the church of la Madeleine, also under construction. It was bordered to the east by the Tuileries gardens with its ironwork gates. Access to them could be barred by a swing bridge. Neither the Rue de Rivoli nor the Concorde bridge existed yet. To the west the Place looked out on the embankment and the Cours-la-Reine, which was still in the countryside.

fairground stalls. Everywhere there were buffet tables groaning with rustic fare and fountains of wine for the taking. There were light shows and dancing. Many courtiers crowded to the best-placed windows. The Seine was covered in boats. The king unfortunately decided not to attend, and the dauphin had no desire to, but the dauphine insisted on going, and her wish was granted. It was agreed that she could go in her coach toward the end, accompanied by Mesdames her aunts, once the fireworks were over and traffic was a bit more manageable.

They were in time to see the last of the display, but just then there was an unnerving noise. Their coach stopped. The women watched helplessly as terrified people came running in their direction. They were told as little as possible and were sent back to Versailles in all haste. An enormous stampede had developed in the Rue Royale. The bridges were closed off so that all the construction, the ditches, and the garden gates had turned the northeast corner of the Place Louis XV into a fatal trap, a tangle of bodies and vehicles. According to some witnesses a small fire broke out, aggravating the panic. The death toll reached 132. Most victims were suffocated, run over or trampled to death. They were buried in the nearby La Madeleine graveyard. Distraught when they found out how horrendous the disaster had been, the dauphin and the dauphine, in whose honor the deadly festivities had been held, hastened to donate their monthly stipend to the victims' families.

Such was Marie-Antoinette's first contact with Paris, and more precisely with this Place Louis XV, built in honor of the monarch and the monarchy. At the time perhaps a few superstitious minds saw in this dramatic event a shadow cast on her married life. But who could have guessed that less than a quarter of a century later, on this very spot, by then called La Place de la Révolution, she herself would be brought to the guillotine, and that in La Madeleine's potter's field her body would join the corpses of those whose blood had flowed at her wedding festivities?

Eventually court life returned to its usual rhythm. These outrageously expensive weeks dug a huge hole in the treasury's finances, but Louis XV had demonstrated that he knew as well as his great-grandfather the Sun King how to make of France the resplendent paragon of taste, luxury and elegance for all of Europe to admire. The festivities were among the most striking any monarchy had ever put on. Along with the famous *Pleasures of the Enchanted Island* of 1664, they remain to this day the most memorable. The royal residence of Versailles never equaled these two, the first and practically the last of its splendorous festivities.

In Vienna the empress was happy with her daughter. The child had followed orders. But once does not a habit make. She acquitted herself brilliantly during these rites of initiation, much better than her chaperons had hoped. There were no missteps, or so few. Starhemberg declared himself happily surprised by her perseverance, her presence of mind, her ease and her grace. That's because her mother's advice was not hard to follow: she was good at pleasing, shining, winning hearts. A murmur of admiration accompanied her every step. Would the miracle continue? Maria Theresa feared that the task might be difficult for her. For despite the good feelings aired in her letters, she knew full well that relations between Paris and Vienna were not at present very stable, if they ever had been. The marriage that she fought so hard for was of her making. Would her daughter be able to do what was expected of her?

CHAPTER 2

DAUGHTER OF THE EMPRESS-QUEEN

It was not easy being the daughter of an exceptional woman endowed by fate with supreme power. Marie-Antoinette was attached to her mother by a close network of ties, which circumstances would reinforce rather than weaken. Surviving the bumps, the misunderstandings and the quarrels, their relationship would continue by correspondence until the empress passed away in 1780. Upon her death, the empress became larger than life and would remain so, the absolute reference, the model that had to be lived up to and be seen as worthy of. It is useful therefore to become acquainted with this exceptional mother in order to understand all that her daughter owed her.

A passionate woman

Looking at what she accomplished politically both at home and in Europe, one is tempted to accentuate her wisdom, level-headedness and prudence. Thrust at the age of twenty-three into ruling over disparate possessions coveted by her neighbors, she managed through clever maneuvering to divide her rivals, and through sheer energy to rally around her even the most recalcitrant of her subjects. Ever after, she would rule with a firm hand over her husband, her children and her states, imposing herself on the European scene as a sovereign of foremost grandeur.

It is a bit surprising therefore to discover in her an impulsive and ardent woman at times prey to extreme passions. But she remained on an even keel thanks to a deep Christian faith that helped her avoid the traps laid by pride; and thanks to her open mind and heart, she was able to see things from others' point of view. She was exceptionally clear-sighted thanks to a sense of humor and a sound instinct for the truth. Very strong-willed, she pursued with extreme tenacity any objectives she set, like getting back Silesia, snatched from her one fine day by the king of Prussia. But faced with hard facts, she never fell into self-destructive obstinacy: she would relent in time – at the last possible moment – but in time. She knew how to make a quick decision and stick to it. Her broad and vigorous intelligence, capable of grasping complex realities, exercised rigorous control over her passions. Her strength, and her originality too, came from this rare balance between the contradictory demands of her temperament.

Fetters dissolved before this powerful temperament. Starting in adolescence, she proved that she would not bow to what others expected of her. When it came time to marry, Francis of Lorraine was not her father's first choice. But she got her own way, helped by the fact that her choice did not present any overwhelming objections. Her ascension to the throne at the age of twenty-three did not diminish her vitality, far from it. She had received the rigorous and straight-laced education reserved at the time for young women. She loved horseback riding, so much so that even during her pregnancies she refused to give it up, conceding only to ride sidesaddle rather than straddling the horse like a man. When she went to be crowned queen of Hungary, her masterful horsemanship impressed the noble Magyars, themselves peerless horsemen. She threw herself completely into her favorite entertainments like dancing and gambling, especially when Vienna got caught up in the frenetic pre-Lenten festivities. "Sometimes in winter," wrote one of her biographers, "upon leaving the gaming tables, she would throw a domino over her shoulders and go into town with her entourage to the Dance Hall and stay until it closed. 'She thought,' one courtier remarked, 'that the mask would prevent her being recognized; just to please her, we played along, although her quick and easy gait betrayed her immediately.'"

She was young. She was beautiful. She could have let it all go to her head. But she didn't. She never let her pleasures interfere with her duties to the state. After nights of partying, daybreak would find her at her desk, ready to deal with whatever ministers needed her for that day. She enjoyed cast-iron health. Over the years, however, she adopted more regular schedules. With age and the birth of her many children she settled down; her exuberance disappeared. But her naturalness was never far from the surface. It can be called her defining feature. She remained quite unconventional. For her, how things should be never clouded how they actually were. She was so naturally imposing that she needed no trappings of power to gain respect. At any given moment the living woman would burst forth unexpectedly from behind the empress. Just reread her letters. They contain a *tone* all her own. Although she shunned evasiveness, waffling and euphemism, she was insouciant about grammar, and expressed herself forthrightly, personally, without fear of leaving herself open. She needed neither show nor mask. She didn't protect herself. She let herself be seen as she was. That does not mean, however, that she expressed *everything*, even less that she gave in. She would show only a part of herself. But the part she showed had the ring of truth and was therefore persuasive. In 1755, when she made Louis XV her surprising offer to become allies, nothing convinced the king more of her sincerity than her direct way of getting to the point. As the abbé de Véri put it, "she had to a superior degree the art of honest seduction."

For she realized very early on that this royal simplicity paid off. When she acceded to the throne, she exercised this simplicity to win over her Hungarian subjects. Throughout her reign she would use it to gain the loyalty of those who served her. Her relationships with her counselors were most unusual; she confided in them, solicited their help, accorded to each of them great freedom of expression and criticism. She treated each one like a personal friend, without their respect for her diminishing in the least. Quite the contrary, the honor thus bestowed on them inspired unconditional devotion. The only one not susceptible to her charm, at least to some degree, was her principal advisor and accomplice in everything, the old fox Kaunitz. He played the flattery card too often himself to be duped by it.

Her aversion to needless complications was clear in her lifestyle. In Vienna the way of life was always less stilted than in Versailles. You were not perpetually on show there, the way you were in France. The efforts of the Madrid refugees to impose Spanish etiquette lasted a while. And Maria Theresa took simplicity a step further. At table no one had to be on their knees to serve her. People did not come to pay court to her ritualistically on a fixed timetable just because that's the way it was done – that would be wasting her time and theirs. Except for the many dazzling parties, or during the state receptions, which afforded all the necessary solemnity, the imperial family led a rather simple daily life centered on their work. Was theirs a bourgeois existence? Let's not go too far. A youthful gouache drawn by the archduchess Maria Christina shouldn't fool us into thinking that the emperor liked to have his breakfast by the fire wearing his nightcap, nightshirt and slippers, surrounded by his wife who pours his coffee and his children all playing with their toys.

This is a sketch of Christmas morning. The clock says it's five to nine. The little ones have just received their gifts (a doll for Marie-Antoinette) except the one who was naughty and found switches in his slipper – our equivalent of his stocking. It's a holiday, after all, not a sketch of daily life. Usually Maria Theresa rose earlier; she hadn't her children under foot; they lived in the children's quarters where they could be left quite a while without seeing their mother.

In any case, how could she ever have managed to take care of them all? She gave birth to sixteen children, with no twins, within just twenty years! Repeated births became routine, interrupting business for only a few hours. Hardly had the new baby belted out its first cry when she was again reviewing and signing state documents. "It is not her majesty's habit to remain long abed," Kaunitz wrote to Starhemberg, who feared that the arrival on November 2, 1755 of Maria Antonia Josepha Johanna – the future Marie-Antoinette – would dangerously delay the talks on the switching of alliances. Of course, not all of her children survived. Among the eleven daughters, three died in childhood and two in adolescence. Of the five sons, one passed away at the age of six. There remained ten children who survived her. Antonia, or Antoine as they called her, was the next to the last of the brood, and the last girl.

One can easily see why she had to entrust the job of raising her sprawling brood to teams of servants, on whom she imposed very strict orders: there were principles to apply, accounts to render. The children's health and moral development were one and the same. They would in no way be coddled, nor would their whims be indulged. They were fed healthful food, including a light meal before bedtime, but their tastes were not consulted, nor were they ever given sweets. In their moderately heated and reasonably comfortable bedrooms, they got used to falling asleep without lullabies or nightlights. Habits of cleanliness were inculcated, but no undue attention was paid to their bodies: the person in charge of washing them performed the task "with decency to inspire modesty right from the start." In speaking to them their caregivers refrained from the baby talk that nannies adopt to facilitate their task. When they were learning how to walk properly, less use was made of the uncomfortable "braces" resorted to at the time. They would learn to walk better and more quickly if they didn't feel fettered. The usual childhood fears of storms, fire, or witches and ghosts and other such silliness were not tolerated. They were to treat their servants with respect but without familiarity; they had to learn that their rank imposed a gulf between them. In the hope of dampening down the vehemence she saw in many of them (because she recognized it only too well in herself) she insisted that they learn from a very early age to control their feelings, showing aversion for no one and nothing. She believed that by seeping in little by little through daily practice, religion would transform the habits inculcated in early childhood into lifelong rules.

It was a bold and original educational regime, that we are tempted to call modern. Its aim was to make them strong and free. It should also be pointed out that it was applied to the entire brood. We could perhaps say it was "unisex" but where the male clearly dominated. The girls' education was fashioned on the boys'. Maria Theresa only distinguished between them when it came to schooling, which was reserved for her sons only. It is ever surprising that this woman, who had suffered so much when she came to power from the lack of an education worthy of the name, never gave her daughters anything better, on the assumption that they had no chance of acceding to the throne. They were born to obey and they'd better get used to it early. They must be prepared for the role of obedient wife. But how could she not see that in forging in them a steely character she prepared them for anything but obedience?

All the more so as this regimen afforded vast stretches of free time during which futile pursuits were forbidden. Only the boys from the age of seven onwards slogged away under the rule of their tutors. In the children's quarters, freedom reigned. There was constant merriment in this troop that kept replenishing itself as the departing older ones gave way to the little ones. It was lots of fun, but that didn't bother Maria Theresa at all. She even encouraged certain amusements we would now call educational: the children danced, sang, played instruments and put on shows. To inspire them she invited the young Mozart to Shönbrunn in 1762. He jumped onto her lap between stints at the piano then frolicked on the floor with Marie-Antoinette, whom – according to unverifiable legend – he promised to marry when they grew up. Their shows were so commonplace that the minister Khevenhüller worried that the children would turn into mere harebrained puppets. He kept his disapproval for his personal diary, however. Who would dare contradict the empress, who so enjoyed marveling at her babes? She even asked the painter Weickert to immortalize on canvas a January 1765 musical performance of Gluck's *Parnasso confuso* with libretto by Metastase – no less! – with Maria Christina, Maria Elisabeth, Maria Amalia and Maria Carolina as the Muses and Leopold at the harpsichord. As for Marie-Antoinette, she played the starring role in the final ballet, accompanied by her two youngest brothers.

Marie-Antoinette had her mother send this charming painting

to France in 1778. She hung it on the Trianon dining-room wall where it remains today, a poignant testament to how fondly she recalled her happy childhood.

A very close couple

The empress had two great passions: one was her husband and the other the Hapsburg dynasty, whose destinies she held in her hands.

As an adolescent she fell head over heels in love with the young heir of Lorraine who'd come to Vienna to fine-tune his education. The dukes of Lorraine, coming from an area too close to France for comfort, had always had ups and downs in their relationship with their powerful and intimidating French neighbor. At the end of the 17th century, the marriage of Louis XIV's niece to duke Leopold seemed to strengthen the bond. But the Lorrains took it very ill in the next generation when Poland's Marie Leszczynska was preferred over their daughter as Louis XV's bride. They then turned to their nominal sovereign, the emperor, and confided their two sons to him. As we know, Maria Theresa wed the older, Francis, and her sister Maria Anna the younger, Charles. The vicissitudes of the war provoked by the young woman's accession to the throne brought a hodge-podge of territorial disputes: the Lorraine was handed over to Stanislas Leszczynski and then promised to France. Francis got in return the Grand-Duchy of Tuscany, over which he exercised but distant authority. Completely acculturated to Austria, he made Vienna his home, becoming a sort of prince-consort.

His wife succeeded, not without difficulty, in getting him elected emperor – a prestigious title, but purely honorific, which afforded him no authority whatsoever over the various Germanic states owing him allegiance. As for the states inherited from the Hapsburgs, she was the sovereign. She agreed to have him named co-ruler, knowing full well that she would get no help from him at all. He had no talent for governing. It was better that way, as she'd have borne no contradiction on his part. She loved him just as he was: handsome, uncomplicated, light-hearted and easy to live with. She felt she could, however, grant him prerogatives in the only area beyond her competence, running the army. Her passion blinded her for a long time to his military ineptitude, until the accumulation of mistakes and defeats forced her to face the facts. She loved him none the less for it. She let him lead the easy life of a grandee given over, within reason, to life's pleasures. He enjoyed gambling, hunting, good food, the theatre, and works of art. He'd have liked pretty women too, but she was not compliant. She was as jealous as a tiger. At the most, she would tolerate flings with actresses or bourgeois ladies, but she bore with difficulty his intermittent liaison with the beautiful, cultivated and dazzling countess Auersperg, who held court over a small band of worshippers that included the emperor, although he remained only one of the group's gems. Unable to get him to break with her, the empress kept her on the sidelines – the countess was not allowed in her presence, each woman remained in her own sphere. She held on to her husband, and she held on tight. She quarreled with him and made scenes followed by tears and reconciliations on the pillow. He would accede to her wishes. When he dared at a certain age to suggest separate bedrooms, she saw red, bursting out in a screaming fit, vowing eternal hatred to the impudent fool who had given him such silly advice. Sacred was the vast marital bed where she had conceived and given birth to their sixteen children.

The children were a powerful link between them. He was an excellent father, very tender – more than their mother perhaps, because he was of a sweeter disposition. He gladly pampered his daughters, especially the littlest ones. His cheerful piety imparted reassuring lessons to them all: God saw to the happiness of all those who obeyed his commandments. As retiring as he seemed in his wife's presence, this very reticence gave him an essential role in the family. He brought balance, serenity and peace. This became all too clear after his sudden demise.

The 5th of August 1765, Austria was in a celebratory mood. Leopold, the imperial couple's second son, was getting married. The entire court had gone to Innsbruck for the occasion. But the celebrations were interrupted first by the news of the death of the duke of Parma, their eldest son Joseph's father-in-law, and then by the young groom's coming down with a violent, life-threatening fever. As soon as he was out of danger, the parties recommenced. Although he was tired, the emperor felt he should make an appearance at an Italian comedy on August 18th because the empress couldn't. He felt dizzy, so he left with his son Joseph. Leaning on a door, he pulled himself together long enough to say it was nothing before falling to the ground, dead. He was only 57.

Maria Theresa, summoned in haste, found his body. She at first fell into a kind of stupor. She could not absorb what was happening. They had to bring her back to her bedroom where she spent a whole night shot through with spasms of weeping before she came to. As the days passed she began to hark back constantly to her lost happiness. She tried to recapture it, obsessively counting it all up, breaking it down into the tiniest parcels:

> My happy home life lasted 29 years, 6 months and 6 days, and just as the memorable hour when I gave him my hand was a Sunday, so was it a Sunday when he was taken from me. That makes 29 years, 334 months, 1,540 weeks, 10,781 days or 258,744 hours. *Pater Noster, Ave Requiem, Gloria Patri* and much alms giving.

The calendar, strewn with memories, gave her ample opportunity to revisit the past. Thus, on the following February 12th, the anniversary of their marriage, she wrote to a friend:

> Last year I was celebrating this day as the happiest of my life, but actually it still is, for the memory of my happiness is too deeply anchored in my poor heart where it is now fastened to the most atrocious pain. I spent all this day in utter solitude, shut up in my office surrounded by portraits of our beloved sovereign. For long hours I was lost in my vanished happiness, not without feeling some remorse for not having sufficiently enjoyed it when there was still time.

In the meantime, they should do away with her wifely wardrobe! She wrote, "What I'm looking forward to impatiently are my shroud and my coffin. They will reunite me with the sole object of desire my heart has ever known."

In the meantime, she decided to dress only in black and admitted into her court only women dressed in black as well. She had her bedroom draped in black and in future would use only black-bordered notepaper for her correspondence. She cut the magnificent mane of blond hair of which she had been so proud. Refusing any kind of make-up, she went so far as to enjoin all the noble ladies to do likewise. But on this last point, the petulant countess Auersperg had the last word: "Am I not mistress of my own face? It was given to me by God, not the government!"

Her sorrow was not unmixed with something of a guilty conscience. Had she not smothered her husband, depriving him of opportunities to show his mettle? It was discovered after his death that this man deemed inconsequential by the day's standards had unbeknownst to everyone a remarkable talent: he had a gift for finance. She'd given him a free hand in this domain. He'd taken advantage of it and increased his holdings. He had earned a considerable fortune – 18,978,178 florins – and the admirable art collection he amassed is to this day the pride of Austria. In our times he'd have become a world-class magnate. Posthumously, his reputation grew. He too had been, in his own way, a great man.

Marie-Antoinette was not yet ten when her father died. She no doubt missed him. But the worst of it was that she would have to bear the full brunt of her mother's mourning. She spent the crucial years of early adolescence in the company of a mother obsessed by the memory of her lost happiness, whose joy in life had dried up, and who retreated into a narrow religiosity. Maria Theresa had even entertained the notion in her early widowhood of abandoning power to live out her days in a cloister. But she quickly changed her mind. She no doubt realized that the contemplative life did not suit her temperament, much given to action and movement. But above all, she had excellent reasons for staying in power. After all, as a good mother, she needed to set her children up in life. Most of them had not yet settled down. And she harbored the greatest worries about her eldest son Joseph's ability to succeed her.

And it is here where we see at work her second great passion: that for the Hapsburg dynasty*.

Matrimonial strategies

By the middle of the 18th century, the house of the Hapsburgs had seen better days. It had lost Spain. In Madrid her cousins no longer reigned. In their place were those of the king of France, the Bourbons. However, the surviving branch in Vienna had got in return the ex-Spanish Low Countries (present-day Belgium); and although it had to give up the Kingdom of Naples, it retained two powerful provinces in Italy, Lombardy and Tuscany. Her father, the emperor Charles VI, had for a long time cherished the hope of reconquering the Spanish throne, and then at least of recovering the lost Italian territory. He therefore competed relentlessly, but in vain, with the Bourbons. Maria Theresa quickly learned that her

---

* This terminology is indicative of the role reversal between Maria Theresa and her husband. Logically, the children should have been called "of Lorraine" or "of Lorraine-Hapsburg" or at least "of Hapsburg-Lorraine" to include their father's name. This was sometimes the case in France when Marie-Antoinette's Austrian descent was to be overlooked. But after the transfer of the Lorraine, the heritage was purely Hapsburg. The literature thus ends the Lorraine line with duke Leopold, and all the descendents of the Emperor Francis I appear under the Hapsburg column.

real interests lay elsewhere. The war following her accession to the throne had cost her Silesia, which King Frederick II of Prussia had snatched in a surprise attack. She realized she was at the mercy of her insatiable neighbor's appetite for land grabbing. And, horror of all horrors, her neighbor's states harbored a den of Calvinists, and he himself was an avowed atheist! She felt she needed to strengthen the ties with the other great Catholic dynasty against the man she called "the monster" in whom she saw the devil incarnate. Yesterday the Bourbons were her enemies; tomorrow they would be her friends.

Even before the spectacular switching of alliance to France that she got rolling in 1755 – while she was pregnant with Marie-Antoinette – she had already begun to infiltrate the Bourbon dynasty by a series of marriages. She killed two birds with one stone. Catholic Europe did not offer many choices when it came to marrying off her many children. By setting her sights on the marriageable Bourbons, she acquired thrones for her sons and daughters, and thus also got an insider's view of the various sovereigns' foreign policy. And if all went well, if all her offspring applied themselves to procreating as assiduously as she had, by the next generation all the masters of Catholic Europe would be of her blood. This peaceable annexation was preferable to the fragile conquests won at too high a price through war. And she hoped thereby to gain for herself a type of immortality: "You would like to see yourself reborn in a hundred different branches," her son Joseph would say to her.

She would have been shocked to learn that she was using her children for political ends. After all, it was the custom at the time; that's what royal families did. But her situation was particularly ambiguous. While she sought at will, without seeking their opinion, possible marriage partners for them, trying to hit upon the most advantageous matches, she forgot that she herself had held out for her own choice of husband. What is more, since her own marriage was so successful, she imagined that all were like hers. She was imprudent enough to promise her daughters happiness, forgetting that her own home life, because of its role reversal, was perfectly atypical. Docility toward an imposed spouse who is master in his own home obviously was no guarantee of success. Actually, she was intelligent and honest enough to admit that if push came to shove, for her the interests of the dynasty took precedence over the happiness of the individuals who composed it. But this was the type of question she did not like to think about and that she faced only when absolutely necessary.

She therefore deployed her vast stores of energy to acquire Bourbon spouses for her children, both boys and girls.

In 1760 her eldest son Joseph at first married the exquisite Isabel of Parma, doubly a Bourbon, as her grandfathers were Philip V of Spain and Louis XV. He was madly in love with her. When she died three years later, he said he would not remarry unless he was given her youngest sister Maria Luisa. But she was already promised to the prince of Asturias. The empress moved mountains to convince the king of Spain to break this engagement, but in vain*. Joseph had to make do with a Bavarian.

For her second son, Leopold, Maria Theresa managed to sweep up an infanta: Maria Luisa of Bourbon. She acquiesced without regret to the condition imposed by the Spanish king: that Tuscany, detached from Austrian inheritance, would be attributed to the young man's individual sovereignty. This was a couple after her own heart. They were a well-matched pair, close and fertile, and dedicated to the prosperity of the archduchy. They did just as much as she had for the dynasty's future; in twenty-seven years they gave her sixteen grandchildren.

As for the daughters, the oldest, Marianne, was not marriageable as she was handicapped from birth and a chronic invalid. The next, the lovely Maria Christina, was unusually intelligent, and had inherited all of her mother's best qualities. The empress kept her useful, having her marry a younger son of the house of Saxony. The couple would govern Hungary in her name, then the Low Countries. For those who followed, she went hunting for Bourbons. Louis XV, recently widowed by Maria Leszczynska's death, was put forward for Elisabeth. He wasn't the least bit interested. But he did ask if she was pretty. She certainly had been, remarkably so, but smallpox had just the year before disfigured her forever.

For the rest of them – four in all – Maria Theresa poured over the list of candidates. It contained only three possible princes, all very young: the duke of Parma Ferdinand de Bourbon; the king of Naples Ferdinand I, both born in 1751; and the dauphin of France Louis Auguste, born in 1754. They were the right age for her three youngest daughters. She risked having Maria Amalia, born in 1746, passed over, but managed to get her engaged to the duke of Parma, having to wait, of course, until he came of age. In

---

* Joseph had a narrow escape. Maria Luisa of Parma became the queen of Spain as the wife of Charles IV. Her capriciousness and violent temper, and her liaison with her favorite Godoy were so scandalous that Napoléon could later use them as an excuse to intervene. Goya painted an impressive portrait of her.

the artful network of royal alliances, this marriage took up where Joseph's had dropped off. In order to safeguard the links with Spain and France, the brother replaced the dead sister. For the king of Naples, she reserved Maria Josepha, born the same year. When smallpox carried her off on the eve of her departure for Italy the empress quickly substituted the next in line. The year younger Marie-Charlotte would become queen of Naples under her more familiar Italian name of Maria Carolina. All she had to do now was conquer for her baby daughter the most prestigious throne, the one indispensable to the house of Austria's security, that of France. It would not be easy.

Pawn of a political alliance

The French-Austrian alliance was fragile and Maria Theresa knew it. She also realized that up until then she was its principal beneficiary. It was vital to her because of the continuing threat of imperialist Prussia. In France, on the other hand, people began to see the alliance as shoddy goods. Already when she originally switched allegiance to France in 1756, Louis XV's decision to accept it met with a lot of resistance. Upholders of tradition, obsessed with the memories of the 17th century wars, still saw the Hapsburgs as a threat. And la Pompadour's enemies were against the negotiations just because she was for them. Within the royal family itself, the dauphin son of Louis XV was hostile to it, for these same reasons and because his Saxon wife had suffered at the hands of the Austrian court. There was only one argument in favor of a treaty: it would perhaps help prevent war in Central Europe, thereby letting France off the hook to devote all its energies to countering England's influence overseas. Wrong. It instead brought on the Seven Years War, seven long years of exhausting warfare that financially ruined both France and Austria with nothing to show for it but a return to square one – small consolation for the Austrian court. Prussia came out of it in a pitiful state too. But for the French, the results were abysmal. After waging war on both land and sea, they saw their efforts paid off by having the English grab most of their colonies. Why hadn't they cultivated Prussia's friendship rather than fight a war simply to please the empress?

With the exception of Louis XV, who'd wanted the Austrian alliance because he believed in its long-term advantages, there was hardly anyone to defend it but Choiseul's faction. At the time, Choiseul was the head of foreign affairs and had made the alliance one of the pillars of his foreign policy. When Maria Theresa put out feelers about a possible marriage between her daughter and the heir to the throne, he lent his enthusiastic support. After all, he had his own future to consider. If the king should die, what a trump card it would be if he had the new queen on his side! He swore he'd make the match.

It took a lot of doing to persuade Louis XV: having Austrian archduchesses for Naples and Parma was all well and good. But for the throne of France? The matter had to be studied. Would it not be better to secure the house of Savoy, less prestigious to be sure, but which held key border positions? In Vienna only one candidate got his vote: Joseph II's daughter by Isabel of Parma, another Maria Theresa, who, it turns out, was his own great-granddaughter*. She was eight years younger than the dauphin. But there was no hurry to procreate, as there were heirs to spare, so the difference in age was not a major concern. The aging king was made of paternal stuff; he took tenderly toward the idea of finding in her something of his departed daughter and granddaughter. Alas, she too died before the project could get under way.

That left Marie-Antoinette's candidacy, for which there was no particular sentimental attachment. She was up against a formidable adversary, the dauphin's own mother, Marie-Josèphe of Saxony, who shared her late husband's aversion for Austria, for Choiseul and for the archduchesses, and who in any case had her own ideas about who should marry her son: she wanted one of her own nieces. Louis XV liked and admired his daughter-in-law, and the feeling was mutual. He did not press his authority; he preferred persuasion. Since she wanted to be agreeable to him, she let herself be persuaded. But she advised him to keep the prospect dangling before the empress to take maximum advantage of the situation. She perhaps was hoping he would eventually change his mind, but her own passing in March of 1767 tolled the death knell for Saxon hopes. The cause of Marie-Antoinette was won.

Louis XV found it no less judicious to follow Marie-Josèphe's advice all the same. As she'd suggested, he refused to follow the ancient custom of inviting the girl to Versailles to finish her education in the vicinity of her fiancé. She had noted, "Once the archduchess was in Versailles, the French would surely not have the effrontery to send her back, so the Viennese court could prove all the more

---

* Louis XV's oldest daughter had married the duke of Parma. She'd given him three children, of whom the oldest, Isabel, had married Joseph. Isabel died at the age of 23, leaving the daughter in question.

churlish about accommodating the king in any small favors he might ask of them." In order to keep the empress "between fear and hope" he let the negotiations drag on. France's ambassador to Vienna was ordered to remain extremely circumspect. So Maria Theresa embarked on a coy game of cat and mouse with Durfort. She would try to wheedle him into uttering any word that could pass for a commitment; he would reply with an evasive move worthy of the best fencing master. She showered him with kindness, as if the deal had already been concluded. She spoke of her daughter as the future dauphine, as did her ministers. "How do you find the archduchess Antoinette?" Starhemberg asked Durfort point-blank. "Perfectly fine," came the ambassador's concise reply. The other persisted, "The dauphin will have in her a charming wife," which drew the cagey and discourteous reply "The morsel is tasty, and will be in good hands, if it comes to pass." This was surely not the way an ambassador speaks of his future queen.

The empress grew impatient. Her Paris representative, the count de Mercy-Argenteau, reassured her: according to Choiseul it was a done deal. She discreetly began to prepare her daughter for her future role. But she had to wait until June 1769 to receive the proposal through proper diplomatic channels. She then single-mindedly went about hastening events.

It was about time, after all, because worries about the future of the alliance were no less severe at the Austrian end. At twenty-three her oldest son Joseph had inherited his father's imperial crown, a glittering but empty distinction. He would have to wait to inherit his mother's real powers. She saw fit to bestow on him the title of co-ruler, which his father had used with so much discretion. She quickly saw that Joseph did not view things the same way; the role of a decorative figurehead did not suit him. He took initiatives, thwarted her efforts, and quietly resisted her, poisoning their relationship. What's worse, she saw that he had his own ideas and meant to apply them, and these ideas were totally contradictory to all the values she had always defended.

He had taken a keen interest in Frederick II and admired him despite his hatred for what he'd done to Austria. The little kingdom of Prussia was a parvenu on the European stage*, but in the hands of this man of steel, it had come a long way. Joseph dreamed of wresting Austrian hegemony back from Frederick II, but by using Frederick's methods. He too wanted to be an "enlightened despot"

---

* The Elector of Brandenburg, also ruler of the duchy of Prussia, had obtained the title of king only early in the century.

as the fashionable phrase went. He drew up plans for radical reform based on the prevailing rationalism. The nobility and the clergy would pay the price for this monarch's revolution, supported by the common people, on whom he would bestow the benefits of learning. As a reformer he was impatient, a man in a hurry. Between the rigorously logical conception of his plans and their execution he saw no need to wait. His mother, to whom he communicated his plans, went into a panic. She was not so upset by the projected reforms themselves; she'd put into effect some of her own, and would have liked to see more. What she could not countenance was the belief system behind them, the refusal to take into account the weight of tradition and the highly complicated situation on which the reforms were being imposed, as well as their disregard for people's differences and vulnerabilities. His plan showed an arrogant contempt for human beings; in it men were simply the stuff of political experimentation. And where was the place of the Christian faith in all this? Joseph no doubt remained at heart a believer, but he seemed to lack charity.

She also understood that his resentment of Frederick II would not last. If he met him, he'd fall under the spell of his magnetic personality. Already in 1766 he'd planned to meet him, using a journey to the battlefields of Bohemia and Saxony as an excuse. She put a stop to that, deciding that if you are going to sup with a "devil" such as the king of Prussia, you'd better have a very long spoon, and her neophyte son did not. He would say with regret "I lost a unique opportunity to see and get to know a man about whom – I cannot deny it – I am most curious." She gave in to his desire in 1769 because the Russian-Turkish conflict was endangering Eastern European stability and she needed to know how Frederick saw the situation. "The man is a genius," Joseph enthused after their meeting, when he'd been treated with the greatest courtesy, "he is remarkably well-spoken, but every one of his sentences hides a ruse." He also told her he was a "scoundrel." But was he not lying to his mother? She had the feeling he could be dragged into the most dangerous adventures either for Frederick or against him, but again, in imitation of him. And she was right, as we shall see. Upon leaving the interview, Frederick was of the same opinion about him: "He's consumed with ambition, and I have no idea whether he's aiming for Bavaria, Venice or the Lorraine, but Europe will surely be in flames as soon as he comes to power."

Fearing the political turbulence that might ensue, the old empress desired more than ever to strengthen ties with France, where this time she saw a genuine possibility of peace. Marie-Antoinette would be the "most tender guarantee of the unity that so happily exists between our two States," she wrote to Louis XV.

A very imperfect education

As soon as the marriage was certain, Maria Theresa started to prepare the girl for her great destiny. As a matter of fact, she did not know her daughter well at all. Upon closer acquaintance, what she learned was of some consternation to her. Marie-Antoinette had had no upbringing.

As is often the case with large families, the adults' energy gets blunted over the years. The overworked governesses demanded less of the youngest ones. In time they lost faith in the outcome of their efforts. All the more so as the children, coming one after another almost every year, blocked those efforts, supporting each other in their common resistance. The two youngest, "Toinette" and Maximilian, got the benefit one might say of their elder siblings' protection. They would do their homework for them and hide their mistakes. The girls especially evinced a clear-cut solidarity. Maria Carolina, three years older, adored Toinette, and showered her with an almost motherly affection. The two little girls were forever chattering and laughing, usually at others' expense, for they liked to poke fun. Rather than struggling to impose discipline on the little girl, the governess Madame von Brandeiss took the easy way out. She closed her eyes to it all, doing what she had to do to show the empress the results she wanted: faultless homework, in impeccable handwriting. Alas, the child, invited to take pen in hand by her mother, could only produce a horrible scribble, and had to admit the deception: all she did was trace in ink what had been previously penciled in. The child knew nothing. She would stumble through a reading passage; both her French and her German were more than questionable, and she could hardly string two words of Italian together. As for her general knowledge, better not even mention it! To this must be added the fact that her bearing left much to be desired. She had a freedom of movement out of keeping with her new status. In short, her education had to be redone from A to Z.

And there was very little time left. Maria Theresa went about it methodically. She broke the counter-productive complicity between the sisters by separating them, and did everything possible to fabricate an accomplished dauphine – the way in more recent times they manufacture movie stars. It was in France that she would have to shine, so it was France that she called on for help. Choiseul was asked to supply the needed personnel.

Thus the court witnessed the arrival of one Larseneur, a "curler" recommended by the minister's sister. There was a delicate problem: her excessively wide forehead had to be camouflaged. He did a marvelous job: "The style is simple, suitable, but at the same time very flattering to the face," the councilor Neny informed Austria's ambassador to Paris, "I'm convinced that our young women, who have for so long been piling mountains of curls atop their heads, will soon abandon them to be coiffed like the dauphine." Another Frenchman, the dentist Laveran, managed more or less to straighten her teeth, at the cost of extracting too many of them, much to the indignation of his counterpart later on in Versailles. As for poise and dance lessons, they recruited the best. The well-known dance instructor Noverre was the only one qualified to teach her the subtleties of the steps and configurations currently popular at court balls. She was good at it. To these lessons she owed her much admired goddess-like bearing and ethereal gait. And as for music, Vienna could easily compete with Versailles; they had everything they needed right at home. She was placed in the care of Gluck, who couldn't do much with her – she hadn't her mother's talents – but who left a big impression.

There was much to be done as regards French language and culture. To improve her pronunciation and help get rid of her accent, Maria Theresa thought she should hire diction coaches, and chose two French actors from a visiting troop. Choiseul talked her out of it: she must not expose the future dauphine to persons considered immoral, as actors were at the time. So she decided to kill two birds with one stone; she would entrust to a single tutor the tasks of teaching her French, of inculcating in her what she absolutely needed to know about French literature and history, and of introducing her to court etiquette. She gave the job of finding this rare bird, preferably a clergyman, to her ambassador. The ambassador consulted the minister Choiseul, who jumped at the chance, and asked his friend the bishop of Orleans to find him the right man, by which he meant of course someone from his own faction. They enlisted the support of a top curate in the service of the prominent archbishop of Toulouse, Loménie de Brienne, a man of questionable morals who dabbled in *philosophie*, a fact they naturally hid from the empress. But the candidate they chose was perfect: "Educated, straightforward and modest," the abbé de Vermond was a doctor of the Sorbonne, librarian of the College of the Four Nations, and according to Mercy, had all the necessary intellectual and moral qualifications. However, he had no teaching experience whatsoever and at the age of 33 was perhaps a bit young for the job. As soon as he arrived in Vienna in December 1768, he immersed himself in his work with a neophyte's zeal, and very quickly gained the affection of his pupil and the esteem of the empress.

The results were altogether a different matter. His little pupil was a darling, but rebelled against any kind of effort. It was impossible to hold her attention for more than five minutes. She may seem to be listening, but her mind was wandering. Vermond was obliged to admit his first disappointments to Mercy:

> She has more intelligence than was thought for a long time. Unfortunately this intelligence was not challenged until the age of twelve. Some laziness and much lightness of mind have rendered educating her more difficult. For six weeks I introduced literary principles. She understood when I presented clear ideas; her judgment was almost always correct, but I wasn't able to get her to deepen her understanding, even though I felt she was capable of it. It seemed to me one could only engage her mind by amusing her.

So he quickly gave up on assignments and highly structured lessons. He'd make do with chatting about this and that.

We mustn't be so naïve as to find in the solutions he adopted some forerunner of modern pedagogical methods. Just like Madame von Brandeiss before him, the abbé simply gave up. All his pupil had to do was turn on the charm – that winning charm inherited from her mother. She stole his heart, like so many others, with her gaiety, her smiles, her embarrassment when she did something silly, and even her simpering excuses. The poor cleric, for too long fed on dusty books, discovered for the first time all the enchantment of childhood. He would forgive her anything. And she was delighted with her conquest. The abbé arrived just at the right time. She was bored now that her beloved confidante-sister has been packed off to Naples. She couldn't do without him. She dragged him everywhere she went all day long, and included him in all of her amusements, to such an extent that her mother admonished her: "You are overwhelming the poor abbé." "No, mamma, can't you see he's having fun?" she replied.

They were both having fun. As a result, this singular style of education produced better results than one would have expected. The child in fact made considerable progress in French. With the abbé she heard a much purer French than that spoken in Vienna. He corrected her accent, pointed out her grammatical mistakes and told her how to avoid them. Compared to this significant progress, her shortcomings in spelling and handwriting didn't seem terribly important because he was sure that "she would hardly make any mistakes at all if she could just pay more sustained attention." She would arrive in Versailles speaking a more or less correct French with ease. But he did more than that; he trained her in the art of conversation, the life-blood of court society. He was intelligent, lively and witty, and he stimulated her sense of repartee, which would become one of her dominant traits.

But there was still the matter of her general education. After all, a princess needs a minimum of baggage in this domain. Unfortunately, the student was incorrigible. She would not read. The abbé gave up, which was a shame. Short on time, he would give her a mere glancing acquaintance with literature. He put his foot down about French history though. He managed to slip into their conversations enough anecdotes to give her the bare essentials of what she needed to know. No politics, of course. All they inculcated in her was one simple point of dogma: there was no salvation outside the French-Austrian alliance. Actually, she only learned the history of the most recent kings and the great families she would be living amongst at court. She was told how to greet each one with the appropriate title, but nothing that would enlighten her about the nature of their relationships: no overview, no perspective. As a result, she only saw the small picture. She developed a simplistic, Manichaean view of the world, seeing it as divided between those who are good and those who are evil. Thus everything became personal. She hadn't a clue of just how complex reality is. And worst of all, she had a habit of fluttering from one idea to the next without pursuing any of them.

It could be said that this type of education, which is supposed to be adapted to the child's mind, is only a first stage, needing to be deepened. But the problem is that it didn't come in time. Every stage of a child's education has its proper moment, and it was too late to get Marie-Antoinette started on her lessons and homework, too late to impose intellectual discipline. The abbé wasn't up to the task. In order to broaden her knowledge he would have had to make her read. But he couldn't; he lacked the necessary authority.

Such a waste. Whose fault was it? Everyone's and no one's. Maria Theresa was angry with herself for not overseeing her education closely enough, for having depended too much on the educational staff. But she also wondered about her daughter's character. She saw in her the same appetite for pleasure she herself had in her youth, along with the same formidable energy, using whatever means necessary to get what she wanted. But she lacked the counter-balancing traits of an open mind, attention to others, and quite frankly, intelligence. Not that she was stupid. She was of average intelligence, no more. But her mind was not trained early enough. She was only interested in herself and in her childish universe, which she refused to leave. When they tried to oust her from it, she slipped away. When her powers of seduction failed, she deployed prodigious amounts of energy to escape from what she didn't want to do. She was what we call a spoiled child.

Which doesn't mean she was a liar. The biographers who are enraptured by her sparkle and spontaneity are not wrong. Dissimulation did not come naturally to her. But she did tend to chatter on about nothing, without thinking first. It wasn't that she never lied either. Her mother witnessed that with the little homework-copying incident. But she didn't lie gratuitously. She resorted to it, like all children and other powerless people, in order to escape punishment. We can hardly fault her for that. Telling the truth is an adult luxury. And she was far from being an adult. Maria Theresa was riddled with anxiety. Nothing that she found out encouraged trust in the child or inclined her to loosen her hold on her, quite the opposite. She would perhaps look good in the court of France, thanks to the thin veneer of education she hurriedly acquired. But she was prepared neither psychologically nor morally to take on her new role, nor physically for that matter, as we've seen. At fourteen and a half, she had the body of a twelve year old. And she was about to enter those difficult teen years.

Last bits of advice

Maria Theresa was understandably in anguish as her daughter's departure date neared, all the more so as she now had added reasons to worry.

For a while now she'd been receiving upsetting news from France. She had always disapproved of Louis XV's personal life, scandalized not that he had mistresses – she'd long since lost any illusions about men on that score – but that he kept them under the same roof as his family. After la Pompadour's death, he could have been expected to settle down a bit. But there he was at it again, despite his sixty years, and with a woman of a more than dubious background. Maria Theresa's puritanism, exacerbated by widowhood, made her fear the worst for her daughter. In her unsettled imagination Versailles became a sink of perdition. As she would write a bit later to Mercy, France for her was "a nation with no religion, morals or feeling."

She made one last attempt at Marie-Antoinette's spiritual development. She thought better of sending her to meditate on the tombs of her ancestors, as she'd required of Josepha. Three years earlier when she was engaged to the king of Naples, Maria Theresa sent a terrified Josepha down into the lugubrious crypt of the Capuchin convent. She came back only to be confined to her deathbed, where she succumbed to smallpox. For Marie-Antoinette, a three-day retreat during Holy Week, under the direction of abbé de Vermond who'd since become her confessor, would do. Lacking the time for her daughter during the day, she had her sleep next to her on a folding bed at night so that she could instruct her. We can be sure that lessons in morality took up most of this time. But there were also topics that are more easily broached between mother and daughter in the darkness of a bedroom. Did she speak to her about married life, until then wrapped in the deepest mystery? Probably, for she must have sensed her apprehension. The young queen of Naples, traumatized by a first week of trying marital relations, had written to Madame von Brandeiss to tell her about her difficulties, recommending that she pamper her little sister, who herself would soon be undergoing similar trials. Surely no one said anything to Marie-Antoinette, but an intense solicitude and lots of veiled references must have troubled her. Maria Theresa tried to nip any sentimental illusions in the bud: "All happiness in a home comes from trust and mutual giving. Mad love doesn't last." Did Toinette dream of marrying Prince Charming? Most likely not, given the number of disappointing experiences among her sisters and sisters-in-law. If we can judge from the last three, the archduchesses mostly dreamed of the day when they could exchange their mother's authority for the presumably gentler rule of their husbands, whom they counted on subjugating. Then they'd be able to lead them a merry dance!

Maria Theresa must have suspected her daughter of harboring such hopes, so she took some preventive measures. In a letter given to her daughter upon arrival in France, she recommends obedience:

> Madame, my dear daughter,
> Thus you have arrived where fate has ruled you live. At least in terms of the loftiness of your state, you are the happiest of your sisters and of all princesses. You will find a tender father

who will also be your friend, as long as you merit it. Trust him completely; you will not regret it. Love him, obey him, try to guess his thoughts, I cannot overstate the matter at this moment when I'm losing you. It is this father, this friend, who consoles me and bolsters me, who is my only consolation, hoping that you will follow my advice to dedicate yourself to him and obey all his orders and instructions. About the dauphin I will say nothing. You know my delicacy on this point. A wife is entirely subject to her husband and must have no other concern than to please him and fulfill his wishes. The only real happiness in this world is a good marriage; I know whereof I speak. Everything depends on the wife, if she is pliant, gentle and cheerful.

A curious letter. A good one for Marie-Antoinette, who surely needed a sermon on obedience. It seems also, however, to be written for the king's eyes, just in case it came to his attention. The same dispatch contained a missive for him as well. For it is certain that Maria Theresa, whatever she said, had no intention of abandoning authority over her daughter to Louis XV.

As was the custom at the time, the girl brought with her a list of very precise parental instructions. The emperor, for instance, had left a sort of moralizing will entitled, *Instructions for my children, for their spiritual as well as temporal lives*. Overflowing with good intentions, it was merely a long-winded exposition of religious and moral commonplaces. It was addressed to no one in particular. Maria Theresa's advice on the other hand was striking, as it was always so carefully targeted. For each of her daughters on the eve of their departure, she drew up a thorough list of clear and concise recommendations adapted to each individual case.

The young bride thus received a long letter in two parts, clearly one more important than the other. The first, *Rules to be read every month*, concerned her religious duties: morning and evening prayer with examination of conscience, daily attendance at mass as well as vespers and benediction on Sundays, an attitude of reflective composure in church, devotions every six weeks. There should also be a quarter of an hour of spiritual readings every morning – "You will always inform me of what book you are using." And she must open no other book without her confessor's permission. "In France there are many books full of enjoyment and erudition, but among which there are behind this respectable veil [sic] many pernicious ones concerning religion and morals." She could not finish without the inevitable sentimental note: "Never forget the anniversary of your dear late father's death, or mine when the time comes. In the meantime you can take that of my birth to pray for me." And there was a rather unexpected political note about the Jesuits – "You must entirely refrain from expressing your opinion – either for or against."

Much more technical, the *Particular instructions* that followed were a sort of manual of correct conduct at the court of France. It seems to refer point by point to her perceived faults: "Take on no recommendation, listen to no one if you want peace of mind. Be not curious; this is a point about which you give me much worry... Respond to everyone with grace and dignity; you can if you want to. You must also learn to refuse... Suffer no shame in asking everyone's counsel and do nothing on your own initiative... Don't carry tales about our domestic affairs here; they are tedious and of little interest." She was to follow Starhemberg's advice in everything, although he would soon be replaced by Mercy. The rest dealt with their monthly exchange of letters that would enable Maria Theresa to pursue a lively correspondence designed to keep her daughter closely tied to her.

And as she didn't dare hope that her scatterbrained daughter would follow her instructions, she set up a close surveillance network around her to guide her and keep her in check.

CHAPTER 3

AN ADOLESCENT UNDER THE INFLUENCE

In the sobs and embraces of leave-taking Marie-Antoinette groaned: how would she ever live so far away, without news of her family? Her mother put her mind at ease right away on that score; they would write to each other at least once a month. But the others, how would she keep up with them? Maria Theresa took care of everything.

The spider web

Since all the news came through her, she would take care of distributing it all. Her letters to Marie-Antoinette contained all the elements of a family chronicle. During the first year, the empress filled up a good half of the pages she sent with news of births and deaths, illnesses and travels, all accompanied by heartfelt comments. The letters paint an idyllic picture: material difficulties are nothing when mutual understanding prevails, as it does, because sisters and sisters-in-law are, apparently, all in love with their respective husbands. There is one exception, however, which cannot be denied since the French court has got wind of it: Maria Amalia's eccentricities have managed within a few months to turn the duchy of Parma upside down; and she would not listen to reason. Maria Theresa has stopped writing to her, banishing her to silence. The lesson for the dauphine was clear; this is what happens to rebellious black sheep who stray from the goodly path.

Marie-Antoinette showed no sign of sympathy for her sister over her ostracism, of which she dutifully approved. Maria Amalia was nine years older, and they were never particularly close. But her mother's chronicles didn't have enough news about those she loved. She wanted to write to them directly and solicited permission to do so as soon as she left. "I do not believe you should write to your family," her mother replied, "outside of particular circumstances – that is to say for sending your good wishes and letters of condolences – and to the emperor, with whom you must sort things out on this point. Also, I believe you should continue writing to your uncle and aunt, as well as to Prince Albert." Thus she had permission to write only to her father's brother and sister, her oldest sister Maria Christina's husband, and her brother Joseph – who was not only 14 years older but also the emperor, and therefore something of a father figure. None of these figures fulfilled the child's need for affection and intimacy. She asked to correspond with her old governess Madame von Brandeiss, who had saved her from many a chastisement. The answer at first was yes, on condition that nothing personal was discussed. But the fear of indiscretions won out, and permission was denied in the end.

And with her dear Maria Carolina? Yes, of course. The queen of Naples had taken the initiative and manifested her desire to write to her. "I find no difficulty with that," Maria Theresa explained. "She will only tell you what is reasonable and useful; her example must serve as a model and as encouragement, her situation having been and still being more difficult than yours... You may, therefore, write to her, but everything must be phrased in such a way that it can be read by everyone." The two young women could hardly fail to follow this last piece of advice, as the empress soon made it clear that their letters would pass through Vienna, from whence she would redirect them. This was so as to take advantage of the special couriers exempt from the surveillance that regular mails were subjected to; but also so that she herself would be the first to read them. The correspondence with Naples for these years has not been found, so we do not know exactly what the sisters wrote to each other under their mother's watchful eye, but it is unlikely given the circumstances that they exchanged any intimacies.

Did such constraints kill off Marie-Antoinette's desire for epistolary effusions? It doesn't seem so, as in 1773 her mother, trying to reassure her, wrote: "If something should happen to the family or to me, we shall send special dispatch riders; so in future put your tender and charming heart at ease regarding the long delays, which happen so easily; a mishap could occur with any delivery... but, seeing the tender interest you have for us, your desires will be met, and each week you will receive a letter from your sisters and brothers, who do so with great pleasure so that you too will be pleased..." But it seems that the brothers and sisters, even relaying each other, did not keep up the pace.

In thus controlling her children's relationships through their correspondence, Maria Theresa built, with the rigor so characteristic of her, a vast spider web of which she would occupy the center, and hold in its filaments her submissive and cohesive family members. Political motives certainly had their part in this insistence on controlling them. But emotional reasons, some unconscious, were capital. She had always been intensely possessive. The loss of her husband exacerbated her motherly possessiveness. She enveloped in the same imperious and protective love her subjects and her numerous offspring. This woman in whom naturalness constantly bubbled up, felt a carnal, instinctive, vital attachment to her children and her lands. She could not bear for them to be taken from her, not through selfishness, nor even through a desire to dominate, but because they were part and parcel of her. The loss of Silesia was like an amputation for her. She was slow to abandon her daughters to the families she married them into. For her, the preeminence of these families was not a *sine qua non*, each was judged on its individual merits. Didn't she herself remain at home when she married? It was her husband who was uprooted. The exile demanded of her youngest daughter was no reason to cut the cord. Quite the contrary; the reins must be tightened. The child would have two families. But her mother hoped that her family of adoption would take a distant second place in her heart, well behind the only real one, that of her blood.

Keeping two sets of correspondence

In this motherly spider web, Marie-Antoinette, because of her tender age, was given privileged treatment. The gaps in her education gave Maria Theresa an excellent excuse to follow her closely, and she set up a sophisticated double-entry correspondence to do so.

First of all she demanded of her daughter a monthly exchange of letters on a fixed schedule: "At the beginning of every month I shall send post to Paris; in the meantime you can prepare your letters and send them off as your post arrives." These letters would not go through the ordinary mails, which were uncertain. Maria Theresa knew this only too well, as her own censors assiduously snooped. Occasionally there might be an entirely trustworthy Paris-bound traveler to carry the letters; otherwise the letters would go via special courier. Austria's ambassador to Paris, count de Mercy-Argenteau, would be responsible for transmission. He would pass on her mother's letters and take hers in return. They quickly saw that by having them pass through Belgium, where they were added to the secret mails from the Belgian Low Countries, they didn't have to finance the remainder of the trip. This detour did not affect the tempo of the exchange; if all went well it only took nine or ten days for the post to get between Vienna and Paris. As it turned out, it was not necessary to prepare her replies in advance; this way she had about five days to write at her leisure, taking into account all the fresh news just received. Thus a regular exchange of letters was set up; as a general rule one letter dated at the beginning of the month, and the other at the middle.

Maria Theresa wanted very precise details about her daughter's doings: her assiduousness as concerns religious duties, her readings, her health, and even details about her menstrual cycle[*]. She demanded to know the titles of the books she was reading. Anticipating today's correspondence courses, she wanted to check that she had read them, so she required book reports. Clearly, this already smacked of an inquisition. But she did realize that the child would not tell her everything; and besides, she needed to see things otherwise than through the eyes of a scatterbrained child. So she had two reliable men, the abbé de Vermond and the count de Mercy-Argenteau, watch her daughter very closely.

They agreed that Mercy would add his own reports via the same special couriers carrying the dauphine's letters. Totally distinct from the mostly political, official dispatches in German, these purely private accounts had to escape the notice of the Austrian ministry. Only the Chancellor Kaunitz knew of their existence, but he paid them no heed. It was "an innocent pleasure" that his sovereign indulged in to satisfy her maternal passion. Mercy had to address them as simple private letters to *The Empress-Queen* and send them, duly sealed, in another envelope to the counselor Neny, who would deliver them to her unopened. "Not that I have the least doubt as to his fidelity," she made clear, "but... one can never be too cautious, because anything can happen; I just wanted to be sure that you and I alone would be the recipients." Better yet, she required him to divide his private reports into two parts, on different sheets of paper. Highly confidential information would be indicated by the Latin phrase *tibi soli*, "for you alone," and thus would not even be read by her faithful Pichler, to whom she dictated her letters, even though he was as silent as a tomb. "Every two or three months you will send me a special report that I can make public, but the logs

---

[*]   The 19th century publishers Arneth and Geffroy, in conformity with their sense of decency, eliminated these passages, without informing the reader.

will be for me alone. I will personally burn them, as they will surely contain details that could offend."

In effect, she demanded of Mercy a minute daily log of everything Marie-Antoinette did and said. It was a lot to ask. He was therefore at pains to tell her that it would not always be possible to meet her expectations. He must "alternate between the logs and the detailed accounts." When the court was in Compiègne or at Fontainebleau, for example, where the ambassadors were invited, he was able to observe her himself and would adopt the log method. But when the court was at Versailles, where he only had access to her through a limited number of protocol visits, he had to resort to looser accounts. Unfortunately, the court was often in Versailles. However, to compensate for this handicap, he luckily had a trick up his sleeve: an informer on the inside.

This informer was none other than the abbé de Vermond, taken into the dauphine's household thanks to his new job as her reader. He was the lynchpin of the surveillance network, as he would live in close contact with her. This appointment, arranged long in advance on Choiseul's advice, almost foundered at the last minute. The empress knew that it was an inviolable rule that a foreign princess could bring with her none of her previous servants. Well-loved nurses or governesses had to go back home. This rule accomplished two things: the newcomer would more quickly become acclimated to France, and it helped prevent a spy network from being formed around her. However, an exception was made for confessors, because it was customary to respect the newcomer's religious needs. Maria Carolina, for instance, had brought hers to Naples.

To get around this rule and keep one of her servants with her daughter, the empress found the ideal candidate in Vermond. Not able to propose him as her tutor, as married women were presumed no longer to need one, she sought for him an appointment as a reader. Since he was not Austrian but French, he would perhaps be exempt from the exclusionary rule. And to make doubly sure, she had him made confessor to the future dauphine. Since in any case the child had to change her confessor because the Society of Jesus had just been banished from France, she cleverly gave her this French clergyman, one she assumed was well regarded at court. She was wrong about that. Although Vermond was of impeccable morals and unimpeachable faith, he belonged to the faction of Choiseul and Loménie de Brienne, archbishop of Toulouse. The dauphin's entourage warned the archbishop of Paris Christophe de Beaumont of this, and he vetoed the appointment, on the perfectly legitimate grounds that being something of a scholar, Vermond had no credentials whatsoever as a director of conscience. A flustered Mercy sent Marie-Antoinette off to ask her "dear grandfather" to intercede. Louis XV, caught between his grandson and granddaughter, took a page from Solomon's book and cut the fruit in half: Vermond would not hear Marie-Antoinette's confession, but he would be her reader.

Maria Theresa and Mercy breathed a deep sigh of relief. Over the years they would tremble at the mere thought that Vermond might resign or be dismissed. "His loss would be irreparable, and make things very difficult for me," Mercy confessed. It was from him, after all, that he got most of his concrete information about the dauphine. In order for Mercy not to be seen too often in Versailles, the abbé traveled almost every day to Paris to bring him his daily harvest of news. If he couldn't go himself, he sent a letter, by special courier of course. So Mercy's correspondence with the empress was based on his with Vermond. Once in a while one of the abbé's letters would get as far as Vienna; but most often these verbal or written reports were simply harvested for what Mercy called his "accounts."

Vermond was not the ambassador's only supplier, however. In the *tibi soli* of 16 November the ambassador explained, laying it on rather thick in order to make himself look good, how he managed to find other informers:

> I secured the services of three of Madame the Archduchess's lower-echelon personnel, one of her chambermaids and two chamber boys who report to me exactly what goes on inside; day by day I am informed of H.R.M.'s conversations with abbé Vermond from whom she hides nothing; the marquise de Durfort tells me down to the most minor detail what is said among Mesdames her aunts; and I have yet other individuals and means of finding out what is said when Madame la dauphine visits the king. To this I add what I see personally, so that there is not an hour of the day about which I am unable to report what Madame the Archduchess might have said, or done, or heard...

Marie-Antoinette was thus subjected to what can only be called systematic espionage. She couldn't lift a finger without its being known in high places. The least little prank on her part was greeted with double or triple reproofs. To Vermond's criticisms Mercy's were added; after which orders arrived from Vienna that somehow tallied with the two colleagues' reprimands. She wondered how word of these little peccadilloes ever got to her mother's ears. Travelers returning from France were blamed, or the royal-watching press, or even the king of Prussia's spies. But we who have access to most of their correspondence see the hand of Mercy at work. Not satisfied with merely betraying her daughter's trust and reporting all her doings, he commented on how she reacted to her mother's letters; and according to whether she was fearful, tearful or annoyed, he suggested to the empress how she should respond. But care must be taken! She must do nothing to "out" her agents. If she were ever to allude to something that only Vermond and Mercy knew about, the child would figure it out, and they would lose her trust.

And the reprimands came raining down harder and harder on the dauphine's head. Even at this distance, she could not escape the inquisitorial gaze of a mother who was never satisfied, who redoubled her surveillance, her advice, her orders and her warnings. She preached, she scolded, she sermonized and she stormed. Far away, invisible but omnipresent, Maria Theresa hovered like a supernatural presence from whose gaze, like God's, it was impossible to escape. She took on the mantle of a terrifying supreme judge, ready to cast her daughter into the penumbra, making her feel all the more guilty through constant emotional manipulation. The least show of negligence was more than merely failing at a given task; it was a betrayal of her mother. More than a mistake, more than a moral failure, it was like a crime of *lèse-maternité*. The unhappy child moaned, "Is there nothing I can possibly do to prove to my mother that I love her?" "I love the empress, but I fear her, even from afar; even in writing, I am never at ease with her." She convinced herself that her mother didn't love her. And Maria Theresa wondered why her daughter's letters rang false and inconsistent, as she complained to Mercy! It would be surprising if it were otherwise. Things got to such a point that Mercy, who was little given to tenderness but eager for efficacy, pointed out to his mistress that a few compliments might be in order to encourage the poor child's willingness to comply.

Reading the three heavy tomes published by Arneth and Geffroy, we can't help feeling very uncomfortable. It is astonishing that the publishers did not feel the same discomfort[*], no more than did Stefan Zweig, who reserved his indignation for the unfortunate Louis XVI. It is clear from this deliberately rigged correspondence,

---

[*] Our discomfort is shared, however, by Georges Girard, who published in 1933 the complete, unexpurgated *Correspondence between Maria Theresa and Marie-Antoinette.*

written with a sort of blithe obliviousness, that the child was being set up. They constantly lied to her; they swaddled her tightly in a network of checks and controls at every juncture, and what is more, they even went so far as to use her as a pawn on the political chessboard when necessary, as we shall see.

Actually, the three collaborators did not have the same motives, so they didn't all push their demands to the same point, and therefore did not all bear equal responsibility for the perverse results of their efforts.

We mustn't blame Maria Theresa too much. It was entirely natural for her to want to surround her child with wise counselors to guide her and help her avoid making silly mistakes; we cannot fault her for that. But anxiety increased her severity. She had been sorely tried by the disappointments both Joseph and Maria Amalia caused her. Had she failed in educating some of her children properly? She was terrified that her youngest daughter's thoughtlessness could compromise her brilliant future. She knew only too well that Marie-Antoinette was not ready, and that it was her own fault. She castigated herself. She should have molded her character, let her make her own mistakes and suffer the consequences; she should have slowly instilled in her a sense of responsibility. But it was too late. It would take too much time, and above all, now that she was dauphine, it was too risky to give her that freedom. She couldn't help being fearful, "I know her laziness, her lack of discipline and application." Later on she would look back and see in her daughter's letters so many warning signs – she was in danger; she was losing her way; she was heading for disaster...

For her, the straightjacket around her daughter was only the lesser of two evils, and a makeshift effort at that. She would like to limit the pressure she was putting her daughter under. She would not ask the young dauphine more than she was capable of. She correctly saw that she was incapable of understanding the first thing about the aims of the various groups that vied for the king's attention. She would like to protect her from the intrigues, the cabals and the corruption, to keep her pure and innocent. She sent her off to France without giving her the most minimal information about the world she was about to enter. Unlike the young duchess de Bourgogne, whose father had given her a complete run-down on Louis XIV's court, Marie-Antoinette knew nothing. Above all else, she should stay away from affairs of state. She must apply herself to pleasing the king by her grace and cheerfulness; as for the rest she must blindly obey Mercy's orders and ask no questions. But Mercy should make political demands, according to the empress, only if and when serious situations arose where Austria's interests were at stake, and even then only with the greatest caution, for she did not want to compromise her daughter's position and therefore her happiness. She would like her to remain on the sidelines most of the time. She forgot that in courts like that of France, everything was political. Even a choice of a lady-in-waiting or a lady of the bedchamber was political; and a simple gesture – a smile, a word, even silence – could set off storms. She forgot also that the choice of ministers was crucial for Austria.

Things therefore did not go exactly as she'd planned. Especially since her two agents saw their roles differently, and of course their personalities inevitably came into play. It is worthwhile looking more closely at these two men set in place between her and her daughter, because they would outlive Maria Theresa and accompany Marie-Antoinette throughout her life, until the Revolution, and even a bit beyond.

The abbé de Vermond

Among Marie-Antoinette's servants, no one triggered more criticism from both contemporary observers and future historians than Vermond. His constant presence in the young lady's company earned him the jealousy of all the other candidates to her exclusive trust, like Madame Campan, who painted a ferocious portrait of him. Not only that, the fact that he belonged to the Choiseul-Loménie de Brienne faction earned him the reputation of being sympathetic to the new Enlightenment ideas, and the enmity therefore of the religious party, and more seriously, of the dauphin himself. As for the historians hostile to *"l'Autrichienne"* ["that Austrian woman"], they denounced the services he rendered to a foreign power and accused him of treason.

Vermond's misfortunate was finding himself in a false and precarious position that he neither foresaw nor could control. Insofar as we can guess, for we only know him through those of his letters Mercy kept and forwarded to Vienna, he seemed to be ill at ease in his job. He was not a very ambitious man. Quite ugly, he had neither suavity nor an easy manner; in other words, he did not fit the picture of the usual court abbé. Because of the modesty of his origins – he was the son of a village surgeon – he could not aim very high. A pure stroke of fate tore him away from his quiet library to throw him into the Viennese court, into the inner circle of the empress and the archduchess. Was his head turned by such high favor? No doubt. But he took his role as educator very seriously and was attached to his pupil. He was delighted to learn that he would continue in his post in Versailles. Can we reproach him for taking advantage of this to solicit benefits from the church? Just about everyone in a similar situation did. He asked for and obtained two abbeys together worth an income of 50,000 pounds. This was not enough to enrich his family. But it was some protection; he would have somewhere to go if he fell out of favor. Even better, if he found it impossible to remain at court, he could leave, for his two abbeys guaranteed him a degree of freedom.

Unlike Mercy, he was a dependent of the French court, not of the empress. If his spying activities were discovered, he could wind up in the Bastille. If he lost favor, he could be summarily discarded. And sure enough, after the fall of Choiseul, he would soon have only Marie-Antoinette's support in the court of France. Without her trust and backing, he would be lost. His job, after all, consisted in imposing lessons on her, getting her to do her homework, and making sure she stayed on the straight and narrow – enough to make anyone irksome. In February 1771, less than a year after her daughter's marriage, Maria Theresa wrote to Mercy: "Perhaps my daughter would be rather glad to be rid of a man who could prove inconvenient during her moments of self-indulgence." The unfortunate man was well aware of this, and did everything he could to keep the favor, not of his ex-patroness in Vienna but of the teenager who would one day be queen of France. The one he served was Marie-Antoinette.

He did so without servility, and in her interests. He undertook to perfect her education. He tried harder than ever to get her to read. He had a considerable trump card: the threat of his being fired. If she didn't read, what need had she of a reader? Very early on, Mercy explained to her that if that were the case, "He could not remain at court without his stay smacking of intrigue." She replied to him that, "for nothing in the world would she consent to the abbé's being sent away" and promised to hit the books soon. She would devote every afternoon between three and four to the task. Vermond managed to get her to absorb Hume's *History of England*, the *Letters* from the count de Tessin to his student the prince of Sweden, some *Bagatelles morales et dissertations* by one abbé Coyer, and a non-identified text by Bossuet. But the reading hour was often shortened by a visit to her aunts, or dropped altogether in favor of a walk in the fresh air, and there was no question of studies at all during carnival season.

He could not get her to write the book reports her mother

required. "What shall I do? Mamma demands that I write about what I've read," she pleaded with him; to which he replied, "Surely, you will tell her the truth, Madame." And he "took the opportunity to remind her how little reading she had done. She agreed, but thinking about a way to satisfy H.M. in the future, she pointed out to me a number of difficulties." The main one was that a reader is not supposed to teach basic writing skills. It would be surprising if he were present while she wrote. As she put it, "It would get about that you are dictating my letters." It was unthinkable to admit that she was still at the stage of childish writing exercises now that she was a married woman! The abbé concurred with this reasoning and added some of his own. The confidentiality imposed by her mother obliged her to keep their letters secret, which made it hard to send detailed book reports. And she would never apply herself to it without him. Would the empress perhaps make do with a "shortened report"? Needless to say, she never received a single one.

What Vermond was careful not to say is that he wrote his pupil's correspondence, or at least edited it. The dauphine knew that her mother would examine her letters for their language, style and spelling as much as for their content. Vermond's intervention is quite clear in the first few months. As she made progress she became more autonomous and finally wrote to Maria Theresa herself. But for all official correspondence – letters of congratulations, well-wishing and sundry notes, and for her requests to Louis XV, who preferred that people write to him rather than address him personally, she could not do without the services of this secret secretary. He was indispensable.

She also knew that she could count on him to answer the thousands of questions that her new life could pose at any given moment. And she sensed that he wanted to protect her. He never ceased to praise the goodness of her character; he played down the neglect of her duties, and found excuses for her weaknesses. "Until now she has made no major errors," he wrote to Mercy in October 1770 in a letter clearly meant for the empress. "Y.E. knows himself how she listens and tries to correct her own missteps. Each day I admire her gentleness, and I dare say, her docility." Was the abbé over-indulgent? Assuredly. Should we therefore accuse him, as Madame Campan did, of having "left his pupil in ignorance by clever but culpable design" so as to ingratiate himself to her? More energetic educational methods might have produced better results. But would they have given her what she needed most in those first few months of exile, tried and true affection? It would later prove necessary for him to be more critical, when the queen's self-indulgence would take a dangerous turn, but even then he would express himself in mild terms, with "a gentleness full of compassion and pain," that would not alienate the queen's friendship.

Vermond confided in no one; we only know him through Mercy's reports. The ambassador was quick to affirm that they were of a like mind. But was their understanding as complete as he would have us believe? When he took on the reader post, the abbé thought his duty would be confined to completing Marie-Antoinette's education. As time passed, he realized that his spying took precedence over his pedagogical functions. He was not terribly proud of this. He often spoke about resigning, with the hope, perhaps, that she would keep him on, which in fact she did; she insisted on it. And he stayed. But the repetition of this scenario five times between 1771 and 1777 attests to his malaise. And in 1778 during the Bavarian affair, when there was question of getting Marie-Antoinette to intervene on Austria's behalf against the advice of the king and his ministers, and clearly against the interests of France, he bucked up his courage and left for Paris, leaving the queen a letter of resignation saying that he did not want to give cause for anyone to suspect that he influenced her actions because of his attachment to the Austrian court. Between espionage and treason there was a step he was not willing to take. His detractors would say that he just wanted it to seem he would not take the step, as he did in fact return. Was this evidence of genuine scruples or a calculated maneuver? We don't know. From then on he prudently refrained from intervening in the queen's relations with her family. He would stay by her side until July 14th, 1789, when he emigrated to Vienna, where he died.

He served two masters. He was pushed farther than he would have liked, but unable to escape Mercy's demands or return to an obscure existence, he hedged his bets. He was weak. He was not made of the stuff that heroes are made of, nor that scoundrels are made of either. He felt only fondness for Marie-Antoinette and seems never to have hurt her even inadvertently. The same cannot be said of his direct superior, Austria's over-zealous ambassador to Paris.

Count de Mercy-Argenteau

Florimond-Claude, count de Mercy-Argenteau, was not an Austrian. His roots lay in Liège, Belgium, where he was born in 1727. But he had no doubts about where his allegiances lay; he served the

Hapsburg dynasty. When the Spanish Low Countries came under Austrian control, his father the count d'Argenteau, quite naturally decided to make a career in the imperial armies. Fostered to a childless cousin who then adopted him, he added Mercy* to his name, and inherited the magnificent lands of that name in the Lorraine's Longwy region. Our Mercy-Argenteau, therefore, had one foot in Wallonia and one in the Lorraine, which became French in 1766**. He also had a foot, one might say, in Högyesz, Hungary, where the aforementioned cousin had acquired for a song a vast domain in the lush plains near Lake Balaton, which needed refurbishing after the retreat of the Turks. He could take his pick of where to settle. If need be, he could have chosen Louis XV as his master and entered into his service. Allegiance to the Hapsburgs won out, but he did not want to stray far from his birthplace. His mother died when he was born, and he was raised by aunts and uncles in the Liège area. His father sent him to Hungary where he felt like an exile, which undermined his already fragile health. A military career was out of the question, so he gravitated toward diplomacy. After a trial run with Kaunitz in Paris, he became the minister plenipotentiary to Turin; he then attained the ambassadorship to Saint Petersburg. There was a brief stay in Warsaw that a civil war put an end to, then it was on to the court in Vienna for two years. In 1766 came the big prize: the ambassadorship to Paris, which had remained vacant throughout the Seven Years War.

This rise in power was not due to any exceptional merit. In a private note, Kaunitz had agreed that his young colleague possessed "good morals, prudence and a mild manner," but found him "timid, taciturn and ill at ease in his mannerisms to the point of being dull." "He will never be a shining genius," he concluded, "but his good character, his zeal and his application will make up for what he might lack on that score, and will surely place him in the ranks of those capable of being used to good effect." In short, he would do what he was told. This opinion was shared by the Frenchman Chauvelin, a colleague of his in Turin. Fifteen years later, Chancellor Kaunitz was still of the same opinion: Mercy had gained ease and good manners, but no panache. However, as it turns out, this lack of flair served him well. For Kaunitz the Paris posting had been, as it had

---

* This Florimond-Claude de Mercy was the grandson of the famous warrior captain who distinguished himself in the imperial ranks during the Thirty Years War, in particular at Nordlingen.

** Legally, he was actually a French national. For, having requested naturalization in the Lorraine to escape the heavy inheritance taxes levied on foreigners, he automatically became French upon annexation.

for Starhemberg, a steppingstone to the ministry. Now that he was getting on in years, he had no desire to give his support to some pushy young upstart.

Mercy couldn't be happier. All he wanted was to stay in France. The last thing he wanted was to go to Hungary to be bored stiff and racked with fever, or subject his rheumatism to the rigors of a Saint Petersburg winter. Even the Viennese winters were too much for this Walloon accustomed to the more clement western European climate. He had taken a shine to Paris where he could finally, now that his father's death had put an end to his financial woes, lead the easy life of a well-to-do bachelor to whom high society opened wide its doors. He was a good-looking man, pleasant, cultivated. His French was flawless – it was his native tongue after all. People flocked to the receptions he gave at his residence in the Petit-Luxembourg and then in the private mansion built for him by the *fermier général* Laborde (a tax and customs officer) over by the boulevards, almost at the corner of the rue de la Grange-Batelière*. There was another reason he wanted to stay in Paris. From 1770 on he had a beloved mistress, Marie Rose Josèphe Levasseur, a 20 year-old opera singer who became a great prima donna known as Rosalie. She would play the role of Amor in Gluck's *Orpheus and Euridice* and go on to do *Alcest*, *Armide* and *Iphigenia in Tauris* before altogether losing her voice and being obliged to leave the stage. This strong, lasting attachment – he would finally marry her during the Revolution to legitimize their child – would remain discreet; not a hint of scandal would stain the ambassador's reputation. But leaving Paris was out of the question.

Thanks to Marie-Antoinette, he became indispensable. For the role to which Maria Theresa assigned him, his mediocrity was an advantage. Had he had Kaunitz's flamboyancy, his visits to Marie-Antoinette would less likely have gone unnoticed. Also, the empress believed that his intellectual near-sightedness would guarantee his trustworthiness: he would be her eyes, ears and voice. Nothing would be left out of his reports. She felt he would take no initiatives or inject anything of his own into his briefs. She was right about his thoroughness, as his reports were very detailed, but not about the rest.

Not that Mercy opposed her wishes. He was the tool of no faction; he took part in no conspiracy, whatever some historians

---

*   Nowadays the Richelieu-Drouot crossroads. The house he inhabited from 1778 on still exists, at 16 Boulevard Montparnasse.

might have led us to believe. He went hand in glove with Choiseul as long as Vienna ordered him to, but abandoned him when he was disgraced, as soon as the empress let him know she did not want him reinstated. For the French royal family, and notably for the dauphin, he had no particular animosity, just a crushing contempt. Serving his Austrian sovereign faithfully, he hoped to distinguish himself and hoist himself up to become the highest-ranking ambassador, greatly appreciated by his masters, an adviser who had the ear of the future queen of France. He therefore gave his all.

When it came to getting information about her daughter, the empress was insatiable. He would give her her money's worth, as they say. To his protector Kaunitz, with whom he kept up a more casual correspondence, he admitted: "By today's post [20 October 1770], I'm sending the empress a report as voluminous as it is inconsequential on Madame la dauphine's daily activities. It would be quite easy to report them in just a few words, but H.M. wants details, and I notice that the longer the reports are the better." On November 15th, he added, "If my dispatches... were as interesting as they are long, H.M. would have reason to be happy. Today I'm sending her a 50-page report that I'm really ashamed of, because it contains a mere two or three items of any interest." We can thank Maria Theresa's anxiety, coupled with her ambassador's zeal, for these interminable letters. They are repetitive to the point of being unreadable, going over the same events, in virtually the same terms. The same is true for the *tibi soli*; we wonder why they had to be written at all, as they simply rehash what was already said in the reports.

Like any self-respecting ambassador, he inflated anything that might be agreeable to his sovereign. So he played on her motherly love. His correspondence for the first four years, before Marie-Antoinette became queen, was simply an encomium to her merit and her successes.

Her merit? He did not go so far as to pretend that she was perfect; he knew her mother would not fall for that. But he tempered his criticism. Yes, she is inattentive, but by no means stupid – when you explain things, she understands! She is not so recalcitrant as one might fear. She promises, "I will make the fewest possible mistakes; and when it does happen that I make them, I shall always own up." She makes good progress; due, of course, to the judicious counsel of the ambassador who knows everything, notices everything and sees to everything, at least according to his reckoning. And he works in the shadows to guide her every step.

Her successes? This was a point Mercy enjoyed expounding upon, emphasizing the goodwill she inspired. The "charming dauphine" so lively and gay and kind, has conquered all hearts. Versailles reacted with tenderness and admiration to the compassion she showed for the poor coachman who accidentally fell under her carriage wheels. "On such an occasion," he enthused, "Maria Theresa would certainly have recognized her daughter, and Henry IV his heir." As for her first visits to Paris, Mercy could not find words strong enough to describe the enthusiasm she aroused in the people. Is that not the most essential asset of a future queen? Nothing could please the empress more; she knew from experience that one wins over peoples, like individuals, through seduction. In orchestrating this campaign to highlight the dauphine's merits among his diplomatic colleagues and in the Parisian salons he attended, Mercy manufactured her image in ways that would not be sniffed at by our modern public relations moguls.

There's nothing particularly wrong with this. But Mercy made one fundamental error: while he overestimated the dauphine, he seriously underestimated the dauphin. He lacked subtlety, and once he settled on an opinion, he rarely changed it. The dauphin's hopeless incompetence was a given – to believe him useless puffed up the ambassador's sense of importance. On the dauphin's supposed incompetence he built a dream of a radiant future: "Given the character and personality of Monsieur le dauphin, it is virtually inevitable that Madame la dauphine will one day be governing France." He ruminated over it so much and repeated it so often to Maria Theresa that he wound up believing it. What he did not add of course was that he was convinced he was the one who would be governing Marie-Antoinette. He already saw himself as the kingpin of French policy, the irreplaceable tool of Austria's imperial house, which was some sort of revenge perhaps against his ex-patron Kaunitz, whose protection smacked a bit of condescension. He went from spying to playing for power.

He thought he could guess the empress's wishes and tried to oblige her. For example, he didn't feel he was going too far when he explained to the dauphine what her future role must be, and concluded in a letter to the empress on July 14, 1770, just two months after her wedding, "Y.M. will deign to judge thanks to this detail how much influence Madame the Archduchess has gained over the dauphin. There is no doubt that with a bit of prudence she will succeed in subjugating him entirely, and I base this hope on the rare and natural talents of this princess who, by the way, understands perfectly and heeds the advice given to her when she sees that it is dictated by reason and eagerness for her well-being." But Maria Theresa did not share his enthusiasm. There was a strong dose of skepticism in her. She believed her daughter to be incapable of governing and thought it pointless and even dangerous to prepare her for it, as it could compromise her happiness. Far from subscribing to her ambassador's plans, she considered them mere chimerical ramblings. But too concerned with concrete reality and too immersed in daily events, she didn't take them seriously enough to put a stop to them. A pity. She let Mercy nurse his ambition. This mission was his chance of a lifetime. He didn't let it go. He was something of a Pygmalion. He would model and chisel the raw material presented to him by the adolescent girl in order to produce his masterpiece. But unlike the Greek sculptor of legend, he didn't fall in love with her. She was merely the instrument of his ambition. His protective affection grated on her, for her chimera was independence.

When she escaped from him and he realized how wrong he'd been, he would prove excessively harsh.

In the kingdom of distrust

The road to hell, as we know, is paved with good intentions. Maria Theresa sincerely believed that she was "a good mother, who had only [her] salvation and happiness in mind," as she was fond of telling her daughter. Did she see the consequences of the surveillance network she set up around her?

First of all, there was the obsession with secrecy. The correspondence between mother and daughter had to be shielded from prying eyes. We have seen the enormous care taken in delivering the letters. But there was no point in trying to write in code, as was often done at the time, because decoding letters once they got to Versailles would have required adding yet another transit point without solving the biggest problem, Marie-Antoinette's negligence. So in her long *Instructions*, Maria Theresa said to her, "Tear up my letters; this will enable me to write more openly to you; and I will do the same with yours." Or burn them as soon as they'd been read. She ordered Mercy to hand them to her daughter personally, and specifically told her that if she could not burn them she must give them back to him resealed so that he could expedite them back to Vienna.

However, Louis XV had to be aware that Marie-Antoinette was

receiving letters from her mother. Should she offer to show them to him? A month after the wedding, it was spelled out, "H.M. agrees that if necessary and if it puts Madame la dauphine's mind at ease, she can communicate the contents to the king alone, but not to Monsieur the dauphin, nor to the abbé de Vermond* nor to any other person." But it soon became clear that she "could not show him one letter without taking on some sort of obligation to show him all future ones." Besides, her peace of mind could allow for nothing of the sort. Louis XV took a kindly attitude to the whole thing, and never showed the least interest in interfering with their correspondence. Ignorant of the grievances Maria Theresa harbored against him, and won over by her direct and unconventional ways, he trusted her. He saw Mercy as a sort of harmless guardian. He counted on him to reason with the restive girl, and facilitated his access to her by granting him the privileges reserved for ambassadors "of the family," that is, representing the Bourbon sovereigns. Mercy could therefore see her at any time without having to petition for an audience. He had permanent right of access, which he was careful not to abuse.

So it is that neither the empress nor her ambassador was subject to the rules that they imposed on others. They both took care to keep originals and copies of the correspondence, today deposited in the Viennese archives**. Warnings about prudence are only for those who risk betraying or being betrayed. Under constant pressure, Vermond and Marie-Antoinette must have trembled at the thought of having their secrets revealed. Very often the dauphine burned letters in Mercy's presence. She would also hide in order to reply, which explains why she didn't always answer questions properly, and why so little attention was paid to how they looked. "I ask her*** pardon if this letter is stained," she wrote on July 12th, 1770, "but for two days in a row I've had to write in the bathroom, having no other time to myself, and if my replies are not exact, I hope she understands that is because of too much exactitude in burning her letter." A few months later, nothing had changed; if anything, the climate had deteriorated. "The quality of Madame la dauphine's

---

*   Not to hide the contents from Vermond – Mercy informs him of it all – but to prevent Marie-Antoinette from figuring out that he is in league with the ambassador.

**   Except for the *tibi soli*, which Maria Theresa got rid of, and which we know about only through copies Mercy made in the early days.

*** Her being Maria Theresa. Frequently, especially in the beginning, she goes from the second to the third in addressing her "dearest mother."

writing is never so bad as in her letters to H.M.," Mercy reported,
"because she writes them much too precipitously for fear of being
discovered either by Monsieur the dauphin or by Mesdames her
aunts to whom she has so far said nothing of her correspondence
with H.M.". According to Vermond, "Madame la dauphine believes
that no paper is safe in her quarters; she fears that others have copies
of her keys or that they might be taken from her pockets during the
night. Whether this fear is well founded or not, it is firmly rooted
in her mind. She wanted to reread H.M.'s last letter and thought
she could only keep it overnight by placing it in her bed." And the
abbé, who had to hide the fact that he was writing first drafts and
correcting her texts, and terrified as well that he could be caught
spying, did nothing to save her from this psychotic bind, which he
suffered from as well.

She was afraid of being watched. She was afraid of being found
out. Writing became a dangerous, clandestine activity that she
could only practice in secret, in fear and trembling. Did Maria
Theresa realize that this obsession with secrecy would harm
her daughter's ability to settle into her new family? Of course
she did; but that was exactly what she wanted. Her prejudices
against France, nourished by Mercy, remained unbending.
Their correspondence oozed with contempt for the libidinous
sovereign subject to the whims of his "creature," and for the
stupid, inadequate dauphin devoid of any sensibility, crushed by
an "inept and vice-ridden" tutor. Around them there was a bunch
of highly dangerous "bad guys" – in which were included any and
all who might remove her from the ambassador's influence – who
could trap the dauphine in their "diabolical intrigues." It must be
admitted that her mother's own psychotic bind was a match for
Marie-Antoinette's. With widowhood and the passing years she
seems to have lost some of the solid good sense that had been her
strength.

In this despicable country, faced with these inconstant and
frivolous French, Marie-Antoinette was bidden to become a beacon
of the solid Germanic virtues of "vigor and truthfulness." "Take
not on this French frivolity, remain a good German, be proud of it,
and a friend to your friends." They required her to give preferential
treatment to her compatriots visiting Versailles, to protect and defend
them. She must demonstrate what queenly comportment means to
a contemptible and despised royal family that has lost its sense of
duty and "does not know how to earn the people's love." "Do not let
the least nonchalance be betrayed in your face or in your behavior...
On this one point follow neither the advice nor the example of the

family; it is you who must set the tone in Versailles; you have achieved perfect success; God has showered you with so many blessings, has made you so sweet and amenable that everyone has to love you; this is a gift from God; you must keep it..." Maria Theresa was certainly not wrong to push her daughter to insist on her rank in the court's ceremonial functions. But how could she imagine in November 1770 that the child could possibly *set the tone* in Versailles? Mercy's gushing reports must really have gone to her head.

Perverse effects

Of all the constraints that intemperate motherly affection put on her daughter, the obsession with secrecy was one of the most pernicious, as it was tied to her mother's desire to keep Marie-Antoinette under her thumb. From it flowed a whole series of redoubtable perverse effects. To recapitulate:

First of all, they forced the dauphine to live in a climate of suspicion which could quickly have become unbearable had the correspondence not been limited to one letter a month. But it was just one more source of tension in a life that necessarily brought with it a lot of its own.

Also, and more seriously, the need to hide her writing contradicted the moral and religious principles that had been inculcated in her, not to mention the advice given to her upon her departure. The little girl had been told to obey the king, to trust him, to see him as a protective and affectionate grandfather. In other words, they were preaching deceptiveness. She had always been told not to lie. But here they were making fine distinctions; truthfulness was *de rigueur* with her mother, but not with Louis XV or the dauphin. They were teaching her to be hypocritical.

That is one of politics' golden rules, one might object. But she was precisely not being schooled in politics. She must blindly obey Mercy. He would direct her each and every step, without explaining the whys and wherefores. Instead of educating her, they were keeping her in a state of infantile submission that would soon suit neither her age nor her station. They were preventing her from becoming an adult.

By constantly criticizing France and its inhabitants' supposed perversions, they were preventing her from becoming French.

Finally, worst of all, they were teaching her to despise the dauphin, her husband. The ambassador pushed her to do everything possible to impose her will on him. He kept telling her that if she succeeded in dominating her husband – an easy job according to him – she would one day govern France in his place.

The regrettable effects of these contradictory demands would soon become clear.

Marie-Antoinette always hated constraints. As she did when a child, she resorted to diversionary tactics to escape from them. Any excuse was good to avoid reading. Writing to her mother became such a painful chore that she dashed off her letters just to be done with them. She only half listened to reprimands; and in any case, they went in one ear and out the other. She threw herself into any entertainment that offered itself. She was taught to sidestep, and learned the lesson well; she pitted her mother's wishes against those of the king. One forbade, the other allowed; what better argument was there for her doing exactly as she pleased? She slipped through the fingers of those who would want to hold on to her. Soon enough, exasperated by being forever treated like a child, she would go from sidestepping to open revolt.

She began to keep Mercy at a distance; he scolded her too often, and she was loath to obey his orders. Had she figured out that he was spying on her? He kept insisting that she suspected nothing, but he took further precautions with the empress. It was natural that the young dauphine freshly arrived in Versailles should give him her full confidence, but it is hardly imaginable that suspicions didn't arise as the days went by. She didn't lack subtlety; she could intuit what was going on. Betrayal is something you sense*. Besides, there must have been in her entourage people who could open her eyes. But if she did figure it out, one can well image that she would not go complaining to her mother. The only way to have any peace was to act as though she suspected nothing, while hiding as much as possible from Mercy. Far from guaranteeing Maria Theresa's control, the cords that she thought would bind her daughter only served to strengthen her revolt, thereby undercutting even the empress' most useful advice.

What is more, the climate of suspicion isolated Marie-Antoinette. She was taught to suspect everyone around her. By insisting that she only trust her two advisers, they bound her in a fearful solitude that she would try to break out of by developing passionate friendships, whose consequences we will see later on.

Finally, Mercy's constant leitmotif was not lost on Marie-

---

* Did she suspect Vermond as well? Was he better at fooling her than Mercy was? We don't know how he maneuvered between his bosses and the child he was supposed to spy on and protect at the same time.

Antoinette. The flattering thought that she would be called one day to rule France was implanted in her mind. While she was still only the dauphine, her fear of Louis XV held her back, but once she was queen she would not be stopped. Not that she had any notion of herself exercising power. She had no taste for it and no desire to do the kind of hard work it required. But as she was fond of repeating, she did not want to "be governed." She hated obeying orders. She could not bear obstacles to her desires. She imagined her role as queen as a kind of control she would have over the king and his ministers to bend them to her demands or her whims, a point of view derived from the ambassador's rash insinuations.

Everything was in place therefore, from the very first months, to greatly compromise Marie-Antoinette's relationships with the husband, the family and the country that would now be hers. Is that really what Maria Theresa wanted? Most assuredly not. Had she been less anxious, she would have understood perhaps that any worthwhile education requires granting a minimum of trust, freedom and responsibility. Had she been better informed, she perhaps would have understood that Versailles, while not a model of virtue, was not the den of iniquity that she feared.

CHAPTER 4

VERSAILLES UNDER DU BARRY'S SPELL

What would Marie-Antoinette find when she landed in Versailles? Maria Theresa's worries were excessive. No, libertinage did not reign supreme; it was possible to meet people just as demanding as she was regarding morals and manners. But there was room for scandal too; and scandal started in high places, very high – for Louis XV had a new favorite. Yet again, he had passed over ladies of the high-ranking nobility, not even for a woman from "the middling classes" like la Pompadour, but for a shady lady with a dubious past. The sudden appearance of Madame du Barry startled the court out of its somnolence, and revealed the personality of each courtier. It reshuffled the deck in this little world of clans and coteries. Everyone felt obliged to take sides for or against her. Unforwarned, Marie-Antoinette arrived in a family racked with tension.

Jeanne Bécu, countess du Barry

After Madame de Pompadour's death in 1764, Louis XV seemed to settle down. No official favorite had come to replace her, and resorting to passing mistresses became more rare, or at least more discreet. Nonetheless, in 1768, the imminent death of his wife Marie Leszczynska did not stop him from falling for the charms of a newcomer. Right after her death, during the court's stay in Compiègne, a mysterious woman was noticed. Although she was lodging in a house in the city, each night during the month of July she arrived at the chateau around midnight and went back to town the next morning in a litter accompanied by liveried servants. At least he had the decency to keep her hidden during this period of deep mourning. It was thought to be a passing fancy – yet another one; everyone had lost count – and nothing was made of it.

Choiseul, who at the time was *de facto* prime minister, thought it prudent to find out what was going on. The count de Saint-Florentin, secretary of state for the king's household and therefore head of the police, had already investigated, and was happy to tell him what he'd found out. The young woman, a top-shelf prostitute, was living with an adventurer by the name of du Barry, well known in the Paris underworld. Their "salon," part gambling den and part house of ill repute, was the meeting place of scalawags of all sorts, some of whom were high-ranking lords tired of twiddling their thumbs at Versailles. Choiseul found the news more reassuring than not. He would write in his memoirs, "We deplored the low creature the king had taken up with, but otherwise we merely thought that such a base liaison could only end as such fleeting fancies do. Amongst ourselves we hoped that it would do the king some good and that it would be the last instance we witnessed of his taste for dubious company."

Come autumn in Fontainebleau, however, the lady would reappear on an entirely new footing. "She is housed in the chateau," Mercy informed the empress, "in what they call the Court of the Fountains, next to the apartment that Madame de Pompadour occupied; she has numerous attendants; her liveried servants are extremely well dressed, and on holidays and Sundays she can be seen at the king's mass in a chapel on the ground floor that is reserved for her." Louis XV was obviously taken with her. Who was she exactly, and by what hidden paths had she been hoisted up to such favor? It is hard to make out what's true and what's false between on the one hand the half-truths and lies she helped spread in her attempt to prettify her past, and on the other the torrents of muck libelously dumped on her. But the archives have handed down some evidence.

Although lying about her age was one of the tricks of the trade so to speak, we know when she was born: on August 19, 1743, in Vaucouleurs. She was baptized under the name Jeanne Bécu. It was her mother's family name; no mention is made of a father on her birth certificate. Tradition has it that her father was a monk of the Picpus order, Brother Angel, or Gomard de Vaubernier; but this cannot be verified. Where had her mother the young Anne Bécu met him? What had led this child of a Parisian tradesman to abscond to this little village in the Meuse? We have no idea. She remained there for another five or six years until an arms dealer traveling in the Lorraine noticed her and brought her back to Paris. Preferring not to impose her on his official mistress, he married her off to one of his employees. Her little girl Jeanne was bright, pretty and charming. The arms dealer or some other friend of her mother's decided she was worth being given a proper education and sent her off to the Sainte-Aure convent on the rue Neuve-Sainte-Geneviève. The nine years she spent there gave her a veneer of religion and some intellectual baggage more than worthy of her station in life. She could read and write, and did a bit of drawing and music. But by the age of fifteen it was time for her to think about making a living.

From the first jobs she tried her hand at, as a hairdresser and then a professional companion, she learned above all the power of her charms. What wife and mother would keep a ravishing beauty like this one who could lead her sons or friends astray? She was better suited for a position in a clothing boutique where her pretty little face could attract clients. So she went off to work for a certain Labille at *À la toilette* on the rue Neuve-des-Petits-Champs, where she sold ribbons, laces, handkerchiefs, shimmering textiles, perfumes and silk flowers to grand ladies. She changed her name from Jeanne Bécu to the more flattering Mademoiselle Lange. Her luminous blue eyes with their lush dark eyelashes, her head of copious blond curls, her rosy complexion dotted with a beauty mark or two, and her long, slender, alluring form also attracted some customers, whom she did not treat cruelly during her off hours. There was pleasure to be had in this good life. Carefree, she intended to partake of it with gusto.

That is how she was spotted by Jean-Baptiste du Barry, offspring of a bona fide if impecunious family of the minor Gascon nobility. He left a wife and child behind in the Gers region to seek his fortune in Paris. Quickly learning that honest means would not bring the success he was counting on, he tried his hand at gambling, but found that pimping was less risky and more profitable. His title of count and his distant Gascon relations almost made him acceptable company for the court libertines in search of fresh flesh. They called him "The Rake" after the regent's partners in debauchery[*]. He understood when he first laid eyes on her that she was worth infinitely more than her peers. He even fell in love with her. So he was careful not to overuse her. Under a version of her presumed father's name he set her up in luxurious surroundings and kept her for his choicest clientele. A police report stating that he was displaying her charms at a box in the *Théâtre Italien* bluntly concluded: "He is clearly trying to traffic her to advantage. When he begins to tire of

---

[*] *Translator's note: reference to Philippe d'Orléans, regent during the early reign of Louis XV.*

a woman, he always does this. But you have to admit that he is a connoisseur and that his merchandise is always in demand... The count du Barry and Mademoiselle Beauvarnier lead an infamous life together. She is his cash cow. He offers her to all comers, as long as they are people of quality or means."

How did the idea of "trafficking" her to the king come to him? We don't know. But it would not have been possible for him to do it alone. In all likelihood, the master planner of the enterprise was the marshal-duke de Richelieu. An old accomplice in the king's amorous exploits, in former times he had thought he could attain power with the help of his nieces, the Nesle sisters, the sovereign's first mistresses. Their death undid his plans, and the arrival of la Pompadour, who came from another milieu altogether, relegated him to a second-class role once a few military victories were over. Power fell to Choiseul. When the position of favorite had been vacated and the aging king suffered a series of other deaths, he was lonely. The time was ripe to furnish his bed with a young woman who was lively, knew what she was doing, and how to show gratitude.

There was one big problem, however: the king hated prostitutes. Fearing disease, he would only take on girls whose favors he would be the first to enjoy. Thus it was arranged for the king to come across her as if by chance. The story is told in a number of versions. According to the best known of them, his usual supplier, the *valet de chambre* Lebel, arranged for the king to see him in conversation with her, and the awestruck king asked no questions. He was smitten right from the first night, perhaps as never before, madly in love at nearly sixty years of age, in thrall to the delights of a December passion. Miraculously, Jeanne had kept the freshness of a child of the people. She was uncomplicated, without pretensions, and made love as if it were the most natural thing in the world. But as a professional she was also able to introduce him to pleasures that he could not even have imagined with his devout wife and overly well-mannered mistresses. The duke d'Ayen, to whom the king had confided his stunned surprise, apparently responded crudely, "It is clear that Your Majesty has never been to a brothel." When pious souls tried to enlighten him about his conquest's doubtful past it was too late. He played deaf and blind, as long as he could find in his arms every night the cure for the melancholy that was eating away at him. It is said that when he asked the same duke d'Ayen about one of those who'd enjoyed the beauty's favors before him, "It is said that I'm succeeding Sainte-Foix?" the duke made bold to reply "As you are succeeding Pharamond." True or false, these anecdotes convey the tone of the sarcastic comments that were making the rounds. Choiseul, whose expertise in the matter was much greater than his master's, had understood the source of her success, "I thought she was more pleasing to the king than the others because of her experience in the avenues that he needed to explore; but I was convinced that he would tire of her..."

No, he didn't tire of her at all. "He seems younger," observed the duke de Croÿ, "and he's never been more cheerful." By December Jeanne was housed in Versailles, on the ground floor of the central building, just below the king's bedchamber. He would soon put her just above him, in the apartments on the third floor where he'd housed the dauphine of Saxony when she was widowed. She thus found herself in the bosom of the private quarters where he had all he needed to live sheltered from view. She led a quiet existence there. But held at a distance from court functions, she would die of boredom waiting for her lover in the company of The Rake's sister "Chon" whom he'd placed with her for company and surveillance. She could not rest until she was received at court. Unlike la Pompadour, however, she was without worldly ambition. She had no desire to rule over the court, even less to decide the fate of ministers. All she wanted to do was enjoy life, to take full advantage of the sudden luxury she was surrounded by, the clothes, jewels, expensive furniture, assiduous servants, and entertainments of all sorts. More than anything else she wanted to escape forever from poverty, which was all too familiar to her. Like a good little Cinderella who knows that her coach can turn back into a pumpkin, she worked at consolidating her position to ensure her livelihood, at least as long as the king was alive. But he was, after all, 33 years older than she was. To protect her from any eventual loss of favor she would soon be given, without even asking for it, the chateau of Luciennes – today Louveciennes.

For the immediate future, the first thing she needed to do to take full advantage of her situation was to be presented at court. Her ex-protector took care of everything. During the summer, as soon as he saw that the king was well and truly hooked, he went to work finding her a presentable station in life. Not able to marry her himself without being accused of bigamy, he gave her hand to his brother Guillaume whom he summoned from the Gers for the purpose, just long enough to have him appear in front of two justices of the peace and a priest, before packing him off home again with a pension and orders never to show his face again. A false baptismal certificate makes her two years younger and calls her the daughter of one Jean-Jacques Gomard de Vaubernier, deceased, of course. Since kid brother Guillaume was supposed to be a count, that made his bride a countess. The title of nobility was the only non-falsified thing in this whole farce*. But since the du Barrys of Lévignac alone appeared to be of too meager nobility, The Rake put out that they were related by blood to some noble Italians from Bari and the English Barrymore family. Whatever the truth of the matter, the papers appeared to be in order. To present her at court, the king would have no need to buy her a name. He just had to buy her a sponsor.

Received at court

The great titled ladies were not pushing and shoving to be the first to carry out such a humiliating task. So a certain countess de Béarn was unearthed. She was a widow laden down with children and deeply in debt, willing to do anything to stay afloat financially. Alas, although she had been well coached, the countess at the last minute committed a diplomatic blunder. And the right-thinking courtiers took advantage of it to put more pressure on the king, informing him of his mistress's turpitudes, while unscrupulously adding a thing or two of their own. However, Mercy-Argenteau had no illusions: "His passion wins out over shame." A fall from a horse, which at first was thought to have broken his arm, seemed to lead the king back to a more Christian perspective, as had happened each time he fell ill in the past. But he was not even completely recovered when he announced one fine evening, before the machinations could properly develop, that Madame du Barry would be presented the following day, a Sunday as per custom. Her husband's Gascon family of course would have been at great pains to produce the required titles of nobility going back to 1400. Jeanne was therefore granted the right of presentation "*par grâce.*" This special privilege infuriated all the ladies who had met the proper requirements, as well as those who hadn't, and as a result were excluded from the court's holy of holies, which added up to quite a lot of ladies...

That evening of April 22, 1769, after vespers, the court gathered in the king's large reception room and gleefully awaited the *faux pas*, the gaffe, the slip-up that "the creature" could not fail to make in the ceremony's highly codified ritual. Jeanne was late. With his arm still in a sling, the king nervously wondered if she hadn't succumbed to the panic that was consuming her. But

---

* Although one might ask how Guillaume du Barry could hold the title as he was the younger brother of Jean-Baptiste, who also claimed to be a count.

her coach at last came to a halt at the foot of the grand staircase. The doors opened and Madame de Béarn appeared, followed by Jeanne, who was so beautiful that her detractors were speechless. Louis had her sent 100,000 pounds' worth of diamonds, so she was covered in them from head to toe. She advanced lightly in her sumptuous white ball gown with just enough décolleté to hint at the sublime contours of her bust. Smiling, she comported herself with such ease that it seemed she'd done this all her life. Gracefully holding aloft the enormous panniers of her gown, she correctly executed the three required bows, bending very low before her lover, who hastened to lift her. She then drew back, as per custom, without tripping over the gown's cumbersome train, which she swished gracefully to the side. There, it was done. The hardest part was over. But she still had to confront the royal family, Mesdames aunts and the dauphin, who managed to maintain an icy countenance without giving outright offense. Let's admit it: she made a success of her entrance. The king could discern something resembling envy in the faces of the men, whereas the women, with a twinge of resentment, sought in vain to find something to criticize. Did not such perfect beauty justify a dispensation from the requirement of aristocratic birth?

Clearly, Jeanne was not the low-life that her detractors denounced. How could she have ever wallowed in the gutter? Her convent school days left her with excellent manners and bearing. The Rake, who had banked a lot on her, perfected her education; and she became more refined and polished through contact with the great libertine lords who frequented their house. But she herself also had incontestable personal charm. She was blessed with a great natural grace that all the lessons in the world on how to make a correct curtsy could not alone have inculcated in her. She was a woman of taste; she knew how to dress and would make her living quarters quite elegant. She was quite bright, but she was more instinctive than intellectual. She knew, however, that only knowledge nourished conversation. So she read a great deal. Her speech quickly lost any trace of her origins. She developed her mind but never fell into that favorite sin of the courtiers, ironic derision, for she was naturally kind, generous, and attentive to others. In short, her worth went far beyond her talents in the bedroom; her lover need not blush on her account. She was infinitely seductive. Everyone would like her if they set aside their preconceived notions. Now that she was received at court, the question would be whether the courtiers could overcome their prejudices.

Louis XV's strong-arm tactics got the results he wanted, for they *were* strong-arm tactics. If he was determined to raise her to the status of his official mistress, it was not only to please her. He was flying in the face of all those who were trying to dictate to him how he should behave. What business was it of theirs? For the first time in his life, he was free. Widowhood had freed him from the sin of adultery. And he hadn't stolen Madame du Barry from anyone, as her phantom husband went back to his province as soon as the wedding was over, renouncing any claims on her. All that was left was a sin of the flesh. But who, when it comes to that, can cast the first stone? His conscience was quite clear in imposing his desires. He wrote to Choiseul, "The unleashing of invective against her has been atrocious, and mostly undeserved. Everyone would be at her feet if... So goes the world. She is truly lovely. She is pleasing to me. That should be enough. What do they want me to do, take on a girl of high birth?" For years now he had seen his authority being chipped away. He was losing his grip on his kingdom and even on those closest to him, his family and the court. Politically his fiscal reforms had come up against insurmountable opposition from the clergy and the Paris Parliament. Measures he'd disapproved of had been imposed on him. Concerning his affairs of the heart he was under constant pressure from the Church, his inner circle and even his ministers. Most often he gave in, although there was an occasional outburst in an attempt to get his way. Would it be impertinent to point out that up till then he'd better defended his love life than his political goals? This time he was determined to impose his mistress *and* crush Parliament. To those who find this juxtaposition outlandish, one just has to point out what happened next. The new favorite, entirely indifferent to politics as she was, would be at the heart of conflicts to come.

A surprising clash

As soon as she became the official favorite, the powerful duke de Choiseul rose up against her. For ten years now, having taken on the portfolios of foreign affairs and the war ministry, Choiseul had been at the head of the government, aided by his cousin Praslin, for whom he obtained the ministry of the marine. His keen, lucid intelligence, his energy and capacity for work rendered him indispensable to the king. But they were not always in perfect agreement, far from it. As regards foreign affairs they both saw England as posing the greatest threat, and judged it essential to maintain the Austrian alliance. But as concerns domestic policy, Louis XV would have preferred him to be less compliant with the Paris Parliament. In order to have his fiscal edicts accepted, for example, was it really necessary to expel the Jesuits? And Choiseul's professed albeit discreet agnosticism offended the king's deep religiosity. But no matter, their partnership had withstood the test of time and the minister believed he was untouchable.

It is somewhat surprising to see him take the lead in opposing du Barry. Was this unrepentant Don Juan, who would be hard pressed to list all of his innumerable mistresses, in any position to point the finger at the king? It seems he thought so. Mercy wrote to Kaunitz: "Monsieur de Choiseul is resolved to grasp the moment to have a few words with the king about his latest mistress, to unmask the creature for what she really is, and to suggest to him the great harm it would do to the monarch's dignity in the eyes of the people if he displayed his favor for a woman who can only reasonably serve to gratify the most hidden pleasures." Why couldn't he behave like Choiseul himself, who as dissolute as he was, could hold his head high because he did not offend convention, making sure to be seen with none but mistresses of quality! Assuredly the minister gave excellent advice in reminding the king that among other constraints imposed on him by the crown, there was the necessity of preserving his public image. But Louis XV felt less and less inclined to bear those constraints.

To be exact, concern for royal dignity alone did not explain Choiseul's animosity. First of all, his sister Béatrix de Gramont was quietly putting pressure on him. She was incensed that the position of official mistress had been usurped – she'd been angling for it for years. She was not the only one. Her former rivals, united in common indignation, joined her in scandalized protest. But above all, Choiseul quickly recognized in the young woman's stupefying rise the hand of marshal de Richelieu, his age-old enemy, master of intrigue and underhanded tricks. Unless he could nip this thing in the bud, he was convinced Richelieu would use it against him. Engaging hostilities is of course not without risk. But he was a gambler and he went for broke. Since the king would not heed lectures on morals, perhaps a public opinion campaign would make him listen to reason. Versailles was humming with gossip. In Paris, songs and pamphlets offered for ridicule "How the Young Stylist Learned Her Trade" and "The Apotheosis of King Pétaud*" and people hummed to a well-known tune the scandalous adventures of "The Bourbon's Lass at the Dance Hall."

---

* *Translator's note: a figure of legend known for his utter inability to keep order.*

He wasn't entirely mistaken in sensing danger in du Barry's sudden rise. But he ascribed to her ambitions she didn't have. She was kind-hearted. All she wanted was to be on good terms with everyone. Just a bit of consideration would have been enough to win her over. Instead of which, he took up the gauntlet, forgetting that he too had many enemies, above and beyond those of the Richelieu clan. He himself was as controversial as his policies. There were many aligned against him: the religious faction who denounced his close ties to the *philosophes*; all those against the Austrian alliance who at this stage had no trouble pointing out its disadvantages; all the partisans of a strong monarchy who saw excessive tolerance in his concessions to Parliament; plus all those who objected to his insolence, his off-hand manner, his caustic wit and his lavish life style. These scattered but numerous adversaries found in his violent attacks on the favorite an excuse to challenge him.

After her presentation at court, Versailles at first turned a cold shoulder on du Barry. Then slowly, more and more people rallied to her support. Marshal de Richelieu's friends and family came first. Well-behaved courtiers fell into line. Why snub the new star and incur the king's disfavor? Then came the administrative offices. She was granted visits to the stores of the *Menus-Plaisirs** and backstage at the new opera house. The ever-active members of the religious clan quickly saw what a precious resource they had in their bête noire Choiseul. Thus the paradoxical situation arose that the staunch defenders of morality and religion warmly welcomed a liaison that the libertine minister condemned. Of course, as the duke de Croÿ pointed out, "the wise ones who loved the king wept, prayed and closed their mouths." But the determined ones, rallying round the flag of religion, claimed to recognize in the king's new mistress, however shameful she was, the instrument of Providence. They saw in her elevation the hand of God "who permits one evil to remedy a greater one." An indignant Mercy explained to Kaunitz that this greater evil was none other than the religious faction's enemy Monsieur de Choiseul. And they went so far as to invoke the bible, Racine's tragedies and the example of Madame de Maintenon to celebrate in Jeanne du Barry the new Esther, sent from heaven to smite the sovereign's sinister adviser Haman, and bring him back to the path of righteousness.

Of course la Pompadour had encountered even less good will. She did after all personify the powerful class of financiers that aspired

---

*   *Translator's note: the office that organized the king's "minor pleasures:" plays, dinners, etc.*

to a social status denied them by the nobility. She was a danger to the established order. It is also true that she was open to the new ideas and was therefore a threat to religion, or so it was obstinately believed. Du Barry on the other hand, a simple daughter of the people who had been hoisted up to the highest ranks by a royal caprice, represented nothing and no one. She was an anomaly; she could not tip the balance and upset the monarchy and its social order. She had no pretensions to rule; she would have but little influence. And given Louis XV's age, his reign would surely end soon. All this explains why in the end she would be more accepted than her predecessor.

For the time being however her presence created two camps at court in which everyone was forced to take a position, the royal family, i.e. Mesdames the king's daughters and the dauphin his grandson, the first among them.

Mesdames

Of the king's eight daughters, four were still living, ranging in age from 46 to 41. All four remained unmarried for want of partners worthy of them and because they were reluctant to go, like their sister Élisabeth, languish in some obscure Italian or German principality. Two of them were quite strong-minded: the eldest Adélaïde – the only one authorized to bear the honorific title of simply "Madame," and Louise, the youngest. The other two went along with whatever their tempestuous older sister wanted. The kind and beautiful Victoire had a smile for everyone. The frightfully ugly Sophie was so shy that she could be seen day in and day out for years without being heard to utter a word. Madame Campan would say of her, "She walked extremely quickly, and to discern without looking at them those who stepped aside to let her pass, she had taken to glancing sideways out of her eyes, much as hares do." Only storms, of which she was terrified, would render her communicative; once fair weather returned, she retreated back into her fiercely timid silence.

Since their mother's death, the four sisters had dug deeper into their isolation. Madame Campan was hired as a reader at this time, and as an eyewitness, wrote a vivid account of their cheerless daily life. Louis XV saw very little of his family; every morning he went down a hidden staircase to Madame Adélaïde's apartment. He would often bring and drink a coffee he had made himself. Madame Adélaïde would pull on the bell rope to alert Madame

Victoire to the king's visit. Rising to go to her sister's, she would ring for Madame Sophie who in turn would ring for Madame Louise." The apartments were vast; the king did not linger. Louise, the last to rush in, hardly had the time to embrace her father before he went off hunting.

Madame Campan would further relate:

> Each evening Mesdames would interrupt my reading to join the princes in visiting the king: this ceremonial visit was called "removing the king's boots," and had its own little ritual. Each princess would don an enormous hoop skirt shimmering with gold or embroidery. They tied to their waists a long train and hid the rest of their insufficiently elegant attire with a long black taffeta cloak, which was wrapped around them up to the chin. The knights of honor, the ladies, the pages, the squires and the ushers bearing sizeable torches, accompanied them to the king's apartments. In an instant, the generally quiet palace would be all astir. The king gave each princess a kiss on the forehead, and the visit was so short that the reading, interrupted by this business, often got started again after a quarter of an hour. Mesdames came back to their quarters, untied their skirt strings and their trains, and resumed their handiwork and I my reading.

If by chance the king showed up unexpectedly and found neither *Loque*, *Coche*, *Graille* nor *Chiffe*, as he nicknamed them, he merely turned and left.

The sisters were not malevolent; they overflowed with good intentions. But they were bored stiff. Fulfilling religious duties and nibbling treats were not enough to fill up their days. The evenings alone lent them a bit of luster. Madame Adélaïde, the highest-ranking lady in the hierarchy, took on the late queen's crucial role of entertaining the courtiers at her gaming tables. But they played only games authorized by the Church, and kept the stakes, and therefore the thrills, to a minimum. The rest of their time was spent keeping a watchful eye on things, making sure that there was strict adherence to custom and etiquette – a domain in which Adélaïde could show even the most seasoned expert a thing or two – and commenting without excessive benevolence on all the goings-on at court. Their apartments were the focal point for all court gossip. One can well imagine that they were not the last to rue their father's fall back into a state of sin and to ferret out information on his new conquest.

What with upholding the honor of the family and the tortuous casuistry of marshal de Richelieu's devout faction, the four sisters didn't have a moment's hesitation about whose side they were on. But it should be acknowledged that they also had a few less noble reasons to be outraged. Already in 1768, in order to accommodate his private life more comfortably, the king had evicted his eldest daughter from her superb suite on the second floor and deprived her of her library on the third in favor of his new mistress. Relegated to the ground floor, Madame Adélaïde was livid. It seemed she had gone back in time to when she led the attack against la Pompadour. She remained combative, not the least discouraged by her previous failure to win over her father, although at least she no longer believed that the warmth and affection of his daughters could replace the love of a mistress. But why not try to discourage the intruder by making her life miserable? The four sisters therefore resorted again to the silent treatment. Neither a glance nor a word from them would help the creature emerge from the void that she should never have left in the first place.

Their hostility toward du Barry won out over their antipathy for Choiseul; so they were now in league with their former adversary. They might even be willing to overlook their anti-Austrian convictions. Mercy-Argenteau arranged for Madame de Durfort, Adélaïde's mistress of the wardrobe, to suggest that the simple solution would be for the king to marry again. As a matter of fact, there was a princess in Vienna who might just be right for him. To Kaunitz he wrote, "I will send details on the advantages for Mesdames of gaining the solid friendship of this archduchess who in harmony with them at all times could ensure the royal family's happiness through the natural influence she would exert over the king, the dauphin and the future dauphine." It didn't seem to occur to the ambassador how ridiculous it would be for the king and his grandson to marry two sisters. After debating the issue, for Adélaïde was hesitant, the four daughters agreed to plead the cause of the archduchess Elisabeth whom we met in the previous chapter. As usual, the king said neither yes nor no, promised to think about it, waited for them to bring the subject up again, and even enquired in Vienna about getting a portrait of her and some information about her character. Most likely he was merely buying time and peace of mind both from his daughters and the Austrian ambassador, because indications were that he was not about to give up Madame du Barry.

There was however one unknown factor: his conscience. And that is where his youngest daughter Louise comes in.

A Carmelite princess

The youngest daughter of Louis XV and Marie Leszczynska was short, frail and in delicate health. She had no doubt contracted tuberculosis like so many members of her family, as she would sometimes spit up blood. Her back was so deformed by scoliosis that she wound up a hunchback. But this did not faze her in the least. Her face beamed with strength and intelligence. There was nothing about her of the old maid embittered by her fate, because she had never envisaged any future but life in a convent.

She'd always had a vocation. Torn from the Fontevrault convent where she'd been relegated with three of her sisters to disencumber Versailles of its too numerous royal offspring, she never got used to court life. To her it was all so artificial. She saw the great formal court gowns as "the devil's hair-shirts." At the age of fifteen in the Carmelite convent on the rue de Grenelle, she watched as the young and beautiful Madame de Rupelmonde took the veil. The latter, having suffered the loss one after the other of her son, her husband and her father, left the world behind and entered the most demanding of the religious orders. Louise would later say, "During the ceremony I resolved to ask God every day to show me the way to break the ties that bound me to the world and to one day become, if not a Carmelite, as I didn't dare flatter myself that I had the strength for that, at least a religious in a well established house." She asked so many questions that the assistant mother superior observed, "It would truly seem that Madame is dreaming of becoming a daughter of Saint Theresa." To which she replied, "And why not, since the daughters of Saint Theresa are so happy?" But when she broached the subject with her father, he replied smiling "that she had to wait until she was twenty-five or a widow," in other words until she had legally come of age.

She'd long since turned twenty-five. She had not given up her hope of serving God, but continued to wonder where she could be most useful. Her mother's death freed her from the duties she felt she owed to the poor Marie Leszczynska. And when her father installed Madame du Barry in his life she thought that nothing short of supernatural means could save him. She felt that through her prayers and sacrifice she could reverse his fate and bring him God's forgiveness. The time had come to join the convent. She informed the archbishop of Paris, Christophe de Beaumont, and asked his support in getting her father's permission. Louis XV was overwhelmed. "How can you bring me such news?" the king asked the archbishop. His head in his hands he moaned, "This is cruel... cruel... cruel... but if God asks it of me, I cannot refuse." He would give his answer in a fortnight's time, to give him the chance to get used to the idea, but he already knew he would acquiesce.

Two weeks later on the 16th of February 1770 he informed her in a very moving letter that he felt it was not his right to oppose God's will or hers. He made only one stipulation: she must not join the Carmelite convent near Compiègne for it was too close to the court's spring residence for her to be at peace there. He ended, "May God give you the strength to bear your new condition, for once the step is taken, there is no turning back. I embrace you with all my heart, my dear daughter, and I give you my blessing."

She chose the house at Saint-Denis, which she made haste to join in the greatest secrecy so as to avoid a fuss. Madame Campan again is worth listening to: "One evening while I was reading, someone came to tell her that Monsieur Bertin, the minister responsible for the sale of offices, had come to have a word with her. She hurried off, came back, went back to her silks and embroidery, had me start reading again, and when it was over she ordered me to be in her office at eleven o'clock the next morning. When I arrived the princess had already left." Louise later admitted to Madame Campan that the visitor had delivered her father's permission. "She was justifiably proud of the fact that she had returned afterwards without the least sign of agitation, although she was feeling so deeply agitated that she could hardly make it back to her seat."

It was the king himself who, having come downstairs to have his coffee as usual in Madame Adélaïde's apartment, explained their youngest sister's absence: "Do not call her; she is no longer here; you will see her no longer. She is at the Carmelite convent in Saint-Denis where she intends to take the veil." At first, Adélaïde was angry not to have been in on the secret, but her anger quickly turned into admiration. Victoire shed silent tears; Sophie did too, although Madame Campan neglected to say so. Soon after her departure the postulant wrote to her father, "Let there be no more talk of me." She would soon change her name from Louise to Sister Theresa of Saint Augustine. But in this case there was no radical separation from her loved ones and the world. It's not for nothing that one is daughter to the king. The princess adjusted quickly and easily to the rigors of convent life, but she would receive many visitors, and keep up a voluminous correspondence. Once she took the veil she could not shirk her responsibilities. She would thrice be elected mother superior, and would lead the convent energetically.

But let's not get ahead of ourselves; let's get back to Louis XV. Louise's sacrifice did not wrest Louis XV from du Barry's arms. As a result, he was reluctant to go see her, even though she repeatedly asked him to. Then suddenly on May 4th he steeled himself to make an unannounced visit in a state of "extreme sadness," and behaved rather aggressively to hide his discomfiture: "I know that nuns like to preach to their parents, but Madame, I want none of your sermons." Her answer came, "Oh, papa, I will respect your orders, but at least please accept my prayers and good works." We know nothing of the rest of their conversation, but according to one nun who saw him leave, he was as cheerful then as he'd been mournful upon arrival. He couldn't get himself to attend her veil-taking ceremony in September and later got a shock when he saw her dressed in the brown homespun habit, her face encircled by a white veil. "Her habit is quite ugly," he would write to his grandson in Parma. He returned pretty regularly, about once a month or more. He was granted the exceptional privilege of access to her cell through a door made for the purpose directly from the parlor so he need not see other nuns except when he wanted to attend mass or benediction. Most of the time he entered with his own key and sat on the humble straw mattress. Sometimes he would look out the window and contemplate the nearby royal burial place and say, "That's where I'll end up, over there." He would make his own coffee and chat with Louise for an hour or so. It is unlikely that she tried to preach or convert him, knowing how resolute he was. She was happy enough just to be her easy, natural, happy self: her radiant serenity was the best of sermons. His visits with her were a welcome respite.

How did he reconcile his nights with his mistress and his regular visits to the Carmelites? That is the mystery of this secretive and tormented man, equally sincere in his very contradictions, on whom the crushing burden of power weighed so heavily. Did Louise take part in an attempt to have him marry Madame du Barry in the Church? In 1771 rumors of such a scheme got as far as Austria. Mercy-Argenteau received a request from Vienna to investigate: "We hear that the king and the duke d'Aiguillon are in frequent talks with the Carmelite Madame Louise who is apparently working hard to get the pope to annul Madame du Barry's marriage so that she can marry the king." But in his answer the ambassador only mentioned some obscure intrigues, the secrets of which the princess remained unaware. If there was such an attempt, it didn't get far – perhaps not beyond idle speculation about similarities with

Madame de Maintenon*. Louise would undoubtedly have scruples about taking part in such a scheme and she must also have known that her father would have none of it. As he once said to Choiseul à propos of marrying an Austrian princess, "If the archduchess were such as I desired her, I would take her as my wife with great pleasure, for I must settle on someone, otherwise I will forever be troubled by the fair sex. And most certainly you will not see me with a Madame de Maintenon." He meant it. He had infinite respect for his family. Unlike Louis XIV, he never wanted to legitimize his illegitimate children, nor even have them brought up at court. He was intent on imposing Madame du Barry as his official favorite, but not on making her his wife in the eyes of God.

Such was Louis XV, ferociously defending against all odds his right to a private life of his choosing, but respecting to a far greater extent than his great-grandfather Louis XIV the duties imposed on him by his state and place in the dynastic chain.

The family dolt?

The crisis that Madame du Barry's arrival provoked within the royal family could not have come at a worse time for the young heir to the throne. He was a vulnerable adolescent who had already had more than his share of sorrows.

The young Louis Auguste, born on August 23, 1754 with the title Duke de Berry, was not preordained by birth to be king. He was but the second of the four sons of the dauphin Louis Ferdinand, Louis XV's only son. He was three years younger than the heir apparent, Louis Joseph. Two other boys followed: the count de Provence, Louis Stanislas Xavier, born in November 1755; and the last male Charles Philippe, count d'Artois, born in October 1757. Being somewhere in the middle in birth order, as we know, is always problematic. But in this case, Louis Auguste had an additional handicap. With his blond hair and porcelain-blue eyes, he took after his mother in every way except in her energy. He promised to resemble his Saxon ancestors whose tall and corpulent figures populate Dresden's museums. Like them, he was slow moving, placid, taciturn and stubborn. His three brothers on the other hand had the dark eyes and brown hair that their father and grandfather inherited from Louis XIV. They were spirited and full of life, with

---

* *Translator's note: Madame de Maintenon was Louis XIV's morganatic wife. See* Les Femmes du Roi Soleil, *by Simone Bertière.*

just enough impudence to seem blessed with vigorous characters. They had the art of attracting people's attention and capturing their interest, of being liked and admired wherever they went. Their father saw more of himself in them than in the awkward little ugly duckling who quietly kept to himself. The eldest especially, who had been very well trained by his tutors, showed signs of becoming an outstanding king, already demonstrating great seriousness, authority and piety. He already played at being king, much to his parents' delight. Neither Madame de Marsan, governess to the four princes when they were little, nor the duke de La Vauguyon, who succeeded her, was exempt from the infatuation that everyone felt for the eldest, to the detriment of the second. What is more, he was quickly followed by the more precocious third son, and thoroughly eclipsed by the cheerful and cheeky fourth. Louis Auguste got a minimum of care and attention; no one seemed to notice him. Naturally, therefore, he was in great need of affection.

When his elder brother came down with tuberculosis of the bone, his life was suddenly turned upside down. The ailing child soon could not move, and wasted away. To give him a companion they decided to send his next brother "among the men" a year before his time. So Louis Auguste was taken out of the nursery to endure the affectionate tyranny of a future sovereign – they refused to give up hope! – who had no other subjects over whom to exert his authority. Louis Joseph set himself up as his younger brother's instructor and lectured him on how to escape the temptations that he himself had vanquished: "Come learn how they dealt with me so as to correct me of my faults, it will do you good." He had his obedient tutor read his brother the edifying story of his road to virtue, and commented along the way: "Of that particular weakness I do believe I am cured." Blind faith in the eldest son's genius and moral superiority prevented his parents and educators from wondering what harmful effects this behavior might have on the younger son. In any case, the little patient, who proved to be very brave when faced with death, should have his way in everything, shouldn't he? When the end came, nature would spare the poor Louis Auguste the ultimate ordeal; he would not witness the death of his well-meaning and captivating tormenter. Himself racked with a cough and burning with fever, the child was so ill that he had to be isolated. This was no psychosomatic illness, as we would say today; he had really been contaminated.

At dawn on Easter Sunday 1761, a messenger arrived with news for the child's parents: "The duke de Berry is doing well, but..." His face did the rest. Slumped in atrocious pain, the parents could not shake the idea that death had chosen the wrong child. He was not the one who should have survived; he couldn't help but seem like an unworthy usurper. But there was nothing to do but resign oneself. Now the eldest brother at seven years of age, the little duke de Berry was subjected by his father to an extremely arduous education designed to hoist him up to the level required by his unwonted promotion.

Contemporary and subsequent historians have handed down the most contradictory opinions of the royal sons' tutor and the education he gave the future Louis XVI. Was he an honest defender of morality and the Christian faith against the rising tide of irreligion, or was he a monstrous conniver covering his hypocritical ambitions with a veil of piety? The truth no doubt lies somewhere between the two. Antoine-Paul-Jacques de Quelen et de Caussade, duke de La Vauguyon, was inordinately proud of his long ancestry. One of his forebears had stood out among Henry III's favorites before perishing by the sword of a henchman of the duke de Guise whose wife he had seduced. In keeping with tradition among the nobility of the sword, the tutor was a man of war. Although he did not rise to the highest levels of military command, he proved remarkably courageous at the battle of Fontenoy. His piety, his hatred of the *philosophes*, and his ties to the religious faction won him the esteem of Louis XV's son, so in 1758 he entrusted his sons' education to him.

Having no pedagogical experience at all did not disqualify him from such a position. The everyday tasks of instructing the young princes were relegated to schoolmasters. The tutor as a rule oversaw his students' moral education. But in this case, as the parents kept an eye on things, La Vauguyon got his charges to produce results that would impress their parents and show him in a good light. Louis Auguste was therefore subjected to an educational regimen worthy of Gargantua. The most reputable specialists were hired for him. Gone were the days when the great lords, contemptuous of puffed-up scholars, gloried in their ignorance. An eighteenth-century sovereign must excel in every discipline; history (still seen as a mere illustration of moral precepts), Latin, living languages, mathematics, physics and geography were part of a program that left no time for leisure. The dauphin Louis Ferdinand was a man of principle; he could not be less open to the indulgent methods promoted in Rousseau's *Émile*. Children must be brought up the hard way. To build character, education must be forbidding. "The frivolous being, accustomed to taking his early studies lightly, will bring this lack of seriousness to his subsequent affairs, will make a game of the most important matters, and will abandon them as soon as they are no longer amusing." Before dismissing this austerity as repellent by today's standards, let's think for a moment of Marie-Antoinette and the effects of her education devoid of any constraint...

Contrary to received wisdom, the future Louis XVI was an excellent pupil; he was willing, he applied himself and he studied. Compared to the younger Provence, who studied with him, he was a slow learner. The other grasped things more quickly and demonstrated more readily what he knew. Louis Auguste concluded therefore that he could not compete with him at this level. Besides, he hated high-minded phrases, wordiness and verbal jousting. He had a precise, meticulous but dry mind, and was fond of the sciences. He was enthusiastic about the physics experiments of Abbé Nollet, who broke out into a cold sweat whenever his pupil took apart his teaching materials. He adored the geography maps that provided him an endless field where he could wander, lost in his dreams. He knew a great deal, but since he didn't say anything, no one was aware of it. His silence passed for stupidity, to such an extent that his father consulted a Jesuit about his son's intellectual abilities. Like all Jesuits, he was an expert on education. His verdict on Louis Auguste was not too severe: he isn't brilliant, but he would be sound. The anxious father exclaimed, "I'm delighted by how you view my oldest son. I have always seen him as one of those unadorned naturals who can only hint at what they will one day ably produce; but I feared that I was taken in by fatherly love." Deep down, however, his doubts remained.

Was Louis Auguste raised properly or not? The debate is still going on. What was unfortunate about the education of this future king was how abstract and theoretical it was. Rote learning predominated, and he was not expected to think for himself. There was no contact with the outside world and no curiosity about it, nor was there any sort of physical exercise. His father, the dauphin Louis Ferdinand, lived in his books and hated to hunt or stroll in the fresh air – everything his own father Louis XV loved.

Two aspects of his education would prove to be disastrous.

First of all, against all tradition, the future king was given no military training. The days when the sovereign was expected to risk his life and lead the charge on the battlefield were over; the leading generals had long since preferred to be left to develop their tactics quietly on their own. But the king necessarily lost prestige if he was not the head of the army. The military maneuvers held in Compiègne during his yearly visit had the advantage of offering the kingly presence for the admiration of the troops. Also, in direct contact with his soldiers he could deepen the mysterious relationship that inspires devotion. The future Louis XVI duly learned the science of fortifications and sieges, and his interest in the navy was so keen that he would acquire a degree of competence that would even surprise seamen. But he would never be a leader of men. How can this inability be explained when his father made a veritable cult of the military and his tutor was a seasoned soldier? Did they find the boy wanting? To this day the question has not been answered.

The other grave mistake of his education had to do with his youthful idealism. Exploring the literary tradition of the Christian prince, borrowing pell-mell from Bossuet and Fénelon, La Vauguyon inculcated in his pupil an irenic view of government, in which effectiveness springs solely from virtue. "The famous Monsieur Bossuet used to say that all of the king's duties could be summed up in these four words: piety, goodness, justice, resolution." To these four duties the zealous tutor added a fifth: chastity. The child would only have to respect them in order to reign in peace over the best of all possible kingdoms. He was made to write, "I feel that the example of my morals, my respect for religion, my love of virtue, my horror of vice and my contempt for any kind of baseness and indecency will constitute a kind of legislation that is more powerful perhaps than laws." In all of this, real politics, those founded on what's possible, that take into account man's diversity and teach the art of wise compromise, were notably absent.

His was a thorough education, but it was too theoretical, and more suited to train a cleric than a man called to exercise supreme authority. He was taught nothing about the exercise of concrete power; this was not how to educate a future king. Louis XIV was far less knowledgeable, but he learned on the job with his mother and Mazarin how to face down a mob and lead an army. He also knew how to dance. Alas, they also forgot to teach Louis Auguste what marshal Villeroy had so well inculcated in his grandfather, the art of walking with grace and distinction, and gliding with measured steps over a waxed dance floor. The unfortunate child was therefore seen as boorish and unsociable, one of nature's oafs, practically an idiot. His father, already riddled with fatal pulmonary tuberculosis, was increasingly hard on the boy, causing tongues to wag. On the feast of Saint Hubert November 3, 1765, for not having mastered a lesson, his father didn't let him take part in the highly popular hunting event in the saint's honor*. Everyone concluded therefore

---

* *Translator's note: Saint Hubert is the patron saint of hunting.*

that the child was really good for nothing. "What a shame that the brilliant Provence is not the older, he would make a much better king," was murmured in the corridors of Versailles.

Terrible loneliness

On the following December 20th, the dauphin Louis Ferdinand rendered his spirit, leaving his wife inconsolable. Before dying he made her swear that she would change nothing about their children's education, something Louis XV would have wished. The king and his only son had never understood each other, and over the years the gulf between father and son had widened. Louis Ferdinand was furious at his father's infidelities and never accepted la Pompadour. Very close to his mother, he supported the religious faction and was indignant at the expulsion of the Jesuits. Of great piety and exemplary family life, he was a living reproach to his father. Although he never lived to exercise power, he was thoroughly imbued with a sense of sovereign authority and took a hard line against the rebellious magistrates. Participating in the King's Council meetings but excluded from the decision-making process, he champed at the bit. He discreetly put himself forward as an alternative; after all, he was going to be the next king.

When La Vauguyon tried to get rid of Choiseul, accusing him of having led the Jansenists' underhanded offensive against the Jesuits, Louis Ferdinand had a violent confrontation with the minister. Unable to get to the bottom of the whole business, Louis XV just buried it. Choiseul survived the attempt, but he jeopardized his future by unwisely uttering words he could not take back about the heir to the throne. Knowing that he was dying, the dauphin Louis Ferdinand wanted to pass the gauntlet to his oldest surviving son; thus the promise he demanded of Marie-Josèphe.

Louis Ferdinand's worries were in vain. Louis XV would never have interfered in his grandsons' education. Like many fathers conscious of their own weaknesses, he wanted to protect his offspring from them. And he suffered too much from the misunderstandings that had separated him from his only son to go against his last wishes. All the children gained from their father's death was permission to take a few walks in the park and a bit of exercise.

So the boy's education did not change, quite the contrary. His late father became his new role model as the memory of the little dying prince waned. La Vauguyon made a cult figure of him. He had to imitate his father's virtues, espouse his enmities and adopt his political viewpoint. The tutor used the memorials to his father to make solemn admonitions in the histrionic style of the period: "Promise me that you will strictly follow his example; meditate before his likeness; each day choose one of his virtues to emulate and be such that in my dying days I can exclaim tenderly: 'God took from me the most virtuous of men; he deprived France of the greatest of princes; but he gave him back to me, and to the nation, in the person of his son.'"

Weakened by the disease she contracted at her husband's bedside, Marie-Josèphe of Saxony, who might have been able to provide her child with a bit of warmth and tenderness, hovered between life and death, only mustering enough energy to fight the Austrian marriage that Choiseul was arranging for him. She died on March 13, 1767. Her mother-in-law Marie Leszczynska, overcome with grief by these successive losses, was the next to succumb. Around the orphan there was no one – except the king, who for the moment remained aloof. Louis Auguste was alone.

A much-recounted incident gives an idea of his emotional isolation. At a little party that the governess Madame de Marsan held for the royal children, she organized a raffle as an educational tool. Instead of keeping the prize from the winning ticket, each child had to offer it to "the person you love the most." Everyone joined happily in the game. When it was Louis Auguste's turn to draw a winning ticket, he quietly pocketed the prize. La Vauguyon stepped in to remind him of the rules. The adolescent pointed to the gifts piled up at the other children's feet while at his there was nothing: "Well, sir, whom do you expect me to love the most here where I am loved by no one?"

During those crucial years when the personality is formed, this naturally kind and contented child shut down; he became secretive, introverted and closed-off. But the raffle incident revealed more than that.

First of all it shows that he felt like a stranger in his own world. He disliked court life. Finding it artificial and hypocritical, he rejected its language and manners. His indifference to how he looked, his preference for extremely plain clothing, his absent look that made him seem near-sighted, his heavy peasant-like tread and even his long silences were all put down to some sort of inborn boorishness. But they were all deliberate on his part, born of his rejection. He rose early and climbed up to the roof to chase the cats around the drainpipes; he gazed at the heavens and inspected the surrounding countryside with his spyglass. He enjoyed talking to ordinary people. He could hold on tight to a farmhand's plough and climbed up the ladders used by the plasterers and painters repairing the chateau. For a relaxing hobby, he chose not wood- or ivory-work like his grandfather, but lock forging, which dirtied his hands and required him to tame fire and grapple with metal, using extremely precise movements. Confined to life in a hostile environment, he protected himself by secreting a shell of silence, which was taken for insensitivity. For now, he was skinny. Later on corpulence would provide a protective layer, a sort of aggression-absorbing quilt. His public image would become that of a mild-mannered and flaccid fat man.

The other thing the raffle shows is that he was not timid. A timid boy would not have responded to his tutor's question. Within, he had a sort of steely resolve, and a block of certitudes. His fervent and deeply held religious faith seeped into every aspect of his being and in his particular case, because he was heir to the throne, it provided serenity. He looked forward with confidence to the future. It was not at all that he was prideful. But he believed that God would grant the blessings needed by him whom He had chosen to be his representative in the earthly kingdom of France. Unlike Louis XV, he did not find kingly duties abhorrent, and he readied himself to carry them out as conscientiously as he did everything. But La Vauguyon was perhaps not wrong in warning him against stubbornness. Obstinacy is not the same thing as firmness; and he was not the least bit flexible. He could not adapt. Faced with obstacles, he retreated into his shell and awaited his hour, which could not but come, or so he believed.

Grandfather and grandson

Only his grandfather, with a bit of love and attention, could have opened his eyes and planted his feet firmly on the ground. But each had a long way to go to meet the other, and they wouldn't have enough time to complete the process.

His son's death had overwhelmed Louis XV and left him consumed by remorse. Yet again, the grief-stricken survivor was desolate. He moaned, "I cannot get used to no longer having a son, and when they bring my grandson to me, what a difference – especially when I see him walk in!" The king deplored the adolescent's lack of elegance and grace; but above all he perceived that his grandson was ill at ease with him. The reason for this was clear. The new dauphin, raised to abhor vice, could not have been unaware of the disapproval that weighed on his grandfather. Of course only veiled comments would be made about his dissolute life, but he was undoubtedly urged to pray for the salvation of his soul. And the history books, awash in moralizing certainties, taught him to see in the moral failings of kings the direct cause of the misfortunes visited upon their people.

A very revealing incident illustrates the awkwardness between them. As was a common educational practice at the time, LaVauguyon had his pupil summarize the most instructive passages of Fénelon's *Telemachus*, and then had him typeset and print the text himself on a small printing press. As per custom, Louis XV was the first to be honored with a copy of these *Moral and political maxims [...] on the science of kingship and the happiness of peoples.* The king could only have been put off by the name of Fénelon and the title of the work, because the theories of this archbishop of Cambrai, although outdated, still retained a whiff of subversion. He read it, however, and what he found displeased him, as he felt indirectly attacked by Maxim XIII: "... The prince must distance himself from and mark his disapproval and contempt for those who, having suffocated the voice of religion, modesty and decency, publicly display their vices and glory in what should cover them in shame and opprobrium." Instead of the hoped for compliments, the budding printer received the reply, "Monsieur le dauphin, your work is finished; break the plate." The king didn't dare punish the tutor, but he was hurt. He could not help but see a reproach in his grandson's bright eyes and innocent remarks.

The dauphin would soon be fourteen, an age when one is expected to understand certain things. Madame du Barry's sudden arrival in his grandfather's life deeply troubled him. Madame Adélaïde recruited him to her crusade against the new favorite. Like his aunts, he turned a cold shoulder when she was presented at court. But his tutor's attitude must have puzzled him. Hating Choiseul so much, the duke de La Vauguyon took the side of the temptress on whom the religious faction was counting, and all of a sudden he was holding forth to his pupil about the king's virtues. Fortunately, someone understood the boy's anxiety and proposed a simple, clear and forthright solution, which cleared up any confusion. Abbé Soldini had been Marie-Josèphe's confessor, and she had him appointed her son's director of conscience. This priest of Italian origins was of an uncommon intelligence. He stayed away from the infighting of the clans and coteries, but cast a lucid eye on society, and piety did not prevent him from encouraging his ward to guard against the clergy's attempts to encroach on royal prerogatives. This was far more concrete and realistic advice than anything in the *Telemachus* maxims! Without trying to minimize Louis XV's undeniable faults, he explained to his grandson that it was not his place to judge him; that his duty was rather to silence the rash zeal of the Pharisees:

> Regard as your personal enemies those who would dare to make in your presence the most minor criticism of him, whoever they are. If children are supposed to throw a cloak over their father's faults, as Shem and Japheth did, so as not to incur the curse of Sham*, how much more is it incumbent on the children of kings to do so... Rise up sharply against those who would have the temerity to censure your amiable father in your presence.

Going further, he encouraged him to take the first step:

> You are his right arm; he needs you with him. Arrange it so that regardless of your various occupations he sees that he is always welcome in your presence, always well received, and that you are desirous of his company. If he visits you or calls for you, drop everything with joy and promptitude... The hunt is truly a kingly pleasure; go with the king when he requires it of you, you will even desire to accompany him always and you will show him your eagerness to do so.

These remarks were included with others in a long letter given to the dauphin on the eve of his wedding**, and thus take on a solemn aspect. They are similar to Maria Theresa's instructions to Marie-Antoinette – guidelines on how to behave in the years to come. Their effect was immediate. The abbé had the right idea in betting that the hunt would break the ice between the king and the dauphin. For a long time deprived of physical exercise, the adolescent developed a passion for riding as soon as he was allowed to mount a horse. Although he had grown a lot and his health was still fragile, he was doing better, and he blossomed in the heady pleasures of the chase, soon demonstrating remarkable courage and skillfulness in hunting down the prey. The king, himself a great hunter, was delighted to find in his grandson something other than a scribbler of moralizing maxims. They grew to trust one another.

---

*   A reference to Noah's drunkeness in Genesis IX, 20-27.

**   The text of this letter is kept at the National Library of France, French manuscripts, 14714, folio 20.

As a rule, once the hunt was over the men would have supper, sometimes alone, but most often in the evening Madame du Barry would preside as mistress of the house in one of the hunting lodges – Saint-Hubert or La Muette – in the forest. The king, a bit embarrassed and fearing a refusal, did not invite his grandson to join them. So he himself took the initiative and quietly gave Madame du Barry to understand that he'd like to be included. It would take a bit of doing to hide the fact from the courtiers. One evening, he was just taking leave of the other hunters when Madame du Barry cried out, "Oh, silly me! I forgot to pray the king to allow Monsieur le dauphin to take supper here, but I will do it another time." And thus the grandson began to sup regularly in her company after the hunt. The homage he thus paid to his grandfather, at a time when the rest of the family were castigating him, profoundly touched him. Invoking the memory of his late son in a letter to the infante of Parma, he wrote on June 16, 1770: "Fate has given me another who seems able to render the rest of my days happy. I love him with all my heart because he loves me in return." And later, on June 24th, "I am very happy with my grandson because of the friendship he shows me both inwardly and outwardly, and it is the latter that pleases me more, as I was already sure of the former." In the battle that raged around the favorite, the heir to the throne publicly took the king's side.

Such was the climate reigning at the court of France when Marie-Antoinette landed there in all innocence, directed from Vienna by her mother. Such was her spouse who, she was told, was an ignorant boor, a religious zealot, and a clumsy oaf whom she would have no trouble dominating. She would find this scenario way off the mark.

CHAPTER 5

THE FIRST LADY OF THE KINGDOM

When Marie-Antoinette arrived in France neither Marie Leszczynska nor Marie-Josèphe of Saxony was alive to welcome her. She was therefore the first lady in the kingdom; but she was still just a little girl who had neither the physical appearance nor the psychological maturity of an adult. She was just entering that awkward stage between girlhood and womanhood. The time could not be less propitious for completely changing one's universe, not to mention being thrust into the highest echelons of society. Three-quarters of a century earlier in similar circumstances the duchess de Bourgogne was firmly taken in hand by Madame de Maintenon, who finished her education. This duty would now fall to Madame Adélaïde, but she had neither the ability nor the authority for the task. We can understand why Louis XV judged it preferable to have the empress direct her daughter through her ambassador. At the time he could not have suspected the untoward consequences.

The dauphine landed in the middle of the war between the conservative faction led paradoxically by la du Barry, and Choiseul's faction, which felt threatened by them. Even if Marie-Antoinette wished to maintain a strict neutrality, it could only be interpreted as an asset for Choiseul, because she was the lynchpin of the Austrian alliance that he initiated and that his enemies were challenging. Whether she liked it or not, therefore, she was an integral part of the conflict. And since the king's age led everyone to believe that she would soon be queen, she was a crucial element, fought over in this end-of-reign climate, a stake in a major political game. She would play her part and show some verve. Not able to neutralize her, everyone competed to flatter and cajole her, exacerbating the natural pride she already took in her high birth. It would be enough to turn the most sensible of heads. If we add to this the fact that her mentors never stopped repeating that she must conquer the entire court, get her husband under control and win over the king, we get an idea of the immensity of the task ahead of her.

She did not immediately take up the gauntlet against the favorite. But right from the start she formed an opinion of her that would not change one iota. As early as July 9th she wrote to her mother, "The king shows me a thousand kindnesses and I love him tenderly, but it's pitiable the weakness he has for Madame du Barry, who is the silliest and most impertinent creature imaginable." But we'll leave their clashes for the next chapter; for the moment Marie-Antoinette had more important things to do. First she must get her bearings; she must settle in and get used to Versailles' ways and habits, organize her life and learn her role. She had hardly managed to carve out a place for herself when two events upset the delicate balance. The first was a political turnaround in internal affairs that ended in the dismissal of Choiseul, her mother's principal ally in France. The other was the marriage of her two young brothers-in-law to princesses of Savoy, which altered foreign affairs by creating a counter-weight to the Austro-French alliance. Her first years at the court of France therefore were full of all sorts of potential pitfalls. Being first lady of the kingdom put her squarely in the limelight and exposed her to many more risks than her husband, sheltered as he was in the king's shadow. All eyes were on her; the least word or gesture on her part had consequences.

Difficult relations

Marie-Antoinette surely did not expect to marry Prince Charming. During the journey to France, Vermond found her "quite concerned with what she had been told about Monsieur le dauphin's sternness and dark moods." She anxiously broached the subject and Starhemberg feared for "the distaste that any extreme unattractiveness could cause her" on the part of her highly unprepossessing spouse. As she was not in the habit of changing her mind once it was made up, when she met him she looked for nothing but confirmation of her preconceived notions. She saw neither his modesty nor his gentleness, only his awkwardness and lack of sparkle, which she took as proof of his oafishness. His reticence she took for stupidity. Clearly there were flagrant incompatibilities between them. He was as slow moving as she was quick, as plodding as she was flighty, as introverted as she was extroverted. He enjoyed peace and quiet and solitude; she couldn't sit still. She needed people and commotion around her, wanted to be entertained. Anything bright and shiny fascinated her; he was distrustful of appearances. She delighted in clever word play; he only liked language that was straightforward. He tried to get to the bottom of things; she happily flitted about the surface. She was only superficially pious whereas he lived his faith intensely.

Although they both liked to laugh, it was not at the same things. His humor was a bit coarse and down to earth, and when he found something funny he guffawed, which she not unreasonably found vulgar. He still enjoyed schoolboy antics, while her sense of the comic was finer, more hurtful too, taking aim at others' faults. His penchant for manual labor offended her aristocratic prejudices. She disapproved and complained to Mercy: "This proclivity could lead him to too much involvement with the lowest orders." She was ashamed of this husband who "looks like a peasant who's just ploughed his fields." In short, they were not predestined to get along.

Far from trying to help them overcome their differences, people did everything possible to make them distrust each other. From the very first day they differed on whether to keep Vermond on or not. The dauphin's dislike of the abbé was immediate and intense. He didn't need his tutor La Vauguyon to tell him the role this protégé of Choiseul and Austria would play; he'd figured it out for himself. But it was La Vauguyon who brought the religious faction into play in an attempt to get rid of the intruder. We saw above how the king had allowed Vermond to become her reader while refusing him the position of confessor. However, he had refused to grant the confessor post to the archbishop's choice abbé Soldini, and instead imposed his own confessor, abbé Maudoux, a decent priest who would have no truck with coteries but had a lot of time on his hands, being the king's director of conscience. The dauphin backed off but remained highly resentful of Vermond, who didn't help matters by trying to insinuate himself into the dauphin's daily visits to his wife. He managed not to utter a word to him for months, even years, and no matter what Mercy might write to Maria Theresa, it was not "through timidity and inattention." The ambassador came out the big winner in this little war. His informer kept his job, and increased his ascendancy over Marie-Antoinette; for it wasn't difficult to convince her that the whole affair only proved that La Vauguyon was a "nasty man" and a "hypocrite" who had subjugated his pupil, and fancied that he could "govern" her through him, "subjugate" her, and "bend her to his wishes." Nothing could have infuriated her more.

Did she plead Vermond's cause with her husband? We don't know. But she could not hold back her disparagement of his former tutor – with remarkable clumsiness. When she told him that

La Vauguyon and his son were a pair of rogues, he merely "shook his head without replying," and she naively took that to mean she had "straightened him out" on that score. She flattered herself that she had "uncovered" the tutor's secret, and that her husband admitted that he "didn't pay him any mind." This was a vague phrase really, as it could simply have meant that he was protesting against her criticism that he was too much under his influence. "It is clear that he does not like Monsieur de La Vauguyon at all, but he fears him," she secretly wrote to her mother. "She was persuaded," Mercy added, "that the dauphin's attachment to the duke de La Vauguyon was one of habit and fear, by no means one of affection and trust, and besides, this prince was so reserved that on the subject of the people around him, despite some discreet prodding on her part, she was never able to get from him a single word to enlighten her." In truth, the young man was not fond of his tutor. He seemed already to have grasped his intellectual limits, and much later on would claim to have been badly educated by him. But he did not like Marie-Antoinette's meddling and lecturing him on the matter. The conclusions she drew from his evasive answers were at very least premature. That she was "always heeded without suffering any contradiction" proved nothing, unless it's that he took what she said with a grain of salt.

Their first contacts were fraught with mutual incomprehension. They did not understand each other; had nothing to say to one another, and nothing they felt like doing together. No, there was one; the week after their wedding they read Sully's memoirs. The choice of this text, one of the books his parents had enjoyed reading together, might indicate that the dauphin suggested it in the hope of replacing Vermond as her reader, but if so it failed. Starhemberg* had to admit that they spoke not a word to each other in public. She tried, however, to turn on the charm with him; it worked so well with others. She smiled at him, asked him questions, sought his opinion, and needled him. Prickly and secretive, he was careful not to tell his little chatterbox of a bride what he thought of this one or that one. He withdrew into his shell, leaving her to believe that in his taciturn way, he'd told her all she wanted to hear. Did she imagine that she'd won him over? She boasted that she had to Mercy, who could then crow: "She treats him with such gaiety and charm that the young prince is subjugated by her. He confides in her things about which he never spoke to anyone before. His

---

* Starhemberg spent nearly two weeks in Versailles after the wedding and wrote the first accounts to the empress before ceding his pen to Mercy.

somber and reserved character has made him impenetrable until now, but Madame la dauphine gets him to say anything she likes." Nothing could be farther from the truth.

The distrust between them did not facilitate their marital relations, already made difficult by their youth and lack of maturity. The entire court was aware of their failure, and prattled on about it. Starhemberg wrote that all were surprised by "the incredible behavior of this young prince so recently married to such an attractive princess who is pleasing in every way to everyone..." Two days after the wedding, the dauphin took up his morning hunts again. "That's leaving rather early," it was said. He visited his wife on his return, she having just emerged from sleep: "Have you slept well?" "Yes." That's all. It wasn't much. Of course, Vermond had only just stepped out of their way – standing in the doorway, he could hear what they said – which didn't encourage effusions on their part. Did they really sleep every night "in the same bed and under the same covers" as Starhemberg affirmed to Maria Theresa? Let us recall that the custom at the court of France, very different from that of Vienna, assigned royal couples separate apartments and granted to the husband the right either to remain in his own or go to his wife's bed, as he saw fit. The evidence we have at our disposal does not permit us to know exactly how the young man used this prerogative during those first months. The only thing we know for sure is that the spouses remained strangers to one another. They did, however, keep up appearances. It helped that the rhythms of court life were as ruled as sheet music.

A dauphine's daily life

As Maria Theresa expressed her desire to know how her daughter spent her day, the latter applied herself on July 12, 1770 to writing a long letter, most of which follows:

> I rise at ten or nine o'clock, or at nine-thirty, and having dressed, I say my morning prayers; then I breakfast and from there I go to see my aunts, where as a rule I find the king. That lasts until ten-thirty, then at eleven o'clock I have my hair dressed. At mid-day the attendants are called and everyone can enter, and they are certainly not of low rank. I apply my rouge and wash my hands in front of everyone, then the men leave and the women stay and I dress in front of them. At mid-day there is mass. If the king is at Versailles I go with him and my

husband and my aunts to mass; if he is not, I go alone with Monsieur le dauphin, but always at the same time. After mass we dine the two of us in front of everyone, but that is over at one-thirty, as both of us eat very quickly. From there I go to Monsieur le dauphin's rooms and if he is busy I come back to mine; I write or I work, as I am making a waistcoat for the king, which is not getting very far, but I hope that with God's grace it will be finished in a few years. At three o'clock I go back to my aunts' where the king comes at that hour; at four o'clock the abbé comes to my quarters; at five o'clock every day the clavichord or voice master until six. At six-thirty I almost always go to my aunts' when I do not take a walk; you should know that my husband almost always goes with me to my aunts'. At nine o'clock we have supper at home, but when the king is here, we go after supper to see our aunts; we wait for the king who usually comes at ten forty-five but while I'm waiting I sit on a large couch and sleep until the king's arrival, but when he is not there, we go to bed at eleven. That is our entire day.

About Sundays and holiday activities, the little one promised to inform her mother another time; but Maria Theresa would never receive the report. We can therefore only imagine her on those days, which were even more strictly timed than the rest, with their multiple religious duties and the public supper offered as a spectacle for the Sunday visitors.

This very childlike letter evokes better than any report can what Marie-Antoinette was like at that point – a little girl unable to stay up until eleven at night and who falls asleep on a sofa like a baby who can't keep its eyes open. We can guess from it just how much pressure she was under from this highly formalistic court where she was struggling to be accepted.

Her lady-in-waiting, Madame de Noailles, very well disposed to her as she was a Choiseul friend, wished fondly to make a polished young woman of her. Unfortunately, although quite an honest woman, she was snobbish, rigid and not terribly bright. For her, the customs of the court, where she had always lived, were categorical imperatives that she strove to inculcate in the dauphine, but she was not able to impart their spirit, or separate the essential elements from the non-essential. She had her work cut out for her. The child rebelled against brushing her teeth and obstinately refused to wear a corset, even though she was told that this could ruin her figure and deform her back. But she fought to avoid this whale-boned garment that stretched like armor from her hips right up to the top of her shoulders. She would go so far as to tell her mother the barefaced lie that no one in France wore such a thing. She would eventually resign herself to it, and it is to the corset that she would owe the wasp-like waist of which she was so proud. In fact, there would come a time when she would not do without it. But for the moment, she found the right nickname for her lady-in-waiting: Madame Étiquette! She continually aggravated her, in the secret hope that she would resign. Mercy had to deploy a whole treasury of eloquence to convince her that she could be replaced by worse.

She loved children. The ambassador complained that she spent much of the day with those of her domestics, who "ruin her clothes, scratch and break the furniture, and cause mayhem in her apartments." And the lady-in-waiting nearly had a fit when she found her, completely forgetting her rank, on the floor romping with them on all fours. Why didn't she play with the little girls in her own family? There were two of them, the dauphin's two young sisters, Clotilde twelve, and Élisabeth six. She preferred the younger Élisabeth; she was much prettier than Clotilde, who was so fat they called her Fat Madame. Their governess Madame de Marsan was indignant at this: it should be the other way around; the dauphine should show greater affection for the one "nature treated less favorably." Nothing terrible about all that, as Louis XV willingly admitted; after all, she was still but a child herself.

There was however, a more serious reason for reprimands – her taste for mockery, which startled everyone right from the start. But this too was appropriate to her age. Most of the ladies who made up her household were the survivors of the days of Marie Leszczynska and Marie-Josèphe of Saxony, both of whom had been rather stern. They were all at least twenty-five years older than she was, so to her they looked like fossils. There were however a few young ladies at court who'd like nothing better than to have a few laughs, so it was with them that she chatted. She whispered in their ear. She scoffed with them at "everything that's ugly or gloomy." Mercy complained: "Purely to have fun, without any bad intentions, she takes to joking about people's peculiarities." He added that she made things worse by giving her remarks "the spice that makes them saucier." The old ladies were indignant that she openly mocked them and laughed in their face.

Even so, as she was the first lady in rank, it was her duty to hold court during the evenings, which at the time merely meant inviting the courtiers to her quarters to join her at the gaming tables. Later she would have to comply with the custom that was still improperly named "the circle." Luckily for her, what had been known as "the queen's circle," as it was practiced by Louis XIV's mother Anne of Austria, had fallen into disuse. There were no longer queens or dauphines capable of leading an elegant and refined conversation amidst a bevy of duchesses sitting in a circle on their stools (called *tabourets*) with the high-ranking lords standing nearby. By this time "the circle" was nothing more than a group of courtiers come to pay homage to the dauphine, who walked among them addressing to each a few pleasant remarks.

Until her arrival these prerogatives fell to Madame Adélaïde as the highest-ranking lady at court. Once she got over her initial jealousy, she took on the role imposed by her age and station. She took the child under her wing with the worthy intention of teaching her how she must play her role, but not without ulterior motives. She would thus maintain her influence over her and delay her own loss of prestige and place. And besides, was it not a work of piety to protect her from an entourage widely infiltrated by Choiseul's clan? Mesdames aunts therefore invited her to their quarters, gave her a key so that she could come and go as she pleased; they fussed over and monopolized her. And, noticing that holding court every evening was a chore for her, they offered to help. Why, one could just as easily hold the games at Madame Adélaïde's! Mercy saw that this was a trap, and warned Marie-Antoinette that "etiquette and custom, in the absence of a queen, assign all entertainments to a dauphine." Even if she was bored to death by Marie Leszczynska's beloved card game *le cavagnole*, it was her duty to preside over it.

Relations with Mesdames aunts had begun on an optimistic note with Maria Theresa's blessing: "These princesses are full of virtue and talent," she wrote to her daughter on May 4th, "this is an asset for you; I hope you will be worthy of their friendship." They quickly soured, however, once the ambassador saw that their influence tended to thwart his own. He denigrated their pettiness, their gossip, and their desire not only to think and speak for her but also to shut her up in their narrow, old-maidish world. Unfortunately, these criticisms, although well enough founded, were not made for the dauphine's benefit; they merely reflected the conflict between the different clans clamoring to control her.

Yearning for independence

What with the instructions from her mother, the reprimands of her lady-in-waiting and the aunts' advice, Marie-Antoinette was suffocating and champing at the bit. What good was it to be married and occupy the highest rank in Versailles if she was going to be treated like a schoolgirl? But Maria Theresa did not let go. In January 1771 she wrote to her, "Try to adorn your mind a bit with some worthwhile reading... Do not neglect this resource, which is more necessary for you than for others, lacking as you are in other accomplishments, having neither music nor drawing, dancing nor painting, nor indeed other agreeable skills." But the dauphine detested "worthwhile reading," and wriggled out of it as best she could. She could not bear the duties imposed by holding court. Although she couldn't get out of hosting the evening games, she could relieve her boredom by substituting another game for *le cavagnole,* at least at her table. Eating before the assembled court ruined her appetite, which was not hearty to begin with. So she speeded up the service. The dishes passed in front the dauphin so quickly that he hadn't the time to get at them. The courtiers eagerly awaited his reaction, but he laughed about it good-naturedly.

She took advantage of any opportunity to impose her will. And she started to play the various contenders for dominance off against each other in order to come out the winner.

Some examples? Theoretically, she had no say in the matter of who made up her household staff. But at one point a chambermaid had to be hired. The dauphin had a candidate, Madame Thierry, wife of his own *valet de chambre.* Madame de Noailles, to whom the king had granted the privilege of recruiting household staff, protested against the appointment of a woman from the opposite clan. However, Marie-Antoinette had seen Madame Thierry's two children and was enchanted by them; she wanted them with her. She prevailed, against Mercy's strict orders. Another example, in which she sided with the opposition: her aged mistress of the wardrobe, Madame de Villars, had soon to retire and be replaced. The dauphin would like to see her replaced by Madame de Saint-Mégrin, his tutor's daughter-in-law. This time, Marie-Antoinette shared Mercy's apprehension. Not daring to confront the king personally, she wrote to him: "It would pain me greatly to have Madame de Saint-Mégrin in my household, especially in such a position. I have too much confidence in my dear papa's friendship to think that he would want to grieve me this way; I beg him forthwith to spare me this." The king conceded, but took the opportunity to remind her of her duties: "When positions are vacated by death or resignation, I hope that you will accept the persons I propose to you." And the following year, without consulting her, he would appoint Madame de Cossé.

When possible, however, he was happy to grant her wishes. She took advantage of this to invoke his authority against her mother's interdictions, an instance of which was his decision on horseback riding. She was fidgety and bored in the chateau. She never missed a chance to go for an outing, up till now on foot, or in a light coach. The others went riding, however, even the women. To prevent her from doing so would be like refusing to let someone drive today. But the empress wouldn't think of it; she feared that riding could compromise pregnancy. Any hope of one was at this point quite premature, with good reason. But Maria Theresa, while she awaited the hoped-for moment, would prefer her daughter avoid temptation and not learn how to ride. She found an excuse – riding ruins the figure and harms the complexion – but it would take a lot more than that to discourage Marie-Antoinette. She got around the problem. Mercy had Choiseul warn the king of the disadvantages that riding could present "at such a tender age," so when she solicited the support of her "dear papa" she was met with a refusal. But to console her, he allowed her to ride on donkeys. Some "very gentle and calm" ones were found on which to ride safely in the forest with her ladies. She quickly got tired of these rustic mounts; so with the help of Madame Adélaïde, who at her age had been an outstanding rider, a little plot was hatched. A horse was waiting in a clearing in the woods, and there she exchanged it for the donkey. A groom held the animal on a tether and was followed by a number of people ready to catch her if she fell. That evening she did not hide her joy and confided in one of her ladies that she couldn't wait to see the look on the ambassador's face. When he arrived the next morning with reproach on his lips, she triumphantly informed him of the king's consent and his desire "to please Monsieur le dauphin by this sharing of his taste for riding." What could he answer to that?

As she admitted to Mercy on December first, Maria Theresa knew her daughter well enough to be convinced that "she would achieve all she desires and be bold in the pursuit." She therefore pretended to give in so as not to lose credibility: "You tell me that the king approves, as does the dauphin; nothing more need be said." But she did not admit defeat, and for months on end the epistolary soap opera dragged on. The girl showed talent for riding; she made spectacular progress. So they split hairs about how she should mount (she could ride side-saddle but not "like a man"), for how long she could ride (no more than two to three hours, and not many days in a row), and above all no hunting, which was categorically forbidden. "I will take you at your word," her mother said, "a great princess would never break it... you will promise me 'Never will I go hunting on horseback.' I accept the offer you are making me... there shall be no excuses or subterfuge on this point."

Throughout the winter "The passion Madame the Archduchess has for riding is still strong, she rides at the riding school when the weather does not permit doing so outdoors." Freezing weather and snow afforded the opportunity to thoroughly enjoy sleigh riding, where she could show off the skills she learned in Austria. But the fine days brought horseback riding back, and two paintings were in the making, one an equestrian portrait and a smaller one of her in riding habit. The promises have gone out the window. Mother scolds, "I am terribly disturbed to learn that you have not kept your word and have taken part in the hunt." She was wasting her time. Over the next months she reproached her for her "lack of candor" which she told Mercy she feared would spread to other matters: "My daughter could be demonstrating as little good faith in what she confides to you as she did to me about hunting." In December 1772 she again caught her in a boldfaced lie and the lamentations recommenced, this time playing on her emotions: "A bit of candor and tenderness on your part might have mitigated the little lie, but condemned to learn about it by the gazettes – (it was actually from Mercy) –, I admit this is hard for me, and in future will cast a shadow over your truthfulness toward me." But the guilty party had an unbeatable argument: "The king and the dauphin enjoy watching me ride... they were delighted to see me dressed for the hunt." And besides, what is a horse for, if not to run?

There was another field in which she revealed her impatient and imperious temperament that tolerated no resistance, her dealings with the buildings department. Historians have neglected this area, as Mercy doesn't mention it. Pierre de Nolhac investigated the pertinent archival evidence. We have him to thank for showing what happened when the newly arrived little fourteen-year-old dauphine came up against Gabriel, architect to the king.

Custom had it that the dauphine, having queenly functions, occupied the sumptuous apartments on the second floor opposite those of the king. In 1769 much-needed renovations began, but the treasury was empty and the works lagged behind. As we saw, her bedchamber was not ready for her wedding. Temporarily housed on the ground floor in rooms that were too modest and confining for her tastes, she was impatient. Works were hardly recommenced when the ceiling in the famous bedroom showed signs of collapsing, requiring complete renovation and causing the costs to soar. So it was decided to skimp a bit on decor, to make do with a flat, square white ceiling adorned with a simple rose in the center. Gabriel protested: such a ceiling would present "a prodigious dissonance" with those around it, which were much more richly decorated. Marie-Antoinette, whose tastes were not yet formed, opted for the simpler solution, not for economy's sake, but because she wanted to take up as soon as possible the sumptuous apartments she had a right to. The delays exasperated her. Deaf to the workmen's difficulties and Gabriel's artistic torments, she made threatening noises. But the architect had his way; all she gained by way of consolation was an eye-catching homage to the house of Austria: a ceremonial bowl mounted on the cornice holding a two-headed eagle above which fluttered two cherubs bearing a crown. The imminence of the count de Provence's wedding required that the ground-floor rooms be vacated, so the works were speeded up and she was able to take possession of the bedchamber by the end of the year.

Two years later she got worked up once more when her library was being installed. Yet again, she was in a hurry; everything had to be done while the court was in Compiègne. Yet again, money was lacking. Madame de Noailles took it upon herself to have simple wooden shelves put up. But upon her return when the young woman found the shelves, she protested loudly, got them taken down right then and there, and demanded "a set of armoires with mirrors and carving." Despite the cost, Louis XV consented.

Marie-Antoinette changed over her first two years in France. She grew considerably; she "put on a bit of weight" – quite enough for her tastes. She was leaving childhood behind. Her personality was asserting itself. She became more self-confident. Louis XV's good graces freed her somewhat from her mother's domination, although they didn't help to assimilate her into the family. It's not that she conquered him – in the end he found her demands and inappropriate handling of things irritating. Her smiles and wiles lost their effectiveness. If he often gave in to her, it was through weakness. Could Maria Theresa hope that he grant her the same consideration that he had showed his daughter-in-law, the cautious dauphine Marie-Josèphe of Saxony, with whom he used to visit and chat every morning over a cup of coffee? No, it was not a prerogative of the dauphine to receive such visits but an honor he paid his daughter-in-law, whom he loved dearly. Marie-Antoinette fell far short; she was therefore very much left to her own devices, to her own desires, infatuations and dislikes, and this at a time when unforeseen circumstances made her position at court more precarious.

Choiseul's fall from grace

In the morning of December 24, 1770, the duke de La Vrillière brought a highly official message to Choiseul from the king. It was terse: "I order my cousin to proffer to the duke de La Vrillière his resignation from the post of Secretary of State and that of Postmaster, and to retire to Chanteloup until further notice." Chanteloup was the property near Amboise that Choiseul had purchased and beautified with his wife's millions where, come summer, he enjoyed playing the grand country squire. Its famous pagoda, the only remnant that still survives, was a concession to the *chinoiserie* style then at its height. Had it not been for Madame de Choiseul's much appreciated charm and virtue, he would have been sent even farther away. But he was allowed to receive no visitors. "He will only see his family and those whom I shall permit to go there," specified the king.

The minister, too confident of his own genius and luck, was the only one who hadn't seen it coming. Well not exactly: Marie-Antoinette was also thoroughly taken aback. In Vienna on the other hand, Maria Theresa had seen it coming since August. Her first reaction was one of consternation. "Vermond will be next," she wrote to Mercy, "I think it's inevitable, and my daughter's downfall... I must tell you that I regard this as decisive for my daughter." For her daughter? Maybe. But especially for Austria, since the party hostile to the Franco-Austrian alliance was triumphant. And Austria could lose its ability to maneuver in France if Marie-Antoinette were isolated from her advisers.

As it turns out, she was wrong; nothing of the sort happened. Choiseul's fall from grace was not the result of the quarrels between the opposing coteries; and despite court gossip, Madame du Barry's animosity toward him had little to do with it. It was Louis XV himself who long ago had decided to eliminate him because he wanted a shake-up in domestic affairs.

Choiseul had been in many ways an excellent minister. Although he'd supported the Franco-Austrian alliance, he deplored the fact that the treaties had obliged France to support Austria for little in return. The fault lay with the negotiator Bernis, but more so with Louis XV, who finally caved in to pressure. The Seven Years War had been fought in the interests of Maria Theresa to the detriment of those of the French, who really needed support against the English in a ruthless colonial war. Choiseul had done his best to limit the damage; he'd been obliged to sign the disastrous Treaty of Paris, and busied himself afterwards in actively preparing France's revenge on the English. He strengthened family ties with Spain; he bought Corsica from Genoa; he reorganized the army and speeded up efforts to develop France's maritime might. But rebuilding the fleet was terribly expensive. To get parliament to register the fiscal edicts[*], the minister had made many concessions, including sacrificing the Jesuits to Jansenist vindictiveness. He was known to harbor the conviction that the monarchy would one day have to relent and allow some sort of control over its finances. His presence in the ministry incited insubordination among the most fanatical magistrates. Over the years Louis XV distanced himself from Choiseul. He became less and less tolerant of his irreligion and relative weakness in the face of internal opposition.

The problem was that since his son's death, the king had been ridden with anxiety. They never agreed about much, but he knew that his son was energetic and sufficiently knowledgeable in the affairs of state. Alas, his grandson, the young Louis Auguste, would not be ready to govern any time soon. What would happen if he were suddenly thrust onto the throne? His grandfather at least wanted to leave him a functioning kingdom. The last years of his reign were therefore marked by a series of brisk measures to prop up the monarchy. Above all, he had to subdue the parliaments. The famous *Flagellation* speech did not succeed in making them compliant. A long conflict ensued pitting the governor of Brittany, the duke d'Aiguillon, against the Rennes parliament's public prosecutor La Chalotais, the upshot of which was to call into question royal power itself. When Louis XV intervened to defend his governor against the parliament's accusations, agitation was such that he finally decided to enact a long-contemplated measure: abolishing the parliaments.

René de Maupeou had been the chancellor since September 1768. He well understood the magistrates' mind-set as he'd risen from their ranks. He worked on abolishing venal offices[**] and

---

[*] Parliaments, which existed in most big cities throughout France, were not like today's elected legislative bodies, but courts composed of magistrates who had bought their positions. The Paris Parliament had a very wide purview. Among others, its function was to *verify* royal edicts, that is, to make sure they did not contradict existing legislation, and to *register* them, which was indispensable for them to be executed. Without any legislative powers whatsoever, as this was purely a royal prerogative, it still could paralyze the sovereign's actions, and it didn't hesitate to do so.

[**] "Venal offices" had been the common practice since the end of the 16th century. It referred to the sale of positions in the army, the judicial system and government administration. The king was thus kept in a ready supply of money, but also had to relinquish some of his power. The owners of these permanent positions, who became even more powerful when they managed to make them hereditary, could flout royal power without much risk.

replacing the parliaments with courts made up of bureaucrats chosen and salaried by the state. This costly reform (the abolished positions had to be bought back) could not happen unless public finances were in a fit state. A seasoned politician, the abbé Terray, appointed Controller General in September 1769, took on the rude task of getting them back afloat. Only a complete overhaul of the tax structure could have solved the problem and satisfied those members of the bourgeoisie who aspired to greater equality. This he could not do; it was too risky to take on all the powerful interests at once. But he did manage through tried and true methods to reduce the deficit.

At the end of 1770, therefore, Louis XV felt able to strike a decisive blow. But first of all he had to get rid of Choiseul. A foreign-policy matter triggered the crisis that was brewing between them. A conflict had just broken out in the Malvinas in South America upon the arrival of British troops there. These islands had been discovered and colonized by Bougainville with the help of shipping magnates from Saint-Malo, after which they were named. These islands off the coast of Patagonia had to be abandoned to the Spanish who reigned over that part of South America. But the English, more powerful on the high seas, disputed Spanish possession. The Spanish in turn sent in troops and called upon France to support them in the name of the Family Pact. Choiseul took it upon himself to ready the fleet. Was this a mere show of force to reassure Spain and intimidate the English, as he later claimed? Or did he want to force the king's hand and set off a conflict that would make him indispensable to the ministry? We don't know. But we do know that Louis XV took it very badly: he would consent to a war only if he were sure to win it, which could only be much later if ever. The ax fell, brutally and irrevocably. He fired his imprudent minister. He himself headed Foreign Affairs for six months, the time it took to impose a mediated solution in the Malvinas, after which he assigned the ministry to the duke d'Aiguillon. Thus was put in place the famous *Triumvirate* of Maupeou, Terray and d'Aiguillon that tried to help the French monarchy climb back up the slippery slope it had been sliding down for years.

The excuse for Choiseul's dismissal – that war was to be avoided for now – is a clear indication that Louis XV's absolute priority was domestic affairs. He was not contemplating abandoning the Austrian alliance. He couldn't care less about the abbé Vermond's presence in Marie-Antoinette's life, completely absorbed as he was in the gradual suppression of the Parisian and provincial parliaments and in setting up a new judicial system. Once the initial shock of

Choiseul's dismissal was over, Maria Theresa quickly grasped that fact. For his part, Kaunitz did not mince his words: the disgraced Choiseul had got what he deserved. He merely hoped his successor would prove more manageable. Vienna rather felt that d'Aiguillon was a better deal. True, the new foreign minister was reputed to be anti-Austrian, but he greatly lacked experience. The empress, who was constantly maneuvering between Prussia, Russia and Turkey to maintain her Eastern European positions, preferred to keep France out of it all. She knew that the wily Choiseul would not have given her a free hand without demanding something in return. She was banking on d'Aiguillon's incompetence to do as she pleased. The exile's efforts to remain in contact with Mercy ended in failure. Choiseul had been unceremoniously dumped.

However, the reasons for this change in tactics were kept from Marie-Antoinette. At first she was merely told to be careful, and then to remain strictly neutral. How could she understand that the constantly harped on debt of thanks she owed to Choiseul was all of a sudden gone with the wind? Choiseul had negotiated her marriage, he constantly sang her praises; he got her to proclaim that "in life and in death," he remained at her orders. And he'd got public opinion on his side. He was missed. She stayed deeply devoted to him, and began to detest the unfortunate man's enemies. She promised to work for his reinstatement as soon as she was in a position to do so. Her entirely pro-Choiseul entourage incited her to resist; they dangled in front of her the mirage of her stunning victory when he inevitably returned, wrapped in the aura of the unjustly persecuted martyr. She was well aware that by resisting she was in direct opposition to the formally stated wishes of her grandfather the king and her husband. But this was all the more reason to defend what she considered a just cause. Did she see that she was also going against her mother's wishes? It would take more than that to discourage her. Choiseul's dismissal therefore left the dauphine head to the wind, alone against her two families, and proud of it.

Two sisters-in-law from the Savoy

Louis Auguste's two brothers were reaching marriageable age. Louis XV was very concerned about the future of the Italian principalities, especially that of Parma where a son of his eldest daughter reigned, and he dreamt of annexing the Savoy, which with its Alpine passes controlled access to the Italian peninsula. For centuries the dukes of Savoy had switched their allegiance back and forth between France, which encroached on Savoy from the west, and Austria, which weighed heavily upon it through Lombardy in the east. This earned them a solid reputation for deceit and double dealing, but it enabled them to keep their states and even to gain access to the world of the high and mighty: the treaty of Utrecht had conferred royal status on Victor-Amadeus in 1713. His descendents, after some territorial redistribution, bore the title of kings of Piedmont-Sardinia. They were quite prolific and therefore never lacked for princesses to propose for the various thrones of Catholic Europe. So it was to Turin that Louis XV turned to marry off the dauphin's younger brothers.

One Savoyard princess in Versailles was one thing, two quite another. Maria Theresa cast a very cold eye on this diplomatic balancing act. What is more, she saw it as a double danger for her daughter. Would the newcomers cause her anxiety and try to overshadow her at court? And would they beat her to it at giving the king his first great-grandchild? Despite her fears, she wisely advised her daughter to work toward family harmony and to put her best foot forward with her sisters-in-law. As long as she remained childless she must handle them with care. Mercy also preached moderation. When the young woman revealed that she was determined to give the older one the cold shoulder, and to make enough trouble for her that her debut would not be terribly brilliant, he managed to convince her that her rank, her spiritedness and her "graces" would be enough to ensure her preeminence.

Born on November 2, 1753 and therefore two years older than her future spouse, Marie-Joséphine Louise of Savoy, the oldest daughter of the Piedmont heir, left Turin duly married by proxy on April 22, 1771. She took leave of her parents the next day at Avigliana and via Mont Cenis traveled toward the Savoy where she crossed the border at Pont-de-Beauvoisin. The Guiers river was not wide enough for an island structure to be built for the hand-over so by joining a number of houses by wooden walkways a suitable place was arranged. In the middle of a great central hall hung with crimson damask cloth, a line was drawn on the floor to represent a totally imaginary border because the whole building was in France. Louis XIV hadn't done as much for the young Marie-Adélaïde when she came to marry the duke de Bourgogne; that hand-over was a bit of a rushed affair in the middle of the bridge. But now as the spirit of the monarchy was waning, Louis XV clung all the more to its forms.

On May 12th he was in Fontainebleau with the entire court to welcome the newcomer, breathless with curiosity. One thing's for sure: she was no blond. At least there was that to reassure Marie-Antoinette in those times when only blond hair was prized. Naturally, upon viewing the young lady's portrait, Louis XV had declared his satisfaction. But everyone knew that he didn't like to retract an opinion; once he took the decision, he would rhapsodize over the ugliest of ugly ducklings. Not this time, however. Bachaumont says that a letter from Lyon affirms "that her hair is not black but brown, that she has very beautiful eyes, that her physiognomy bears the mark of the nobility that inspires it, and that her shape is attractive." Seeing her up close the king was disappointed if Mercy is to be believed, and admitted that he found her "quite ugly." All the same, he wrote to the infante of Parma, "She is very shapely, not tall, with very beautiful eyes, an unattractive nose, a nicer mouth than it was [in a portrait?], dark brown hair with matching eyebrows and perfect skin for a brunette." And he added, "If I were a few years younger... I would have taken her myself." Public opinion on the other hand would only grant her beautiful eyes, which were indeed quite large and animated. But her uncommonly thick eyebrows nearly met at the top of her wide and turned-up nose, taking too much space on her forehead. Her upper lip was topped by a pronounced fuzz, and it would be said later that her chest itself was not spared this over-abundance of hair. A delighted Marie-Antoinette could write to her sister in triumph: "Monsieur le dauphin does not find her to his liking at all, and complains that she has a mustache."

Her lucky intended put up a brave front. During the wedding ceremony two days later, he fairly shouted out an emphatic "I do." When it came time to bed her, he replied playfully to his grandfather's bawdy encouragements, and the next day he cheekily boasted that he was "four times fortunate." He clearly annoyed his older brother when fishing for a compliment, he asked him his opinion of her. His reply was blunt: "Not that attractive. I would not have cared to have her for my wife." To which the young groom stiffly replied, "I'm glad that fortune granted you someone more to your liking. We are both happy, therefore, as mine is infinitely pleasing to me."

The tone was set. This instinctive, irrepressible rivalry between the two couples would be life-long, sometimes unleashed in fiery outbursts, but more often hidden behind a veneer of hypocritical and self-interested civility. Better-looking and with more sparkle, Marie-Antoinette felt safe in her own superiority. And she was also quickly reassured about the other's likelihood to reproduce. Court gossip made short work of the count de Provence's amorous boastings: the adolescent was already quite chubby and no doubt beginning to suffer the effects of the diabetes mellitus that would afflict him all his life. His wife's letters to her family in Turin leave no doubt that he was just as incapable as his brother of consummating his marriage. Marie-Antoinette had nothing to fear, the countess de Provence would not assure the dynasty's continuity before she would. So she could afford to be pleasant to her poor homely sister-in-law whose complexion besides had been ruined by smallpox. Her mother advised her to treat the Savoyard gently for charity's sake: "You have no reason to be jealous of her, but to take pity on her and look after her. That will be seen as worthy and right, not to govern her – that would be just as unsuitable as jealousy – but to help her get over her difficulties." But Marie-Antoinette would taint all the attention she poured on her with a hurtful condescension that precluded any good effect coming from the mail-order goodwill.

She made a big mistake in underestimating her, however. Marie-Joséphine lacked neither personality nor character. She was wise enough not to engage in any beauty contest. That, she knew, was lost in advance. She balked at smearing her cheeks with rouge and emphatically refused to pluck her eyebrows. It was even said unkindly that she refused to bathe or wear perfume. She relied on her spiritedness – for she had plenty of that – and on her excellent manners to win over public opinion. Besides, she could hold her own in society. During the grand ball, it was discovered that she was an admirable dancer – and *she* danced in step! Judging the book by its cover, Marie-Antoinette foolishly concluded that she was stupid. And since her sister-in-law maintained a facade of prudent reserve, she found in her an inoffensive timidity. "She follows her husband in everything," she wrote to Maria Theresa, "but that's only through fear and stupidity." Actually, the infinitely more mature and clear-thinking Savoyard quickly understood that solidarity with her husband was her only chance of survival in this hostile court. She didn't forget that her husband was second in line for the throne. Should the dauphin die childless, he would succeed Louis XV. The count and countess de Provence, childless themselves, kept a close eye on the conjugal relations of the older couple.

While awaiting this very hypothetical elevation, Marie-Joséphine went her own way, for she hated vacuous gossip and the court's rumor-mill. In vain her mother reminded her that she was now living "in a country where people prefer to talk about nothing than to keep their mouths closed" and that her reserve could be taken for pride. She would never try to fit in with the frivolous set around the dauphine, who would accuse her of hypocrisy. Everyone could see through her forced friendliness. But Marie-Antoinette's was just as forced.

The daily life of these young people cannot be seen as overly starchy, however. They were capable of indulging in merry horseplay, like on the spring day in 1773 as they packed their bags for Compiègne. Marie-Joséphine wrote to her parents:

> I don't know why I haven't gone mad... Here I am, surrounded by cases and papers, books all over the floor... I'd already packed my case. Crash! It's upended. I have to start all over again. You know me. Madame la dauphine kindly dumps a pile of books on the floor, I get angry, we laugh; they tear the paper from me and doesn't the count de Provence start singing at the top of his lungs and admirably off key... Good Lord, what a ruckus! I'm thoroughly fed up. As I was saying, here I am still in my little corner surrounded by luggage. Madame la dauphine is turning everything upside down, the count de Provence is chirping away, the count d'Artois is telling this story for the tenth time, shouting and laughing his head off, and to top it all off Monsieur le dauphin is loudly reciting a tragedy... And there are two birds singing and three dogs. One is mine, two are the dauphine's, and they're making such a racket that we can't hear ourselves think.

The marriage of the youngest brother would soon widen the family circle. Marie-Joséphine in her desire to strengthen her homeland's ties with France made a strong case for either one of her two sisters to be chosen. Back in Vienna Maria Theresa protested. Two sisters from the same house when there was a princess of Saxony available! "That's a bit much," she wrote to her daughter, "you will have to be all the more careful and overlook nothing that could be used against you." Marie-Antoinette agreed wholeheartedly, especially as there was yet another Savoyard wedding in the offing: her young sister-in-law Clotilde had been betrothed to the prince of Piedmont. Neither the dauphine nor her husband had anything to say in the matter, so a choice between the two Savoyard sisters it would be.

The other two sisters were tiny. The king couldn't decide. He enquired about their size, seemed to favor the younger one. Marie-Joséphine intervened. Wouldn't it be cruel to choose this one and leave her older sister on the shelf? Tradition had it that the order fixed by nature and providence should be respected. She got her way. On the 16th of November 1773, the count d'Artois, sixteen years of age, married Marie-Thérèse of Savoy, who was seventeen. "She's quite attractive," the king wrote to his grandson in Parma, "a bit short, with beautiful skin and a fine bust, quite a long nose..." Mercy-Argenteau painted a less flattering portrait: "She is quite short, somewhat unshapely, although lacking in any downright shocking defects; her complexion is rather pale, her face thin, a nose that is too long and comes to an unfortunate point, badly turned eyes, a large mouth... she does not know how to pronounce a single word... she dances very badly and everything about her proclaims either the lack of natural aptitudes or an excessively neglected education." Since she received the same education as Marie-Joséphine, we must deduce that the lack of natural aptitudes was what he was really talking about. If she was a bit less ugly than her older sister, she was infinitely sillier, so much so that Marie-Joséphine found that the fond task of initiating her sister into Versailles' mysteries was daunting. She was a hopeless case; she would be good for nothing save making children. Her husband, the youngest in the family, devoted himself to that task with zeal. He was the only one to inherit his grandfather's warm-blooded temperament and no one would dream of doubting his exploits in this domain. So Marie-Antoinette, who feared no competition from her at court, could expect to see her waist thickening in short order. But for now the greatest danger was averted; the two Savoyard sisters, devoid of any prestige, would remain in Marie-Antoinette's shadow.

Artois' vivacity also helped lighten the atmosphere among the three couples. They were young and gay. They arranged to take their meals together on days when they didn't have to dine in public. Keeping her rustic tastes, the countess de Provence treated her companions to a soup with herbs that she'd prepared herself from a recipe she'd brought from Turin. They had fun together. They created their own little theatre troop. Did the king really refuse them authorization, as Madame Campan supposed? He was not even consulted. The secret added a little spice to the enterprise. They performed in a forgotten little room on a mezzanine. Marie-Antoinette's librarian, Monsieur Campan, acted as their director and played the grand old man roles. The princes and princesses shared the leading roles. "The count de Provence would always perform imperturbably, the count d'Artois rather well and gracefully; the princesses not well at all. The dauphine acquitted herself in some roles with finesse and feeling." The dauphin, who was their only audience, acted as theatre critic. The repertoire was varied, and included "good comedies from the French theatre," some classics, a little bit of everything. The petulant count d'Artois made a superb knight errant with his helmet, lance and shield. The tiresome count de Provence was better at character acting. Rumor had it that the future Louis XVI applauded him in the title role of *Tartufe*, and exclaimed – whether mischievously or not we don't know – that he played the role "quite naturally."

Whether true or not, this anecdote shows the fragility of the apparent harmony between the older couple and the next in line. These shared activities masked but never extinguished the muffled animosity between them caused by their respective positions on the dynastic chessboard. If Mercy can be believed, the brothers once came to blows over a broken vase. Another less often cited incident also exemplifies this latent animosity. One day the dauphin was hitting his brother's arm with a stick, either to annoy him or distractedly perhaps, but the latter reacted furiously, and tried to grab it from him. Marie-Antoinette snatched it away and broke it into pieces, putting an end to the dispute. But she herself was not immune to outbursts of anger. She flew off the handle when she learned that a party given for Marie-Joséphine by her lady-in-waiting ended with a tribute to Madame du Barry's beauty. Beside herself, she made straight for La Muette where her sister-in-law was convalescing and demanded an explanation. Marie-Joséphine told her she was just following her husband's orders, so she rushed to Versailles, found the count de Provence at the aunts' quarters and publicly rounded on him for the "duplicity of his character."

It was decidedly difficult in Versailles to exercise the kind of restraint recommended by Maria Theresa in far away Vienna.

Finally, Paris!

The spring of 1773 brought some much-needed balm to the dauphine's wounded spirits. As yet she had not set foot in Paris. We recall that her first contact with it was ruined by the deadly stampede that followed the fireworks in honor of her wedding. Since then confined to Versailles, Fontainebleau and Compiègne, she was always temptingly close to the marvelous amusements that, she was constantly reminded, one could enjoy there. The sweet little balls organized by her lady-in-waiting or her sister-in-law could not compete with those at the Opera. She kept imploring the king to let her go there, duly accompanied, and in February, with carnival season in full swing, he gave in. The little outing was authorized, and she could therefore admit to her mother, "Last Thursday, Monsieur le dauphin, the count and countess de Provence and I were at the Opera ball. We kept it most secret. Although we were all wearing masks, we were recognized within a half an hour. The dukes de Chartres and Bourbon, who were dancing at the Palais-Royal, which is quite nearby, came looking for us, and they tried hard to get us to go dance at Madame the duchess de Chartres' place; but I excused myself, having the king's permission only for the Opera. We arrived here* at seven o'clock and heard mass before going to bed. We are all delighted with Monsieur le dauphin's willingness to participate, as we all thought he was against it."

A few months later, on June 8th, she finally received the consecration required of all the young women destined to the throne of France, her solemn entry into the capital. Three years after her marriage, it was high time.

Greeted at 11 o'clock in the morning by cannon salvos at the Bastille, the Hôtel de Ville and the Invalides, the dauphin and his spouse entered Paris at the Conference gate in a gilded ceremonial coach. They followed the quays up to Notre-Dame where they heard mass. They then received the tributes of the nuns at the Hôtel-Dieu and the clerics of the Louis-le-Grand school, before going to bow before the reliquary of Sainte-Geneviève. They eventually found a bit of respite at the Tuileries; but they dined there in public, where etiquette dictated that the young prince be the only male in attendance**. In the afternoon they appeared on the balcony, raising thunderous applause, and the duke de Brissac fashioned a gallant compliment for the dauphine, "Madame, you have here two hundred thousand men in love with you!" In the gardens where she later dragged her husband, she gave in to the contagious popular excitement. Freed from the monotony of Versailles' court rituals, she felt real life coursing through her veins; it was intense, exhilarating, and a bit wild.

Mercy wrote an account of the festivities for the empress. As one might expect, it overflowed with praise for the dauphine and was dotted with acid remarks about the dauphin who was supposedly seen merely as "an accessory" to the star of the day. Marie-Antoinette was over the moon. She fairly melted with gratitude for her mother who had procured for her such a brilliant "establishment." "I was the last of them all, yet she treated me like the eldest, and my soul was therefore filled with the most tender gratitude." Her version of the ceremony, more spontaneous and believable than the ambassador's, vibrates with candid, youthful joy:

---

*   Versailles, where the letter was dated 15 February 1773.

**   No man except her husband was allowed to sit at the table of the queen or the dauphine.

As for honors, we received all anyone could imagine; all of it, although wonderful, was not what touched me the most; it was the outpouring of tenderness of these poor people, who as burdened down by taxes as they are, were overjoyed to see us. When we went walking in the Tuileries, there was such a crowd that for three-quarters of an hour we could move neither forward nor back. Many times Monsieur le dauphin and I advised the guards not to strike anyone, which made a very good impression. The day was so orderly that despite the enormous crowds that followed us everywhere, no one was injured. After our walk we went up on a balcony where we stayed for half an hour. I cannot tell you, my dear mamma, the transports of joy and affection for us that we witnessed during that time. Before going inside we waved to the people, much to their delight. How lucky those in our position are to earn the friendship of a whole people at so modest a price! And yet there is nothing more precious; I could feel it, and I shall never forget it.

And she didn't forget to pay homage to her husband: "He answered all the speeches beautifully, acknowledged everything that was done for him, and especially the great joy expressed by the people, to whom he showed much good will." Returning to Versailles, she tactfully shared their success with the king: "Sire, you must be much loved by the Parisians, for they greatly celebrated us." But the truth was, and everyone knew it, that the king was very unpopular. What the Parisians were celebrating was the promise of a brighter future with the young couple who would soon ascend the throne.

Having yearned to spend time in Paris for such a long time, Marie-Antoinette fell madly in love with it. Her euphoria only grew in the days that followed. She went to the Opera, where she was given a standing ovation. At the Comédie-Française, where *The Siege of Calais** was playing, she and the dauphin initiated the applause, which was quite contrary to convention**. At *les Italiens* the stalls joined the chorus as it chanted "Long Live the King!" An actor threw his hat into the air towards the young couple crying

---

* This tragedy by Dormont de Belloy about a famous incident involving bourgeois gentlemen of Calais, owed its success to the anti-English feeling that was running high in France after the Seven Years War.

** In the 18th century, the public was forbidden to applaud during a performance in the presence of the king, the dauphin or the dauphine. And these respectable personages risked demeaning themselves by clapping.

out "Long Live the King and his Dear Children!" The dauphine, thoroughly intoxicated by Paris, found clever ways to make up for lost time, dashing from monuments to manufacturers, and from fairground stalls to open-air dances.

The following spring Gluck's arrival made her the arbiter of musical taste. The "German Orpheus" wanted to crown the glory unanimously accorded him in Germanic Europe by conquering Paris. He offered the Royal Academy of Music an opera he'd composed based on a French libretto of Racine's *Iphigenia*. Fearing competition from him, his rivals tried to drag out the negotiations, claiming that such a work "was likely to kill off all the old French operas." The relationship between the action, the text and the music was, in fact, greatly changed, making it more powerful dramatically and emotionally. Gluck called upon Marie-Antoinette, who back in Vienna had toiled at her first harpsichord lessons under his direction. She welcomed him with open arms. The maestro was not easy to work with and was soon exasperating singers and instrumentalists alike, especially those on whom he felt entitled to impose the rigors and flourishes of the Italian lyrical tradition. To one capricious diva he is said to have remarked, "I am here, Mademoiselle, to produce *Iphigenia*. If I cannot count on you, have it your way, I will go to Madame la dauphine and tell her 'It is impossible for me to put on my opera.' Then I shall get into my carriage and take the road back to Vienna."

Everyone made sure to get a ticket for the opening night on April 12th; not a courtier was missing. Unfortunately, the night before, the singer in the role of Agamemnon came down with a cold and lost his voice. Not to worry – he could be replaced by his understudy. But the composer vehemently protested; the performance must be postponed. What? They all must rearrange their schedules on the whim of this madman? The "madman" held firm, and thanks to the dauphine's support, got his way. *Iphigenia* opened on April 19th. With the exception of the king and his favorite, the entire court was in attendance. The public was scandalized by Gluck's behavior and paid a fortune for tickets. Reviews were mixed; the work was disconcerting to French ears. But the dauphine's enthusiasm ensured its success. According to Bachaumont's *Mémoires secrets,* "We can attribute a lot of the applause for it to the public's desire to please Madame la dauphine. This princess seems to have hatched a plot and never stopped clapping, which obliged Madame the countess de Provence, the princes and the whole house to do the same."

Thus Marie-Antoinette defied tradition in order to ensure

Gluck's success. "It was a great triumph..." she wrote to her sister Maria Christina, "I was transported by it; no one talks of anything else; there is an extraordinary fermentation going on in everyone's head over this event; it's incredible, everyone is taking sides and attacking each other, as if it were some sort of religious dispute; at court, even though I've publicly declared myself in favor of this work of genius, there are sides taken and discussions of a singular intensity. And it appears that it's even worse in the city..."

There were two important aspects of Gluck's triumph, which was also Marie-Antoinette's. First of all it took place in Paris, not Versailles. It is true that in Versailles the cost of running the brand new theatre inaugurated for her marriage was so high that it was reserved for the most important occasions. It was therefore Paris – as the *Iphigenia* affair proves – that had become more than ever the center of theatrical life. Secondly, neither the king nor Madame du Barry was there. Their abstention, whether out of indifference or umbrage, left the field open to the dauphine. She was the heroine of the day. And her love of Paris grew accordingly. In Versailles she had to deal with the favorite, who rivaled her in preeminence. In Paris she reigned supreme. Where else could she find real enjoyment? For a long time she would remain as attracted to Paris as a butterfly to flowers.

In crowning her queen of the ball and the theatre, by taking her away from Versailles and her duties there, fashionable Paris gave her a poisoned apple. She was not aware of it, however. She would learn too late of its deadly effects. In that spring of 1774 she believed she was the stronger in the conflict that had pitted her for three years against the powerful favorite. To examine this conflict, we must take a few steps back to retrace its different phases, which would have been more laughable than tragic had it not been for its consequences.

CHAPTER 6

DAUPHINE VS. FAVORITE

"I shall be her rival!" the dauphine is supposed to have exclaimed the evening of her arrival when she spotted Madame du Barry at the state dinner. This outburst described too well their future relationship to be believable but was, like so many phrases coined after the fact, blindingly true. Rather than going back and forth between the scenes of daily life evoked in the preceding chapter and the episodic battles between the two women, we have chosen to devote a whole chapter to them. First of all because with all their twists and turns, they make up a hilarious comedy something like that of an Italian farce, only to end more like a tragedy. Secondly, because they reveal Marie-Antoinette's personality, and lay bare her intransigent pride, her refusal to buckle under, and her reckless behavior. Finally, because they make it clear just how much she was the victim of forces she could not understand.

So on to the mock-heroic comic war that the dauphine led against the favorite for four years, during which the court reveled in counting the blows.

Peaceful coexistence?

Louis XV had suffered from his wife's jealousy and found it especially hard to bear the disapproval of his children, who refused to accept Madame de Pompadour's presence in his life, and consistently championed their abandoned mother's cause. Even though she was no longer alive, his daughters froze Madame du Barry out. But he could have hoped that his grandsons, who had not witnessed the trials of the deceased queen, might prove to be more understanding. Since he and the dauphin had become close, he assumed the dauphine would follow suit. Once his two other grandsons were married, the younger generation could bring back the kind of warm family environment he craved. Unfortunately, he hadn't reckoned with Marie-Antoinette's heedlessness and stubborn streak, or with the strength of the coteries that divided the court.

Her first two months in Versailles seemed to live up to his hopeful expectations. She wisely followed the empress's orders to be pleasant to everyone. In mid-June 1770 the ambassador wrote, "Madame du Barry thought it incumbent upon her one morning to go pay court to H.R.H. The princess received her without affectation; it took place with dignity and in such a way as to displease no one." To get the dauphine used to frequenting the favorite, Louis XV organized visits to smaller castles than Versailles where the etiquette was less rigid. At Marly in particular one could live on closer, less formal terms. It all went smoothly. But her relative good will could not be put down to her presumed naivety. She had been duly put on guard. She was not so innocent as to be unaware of Madame du Barry's real role. She deplored the influence over the king of this "silly and impertinent creature." But her contempt above all was aimed at the woman's low rank. She does not seem to have any overwhelming moral objections to her. She wrote to her mother, "She joined in the games with us every evening in Marly; twice she sat next to me, but she didn't speak to me and I of course did not try to converse with her; but when it was necessary I did speak to her, however." And she added, "Last night I wrote to the king for the first time; I was quite frightened knowing that Madame du Barry reads them all, but you can be assured, my dear mother, that I shall never make any misstep either for or against her."

A few days later, however, an incident broke out in Choisy that had nothing to do with Marie-Antoinette but that required her intervention. The chateau's theatre was a bit small and there were not enough seats for everyone. When Madame du Barry arrived with her two friends the duchess de Mirepoix and the countess de Valentinois, the dauphine's entourage had already taken over the first rows and refused to share them. An exchange of "testy remarks" ensued, especially from the countess de Gramont, a cousin through marriage of Choiseul. The victims of the insult complained to the king, who promptly exiled the countess. To keep her ladies' respect, Marie-Antoinette had to intercede on their behalf. All worked up, she was about to demand the guilty party's recall. Fortunately the cautious Mercy took her aside and proposed the smartest solution. She thus went and told the king that "she was saddened by the fault committed by a lady of her palace; that she did not seek to learn H.M.'s motives for punishing this lady" but that she was surprised that she hadn't been informed of this measure taken against someone in her service. Embarrassed, the king was at least relieved that the crux of the matter was left unsaid. He would sanction the duke de La Vrillière* for his negligence and promised that such a thing would not be repeated. The dauphine had proven to her household staff that she was ready to defend her prerogatives, without displeasing the king. For once, she behaved diplomatically. But her entourage, made up of Choiseul recruits, wanted nothing better than to drag her into the war he was waging against the favorite, and Mesdames aunts threw themselves into the effort. Remaining neutral would be difficult.

The dauphin on the other hand continued going to the little post-hunt suppers attended by Madame du Barry. His wife complained to him about it, claiming that it smacked of wanting to separate him from her and to introduce him to unsuitable company. She got him to say he "regretted" it, but not to give up going. The countess de Noailles therefore suggested she too ask to be invited to these suppers. Mercy did not take the risk of deciding on such a thorny issue himself, and proposed bringing the matter to Choiseul. The latter however had no wish to see any rapprochement between the dauphine and the favorite, so he advised against it. All she should do, if the king proposed it, was to "accept with a semblance of pleasure." He knew however that the king would never take such an initiative. So the dauphin continued to take part in the little suppers, as his diaries attest. But helped by Mercy, Marie-Antoinette tried hard to convince her mother that he'd stopped, or if not, that he did so against his will and because she encouraged him to show his grandfather this mark of respect – anything but admit that she had absolutely no influence on him.

Already her neutrality toward the favorite was weighing on her. In her quarters and those of Mesdames aunts, the tongues were wagging. No one had anything better to do than indulge in malicious gossip. And la du Barry furnished an endless supply of that. Already by October the tittle-tattle had reached Vienna, and for once not from Mercy. "People here are prattling on about my daughter's misbehavior... They say that the king is becoming reserved and uncomfortable with her, that she is openly confronting the favorite..." That's all nonsense, Mercy protests: "There has never been anything but a few little remarks against this woman, ones which Mesdames aunts were always the first to instigate;

---

* In charge of the king's household, it was he who conveyed the orders of exile.

why even at present, Madame la dauphine holds her tongue better concerning the remarks in question, to such a degree that whole weeks can go by without anyone being able to cite a single one." Ah ha. So there were then times when she did go at it quite happily? The ambassador's assertions were really an unintentional admission of guilt.

In November Marie-Antoinette took up the charge again on behalf of the countess de Gramont who, gravely ill, asked permission to go back to the capital for medical treatment. "Papa, quite apart from questions of humanity and justice, imagine the sorrow I would feel should a lady in my service die out of your favor!" The king smiled, promised to respond favorably, and having obtained medical certification, allowed the countess to come back to Paris as long as she never showed her face at court. For the dauphine this was only a partial victory, humiliating really, as she only learned of it through "public rumor." She took it out on the poor La Vrillière, who was helpless in the situation, but nonetheless was told: "I should have been the first to be informed, and by you, of the action the king would take... but I see, Sir, that you treated me like a child, and I gladly tell you that I shall not forget it."

In town and at court, everyone was expecting a face-off. A heated altercation had taken place between Choiseul and marshal de Richelieu, pillar of the opposing clan. Storm clouds were gathering. But between Marie-Antoinette and Madame du Barry peaceful coexistence limped along until year's end, thanks to the care they took to avoid each other: "Madame dauphine is hardly ever anywhere where she can come into contact with the favorite, who comes neither to the circle nor to Mesdames aunts', and in the very rare cases where this woman was in Madame the Archduchess's presence, H.R.H. never treated her haughtily." All the same, his granddaughter did not show the king the spirit of reconciliation that he'd hoped for; he was not terribly happy with her. And at the end of December 1770 the situation deteriorated all of a sudden. Choiseul's disgrace changed the equilibrium of the various court factions to the detriment of Marie-Antoinette, who reacted vehemently.

Palace revolution

When Choiseul returned home rather crestfallen on Christmas Eve, his gracious spouse welcomed him with a smile: "My good friend, you indeed look like a man exiled, but come sit down, our dinner will be no less good for all that." The crowds who flocked to their door despite the king's orders soothed his wounded pride. He left for Chanteloup displaying the detachment of a philosopher immune to adversity. He was sure that his purgatory in the provinces would soon end with a triumphant return. Five months later, however, the appointment of the duke d'Aiguillon, an intimate of Madame du Barry's, to the ministry of foreign affairs, completed the palace revolution. Decidedly, his adversaries were winning this battle. And they could look forward to some support within the royal family itself, since the king had chosen Savoyard wives for the dauphin's younger brothers. Power had well and truly changed hands. The "dominant party," as Mercy then called it, was made up of men notoriously hostile to Austria.

This change in no way affected Louis XV's foreign policy, as he was personally invested in the Austrian alliance. Maria Theresa had nothing to fear from that quarter. On the other hand, it was a great blow to her daughter's position in court. The rout of the "Choiseulites" was seen as a victory for the "Barryites" and resulted in bringing those sitting on the fence into the favorite's fold. At the same time it hardened the opposition. Marie-Antoinette, friendly and beholding to Choiseul, swelled up again with resentment against du Barry, whom she held responsible for his banishment. What is more, Choiseul's friends saw her as the instrument of his eventual return to favor. Pierre de Nolhac noted, "invested in her were the hopes of a whole party" – a powerful party that went way beyond the confines of the court and was supported by public opinion outraged by the suppression of the parliaments. It was a party that pinned its hopes on the idea that in the near future – the king was not getting any younger after all – she would be able to impose on her freshly crowned husband the great man's return to power. Despite instructions from her mother who ordered her more than ever to keep out of politics, she could not escape from it by the mere fact that she was Austrian and therefore pro-Choiseul, and because no one else at court had sufficient rank to stand up to the favorite.

Her entourage therefore incited her to go on the warpath. So did her pride. For Madame du Barry acquired a new kind of prestige from her friends' triumph. Not that she was vindictive or unkind. Although not wanting to make her enemies pay for their earlier expressions of contempt, she couldn't help but show her pleasure at the recognition she now enjoyed from this stunning display of her power. She could make and unmake ministers. She was feared; she was honored. She was not ambitious; she hadn't sought this situation. But since the hosannas were there, she savored them. She was called upon to solicit pardons, favors, positions, and she was always successful, to the detriment of the dauphine's candidates. She filled the two Turin princesses' households with her friends. She was consulted about all the court parties, performances or little excursions. And taking a page out of la Pompadour's book, she found work for artists, and furnished her apartments with pricey furniture of the latest fashion – already "Louis XVI" before the fact. Fragonard occupied on her walls the same place that Boucher had on her predecessor's, and Pajou immortalized her features in marble. The heir to the throne of Sweden paid her a visit and left as a souvenir a diamond-studded collar for her dog. In the autumn of 1771 it was to her that Grétry, one of the dauphine's favorite musicians, dedicated his comic opera *Zemire and Azor.* At Fontainebleau, enthroned in the first row of the royal box, the lady thus honored, arrayed in sparkling jewels, received her share of the praises with which the play was greeted. "The lady is more sovereign-like than her predecessor or even the cardinal de Fleury," lamented the marquise du Deffand, Choiseul's faithful friend. "The grip that the countess du Barry has on the king's spirit now hardly knows any bounds," Mercy would confirm. In truth, the queen of the court was Madame du Barry, not the dauphine, whatever etiquette, precedence and prejudice might dictate.

It was all too much for Marie-Antoinette, who was seized with an uncontrollable, visceral hostility. It would be wrong to assume that the source of this reaction was some dark jealousy of one woman for a more beautiful and dazzling rival. She was still too young for that; she as yet cared little for her appearance, and did not pretend to be more beautiful than women in the fullness of their maturity. Neither did she reproach Madame du Barry with monopolizing the king at her expense, for she didn't like Louis XV; she was afraid of him. However much Mercy might harp on her need to do everything she could to please him; she did the bare minimum. As for any disgust a "chaste young lady" might feel for a "depraved creature," it is hard to explain the fact that it only appeared after the favorite's political triumph. No, the key to understanding her violent reaction is elsewhere, in her keen awareness of the hierarchical order upon which the monarchy was founded. It was her prerogative alone to occupy the highest rank. The other's pretence at royalty was a breach of her dignity even more than an offense to her pride. It was nothing less than usurpation, and that was intolerable. Despite Madame du Barry's efforts to win her over, the dauphine took the initiative in a battle where she was quite obviously the aggressor.

And where did Mesdames aunts stand in all of this? It has forever been repeated after Mercy-Argenteau that Marie-Antoinette was a passive recipient of their influence and that they were entirely responsible for her escapades. It is true that the ambassador never stopped criticizing the dowdy old spinsters, to the point where Maria Theresa, who once couldn't praise them enough, now saw them merely as "an abominable clique." Perhaps Mercy was fooling himself. But if he did guess the truth, how could he admit it to the empress without also admitting that he had greatly exaggerated the successes of her daughter; that the child did not play the eminent role in court that he claimed, and that her obedience to him was far from complete? Better to deflect onto the aunts the suspicions that had started to torment the empress.

They made it easier by being willing partners in this war. It was in their quarters that the strategy was mapped out. But they lacked imagination as well as means. They therefore fell back on the weapon they'd used against la Pompadour – the silent treatment. But there is silent treatment and there is silent treatment. In the close quarters of the gaming tables, Marie-Antoinette continued to behave toward the favorite with "neither distaste nor distemper." She spoke to her "willingly, without affectation" because the humdrum conversation was inconsequential. The same does not go for pleasant remarks made in public during the "circle" or a ceremony – when they become charged with meaning. For etiquette forbids that those who come to "pay their court" speak until they are spoken to. We can well imagine what a trial it must have been for Madame du Barry to wait for the dauphine to finally approach, and grant the hoped-for smile, a few meaningless words – anything; the kind of thing she accorded to everyone else, and instead to see her suddenly turn icy, her lips resolutely closed, her glance lost somewhere in the distance in back of you, as if you were entirely transparent, an absolute non-entity. As much as she avoided occasions where she must suffer this contempt, Madame du Barry was offended all the same. Soon, all those considered her friends were subjected to the young woman's hurtful treatment. The duchess d'Aiguillon, come to render homage, was furious when she did not get the recognition that her birth and court rank should have guaranteed her, and she made no secret of her displeasure.

The situation was getting out of hand. Louis XV had to intervene, for his own sake.

The king gets involved

He was, however, careful not to get directly involved. He always hated having to confront people face to face, because he lacked the talent for clever riposte and was afraid of being caught short. He preferred to be informed of things in writing so as to have the time to reflect – thus his peculiar habit of communicating through notes, even with those he saw every day. Mercy warned the empress very early on that she should not count on him to guide the dauphine: "Everyone knows that the king has never been able to advise his children or to correct them in any way whatsoever." He later added that his way was never to upset them in any way, but "to put up with what he doesn't like rather than remedy it," which risked leaving the dauphine free to impose her will. For him to take the decision to act, therefore, he had to be exasperated, and the favorite very insistent.

His oft-repeated interventions that had no tangible results, puffed up in lofty phrases that disguised the nature of the offense and the name of the victim, could have been made into great comedy in the hands of a Molière:

Act I. Starting in mid-March of 1771, in an attempt to put a stop to the gossip, the king takes things in hand and summons Marie-Antoinette's lady-in-waiting Madame de Noailles to inform her of his grievances. He starts by praising the dauphine's good points before proceeding to his reproaches. She is too spirited and lacks the proper reserve when she holds court. He criticizes her habit of bringing food with her when she follows the hunt and handing it out to people from her carriage, which entails too much familiarity "especially among young people." He finally gets to the crux of the matter: she speaks too freely "about what she sees or thinks she sees." "Her loose remarks could have deleterious effects within the family." Perhaps it is a matter of her getting poor advice. Madame de Noailles prudently refuses to address the matter "out of respect for the place where this advice was coming from." "I know where it is coming from and I am greatly displeased," replies the king. Neither the names of Mesdames aunts nor that of Madame du Barry are uttered.

Finding out about the message, Mesdames aunts become indignant, knowing that they are obviously being singled out. Why is the king implicating the lady-in-waiting in what is strictly a family matter? Why does he not address his displeasure directly at the interested party? The answer they know only too well; for years now they have seen their father flee from confrontation. They push the dauphine into asking him for an audience, from which they know she would come out the winner. Duly coached by Mercy, she goes on her best behavior to tell him how pained she is that "her papa had not enough friendship or trust in her to speak directly to her about what he found agreeable or not." As expected, the much-embarrassed king says that he loves her with all his heart and sends her away with a kiss. Very proud of her success, Marie-Antoinette redoubles her slights against the favorite's friends.

Mercy however is well aware of the danger she is incurring and lectures the impetuous girl. Why give these people the "impertinent satisfaction" of believing she cared a fig for them? That would be giving them too much credit. The best way to punish them would be "to speak to them from time to time with an easy, indifferent air." He cleverly follows up with, "Had Madame la dauphine wanted just once to address a word to the countess du Barry herself" the whole cabal would have been disarmed. Just one word, a single word, and things would be a lot different! The headstrong girl quibbles, hiding behind the supposed advice of the aunts. Speaking to the favorite is out of the question. She does wind up compromising on some of her friends. She speaks a few words with the countess de Valentinois and the duke d'Aiguillon. But the latter's appointment to the foreign affairs post revives her anger; she says not a word when upon taking office he is presented to the royal family.

Act II. This time the king makes use of two intermediaries. Around mid-June it's d'Aiguillon who must contact Mercy, even though he hardly knows him. Though no more names are mentioned than with Madame de Noailles, the criticisms are harsher, more precise. The king "observed with displeasure Madame la dauphine's too obvious signs of aversion for people in [his] company. Madame the Archduchess not only refused them the treatment due to members of the court... she went so far as to make hateful and satirical remarks." This "fanned the flames of partisanship at court." Very worried, the ambassador strives to blame Mesdames aunts for his protégé's behavior. And he calls Maria Theresa to the rescue, who writes right back admonishing her guilty daughter rather mildly, because she still believes that it is the aunts who are instigating the trouble. Marie-Antoinette must stop imitating them. She must agree to treat decently, with neither "wheedling" nor "hurtful behavior," all those whom the king honored with his favor. She is not supposed to be aware, adds Mercy, " of the nature of the function Madame du Barry fulfills here," and therefore has no reason to treat her differently from the other ladies received at court. And he tries hard to get her to say to the favorite, in public, one word, just a single word, "about her gown or her fan" to put a stop to all the nonsense.

Thus begins Act III containing two scenes, each of which warrants being recounted in detail.

It almost happens

Act III, scene i. The count de Mercy-Argenteau gets quite a surprise at the end of July. Invited to supper by the countess de Valentinois, he finds amongst other guests the duke d'Aiguillon and a very attentive and solicitous Madame du Barry. At the end of the meal the duke takes him aside and informs him that the king would like to have a very confidential meeting with him. But where? The sovereign is supposed to have said, "You know that I am not housed here in such a way as to make it seem as if we just happened upon each other," referring to his official apartments, "so get him to come see me at Madame du Barry's."

The next evening at seven o'clock, the duke brings Mercy to the favorite's home. She proves even more solicitous as she gives him a long talk about how pained she is that the dauphine treats her so harshly; this could only be the result of "atrocious calumny." She is counting on him to clear up the misunderstanding. Then Louis XV makes his entrance. Mercy writes to Kaunitz, "Although I spend my life here watching extraordinary things, it often seems that they are only happening in a dream. I saw the king in the company of Madame du Barry; she calls him *Monsieur* and treats him like an equal. He finds this quite acceptable and even in my presence, didn't seem bothered that his favorite behaved this way." She soon finds an excuse to slip away, leaving the two men alone. The king blurts out heatedly: "Up until now you have been the empress's ambassador, but I pray you now to be my ambassador, at least for some time." He "really didn't like having words with his children," he admits to the ambassador, and he therefore asks him to "take the matter in hand." We will spare the reader the topics developed by each of them, as it would be repetitious. Despite the allusions to "bad advice," each avoids naming Mesdames aunts. Mercy manages to convey to the king that he would not mention the name Madame du Barry in the dauphine's presence, as the king himself could not do so. He has to promise to keep the king informed of his progress. He comes out of this meeting wearing two hats, but luckily for him at least the two sovereigns he has to serve are in agreement: Marie-Antoinette has to be brought to heel.

He never does convince her to have another talk with the king. She no longer dares to confront him. But she finally promises to grant the favorite the much-anticipated word.

Act III, scene ii. On August 11th everything is in place for the fateful event. Duly warned that the countess would attend the circle that evening, the whole court gathers and lies in wait. The dauphine insists that Mercy be present. They have agreed on the scenario. He writes, "At the end of the game, I was supposed to go over and chat with the favorite; Madame the Archduchess, making her rounds, was to stop near me and, as if coincidentally, say a word to the countess du Barry." She needed this set-up "to steel her against the fear she was feeling." As for the aunts, they were not in on the secret.

At first, things go without a hitch. Mercy relates:

> I appeared at the circle; Madame du Barry was there with her companion; Madame la dauphine called me over to tell me she was nervous, but that things would go according to plan. As the game was about to finish, H.R.H. sent me over to the favorite, with whom I struck up a conversation. At that moment all eyes were on me; Madame la dauphine began to chat with the ladies; she arrived beside me, a mere two paces away, when Madame Adélaïde, who had not taken her eyes off her, raised her voice and called, "It's time to go, come now. We shall await the king at my sister Victoire's." Whereupon, Madame la dauphine walked away, and the whole thing fell through. This little scene was followed by a lot of talk at Mesdames' quarters; they greatly criticized my guidance. However, Madame la dauphine was good enough to take my defense, especially after Monsieur le dauphin told them with great composure, "I do believe that Monsieur de Mercy is correct and you are wrong."

"Well, Monsieur de Mercy, did you see Madame la dauphine's performance? Your counsel has been less than fruitful; I shall have to come to your rescue!" exclaimed the king. But Mercy knew full well that Louis XV would never approach her about it, that he'd keep quiet and simply freeze her out. The situation could only get worse. For although the ambassador would not say so, he saw that hostilities had escalated: Marie-Antoinette had publicly insulted Madame du Barry.

It was probably not premeditated on her part; her pre-performance jitters have the ring of truth. But it is too easy to attribute her abrupt about-face to any fear of her aunt. Madame Adélaïde's butting in was the green light that gave her the excuse she needed to indulge her revulsion for the favorite. The little scene recounted by Mercy is an excellent example of what psychiatrists call the *acte manqué* or parapraxis: in her innermost depths she refused to buckle under and subject herself to what she considered a humiliating act. This was typical of her: the more people insisted, the more she resisted. Henceforth, it was not simply a matter of snubbing the favorite. A word for Madame du Barry became a bone of contention between her and those who wanted to extract it from her. Rather than capitulate, she was ready to defy Mercy, Louis XV and Maria Theresa herself. Because this time, the empress was well and truly peeved.

The empress is furious

In Vienna the ambassador's tale caused great consternation. A forceful letter from the empress dated September 30th put Marie-Antoinette squarely in front of her duties. Behind the fiction of the bad advice from the aunts, criticism of her daughter is clearly visible:

> I esteem them, I love them, but they have never learned how to be esteemed or loved, neither by their family nor the public, and you want to go down the same road. This embarrassment and fear of talking it over with the king, the best of fathers, of speaking to people you are advised to speak to. Admit that this embarrassment, this fear of uttering a greeting, or a remark about a garment, any little thing, costs you so much posturing, pure posturing, or worse. You have thus let yourself be dragged into such servitude that reason and even your duty have no power to convince you... You must see and recognize in Madame du Barry nothing other than a lady admitted to the court and the society of the king. You are first among his subjects; you owe him obedience and submission; you must show the court and the courtiers through your example that your master's wishes are to be executed. If one were demanding of you chumminess or some affront to your dignity, neither I nor anyone else would advise it, but an insignificant word, a bit of regard, not for the lady, but for your grandfather, your master, your benefactor! ... Your appearance, your judgment, when not directed by others,

is always proper and for the best. Let Mercy guide you: what interest have I, or he, but for your happiness alone and that of the State? ... You are afraid to speak with the king, yet you are not afraid to disobey and disoblige him. I can permit you for a short time to avoid talking things over with him, but I order you to convince him by everything you do of your respect and tenderness... You have but one objective, that is to please and carry out the wishes of the king.

Maria Theresa then pulls out all the stops. She knows how proud her daughter is, how she hates to appear "governed." "Start acting on your own account," she tells her, without realizing that she is inviting her to shake off the aunts' yoke only to obey the injunctions of others. True to form, she resorts to emotional blackmail: "Think how affected I must be, and how much I would wish, at the expense of my life, to be useful to you and pull you out of the relinquishment into which you have cast yourself." And she threatens: "I foresee great unhappiness for you: nothing but terrible vexations and little cabals that will be a blight on your days." When Marie-Antoinette received this warning, she was at her toilette, according to Mercy. "She read it rapidly and I saw that she was quite shaken; but as I have learned to read her gestures, I was disturbed by what they seemed to portend on this occasion. H.R.H. spoke few words, in a tone that bespoke more impatience than obedience or a change of heart: that was enough to predict more or less what her response would be."

Dated October 13th, Marie-Antoinette's reply to her mother owes nothing, in effect, to the advice of anyone at all. Neither her aunts' – she explicitly states that she didn't consult them – nor especially Mercy's, whom she accuses of betrayal now that he's frequenting du Barry. She is clearly writing "on her own account," but it is in order to express her revolt.

You will permit me to exonerate myself on all the points you send. First of all I am in despair that you give credit to all the lies that are sent to you from here, as opposed to what Mercy[*] and I are saying. You seem to believe that we want to deceive you. I have many reasons to believe that the king does not wish

---

[*] It seems impossible under the circumstances for her not to suspect Mercy of having informed Maria Theresa about her latest escapades. The care she takes here in exonerating him suggests that she prefers to pretend that she is taken in by him, which obviously serves her interests.

for his own sake for me to speak to du Barry aside from the fact that he's never mentioned it to me. He shows more friendship to me since he knows that I have refused, and if you were in a position to see as I do everything that goes on here, you would find that this woman and her clique would not be contented with a word, and nothing would be gained. You can rest assured that I have need of no one's guidance when it comes to matters of honesty.

She adds at the end of her letter:

To show you the injustice of du Barry's friends, I must tell you that I spoke to her at Marly; I do not say that I will never speak to her, but I cannot promise to speak to her at a specific time or place so that she can go telling everyone in advance and declare a great triumph. I ask your pardon for my force-fulness on this subject; if you could have seen the pain your letter caused me, you would have quite excused my troubled language and would quite understand that in this moment as in all my life I am shot through with the greatest tenderness and the most respectful submission to my dear mamma.

Astonishing letter, markedly different from the childish meanderings of those that preceded it. Marie-Antoinette's intelligence here cannot be denied. What's at stake is clearly defined: the argument isn't over just a single insignificant word asked of her; she is being asked to capitulate. As she quite rightly notes, nothing would be gained, for Madame du Barry's intention is to be accepted in society on a par with all the ladies of quality. She is also clever in implying that her mother would treat her the same way if she were there. She knows that women of easy virtue are hounded out of the Viennese court. But she is surely lying when she interprets the king's silence as approval. She cannot ignore the fact that aside from a few amiable remarks made in the hope of winning her over, he has turned his back on her – which is precisely why she no longer dares to speak to him.

But what is the most striking in this letter is a surprising strength of character. The dauphine is no longer a child; the butterfly has come out of its chrysalis. For a long time her tenacity and forcefulness have been just under the surface. They now burst out with blinding clarity. The aunts are just second-rank allies in a battle she intends to lead herself, with motives that are hers alone. Facing off against the favorite, the king, her mother and Mercy, she looms up intrepid and sure of herself. The only thing she has not properly gauged is the balance of power here; she is up against some formidable adversaries.

In a new maternal epistle dated October 31ˢᵗ the empress heeds Mercy's advice: excessive severity will only get the dauphine's back up: "I did not take ill your lively self-defense in reply to my last letter. Anything that marks your sensibility and candor is dear to me." The rest of the letter contains merely a fresh diatribe against the aunts and a small bit of advice: speak to the king as often as possible in order to reestablish contact. It's up to Mercy to get the dauphine to see that it is in her best interests to oblige the "dominant party," as he himself does to good effect, for purely political objectives. And he finally does get modest results, but they would prove capital.

On New Year's Day 1772, the traditional wish-exchanging audience was to take place. Madame du Barry would of course be present. Mercy lectured the dauphine and managed to extract a promise. At the event, she slowly made her way among the rows of presented ladies, and reached Madame du Barry who had the duchess d'Aiguillon and marshal Mirepoix's wife beside her. "She first addressed the former; then passing in front of the favorite and looking at her without embarrassment or affectation, said to her, 'There are quite a few people in Versailles today,' after which H.R.H. spoke immediately to the duchess d'Aiguillon and the marshal's wife." Looking at her and addressing a short, impersonal phrase were enough to lift Madame du Barry out of the non-existence to which Marie-Antoinette had relegated her. The event was seen as a miracle, and the king responded by showing more than his customary affection. However, the dauphine had only half conceded; rather miffed, she told Mercy, "I've followed your advice; Monsieur le dauphin will attest to my conduct." But she immediately added, "I have spoken this time, but I am determined that it will be the last; the woman will not hear the sound of my voice again." The ambassador felt obliged to write to Maria Theresa, "I can give Y.M. most positive assurance that there is no danger of Madame the Archduchess's overdoing it as regards treating the countess du Barry favorably, and that on the contrary, H.R.H. will always need rather to be pushed to it than prevented from it." Could Monsieur de Mercy-Argenteau actually have had a sense of humor?

Save the alliance!

While this ludicrous courtly vaudeville show was going on at Versailles, in Vienna the empress was worried sick. Was Madame du Barry going to be the grain of sand that derailed the destiny of her august house by depriving it of French support at a time when she most desperately needed it? Trouble was brewing that threatened the survival of two countries with which France had always had friendly relations, often concretized by treaties of alliance: Poland and the Ottoman Empire. What would happen to Austria if war broke out? So much depended on Louis XV's reaction that Maria Theresa was willing to set aside her virtuous disapproval of his peccadilloes. She had powerful motives for encouraging her daughter to do everything possible, including being gracious to the favorite, to win back and strengthen the king's affection.

It is impossible to relate here the entire history of the negotiations that brought about the partition of Poland, but substantially it was this.

Balance of geopolitical power in Central Europe had been greatly modified over the course of the century by the rise in power of two countries thirsting to expand, Prussia and Russia, with the concomitant decline of Turkey and Poland. It was Catherine the Great's ambition that ignited the fire in the late 1760s. She thought she could gain sovereignty in Poland by getting her favorite and lover Stanislas Poniatowski elected king. But because the Polish had remained restive, she sent her troops to occupy the country, turning it into a Russian protectorate. Unable to intervene directly because they had not yet recovered from the wounds of the Seven Years War, France, because it was Poland's long-time friend, and Austria, because it was unnerved by the Russian advances, had both tried to dampen things down. Turkey was exasperated by Cossack incursions on its territories to the north of the Black Sea. At the instigation of France and Austria, it declared war on the czarina in October 1768. Unfortunately for them, in the summer of 1770, Russian troops took over Azov in the Crimea and crushed the Ottoman army at Ismail on the Danube, while the Russian fleet sank that of the Turks at Fort Chesme in the Bay of Chios in Asia Minor.

Frederick II of Prussia did not wait for these disasters to work out his plans for the future. Although allied to the Russians, he had no desire to see them crush the Turks, as he found the latter useful in containing Austria's desire for southward expansion. He himself had nothing to gain from carving up the Ottoman Empire; it was too far away. On the other hand, he'd long cast a covetous eye on a few scraps of Poland. With them he could realize his dream of joining his Brandenburg possessions to those of eastern Prussia. Twice he contacted Joseph II, and the second time did the trick: they agreed to offer to mediate. Chancellor Kaunitz, who had led the talks with his boss Joseph II, wished to support the Turks, and in return for his efforts to get a part of Wallachia. But Frederick had other ideas. Taking advantage of a crisis in Polish internal affairs, he persuaded Joseph II to intervene, and while the latter occupied Galicia on the borders of Hungary, he helped himself to the coveted region around Gdansk that would bridge the gap between his states. But they still had to make these annexations official by offering Russia her piece of the pie in order to dissuade her from exploiting her successes in Turkey. Thus originated the first partition of Poland: a partial amputation that was met with no resistance from the rest of Europe, a prelude to its subsequent annihilation.

The whole thing was horrifying to Maria Theresa. This unjustified aggression against an innocent country profoundly disturbed her moral and religious sense, and badly contradicted her idea of how international affairs should be conducted. Frederick II's "co-partnership" system, which consisted of shamelessly dividing up the victims' spoils, was for her nothing other than thievery. Even the hope that she briefly entertained of getting her dear Silesia back in return was not enough to reconcile her to this "Prussian" behavior. She had the added woe of seeing both her son and her chancellor unscrupulously supporting the operation, the one because he wanted to enlarge his states, the other through sheer cynicism. On August 21st she wept as she signed the treaty sent from Saint Petersburg, where the final negotiations had taken place. In the official communiqué published by *Wienerisches Diarium* announcing that the powers had the satisfaction of seeing that "their legitimate demands" had been met, she tried to have the word "legitimate" removed. But Joseph got her to put it back. This treaty was a heartbreaker, not only for the sovereign but also for the mother that was Maria Theresa. And as if that weren't bitter enough, she became the laughing stock of Europe. For while her negotiators were at it, they demanded the maximum: the share allotted to her was by far the biggest both in terms of land and population. Frederick was able to ridicule her hand wringing, "The more she wept the more she swept up." In humiliation and remorse, she wept all the more: "This dreadful outcome has taken at least ten years off my life," she wrote to her other son Ferdinand.

She had been careful to keep these dealings from Louis XV. She was very fearful of how he'd react when the treaty became public. Not that she feared any military intervention on his part; she knew full well he hadn't the wherewithal. But he could at least protest. And above all, he could denounce their alliance. After all, it was conceived and negotiated against Prussia; it essentially served to protect Austria from the appetites of its powerful neighbor. There had been nothing in it for France, quite the contrary; and France could expect no help from it in its conflict with England. But then Austria had made friends with Prussia and carved up Poland without informing her ally, friend of this unfortunate country. Why should France respect its one-way alliance with a partner of shaky good faith? France could be tempted to withdraw from it and renew relations with Prussia, which had been making repeated overtures in its direction. What would France have to lose? Nothing. Austria on the other hand would find itself at Frederick's mercy. And Maria Theresa had very little faith in him. If he took it into his head to send in troops to help himself to an Austrian province or two, who would stop him? He had the czarina's support. Austria would stand alone against him, and he'd make short work of her. Such were the grim perspectives that the empress could not help fearing.

But the mother did not wish to explain to her daughter the ins and outs of such complicated business, in which she was ashamed of the role she'd been forced to play. Better to keep her ignorant and bid her to obey unquestioningly, "I repeat, my dear daughter, if you love me, you must follow my advice, that is follow without *hesitating* and with *confidence* all that Mercy says and requires of you... *You must without exception follow all the advice he gives you**.*" These instructions were not new. They were like water off a duck's back, for the child had no idea of what was at stake. "You can be well assured," she wrote the day after the New Year's encounter, "that I always surrender all my prejudices and abhorrence as long as I'm not asked to do anything outlandish or against my honor. It would make me very unhappy if my two families where at odds with each other; my heart will always be with mine – by that understand that of Vienna – my duties here will be hard to fulfill. I tremble at the idea; I hope it never happens, and at least that I shall not furnish the excuse for it." But she continued to resist and believed that it was enough to spout a few words for her duty to be done once and for all. And Kaunitz, discouraged but clear-sighted, wrote to Mercy, "As long as she continues to act without conviction or principle,

---

* Written February 13, 1772. The words in italics are underlined in the text.

I shall regard Madame la dauphine as a bad debtor, from whom one is happy to extract whatever one can." No, Mr. Chancellor, Marie-Antoinette did have convictions and principles; they were just not yours. And she held on to them very tenaciously!

The months passed; the treaty would soon be public knowledge. Maria Theresa was tearing her hair out. On July 2nd she wrote Mercy a long letter in which she admitted her faults in the Polish business. She had still to save her alliance with France from drowning. No prejudice could hold up against such a danger:

> France's minister is a good Prussian...We know for sure that England and the king of Prussia want to get du Barry on their side. The king is constant in his friendships and I dare appeal to his heart; but he is weak and his entourage leaves him no time to think and follow his own counsel... To prevent these evils... we must take every means and there is only my daughter... who could render this service to her family and her country. Above all, she must through care, attention and tenderness cultivate the king's good graces; she must try to divine his thoughts, she must do nothing that could shock him, and treat his favorite kindly. I am not demanding that she humble herself, much less any familiarity, but the necessary attentiveness due in consideration of her grandfather and master, and for the good that can come of it for us and the two courts: the alliance itself may depend on it.

At this point her mother's and Mercy's joint efforts succeeded in shaking up the obstinate girl, whom they had partially let in on the affair. She promised to be amenable in everything. On July 26th she took advantage of a fortuitous encounter with Madame du Barry to address to her and Madame d'Aiguillon "a few remarks on the weather, on the hunt," vague enough for the favorite to read into them what she liked without being able to claim that they were directly made to her. Right away the king showed his gratitude. But, predictably, Madame du Barry wanted a public demonstration. Mercy had to deploy a treasure trove of eloquence to convince Marie-Antoinette. On the morning of October 27th, the day appointed for the ordeal, he went to her apartments for one last exhortation: "She was coming back from mass. 'I have prayed hard,' she told me 'I said my God, if you want me to speak, make me speak; I will act upon what you deign to inspire in me.'" But the ambassador put no trust in divine intervention, and replied firmly, "that the voice of her august mother was the only one that could interpret for her God's will with regard to her conduct, and that she was thus already inspired as to what she had to do for the best."

The result? When Madame du Barry came along accompanied by the inevitable duchess d'Aiguillon, the dauphine first spoke to the latter, then said while looking at the favorite "that the weather was bad, that it would not be a day for going out for a walk." *Bis repetita non placent*. This time, the "dominant party" was disappointed. They'd expected better than that.

The dauphine goes back on the offensive

The months passed all the same and nothing drastic happened. Public opinion, for a time ferociously in favor of Poland, turned to other concerns. Absorbed in getting the realm's internal affairs back in order, the king put foreign affairs on a back burner. Steadfast in his friendships and sharing Maria Theresa's mistrust of Frederick II, he remained deaf to the sirens' calls coming out of Prussia and did not repudiate his alliance with Vienna. The empress breathed a sigh of relief. The pressure on Marie-Antoinette was off, and she took advantage of the fact by again keeping du Barry at a distance.

Besides, time was on her side. In the beginning of 1772, there was alarm over the king's health. Mercy enjoined her to make herself available to him. Would she please give up a few of her pleasures to go see him, and not make it so obvious how bored she was in his presence? For illness and thoughts of death would surely soon release him from the arms of his mistress and bring him back to "a more ordered and Christian life." At that point it would be easy, very easy, to govern him. "My great objective," Mercy wrote, "is for Madame la dauphine to seize the moment of any possible change, and that no one but she get control of the king, should he come back to himself." Of his possible death he was careful not to speak, but it is clear that he was considering that too. It was just a matter of time.

While waiting, Marie-Antoinette went back on the agreed-upon concessions. During the 1773 New Year's ceremonies she took advantage of the crowded conditions to speak only "generally," drowning the favorite in the sea of anonymous courtiers. Madame du Barry resented the insult all the more as the dauphin for his part had received her quite cordially. To Mercy's reproaches, the guilty

---

* *Translator's note: the author's riff on Horace's* Bis repetita placent, *or "What is repeated is pleasurable."*

dauphine justified herself by citing her dislike at going back on her opinion. She admitted that things would have been easier had she behaved better from the beginning, "but the damage having been done, and having taken the stance that everyone saw, you must admit that it is quite difficult to go back on the matter and contradict oneself!"

She thus did not contradict herself when in the month of August the presentation took place of one of Madame du Barry's nieces. She gave a very chilly reception to the poor young lady, of excellent provincial nobility, who'd been married to The Rake's son without even being consulted. As she explained to her mother, "I was told right before they arrived that the king had said nothing either to the aunt or the niece, so I did likewise. But aside from that I can assure my dear mamma that I received them quite politely: everyone who was at my home agreed that I was neither embarrassed nor in a hurry to see them go. The king was surely not unhappy for he was of excellent humor with us during the whole evening." Maria Theresa was not taken in by this charade. She was all the more annoyed, knowing that the countess de Provence was kind to the newcomer. "If my dear mamma could see all that goes on here, she would judge that the king's good countenance was sincere," protested the unconquerable girl, who behaved likewise in October when another relation of the favorite was presented.

Madame du Barry, although she shone "like the sun" at the count d'Artois' wedding the following month, was starting to get worried. She was better placed than anyone to see that the king was failing before their very eyes. She redoubled her approaches to the dauphine. She tried in vain to get her to come along to the king's little journeys to his various residences. She got negative replies, but no "mortifying remarks," nothing "that could be interpreted as aversion or revulsion." All the same, she and her relatives continued to be kept at a distance. She therefore made a desperate and highly awkward move that only served to irritate the dauphine. "A Paris jeweler," writes Mercy, "has in his possession earrings made of four diamonds of extraordinary size and beauty; they are estimated to be worth 700,000 pounds. The countess du Barry, knowing that Madame la dauphine loves precious stones, persuaded the count de Noailles to show her the diamonds in question and to add that if H.R.H. found them to her liking and wished to keep them, she should not in the least be concerned either with the cost or with payment because a way could be found to have the king present them to her as a gift. Madame the Archduchess simply replied that she had enough diamonds and had no wish to augment their number" – a courteous reply after all to an offer that was uncalled for, even unbecoming by the norms of the day. One does not try to bribe the dauphine.

The year 1774 began in an end-of-reign climate with the concomitant increase in popularity of the heir and his spouse. The king's morale was low. He was deeply affected by the sudden death of one of his circle, Chauvelin, who collapsed in front of him at the table where he'd just had supper. He was not at all pleased with the Lenten sermons, which were particularly energetic that year. He had to endure the bishop de Beauvais' vituperations from the pulpit: "In the end the monarch, cloyed by sensual pleasures, spent from having offered his withered senses all the delights the throne can bestow, ended up trying to find novel ones in the vile remains of public licentiousness." Of course, he was speaking about King Solomon, but the allusion was clear. Louis XV pretended the sermon was aimed at Richelieu, the old accomplice in his amours, whose concupiscence had not been quenched with age. "It seems to me that Monsieur de Beauvais has thrown many stones into your garden," he remarked. "True," shot back the other, "and so vigorously that many of them bounced into the park of Versailles."

The king was jesting, but he remained somber; his taste for life was waning. On Holy Thursday, he listened as the preacher went at it again, still through the smokescreen of the bible: "In another forty days Nineveh will be destroyed." An unpleasant prophesy to hear for someone who has just turned 64 and sensed that his body was betraying him. He did not know it, but he had less than forty days left to live!

The death of Louis XV

When he left for the Trianon on Tuesday April 26th with Madame du Barry, he'd been looking terrible for a good week. He was supposed to go hunting the next day with the dauphin, who joined him for lunch. He felt feverish and was shivering but he did not want to give up his favorite pastime, so he traveled in a carriage instead of on horseback. The stag got away we are told in his grandson's diary. He slept very badly and had to remain in bed on the 28th. During the day his fever went up and he became nauseous. The favorite hoped she could take care of him there, away from the family and the crowds of courtiers. But the chief surgeon, La Martinière, called to the rescue, huffed and puffed: "Sire, it is in Versailles that one must be ill!" They wrapped him in a coat and lifted him into a coach. "With all possible haste!" he cried. Three minutes later the king was in his castle and quickly brought to his bedchamber. He spent an agitated night. Now, besides the fever and nausea, he had a violent headache. In the morning of the 29th, after an ineffectual bleeding, an illustrious colleague and Madame du Barry's doctor the celebrated Bordeu was called in. The king was seriously ill. And the political implications became obvious.

We know that Louis XV, whose private life had kept him from the sacraments since 1736 but who remained deeply religious, had always intended to put his conscience in order before dying. His return to the bosom of the Church required the dismissal of his mistress. Thus at his bedside a sordid tug-of-war ensued between those whose fate was tied to that of the favorite, who tried to minimize the danger, and those who wanted to see him return to the decency of a Christian life. Each side could not help but speculate as to the outcome. If he died it was simple – the fate of the favorite was sealed. But if he recovered after having made honorable amends, would he keep his promise to renounce her or revert to his old ways? His family hoped of course that he would recover and come out of the ordeal morally regenerated. But with him you could be sure of nothing, for there were disquieting precedents. He had already made two false starts. The first time at Metz in August of 1744 when he ceded to the berating of his confessors who then made a great show of his contrition with untoward consequences: once out of danger, he lost no time in recalling his favorite, Madame de Châteauroux, who had been jeered and hounded out of the city, and he exiled those foolish enough to have humiliated her so. The other time, after Damiens' assassination attempt, and even though he was not in danger of death, he underwent similar pressure, with the same results: Madame de Pompadour, who'd been briefly threatened by what she called "Metz, Tome II," came out of it more powerful than ever. Were they now facing a "Tome III" with a similar outcome? He was older now, so the probability that he would fall into line was stronger. Madame du Barry would prefer for the question not to be posed; all she wanted was to see him recovered without having confessed. Her adversaries on the other hand were hoping that a return to the sacraments would make him see the light once and for all. Since everyone knew how sensitive he was to the influence of his entourage, each party stood their ground, in the literal meaning of the term. The favorite and her friends tried to keep the family and confessors away. They took over his bedchamber and refused entrance to the opposition party. As the prognosis worsened, however, they lost their footing, and eventually ceded their place.

But by April 29th things had not yet reached that point. Court ritual remained intact, with only a few exceptions: there was no longer any "*grand lever**" because the king could no longer get up out of bed. The procession of "grand entrances," the conversations with his ministers took place in his personal bedroom and not the great formal bedchamber inherited from Louis XIV, which was ice cold. Seeing the condition of the patient about mid-day, his doctors wondered if they should keep it down to one more bleeding or perform a third. A third bleeding would send the message that there was danger of death, and therefore the priests would be called in. To avoid this, they expediently bled him only once more, but more abundantly this time. The only result was to make him perspire more. They had to transfer him to a camping bed because his was soaked. Not very reassured, he barked at his physicians, "You say I'm not doing poorly and that I'll soon recover, but you don't believe a word of it." Around five o'clock he received his children. The duke de Croÿ, who saw him about nine o'clock, was struck by his agitation and hoarse voice. A little later, when they gave him something to drink, they thought they detected red spots on his face. "Bring some light over here, the king cannot see his glass," said one doctor leaning over him, closely surrounded by his colleagues. They all recognized the symptoms: he had smallpox. This diagnosis calmed them a bit, for it exonerated them from any responsibility and dispensed them from taking any initiatives. The illness was well known. They could do nothing but let it run its course. They knew that by the ninth day he would either be over it or dead. The sharpest ones, like Bordeu, knew that given the king's age and already shaky health, they had to fear the worst.

Should they tell him the truth? Du Barry's friends, notably the dukes d'Aiguillon and Richelieu, did not want to give this advantage to the opposite faction, so preferred they didn't. They said that revealing the situation to him risked dealing a fatal blow, the emotion could "keep the venom from leaving the body." They discussed the matter and came to a decision: it was agreed that they would tell him nothing, but that if he guessed the truth they would not deceive him. Since in 1728 he'd had a skin infection that was taken for smallpox, he believed he was immune to it. Now the disease seemed to be taking a satisfactory course, the pustules appeared. The time to tell him the truth would be once he was over it. When on the first of May the very pious archbishop of Paris, Christophe de Beaumont, asked to see him, Richelieu managed to dismiss him repeatedly and then, faced with his insistence, lectured

---

* *Translator's note: the first formal audience of the day at the king's rising from bed.*

him at length and convinced him that any allusion to mortal danger would compromise his recovery. Their conversation was therefore not of any import. There would be no confession or receiving of the sacraments.

The physicians took care to keep away anyone who was not immune to the disease through prior infection. The French royal family, unlike those of London or Vienna, had not wanted to undergo inoculation*. The dauphin and his two brothers, whose lives were particularly precious, were kept at a distance. Mesdames, who had never had the disease, in theory should have been treated likewise. But an ancient custom required the women of the royal family to take on the role of nurse for their ailing spouses and fathers. Adélaïde, Victoire and Sophie heroically decided to risk contagion and remain at the king's side. As for Madame du Barry, who also had not been immunized, she wouldn't dream for a second of leaving her post. The king's bedchamber therefore witnessed a most peculiar time-share. During the day it belonged to Mesdames; but when they withdrew to bed each evening, the favorite took back possession of it and she watched over her lover until dawn. One can well imagine what the Romantics, who always went in for symbols, must have made of this alternation of shadow and light, of good and evil, of the call of the earth and of the heavens!

More prosaically, Mercy-Argenteau kept wondering what role Marie-Antoinette should play. She'd had smallpox in 1767. It would have been unseemly not to offer her services at her aunts' side. But truthfully, she had no desire to help whatsoever. We can hardly hold it against her. As is normal at her age, disease filled her with fear and revulsion. Besides, she knew she wouldn't be welcome either by her aunts, with whom she'd had rather chilly relations of late, or by the favorite, whom she'd humiliated. She would only get in the way while not pleasing the king, who was no longer very fond of her. This was also Mercy's opinion. He knew that should the king survive there would be little benefit for the dauphine, as she was unable to influence him. If he were to die on the other

---

* Inoculation, imported from Turkey to England in 1717, consisted of cutting the skin in three different places and putting in the cuts a bit of the puss from a smallpox sufferer. The method was not without risk. But despite a certain percentage of deaths from it, the number of people effectively protected was infinitely superior. Some countries adopted the practice more swiftly than others. The empress had her family inoculated only after the disease had ravaged them. France was the most hesitant. Thanks to Jenner, inoculation was replaced at the very end of the century by the less harrowing vaccination, which became widespread.

hand, her usefulness was at the dauphin's side where she might guide his first steps into kingship. Taking care of the dying king would have required her being quarantined, which would separate her from her spouse at the crucial moment. It was therefore out of the question to let her be shut in with the aunts. Virtually certain however that her services would not be required, Mercy preferred she get credit for proposing them. Through Vermond, who was never to let her out of sight, he tried in vain to convince her. But the abbé tells him, "Madame la dauphine continues to refuse to leave Monsieur le dauphin." He therefore took it upon himself to make as big a show as possible of the so-called devotion that she did not have and boast to the empress about it: "I tried to get Monsieur le dauphin's opinion on the matter... I do not yet know what will have been resolved... but be that as it may, it will have been noted that Madame the Archduchess offered to be shut in with the king and she will at least have received recognition for this act of good will." As for the rest, Marie-Antoinette played her part very well. Mercy's advice coincided for once with her own sentiments. She cloistered herself in her apartments with her husband, refusing all visits and getting news at regular intervals, earning herself a concert of unanimous praises.

In the afternoon of May 3rd, the king finally understood what was happening. "He looked carefully at the spots on his hand and said 'This is smallpox!'" recounted the duke de Croÿ. No one replied, and he turned over in his bed, saying, "This is indeed surprising." That night his face seemed quite swollen and red, but his voice retained its usual timber. He waited until about midnight to speak tearfully to his mistress, "Now that I am aware of my state, I cannot repeat the scandal of Metz. Had I known before, you would not have been admitted. I must give myself to God and to my people. You must therefore withdraw tomorrow." The next morning he had the duke d'Aiguillon arrange Madame du Barry's discreet departure. She took refuge in the minister's country home at Rueil.

Two days passed. The doctors kept a close eye on the suppuration, which was too slow for their liking. The king withdrew into a state of silent meditation. Finally on the 7th of May in the depths of the night, at 3:15, he called for his confessor. Their conversation lasted 16 or 17 minutes; then he prepared for seven o'clock mass. The dauphin and his brothers had to remain at the bottom of the stairs, on their knees. Marie-Antoinette, admitted into the Council chamber, was able to watch the ceremony through the bedroom's open door, near which the aunts had gathered. The patient received communion from the hands of his principal chaplain, the cardinal de La Roche-Aymon, who then went to the Council chamber door and declared, "Gentlemen, the king has enjoined me to tell you that he has asked God's forgiveness for having offended Him and for the scandal he has given to his people; that if God grants him renewed health he will see to doing penance, upholding religion and relieving the sufferings of his people." The king could be heard to murmur, "I would have wished to have the strength to say it myself." Shortly afterwards he confided to his daughter Adélaïde, "I have never felt better or more tranquil."

The next day, May 8th, the disease reached the critical point where it had to swing one way or the other, and at this point he degenerated rapidly. The king was dying when he was given extreme unction on the evening of the 9th. According to de Croÿ, he was a ghastly sight. The pockmarks had dried. Crusted scabs had sealed his eyelids closed and blocked his throat. They were so close together that they formed one continuous blackish crust, turning the face into a bronze mask with a gaping mouth, "swollen and coppered, like a black man, a Moor's head." The stench was unbearable. He lived another twenty-four hours, suffocating, gasping atrociously. He lost consciousness only toward noon, and expired at 3:15 in the afternoon of May 10th.

The new king, "learning that his grandfather had passed from this life to the next, let out a great cry, clearly in the greatest grief... and made it quite plain that he was really distressed to be king so young and with such little experience." Undoubtedly this was the source of the historic remark he and his spouse were supposed to have uttered, "My God, protect us! We reign too young." But Marie-Antoinette didn't have a clue about the burdens or dangers of power. As always, she simply dealt with the present moment. If Mercy can be believed, the whole court was edified by "her countenance, her remarks, her care for the young royal family, and the easy and noticeable way she showed her filial piety and feeling for the king" – "the sentiments of her beautiful soul were painted on her physiognomy." Simply put, she behaved better than the ambassador had expected. Although she was much less attached to the deceased than her spouse had been, she shed real tears with him, because she was easily moved, and contact with death is always affecting, even if it isn't the first. At 5:15 they all got into the coach that was to bring them to Choisy, for custom forbade them to stay in any place touched by death. Mesdames followed in another coach, as they had to be sent into quarantine.

Louis XV was not much missed. At 10 o'clock at night on May 12th his half-decomposed cadaver was hastily placed in a heavy leaded casket. It had been impossible to extract his heart*. Forty torch-bearing bodyguards and thirty-six pages from the great and lesser stables brought him swiftly to Saint-Denis. All along the route insulting gibes rose up, tarnishing the memory of the monarch. They were still ringing out at the entrance to the necropolis and could be heard behind the walls of the Carmelite convent where Sister Theresa of Saint Augustine, that is Madame Louise, was trying to collect herself. "I bore up well the horrible night of yesterday and today when the king's body was brought to the abbey. They put me in the quietest part of the house, but I still heard everything... I cried and I prayed."

Paris in the meantime was ringing out with satirical couplets:

> *Now Louis this world he's aleavin'.*
> *And is meetin' his sorry fate.*
> *So flee all you who're whorin' and thievin',*
> *For you've lost your very best mate.*

People celebrated and dreamed of the radiant future about to open up. The country's hopes were invested in the young couple. The new king was twenty, the queen nineteen. Here she was, at the top of the hierarchy, with no rivals. Now no woman could vie with her for first place; she would see to that. Beside a husband presumed to be manageable, she alone would set the tone at court, in Paris, in France – she alone, without the lightening rod of a favorite to deflect criticism. She was exposed to all the risks inherent in this exclusive preeminence, which she could not protect herself from, because she didn't even suspect they existed.

---

* By tradition, it should have been sealed in a special urn and deposed at the church of Saint-Louis des Jésuites.

Archduchess Marie-Antoinette prior to her wedding,
by Jean-Baptiste Charpentier the elder, after a portrait by Ducreux.
Chateaux of Versailles and the Trianon.

Saint Nicolas morning, 1760 at Hofburg:
the emperor and the empress with their youngest children.
Gouache by the archduchess Maria Christina.
On the left Maria Christina explains to Ferdinand why he received only switches
In the center, Marie-Antoinette proudly shows off her brand new doll.
On the ground in front is the little Maximilian.
Vienna, Kunsthistorisches Museum.

Marie-Antoinette dancing with her brothers Ferdinand and Maximilian,
at Schönbrun, in *The Triumph of Love*,
at their brother Joseph's second wedding, 25 January 1765.
In 1778 Marie-Antoinette asked her mother to send her
this painting (attributed to G. Weickert), which is now in the Trianon.
Another copy is kept in Vienna at the Kunsthistorisches Museum.

The empress Maria Theresa in her widow's dress
surrounded by some of her children.
On the left her eldest Joseph II.
On the right the Saxe-Teschen couple.
Maximilian in the background.
Vienna, Belvedere.

Louis XVI at the age of twenty,
shortly after ascending to the throne, by Joseph Siffred Duplessis.
Chateaux of Versailles and the Trianon.

Marie-Antoinette in hunting costume,
by Joseph Kranzinger, 1771.
Maria Theresa tried in vain to prevent her daughter
from horseback riding, but wound up having to capitulate.
She liked this portrait, which she found to be a good likeness.
Vienna, Kunsthistorisches Museum.

The countess du Barry,
after a portrait by Madame Vigée-Lebrun.
Louvre Museum.

Marie-Antoinette wearing a famously simple muslin dress.
Shown at the Salon of 1783,
this portrait by Madame Vigée-Lebrun caused a great scandal.
It was said the queen was dressed "like a chambermaid."
The artist had to do another version where the queen is seen
in the same stance with a rose in her hand,
but wearing a stunning court robe of blue silk.
Darmstadt, Schlossmuseum.

The Hamlet at Trianon. Gouache by Richard Pique.
The lake in the forefront. To the left the Marlborough Tower, today restored.
To the right the Queen's House
and the Billiard House, joined by an aerial passageway.
Modena, Biblioteca Estense.

Marie-Thérèse de Savoie-Carignon, princess de Lamballe,
Marie-Antoinette's first favorite.
Miniature on ivory by Joseph Boze.
Louvre Museum.

Yolande de Polastron, duchess de Polignac,
"the most charming face to be seen,"
by Madame Vigée-Lebrun.
Chateaux of Versailles and the Trianon.

Marie-Joséphine de Savoie, countess de Provence,
shown before a portrait of her father,
by Gautier-Dagoty.
Chateaux of Versailles and the Trianon.

Marie-Antoinette and her children, by Madame Vigée-Lebrun, 1787.
Standing to the left, Madame Royale, to the right the dauphin Louis Joseph.
On his mother's knee the duke de Normandie, the future Louis XVII.
In the empty cradle Sophie should have appeared,
but she died before the painting was finished.
Chateaux of Versailles and the Trianon.

Madame Élisabeth, Louis XVI's younger sister.
Having remained single, she chose to follow her brother into captivity,
and died under the guillotine fifteen months after he did.
18th century French School.
Chateaux of Versailles and the Trianon.

Louis Charles, duke de Normandie,
younger son of Louis XVI and Marie-Antoinette,
became Louis XVII after his father's death.
After a color drawing done at the Temple by Kucharski in 1793.
Chateaux of Versailles and the Trianon.

Marie-Antoinette dressed as a widow, by S Prieur.
After a sketch made in the Temple by Kucharski,
of which many copies were made.
These either accentuated or attenuated the subject's ravaged features.
Paris, Carnavalet Museum.

Part II

The Queen

CHAPTER 7

THE QUEEN'S INFLUENCE

Mounting the throne had a very different effect on each spouse. The king, deeply committed to his duties, educated himself, worked hard. He reflected on how best to govern. For her part, his young wife saw opening before her a realm where she could do as she pleased; she was quite determined to throw off all forms of supervision and impose her own will. Louis XV was no longer there to rein her in. She was convinced she could extort whatever she liked from her husband. She could sidestep her dear mother's reproofs with the rationalization that by the time they got to her, it was already too late. The Austrian ambassador saw things differently. He believed that the hour had come for her to rule France through her husband. The empress, more clear-sighted, worried about her daughter's fate, "which can only be thoroughly magnificent or quite unhappy" – the latter being by far more probable, for "I dare say her happy days are over."

Fond hopes of the Viennese court

Marie-Antoinette's tears dried quickly. But who could fault her? Here she was, at eighteen and a half years of age, queen of France. To mourn over a grandfather who preferred the company of a du Barry to hers would be hypocritical. Unalloyed joy burst from the first letter she sent to her mother after his death, only four days later: "Because I am queen, the king leaves me free to choose the new disposition of my household... Although God destined me to the rank I occupy today, I cannot help but admire the workings of Providence that chose me, me the last of your daughters, for Europe's most magnificent realm. I feel more than ever how much I owe to the tenderness of my august mother, who took so many pains and worked so hard to procure this excellent situation for me. I have never desired so much to be able to place myself at her knees, to embrace her, to bare my soul to her, and to show her that she has my utter respect, tenderness and gratitude."

This childlike devotion does not, however, entail any increase in compliance, quite the contrary. She is no longer the little girl who must sit through her lessons. Maria Theresa would do well to change her tone, explains Mercy. "This is a decisive time for the queen's happiness. She has never before had nor will ever again have greater need of her august mother's words of counsel; but Y.M. will know the right turn of phrase to give them. Some perhaps will demand nothing more than a hint of kindliness and friendship; others are likely to carry the weight of maternal authority. The queen used to fear being scolded (the term is hers) on the subject of her little doings and amusements. Y.M. will deign to judge if now an indulgent and gentle tone might not be more suitably applied to such things." A little later, Kaunitz would echo the same sentiments in a more polished style: "Instead of keeping her trust, we would distance her from us, were we not to imbue our advice with all the care and attention that are due to a queen of France, who knowing herself to be queen, is no longer, or at least believes she is no longer, a child." In other words, she must be handled with care. They must put their foot down with regard to essential matters only, i.e. politics.

Caution, caution at all costs. Even more so than in the past, correspondence with Vienna would have to be free from indiscretions – regarding the king in particular. Maria Theresa specified that the letters addressed "To the Queen" would be handed to her personally and she must hand them back to Mercy for fear that they could go astray: It was like a *tibi soli*, for neither Maria Theresa nor her chancellor had given up the hope of using their correspondence to direct the young woman's political dealings, so that she in turn could direct her husband's. They were hoping finally to reap the rewards of their efforts. Their underlying assumption of course was that the king was a total incompetent. Although he had "sense and some good qualities in his character," Mercy affirms, "[he] will probably never have the strength or the will to rule on his own. If Madame the Archduchess does not govern him, others will." It was therefore imperative right from the start of his reign that she seize authority as quickly as possible.

They discussed in detail just how she should go about it. Kaunitz had jotted down his observations in a memoir that he presented to the empress. If the queen played her cards right, she would have an input into all of the king's decisions; however, she must be careful not to make a show of her influence. Quite the contrary, she must give the public the impression that he did everything on his own. She must be very careful how she handled the whole royal family, especially her brothers- and sisters-in-law. "To respect the memory of the late king," she must do her bit in treating Madame du Barry "with generosity and greatness of soul." She must avoid court intrigues and reserve intervening purely for important occasions, above all as concerns the choice of ministers; for if they know that it is to her they owe their appointment, they can deny her nothing. The foreign affairs office is a key post; if she could get Cardinal de Bernis appointed to it, Austria would benefit; if not it would be better to keep the duke d'Aiguillon, whose mediocrity renders him harmless. Kaunitz even concludes that given the new king's age, perhaps it wouldn't be a bad idea if he took on a prime minister. Mercy doesn't agree. "The job of prime minister in France has always been to cut off and destroy the queen's influence. History is full of striking examples of it*; the queen is aware of this, and if she chooses to take the necessary measures, it will be very easy for her to dismiss the idea of a prime minister, who could prove in future to be too inconvenient a character." As for the rest, the chancellor's words are golden.

A debate arose about certain practical aspects, however. Maria Theresa was very skeptical about her daughter's abilities, and would not like her to interfere in government matters or accept to transmit any "recommendations." She must limit herself to preventing any "squabbles" from developing between the two families. "How can I prevent them if I can never get involved in anything?" the young woman quite sensibly asked Vermond. Maria Theresa wished to see her become "the king's friend and confidant." Was that possible if she remained unaware of what was going on? Mercy deplored the fact that she hadn't the taste for the affairs of state; he'd prefer she took a minimum of interest "in order to maintain and augment the trust of her august spouse." As for recommendations for government posts, Vermond showed in a nuanced letter that it was impossible for a queen of France not to deal with them: by custom she had the privilege of dispensing a good number of favors and positions; if she refused to do so, the posts would not be better filled, and she would still be criticized because her "bounty is dispensed on frivolous things." All they could hope for was that she didn't abuse the privilege. Maria

---

* He was thinking no doubt about Richelieu and Anne of Austria or more recently Fleury and Marie Leszczynska.

Theresa therefore had to modify her instructions; and she took great pains not to seem to be contradicting herself.

In the end Mercy despaired that the most minimal political lesson would ever enter such a frivolous head. "Although, through her intelligence, the queen grasps the different matters one presents to her, her natural temperament does not allow her to register even the clearest overall plan or to put it gradually into operation. I have even noticed that her mind wanders and she gets things mixes up, so she becomes indecisive and is easily discouraged." They therefore gave up on the idea of involving her in any sustained plan of action and agreed that they would merely use her to influence ministerial appointments. For if ideas bored her, they knew she was passionate about people; she would fight tooth and nail for the candidates they chose. As for the rest, the ambassador would guide her on a point-by-point basis. Which really only meant that they would continue doing what they had done when she was still the dauphine.

Two essential components escaped those promoting this plan. One was that Louis XVI was far from being the incompetent they supposed; the other that Marie-Antoinette was now conscious of her power. She very much wanted to get involved in affairs of state. But she saw them in her own way; she had her own candidates, her own sympathies and grudges, and she was not willing to blindly follow her ambassador's advice, which she didn't even bother to try understanding, because it bored her. In politics as in every other domain, she only wanted to do things her way. It also could be that Monsieur de Mercy-Argenteau was not the best teacher...

The new reign gets started

Before leaving Versailles on the evening of May 10th to go to Choisy with his family, the new king let it be known that he would take the name Louis XVI. He also set up an appointment for the following week with the ministers who had to submit to nine days of preventive quarantine. He was alone. His first step was to look for an advisor. Two days later, he sent the count de Maurepas a note of moving simplicity:

> In the fitting grief that has overcome me and which I share with the entire kingdom, I have great duties to accomplish. I am king: this name encompasses many obligations; but I am only twenty years old*. I do not think I have acquired all the knowl-

---

*   He would reach twenty the following August 23rd.

edge I need. What is more, I cannot work with the ministers, all of whom were cloistered with the king during his illness. I have always heard tell of your probity and the reputation that your profound knowledge of affairs of state has justly earned you. That is why I pray now your willingness to assist me with your understanding and counsel. I would be obliged to you, Sir, to come with all haste to Choisy, where I shall see you with the greatest pleasure...

A persistent legend has it that Louis XVI first wrote this letter to Machault d'Arnouville*. The page who was to bring it to him having noticed that one of his spurs was broken, is said to have delayed his departure in order to fix it, which left Madame Adélaïde the time to intervene. In a hastily called family council meeting, she is supposed to have produced a list that the dauphin, the king's father, had drawn up before his death. Maurepas' name was at the top of this list of the trustworthy men capable of granting useful counsel to Louis XV's successor. So, it is said, the page was called back in the nick of time and sent off again with a change of address. Modern historians agree that this is improbable. Mesdames, who had cared for their father, were lodged elsewhere. Madame Adélaïde was already complaining of chills and a fever. It was out of the question that she go near her nephew**. It therefore seems certain that Louis XVI never had anyone else in mind but Maurepas. It is probable on the other hand that he did ask Madame Adélaïde's opinion. It is not impossible that Marie-Antoinette herself, who had no fear of contagion, acted as intermediary. At least we can infer this from Mercy's recriminations. He was unhappy that Marie-Antoinette let her aunts follow her to Choisy instead of being sent to the Trianon: "And thus it happened just as I'd predicted: right away Mesdames started interfering in governmental matters, giving advice, proposing that the count de Maurepas be sent for, and the queen, going along with it all, herself served as the go-between so that Mesdames' opinions could reach the king."

---

* Louis XV's former minister, who was owed a debt of gratitude although he had failed to get the clergy to adopt the fiscal reforms, and then tried in vain to reduce the Paris Parliament to obedience.

** Other unlikely elements: the page would have had to spend an inordinate amount of time replacing a broken spur; what is more, this sort of message required a more important emissary than a mere page. Madame du Deffand mentions that it was carried by La Vrillière. Finally, it was impossible simply to change the address on a letter as it was on the back of the letter itself. It would therefore have been necessary to rewrite the whole thing.

Oh, if only the ambassador had been there to guide the scatterbrain! The empress would have been spared being "surprised" not to mention upset, by Maurepas' entrance on the scene. Alas, Marie-Antoinette, left to her own devices, cared little about who her husband wanted to consult on decisions he had to make. She had only two things on her mind. First, it was to make the horrible "creature" and her acolyte the duke d'Aiguillon pay for the humiliations she had to suffer on their account. Even Maria Theresa found her vehemence misplaced and felt sorry for "the poor du Barry." The young woman could easily have remained neutral for the favorite was so unpopular that it was impossible not to make an example of her. She was packed off for a while to the Pont-aux-Dames convent near Meaux and forbidden to leave, and all of her relations were chased out of Versailles. Chastising the duke d'Aiguillon, Minister of Foreign Affairs and of War, was another matter, which the king wished not to bring up for the moment; he would find out soon enough what was in store for him. The queen's second objective was to reinstate Choiseul.

These first initiatives could therefore only have irritated Mercy. He did have one consolation, however: Maurepas would not become prime minister. At least it seemed that way. Born in 1701, he was by now an old man, something of a ghost who reemerged after a quarter of a century of an exile that was supposed to last forever. Under Louis XV he had brilliantly occupied the post of naval minister, but a great fan – and scribbler on occasion – of satiric couplets, incapable of resisting the pleasure of a *bon mot*, he had gone too far in his campaign against la Pompadour, and the king, upset by his favorite's complaints and feeling himself under attack through her, sent him packing in 1749. He was at first under house arrest in Bourges then sent to his chateau at Pontchartrain near Rambouillet, before being allowed back to his townhouse in Paris. In each place he led the ordered life of a man of intellect and great culture, curious about everything that was new, receiving visitors, amiable in every way. Intelligent and subtle, he knew better than anyone the history of the previous reign, including its underside. A friend of Marie Leszczynska, he supported the religious faction without being religious himself. He chose to see himself as above the political fray with its clans and coteries. But he understood the motives of those dividing the court. No one was better able to answer Louis XVI's questions. Perfectly honest, he was seen among other things as devoid of ambition – otherwise such a long spell in purgatory would have killed him! And besides, his age precluded any long-term designs.

For the freshly minted twenty-year-old king who'd just lost his grandfather, he was a father figure, a teacher.

He understood that Louis XVI wished to rule in his own right. It had become a dogma among Louis XIV's descendents: no prime minister! The less they were capable of governing on their own, the more they wished to appear to be doing so. The veteran courtier was clever enough to guess what he had to do. He invoked Cardinal Fleury:

> He was accused of having prolonged your grandfather's childhood in order to remain the master. I do not wish to merit this reproach and if you deem it right, I will not exist in the eyes of the public. I will be for you alone: your ministers will work with you, not me. I will never speak to them in your name nor will I ever take it upon myself to speak to you in their name. Merely refrain from taking an immediate decision on extraordinary matters requiring further consideration; let's have a meeting or two a week, and if you have acted too quickly, I will let you know. In short, I will be your man, yours alone, and nothing beyond that. If you wish to become your own prime minister, you can do so by dint of hard work, and I will back you up with my experience; but do not lose sight of the fact that should you not want to or cannot be, you will be obliged to choose one.

The king answered, "You have understood me; this is precisely what I desire of you."

Maurepas thus acted as *de facto* prime minister while managing to avoid much of the routine work the position usually entailed – at his age this was not unwelcome. And it gave the impression to outsiders that he was of little account. People in the know however noticed that he enjoyed a privileged position. The king granted him and his wife some of Madame du Barry's rooms, above the royal suite. A little staircase enabled the king at any time to go up to consult with the one who soon got the sobriquet of Mentor, after the illustrious counselor of the young Telemachus. Marie-Antoinette and even Mercy would soon feel the consequences of having underestimated him.

Another dogma inherited from Louis XIV but not always applied held that women – wives and especially favorites – were to be kept out of government. Louis XVI declared his agreement with this policy. As he had no mistress, the declaration was aimed at his wife. "[He] told Monsieur de Maurepas in no uncertain terms that he never spoke to the queen about affairs of state any more than he did to his brothers." And the abbé de Véri was more specific: "[The queen] will have no influence... on the decisions regarding two such important points: the make-up of the other ministries and the business of Parliament, both old and new." Louis XVI had his own reasons for keeping her out of things. He was aware of her intellectual limitations, her flightiness and her vehemence. But above all he had for a long time known what role Mercy and Vermond were playing and how the Viennese court kept trying to manipulate her. He didn't have his grandfather's attachment to the Viennese alliance, but he realized it was too late to try to sever Marie-Antoinette's ties to her mother. That would be to invite serious diplomatic incidents, much better to pretend to know nothing while keeping an eye on the situation. He noticed also that she showed no hesitation in spearheading the cause of Choiseul, whom he had every reason to mistrust. Mercy-Argenteau was not alone in seeing that she had become impossible to handle. The king saw it as well. And he'd have to do something about it.

To neutralize her, he did not want for resources. Her own personality was his foremost ally. Just get her mind off politics and onto other things. Let her get her fill of all the amusements she wanted. She had begun to build friendships with people of her age or disposition who shared her tastes and pleasures. Their initiatives would be encouraged, as their influence could counteract that of her mother's agents whose endless sermonizing had begun to grate on her. As for her recommendations for government posts, which she made right and left, there was a simple enough way of getting around them: give in for the inconsequential jobs so as better to dismiss the major ones, which they'd make up for with other compensations. As a general rule, they would make a pretense of consulting her whenever possible, discreetly warn her of measures about to go into effect, pretend to include her in decisions to which she actually had no input but with which she would agree. It came down to giving her the illusion of power without its substance.

That there was a strategy for neutralizing Marie-Antoinette is clear. Of course there is no written record of it; but it is the only explanation for a whole series of events that took place during the early years of the reign. Louis XVI was too young, unsophisticated and decent to have elaborated it himself. It bears the hallmark of that old fox Maurepas who was psychologically astute enough to design it and get his master to apply it when needed. It explains why the two men who enjoyed the king's trust – Maurepas and soon Vergennes – managed to deal with the queen's outbursts with as much equanimity as they did the vagaries of the weather. They would just open wide their umbrellas and wait for the storm to pass. The king himself joked about it: "Oh don't go today, the weather is not good over there," he said at one point, laughing with his old Mentor who was getting ready to visit the queen. Marie-Antoinette's smiles had no more effect than her lamentations on the man whom Madame Adélaïde had nicknamed "the sleek cat." And we'll see later how Vergennes would resist all her efforts, with less dexterity but equal determination.

We can see just how blind Mercy was therefore when he wrote in all seriousness on 31 July 1774: "The king shows great willingness to consent to his august wife's amusements, and he will certainly do the same in more serious matters when the queen demonstrates that she is interested and involved." He doesn't get it. The king's complacency regarding her amusements was the price to pay for keeping her out of politics. Marie-Antoinette's rise to power, which he'd been planning for a long time, was a patent failure.

"The Saint Bartholomew's Day of the ministers"

The entire country excoriated the previous reign. There was a general wish to name the new king "Louis the Desired." At Saint-Denis the inscription *Hic jacet, Deo gratias* was found at the foot of Louis XV's sarcophagus and on the Pont Neuf *Resurrexit* at the bottom of Henry IV's statue. Miracles were expected of the young man in whom the good king of "a chicken in every pot" was reincarnated. Enthusiasm greeted his decision to do away with the traditional tax called the *free gift at a joyous accession* while his spouse refused to collect the tax known as *the queen's belt*. It was politic to give up these practices that came from another age. The young woman inspired great enthusiasm when she declared smilingly, "What need have I of it? We no longer wear belts." There was only one sore point: no pregnancies in sight, and for a good reason it seems; it was murmured that the marriage wasn't even consummated yet. But they were young; they'd get the job done.

Louis XVI also showed his modernity by supporting anti-smallpox inoculation, to which his parents had been opposed. Was it wise of him to get his two brothers involved, exposing at once all three heirs to the throne to a calamity that was always possible? Maria Theresa disapproved, but it didn't matter to Marie-Antoinette. When her mother's criticism arrived the three brothers were already perfectly recovered.

Political changes were expected. No one liked the ministers in place. The king knew he couldn't keep them, but he did not want to act hastily. The duke d'Aiguillon was in the most danger. Although he was Madame de Maurepas' nephew, his uncle didn't think he could save him. The king was hesitant: he was a good minister, but the source of his wealth was "tainted" as he owed it to du Barry. And above all, he'd been involved in a great number of conflicts in which he was not necessarily in the wrong but where he'd behaved with such ferocity that he only aroused passions and made things worse. The man was trouble. Very wisely, he took the initiative and resigned at the beginning of June. It would have taken more to satisfy the queen however, who wanted nothing less than his being stunningly and immediately disgraced, and she was in a huff that she didn't get her way.

She also wanted Choiseul to replace him, and nagged her husband on his behalf. But Louis XVI felt nothing but "horror" for this proscribed individual who had outraged his father and hounded him with such hatred that he was suspected – wrongly – of having poisoned him. Marie-Antoinette made it her personal business to have him returned to favor and she *demanded* the king's indulgence, "saying that it was humiliating for her not to be able to obtain this pardon for the man who had negotiated her marriage." He pretended to give in, but on June 12th he received him with deliberate hurtfulness: "Why, Monsieur de Choiseul, you have grown quite fat and have lost your hair; you are going bald." The Parisians who'd applauded him, believing he'd be the next minister, were disappointed. Quite undone, he scurried back to Chanteloup. Madame du Deffand remarked about this old friend of the *philosophes* that he had returned to Paris in triumph, but he left again with his tail between his legs. He had all the more need of philosophy as the loss of his post of colonel-general of the Swiss Guards the year before had put a hole on his finances that he would never recover from – he was reduced to selling off his art collection piece by piece in order to maintain his lifestyle.

Perhaps to stave off Marie-Antoinette's bitterness at her double failure, at the beginning of June the king gladly granted her a different kind of wish. She had long desired a country retreat and had set her heart on the Petit Trianon. Had she forgotten that a scent of libertinage hovered about this charming pavilion, which had been built for Madame de Pompadour but who had died before she could enjoy it, and which had subsequently harbored the late king and Madame du Barry's trysts? But then, offering it to the young queen might cleanse it of its unsavory air. Remodeling the gardens was her first undertaking. The flowerbeds designed in Le Nôtre's era to show how nature can be disciplined to reflect a higher order, offended modern sensibility, smitten as it was with freedom and spontaneity. English-style copses and flower gardens were all the rage. Even the botanical garden lovingly created and maintained by Louis XV, full of exotic plants that were pampered in greenhouses, found no charm in her eyes. Thanks to the protests of those who had seen its birth and growth, however, a good part of it was saved, with plants transferred to the Jardin des Plantes in Paris. Marie-Antoinette could then indulge her whims. She devoted to it the same feverish ardor that she had erstwhile invested when still dauphine in furnishing her apartments. She visited the garden of the count de Caraman, which had the reputation of being a masterpiece of the new style. Natural or not, the count had to quickly gussy up his lawns and flowerbeds ruined by a draught. He even had to rent flowers in pots that were hastily buried in the ground to make it seem they'd grown there. A delighted Marie-Antoinette named him director of her gardens. She was in her element in this kind of decorative work; she was competent and happy, with excellent taste. Why should she be thrown into politics for which she had no gift whatsoever?

This diversionary tactic was costly but effective. The king was able to go about reshuffling his ministry in peace. The foreign affairs post was assigned "almost entirely without the queen's being informed or involved at all." Vienna would have preferred Bernis and she herself was leaning toward Breteuil, but she showed no ill humor when Vergennes was chosen, and even facilitated his wife's presentation at court*. His nomination was only the first stroke in a great cleaning out of the stables, a prelude to the restoration of the former parliaments, to which was given the name "the Saint-Bartholomew's Day of the ministers," because it occurred on August 24th. "Yes," the Spanish ambassador Aranda quipped, "but it was not the Massacre of the Innocents." This is not the place to pass judgment on this political about-face, which cancelled out Louis XV's last efforts to restore his authority. Perhaps, had he lived, he could have brought his "royal revolution" to fruition and saved absolute monarchy; but nothing is less sure. If Louis XVI tried to keep in place magistrates whose legitimacy was questioned – "bogus judge" the pamphlets called them – without being able to compensate those who'd been deprived of their functions, he would be going against almost unanimous public opinion, supported by

---

* Vergennes met his wife when he was ambassador to Constantinople. The widow of a mere tradesman, she had a long liaison with him before he married her.

the princes of the blood. He had his heart set on governing in accord with his people and his first gesture was to show that he had taken their wishes to heart.

Maria Theresa, as a good autocrat, judged it "incomprehensible that the king or his ministers should destroy Maupeou's work." But Marie-Antoinette was delighted about it, believing that "the authority of the king would be greater and more solid than in the past." The departure of Maupeou and Terray left her indifferent. The nomination of Turgot to the naval ministry and then to controller general in the finance ministry elicited from her only clichés: he was "a very honest man, that is quite essential for Finance." Turgot wished to loosen control on grain circulation and he'd experimented in the Limousin region with granting taxpayers some control over where their money went, but nothing of the sort ever came to her attention. She admitted that she knew nothing about the minister of justice Miromesnil. On the eve of the November 12th *lit de justice* where the restoration of the former parliament was to be announced, the king took the precaution of writing down for her in his own hand the ceremony's program and the text of his speech, a token of his trust that she gloried in sending to her mother. But the precious document contained no secrets really. He also doubled, unsolicited, the contents of her purse. Mercy took care of it without her knowledge. Louis XVI honorably withstood the ordeal of the *lit de justice*. "We were surprised," notes the abbé de Véri, "at the firm tone and personal authority of the king's speech. The ministers... had been so used to his grandfather's natural timidity in such circumstances, where he could hardly read four sentences together, that they had wanted to coax him into firmness. 'And why do you think I'd be fearful?' he replied." Such was the young king at the dawn of his reign, convinced that justice and goodness would enable him to surmount all obstacles.

It was of little consequence to him that Marie-Antoinette got worked up about one person or another, as long as he paid her no heed. But he must be vigilant. Egged on by one of her courtiers, Besenval, she tried to patch things up with Maurepas so that he might advocate for her with the king. She would like to take part in the little committees where the business of the realm was discussed. Had not the queens of old the right to take part in the King's Councils before Louis XIV put an end to the custom? As we can imagine, the reply was a decisive no. However, while her efforts in favor of various protégés were almost always rebuffed, she did have one consolation: her friend Madame de Lamballe would be reinstated in her perfectly superfluous title of household superintendent.

How Marie-Antoinette busied herself in Reims

When the grain trade was deregulated and wheat prices shot up, riots shook the region around Paris. Nonetheless, a few weeks later on June 11ᵗʰ 1775, Louis XVI was anointed and crowned in triumph. Mercy had hoped Marie-Antoinette would be included. He had read in a serious study that in the past, queens were anointed in Reims at the same time as their husbands[*]. He arranged for the king to see this manuscript and had Vermond alert the queen to the possibility. He reasoned correctly that if she were included in the ceremony she would be in a stronger position, which remained fragile as long as she hadn't blessed the dynasty with children. When the empress was consulted, she expressed doubts about the success of the enterprise. The queen remained supremely indifferent to the idea, and the king did not take the trouble to reply. Marie-Antoinette would be a mere spectator at the event.

The cathedral was turned into a theater, hung as it was with tapestries and enhanced with golden colonnades so as to destroy any vestige of the "barbaric" and coarse Gothic style. Viewing platforms were set up for the persons of quality. In one the queen was ensconced, collapsing under the weight of her jewel-incrusted robes. Behind it was a veritable apartment containing all the required comforts. The ceremony promised to be a very long one. About eight o'clock in the morning the two bishops who had been at the king's bedside to wake him brought him to the nave, where all the dignitaries in full regalia awaited him, along with the prelates and princes chosen to represent Charlemagne's twelve peers. He made the traditional oaths and received the nine ritual anointings. Then the coronation took place. The peers lifted the heavy crown to put it on the sovereign's head. "It's uncomfortable," he murmured. Draped in the great ermine-edged mantel decorated in *fleurs de lis*, he was brought to his throne mounted on a platform topped by an enormous canopy, equally decorated in *fleurs de lis*. The doors were then thrown open and the people burst into a tumultuous roar, drowning out the sounds of the trumpets.

---

[*] Anointed or crowned? The term designated two successive ceremonies as regards the king. As concerns the queen however it seems that the two were sometimes combined, as was the case for Marie de Médicis. There, the terms coronation and anointing have both been attested to, but only the first was relevant. She was crowned or anointed in Saint-Denis on May 13ᵗʰ 1610.

At the moment of coronation and enthroning*, Marie-Antoinette was overcome with emotion and shed such "an abundance of tears" that she had to leave the viewing platform temporarily. When she reappeared, Mercy said, "the whole church rang out with shouts and applause." And the king, raising his head, looked at her with "an unmistakable air of contentment." For the rest of the day he regarded her "with a look of adoration that one would be at pains to describe." In other words, the ambassador was trying hard to depict them as a couple deeply and truly in love. Marie-Antoinette's letter to her mother, riddled with platitudes, mentions the tears only to say that the people were gratified by them. All she retained about the ceremony, or indeed about the whole journey, was the roaring of the people. "It is an astonishing thing and fortunate at the same time to be so well received two months after the revolt and despite the high cost of bread, which unfortunately still continues... Truly, seeing people who in hardship treat us so well, we are even more obliged to work toward their happiness." And she concluded this account that any eight-year-old could have written by saying, "I shall never forget for all my life (even if it lasts 100 years) the day of the anointing." Her feelings were undoubtedly sincere, but thoroughly shallow. The religious significance of the ceremony escaped her entirely.

In contrast, she used the trip to Reims to disobey an order. She knew full well that the empress disapproved of her efforts to recall Choiseul. She also must have heard that the king, solicited in favor of the former minister, replied brusquely, "No one is ever to mention that man's name in my presence!" Was it sheer contrariness, a desire to scoff, or a taste for provocation? Choiseul was in Reims. She wanted to see him. She didn't dare do it behind the king's back, so she found a way of getting his indirect authorization. And she was foolish enough to boast of it two days later in a letter to the Austrian diplomat count von Rosenberg, a friend of her mother's of whom she had long been fond.

> You will perhaps have found out about the audience I granted to the duke de Choiseul in Reims. There was so much talk about it that I wonder if old Maurepas doesn't fear going home to rest**. You can be sure that I would not see him without speaking to the king about it, but you'll never guess

---

* Etymologically speaking, this ceremony consisted of installing the king on his throne.

** Meaning that she hoped to see him replaced by Choiseul.

how cleverly I managed not to appear to be asking permission. I told him that I felt like seeing Monsieur de Choiseul but just didn't know which day. I pulled it off so well that the poor man himself arranged the most convenient time for me to see him. I believe that I exercised my feminine wiles rather well on this occasion.

Already the previous April she'd sent the diplomat a letter in which she complained about unwarranted "tales" being spread about her in Vienna, while at the same time making quite careless remarks about her husband: "My tastes are not those of the king, who likes nothing but hunting and making mechanical devices. You will agree that I should cut a rather unbecoming figure in a forge; there I would be no Vulcan, and the role of Venus might well displease him much more than do my fancies, of which he does not disapprove." At the time Rosenberg said nothing, but when he received the letter about the Reims meeting, he panicked and showed it to Joseph II, who showed it to Maria Theresa.

One can well imagine their indignation and anger when they saw the tone the queen dared to take in speaking about her husband. Joseph took advantage of the situation to draw up an extremely harsh and thorough indictment in which he reproached her for everything from her laziness to her ignorance, from her frivolity to her indulgence toward her flattering coteries, and her mania for interfering in things that were none of her business. "What do you think you are doing, my dear sister, getting rid of ministers, having another one packed off to his lands, giving one department or another to this one or that one, helping someone else win a court case, creating a costly new position at court... Have you ever once asked yourself by what right you are interfering in the affairs of the government and the French monarchy? Where did you do your studies? What knowledge have you acquired to dare imagine that your opinion is worth anything...?" Then he got to Rosenberg's letter. "Is it possible to write anything more imprudent, more unreasonable, more improper? ... If ever a letter like this one got into the wrong hands; if ever, as I almost believe you perfectly capable of, you let slip such remarks and phrases within your most intimate circle, I can only imagine what hell your life will be..." Try to merit the king's friendship and trust, he concluded; never discuss politics with the ministers and in all matters consult with the king, who alone must have the final word.

Maria Theresa opposed sending this incendiary missive. She

prevailed upon her son to write a second, less harsh version that has not survived. She had a guilty conscience. She saw that they were reaping what all four of them had sewn: herself, her son, chancellor and ambassador. How could they blame Marie-Antoinette for trying to influence ministerial appointments when they had explicitly told her to do so? How could it surprise them that she despised her husband when they had been telling her for years that he was a simpleton that she could lead around by the nose? As for what Joseph said about her letter to Rosenberg, it implied that he cared little what the queen thought about her husband, as long as no one found out about it. In short, he was implicitly preaching hypocrisy. The empress preferred to take a different tack. She appealed to her feelings, to her pride:

> ... I cannot hide from you the fact that a letter written to Rosenberg has given me the greatest consternation. What style is this? What light-headedness? Where is the good and so generous heart of the archduchess Antoinette? All I see in it is intrigue, base hatred, a spirit of persecution, derision; intrigue like that a Pompadour or a du Barry might have indulged in, but in no way that of a queen, a great princess of the house of Lorraine and Austria, full of goodness and decency. Your easy triumphs and the flatterers have always made me tremble for you... Such language! The poor man! Where is your respect and gratitude for all he has given you? I leave you to your own reflection and will say no more, although there is much more that could be said... I pray God to end my days forthwith, no longer being useful to you and not being able to bear to lose and see my dear child unhappy, my child that I will always love tenderly till my last breath.

Marie-Antoinette reared up under the onslaught:

> I would never dare to write to my august mother if I felt half as guilty as she seems to think I am. To be compared to the Pompadours and la du Barrys of this world, covered as I am in the most atrocious epithets, does not sit well with your daughter. I wrote a letter to a man of merit who enjoys your trust and to whom, by such respectable authority, I thought I should give mine. Since he came to this country and knows the value placed here on certain figures of speech, I should not have had to fear any harm in doing so. My dear mother believes otherwise, so I must bow my head and hope that in

other circumstances she will judge me more favorably and, I dare say, as I deserve.

How did she reply to her brother? With a letter that was "more than cold" according to Mercy, about which we know nothing else. With her mother she avoids the fundamental issue, saying only in substance: with a man like Rosenberg I thought my letter would not be misinterpreted or divulged. Mercy senses that he is losing control of her and tries to calm her down, and since he feels guilty for having so poorly kept her in line he tries to excuse her to the empress and minimize the offense. The incriminated passages, he says, can be put down to a "bit of vanity in wanting to appear in a position to govern the king." And, "the queen had no intention of giving the terms she used, and notably 'the little man,' the joking implication that they can be seen as having..." Alas, the empress, even if she made a hash of French syntax, understood full well the nuances when it came to vocabulary. "It is not the epithet of 'little' but of 'poor' man that she bestowed upon her husband." That having been said, it was better to humor her for her own sake even more than for Austria's. Because suffering from wounded pride, she might try even harder to throw off the yoke. Maria Theresa half apologized therefore and Marie-Antoinette breathed a sigh of relief: "Your dear letter brought me back to life; the idea of being out of my tender mother's favor afflicted me greatly..." All's well that ends well; the incident was hushed up. No one would know anything about it until historians unveiled the secrets of the archives.

The obstinate girl did not give up on seeing Choiseul for all that; she would later spend a good hour with him at the Opera ball. But damage in public opinion was kept to a minimum, for everyone sensed that the king's veto was cut and dry: he knew how to stand firm against his wife. There was however another matter in which Marie-Antoinette's sympathies and antipathies were so enmeshed in political issues per se that she was believed, not entirely correctly, to have gotten the ministers to dance to her tune and procured for one of her protégés unwarranted favors. And the king's image would come out of it tarnished.

The Guines affair

There were in fact two Guines affairs, the first of which Marie-Antoinette managed to tie to the duke d'Aiguillon's exile, and the other to Turgot's dismissal.

The first of the two had its beginnings in early 1771 during the Malvinas conflict back under Louis XV's reign. At the time France's representative in England was a Choiseul protégé, Anne-Louis de Bonnières, the count de Guines, a high-living and high-ranking lord who affected off-handedness, spoke with lofty self-regard and played his role to the hilt. He was better known for his public exploits than for his diplomacy. At his previous posting in Berlin his virtuosity with the flute had earned him the favor of Frederick II, who was no mean flutist himself. In London he pranced about the salons cultivating, not without a degree of scandal, a reputation both as a wit and a womanizer. He was all the same savvy enough to play the stock market – usually quite well, thanks to first-hand information – the term *insider trading* had not yet been coined. When rumors of war in the Malvinas started to spread, speculators' temperatures rose. If war broke out, government bonds would go down; if it were avoided, they would go up. Forward buying was nothing other than betting on what might happen.

It is possible that Guines himself passed information, or had someone acting in his name pass information, to some London brokers, but no one has ever gotten to the bottom of it all. In the spring of 1771 however, he sued his secretary, Tort de la Sonde, who had left London precipitously, accusing him of having misused his name in order to trick dealers who'd played the market and lost. Sent to the Bastille, Tort willingly admitted – for it wasn't a crime – that he had been mistaken in advising dealers at their risk and peril to bet on their going down, and he was freed. But Guines did not relent: Tort's fault lay in using his name. Arrested and interrogated again, Tort accused his master: after all, he was acting on the ambassador's behalf; and sued him for defamation of character, which entailed criminal proceedings.

The complex proceedings were drawn out over many years, during which time Choiseul's sworn enemy d'Aiguillon had become minister. The new minister did nothing – and that's an understatement – to help Guines clear his name. He let matters slide, affording Tort the time to poison the well. Guines, who had to go back to Paris to plead his case, grew impatient. His arguments were all variations on the one theme: he had not bet on bonds going down, because he was sure war would be avoided. If he had wagered at all, it would have been that they would rise, and he would have earned money. But how to prove that at the time in question he knew the outcome of the peace talks? He would have to admit he had access to diplomatic correspondence containing what we would call classified information. Louis XV refused to take sides, and tried to bury the whole thing. He let Guines go back to London, which seemed to vindicate him, but he also freed Tort, which seemed to exonerate him too.

Neither of the two was happy with this decision of Solomon. They recommenced their legal battles and continued their investigations. Guines believed that d'Aiguillon had hidden elements of the judicial proceedings from him that could have strengthened his case, and struck out at the minister. Thus, the Guines vs. Tort affair became the Guines vs. d'Aiguillon affair, getting all and sundry riled up both on the Choiseul and la du Barry side. At this point Louis XV died, and thus it fell to Louis XVI to unravel the whole mess, which had grown devilishly complex. To make matters even worse, Guines, who had no faith in the justice system, took his case to the public forum in France and beyond. This was when Marie-Antoinette was pushed by her entourage to intervene on his behalf, even though she didn't know him, and to get authorization to publish some of his correspondence not only with the minister at the time, but with the duke d'Aiguillon as well. The latter did not take it lying down, so the two went at each other with memoirs that were widely read. It all blew up into a big scandal and greatly exasperated the king.

To make a long story short, this interminable business would finally come to a halt on June 2nd, 1775, but with two endings. In court Guines narrowly won his case against Tort, by a vote of seven to six. Whereupon the duke d'Aiguillon, who as we recall had resigned his post but remained in Paris, was ordered into exile. The queen, worked up into a frenzy of "boundless hatred" against him, insisted on making an example of him. In her famous July 13th letter to Rosenberg, she wrote: "His departure is entirely my doing. He went too far; the nasty man was involved in all sorts of espionage and name-calling. More than once he tried to defy my wishes in the Monsieur de Guines affair; as soon as the case was decided, I asked the king to send him away. True, I did not want a *lettre de cachet**, but nothing was lost, as instead of remaining in Touraine as he'd wished, he was asked to continue on to Aiguillon, which is in Gascony." She flaunted her responsibility for it and Choiseul's friends never stopped crowing about it.

It is not entirely sure that the king succumbed to his wife's anger as regards anything more than the place of his exile, for in effect it was difficult for him not to send away the man who'd been the

---

* *Translator's note: the king, as chief justice, could have decisions executed by simply signing a lettre de cachet, bypassing any court of law. Often these ordered the imprisonment of the recipient.*

ringleader of the former "dominant party" and who continued to be a focal point of discontent. He couldn't do so while the Guines affair was unresolved without risking influencing the judges' decision. Did his reading of the evidence in the case convince him that d'Aiguillon had acted in extraordinary bad faith in the whole business and deserved to be punished? Possibly. But as he spoke not a word about it to anyone, while Marie-Antoinette broadcast thither and yon her responsibility for his punishment, the public concluded that she was a maker and breaker of ministers.

The second Guines affair was shorter and simpler, but had a similar outcome. It burst out the following January. Its repercussions are intelligible only if we see that the affair had profound political implications both inside and outside of France.

Two colleagues joined forces with Maurepas and Vergennes. The first was Turgot who had made a name for himself as the *intendant* of the Limousin region, where he had accomplished great feats. He very quickly left the naval ministry to take control of the finance ministry. He brought along the second colleague, his friend Malesherbes, whom he managed to impose on the king's household, despite the sovereign's reservations. The king found it hard to forgive him for his *philosophes* sympathies and the role he had played as the magistrates' spokesman under Louis XV*. The fact that he was chosen above the queen's candidate was for her "what is known in the language of intrigue as a slap in the face." Both he and Turgot were newcomers who had never been household names at court. They were open to reform and full of immense good will. They differed however in that Turgot believed passionately in the tasks he took on, whereas the less starry-eyed Malesherbes only half-heartedly accepted his position. Neither was ready to compromise or make concessions. Turgot was particularly intransigent. "He is of unconquerable integrity;" said his friend Véri, "the good, such as he conceives it, is the only goal his soul will allow. His courage would match his integrity, to the point of obstinacy, should he be in error. He will find it hard to reconcile his opinion with that of others when it comes to issues requiring common consent."

It was precisely his integrity that the king liked, along with

---

* In 1771 when Malesherbes presided over the financial appeals court he wrote his famous *Remonstrances*, denouncing the king's abuse of power in suppressing the parliaments. Malesherbes was not against the monarchy, far from it, but like many of his contemporaries, he did not want to see the king exercise power unrestrainedly.

his program: "no bankruptcy, no tax increases, no borrowing." Turgot had a "mania for the public good." He quickly instituted important reforms: free circulation in the grains trade to strengthen agriculture, the suppression of guilds for freer business dealings, and replacing the *corvée* duty with a tax on all property owners both nobles and commoners. To this he added a hierarchical system of territorial assemblies that at every level would take charge of tax distribution, policing matters, public works and assistance. Needless to say, these proposals raised a storm of protest from those who were hurt or simply inconvenienced by them. But Louis XVI held firm, and forced through a registration of the edicts in a *lit de justice*. He didn't lose his nerve when faced with the "Flour War*" and courageously stood up to the rioters who got as far as Versailles. But the criticism of his entourage got to him in the end. The royal family and the court rose unanimously against Turgot. The king's brothers saw in his reforms, not entirely without reason, attacks on the rigid and sacrosanct social hierarchy. The courtiers fulminated against money-saving measures that ate away at their income. Forced to relent and grant a pension to one of Marie-Antoinette's protégés after all, the minister responded to her thanks with "Don't thank me; I had nothing to do with it," a gruffly frank remark she found insulting. Turgot's intransigent, all-or-nothing personality, his overbearing self-confidence and his inability to accept any criticism irritated the other ministers. And above all, Maurepas became increasingly jealous of this rival who risked usurping his preeminence. Louis XVI himself began to find him invasive: "Monsieur Turgot wants to be me, but I don't what him to be me." After a year in office, the controller of finances had attracted so much hostility that his position was in jeopardy, but he didn't realize it.

It is essential to understand, as well, that while Louis XVI was slowly learning how to exercise power, on the other side of the Atlantic, the inhabitants of the British colonies were learning how to exercise freedom. The famous Boston Tea Party took place a mere six months before Louis XV's death. In 1775 the uprising turned into an armed revolt and England sent in troops to crush it. The insurgents sought help, in France notably. The king was indecisive. The temptation to take revenge on France's traditional enemy by supporting the rebellion in the colonies was strong. But was it not rash of a king to aid and abet subjects in revolt against their master – indeed, subjects who professed republican sympathies!? After all,

---

* The name given to the grain riots in 1775 prior to his coronation.

France had colonies too. However, between total abstention and armed intervention, there were many intermediate solutions. It was decided therefore to clandestinely provide arms and financing before going any further. Better to wait and see more clearly what each side's chances of success would be.

It was just at this juncture that Guines really slipped up. And this time there was no doubt about his guilt. Through the Spanish ambassador, Vergennes learned that Guines was playing his own political game in London, in direct contravention of his orders. He had told the Spaniards that Louis XVI would abandon them in spite of the Family Pact if they dared to settle scores with Portugal in South America. He stated that the English naval expedition was heading for their possessions in Mexico, not the rebellious colonies. He went so far as to promise the London cabinet that France would never help the insurgents. This was very serious. He had to be recalled. For an ambassador a recall means an end to his career. And though all the ministers agreed that he had to go, none of them wanted the queen to blame them for his dismissal. They managed so well to wriggle out of the tight spot that only Malesherbes and especially Turgot consented to openly admit that they had advocated his recall. It was on the latter that Marie-Antoinette unleashed her anger.

Then an idea occurred to Turgot that was so simple it seemed childish. Why not get Marie-Antoinette involved in Guines' interrogation and for that matter in governmental affairs in general? "At the bottom of her heart the queen is honest, if a bit light-minded... The king's difficulty in resisting the queen's ardent wishes will often have an adverse effect on governmental affairs and render ministerial matters uncertain. Deep down the king's interests are those of the queen, and if a woman must have some say about the king's decisions, is it not better that it be she rather than a Pompadour or a du Barry? Our [the ministers'] responsibility is to guide them as best we can and to prevent the dangers that come from foolishness, ignorance and intrigue." In short, they were advocating getting Marie-Antoinette properly involved in the affairs of state rather than throwing a few crumbs her way. The idea made good sense; it was very wise and reasonable. But it should have been implemented much sooner. Things had come to such a point that neither good sense, nor wisdom nor reason could make any difference.

The outcome was absurd and scandalous. The same day, the 12th of May, it was learned that Turgot had been dismissed and that the count de Guines had been made a duke. As for Malesherbes, he had left of his own accord a bit earlier, unable to tolerate the atmosphere at court. The two ministers were popular; the people had invested a lot of hope in them. It was a regrettable loss. There was an outcry over Guines' promotion to dukedom. And it got around that the queen had made the king rewrite the letter informing him of it three times before she found it laudatory enough.

In fact, the decision to sever ties with Turgot was Louis XVI's, for the reasons stated above. Marie-Antoinette had little to do with it, and made it clear that she was disappointed he was merely deprived of his functions rather than being sent to the Bastille. Was it she who pulled off getting Guines the dukedom so that he would appear "as white as snow"? Perhaps she thought so. But Véri's journal suggests another explanation. Guines knew too much, and had proven in his quarrel with d'Aiguillon that the idea that one should keep one's mouth shut did not hold much water with him. He was dangerous. If he were peremptorily disgraced, he could again appeal to public opinion and embarrass the French cabinet, who were busy making secret deals with the American insurgents. In no way could he return to London. His embassy was taken from him, but along with this sanction he received such a dazzling reward that it closed his mouth. That was the end of his diplomatic career. He would soon find employment more suited to his talents – that of court jester in Marie-Antoinette's little circle. Of course none of this could be made public, so the queen got the credit for Guines' promotion. It was credit badly used, in favor of a man not worthy of it. Her coterie made matters worse by hailing these events as their own double victory.

Poisonous influence

Let's sum up: contrary to widespread rumors, picked up by most memoirs and documents of the period, the queen had only minimal input into the big decisions at the beginning of Louis XVI's reign. Her input was not negligible certainly, but it was limited to the distribution of favors, jobs and pensions outside the sphere of government. She undoubtedly had something to do with d'Aiguillon's dismissal, but not with Turgot's. And hers was not a determinant role in the two Guines affairs. As for her attempts to bring Choiseul back into power, they were a complete failure. But it is clear that she greatly exerted herself, and publicly, for some and against others, whatever she might tell her "dear mamma," whose precepts she blithely ignored. Mercy taught her that public perception is a matter of appearances, and that it feeds on itself. The more one is seen to have influence, the more influence one has. Hers was based partly on what one is tempted to call a bluff. She showed off and inflated her least little successes, through childish vanity and because her flatterers encouraged her to. She was seen as much more powerful than she was. And in effect she became more powerful, because people feared her.

This would not have been a problem if she had used the bit of influence she enjoyed wisely. But since she knew nothing about governmental affairs she exercised her authority indiscriminately, according to whatever her whims were at the moment. As Saint-Priest astutely pointed out, "She is naturally obliging, and enjoys flaunting her power." So she wanted to fulfill all requests. She was incapable of resisting solicitations made cleverly or awash in tears: "I don't like anyone to leave me unhappy." So on behalf of her protégés she besieged the ministers; she summoned them and reprimanded them. It took a Turgot to refuse her a favor, for everyone knew that she considered refusals as a personal affront, as attacks on her dignity. "That one got away," she said of Turgot. It was impossible to talk to her, to invoke reason or interests of state. She took everything personally. She invested passionate, opinionated and blind fervor in supporting her "friends" and sinking her wicked "enemies." And the effects of what people were beginning to call her caprices were disastrous.

The least harmful first: She complicated the lives of ministers who wasted a lot of time and energy protecting themselves from her unpredictable moods. And she put off people of exceptional ability. Her animosity, for instance, was one of the reasons why Malesherbes refused for a long time to accept a portfolio and eventually resigned. To quote him, "The queen wants to have influence. It is not my role to say whether or not the king should grant her credibility or even influence in the government and on the selection of ministers. But the fact remains that she wants to have it and will have it. That being the case, it is harmful to public welfare and order to call to a ministry anyone she doesn't like..." She discouraged good candidates and for those in place she was a source of constant worry.

What was more harmful was that she worked to the king's detriment, for the ministers from whom she exacted concessions were *his* ministers. When they gave in to her, when she got an unfair promotion for someone or a costly favor for another, at this time when saving money was so important, people not unreasonably concluded that she had succeeded in bringing her husband to heel. The exercise of "the queen's authority" too often took on the aspect of a power struggle between them. She herself saw it that way, and made light of it, as demonstrated in her notorious letter to Rosenberg. She did it in all innocence, like a little girl who delights in skirting rules and bending adults to her will. But it was a very dangerous game. At each of his wife's "victories" the king's prestige was tarnished; his authority decreased as her influence grew. No matter, one might say, it was all just appearance. But authority too feeds on appearances. Marie-Antoinette's presumed influence on the government was terribly harmful to the king's image. No one knew that in the silence of his office he disregarded her advice. But the concessions he did grant her just to get a bit of peace were very visible on the other hand. He got the reputation of being weaker than he actually was, putty in his wife's hands, unable to get her, and therefore even more so the country, to obey him. Even more than he, his advisers made a terrible mistake in not taking this fact into account. They hadn't the strength to put a stop to this pernicious process. At twenty years of age, Louis XVI could be excused, but not Maurepas. They would pay a high price indeed for the mistake.

The queen herself gained nothing by it, quite the contrary; for the great influence she was thought to have made her seem responsible for all of the government's doings. Opinion would turn against her over the least problem. Less than three months after their accession, hostile pamphlets began to circulate. Louis XV's death and Madame du Barry's eviction deprived the pamphleteers of their targets of predilection, but they hadn't lost their verve. Marie-Antoinette's pretensions to govern furnished them with a new excuse to display it. And as we shall see, the flamboyant lifestyle the young woman adopted during these same years provided them with even richer material.

CHAPTER 8

"AN ILL-FATED WHIRLWIND OF PLEASURES"

Louis XV was barely cold in his grave when Marie-Antoinette got caught up in an "ill-fated whirlwind of pleasures" from which her brother would complain twelve years later that she had not yet totally emerged. The frenzy of self-indulgence gathered momentum from 1774 until 1776 and gradually, if not seamlessly, subsided only after Joseph II's visit in the spring of 1777. But by that time the damage was already considerable. At the heart of most of the queen's behavior there was a single impetus, her refusal to buckle under any constraints, wherever they came from. What with Madame Étiquette's lectures, Louis XV's exhortations that she bend before Madame du Barry and the empress's sermons, the proud adolescent felt that she had to put up with more than her share of pressure. She wanted revenge, and she went about it as impetuously as a prisoner freshly sprung from jail.

In 1776 Maria Theresa received and archived a report from her secretary Pichler regarding the young queen that was so on the mark that it must have made her shiver:

> Already her predominant sentiment seems to be her desire, or rather her iron will, to maintain absolute independence. She has taken every opportunity to let it be known that she will be neither governed nor directed, nor even guided by anyone. This is the point that all the comments she's made so far seem to be pointing to. What is more, she hardly reflects on what she is doing, as the use she has thus far made of her independence proves, devoted as it is to mere amusement and frivolity. But time for reflection must needs arrive, and soon; and at that point, it is clear, her spirit of independence will take on a very different aspect from its present form. A desire to dominate will manifest itself.

This diagnosis accorded with the impression the empress got from her daughter's letters, which became more and more shallow, and from Mercy's as well, which were more and more critical. Frivolity was on the rise; that was certain. In May Maria Theresa scolded, "For over a year now there has been no mention of reading, or of music; I hear of nothing but horse racing and the hunt..." And other amusements, like the *bal de l'Opéra* and gambling, were even less commendable. As for her desire to dominate, it had already manifested itself in politics, and the few obstacles she met only made her shirk her duties more, and increase her thirst for incessant distractions. Alas, she has forgotten something: that a queen of France, whose image is essential to the prestige of the monarchy, has an absolute obligation to fulfill certain duties. Despite appearances, no woman is less free. Maria Theresa understood this perfectly and tried to make her understand it as well. But Marie-Antoinette came back with an unbeatable argument: the king leaves her wide latitude in organizing her pleasures. The reprimands haven't the slightest impact on the young queen reeling from her new taste of freedom.

To the devil with court ritual!

Soon after taking the throne, the queen, according to Bachaumont, "now sovereign and mistress of her ways, can indulge her aversion to boredom and frustration." She "will not be a slave to court ritual, which already as dauphine, she tried to shake off." Because of her innate vivacity she couldn't bear all the etiquette imposed by the court, which by nature was slow moving. It took forever in Versailles to get a glass of water or a handkerchief, because the task of handing the queen the things she might need was shared among a number of people for whom this function was an honor and a privilege. It didn't matter how long it took: she had nothing else to do. Nor did her comfort count either: she was there for the audience, which may be large or small depending on the circumstances. There were always people admitted to her rooms to watch her rise, get dressed and groomed, have her hair done and take refreshment. Here for example, from Madame Campan's perspicacious pen, is the comical story of a chemise that took quite a while getting from one hand to the next before it reached its destination on the queen's person:

> The dressing of the princess was a masterpiece of etiquette; regulated to the finest detail. The lady-in-waiting or the mistress of the wardrobe, or both if they each were present, aided by the

first lady-in-waiting and two ordinary ladies-in-waiting, carried out most of the service; but there were distinctions between them. The mistress of the wardrobe put on the underskirt and presented the robe. The lady-in-waiting poured the water with which to wash her hands and handed her the chemise. If a princess of the royal family happened to be there, the lady-in-waiting ceded this function to her, but did not cede it directly to princesses of the blood; in this case the lady-in-waiting would hand the chemise to the first lady-in-waiting, who presented it to the princess of the blood. Each of these ladies jealously guarded these functions as her right. One winter's day, it happened that the queen, already fully undressed, was just about to have her chemise put on; I was holding it all ready for her, when the lady-in-waiting came in, hurriedly removed her gloves and took the chemise. There was a knock on the door. They open it and there was Madame the duchess d'Orléans; her gloves are removed, she steps forward to take the chemise, but the lady-in-waiting must not present it to her; she gives it back to me and I give it to the princess. There's another knock on the door: this time it is Madame the countess de Provence; the duchess d'Orléans presents her with the chemise. The queen had her arms crossed over her chest and seemed to be cold. Madame notices her discomfort, makes do with discarding her handkerchief, keeps her gloves on, and while putting the queen's chemise on, dishevels her hair. The queen starts to giggle to disguise her impatience but only after repeating several times under her breath, *This is odious! Such an imposition!*

Marie-Antoinette had never experienced anything like this in the Viennese royal family, where daily life was very simple and straightforward. In fairness, Maria Theresa never had to keep close tabs on a rebellious nobility as had Louis XIV. The grandees lived in their own homes and only came to court for visits or official receptions. It is easy to understand how the young woman could get exasperated at what must have seemed absurdly overdone. So she cut short the rising ritual. As soon as she got out of bed she disappeared into her inner chambers to be dressed by her maids who didn't make such a fuss. Did she understand that she was thereby depriving her ladies of the privileges that justified their existence and afforded them their high status?

The queen's strolls on the grounds were no less ritualized. She could not put a foot out the door without being accompanied by ladies who had to follow her, less in order to supervise than to isolate her from contact with the public. During the day they formed around the queen a living barrier something like the equally symbolic balustrade that set her bed apart from the rest of her bedchamber. When out walking these ladies surrounded her, always at a respectful distance determined by their rank. When she wished to go off somewhere, they all piled into a great carriage where each lady had her assigned seat. They moved at so slow and stately a pace that the young woman got pins and needles in her feet. The king at least could find escape in hunting, where even the most robust horsemen had a hard time keeping up with him; whereas Marie-Antoinette was constantly exasperated at being stuck in a life of ceremony that had the added disadvantage of reducing any conversation to an exchange of banalities. But scandal of scandals! She went out without telling anyone whenever the spirit moved her, not at the times set aside for it, and unaccompanied, without even a squire. Or she walked arm in arm with the princess de Lamballe, and the ladies she left behind choked with indignation at this shocking familiarity from which they feel excluded.

And there she goes and abandons her gilded coaches, to jump into a cabriolet, a light two-wheeled vehicle she drives herself that just barely has enough room for one other person! It's dreadful! Those things turn over so easily; she is going to break her neck! But she goes tearing off, in control, free, happy – perhaps it would be comparable to a princess today swapping her chauffeured limousine with bodyguards for a little convertible sports car. She returns when she feels like it in the company of friends of her own choosing. How could her ladies keep up with her when she did everything possible to dodge them? They quickly realized that their assiduousness was getting them nowhere, and adjusted to the situation. Theirs were not full-time, live-in posts after all. With the exception of the lady-in-waiting and the mistress of the wardrobe, six of them worked each shift, which was one out of every three weeks[*]. As most of them lived in Paris, they came to sign in, so to

---

[*] In the days of Louis XIV, all ladies holding posts at court had to reside there despite the discomfort of the cramped living quarters assigned to them. It was not Marie-Antoinette who changed this but the duke de Bourbon at the beginning of Louis XV's reign, to lighten the load of his mistress Madame de Prie who was a *dame du palais*. The king later took advantage of the situation to bring with him the de Nesle sisters on little journeys during the two weeks they were not serving Marie Leszczynska. This measure also made it possible to increase the number of posts, which greatly expanded with the presence at court of Louis XV's numerous offspring. It was no longer possible to house everyone in the chateau.

speak, to justify the salary attached to their post. And when they saw that the queen didn't even glance in their direction, they went off in a huff back to their home, family and friends. And of course they proclaimed for all to hear that the court wasn't what it used to be; it was no longer the center of the universe; real life was found elsewhere. Although it still paid to be in the queen's service, it was no longer gratifying work.

There was no one in Versailles to make the young scatterbrain understand that she was shirking her queenly duties. She didn't even realize it. None of her escapades was a hangable offense and she was not aware of doing any harm. Madame de Noailles tried to inculcate in her, in the name of proper behavior, a myriad of minute rules whose meanings had been lost. Such and such was done or was not done; that's all there was to it. But why shouldn't one have the right to change a few things? The little archduchess from another country could not help but find some of these rules absurd, and they were in fact absurd if taken outside a religious conception of the monarchy of which they were the outward signs.

To make matters worse, Louis XVI was more or less of the same opinion. He had imbibed respect for court ritual from infancy. Through faithfulness to tradition he wished to preserve the ancient ways. But if he had his druthers, he would infinitely prefer to be served with far less formality. It was hard for him to live his life in public. Rising early, about seven or eight in the morning, he would rush through breakfast and go up and wander among the chateau's rafters. "The uneven floors that were intersected with chimneys, pipes and roofs, and where little stairways had been installed to go from one side to another, must have made this little outing rather dull," exclaims a surprised count d'Hézecques, "but the beautiful view, the clean air and the pleasure of looking through a spy glass at everything that was going on in Versailles compensated him for his pains." In fact, finding his way around this maze must have appealed to his hunter's instincts. He would watch the roofers work or chase the cats in the gutters. Why did he like it so much up there, people would ask. Because it was the only place where he could walk around on his own. But at eleven thirty[*] he went back to his state bedchamber, which had been Louis XIV's, to dutifully undergo the rising ceremony. Like his wife, however, he found all the protocol stultifying, and indulged in boyish pranks to relieve his boredom a bit. In the summer curtains would be hung at the

---

[*] Except on days reserved for the hunt or for ceremonies, when it had to be earlier.

windows of the rooms of state and sprayed from pumps with water
to help keep them cool. He "would often have fun pushing people
in front of them to get them wet, especially people who seemed
proud of their enormous hair arrangements that were fashionable
at the time." And one can imagine the laughing fits of the pages
– d'Hézecques was one of them – when he "played tricks" on them
or when he set about "tickling an old butler" who was so ticklish
that the very idea of it drove him into a panic.

Louis XVI was also very young, let's not forget. In his natural
simplicity, he did not understand that a minimum of decorum was
necessary to isolate the person of the sovereign from the masses of
his subjects. "Ceremonies are one of the strongest ramparts of royal
authority," says d'Hézecques. "Deprive the prince of the aura around
him and he will be nothing in the eyes of the multitude but an ordinary
man, for the people respect their sovereign less for his virtues and his
rank than for the gold and the pomp that surround him. I do not
mean that we should forever condemn princes to tiresome display;
they are men, being out of the limelight relaxes them... But in public it
cannot be stressed enough that they must be surrounded by this aura
of majesty that commands respect and persuades the people that the
sovereign is truly the representative on earth of the universal God."
For his part, Louis XVI did not believe in the value of appearances.
Upon accession to the throne the first thing he did was to order eight
gray woolen suits to freshen his every-day wardrobe. The idea that
he might need formal wear did not occur to him. Mingling with the
invitees at a party was not easy for him; people stepped on his feet.
When he wanted to sit down, all he found was a half-empty bench
where the occupier grudgingly shifted to make room for him. Things
were so awkward that Maurepas had to take him aside: "You came
in without your captain of the guards and without being announced;
you entered in a hurry and your chair was not ready for you. We are
not accustomed to seeing our sovereign count for so little in public."

The king also bore his share of responsibility, therefore, for the
degradation of court ritual. That did not mean, however that ritual
lost all its grandeur. Marie-Antoinette's apologists have no trouble
showing that her innovations were minimal compared with the rituals
left in place. Court etiquette had so well withstood all the assaults
upon it that in 1787 the young Chateaubriand, come to be presented
at court, was overwhelmed. "You've seen nothing until you've seen
the pomp of Versailles... Louis XIV was still present." But Monsieur
de Chateaubriand was mistaken. The Sun King was only there on
Sundays, as Madame de La Tour du Pin attests in her memoirs with
an amusing depiction. The future author of *Memoirs from Beyond*

the Grave got from Louis XVI a vague look and a greeting; he was able to get a peek at Marie-Antoinette as she left the chapel "surrounded by a radiant cortege," distributing smiles left and right, looking "enchanted with life." He had the honor of being conveyed in the king's carriages and of going hunting with him, long enough to bring down only one stag and display how clumsy he was. He left determined to go home to Brittany. He did not know that Versailles was deserted the rest of the time and only came to a semblance of life again at the end of the week, because for a long time now the soul had gone out of it. All that was left in place was the public image; inside, the edifice built by Louis XIV was a mere ruin.

It was not Marie-Antoinette's intention to destroy court life. All she wished to do really was to bring it in line with what she believed was modern taste.

To the devil with the old ones and their old ways

Unlike her husband, Marie-Antoinette had a gift for display and thoroughly enjoyed it. Nothing enchanted her more than being the focal point of a crowd of courtiers gathered in the great gallery to watch as she passed by. Her success in this domain was genuine; she fully deserved it. She just couldn't stand the monotony.

Right from the start, Louis XVI granted her full control over court amusements. This was a weighty task that in the hay-day of the previous reign had been shared. Madame de Pompadour presided over the private entertainments, while the queen and especially Marie-Josèphe of Saxony had their say about the theatre and music that would furnish the official evening activities. For the most important festivities, however, la Pompadour was always consulted. Marie-Antoinette on the other hand dealt with everything on her own. She had a free hand. Court life had to be re-established, after being disrupted by the internecine conflicts and then the death of Louis XV. The task did not weigh heavily on her at the beginning. She was delighted with it. But everything had to be done her way.

Her initiatives were often at odds with how things had been done before. Patience was not her strong point. She wanted to modernize court life as quickly as possible, but didn't realize the inevitable untoward consequences. She caused a backlash that was aggravated by a wide generation gap; the difference in age between the late king and his grandchildren was roughly fifty-five years. The generation between them, that of Mesdames aunts, was thrust aside along with the preceding one, without ever having had its day, because its time had never come. Marie-Antoinette cruelly accentuated this sad fact rather than smoothing it over. Around her you had better not be old or ugly. And in her eyes old age set in early. Had she not been heard to declare, according to Bachaumont, that she didn't understand how "anyone over thirty could dare show himself at court"? The countess de Boufflers plaintively echoed, "This is the reign of youth, they seem to think that past the age of thirty everyone is senile."

A revealing incident took place shortly after Louis XV's death, during an event to mark his passing and honor the new sovereigns. Madame Campan recounts:

> Old and young ladies alike hastened to be present on the day of the grand reception: the little black bonnets with their big bows, the wobbly old heads, the deep curtsies as wobbly as the heads, really made some of the old dowagers look grotesque; but the queen, who had great dignity and respect for propriety, did not commit the grave fault of losing proper composure. An indiscreet prank on the part of one of the *dames du palais**, however, made it seem so. Fatigued by the long ceremony, Madame the countess de Clermont-Tonnerre, whose functions required her to stand behind the queen, found it more comfortable to sit on the floor hidden by the hoop skirts of the queen and other *dames du palais*. There, wishing to make a stir and have a bit of fun, she pulled at the ladies' gowns and generally got up to mischief. The contrast between these childish pranks and the sense of occasion that reigned over the queen's entire chamber was disconcerting to Her Majesty. More than once she brought her fan to her face to hide the smiles she could not suppress, and the severe and distinguished assembly of old ladies declared that the queen had made fun of all the respectable persons who'd come to render homage to her, that she was fond only of young people, that she had behaved in a manner most unbecoming, and that none of them would ever make an appearance at court again. She gained a reputation for mockery, and there is no reputation less favorably welcomed in the world.

With due regard for Madame Campan, who was trying to defend her mistress, Marie-Antoinette's penchant for mockery cannot be denied. Her great distaste for old people and her predilection for the

---

* *Translator's note: the "dames du palais" were those ladies of rank who did not have permanent positions in the queen's service.*

young cannot be doubted either. Inter-generational cohabitation has never been easy. For a long time and everywhere it was the rule, however, because the older people most often retained power. But the queen was twenty years old. The old ladies she found ridiculous and called the "centuries" were foreign to her. There was nothing astonishing therefore in the fact that this incompatibility should burst into the open.

So the old ladies took their leave. It was not the stampede they promised in a fit of anger, but a slow disaffection. Among the first to keep their distance were Mesdames aunts. Louis XV's daughters caught smallpox from him. Providence smiled on their dedication, as they didn't die from it. But the illness and convalescence kept them on the sidelines for a while. When they reappeared, their faces spotted with pockmarks, they seemed to be emerging from another world. Marie-Antoinette made them feel that a great distance would thenceforth separate them. "The queen received her aunts with graciousness and friendship but in such a way as to let them know that the days of their dominance were over." She couldn't forgive Madame Adélaïde for having tried to boss her about when she was dauphine. "As for my aunts," she told her mother proudly, "it can no longer be said that they rule me." She treated them like any other courtier. Madame Adélaïde fumed all the more as the king her nephew did not accord her the political trust she had hoped for. She lost all influence and credibility, says Mercy, who would soon remark that she had taken the wise decision to renounce getting involved in anything. Making virtue of necessity, the three sisters fled the court that was rejecting them. In 1775 they took refuge in Bellevue, Madame de Pompadour's castle that had been given to them. They only came to Versailles to fulfill their obligation of paying court to the royal couple. But their heart wasn't in it, and with the help of their sharp-tongued ladies-in-waiting, they would make of Bellevue one of the main gossip mills churning out vilification of Marie-Antoinette.

Whenever there was a resignation or death, a lady of the queen's household was replaced. Each time, it was a young lady who was chosen. Some of the older ones – and not necessarily all that old – felt ill at ease in an environment that was no longer theirs. Marie-Antoinette had long resented Madame de Noailles, but the latter somehow managed to hang on. The queen forced her to resign when she resuscitated for Madame de Lamballe the position of household superintendent. Madame de Noailles could not bear working under another's supervision, and the resulting quarrels over precedence got the better of her. She went off to swell the ranks of the malcontents, which included men as well. One such was the count de Tessé, whose position of grand equerry was coveted by a Marie-Antoinette protégé. He was furious when he was assigned this gentleman as "*survivancier**" without his knowledge. Mesdames took in some of the flotsam and jetsam of "the old court," others returned to their estates. The most tenacious remained in Versailles and flocked to Madame de Maurepas' salon to wag their tongues.

The court was becoming more youthful every day. Not only in age but in style and tone too. For Marie-Antoinette youth was not a matter of years but of fashion and a way of looking at the world. Change was in the air. Anyone was considered young who, like her, champed at the bit of convention, poked fun at the old ways, and made a show of speaking and dressing more freely. Above all, the young were those who valued simplicity and "the natural" over all else, although that was often confused with flippancy and even cynicism. But Marie-Antoinette didn't realize it.

The court was getting younger, and its structure was changing with the emergence of a tiny little group privileged enough to be admitted into the queen's inner circle.

"The queen's set"

Marie-Antoinette dreamed of a life without the faceless courtiers who populated Versailles' antechambers. Like Louis XV, she tried to carve out a private life for herself beyond the court's inner sanctum, in the company of friends of her choosing. Her criterion was clear-cut: those who amused her or whom she felt tenderly toward were admitted; those who bored her were not. Already, the mere fact of making a selection based on personal inclination instead of rank and merit was an infraction of the rules. She compounded the fault by abandoning the queen's traditional activities to devote herself to her inner circle. It must be said that the existence of a circle of friends was nothing new. Every afternoon Marie Leszczynska hosted a little group of friends of both sexes with whom she chatted freely. But no one criticized her because the rest of the time she fulfilled her duty of representing the monarchy, and her friends were all getting on in years if not downright old, and as often as not

---

* That is, someone who, without depriving him of his function, was sure to succeed him. This practice enabled functions to remain in the same family. Custom dictated that the person holding the position be consulted about his successor, even if he had no one to leave it to, but de Tessé was not. It should be pointed out that the grand equerry commanded the troops who protected the queen and her household.

unattractive, the two not being mutually exclusive. This could not be said for Marie-Antoinette's circle.

It was during these crucial years from 1774 to 1777 that what would be called "the queen's set" came together. But the first inklings of it appeared already while she was still dauphine. At the time she was terribly bored and lonely. During the 1771 carnival season she noticed a young woman who also seemed to be a bit lost. Despite her very illustrious lineage, life had not been kind to Marie-Thérèse Louise of Savoy-Carignan. Born in Turin into a younger branch of the house of Savoy, at the age of eighteen she married the prince de Lamballe, who was the great-grandson of Louis XIV via an illegitimate branch*. An unabashed debauchee and already suffering from terminal syphilis, he died, leaving her a highly disillusioned widow after a year of marriage. His father, the duke de Penthièvre had no other sons**. He took in the despondent young widow and brought her to Versailles when he came to pay court.

Blond with gray eyes, Madame de Lamballe, without being conventionally pretty, was not lacking in charm. She seemed quite young even though she was six years older than the queen, and she was touchingly vulnerable. Marie-Antoinette was won over by her gentle face, her shyness and loneliness. No longer having her sister Maria Carolina, with whom she had been extremely close during her entire childhood, she longed for someone in whom she could confide. She thrust herself into the new friendship with the same single-mindedness she invested in everything. Soon after the accession they became inseparable. It was a time of secrets whispered in each other's ear, mutual tenderness, and girlish giggles. From Vienna, Maria Theresa groaned, "Not another Savoyard!" But her hostility sprang from her anger at seeing someone other than her two agents insinuate herself into her daughter's confidence and steal it from her. She had little to fear, however, from this surrogate sister who was less domineering than Maria Carolina. Most people found the new favorite quite dim and lacking in ambition. Marie-Antoinette was the stronger of the two. She would quickly enjoy leading her around by the nose, Mercy remarked with satisfaction, and the

---

*   His grandfather was the count de Toulouse, last son of Louis XIV and Madame de Montespan, who was later legitimized. His father was the duke de Bourbon-Penthièvre.

**   His only remaining child was a daughter, married to the heir to the house of Orléans, at the time the duke de Chartres, who would become known to history as Philippe-Égalité.

other would never try to reciprocate. In the end she tired of her, of her mild manner and blandness, if not to say her insignificance.

Throughout 1775 however their friendship still seemed to be at its zenith. As we have seen, Marie-Antoinette had her appointed superintendent of her household. However sweet-natured the young woman was, she was keenly aware of what she was worth. The duke de Penthièvre, who negotiated her emoluments, had set a high standard, not through cupidity – his was one of the greatest fortunes in France – but as a point of honor. It was out of the question that his daughter-in-law be paid less than the previous position holder*. At the ministry of finance, Turgot protested. But Maurepas buckled under: "What do you say to a queen who tells her husband in front of you that her life's happiness depends on it?" Giddy with her victory, Marie-Antoinette wrote to her mother, "Imagine my delight at making my friend happy" – which would show what a poor prophet she was. And the high price of this dubious delight would furnish public opinion with a very good excuse to condemn her prodigality.

In fact, the superintendence had the ring of a parting gift. Already Marie-Antoinette had begun to get bored with her friend's insipid conversation; the charm had gone out of their intimacy. Through an ironic twist of fate, thanks to Madame de Lamballe she found a more stimulating environment. Before inhabiting the vast apartments with reception rooms that came with the position, Madame de Lamballe brought the queen to evening events at the home of the princess de Guéménée, governess to the royal children. This lady had a lot of free time on her hands; of Louis XVI's two sisters, Clotilde was reaching marriageable age and Élisabeth was no longer a little girl; and it would be a long time before any other royal children would come along. At the princess de Guéménée's, the crème de la crème of the fashionable set gathered. There they could speak freely and gamble for high stakes. It was here that Marie-Antoinette made the acquaintance of the count and future duke de Coigny who as grand equerry could accompany her everywhere, acting as a sort of favorite. She also met a man whose many talents would fascinate her for a year or so, the baron Pierre de Besenval, who apparently won her favor by teaching her how to play backgammon.

---

* Mademoiselle de Clermont, who had been named to the post in 1725. Her brother the duke de Bourbon, at that time prime minister, had given her the considerable emolument of 150,000 pounds. The position, which was extremely costly and perfectly superfluous, died with her in 1741.

He was not a young man; he was fifty at least. But his full face and vivacious look, his easy manners said it all. His father was from the Aosta Valley and a naturalized Swiss. From him he inherited the robustness of mountain folk. His mother was Polish – a cousin of Marie Leszczynska – and from her he inherited the charm of the Slavs. A brilliant military career brought him to France, where he became inspector general of the Swiss regiments, a position he found it wise to give up when his friend Choiseul fell from grace. He seems to have feathered his nest quite nicely, because he was able to set himself up as a sort of likable dilettante. He had "a buoyant disposition, some wit, a body that can withstand anything," a hearty appetite for pleasure, a solid skepticism about "the transports of passion," and the ability to take things as they come. All this, together with his lucky star, made it possible for him to affirm that he was never unhappy. A confirmed bachelor, he collected passing conquests. He prided himself on his writing; he would leave behind a dreadful novel and estimable memoirs. He learned quite young that it was vain to try to change the world; he was content just to carve out a comfortable little niche for himself from which he could observe it with a critical eye. Because of "his handsome and open looks," noted the prince de Ligne, "he would at times risk being impertinent, but he got away with it marvelously." All of it was perfectly designed to appeal to Marie-Antoinette, who herself was much given to irreverence. In 1775, we will recall, he encouraged her to exert her influence to assign ministerial posts. Was it in order to bring Choiseul back to power? Perhaps. But did he really believe it possible? The taste for intrigue and the sheer pleasure of the game counted for a lot in everything he did; failure didn't seem to faze him.

Around this little kernel of friends a looser group was formed, whose members came and went. Esterhazy, d'Adhemar, Lauzun, Guines and a few others would be admitted over the years, and the prince de Ligne would never fail to make an appearance each time that his wanderings brought him back to France. To gain entrance to it, one had absolute need of one's passport: an ability to be gay, open and natural. Marie-Antoinette was fond of saying that among them, "I am not the queen, I am myself." There was no courtly ritual, everyone acted as they pleased; no false politeness, just an agreeable naturalness. There was no conventional or artificial language, just elegance and a light spirit; and above all no weighty discussions, her mentors had completely cured her of that. "No pedant will ever be a friend of mine," she willingly admitted. Any pontificating bores were excluded out of hand; but that didn't mean she'd tolerate imbeciles. She counted on her male friends to keep the conversation lively with their vivacity and verve, and to bring in the daily crop of *bons mots*, anecdotes, gossip, cheerful ditties, and yes, back-biting, delivered with a flair that precluded any vulgarity. With the exception of her young brother-in-law the count d'Artois, none of those who gravitated to her were mediocre. She chose men for their esprit.

But for baring one's soul, nothing could replace a woman. By the summer of 1775, Marie-Antoinette's soul found the princess de Lamballe wanting. She was ready for a new friend. Saint-Priest made the unkind remark, "She looked for a friend the way she would for someone to fill a household position." And then she found herself face to face with the most charming visage one could ever encounter. "In comparing her features," said Besenval, "it would have been impossible to say which was the best." At the age of twenty-six she still had a look of childlike fragility. But, says Madame de Genlis, she radiated a kind of "magical seduction." The transparency of her skin, the fineness of her features, the slightly turned-up nose, her eyes of a pure "expressively celestial" blue, set off the brilliant sheen of her wavy black hair that seemed to have been "bathed in ink." All the same, her looks were less arresting than the engaging, gentle aura that emanated from her regard, her voice, her bearing, from her whole being. She had such an interesting physiognomy, as they said at the time, that Marie-Antoinette wanted to find out more about her. She was the countess Diane de Polignac's sister-in-law, recently appointed to the countess d'Artois' household. Asked why such a charming lady did not come more often to court, she replied without false modesty that her husband's finances obliged them to live in the country. Was this admission as devoid of artifice as it seemed? "The queen was sensitive and liked to repair the injustice of fate," as Madame Campan said; especially, we might add, when it struck charming, good-looking people. To her she opened her heart, her home and her purse – or more exactly that of the state.

Was Yolande de Polastron, countess de Polignac, called the countess Jules to distinguish her from her sister-in-law Diane, a true friend to the queen, or was she an unscrupulous schemer? It's well nigh impossible to judge, as the contemporary opinions about her were influenced by the disastrous consequences their friendship would have for the queen. She can be accused of incurable nonchalance and indolence as well as an aversion for politics that made her declare, as soon as anyone broached the subject, "All that is over my head." Be that as it may, according to Besenval she lacked the energy required of ambition. Others were less indulgent, but everyone pointed out that she was the passive instrument of a corrupt and greedy entourage who used her to exact jobs and gratifications from the queen.

Her severest critic was Mercy-Argenteau, who condemned the new favorite to Maria Theresa even before the Polignacs were showered with gold. The princess de Lamballe had been discreet, but the countess Jules did nothing to hide her liaison with the count de Vaudreuil, whom she got introduced to the queen. Should we share Mercy's disapproval and call her decadent? Wherever they took place, family-negotiated marriages of convenience engendered quasi-official extramarital households, which if they were not exactly in keeping with church teaching, were not thoroughly debauched either. The spouses would seek elsewhere what they could not find at home, but they remained friends and supported each other in matters of mutual interest. This seemed to be Madame de Polignac's case. The pious and prudish Louis XVI did not see her as wanton. Far from frowning upon the largesse showered upon her, he applauded it. Once in a while he would seek out the soothing sweetness of her conversation and even had "a bit of a penchant for her" if we can believe Saint-Priest. Mercy's animosity was not based on moral disapprobation. Madame de Polignac was a Maurepas relative, and Marie-Antoinette "hides nothing from her." He feared that the countess might be the minister's eyes and ears and report back to him some of her royal friend's confidences, especially about instructions from Vienna. It seems he worried more than he needed to. But so did the empress apparently, who could not bear the idea of losing her daughter's mind and heart, as we have seen. For years Mercy and her mother would try to undermine their friendship.

The fact that the unanimous attacks against the Polignacs were muted should not obscure the fact that the queen's predilection for them did her great damage. There were lots of them, and they were often ambitious. The countess Diane and Vaudreuil pulled the strings. Under their influence the queen lost control, and the group lacked the proper balance. It would have been perfectly normal to introduce her friend into her set. But to everyone's indignation, it was she who joined the Polignac set. She thus violated one of the principal rules of queenship. Mercy told her repeatedly, "A queen at the head of a great court must not keep constant company with any particular group." In any collectivity it is never a good idea to play favorites. In a queen it is unforgivable.

Why was she so intent on playing favorites, it was murmured, unless she was up to something she couldn't admit? It didn't take long for the most malicious rumors to spread through the court.

Despite opinions to the contrary, the affection Marie-Antoinette had for one friend and then the other was purely sentimental, more like schoolgirl crushes than forbidden love. But the spontaneity and freedom of her behavior were incompatible with the restraint demanded of a queen, and fed the rumor mill. And the commonly used term of favorite invited confusion with royal mistresses.

What about the men? Certainly some of them, like Lauzun and Besenval, were certified Don Juans. Marie-Antoinette was flirtatious; she enjoyed being admired and had nothing against men secretly pining after her, as in the sentimental novels so fashionable at the time. Of course she hadn't read them. The interminable *Nouvelle Héloïse** if she got a hold of it, must have bored her to tears. But French society at the time, as we can see from the music and theatre then in fashion, was saturated with a sensibility that found its expression in wishy-washy tales like this one, bathed in torrents of tears, where love rhymes with virtue. She breathed it in with the songs she sang, in the dances she danced, and the plays she applauded. She didn't realize that she was playing with fire by making a show of being seen with mature men who had a very different conception of love. Madame Campan would have us believe that two of them, Besenval and then Lauzun, went so far as to make advances that were vigorously rebuffed. Lauzun boasted about it, claiming in his memoirs that she would have given in to him had he not had the wisdom to take things no further. Madame Campan on the other hand heard her mistress shout loudly and angrily, "You must leave, sir," and his subsequent loss of favor seems to confirm her version of events. Besenval did not boast of it, but here again, the account of the former lady of the bedchamber, confirmed by the queen's obvious disaffection from the baron in the beginning of 1776, rings true. He apparently was mad enough to make a declaration of love on bended knee only to get in reply, "Arise, sir, the king shan't hear of this wrong that could cause your eternal disgrace." Madame Campan tells us that the queen accompanied this avowal with reflections on "men's strange presumption and the reserve that women must always employ in their company." This realization should have come earlier, but at the time she still had the reckless confidence that only innocence can bestow. She would be accused of every vice.

---

* *Translator's note: enormously successful novel by Jean-Jacques Rousseau.*

The pleasures of Versailles

When she ascended to the throne, before getting absorbed into the Polignac set, Marie-Antoinette had tried to make official life less tedious and to rejuvenate the court's offerings of evening entertainment. She took her role as organizer of these affairs seriously. Her intentions were good. But here again she upset old ways, exposing herself to criticism.

One of her first innovations concerned meals. It should be pointed out that meal taking as arranged by Louis XIV was one of the most boring things imaginable. Conceived for the public and not for those dining, meals brought together around the king and his family a dazzling array of women in formal dress. As you had nothing to say to the person that hierarchical order placed at your side, music made up for the lack of conversation. No males other than princes of the royal blood were allowed to sit at the queen's table. When the king was away she dined in her own apartments accompanied by her ladies, less formally but still in public. Louis XV disliked all this ceremony and started his "little suppers." He enjoyed taking his evening meals with a small group of choice friends in a hunting lodge or in the hideaway apartments he had fitted out in the depths of the chateau. It was usually his mistress who presided at these suppers where men and women alike would gather around the table, heedless of protocol. There was nothing of an orgy about them, they were simply relaxed evenings that any great lord or bourgeois gentleman could afford. Whenever Louis XV invited a woman of his family, as happened from time to time, protocol was again imposed; there would be two tables, and a lot of the fun went out of it.

Would Louis XVI keep the "little suppers" going? On hunting days he no doubt would have liked to spend the evening with his companions. Dinner with the boys? This risked the possibility of guests bringing women along, perhaps tempting the king to take a mistress. Would it not be better to take the initiative and ask the queen to preside at these suppers? But if they wished to maintain the pleasant atmosphere sheltered from the tyranny of etiquette, they would have to allow men to sit at the same table as the queen. Mercy-Argenteau put forward this idea with the express purpose of making the little suppers morally acceptable. Marie-Antoinette applauded it too, as that was how things were done at the Viennese court. Mesdames aunts protested indignantly, as did all the old people; another good reason to put her foot down. Louis XVI couldn't decide, but finally gave in; so little suppers in mixed company became accepted custom. It fell to Marie-Antoinette to choose which women would be invited. And even though it was up to Louis XVI to choose which men to invite, everyone knew that he wouldn't dare go against his wife's wishes. And since many are called but few are chosen, she made a lot of people unhappy. Unlike Louis XV when he brought guests to Marly, she didn't know how to dole out this privilege according to the rank and merits of the invitation seekers. And when there were guests she found boring or unfashionable, she would ignore them; "she spoke only to the young people," the prince de Croÿ noted. And since she always chose the same ones, she greatly annoyed those excluded.

At the same time, the ceremonial public meals were streamlined somewhat. In order to economize, *le grand couvert* was reserved for the big holidays. Guests who hankered to see the famous worked-gold "vessel"* were disappointed. The *petit couvert*, in which the king was served in his chamber, was still held, but only on Sundays. A restrained Marie-Antoinette merely made an appearance. She hardly touched the food that her husband, blessed with a hearty appetite, "enjoyed with all the forthrightness of his character." She would be in such a hurry to get it over with that she'd push things along in order to go back to her own apartments to nibble on some boiled white meat and drink some cold water. And such was the force of tradition that everyone felt that the dignity of the monarchy had been impaired.

Her involvement caused a stir in the theatre world too. She threw herself into it with passion. To comply with her wishes, Louis XV had brought two comedies a week to Versailles. As soon as she became queen she brought in a third. "The king left it to the queen to arrange for whatever she found apt to make the winter court season pleasurable and outstanding," Papillon de La Ferté wrote in December of 1774. "Consequently, the queen decided on three shows a week, two French comedies and an Italian one." More precisely, between December and Easter, during what was known as "carnival season," there was a tragedy on Tuesdays, a French comedy on Thursdays and an Italian one on Friday. Because of their high cost, operas were performed only five or six times a winter.

Until the Revolution, Marie-Antoinette would reign supreme over

---

* These *nefs or cadenas* were vermilion boxes containing salt, pepper and the dining implements.

court performances in Versailles, and at Fontainebleau during the autumn season. Her impatience and imperious ways sewed discord in the ranks of those who previously had dominated theatrical affairs. Trampling on habits and privileges, she didn't consult the first gentleman of the bedchamber about what programs to choose; she gave orders to the *Menus-Plaisirs* without bothering to find out if they could be carried out within the time available. Although there was already a problem of overstaffing, she brought in one of her protégés, raising a storm of jealousy. She interfered with the selection of actors and actresses without regard for the ladies' respective protectors. During a rehearsal she took it upon herself to reject a play about to be put on because she didn't consider it ready. Upsetting the slow pace and humdrum routines, she brought a gust of fresh air to a sleepy court lulled by the out-dated music of Lully. But she stepped on a lot of toes.

She decided what would and would not get put on stage. Although the king loved tragedies, she didn't. She wouldn't touch them. She rather liked comedy but detested the slapstick kind that made her husband burst out laughing. Her preferences went to the lyric theatre, which only made him yawn; he was tone deaf and sang frightfully off key. Too bad for him. She set about eliminating from the Versailles *Italiens* repertoire the knockabout farces of the traditional *commedia dell'Arte* and replaced them with the musical comedies that satisfied the new tastes. By far her favorite musician was Grétry, followed by Monsigny, Philidor and a few others, all quite forgotten today. A dash of gaiety, gushings of sentiment, a hint of pathos quickly erased by a happy ending, characters of unconquerable morality but who knew how to make virtue seem attractive, with just a dash of magic or the fairytale to bind it all together: such was the recipe enjoyed by a public that prided itself on its sensitive soul and ready tears. Here again Marie-Antoinette was a woman of her times, perhaps even ahead of her times. But her passion for the grand opera brought her to Paris as well. Without giving up what Versailles had to offer, she would seek in the Paris theatres emotions of a higher order.

The balls in Versailles, for a time highly reputed throughout Europe, would also suffer in her eyes by comparison with what the capital had to offer, and this despite the fact that they were quite popular in the winter of 1774-1775, when the mourning period was over and people could again indulge their desire for parties. They took place either in the great hall or in a room on the ground floor that could be made larger by adding on wooden pavilions whose walls the *Menus-Plaisirs* would decorate for the occasion.

They began at six and never went past ten o'clock. The ladies would arrive "wearing dominos or in another costume that suited them," but the men wore their usual attire. Silver and gold could not be added to garments, so as to keep things at a low key. Visiting France, Horace Walpole remembered the dazzling atmosphere of one such soirée. He noted that there were eight minuets and aside from the queen and princesses, only eight ladies took part in them. He didn't find any beauties among them, or perhaps it was just that the queen outshone them all, he said. Since the weather was extremely hot, refreshments were served between sets. The king didn't dance. He watched his wife execute "with divine ease" the first dance steps on the floor. No one could find fault with these balls – nothing more fitting and decent could be imagined.

But the queen quickly tired of the inevitable obligatory sets. So she replaced these traditional balls with dances and quadrilles based on exotic or mythological themes: Laplanders, Indians, the four seasons, one or the other of the arts. From week to week they perfected the entries, took care in creating the costumes and masks; they rehearsed, worked on the steps and improved the choreography. This entertainment could not be criticized either. It placed Marie-Antoinette, perhaps without her even knowing it, squarely in the tradition of Louis XIV.

All the same, these balls were quickly deserted. Mercy tells us why. The "presented" ladies who lived in Paris – and these were the majority – stopped coming to court, not knowing whether or not they would see the queen. Invited to these balls, "they arrive in Versailles and stay all dressed up in their ball gowns until ten or ten-thirty and then go back to Paris at night in search of supper; and since this tiring routine does not grant them admission to the privileged private suppers, the ladies in question are quite put out and dispense with the Versailles balls as much as possible."

For her part, the queen got tired of them too, because the court's sweet little balls were quite insipid compared to what the Opéra de Paris had to offer.

The pleasures of Paris

As we have seen, while she was still dauphine Marie-Antoinette infringed on the rule that outlawed applause in theatres when the sovereigns were in attendance. When *Iphigenia* premiered in Paris, she assured her dear Gluck's success by energetically applauding. She saw this as a great feather in her cap, and tried to introduce the practice to Versailles. But there, this fresh attack on proper behavior produced only a smattering of polite applause amongst the courtiers imbued with respect for tradition. This was altogether different from the fervor of Parisian audiences.

The audience is an important ingredient in any performance; all theatre people know that. In the stalls in Paris the audience was used to applauding; they hated being prevented from doing so by the presence of the queen. When they saw that she took the initiative they went wild. And she thoroughly enjoyed the electricity between the performers and the public produced by the mutual admiration expressed in the applause. She was the one who produced this electricity! And not only that, for she was not just any spectator, she was the queen, and the crowd's acclamation was also for her. The actors developed the habit of turning toward her whenever the play presented an "application." Therefore any homage to the kings and queens in the plays was addressed to her – and heaven knows there were plenty of them! When *Iphigenia* was staged again, the actor Le Gros stepped out of the chorus singing "Lift your voices, celebrate your queen..." and went to the edge of the stage to dedicate to Marie-Antoinette a verse made up for the occasion:

> *Lift our voices, celebrate our queen*
> *May the marriage that binds her*
> *Make us happy forever.*

The box where she was enthroned beneath a gold-fringed canopy became another stage. On that stage it was she who played the dream role, that of a sovereign lauded to the skies by her loving subjects. This was altogether more thrilling than the mechanical-doll curtsies of the ladies at court. Her love of the theatre had its roots in her childhood performances back home. The theatre afforded a few hours of making believe you were someone else, of escaping the life you were trapped in. In Versailles the little family performances were but a pale reflection of the real theatre, which presupposed a real audience. Being queen prevented her from performing – for the moment. But she got a foretaste of the giddy pleasures of the stage when sitting high up in her box like some sort of goddess perched on a cloud in a mythological opera, she intervened by clapping her hands, making it socially acceptable to reward the good and punish the bad.

She was a "good audience," and did not deprive herself. Her enthusiasm was contagious and her applause infused new vitality into the lyric theatre, although not without some epic battles.

When dear papa Gluck had the audacity to compose another *Armide* – how dare he? – on the same libretto that Lully had used, twice in a row she had a hard time putting a stop to the boos and whistles of a bunch of Lully lovers determined to rip it apart. But their tried and true friendship didn't prevent her from occasionally supporting his rival Piccinni. She was welcoming to all musicians, as long as they catered to her modern tastes. Her passion for the lyric theatre would outlive her divorce from Paris, when she would become so unpopular that she had to flee the capital. Right up to the Revolution she would continue putting on performances at Versailles and Fontainebleau. By and large, she greatly contributed to renewing France's musical life. But in order to do so it was necessary to tread on some traditions. She did so thoughtlessly, and ruffled many feathers. A great many of her contemporaries, unfortunately, saw only that.

There was nothing to criticize in her love of the theatre, except perhaps a bit too much exuberance in expressing it. The pleasures she sought in the Opera balls, on the other hand, would be less innocent. They sprang from the same desire to escape from her condition, to become someone else, if only for an evening. She wanted "to enjoy the Opera balls as unhindered as the lowliest woman in the kingdom," the marquis de Bombelles remarked astutely. Masked balls, after all, provided anonymity, or at least she liked to think so.

Of course there were masked balls in Versailles too. At royal weddings for example it was customary for a masked ball to follow the official grand ball. These allowed guests to choose their own partners and mingle anonymously in the crowd. However, the queen was an exception to this rule; she always had to be recognizable. Besides, even if she wanted to, Marie-Antoinette couldn't get lost amongst the masks; the courtiers immediately spotted the haughty cast of her head and her ethereal walk. Not so in Paris. The Opera balls, reserved as a rule to the well to do, attracted a mixed public. Princes and noblemen rubbed shoulders with the cream of the wealthy bourgeoisie, but also with a few adventurers seeking good fortune, in all the senses of the term. People were not there to pay court but to enjoy themselves, and no one expected, at least in the beginning, to see the queen there.

Protected by this anonymity, a few months before Louis XV's death, on 30 January 1774, Marie-Antoinette was able to dash off a few dance steps and chat for a good while, carefree, smiling and happy, with one of the handsomest gentlemen there. Did she recognize this young Swedish officer who had been introduced to her a few weeks before, but who had escaped her notice at the Versailles balls? He in any case was genuinely stupefied when ladies arrived to whisk her away, followed close behind by the dauphin and the count de Provence. His charming dance partner had been none other than the dauphine! He took the wise decision to bury the memory of this dangerous triumph in the arms of his mistress-of-the-moment. The dauphine went back to the world from which she had thought she could escape briefly, but she did not forget his face, or his name: Axel von Fersen.

We shall see later what this chance meeting would lead to, but in the meantime, Marie-Antoinette, who became queen shortly thereafter, threw herself into a feverish pursuit of pleasure. She attended the Opera balls frequently, happy in the knowledge that the king approved, as she loudly proclaimed to her mother. But since he was not accommodating enough to go with her, she needed a family member to fulfill the function of lordly escort. Sometimes the count de Provence and his wife accompanied her. But it was usually her younger brother-in-law the count d'Artois who gladly followed her, or led her, to places where they could have fun. It would be hard to find anyone less suited to be a chaperon. He was seventeen and as light-minded as his brothers were serious. This pretty, hare-brained boy already had the reputation of an out-and-out libertine, given to gambling and womanizing, cheeky, capricious, and emotionally unstable enough to go from fury to hilarity in a flash. Far from keeping an eye on Marie-Antoinette, he encouraged her to misbehave, and it was she who sometimes had to warn him that he was going too far.

It goes without saying that she felt free with such a companion. She attended these balls less to dance than to mingle with people, said Mercy; to exchange with strangers a few words without the constraints usually imposed by her condition. How far could she let herself go during these hectic Parisian nights? Masked, she could hear things and accept behavior that she would have to disapprove of if she were recognizable. It's inconsequential; there is no danger, she thinks. Since people do not know whom they are dealing with, nothing will come of it. She enjoys the heady feeling she gets from the compliments men pay to her as a woman that they would not dare pay to the queen. They are but stillborn idylls, lasting no longer than a sigh; they furnish her stock of dreams. In the long run, however, masks and dominos no longer fooled anyone. When she started to attend regularly, as soon as people suspected she had shown up, they were on the look out for her; they spotted her easily and spread the word. Both she and they kept up the pretense of her not being recognized; otherwise she would have had to relinquish the freedom of speech and manners that was the whole point of these encounters. This tacit complicity made for more racy banter, but at the same time it protected her. For each of her partners knew that if he went too far, the queen in her would come to life. It was just a game, one in which the whole ballroom sometimes took part. "Some sort of scheme would always be found," Madame Campan tells us, "so that the queen could happily maintain her incognito."

The game was a dangerous one, all the same. Marie-Antoinette breathed in the exhilarating air of flirtation, which went to her head. Would she go so far as to abandon her inaccessibility? Even if, as it is almost certain, she did nothing reprehensible, she did compromise herself, more seriously than would an ordinary woman. For she was not an ordinary woman, however much she would like to behave like one when attending a ball. She was the queen. She did not have the right to expose herself to contact with the common run of mortals, alone and unprotected. Try as Mercy might to hide the fact from the empress, she was often unprotected, in a very lax environment. One evening in February 1776, for instance, the ball was very crowded. There was pushing and shoving and a black domino hit the count d'Artois, who violently punched the offending party. The victim complained to the security agents who didn't recognize the count, and hauled him off to the guard post. The affair was bruited about and the empress got wind of the fact – and not from Mercy – that her daughter was alone at the Opera ball for two or three hours "chatting freely with a number of masked figures who even took turns guiding her in their arms." Whatever Mercy said, she remained convinced that Marie-Antoinette was becoming degenerate. She was, unfortunately, not the only one.

Her young brother-in-law also brought her along to the racetrack. Horse races were not new, there were others back in the days of the duchess de Bourgogne at the beginning of the century. But now with anything English in fashion, they were all the rage. They were held on the Sablons plains near the Bois de Boulogne, except in the fall when everyone went off to Fontainebleau. The problem was the betting. It incited almost indecent passion, and the count d'Artois, who placed horses, was not shy about making a noisy show of his feelings. According to Mercy, "they built a structure rather similar to the one at Fontainebleau – in other words a viewing stand – where lunch is served; the men arrive dressed rather improperly and there is much noise and commotion unbefitting the decency and respect that the presence of the court should inspire." At least Marie-Antoinette was not unaccompanied. In the midst of this crowd Mercy could discern around her "Madame, Madame d'Artois, Madame Élisabeth, Monsieur, Monsieur the count d'Artois; the latter was running up and down, betting, moaning when he lost, pathetically giving vent to his glee when he won, jumping into the crowds of people to go cheer on his postilions or jockeys, and presenting the winner to the queen." The ambassador's consternation was all the greater because, he says, "all this takes place before the eyes of a great many Parisians curious to see this sort of spectacle, who then go making the remarks about it, whether true or false, that they feel entitled to make." Neither the queen's prestige nor that of the monarchy came out of it enhanced.

Marie-Antoinette superstar

While she was dauphine, Marie-Antoinette remained faithful to the simple ways of her Vienna days, and paid little attention to her grooming. She would dress in whatever robes her mistress of the wardrobe proposed; she would wrinkle and soil them playing with her little dogs. But with the passing years and male attention, she took more care in her appearance. Must not the queen be the most beautiful of all? At twenty, "she was like the morning star, shining with health, happiness and glory." How could she not swoon from the clouds of incense rising to her from every quarter? At her young sister-in-law Clotilde's wedding, they only had eyes for her. Horace Walpole exclaimed "Hebes and Floras, and Helens and Graces, are street-walkers to her. She is a statue of beauty when standing or sitting, grace itself when she moves." Rivarol would say of her, "Always more at home in her femininity than in her rank, she would forget that she was born to live and die on a real throne; she wanted to enjoy that fictitious empire that beauty imparts to women and makes them queen for a day." She was expected to "set the tone," her mother had reminded her. She concluded from that that she should also set the trends.

In the person of Rose Bertin, she found a devilish temptress. This petite woman from Picardy had come to Paris to seek her fortune, and found a job at a dressmaker's with the firm intention of making it in a trade for which she was talented. Delivering merchandise for her employer, she met the aged princess de Conti who took a liking to her. She gave her some work and was so pleased with it that she recommended her to all of her relations when Mademoiselle de Penthièvre married the duke de Chartres. Her career was launched, and the young seamstress was handed up from the duchess de

Chartres to Madame de Lamballe, and from her to the queen. When she opened her own boutique on the rue Saint-Honoré, she chose a sign depicting the Grand Mogul, since everyone was going crazy over Chinese motifs. A very clever manager, she soon had thirty-six workers in her employ. She not only created patterns for gowns and coats, she also furnished every imaginable accessory. These ranged from bonnets, caps and hats to embroidered bags and slippers, little collars, ribbons and bows, watchbands, hankies and gloves, to name just a few. She also had fans on offer, like the one the queen used at the theatre to compensate for her near-sightedness, thanks to a lens cleverly hidden in its folds.

By 1774 she had made a conquest of the queen, who named her as her official "stylist." But it was agreed that she would not abandon her boutique, which again, was an infraction of the rules. The queen had her own tailors, seamstresses and hair stylists attached to her service; they remained in place and were for her use only. It was scandalous to share Mademoiselle Bertin's services with the fashionable women of Paris. But while her own dressmakers always made the same dresses over and over again with only minor variations, Mademoiselle Bertin kept a keen eye out for anything that was new. Overflowing with imagination, she offered much more tempting creations. She came to Versailles two mornings a week for what she pompously referred to as her "work with Her Majesty." As she was not permitted to enter her bedchamber, she would wait in a nearby office, to which the queen would rush, hastily abandoning her ladies. She would show her drawings and fabric samples; she would empty out boxes of accessories, and the two of them would discuss *ad infinitum* which ribbon to choose, or where a feather should be placed, with stupefying familiarity.

She not only had great talent; she also had a sharp nose for business. She got you to buy, proposing mountains of robes which having been bought and perhaps not even worn were quickly scrapped to make room for others. There were so many of them that to help the queen decide which robes she would wear every day she was shown a sort of color chart with a piece of fabric from each one into which a pin would be placed to indicate her choices[*]. The fact that Mademoiselle Bertin worked both in Versailles and Paris enabled her to play on the two sets – the court and the Parisian

---

[*] The one that has come down to us belonged to Madame Élisabeth; it is of a later date and still has the pinholes. Another, which has no pinhole traces and was used to choose fabrics from which to make dresses, did belong to the queen.

clientele. Marie-Antoinette was the trendsetter. Bachaumont recounts that in the autumn of 1775 she was wearing a gown of a brownish tint. The king remarked, "Why, that's the color of a flea." All the dye-makers pounced; they outdid each other in explaining the variations in color of the unsuspecting flea: "They distinguished between an old and a young flea, and even subdivided the nuances into the insect's body parts: the thorax, the back, the thigh and the head." But Marie-Antoinette was already switching her loyalty to a cindery beige. Her brother-in-law de Provence exclaimed that it "was the color of the queen's hair," and this new shade deposed the fleas. Soon more poetic names were being sought. In the summer of 1776 a lady was seen at the Opera wearing a satin robe of a *muffled sigh* color, garnished with touches of *needless regrets*, and diamond-embroidered slippers the color of *low blows*. This was not Marie-Antoinette's fault, it would seem, but she had started the ball rolling.

For her greatest sensation, Rose Bertin found a clever accomplice in the renowned hairdresser Léonard. Between the two of them, for nearly three years, they got women to perch the most outrageous contraptions on their heads. On a structure called a *pouf*, measuring 32 inches high and proportionately wide and patched together with gauze, false hair, pins and ribbons, they would place ornaments chosen from the stylist's inexhaustible supply. The stroke of genius was tying these ornaments to current events, which of course had the advantage of changing all the time. Thus there were *poufs* on themes such as *Inoculation, The Insurgents*, or *Parliament in Session* dotted with objects whose symbolism verged on the sibylline. When the news was dull, the vast resources of nature and the seasons were called upon. One could spy snow-covered mountains, grape-harvesters, an English garden, lambs drinking from rippling brooks, prairies dotted with flowers. And since flowers faded quickly, their stems would be slipped into little phials of water and hidden in the under wiring – but the beneficiaries of this particular refinement were well advised not to lean over. As Madame Campan recalled, "These headdresses reached such a height from the scaffolding of gauze, flowers and feathers that women could no longer find carriages with roofs high enough to accommodate them." They had no choice but to keep their heads out the carriage windows or kneel on the floor. A few of them even "had their hair arrangement carried in a container like the ones they use to transport double basses and had them placed on their heads at the entrance to the church or ballroom."

Advertising campaigns unscrupulously exploited anything Marie-Antoinette endorsed – it's as if she were a top model; her face appeared in some fashion magazines. And the ploy succeeded beyond expectations. "Every woman wanted to imitate the queen. Everyone rushed to get the same jewelry as the queen, the same feathers, and the same ruffles on which her beauty bestowed such infinite charm. Young ladies saw their expenses skyrocket; mothers and husbands were not pleased; a few foolish girls went into debt; there were family rows and many households were adversely affected. Word got about that the queen would be the ruin of the ladies of France." A scathing rumor was soon circulating in Paris according to which the queen, seeing a woman "less fancily dressed than the others," joked about her parsimony only to be told, "Madame, we have not only to buy our gowns, we have also to buy yours." The abbé de Véri who reported the anecdote didn't believe it himself, but stated that it showed "the nation's overall sentiment." And according to Bachaumont, an indignant Maria Theresa sent Mercy back a portrait of her daughter festooned in enormous feathers with the complaint, "This is the portrait of an actress, not the queen of France." It's an apocryphal story* no doubt, but it goes to the heart of the matter.

Marie-Antoinette would have been astonished no doubt to learn that she was taking on a role usually reserved for royal mistresses, and that she was exposing herself to the same discredit. What was worse, she didn't have the excuse that she was trying to please the king – he had asked her to put a stop to her extravagant behavior.

Debts build up

Parisian ladies weren't the only ones going into debt to keep up with fashion. So was the queen. Not in order to pay for her wardrobe; the household services took care of those colossal invoices, which could not be checked, by the way, because Mademoiselle Bertin did not itemize. Household services didn't cover the cost of jewelry, however, since the queen in theory made do with what the crown put at her disposal and what she was given. But Marie-Antoinette adored jewelry, and all the big Parisian jewelry dealers knew it.

The most sought after of them, a certain Boehmer, "had gathered

---

* We know from her letters to her mother of May and June 1774 that Marie-Antoinette tried to reassure her by sending some engravings of the stylish headdresses. Maria Theresa's only commentary came on June 30th: "I must say, the drawings of what the French ladies are wearing are quite extraordinary; I can hardly credit that anyone would wear them, much less at court."

at great expense six pear-shaped diamonds of prodigious size" and of the most pristine clarity. He had them made into earrings for Madame du Barry, but was left with them on his hands when she fell from grace. For such jewels there was only one client. Toward the end of 1775 therefore he had them presented to Marie-Antoinette. The price – 400,000 pounds according to Madame Campan, 600,000 according to Mercy[*] – put her off. But she had seen them, she was dying to have them and her annual pension had been doubled. She made a deal. The jeweler replaced the upper part of the clusters by diamonds she provided, bringing the cost down to 348,000 pounds. Done deal. She asked to pay in installments. Boehmer got a down payment of 48,000; she would pay the rest from her purse at regular intervals over four or five years, and the king would know nothing about it.

The empress' warnings did not stop her from succumbing six months later to the temptation to buy diamond bracelets. Mercy, from whom she at first had hidden the purchase, estimated their worth at 100,000 écus. She "gave in exchange some precious stones that the jewelers got at a good price; for the rest she had to pay considerable installments." When she looked at her account books she realized that aside from the 100,000 écus in arrears for the pendant earrings, she owed another 100,000, and hadn't a penny left for her daily expenses. "Seeing the difficult situation she was in, with great reluctance she decided to ask the king for 2,000 louis. The monarch received this proposal with his usual compliance; he merely remarked mildly that he was not at all surprised that the queen had run out of funds given her taste for diamonds."

The abbé de Vermond was present when Marie-Antoinette received the letter containing her mother's inevitable sermon. "Reading the letter, the queen said to me in a rather light tone, 'So my bracelets have arrived in Vienna! I'll bet that bit of news came from my sister Maria[**].' Why, I asked. 'It's just envy. She's like that.'

---

[*]   Giving today's equivalent would be nearly impossible and of little relevance. Suffice it to say that enormous sums were involved. Some useful references however: an écu was worth three pounds but a louis was worth eighty pounds. The words franc and louis were interchangeable. The queen's annual purse was brought to 200,000 pounds in 1774.

[**] Maria Christina, then governor of the Low Countries. Marie-Antoinette was not very fond of her, but she didn't generally accuse her of carrying tales to Vienna. The light non-committal tone that she employs here with Vermond suggests that she knew perfectly well who the informers were, the first of them being Vermond himself. Without being blunt, she imparts the message. And the way he tells the story shows that he understood.

I asked if the empress was annoyed. 'Not terribly. Have a look,' and I was handed the letter." In her reply to her mother she swept aside any criticism with an offhand "I have nothing to say about the bracelets; I couldn't believe that anyone would want to bother my good mother with such trifles." Vermond, tired of preaching in the desert, considered resigning.

Did Marie-Antoinette believe that gambling could solve her money problems? Her brother Joseph thought this might be the case, as he said that as a child she had no time for such things. She may well have been encouraged to take up gambling by her friends. Be that as it may, she gave up the usual petty-stakes games played to pass the time, where the losses were proportionately small, for high-stakes gambling, where one could hope to win big, and where the losses were even bigger. In the autumn of 1776, "she usually plays lansquenet." Soon she would prefer pharaoh*. At first she played privately, at the princess de Lamballe's or Madame de Guéménée's, then at her own home. Who played depended on how much money was bet. Many courtiers withdrew for want of ready money. Soon none of Marie-Antoinette's friends could afford to be the banker. Professionals were called in. And traipsing after them came big-time gamblers, adventurers and cheaters. This motley crew gave the court the tenor of a gambler's dive.

In Fontainebleau at the end of October 1776 bankers were brought from Paris to cut the cards. "Mercifully, the game only lasted two nights," noted Mercy. Two nights at the wrong time. The king, who disapproved of these games at court, especially because they were outlawed throughout the kingdom, had granted permission for one session only. The trouble was, the session went on non-stop, with players taking turns relieving each other. "The bankers arrived on October 30th and dealt cards through the night and the morning of the 31st, at Madame de Lamballe's quarters, where the queen stayed until 5 o'clock in the morning. Her Majesty had them deal again in the evening and well into the morning of November 1st, the Feast of All Saints. The queen herself played until almost 3 o'clock that morning. The great harm came from the fact that it took place on the morning of a high holy day, and the public took note. The queen wriggled out of it

---

* A card game where the banker plays alone against any number of players or punters who can bet either to the left or the right. The banker turns up cards alternating between right and left. The best card wins for the side it's on. The banker doubles the ante on this side and takes the cards from the other side. If he turns up two cards of equal value, he takes the stakes from each side.

by joking to the king that he'd permitted the game but did not say when it should end, so they were within their rights to have it go on for thirty-six hours. The king started to laugh and replied cheerfully, 'Go on, you're a worthless bunch!'"

Whatever her initial motivation, the queen got hooked on the strong passions that gambling incited. It was like an addictive drug. Since she played "without thinking ahead" against game-hardened bankers, she lost regularly. And the debts piled up. In January of 1776 she got worried, but since she couldn't figure out how much she owed, she gave Mercy this task, and he came up with a total of 23,303 louis, or 427,272 pounds – more than double her yearly allowance. "A bit surprised to see her finances in such disarray, she realized how short she would come up in her daily expenses, so she made up her mind, not without some trepidation, to sound out the king on how accommodating he might be in taking on at least some of the said debt." Chastened, she approached her husband. But "without hesitation and most graciously" he agreed to pay the whole thing, asking only for a few months time because he wanted to take it out of his own allowance and not from the state.

One would think it all might teach her a lesson, but no. In March Mercy complained, "The sums the king put aside to clear the queen's debts and that he gives her each week are at least in part absorbed by the daily gambling losses, and if this continues the queen will find herself doubly burdened by having increased her debts and abused the king's good offices." The king's generosity remained a secret, while it was common knowledge that gambling was ruining the queen. And her almsgiving and charities suffered as a result. When she was still dauphine, Mercy lamented that she was not terribly given to liberality; but he had managed to convince her that part of her personal monies must go to charity. Alas, all she had left to share with the poor was her debt! To solve the problem she got it into her head to impose a sort of tax on her companions in pleasure.

Madame de La Tour du Pin tells us that she "had at her door one of Versailles' two curates who handed her a purse and she solicited everyone, men and women alike, saying "For the poor, please." The women all had their six-franc écu in hand and the men their louis. The queen pocketed this little charitable tax followed by the curate, who often reported bringing a hundred louis to his poor parishioners and never less than fifty." Some among the worst spendthrifts complained indecently of being forced into this gift giving while they thought nothing of betting sums a hundred times higher. Others not part of her inner circle felt that the queen should have abstained from gambling and given the church the money she would thus have saved.

In her blind quest for amusement, Marie-Antoinette destroyed in less than three years most of the sympathy she had enjoyed upon her ascension to the throne. She was no longer so popular. When she went to the Opera there was less applause. She was held responsible for the court's wasting of public monies. And the rampant slander increased. She was accused of not behaving like a queen. The count and countess de Provence, quick to see which way the wind was blowing, openly distanced themselves from her. Rather than shunning the places where she lent herself to public spectacle, they chose to show up together at the same places. At the theatre, at balls and the races, Marie-Joséphine, by her modest dress and discreet behavior, put herself forward as the living antithesis of her thoughtless sister-in-law, and seemed to be giving her a public dressing-down. Marie-Antoinette's reputation was tarnished. The countess de La Marck expressed the general feeling very well when she wrote to the king of Sweden Gustav III: "The queen is forever going to Paris, to the Opera, to the Comédie; she incurs debts, gets dolled up in feathers and pompoms, and doesn't give a fig about anything."

In Vienna the empress decided that it is high time they intervened.

CHAPTER 9

WHAT JOSEPH II HAD TO DO

For years the empress had been stewing – what on earth was Marie-Antoinette waiting for to give her grandchildren? Every time one of her siblings had a child, the issue of her following suit was raised. This was a natural enough wish in a mother of 16 children convinced that the strength of a family, not to mention a dynasty, resided its in fertility. But not only did the young wife remain childless, it appeared that the marriage hadn't even been consummated. To her mother's repeated questions, Marie-Antoinette made vague references to her husband's "timidity" and "nonchalance," implying that things would eventually work out. Mercy-Argenteau echoed her. Sometimes the possibility was raised of some slight physiological malformation that would require the young husband to seek surgical intervention. But time went by, with no end to the so-called nonchalance, and no operation took place. That's all Maria Theresa knew, but she wondered and worried.

A tenuous position

Marie-Antoinette seemed unaware of the fact that the only thing that guaranteed the status of a queen of France was motherhood. Mercy was therefore given the task of explaining to her "that her position is in jeopardy as long as she hasn't given France an heir." A childless queen can always be repudiated. Certainly it was a cumbersome process to get Rome to annul a marriage. Non-consummation is grounds for annulment, whereas infertility is not. However, experience had proven that accommodation can be found between God and man when refusing an annulment might entail serious political consequences*. Could Marie-Antoinette be subjected to a similar fate? The empress' fears were probably inflated.

This marriage was not easily come by; she had to fight tooth and nail for it. She knew that there were those in France quite opposed to the Franco-Austrian alliance. Since Choiseul's Christmas Eve dismissal in 1770, their party was in power. Her daughter wasn't in any danger as long as Louis XV was alive. In the thick of the international crisis over the alliance, he had teased her by saying, "We mustn't discuss Poland's affairs in front of you, because we don't see eye to eye with your relations on that issue." And when Austria seemed to protest against France's aid to King Gustav III of Sweden, he laughed, "The emperor is against what's happened in Sweden. That will muddy the waters between us, and I'll just have to send you back to Vienna," whereupon he gave her a hug and chirpily blamed her brother's bad advisors. His joking about it made it quite clear that he would not allow her to become a hostage to political vicissitudes. But such a joke says a lot about the designs of the king's entourage and the turn events could take upon his passing.

If the young couple's sterility was painful for Maria Theresa, others rejoiced over it. The possible heirs found their appetites whetted, first among them the envious count de Provence, who believed himself infinitely more able to reign than his older brother. But since he himself didn't seem to be any more prolific, the collateral branches started to daydream. Only the count d'Artois and any sons he might have stood between the throne and the Orléans branch; and they gave full flight to their fancy. But their candidacy would instantly raise the hackles of Philip V of Spain's descendents, who never considered their ancestor's renunciation of the throne of France valid. This situation recalled a similar one at the beginning of the century when the Orléans and the Spanish speculated about the possible loss of the young Louis XV. This time the interested parties were a bit premature in disposing of all of the dead king's descendents**. But it is clear that the conjugal situation of the princely couple led to much sordid conjecture.

---

* Henry IV received an annulment of his first marriage, enabling him to marry Marie de Médicis and have children with her, thus avoiding a serious crisis over a successor.

** Their dream would come true, but much later on. The Revolution saw to that. The three brothers would all have reigned in turn, when in 1830 Louis-Philippe d'Orléans became the "King of the French."

During the first years, it was commonly believed that the dauphin was impotent, either temporarily, in which case an operation would take care of the problem, or permanently. And people sympathized with the plight of the poor little neglected bride. A few different rumors reached the empress' ears, however. She was terribly alarmed at the idea that her daughter could be held responsible. She wrote to Mercy on 6 November 1773, "I am consumed by the desire at present to see her with child for I am not convinced that the fault lies with the dauphin and not her." What did she really think? What had she been told? She didn't make that clear. But we see that she framed the question in terms of blame: whose fault is it? She would greatly prefer that the fault lay entirely with her son-in-law.

Louis XVI's ascension to the throne only increased her worries, for the new king was known to look far less favorably on Austria than his grandfather. And when Marie-Antoinette's blunders alienated the old guard, the inevitable little ditty appeared. Barely three months after she ascended the throne she was treated to the refrain:

> *Little queen of twenty years*
> *You mistreat the people here.*
> *You'll be sent back home, no fear.*

But pretty soon she would be blamed for a lot more than just mistreating some old ladies at court.

The Beaumarchais affair

In the middle of August a most peculiar person requested an audience with Maria Theresa. Had she ever heard of him? We don't know. In any case, at the time a certain Pierre-Augustin Caron de Beaumarchais – originally simply called Caron – was already known to be a man of as many enterprising pursuits as talents. And of talents God knows he had plenty. Tutored in clock making by his father, he had been clever enough to invent an escapement that enabled him to beat out the famous Lepaute for an Academy of Sciences prize. His musical abilities won him the favor of Mesdames, Louis XV's daughters. He was their flute and harp teacher. He had entered the world of business thanks to the very well known banker Pâris-Duvernet, and got involved along with the financier's heirs in a high-profile court case. He wrote about it with astonishing verve, much to the amusement of the Paris reading public. His theatrical successes were still in the future. He was willing to dedicate his flair, his glib tongue, and his gadfly ways to the service of the government, undertaking shady dealings such as negotiating with London printers who specialized in producing *pamphlets à scandale* to have them destroyed before they could be distributed. At the beginning of 1774 he was instrumental in getting one about Madame du Barry suppressed. This time, he had to stop another that dragged Marie-Antoinette in the mud. He succeeded, but he noticed that the presumptive author, a certain Angelucci, had kept a copy of it, which he managed to wrest from him in an outlandish tussle after a hot pursuit through the Low Countries and Germany. The whole thing was probably a set-up. Since it was he who'd notified the police boss Sartine of the pamphlet's existence, there was a strong temptation to believe that he had penned it himself. There was only one counter-indication to this hypothesis, but it was a strong one: the style was deplorably platitudinous.

Be that as it may, our hero had the idea, since he was so close to Vienna anyway, to go see if he could get some money out of the empress. She was given a pamphlet that opened up terrifying perspectives on her daughter's future. Its title was *Advice to the Spanish Branch on its Rights to the French Crown in the Absence of Heirs, which could even be very useful to the entire Bourbon Family, especially to the King Louis XVI.* We won't go into detail here on its opening political remarks, which basically rehashed the arguments of Choiseul's enemies. Suffice it to say that the pamphlet laid bare the framework set up by Vienna to manipulate the queen, and advocated ending any commerce between mother and daughter as well as dismissing abbé de Vermond. But this was nothing compared to what followed: "Because of an almost unbelievably bizarre situation... we have at the head of the nation three princes from whom we can expect no offspring at all. The king especially, the most important of the three since it is he who governs, seems to be so built as to be irrevocably condemned never to be a father." It went on to say that he alone appeared not to notice this and that his ambitious wife, who knew this to be the case, needed to have a son "to whom the crown can belong" should her husband pass away. She would easily find the means to have one, provided she could attribute it to her husband. "The first thing that the empress will advise her daughter," the pamphlet warned the king, "will be to make the greatest efforts to convince you despite all the evidence to the contrary that you can be a father as well as any man... You shall then be one forthwith. They are merely waiting for the right moment for this clever persuasive ploy to make you the fable of all of Europe." In order to avoid having a bastard make off with the crown, the princes of Spain were invited to keep a close eye on the queen's conduct and to convince the king of his irremediable sterility. Thus the Spanish branch would increase their chances of getting back their lost inheritance.

This pamphlet, full of groundless suppositions, was not at all convincing. But the fearful thing about it was that it cast lasting doubt on the legitimacy of any children born to the royal couple. Beaumarchais proposed to have the pamphlet reprinted minus the offending passages about the queen. He offered to make all the changes necessary to preserve her good name. An infuriated Maria Theresa threw him in jail, and it took Sartine's intervention to get him out. "Never before has anything more atrocious been seen and which places in my heart the greatest contempt for this nation without religion, morals or sentiment," she wrote to Mercy in a fit. He replied in kind with a virulent diatribe against "the atrocities that infect this country." Poor Louis XVI! All she found to say about him was: if only the reading of this text could cut him to the quick and incite him to perform his conjugal duty!

It was agreed that nothing would be said to Marie-Antoinette, but she heard about it anyway, through the king, who made a passing reference to it, seemingly without having read it. Mercy put his own slant on it when he summed it all up for her, taking advantage of the occasion to remind her that she must be of "irreproachable conduct" and that it was "essential that she fulfill the commitment she made to the nation," that is, to give it a dauphin. Which came down to admitting, even if implicitly, that she bore some responsibility for the present situation. He was in a position to notice that she did nothing to make herself attractive to her husband. And that's an understatement! The empress would soon discover, through her ambassador's reports and the gazettes she had delivered from all over Europe, that the allegations contained in Beaumarchais' pamphlet were not entirely unfounded.

A husband scorned

Marie-Antoinette always believed herself to be infinitely superior to her husband, as her two mentors never tired of reminding her. She would "govern" him to be sure. The only question was whether it would be through kindness or fear. As dauphine she had opted for relative kindness; she showed him some consideration, she claimed to curb his unsociable tendencies somewhat, and she tried to get him to come along to balls and parties. But she was even then treating him with studied condescension, like some sort of savage she needed to teach how to read and behave in public! Once she was queen and therefore free to do as she pleased, she felt her efforts were no longer necessary and concluded therefore that it was simpler just to keep him in line "through fear." What did she have to lose, since he never complained anyway? And as her mother had guessed upon reading the famous Rosenberg letter, she had taken to speaking of him among her friends with exceeding carelessness. He was nothing more than "that poor man," who could be hoodwinked and mocked at will. "What do you expect from a man made of wood?" she exclaimed when he did not indulge one of her whims fast enough.

Members of her circle, Besenval in particular, encouraged her irreverence. When Louis XVI ventured into their company, he stuck out like a sore thumb. As it was his custom to retire punctually at ten in the evening, reports the count de Tilly, "they would sometimes advance the hand of the clock, and when this had the desired effect, the inner circle would recommence their merriment in the absence of the king." The queen got a good laugh out of this hoax, which would have been completely excusable in a schoolgirl seeking a quick escape from a tedious master. But the target of her ridicule was the man who held supreme power. And this was only one example of the crushing contempt in which he was held.

The queen's disdain for her husband did not remain within the confines of her tight inner circle. It manifested itself in public as well, and the king gradually stopped appearing at festivities where he clearly counted for so little. The abbé de Vermond already noted in early 1775: "It is possible that the low regard for him that the queen displayed at the balls where she set the tone put him off them altogether. Nothing in his behavior, however, indicates that he took any notice, but everyone else saw it, to the point of being shocked." Of course he noticed, but chose to ignore it. And the distance between them widened. As we have seen, she took to going out without him, accompanied by the count d'Artois; and this was when criticism of her, until then confined to the court, began to increase in Paris as well. The Paris masses remained ignorant about the infringements of court etiquette. The king was gleefully applauded when he ventured into the crowds with his wife on his arm. However, people did not like to see Marie-Antoinette showing up alone at the theatre or the races or the

Opera ball. People would willingly have forgiven her a bit of indecorous behavior, putting it down to her youthfulness, had her spouse been at her side. But without him, she caused scandal. And Maria Theresa agreed. "All these noisy entertainments in the absence of the king are not proper. You will tell me, 'He knows about them; he approves,' but that is not good enough." And she was correct, because the public saw the king's approval as proof of weakness, without in the least excusing Marie-Antoinette's lack of decorum.

What is more, it didn't take long for people to notice that she was seeing more and more young men, and men not so young. In any case, they were flocking to her and she was not immune to their admiration. No one doubts today that it was all quite innocent. But she exposed herself to slander. "Each day she gives her enemies weapons against her," Kaunitz wrote to Mercy in May 1775. The royal couple's obvious inability to get along led to all sorts of speculation. It's not that they quarreled; the king handled her with kid gloves. But he rarely went to her bed at night. How could he, when they blatantly kept such different hours? In November of 1776 Mercy complained that "the queen's evening activities have made it nearly impossible for the king to go spend the night with his august spouse." He lived by day; she lived by night. He went to bed at eleven o'clock and rose early, between seven and eight. When she went gambling at one or another of her friends' homes, she could stay out until three in the morning. When she went to the Opera ball she often returned at dawn to emerge from her slumbers at eleven. And sometimes she made matters worse by not going to mass, saying she had already done so in Paris.

Far from hiding this *de facto* separation, as Mercy advised, she told her friends stories she shouldn't have about her husband's inadequacies and his supposed refusal to have an operation. The friends in question ridiculed him and wasted no time spreading the stories about. The poor man became the butt of jokes. And everyone suspected the young woman of seeking and finding consolation in the arms of one of her willing cavaliers. Maria Theresa, who choked with indignation at the text Beaumarchais gave her, found the same topics in the piles of gazettes and gutter-press newspapers that her agents sent her. And she rightly was horrified: "My daughter is running headlong into her ruination," she wrote to the abbé de Vermond, begging him not to abandon her.

The queen's "spleen"

At first Marie-Antoinette pretended to take all the libels against her with a grain of salt. On December 15, 1775 she wrote: "There's been an epidemic of satirical songs here. There are songs about every member of the court of both sexes and this French flippancy has even extended to the king. The need for the operation has been the principal topic about the king. I have not been spared either; people have quite expressly accused me of both preferences, that for women and that for male lovers. Although these nasty things go down well in this country, they fall flat and are of such a poor quality that they have no success either in the general public or among people of quality." She wanted to take the initiative, knowing that her mother would find out about it anyway. But the "nasty things" in question, although they were indeed of very poor taste, did not fall so flat as she claimed; quite the contrary, their popularity cannot be denied. Here are a few examples, though of a slightly later date:

About the king:

> *Everyone wonders though they don't say it,*
> *Can the king do it or can he not do it?*
> *The poor little queen's in a state of despair.*
> *Tra la la.*

> *Some say he can't get it up,*
> *Some that he can't get it in.*
> *Must be he's all cocked up.*
> *Tra la la.*

> *That's not where the problem lies,*
> *The royal clitoris replies.*
> *It's that naught therein but water lies.*
> *Tra la la.*

About the royal couple:

> *The queen, she states rashly withal,*
> *To her dear confidant, Besenval,*
> *"My husband is not a good sire at all!"*
> *The other replies, "My dear queen, all in all,*
> *Everyone thinks it but does not say it,*
> *And you say it but do not think it."*

About the queen (Maria Theresa is supposedly speaking to her):

My child, the king needs an heir.
Whether before or aft the royal chair
Make for the king a little heir,

But before you make a cuckold of the king
Make sure that he is convinced of one thing,
That he too can make a little king.

So the pamphlet's accusations that Beaumarchais said he had nipped in the bud were not lost on everyone. There were many others. The least little thing Marie-Antoinette did was given a malevolent cast. The press went at her with guns blazing. Would the queen like one fine morning to watch the sunrise with some friends? A lampoon entitled *The Rising Dawn* turns the little outing into a saturnalia. Does she feel entitled on a beastly hot evening in 1777 to take some cool air in the chateau's terraced gardens? Right away people are denouncing the orgies that take place under the leafy canopy of the dark and welcoming woods. Counted among her reputed lovers were the duke de Coigny, Besenval, Lauzun, and even her young brother-in-law the count d'Artois, to name but a few. She was accused of having Sapphic relations with Madame de Lamballe and especially Madame de Polignac. It must be said and repeated that these accusations were completely groundless. But they came from the court itself, and contemporaries saw the count de Provence as their chief instigator. The public was only too happy to believe them: after all, she did go out gallivanting without her husband. "Some spineless courtier cooks up a calumny behind her back," reports an anonymous "anti-libelous" publication, "another one sets it to verses and couplets; and through the Ministry of the Serving Classes, sees that they are spread in the marketplace."

Although she affected indifference to these bottom-shelf pamphleteers, Marie-Antoinette resented the attacks. By July of 1774, the abbé Baudeau noted in his *Secret Chronicle*, "The queen came to the boulevards. She was very coldly received there, which cut her to the quick they say." So receptive to praise and admiration, she couldn't bear all the criticism or merely the loss of love. It was painful for her to see that the audience at the Opera was more sparing in its applause. Within three years her Paris idyll was just about over; she realized that the people of the capital no longer loved her. Bachaumont in his memoirs said that privately she let herself go and wept bitter tears about it. In a nearly deserted Versailles in the summer of 1776, she had an attack of "spleen," the word that became fashionable to denote melancholy. More attentive to practicing her religion, she decided to earn a plenary indulgence by doing the required acts of devotion. She told Mercy that she despised her fun-loving friends and that the count d'Artois' bad case of measles left her indifferent. It is also possible that the life she led was badly affecting her health. By September she had no joy in life whatsoever, she brooded and had vapors, fever and crying fits; she shut herself up in her rooms with her closest friends. In October she bounced back, but these bad spells just added to her mother's fears.

Travel plans

The empress was worried, very worried. She had long since stopped believing a word of what her daughter told her. Her tone was too childish and smacked of self-interest, she wriggled out of things; there was too much hair-splitting and evasiveness, too much was left unsaid. Mercy said she trusted him completely, but the empress was not so sure. Already in 1772, when her child was still manageable, she wrote to him, "My daughter could be just as disingenuous about her trust in you as she was about hunting with me." Now she was quite sure he was being duped. And when she compared her daughter's letters or her ambassador's long-winded reports with the gossip of the gazettes, a chill went down her spine: what she read in them about Marie-Antoinette's life seemed to confirm the pamphlets' worst claims. The hypothesis that she hardly dared think about, that her daughter might have taken on a lover, was terrifying, especially if her marriage had not been consummated. Neither her letters nor Mercy and Vermond's sermons were effective in warding off danger – if indeed it was not too late. There were only two solutions to the problem, either she must go herself to see what was happening or send her eldest son.

Once before, at the beginning of 1774, the groundwork was laid for a visit from Joseph; but it was called off when Louis XV died. At the end of the following year, the empress herself thought of going to Brussels, from where it would be easy to arrange a private meeting somewhere on the border. It was to take place within two years, but never happened. In the spring of 1776 Joseph again declared his intention of coming to France. Maria Theresa was not too happy about the idea of entrusting him with such a delicate matter. They saw eye to eye about virtually nothing. She was afraid his acerbic tongue could get Marie-Antoinette's back up and merely drive her deeper into her state of revolt. On the other hand, she feared that the young woman might turn on the charm and wrap him around her little finger. In either case, a visit from the emperor would have gained nothing. Above all, she was afraid of what he'd find out. Will he go or won't he? He can't decide. At first he thought he'd go in time to attend the pre-Lenten festivities, but his mother detained him, citing trouble in Bohemia. Then he used the excuse of bad weather to tell Louis XVI that he wouldn't be coming; snow was blocking the roads. But the king let him know that he was disappointed and terribly keen to meet him. Joseph would finally depart on the 14th of March 1777.

Mercy said he was very relieved, for he had discovered that someone else had tried to address the problem, after a fashion. Marshal de Richelieu noticed at the Comédie-Française that the king took quite a liking to a charming actress called Mademoiselle Contat, and he suggested he take her on as his mistress. The king refused, but did not hold it against this incorrigible old matchmaker. But who knows how long his moral scruples might last? Joseph had to step in immediately.

Marie-Antoinette pretended she was delighted, but she was in fact very distressed. She expected to be roundly upbraided. She confided her fears to her friends, much to Mercy's displeasure; and he tried to reassure her. The emperor apparently "was coming here neither to monitor nor criticize, much less to moralize; that his only goal was to have the pleasure of seeing his august sister, and he wished nothing to interfere with this satisfaction." Yes, yes, of course. But Marie-Antoinette found in a post-script in the letter where her mother announced the visit, a few words that left no doubt: "You will speak to your brother in all frankness about the state of your marriage. I will vouch for his discretion and his being able to give you sound advice. This point is of the utmost importance for you." Not only is she in for a tongue-lashing over her self-indulgence, but it will be time to fess up. As the time gets closer she is more and more anxious. So her mother, brother and Mercy concur to find the best way to soften the blow so as to avoid what the ambassador euphemistically calls "tiffs" – by which he meant the kind of explosion followed by a brutal break-up that had occurred a few years previously in the duchy of Parma.

There is no doubt but that Joseph's real mission was to determine exactly what was going on in the royal couple's bed. But everything is done in Vienna as well as Versailles to keep the public from finding that out. It is therefore put out that he is simply making a courtesy call. This is not a visit between heads of state with its ensuing pomp and political communiqués. Joseph II is coming on a private visit, as a tourist, with the assumed name of count Falkenstein – transparently an incognito, but this way they can dispense with the rules of protocol. He wants simply to embrace his sister whom he hasn't seen in seven years, meet his brother-in-law and see all there is to see in and around Paris. It will be a family trip, a cultural journey with nothing at stake, altogether insignificant.

Marriage counselor Joseph?

Was Joseph qualified to play the role of marriage counselor? Maria Theresa had her doubts. Fourteen years older than Marie-Antoinette, his mother's heir apparent and already emperor of Germany for more than ten years, he certainly had the moral authority to come to grips with the young featherbrain. But he was often unpredictable. Despite the enormous distance between them at an intellectual level, the siblings had much in common. Like her he was given to ridicule, had a taste for mordant irony, and an overwhelming distaste for protocol and etiquette. He was just as quick as she was to make feverish attempts to impose his will. He also wanted to simplify the way things were done, but his reforms concerned things of far greater import than who got to dine at the king's table. In his haste to modernize the old Austro-Hungarian monarchy, he abruptly shook up the most time-honored traditions. To protect the peasants he stopped the nobility from hunting wild boar, because it was harmful to farming. Then he went so far as to abolish serfdom in the domains belonging to the largest property holders in Bohemia, and to take issue with the clergy's privileges. The more Maria Theresa preached prudence and tried to undo what he'd done, the more obstinate he got. He strained under his mother's authority, which he found tyrannical. In his own way, he too was in revolt.

He also rejected his mother's example when it came to married life. His two marriages, although in opposite ways, were marked by the same extremes of emotion. When he was nineteen he married Isabel of Parma, a maternal granddaughter of Louis XV. The marriage was imposed on him, and he only consented half-heartedly. But what a surprise it would be! On seeing her for the first time it is said he became beet-red as he was blushing so, and his eyes filled with tears. He fell hopelessly in love with the brown-eyed, dark-haired infanta of gentle features and fragile, melancholic beauty. It was a vehement, frenetic, all-devouring love that custom would not stale. He could not have found a more perfect spouse. Isabel was docile, devoted, always even-tempered and obedient to his desires. She had the delicacy never to show off in his presence a peerless intelligence, which earned her Maria Theresa's respect and affection. Alas, this marvel of marvels did not love him. Consumed by romantic melancholy before the term was invented, she lamented the fate of princesses married against their will. And she bared her soul to her sister-in-law Maria Christina, nicknamed Mimi, who had just been deprived of the fiancé of her dreams. Isabel then developed for her sister-in-law one of those burning passions that could once be found in convents and girls' schools. Each day she sent her strange and morbidly overexcited letters. Much more grounded, Mimi tried to soothe her and bring her back down to earth. But a desperate Isabel saw no other solution to her forbidden love than death. Her wish was granted three years later after she'd suffered a number of miscarriages and given birth to a daughter. At the end of another exhausting pregnancy, smallpox freed her from a marriage she had borne in silence as a bitter burden. Was Joseph aware of the fact that he was holding a stranger in his arms? The air of mystery she gave off attached him all the more perhaps to this woman whose soul he could not fathom. His despair was extreme, and he never fully recovered from her loss[*].

He actively resisted proposals to wed again. Unable to win the hand of Isabel's youngest sister, he declared he no longer wished to marry. His mother insisted, for dynastic reasons, and leaned toward Cunegonde of Saxony. He managed to wriggle out of that one after a brief meeting, but he couldn't escape from Josepha of Bavaria, whom he married in 1765. He described her to his ex-brother-in-law the duke of Parma as "Twenty-six years of age, but with no youthful grace; shortish and chubby, puffy- and blotchy-faced, with nasty teeth, she has nothing about her that can incite me to take again to the married state in which before I had found someone completely different." So he didn't! "I thought I was strong enough to calmly accept the awful distance I found between us," he wrote a little later, "… but human weakness took over." His new spouse was so repulsive to him that he could not touch her without revulsion. He did try, however, as seldom as possible, but with the pretext of

---

[*]   It has been claimed that Maria Christina, in order to help him get over her, showed him the famous letters, but we really don't know.

a possible pregnancy he abandoned his marriage bed for good. Two years later the poor Josepha was carried off by a merciful death, childless, of course.

An aborted romance with a high-ranking lady in Viennese society put him off love altogether. He became entrenched in his bachelorhood, seeking bodily satisfaction from easy women, but devoted all his energy to planning reforms that his mother hastened to put a stop to. Let his brother Leopold ensure the dynasty's future. By the spring of 1777 when he was getting ready to go to France, his brother's wife the grand duchess of Tuscany already had six sons and was expecting her eleventh child.

At thirty-six Joseph was a free man, self-assured, open-minded and unsentimental. Not having been lucky in love, he nursed a solid distrust of women and their ability to make him happy. He was capable of understanding a lot in life, but little inclined to be sidetracked by evasiveness or kittenish seductiveness. He was enough of a diplomat, however, to put his interlocutors at ease – after all, he had studied how to deal with Frederick II at the Kaunitz school. Maria Theresa could rest assured: the mission was in good hands.

A propaganda effort

To tell the truth, Joseph II's solicitude over Marie-Antoinette's marital problems was not entirely devoid of self-interest. He thought he would soon need her when he sought France's support in the land redistributions he was contemplating, which we'll get back to. Much better that she should be on good terms with her husband at that point so as better to influence him. In the meantime, he hoped to sound out Louis XVI to find out where he stood on various matters, and give a needed boost to their wilting alliance. If he were lucky he would also be able to gauge better the kingdom's vitality, resources and might. The supposed sightseeing trip allowed him to mask these goals somewhat.

Joseph was aware of the weight of public opinion in France and realized that it was largely unfavorable to Austria. Two years earlier his youngest brother Archduke Maximilian's stay had done nothing to improve matters, quite the contrary. Even though he too was traveling under a pseudonym, Marie-Antoinette felt she had to come down on his side in an argument over precedence. She felt it was up to the princes of the blood to come greet him first and not the other way around. She behaved so high-handedly with them that they never forgave her. And people began to whisper that she favored her own homeland over France. As well, the young archduke's lack of refinement led to his committing certain gaffes that earned him the nickname of "archdope." When the famous botanist Buffon was given the task of showing him the king's gardens and offered him as a gift a copy of his works, he refused most politely with the words, "It would pain me greatly to deprive you of it." Paris got a good laugh out of that one.

Knowing that this had tarnished the House of Austria's reputation, Joseph wanted to make his own visit a smashing success. He planned on staying six weeks; that would be enough time. Before getting down to the serious business with his sister and brother-in-law, he wanted to study them, observe how they lived, listen to what their entourage had to say, see how the court operated and generally take the pulse of the capital. He arrived in Paris in very modest style on April 18th, checked in to a hotel run by a German in the Luxembourg area, and went immediately to see Mercy-Argenteau, whom he found in his sickbed. It was the abbé de Vermond therefore who ushered him discreetly the next morning to see the queen via a hidden staircase. It was an idyllic reunion. He made a few gallant remarks, saying that if she weren't his sister, "He wouldn't think twice about marrying again if he could have a companion as charming as she." She brought him to meet the king before going to see the princes and princesses, then the three of them retired to dine modestly together in the queen's chamber, seated on uncomfortable folding stools. But he refused to stay in the apartments prepared for him, preferring to go to a Versailles inn. Dressed simply in a brown suit without military or other decorations, he affected an air of Spartan austerity, saying that authority is not measured in gold trimmings. Above all he wanted to maintain his freedom of movement.

With the ample leisure time afforded between the festivities his sister organized, he roamed the city, not in search of amusement but of instruction. As he had planned his visit carefully, he was able to demonstrate his abilities and have just the right word to say to everyone. He went to Les Invalides, which he greatly admired, and to the Hôtel-Dieu, where he was shocked to see patients crammed four to a bed. He visited the Gobelins and Sèvres manufactories, and the foundling hospital, the Salpêtrière general hospital, and the Bicêtre insane asylum. He also visited the king's private natural-history collection at the Jardin des Plantes, the royal printing press, the Savonnerie tapestry makers, the Palais du Luxembourg, the veterinary school, and the Marly hydraulic works. And that's not all. He was spotted at the French Academy, and the Academy of Sciences, at parliament, at the Palais-Royal, and the archbishop's residence. He strove to meet the best the kingdom had to offer by way of savants, engineers and artists, "anyone from whom he had something to learn." Very interested in the abbé de l'Épée's teaching of deaf-mutes, he asked him to take in two of his compatriots to teach them his methodology. He found the time between the formal suppers and theatrical performances to visit the duke d'Orléans at the Palais-Royal, Mesdames at Bellevue, Madame Louise in her Carmelite convent, and to meet Turgot at Madame Necker's salon. Calculating his every little gesture, he treated Choiseul very coolly, much to his sister's displeasure, and even dared to go as far as Louveciennes to meet Madame du Barry, at the time in the full blossom of her thirty years, in a supposedly impromptu visit. When she declared herself discomfited by this "too great an honor" he declared gallantly, "Do not protest, Madam, beauty is forever queen." Even though he considered himself an enlightened despot, rationalist and modern, he snubbed the *philosophes*, whose way of thinking he considered too subversive. Voltaire, whose Ferney property was on his route home, would have to do without his visit. But that did not prevent him from being the darling of Paris for three or four weeks.

At court he wasn't quite the success he was in Paris, and for good reason. Far from seeking to ingratiate himself there, he went out of his way to be provocative. His simplicity seemed affected, which of course it was. The count de Provence found him "quite cajoling," full of protestations of friendship that could not hide his desire to wheedle information out of people, and judged his learning shallow. His scorn for etiquette, too like his sister's, was shocking. He rebuffed advances from of a few coquettes, who in a twinkling retorted by comparing him to his biblical namesake. He made some disparaging remarks about how extravagantly people dressed and how make-up was overused. He accompanied Marie-Antoinette to an evening at Madame Guéménée's and was shocked at the licentiousness that reigned in this "dive." He was judged haughty and cutting. Whatever Mercy might have reported to flatter the empress, he did not win any hearts in Versailles.

With the king he did not need to resort to subterfuge to get the information he wanted. Louis XVI had all doors opened to him and invited his ministers to share their dossiers with him. The best-implanted mole could not have gathered in a year a quarter of the information he harvested in a month. Before leaving France, he undertook a long journey to Brest and Nantes to evaluate the modernization of the fleet, and then to La Rochelle, Bordeaux, Marseille, Toulon and Lyon. He left with the accurate conviction that France was rich and prosperous, very much ahead of Austria in terms of development. He was also convinced that it was a lot easier to govern and defend a compact, homogenous and centralized state than the mosaic of territories he would reign over. And this observation strengthened his resolve to carry out his as yet secret plan to appropriate Bavaria. But when he tried to sound out the king on extending the Austro-French alliance, all he got were protestations of fidelity that were much too general for his taste. And he found Vergennes on the defensive. It was clear that Louis XVI was not willing, as his grandfather had been, to support on principle whatever his ally undertook.

His political mission was therefore only half successful. On the other hand, his private conversations with the royal couple constituted an undoubted success: he actually managed to get their marriage going.

A most private investigation

He'd kept the most difficult part for last. He did not want to tackle delicate subjects without taking the measure of the partners involved and establishing easy and cordial relations with them. Mercy had warned him that Marie-Antoinette would try to put him off the scent. He therefore showered her with flattery to soften her up. Visibly worried, she had wanted to speak to him at length and in private the moment he arrived. Then she tried her utmost to prevent any tête-à-tête with the king. All the same, on April 30th, she was obliged to leave them alone together for the first time. They had a second conversation on May 9th in the carriage on their way to a hunt, and then a last one on the 29th, the eve of his departure. We only know more or less what was said in the first two from the very lengthy account of the emperor's stay that Mercy wrote for the empress[*]. There are two reasons why we cannot comment here in detail on the ambassador's description of what they said to each other. First of all, we do not know if Joseph revealed to Mercy everything he had learned. Secondly, the two of them probably agreed to tell the aged and worn-out empress a few white lies. Joseph kept what he discovered for his brother Leopold in letters we will get back to in the next chapter. It is enough here to relate

---

[*]   About the May 29th conversation, Mercy himself says that he knew nothing.

the apparent effects of his intervention, which themselves were quite considerable.

For a start, the atmosphere between brother and sister began to degenerate the day after the second visit with the king. Goodbye to compliments and flattery! He clearly took Louis XVI's side against her and made mortifying remarks to her, sometimes before witnesses. Privately, he was even more brutal. He hammered her on her lack of regard for her husband. Why would she want to accompany him on a trip to the provinces? As far as he was concerned, she was "good for nothing." He criticized her for "slighting" him, for her "disrespectful language," her "lack of submission." One evening while she was lingering in the company of the duke de Coigny and the countess de Polignac, he curtly forced her to join the king in his apartments. He wound up telling her in his presence that if he were her husband he would find a way to "direct her willfulness and bend it to what he desired." This was a rather maladroit remark as it implicated the king as well, but it shows that no matter what Mercy said, this sudden severity was not a tactic designed "to sound out the queen's soul" but a sign of his exasperation with a couple whose problems he discovered were not what he'd expected.

Right up to his departure, "great animation" continued to trouble the waters. But Marie-Antoinette had knuckled under and promised to take his advice seriously. True to family custom, he drew up written instructions to remind her of her duties[*]. They are of two types: as a wife toward her husband, and as queen, because she fulfilled neither one nor the other. He invited her to examine her attitude toward her husband, and every question was a stinging rebuke:

> Do you take every care to please him? Do you study his desires and his character, in order to comply with them? Do you try to get him to enjoy, preferably above any other object or amusement, your company and the pleasures you procure for him? Do you make him need you; do you convince him that no one loves him more sincerely or holds his glory and his happiness more dear than you do? ... Can you mitigate your misplaced vanity in shining at his expense, in being outgoing while he is not, in seeming to take care of things that he neglects, in short, in wanting to make your reputation at his expense? Are you tender and winning when you are with him? ... Are you not cold and unresponsive when he embraces you, speaks to you?

---

[*]   We are only familiar with the copy sent to the empress.

Do you not appear bored, disgusted even? How, if that is the case, could you possibly expect an untested man, one who has not tasted the pleasures of the flesh, to approach you, become aroused and in the end love you...?

And he commands her to do everything in her power to give him children. For he is the king after all, he reminds her in passing, and can with one word decide her fate.

The second part of his instructions, which deals with her self-indulgence, merely repeats, but more vehemently, the advice we have already heard from Maria Theresa and Mercy. The emperor ends with the need to change "the system" with all haste. "You are getting older; you no longer have the excuse of being a child. What will become of you if you wait much longer? An unhappy woman and an even unhappier princess." But she felt entitled "because she did not want to appear to be governed" to let some time pass before putting this good advice into practice. Yes, patience would still be required.

The time for farewells came on May 30ᵗʰ between eleven and midnight. Emotions ran high. The emperor embraced the king and asked him "in a tone of friendship" to look after his sister and make her happy. The king replied that it was his greatest desire, while she struggled to hold back the tears. She was sobbing when he accompanied her back to her apartments. He retired for the night to his inn in Versailles and left the next morning at dawn, his mission accomplished. That evening, Marie-Antoinette, exhausted by six weeks of tension and anxiety, had a violent nervous fit from which it took her two days to recover.

There were many surprises in store for Joseph in his conversations with husband and wife, and he could well wonder if his advice would be followed. Concerning Marie-Antoinette he quickly became convinced of two things, about which he told his brother Leopold. One of them was not very pleasant: she had a great deal of responsibility in the failure of her marriage. The other gave them some comfort: she had done nothing irreparable, "her virtue is intact" for the moment; all he found was her frivolity, her thoughtlessness, her childish stubbornness; she was just an "air head." At heart she was still the child he knew in Vienna. What he wrote to his mother must have been balm to her spirit: "I was sad to leave Versailles, really attached to my sister. I found a kind of sweetness in life that I had renounced, but I see that I have not lost a taste for it. She is amiable and charming; I spent hours and hours with her without seeing them go by. She was greatly affected when I left, but she seemed well; it required all my strength to walk away from her." Maria Theresa would have to wait for the detailed verbal account to fill in the blanks. As delighted as she was with this happy outcome, she was astute enough to sense that he was hiding something from her. She kept repeating in the ensuing months that she would only believe in the success of Joseph's mission when she learned that her daughter was pregnant.

What actually happened between Louis XVI and Marie-Antoinette? The documents that have come down to us contain so many contradictions, and the biographies of the young queen have given such romanticized accounts of the matter that it is worthwhile returning to the question, distinguishing between known facts and hypotheses. So we have to go back over those seven wasted years and examine them in the light of what the preceding chapters have revealed about the protagonists of this drama.

CHAPTER 10

THE STORY OF A MARITAL FAILURE

There are things a well-bred man does not discuss. Such was the conviction of historians at the end of the 19th and beginning of the 20th centuries, united in their conspiracy of silence about Louis XVI and Marie-Antoinette's conjugal relations. For these gentlemen, respect for the memory of the two martyred sovereigns, puritanism pushed to the point of extreme prudishness, and dismissal of the secrets of the marriage bed as unworthy of History with a capital H – all combined to cast a veil of silence over them. They knew, however, from contemporary memoirs, gazettes and pamphlets that there was much talk at the time about Louis XVI's presumed impotence. True, these texts contained so much slander that they felt entitled to ignore them. In his very delicate and thorough 1890 study of *La Reine Marie-Antoinette*, Pierre de Nolhac could not get himself to allude to the subject otherwise than as her vain hopes of motherhood[*]. In 1920 the marquis de Ségur, dealing with the same subject, broke ground by devoting two pages to the king's failings.

Their discretion is regrettable, for by throwing a veil of silence over the intimate problems of the princely couple, we sacrifice an important means of understanding the mentality that produced them. The very things about which we refuse to speak, our ancestors spoke of most freely. Physiological truths that we would like to ignore were the subject of conversations, letters, even diplomatic dispatches. Besides, how could these questions possibly remain outside the realm of politics when they concerned sovereigns? For them, the distinction between public and private life did not exist. Misplaced modesty is a poor counselor.

---

[*] When it was reprinted in 1929 he didn't deem it appropriate to change anything in his portrayal of the queen.

Even the publishers of the great fundamental texts that form the basis of all Marie-Antoinette studies were not exempt from this widespread error. We have Stefan Zweig to thank for having so usefully discovered that in their great canonical edition of the correspondence among Maria Theresa, her daughter and ambassador, Arneth and Geffroy had cut certain things from the two women's letters, without advising the reader. With the exception of two of them*, these deletions concerned conjugal relations. Stunned by the revelations in the originals, he built his evocation of Marie-Antoinette upon them.

A woman of Zweig's dreams

This is how Zweig saw it: An innocent maiden, delightful and exquisite, waits in vain for seven interminable years for her imbecile of a husband finally to make a woman of her. Why? Because he suffers from a slight biological malformation and shamefully refuses to go under the knife, which is the only thing that can solve the problem. Seven long years go by during which this bumbling oaf goes at her young body ceaselessly but in vain and everyone at court, and then all of Europe knows about it, ridiculing their compounded disgrace. It would take Joseph II's intervention to get the poor man to make up his mind to undergo the rectifying operation. Too late, the harm is already done. The psychological damage to both of them is irreparable. The political damage as well.

Buttressed by the psychology of Sigmund Freud – his book came out in Vienna in 1932 – Zweig applies to the personality of each of them an impressively coherent analysis based on their sexual frustrations. The man's biological deficiency makes him feel inferior and this has repercussions on everything he does. Incapable of manifesting his wishes in any way, much less of imposing them, the young man tries to appear virile by adopting the air of a Nimrod or a Vulcan. But his awkwardness and timidity are blindingly obvious as soon as he steps out into society. And this highly personal failure explains his remarkable acceptance of his wife's capriciousness. He becomes her slave. She can demand of him whatever she likes; he is always ready to atone through his boundless weakness for the fault about which he secretly feels guilty. He commits the fatal error of

---

*   These deletions had to do with Maria Theresa's vehement scolding of her daughter over her remarks about her husband in the famous letter to Rosenberg, and her daughter's reply.

letting all power pass through and crumble in the hands of a young featherbrain, much to the despair of the ministers, the empress her mother, and the entire court.

While he becomes more and more spineless, Marie-Antoinette abandons herself to a pathological hyperactivity to which Freudian psychology again holds the key. Humiliated by the nightly assaults of an impotent man, she suffers from a "nervous frenzy," springing from a sexuality that is ceaselessly solicited and forever frustrated. From this comes her insatiable need to distract herself from her melancholy, and this thrusts her into a self-destructive whirlpool of pleasures. From this also comes her need for love that drives her to trifle with masculine desire and renders a passionate, scandalous tone to her female friendships. Zweig contends that unless we see feminine despair behind this frenzy for pleasure we can neither explain nor even imagine the extraordinary transformation that takes place as soon as she finally becomes a wife and mother. When her nerves are calmed, another Marie-Antoinette appears. For him she is thoroughly normal. She is very feminine, very tender, designed for ample motherhood, probably aspiring to nothing more than to surrendering herself to "a real man." In short, the kind of woman Zweig himself dreams of. *He* would have known how to make her fall willingly into his arms, as he slowly awakens her to the pleasures of the bed! For her worthless husband he reserves the most atrocious invective in inverse proportion to the posthumous love he bears for Marie-Antoinette. It is this love that gives his book its force, warmth and tenderness, its captivating depth of conviction and superb poetic quality.

It is this love that also leads him – after all he was more a novelist than a historian – to closing his eyes to certain facts that conflict with his interpretation. He developed this interpretation in the joy of discovery and the powerful emotions he felt in the Vienna Archives while reading the unexpurgated letters between the young woman and her mother. And he created upon this initial impetus an inspired book so appealing that the vast majority of those who have ventured to write about her ever since have adopted the same point of view. However, a thorough examination of the documents we have at our disposal today leads us to conclude that Louis XVI never underwent an operation, because he had no need of one. And therefore the whole edifice crumbles. We see that the unhappy young man did not wear himself out with his wife each night to no avail – because they did not even sleep in the same bed. We begin to suspect that over seven years, during which time the spouses passed from adolescence into adulthood, their relationship must have undergone certain changes. If we recall what royal marriages were all about, we can ask ourselves if indeed Marie-Antoinette ever expected marriage to bring her womanly fulfillment. And we must add that the metamorphosis Zweig talks about was not as rapid as he claims, for her "dissipations" continued long after the consummation of her marriage and the birth of her first child.

In short, the secrets of this marriage bed are rich in surprises.

An unnecessary operation

A word first of all about sources. A most important fact seems to have gone unnoticed until very recently*: that is, the correspondence between Maria Theresa and Mercy-Argenteau was also methodically expurgated in the Arneth and Geffroy edition in order to do away with a great number of allusions to Marie-Antoinette's marital life**. It is therefore in the Vienna Archives' originals that we must look for the most revealing texts.

The first reference to the issue isn't from Mercy, however, but from the pen of Louis XV in a letter dated 28 August 1769 to his eighteen and a half year old grandson the infante of Parma. Five weeks previously the young man had married the archduchess Maria Amalia and had not yet consummated his marriage. "Where does the fault lie if your marriage has not yet quite been consummated? Might you have need of a little operation, which your cousin here might also need and which is rather common?" The cousin in question is the dauphin, who had just celebrated his fifteenth birthday and had not yet reached puberty. It is clear that by comparing the two, the king was above all trying to reassure the infante.

Louis XV did not take a serious look at the question until the following year when the dauphin too was married and experiencing similar difficulties. In July of 1770 he took advantage of the fact that a bad cold prevented the young man from following the court to Compiègne to have him discreetly examined by his principal surgeon, La Martinière. The latter is categorical, and even Mercy admits it: "He states that the prince has absolutely no natural defect that could prevent the consummation of his marriage." Two years later when again rumors were spreading about the dauphin's

---

* Cf. Appendix: *Bibliography.*

** The reader is given no indication of these deletions, either through suspension marks in the text or by any reference to them in the Introduction.

supposed incapacity, he confirmed his diagnosis at the king's request to the dauphine's confessor: "He knew with certainty that no physical obstacle prevented consummation." La Martinière was not just anybody; he was one of the best surgeons of the time – and we know that surgeons then were much more advanced in their methods than were doctors. Operations of this kind were known, both for circumcision necessitated by phimosis, and for making the adjustments required to facilitate erections. He was an independent sort of man, known for speaking his mind. If he said that there was no need, he was sure of it. Also, Louis XV was very conscious of the untoward consequences of a prolonged marital failure, and would have ordered him to perform the operation right away had it been necessary. And everything we know about the dauphin leads us to believe that he would have consented, as he was always so obedient and respectful of his grandfather's wishes. Besides, nothing tells us that he would have shied away from undergoing a risky procedure; his decision to be inoculated against smallpox proves otherwise. He surely had some untested courage. He could be called weak, but not cowardly.

So the cause should have been clear. If he presented no congenital deficiency at the time of his marriage, he could not have developed one later. But Maria Theresa kept harking back to the question of an operation; she was not convinced by what Mercy told her. Her doubts arose partly from the contempt in which she held anything French. But that wasn't all. For if there was no physical obstacle, the failure could only be explained by a "delayed puberty" or a "psychic frigidity." Delayed puberty maybe; it was possibly true for the first year of marriage. But afterwards? In 1771 Maria Theresa sent the Dutch doctor Ingenhaus on an unofficial visit. He was not allowed to perform a physical examination but confirmed that the dauphin seemed to him to be in good health, with legs and torso "cut out for potency." She consulted her private physician Van Swieten who begged off with the excuse that "if a young woman, and one who has the dauphine's looks, cannot excite the dauphin, no remedy would be effective." Maternal pride reared its head. Although she had no illusions about her daughter's intellectual capacities, the empress could not admit that her daughter's powers of seduction might be found wanting.

As time goes on the less she understands, and the more the thought nags at her that her daughter could have something to do with it. It's an idea she rejects with all her might because marital failure is always seen, even today, in terms of responsibility. "Whose fault is it?" Louis XV asks the infante of Parma. "I cannot believe that there is something amiss with her," Maria Theresa would say of her daughter. At all costs, she wants it to be the "fault" of the dauphin. Thus, in reply to her questions, the topic of an operation flows periodically from Mercy's pen. He tells her in January 1772 that the doctors are looking at the possibility of "a minor operation, of no great concern," without "the slightest drawback or danger." But he cannot explain, in this case, why the dauphin refuses, and he has to backtrack the following month: "the physicians believe... that consummation of the marriage depends on the young prince's volition." And the same shilly-shallying goes on in the months to come, followed by a new pronouncement, seemingly made halfheartedly, in January of 1774: "Insofar as there can be any evidence in such cases, we cannot help but suspect that there exists no physical obstacle, and that purely non-physical causes are delaying the complete consummation of Monsieur le dauphin's marriage."

But the empress does not give up. As soon as Louis XV dies, the rumors start up again. As can be expected, the public wonders about the new sovereign's capacities. And these rumors spread as far as Vienna. Does she suspect the late king of having tricked her? She takes up the charge again, demanding an examination. And Mercy, who had in November again raised the need for an operation, contradicted himself in December. "The king summoned the physician Lassonne in closed session and after a new general discussion of his situation, he had himself examined on the spot in a most thorough way." Lassonne judged that an operation was not at all called for, attributing this failure to bashfulness, lack of self-confidence, an aloof temperament and late development, which was beginning to blossom, however. In the meantime he was to take some iron to build up his strength. Would it persuade Maria Theresa? Not a bit. "Frankly, unless an operation is resorted to, I hold out no hope for a remedy," she replies a month later. Throughout 1775 the prospect of an operation is on the table. On September 15th Marie-Antoinette reports that she's working on the king toward that end. Mercy goes so far as to claim in mid-November that the king has given his consent and that a date is fixed. But in the middle of January 1776 there is a complete turnaround. Louis XVI called in from Paris a top specialist, the Hôtel-Dieux's surgeon Moreau, who did not mince his words. Marie-Antoinette was terribly disappointed. "I'm no happier than my dear mamma about what the doctors are saying. Yesterday the king brought in Moreau... He said more or less the same thing as the others, that an operation isn't necessary and that there was every hope without one. It is true that the king is changing very much and his body seems to be taking on more substance." And she threw in without noticing she was contradicting herself, "He promised me that if nothing comes of things within the next few months, he himself would go for the operation." After which, the question was never brought up again.

Needless to say, Louis XVI's schedule hardly permitted an operation that would have required at least a few days of inactivity, not to mention the fact that had it indeed taken place and by some miracle escaped public notice, Marie-Antoinette and Mercy would immediately have informed the empress of it. It isn't surprising therefore to find it all confirmed in Joseph II's handwriting, as we shall see: no malformation rendered Louis XVI incapable of consummating his marriage.

The picture painted of Louis XVI by Stefan Zweig, which became something of a doctrine, does not stand up to examination, any more than does the image of a young woman subjecting herself in vain to nightly onslaughts. They simply did not share the same bed. Before getting into what their marital relations were probably like, we should set the stage, for that is what determines the action.

To sleep together or not to sleep together

The empress, inconsolable at the loss of the spouse she adored, would like to see her daughter replicate such a consummate model, without realizing of course that her own meddling had a lot to do with her child's inability to do so. For her, in order to build a solid marital relationship there was no substitute for a common bedroom with a great big bed to which to retire together each night in an intimacy enhanced by habit. A bed that lends itself to embraces and "sweet nothings" and to the promise of fruitfulness, but also to intimacy and free-flowing conversations, which all help the couple to get to know and understand one another. A bed that brought together not only bodies, but also minds and hearts, in true intimacy. As she wrote to Marie-Antoinette, "I regard this as a most essential point, not for having children, but so as to become more united, familiar and trusting, by spending a few hours together every day."

But Versailles was not built to afford princely couples this sort of intimacy. Its layout and scheduling were designed not to bring them together but to allow them to take up as much space as possible on the stage where the cult of the monarchy was constantly played out. They each had their own apartments. They each had different activities during the day and were not expected to spend the night together as they each had their personal bedroom. It was not the done thing to appear to live together. Louis XV's dauphin son and Marie-Josèphe of Saxony did so at their cost. Although they each had their own quarters they spent part of the day confined to their library while the other men joined the king in the hunt and the women accompanied the queen to the park. They were criticized for being bourgeois and were not liked.

Each of the royal partners therefore had an individual suite that could be decorated to their tastes and a bedroom with their own things, their ways, their beloved objects, where they could feel at home. There was one difference, however: marital relations always took place in the wife's bed. It was the husband who went when he so desired to join his wife, never the other way around. She waited until he was of a mind to take the initiative. He was entirely free. He was a visitor in her bedroom; he went there when he was so inclined and stayed only as long as he wished. He could go every night if he liked, as Louis XIV did until his wife Marie-Thérèse's death, or Louis XV for the first eight years of his marriage. He could also not go at all, like the same Louis XV as of 1748. In either case, this practice exposed the princely or royal couple to court gossip, because it was virtually impossible to hide the comings and goings from one bedchamber to the other.

This practice obviously did not encourage the kind of relations Maria Theresa evokes, but it was so rooted in the ways of Versailles that it would have been useless to try to oppose it. Mercy-Argenteau was aware of this, but he didn't dare tell the empress, and Marie-Antoinette even less so. Their correspondence on the issue is therefore stamped with a disconcerting ambiguity. While the young woman was still only the dauphine, it was relatively easy to hide. At first housed next to her husband on the ground floor, she took possession of the queen's apartments on the second floor in the beginning of 1771. In both cases, access between her husband's and her bedrooms was easy, as they were either next to or above one another. The dauphin had just a bit of hallway to traverse or an inner staircase to climb. Valets and chambermaids tended to be discreet. The court couldn't keep a precise record of conjugal visits. But a close examination of correspondence makes it clear that what with Marie-Antoinette's monthly "*générale**," each one's various colds, digestive and other ailments, not to mention the nighttime festivities at carnival time, the spouses spent few nights at each other's side, whatever the ambassador might have said to the contrary.

---

*   Marie-Antoinette's nickname for her period.

But once they were on the throne things went awry, because from then on Louis XVI lived at the other end of the central building. Under such conditions how could they possibly comply with the instructions that Maria Theresa had just emphatically reiterated? "Never sleep apart from the king!" That was clearly impossible. The smokescreen surrounding these matters in their correspondence was no longer of any avail. Everyone would know when he went to visit his wife at night because from then on he would have to cross a whole series of rooms, including the famous "Œil-de-Bœuf" which was the nerve center of castle life with its perpetual courtiers on the prowl to find out everything that was going on. Fortunately, he too wanted nothing better than to escape this type of inquisition. It was therefore agreed that Mercy's idea was a good one: they would hollow out a hidden corridor in the belly of the castle to communicate between the two bedchambers. "I have had a communicating passageway built through which he can come to my quarters and I to his without being seen," Marie-Antoinette wrote to her mother. Mercy was delighted at this, while deploring the fact that the young lady didn't make the desired "customary use" of it. Neither one mentioned the fact that the new corridor – which was quietly built during the coronation – could not change the tradition conserving the king's prerogative to initiate matters. The queen could not use it at night, and during the day she saw no reason to change her usual routes.

The game of hide-and-seek that Marie-Antoinette played with her mother over the bed question would last for years. In mid-February 1777, protesting against the tales supposedly spread by the king of Prussia – they were actually Mercy's reports – she stated forcefully, "Certainly no one here would dare say that I do not get along with the king nor that we sleep separately. There are too many witnesses to the contrary." She would only risk telling the truth once the birth of her daughter had reassured the old empress once and for all. "It's been quite a long time now that we've had separate bedrooms," she would write to her in October 1780; "I thought my dear mamma knew that. It's quite a common custom here between man and wife, and I felt I shouldn't bother the king about it, which would go very much against his way of life and personal taste." But she would not go so far as to admit that the "taste" was also her own.

"We marry them too young"

Now that the way has been cleared, we can attempt to envision what must have occurred between Louis XVI and Marie-Antoinette for the first seven years. But we must be careful. For Louis XVI confided in no one, all we know about his private behavior is told to us by Marie-Antoinette and Mercy. Regarding his attitude toward her, the many allusions to it in the letters are equally subject to caution. After all, she only said what she wanted to say about it, which was perhaps revised or contradicted by the ambassador. In any case, it was all written for "dear mamma's" consumption. As regards how the two felt about each other, convention required that they love each other; it's part and parcel of the image that a princely couple must project to the world. To develop a plausible reconstruction of their tragedy despite the gaps in our knowledge, we must retain a healthy skepticism regarding the partial and partisan accounts of witnesses, and base our findings on facts and concrete situations. We also must give up the common perspective that sheds light only on Marie-Antoinette; there were two of them after all who entered into a marriage for better or for worse. We must try to put ourselves in their position, to guess, thanks to what we know about their respective characters, how each experienced what for both of them was an abominable ordeal.

By June of 1769 when France decided to ask for Marie-Antoinette's hand for the dauphin, neither of them had attained puberty. Choiseul spoke with authority since he presided over the proceedings, when he confided in the Spanish ambassador that the young Louis Auguste, despite a strong growth spurt, was not yet quite mature enough to marry. About Marie-Antoinette the ritualistic question in such cases was of course asked, "Has she had her period yet?" She has not. Her mother was so relieved to see what she took to be her first period in February of the following year that she advised Louis XV of it by special courier. But she was careful not to tell him that it hadn't reoccurred. The dauphin for his part had matured somewhat, his valets could attest to that. However, between the first stirrings of masculine maturity and the ability to consummate a marriage with a girlish virgin there was a large gap, which everyone chose to ignore. He was fifteen going on sixteen, an age at which his grandfather and father were married. She was fourteen and a half, quite old enough to marry by the day's standards. However, nature does not bestow maturity on everyone at the same rhythm: her body was more like that of a twelve-year-old. People refused to see that they were both still children, and treated them like adults. Politics obliged.

The reasonable approach would have been to keep them apart until they were ready, as usually happened in such cases. There had been enough previous examples of this for it not to seem unusual.

But Louis XV had been so hesitant before making up his mind about this marriage that the empress would have found suspect any delay in consummating it, interpreting it as a sign that the French were keeping it as grounds for annulment if necessary, in which case she would have turned it into an *affaire d'Etat*. So he chose the path of least resistance and turned a blind eye to it all. He must have realized that he risked setting the young couple up for failure, but he thought that things would work themselves out soon enough. After all, his son, the father of the present dauphin, took six months to consummate his first marriage, which didn't stop him from being highly prolific later on. When it came to such matters time could be counted on to do its job.

Right enough, the first night was a failure. "Nothing" the dauphin marked the next day in his diary. On this one little word, which merely meant that he didn't go hunting that day, much ink has been spilled in error, for it has been forgotten that the diary remained just as mute when something finally did happen in the marital bed. But it so happens that in this case it was true, nothing happened. Did the young husband even try to make an approach? Perhaps not. Let's not forget they each had received a very puritanical education. Theirs was the shyness "of all those raised in innocence," as Maria Theresa would say. In Vienna, the empress was aging and widowed, and her judgment was clouded by her conviction that morals were going down the drain. She taught her daughters to mistrust their bodies and their sex organs, and to hold nudity in horror. For all of her life Marie-Antoinette would remain extremely modest. Madame Campan reported that she bathed "dressed in a long flannel robe buttoned up to the neck," and avoided being seen by her attendants while she was changing. As for Louis Auguste, he spent his childhood and adolescence in the hands of deeply religious educators chosen by his parents – deeply religious educators made even more rigid by the era's slackening in morals and increase in irreligion, who made it a point of honor to raise their pupil to be the antithesis of his scandalous grandfather. Louise's recent entry into the Carmelites was seen as a sign that one person could make amends for the sins of another, in this case her father. By the same token, the dauphin's chastity could make up for the old king's lustful hedonism. Such was the climate in which both the dauphin and dauphine were raised. They had been taught to consider anything having to do with their sexual organs forbidden territory, and all of a sudden, with no preparation, they were told they should use them. Easier said than done.

Louis XV could do nothing about it. Any intervention from him would have been seen as an attempt to corrupt them. It was no longer considered normal for an experienced woman to take young princes under her wing and give them lessons in what in *Candide* Voltaire so amusingly called "experimental physics." No, Louis Auguste was not "taught a thing or two" in the park woodlands, as is said here and there. He's as virginal as they come, in mind and body: he is ignorant of everything. As incredible as it might seem, Louis XV wrote on 7 May 1770 to the infante of Parma, nine days before the wedding, "The groom seems to me to be impatient to see her and for it all to be over with, *although he does not yet know what he will have to do when it comes down to it*." Needless to say, Marie-Antoinette hardly knew better herself. Her mother taught her more or less what to expect, but her harping on docile acceptance could not have presaged anything good. After hearing about her sisters' experiences, she greatly apprehended the very difficult business in store for her.

Her misgivings were not entirely unfounded. Princes got a brutal sex education, as shown by the militaristic metaphors so commonly used at the time. The marriage bed for them was a battlefield where they would confront a stranger to conquer. Their triumph held no glory, as their victory was a foregone conclusion. No superfluous preliminaries, therefore, since the territory was already handed over. They had a duty to fulfill, that's all, and they'd better hurry up about it. That's the theory, anyway. In practice, everything depended on the temperament of each spouse. And fortunately, harmonious relationships could come of it. But the beginnings were always difficult.

How could two children ever manage to do what's expected of them on such a wedding night? A very intimidated dauphin did not know how to approach a young maiden paralyzed with fear. She was still too much of a child, not yet developed enough to awaken the least desire in an adolescent. Never mind that she didn't feel any herself, to say the least. Neither one of them had the least inclination to engage in the act. At the end of an exhausting day of ceremonies and festivities, overcome with emotion, dead tired, they were most likely happy enough just to try to get some sleep if they were lucky. The nights followed and resembled each other. While telling the infante of Parma that "the thing is not completely done," Louis XV added, "My grandson is not terribly affectionate, but he is fond of hunting." We might ask what one has got to do with the other. Well, the dauphin had been hunting frenetically since his wedding, which allowed him either not to sleep in his wife's bedchamber with the

---

* Italics added by the author.

excuse that he must arise early, or to arrive there at night thoroughly worn out only to fall asleep as soon as he hit the pillow. The fact is, the more the adolescents got to know each other, the less they liked each other. The abbé de Vermond's contentious presence in Marie-Antoinette's life did not help matters either. There was nothing to bring them together, quite the contrary; they really had nothing in common.

We will recall that a bit nervous, Louis XV consulted the doctor La Martinière as early as July. Sure that his grandson presented no physical abnormality, he was happy to wait, especially as he was a bit worried about his health. Hearing his hacking cough brought back bad memories. "Your cousin had me worried there for a few days," he wrote to the infante. Word got as far as Vienna, where Maria Theresa concluded that he was perhaps not long for this world. In the beginning of October there was another scare. "We were terribly afraid your cousin had a certain malady, but it was only aches and pains due to too much hunting, as he is still so young." Besides, his bride was also "quite young, still a child really." It wasn't until that August that her period returned. There's no hurry. Since there is no want of heirs for the throne, why push them to have children too soon and risk losing them? Married at fifteen and a half, Marie-Josèphe of Saxony had to wait three and a half years to bring a pregnancy to term, after numerous miscarriages. Marie-Antoinette clearly needed to mature some more before starting down that path. And it just so happened that Maria Theresa agreed. She wrote in May 1771, "No matter, the two of you are so young; on the contrary, for your own health it's all for the better; you have time to build yourselves up, the pair of you."

It was wisdom itself. But it wouldn't stop court tongues from wagging or pressure from mounting. With the best intentions in the world Madame Adélaïde questioned the dauphine incessantly. Is it done? No? Then when? Twice Marie-Antoinette mentioned a promise from her husband and announced a date. But he didn't come through. Because according to Mercy the fact that all eyes were riveted on him was paralyzing. That's possible, but it would be paralyzing in any case: he had a job to do, and it made him very nervous. Every day his feelings of guilt increased and that in turn made him more inhibited. And the ironic comments about his supposed impotence did not help matters. He had to go to it at some point. Exactly when we don't know. But already Marie-Antoinette had accepted this temporary abstinence and adapted to it quite well.

The unmentionable

"She feels nothing for him," Joseph II would later say. The phrase can be taken at its most literal, and at that it would be an understatement. Not only does she feel no desire for him; he inspires in her nothing but revulsion. No doubt she was totally lacking in "temperament" as Joseph would also say, but it is probable that their first contact put them off each other altogether. And before casting the first stone, let us recall that at the time she was but an immature, still growing girl who had not yet fully developed. The premature discovery of sexual reality must have been a shock to her, a shock that could have produced a violent reaction and caused a psychological block that she never got over. Far from being a wanton, Joseph points out that "she is austere, by temperament rather than reason." Those who knew her well noted, as did Tilly, "her distance and coldness toward young men." Others, like the prince de Ligne, asserted, that "her supposed licentiousness" was nothing but "the general flirtatiousness of a woman and a queen who wants to be pleasing to all." She tended to separate emotion from sexuality, as did the sentimental plays popular at the time. Marital relations for her were too direct and brutal. She dreamed of tender words, compliments, and inconsequential, suggestive banter of the kind she heard at the Opera balls. She would have liked to be romanced, and her husband was utterly incapable of giving her that. As the poor man was in no way capable of rape either, her resistance nipped in the bud any initiative he might have wanted to make. But to say that she refused to give herself to him would be unfair and incorrect, at least in the beginning. Without necessarily trying to shirk her duty, in order to deter him she only had to be herself, a little girl frozen with fear. There was "a lot of awkwardness and ignorance on both their parts," Louis XV would state sensibly. But it would have been better had he thought of that before and waited for sexual stirrings to be awakened in them before he joined them in matrimony.

She knew full well that she was not fulfilling the duties repeated *ad nauseum* in the maternal catechism. She was not compliant, amusing or gentle toward her husband. But she had the advantage that all the attention was on him. It was his fault if he couldn't consummate his marriage. No one asks whether or not she helps him in the effort, because a wife's submissiveness is taken for granted. But as we have seen, she is not submissive. And we already know from Maria Theresa that "she doesn't like to make an effort to overcome her revulsion for things not agreeable to her*." But just to be sure, and to protect herself, and no doubt on Vermond's advice, she assumed the persona of the abandoned wife, forever moaning about the dauphin's "nonchalance." In this she was backed up by Mercy, who wanted to shelter her from any suspicion. How could she openly admit that the idea of sex with her husband was loathsome to her?

But to this primary, immediate and instinctive motive, another one was quickly added, one that she could admit to even less: she did not want to have children. But she loved them, one might protest. Yes, child that she still was, she loved to play dolls with the children of her chambermaid. But between that and having her own there was a big difference. She was barely fifteen and had the mental age of a twelve year old. It was too soon. She wouldn't mind having them some day, but please, not right away! Let her live a little in the meantime.

Before disapproving of the fact that she preferred her pleasures to the joys of motherhood, let us recall what life was like for the queens of France. The fulfilled married life in the arms of a loving husband that Zweig dreams of for his heroine is nothing at all like what awaited her, or her predecessors. What they had to look forward to were marital embraces meant purely for procreation – where pleasure was rare – and suspended as soon as the first signs of pregnancy appeared. Upon the birth of a child they began again, one pregnancy following another year after year if one was lucky enough, or unlucky enough, to be fertile, as was the fate of Marie Leszczynska and Marie-Josèphe of Saxony, unless they died in childbirth around the age of twenty, like Marie-Thérèse Raphaëlle of Spain, Louis XV's first daughter-in-law. In this court of France where Louis XV had taken medical supervision to an extreme, she knew the extent of precautions surrounding the future mothers of dauphins. Marie-Josèphe was not allowed to take the smallest risk; almost complete immobility was ordered. She was ensconced in her cocoon, treated like a precious vase to be handled with the utmost care. But for someone of Marie-Antoinette's quicksilver temperament, who only existed in movement, immobility meant death. Embark upon this relentless breeding cycle? Just thinking about it threw her into a panic. It would mean entering a long dark tunnel out of which she would emerge ten years later aged, used up

---

* The empress made this remark on 31 August 1771 about her refusal to speak to Madame du Barry, but it can be applied to much else.

and perhaps, like so many others, replaced by a favorite. Well, she didn't really see the last eventuality happening; she knew that her husband had his principles. This was not necessarily to her liking; for the time being after all, if he took a mistress, he'd leave her alone. She really doesn't think things through, Mercy laments, distressed that she can't seem to see beyond her nose.

When she first arrived in Versailles she came up against the prohibition of horseback riding, as it was incompatible with hopes of motherhood. We saw how niftily she got around that one. But her mother's obstinacy in proscribing this exercise only drew her attention to everything she would soon have to give up forever. So it was with all the more determination that she rushed into the pleasures offered while they were still to be had. Afterwards everything would be forbidden. Goodbye to horseback riding, the hunt, dancing, the little Parisian sorties, staying out all night – everything she loved. When finally she felt that the ineluctable end was nigh, she threw herself body and soul into them, like a man about to go to prison, taking advantage of every last moment of freedom. As she explained to Mercy in February 1777, "one must enjoy one's youth; the time for reflection will come and frivolities will disappear." That was the period when the king gave up trying to join her in her bedchamber at night because he knew she wouldn't be there; she was at the Opera ball or at one of Madame Guéménée's gaming tables.

Of course she moved mountains to hide what she couldn't admit. She probably didn't breathe a word of her feelings to Vermond, much less to Mercy. She resorted to greater and greater subterfuge. She punctually expressed her delight in all the births in the family, and pretended to envy her sisters and sisters-in-law who procreated like clockwork. But we cannot deduce from this that she was living her lie comfortably. She was ill at ease with it all and unhappy, which explains her emotional outbursts. And her mother was informed. She felt guilty. She knew she was guilty. She took comfort in telling herself that she didn't reject the idea of having children one day. But when? Later, always later. She realized that they must come, and as she matured, there were times when she wanted them. She always had the right words for the family births that Maria Theresa hastened to tell her about, which proved nothing of course. But from time to time we sense that her trepidation or anxiety was coming to the surface. The marriages of her brothers-in-law and then d'Artois' wife's pregnancy, which could well give the dynasty an heir before she did, hurt her self-esteem but also revived her fears: how could the countess d'Artois remain so calm about giving birth; in her situation she would be dying of fear. Sometimes she let something slip that showed her feelings. At the beginning of September 1771 she wrote to her mother about her marriage, "I still live in hope... but I would like it all to be over with." And a month later, announcing that the duchess de Chartres had suffered a stillbirth, she added, "Although this is awful, I would like myself to have reached that point..." It isn't surprising to find in her handwriting words similar to those Louis XV ascribed to his grandson on the eve of his wedding: that he would like "for it all to be over with." Fear was the dominant factor in each one's attitude to marriage. For both of them it was fear of the first time; but for Marie-Antoinette it was also the fear of everything that must follow.

Seven years would pass before it was "all over with," before the ordeal was behind them, and the unknown had become the familiar. Seven years during which everything she feared remained in the future, leaving her prey to an absurd, pathological panic, and pushing her to flee in frenetic agitation. Flee from the court that eyed her suspiciously, flee from her husband especially, who did not know how to help her cross to the other side of the looking glass.

There certainly was a problem in their marital relations, but was it Louis XVI's impotence? No. "Nonchalance" and the late onset of puberty? That explanation could pass when he was sixteen, not twenty. The temptation to lay the blame on Marie-Antoinette is strong therefore. Some of the king's biographers say she refused to give herself to him. This was true, in part, after they acceded to the throne. Is it conceivable all the same that for seven long years she obstinately resisted a husband who was very conscious of how damaging this ridiculous situation was to his public image? Especially since the highly irrational resistance on her part did not spring from any deliberate plan. As time went by, she wanted to abandon this suicidal path.

The real problem lay elsewhere. It sprang neither from him nor from her, but from both of them together.

"Two-thirds of a husband..."

"He's only two-thirds of a husband;" this was the astounding discovery that Joseph II made once he'd got them both to confess. The censored sections of the correspondence published by Arneth and Geffroy allow us to reconstitute the astonishing story of a marriage whose consummation would stretch out over seven years. The first year nothing happened. But by the spring of 1771, word was out that everything was set. The two adolescents were visibly changing. The dauphin, already tall, had filled out; he promised to be of Herculean strength. He would soon prove able to lift a page perched on a digger's shovel. And during the summer of 1772 it was obvious to everyone that Marie-Antoinette had left adolescence behind; her health was better, she got fewer colds, and her sudden growth spurt had rendered her more slender. Favorable comments were heard again; everyone assumed the marriage was consummated. But Marie-Antoinette and Mercy didn't go so far as to say so to the empress; they spoke only of some progress, which "leads one to hope." But a pregnancy must not be counted on, and of course none occurs. Periodically the king sent for his grandchildren, questioned them, and entrusted to the doctors the task of furthering their education. In November of 1772 the young prince told him "that he had made attempts to consummate his marriage but was always stopped by painful sensations." In the spring of 1773 there were more rumors, very persistent this time. "The truth is," writes Vermond, "that the attempt was greater this time and the success more marked than ever before; they both felt some pain and it is still something of a thorny matter... Lassonne esteems and hopes that Monsieur le dauphin will soon grasp the rose."

The rose was grasped some time later, in July. "I can tell my dear mamma and her alone that we have made great progress and that I believe the marriage consummated, although not in the case of being pregnant." And Mercy related a very interesting scene. "Madame la dauphine had come to see the king. Just as the usher swung open the doors, the king having asked who had arrived, Monsieur le dauphin, who was next to him replied, 'It is my wife.' The king, smiling, asked him by what right he could call her such. By every right, was the dauphin's reply. The monarch, touched and surprised, took the young prince and princess by the hand and escorted them into his office, and it was there that Monsieur le dauphin informed him that his marriage was consummated." The news was immediately spread and everyone was very happy about it. That's all well and good, but there is something decidedly odd about this edifying story. The young lady was not sure her marriage was consummated after all; she only *believes* so, and she excludes any possibility of pregnancy. It seems that the rose has kept its thorns.

Let's be frank about it. The dauphin succeeded in deflowering his wife, but the adventure did not go much farther. For this semi-success, or semi-failure, followed by two years of fruitless fumbling, there is only one explanation – there must have been a physical disparity between the two partners. And let's be honest: no text that has come down to us alludes to such a possibility directly, no doubt because they all come from Marie-Antoinette and her entourage, who work hard at placing the blame for the fiasco entirely on her husband. But Mercy himself points us in the right direction when he compares the young man's case with that of his father who, for the same reasons of late development and timidity, did not live with the infanta of Spain for six months when he was married the first time. Although at the time, everyone in Versailles was aware that the difficulties they encountered had nothing to do with timidity or frigidity. The young man was very much in love with the infanta, but had to wait a long time before possessing her because of "the narrowness of the passage." He encountered the same difficulties with Marie-Josèphe of Saxony as well, but having learned from his prior experience, he succeeded more quickly, and no doubt with less tact. One can be forgiven for supposing that the future Louis XVI, who was even more sturdily built than his father, took after him in this respect.

Brutally subjecting the child who was Marie-Antoinette to sexual relations as soon as she arrived would not have been contemplated. The question came up properly when she was sufficiently mature. The dauphin too had grown, but that did not make them any more compatible. That is why consummation progressed in stages, a step forward here, and a bit of an improvement there, as the letters to Maria Theresa indicate. From deflowering to complete penetration there was a whole itinerary to follow, punctuated by Marie-Antoinette's dodging and groaning. The thing was at least as painful for her as for him. Accession to the throne brought about renewed efforts from Louis XVI, who according to Mercy demonstrated "volition" and "ability." But he only managed to get his wife's back up; she proved to be more horrified than ever by her conjugal duty and would from then on do everything possible to avoid it. In 1775 they were still only two-thirds of the way down the road in what became for them both an abominable chore. It was enough to throw Marie-Antoinette off balance, and at this point we can subscribe to Zweig's analysis of the psychic and physiological troubles this disturbed sexuality engendered. And to top it all off, her malaise was worsened by the fact that she realized she herself was partially responsible, for which she felt anguish and remorse. It all went on far too long.

Two years later this was still the situation that a stupefied Joseph II unmasked. Here is "the secret of the marital bed" as he crudely confided it to his brother Leopold in two letters dated May 11 and June 9, 1777:

He's got good solid erections, he introduces the member, stays in maybe two minutes without moving, pulls out still hard without ever discharging, and bids good night. This is hard to figure out, because he does have nocturnal emissions at times, but in bed, and not doing the job himself either, never, and he is happy*; admitting quite openly that he only did it because it was his duty and he had no taste for it at all. Oh! If ever I could have been there, I'd have fixed him! A good whipping would have made him discharge through sheer rage, like a donkey. And with that my sister lacks spirit, and there they are the pair of them, totally inept.

This explanation, which has the advantage of describing the situation in graphic terms, calls for some remarks all the same. Ineptitude does not mean ignorance. After all the lessons the doctors gave them, they knew perfectly well what they had to do. But they neglected to mention that there were some necessary preliminaries. Louis XVI never learned how to earn his wife's trust, and for her part, she only ever approached him with fangs bared. We can easily believe that he did it out of duty with no pleasure whatsoever. As for her, the effort she invested in avoiding him says it all. But having come so far, why did he not go all the way? Joseph doesn't seem to pose the question. The only possible explanation, the key to the whole matter, is that he would withdraw because of the pain it caused him, but even more the pain his wife complained of. However, to admit that Marie-Antoinette had her own part to play in the failure would be to totally dismantle the version of events that the family had so laboriously been piecing together for seven years. These things can be spoken about in person, but not committed to paper. All the same, Joseph's fit of anger at the end is revelatory. Why beat a donkey if it is not to make it overcome an obstacle it refuses to get past? Surely he suggested that Louis XVI work through his own painful sensations and ignore his partner's groaning to finally arrive at normal marital relations. And he gave his sister a mighty scolding, opening her eyes to the dangers of remaining infertile.

By the time he left he had them convinced; they determined to get out of the impasse. It took them another two and a half months to arrive at the desired result. "This most interesting event took place on Monday August 18th," Mercy wrote. On the 30th, Marie-

---

* We must be careful with this word because "he is happy" at the time meant not that he was satisfied but that he made do with what he had and asked no more.

Antoinette, much relieved at last, sent her mother a triumphant communiqué: "I am basking in the happiness most essential for my entire life. It has been more than a week since my marriage was consummated; the thing has been repeated, and yesterday again more thoroughly than the first time. At first I thought I'd send a courier to my dear mamma but I was afraid it might be made much of and cause rumors. I must admit too that I wanted to be absolutely sure of what I was saying. I don't think I'm expecting yet, but at least I can hope to be at any time now." And Joseph can boast to Leopold about the success of his mission: "The king of France, as you know, has finally managed the great feat, and the queen can now become pregnant; they have both written to thank me, and attribute it to my advice. It is true that I saw perfectly well that sluggishness, awkwardness and apathy were the only impediments to the matter."

This letter alone is enough to put the lie to all the allegations about a supposed need for an operation. But the belief in some mysterious physical obstacle to the marriage's consummation explains the fact that recourse to surgery was so often mentioned at the time. And Maria Theresa's obstinate calls for one, together with the secrecy she imposed on her daughter regarding her marital relations, reinforced the legend that Zweig expounded on so eloquently of a soft and spineless Louis XVI, forever recoiling from a harmless operation. But it was in dealing with the groans of his wife that he was weak and timorous. Before closing this chapter on their marital failure, we should investigate the feelings he bore for her.

The "boundless complacency" of Louis XVI

Marie-Antoinette always measured her husband's love by how compliant he was. "He loves me very much and does everything I want," she wrote naively after a year of marriage. While Louis XV was still alive, they gave the impression in public that they were a sweet young couple full of concern for each other, whose private problems no doubt would eventually be sorted out. People knew of course that the dauphin neglected his young wife's bed, and they felt sorry for her. But there were few opportunities for her to clash with him. She solicited his help only for little things, because all the important authorizations came from the king. So it is only after he came to the throne that Louis XVI's extraordinary complacency towards his wife began to shock the public.

In October 1774 Mercy wrote to Maria Theresa that the queen's reputation could not be higher and that her husband was "in love with her in every meaning of the term." To those who might be tempted to take this remark as gold standard, let's quote what follows: "He joins to this sentiment that of esteem, because in effect it is impossible not to esteem the qualities of mind and character this princess is blessed with." Either the ambassador had lost any ability to see things clearly or he was cynically flattering the empress' maternal pride. When it came to love, it would always be impossible to discern in his assiduity towards his wife the part of duty and the part of pleasure. Yes, he did dismiss his aunt Adélaïde's indiscreet curiosity by replying that he found the thing agreeable, but nothing indicates that the consummation of the marriage awoke in him after seven years any hitherto unsuspected appetites. Their relations thenceforth would suggest that he merely wanted children from them. As for the supposed esteem for her mind and character the ambassador mentioned, it rested purely on the conviction of the Viennese court that the young woman was superior to him in every way. It is not certain that the interested party shared the opinion. He was, however, incontestably proud of her when he compared her to his brothers' brides, who were less beautiful and imposing. Mercy was therefore close to the truth when he wrote in 1777, "that the king takes pride in the queen's charms and qualities, that he loves her as much as he is capable of loving, but that he fears her at least as much as he loves her." The abbé de Véri agreed. "The king fears rather than loves her, for he is clearly just as cheerful and even more at ease at events when she is not present."

The fact is that he let the queen take the upper hand in their relationship to such an extent that Besenval could say that his attitude "borders on subservience." Why? It's impossible to fall for the explanation habitually given of his impotence. But even if their marital failure cannot be entirely blamed on either one of them, he did feel some guilt over it and believed he needed to compensate her. She was such a child! Why should he prevent her from enjoying herself just because his tastes were different? Even though he was only a year older, he considered himself to be infinitely more mature. And besides, he was a man and she was his wife in the eyes of God; he had no choice, he must do everything possible to get along with her. At first he thought in time she would come to her senses; that was Louis XV's belief, and his natural inclination was to believe so too. It's so much easier to wait than to risk conflict. But as it happened, the situation didn't ripen, it only got worse. When she began to avoid him, he hoped to win her to him by granting her every wish. This was a great mistake. Far from being grateful, she despised him more for it. The more he gave in, the more she fled him. Because she behaved like an irresponsible child, she needed to be countered by a strong will, but such was not the case.

There were further nuances, however. The king compartmentalized the two domains of daily life and politics. We saw earlier that far from putting a brake on her entertainments, he encouraged them so as to keep her out of his hair regarding internal affairs. We shall see later on that he knew just how to contain her regarding international affairs as well, but as he feared her fits of anger, he avoided clashes with her. His opposition to her was limp, silent, full of subterfuge and volte-face. He rarely said no with any vigor. To get a bit of peace, he gave her the illusion that she could do anything she wanted with him; she boasted of it, and his indulgence of her pleasures gave credence to the idea that he was utterly subservient to her.

So Louis XVI's weakness with regard to her was not so great as it seemed. But since the public saw it as such, the damage was done, especially since it appeared tied to his supposed impotence. Unfortunately, he underestimated the dangerous power of public opinion. So many pamphlets had been published in the previous twenty-five years that in high places they ceased to be taken seriously. Besides, who could have taught him the utility of cultivating his public image? Surely not his grandfather, who'd become jaded, or his tutor, for whom the people were merely an inert mass that the sovereign must make happy, but without consulting them. As for the scribblers, the *philosophes*, and the idea-pushers, they were considered troublemakers with no audience beyond the cafes and Parisian salons. Little by little Louis XV had tarnished the image of the inherent sacredness of the monarchy. How could his successor know that in the Middle Ages and even in the 16th century, the king's fecundity gave the promise of fruitfulness as well to his kingdom's people, animals and harvest, and that a childless king was practically seen as a reprobate? Certainly, in the century of reason, no one would dare to formulate such a notion. But in the collective unconscious, sexual power is linked to all power. An impotent king got no respect, especially if he was seen as hen-pecked. All Louis XVI's Christian virtues were as nothing against this instinctive reaction. Voluntarily chaste behavior out of respect for the marriage sacrament could have done him credit after his grandfather's libertinage. But the years of childlessness would stamp him forever with ridicule, and the queen's image would never recover from her rash flight into suspect pleasures.

Fate hung in the balance for them during the three years between their accession to the throne and Joseph II's visit, but they didn't realize it. Now they were making a fresh start, which before long would be crowned with the birth of four children.

CHAPTER 11

MOTHERHOOD

Joseph II's arguments hit their mark. Marie-Antoinette knew he was right and promised him that she'd take them to heart. But obedience was abhorrent to her, and she asked for a reprieve. "The time will come when she will follow his good advice." Not immediately, because she in no way wanted to "appear to have ceded to his way of thinking" or "to seem to be governed." And she questioned everything; she quibbled with "some ill humor" about some "very essential points" her brother had listed. But there was really only one essential point: she must have children as soon as possible. She admitted the necessity of it and declared herself ready to do whatever it took to accomplish it. But she used this concession as a bargaining chip to get what she wanted in other areas. In other words, she consented to fulfilling her wifely duties, but she was less disposed than ever to sacrificing her pleasures to her responsibilities as queen. And her husband, overjoyed at the prospect of becoming a father, gave in to her more than ever.

Over the eight years in which her four pregnancies took place, people saw a difference in her behavior. There were times when she wavered and her bad old habits returned. But little by little, although sometimes falling back into her dissolute ways, she became more reasonable. Because she changed: she became an excellent mother; her children had a growing place in her life. Also because it seemed to her that Paris was changing. She was reluctant to go there because she was no longer applauded there, and soon enough she would feel hated there. And finally, because she was overcome with powerful feelings – she had fallen in love with a handsome Swedish officer, Axel von Fersen.

Little by little she abandoned the tumultuous thrills of her youth to create a safe haven for herself at Trianon. "I will enjoy the sweet pleasures of private life from which we are excluded unless we take it upon ourselves to claim them." Since her arrival in France she had longed to escape from court life, to be freed from its constraints, its crushing boredom and its hypocrisy. For a few short summers she created at Trianon an idyllic place where she could be a woman just like any other, much more successfully than she could behind a mask at any Opera ball. Better still, a woman who was almost happy.

Motherhood, Trianon and Fersen were three aspects of her life that we were inextricably bound together. But we will examine each of them in turn in order better to understand their importance.

An incomplete metamorphosis

Patience was never her strong point. Now that she had made up her mind, she wanted to get pregnant immediately. She happily gave up horseback riding and dancing in order to do so. But nature was in no hurry and the young woman grew impatient. Clearly marital relations remained a chore for her, and she was irritated at their inefficacy. She found no relief from her nerves except in "dissipation." The 1777 stay in Fontainebleau was marked by a fresh outbreak of gambling, and no amount of criticism stopped her. And no one even pretended that the sessions she held three times a week fulfilled any court functions – people went there to play hard and to win, not to be seen or exchange a few polite words with her. The very high stakes involved in the game of pharaoh obliged her to allow in all sorts of people, in "unseemly disorder." The games, either in her quarters or the princess de Guéménée's, went on so long into the night that the king refused to join her: "It's her fault if he doesn't sleep with her, and staying up all night to gamble is the cause." In her quest to kill time she jeopardized her ability to get pregnant, which was exasperating. What on earth was she looking for? She no longer even knew herself. One night in Fontainebleau, the Piedmontese ambassador along with the rest of the court spied the king sheepishly leaving his wife's apartments, from which he had just been evicted.

Once back in Versailles, they resumed conjugal relations, and Louis XVI promised the emperor a niece or nephew for the coming year. Marie-Antoinette had taken up her old habit again of going to the theatre or to balls. But she'd lost her taste for them. The only ones she enjoyed were the masked balls. Carnival season was approaching, and didn't she face the possibility that this might be the last one she could enjoy? Haunted by the idea that her youth was about to end, she sought a further reprieve. She took up dancing again. And she went back to Paris. As the weeks went by and Lent approached, her appetite for amusement was more frenzied. On Thursday the 26th of February there was a masked ball at the duke d'Orléans' home at the Palais-Royal; she arrived a bit after midnight and stayed until five o'clock in the morning, then entered a box where she could watch the Opera ball* until seven. On Saturday there was a ball at the princess de Guéménée's apartments in Versailles, on Sunday a masked ball at the Opera until six in the morning. On Shrove Tuesday another Opera ball until seven in the morning. Her chaperon the count d'Artois got involved in a violent altercation with the duchess de Bourbon that would result in a duel with her husband – purely for show, of course, but it became a massive scandal. Was it seemly for the queen to be seen in such disreputable company? But Louis XVI did nothing to thwart her whims.

Mercy tried to cut her to the quick: an abandoned husband could take up with a mistress. She laughed in his face, so sure she was of her power over him. Why should she bother being kind to him when he didn't even seem to notice, and when it was so easy just to keep him in line "through fear"? But this was pure bravura, just to show that she hadn't buckled under. In truth, she had other reasons for not fearing a rival, for the king had found the means to parry her wayward ways. Since her evenings out prevented him from sharing her bed at night, he went to her when he rose. "He comes to see me every morning in my private quarters." His assiduousness paid off; by mid-April Marie-Antoinette was certain enough that she was pregnant to announce it to her mother.

Her relief was as great as her earlier fears. Pregnancy was not as awful as she'd imagined. She was fortunate; aside from some morning sickness in the beginning, she was spared many of pregnancy's ills. She was as fit as a fiddle, so she was not condemned to bed rest. Carriage riding was not recommended because of the bumping, but she was allowed to walk in the park or inside the chateau, in moderation for the first three months, but then as much as she liked. The rest of the time it was "conversation, music, a bit of gaming." She would even be seen doing some handiwork.

---

* Performances and Opera balls were held at the time in a theatre that Richelieu had built in his palace, which became the Palais-Royal. This explains why there were boxes overhanging the stalls. The duke d'Orléans used to host private balls in another, smaller room at the Palais-Royal. And it was possible to pass directly from his quarters into one of the boxes in question.

Little by little maternal feelings were stirring and replacing flirtatiousness. She took pleasure in seeing her form blossom outward. In mid-June she measured her waist: four and a half inches wider. Six weeks later: "My baby moved for the first time on Friday the 31st of July at ten-thirty in the evening; since then it has been moving frequently, which brings me great joy... I've become quite a bit fatter, more than one usually is at five months." From Vienna the child's future grandmother set out her views on the care and feeding of newborns: "reasonable care of a natural kind, do not wrap them too tightly in their linens, do not let them get too warm, don't stuff them with mush and pap." And Marie-Antoinette outdoes her: "The way they raise them nowadays, they are much less encumbered; they are not swaddled; they are always in a bassinet or carried, and as soon as they can be taken outside, they gradually get them used to it so they end up by being outdoors practically all the time." She imagined watching her own child grow: "He will be housed downstairs, with a little gate to separate him from the rest of the terrace, which might even get him to walk sooner than on the wooden floors."

Mother and daughter were united in the same love of the child to come and their relationship was restored. Their letters henceforth took on a trusting tone. Eight years of misunderstandings faded away. And it was an added joy for Marie-Antoinette no longer to have to lie and be reprimanded. Motherhood finally liberated her from the prolonged childhood where she had been comfortably maintained. At peace with her mother, she felt at peace with herself, almost an adult. Let's not forget that she wasn't yet twenty-two years old.

The summer that year was beastly hot. The court practically ground to a halt. The men's attention was monopolized by the war that had just broken out with England. In August Marie-Antoinette had to give up the little private get-togethers at Trianon. During the day she dozed in the relative coolness of her apartments, and didn't go out until the temperature dropped somewhat, in search of a bit of air in the gardens while listening to evening concerts. She walked or relaxed on benches beside her sisters-in-law wearing light summer dresses in the semi-darkness that was dotted by terrines[*] and lanterns scattered in the woods, with the illuminated chateau windows in the background. A lot of venomous hatred was needed for the pamphleteers to dress these evenings up as orgies.

In Vienna Maria Theresa was fearful, more blinkered than

---

[*]   Candles planted in glass jars to protect them from the wind.

ever by her anti-French prejudices – a country where "irreligion is pushed to its greatest excess" and where "the most atrocious crimes come cheap." Would they go so far as to use the birth to try to do away with the baby, perhaps even its mother? She pestered her ambassador with advice on what staff to choose to assist her daughter or care for the newborn. Her imagination ran wild. It is true that the count de Provence, disappointed at having his hopes dashed of one day succeeding his brother to the throne, did not hide the fact well. Nor was the count d'Artois happy to see his two sons move back in the line of succession. But that's a far cry from resorting to the dagger or poison! Mercy was wise enough to hide these outlandish musings from the expectant mother. The end of her pregnancy could not have been better; she didn't even develop the famous mask that mars some women's faces as they approach the end of their term.

A delighted Louis XVI showered her with attention and little gifts. The baby was to be born in mid-December. The queen would have to miss most of the season's festivities. "There will be no carnival for me this winter," she remarked with melancholy. So her husband arranged a surprise. All of a sudden one night at the beginning of the month he sent to enquire if she would like to have some masked entertainment. "Most happily, as long as the king comes along too but unmasked." He complied, and came in undisguised, followed by Maurepas dressed as Cupid with his wife as Venus and Sartine as Neptune; Vergennes, a globe gracing his head and a map of America draping his front and one of England on his back, personified foreign policy. And the survivors of the previous court had to do their bit: Soubise was dressed in Chinese costume, Richelieu was Triton, and the venerable wife of marshal Mirepoix was Aurora. A druid, a vizier, a dervish, a sultan, a Bedouin, and many others mingled with them, happily dancing the minuet before going off to enjoy a hot chocolate with ice cream. The layette was ready, the godparents chosen; they would be King Charles III of Spain and Empress Maria Theresa. The prisoners to be liberated had already been selected and the churches churned out prayers, vows and novinas for it to be a boy. Everything was ready except him.

It's only a girl

Around midnight of the night of 18-19 December 1778 Marie-Antoinette felt the first signs. She summoned help and had Madame de Lamballe sent for. Around three o'clock she in turn sent for the king. He remained at her side while the superintendent summoned all the princes and princesses in the family. In no time the news was spread. As royal births always took place in public to avoid any risk of substitution, onlookers were piling in to each room of her apartments by eight o'clock in the morning, the highest ranking in the closest rooms to the queen. This ritual had always been a trial for the poor queen or dauphine. With all her hostility to court etiquette, Marie-Antoinette must have found it barbaric. Installed on her "bed of labor" she grit her teeth so as not to make a show of her pain before the court. Madame Campan said that shortly before noon, when the abbé de Vermond's brother, who was the doctor in charge of delivery, announced that the birth was imminent, the bedchamber was besieged by such a diverse crowd that it seemed like a public thoroughfare. Some people even climbed on furniture to get a better look. If the king had not taken the precaution of having the screens around the queen's bed anchored and tied in place, they would have fallen on top of her.

At first the baby made no sound. Perhaps the queen believed it was born dead. Then, although the custom was not to announce the sex right away, Madame de Lamballe gave her a previously agreed upon sign, and she found out it was a girl. What with the tension of the long ordeal, the mounting din from the crowd, the close atmosphere, the emotion, the disappointment, it was all too much. She was overcome by a convulsive fit and fainted. Vermond shouted for air and hot water and demanded a bleeding of the foot. In order to prevent drafts it had been thought a good idea to caulk the high windows with wads of paper. Madame Campan relates that the king opened them "with strength that only tenderness for his wife could have given him." However, Louis XVI didn't mention this fainting spell in the dry but precise account of the birth he confided to his diary – for once abandoning his usual terseness. By then he had followed his daughter into the large study to watch as they swaddled her. The windows were opened; it doesn't matter by whom. The ushers got the rooms cleared out *manu militari*. The hot water didn't arrive and Vermond performed the bleeding without it. As soon as the blood started to spurt, Marie-Antoinette came to. She was not coming back "from death's door" as Madame Campan reported; she was over-dramatizing a bit. All the same, it had Mercy frightened. So as not to put her off, they decided to hide the incident from her. Nonetheless, this first birth left very bad memories.

She did not hold her daughter responsible for her disappointment.

When they brought the baby to her, she had already dried her tears. It is said that she cried out, pressing the baby to her bosom, "Poor little girl, you were not desired, but you will be no less my daughter. A son would have belonged more particularly to the State. You will be mine; you will have all my care; you will share my happiness and lighten my sorrows." The baby girl, quickly baptized Marie-Thérèse and given the title Madame Royale, was robust; her physical traits were "regular and charming, with big eyes, a nicely formed mouth and the flush of excellent health." Seeing the portraits sent to Vienna, her grandmother was said to exclaim, a bit dismayed, that she looked like her father. The father in question was over the moon. Throughout the whole first week when she was confined to bed to assure her some rest, he only left her bedside to go gaze in admiration at his daughter, for whom he was overcome with tenderness. His mood was so light that he forgot his grievances against the abbé de Vermond, and before he knew it he was chatting happily with him.

The new mother used her condition as an excuse to miss the New Year's Day wish-giving rituals. But she recovered quickly. They were soon playing pharaoh in her room. They then set up a theatre in the Salon of Peace next door, and she was able to attend a comedy reclining on her *chaise longue*. She received ambassadors. She started taking walks again; she made one or two appearances at balls, without dancing, and went to the theatre at court and in town. Even though the child was not a boy, they took advantage of the opportunity to revive popular enthusiasm by an official visit to Paris. On February 8th, accompanied by the king and her brothers- and sisters-in-law, she attended thanksgiving services at Notre-Dame and the Sainte-Geneviève Abbey. The weather was mild and the cortege superb. But the great throngs came more out of curiosity than affection. There was little applause, despite the silver coins being showered on the crowds. They were greeted almost everywhere with silence, which Mercy rightly interpreted as disapproval rather than respect. Even the one hundred couples, married and given a dowry for the occasion, didn't help. Neither did the festivities organized by the municipal authorities. It was a holiday given in honor of the queen, and the queen was not well liked.

Decidedly, Marie-Antoinette only liked Paris by night, and had not entirely abandoned the folly of her ways. The end of the pre-Lenten festivities was approaching and she wanted to soak up a bit more of the atmosphere. She talked her husband into accompanying her to the Opera ball on the Sunday before Lent. As he refused to go again on Shrove Tuesday, she decided to go without him, incognito. She went out with a single lady, left her carriage adorned with heraldic signs at the home of her first equerry, the duke de Coigny* and exchanged it for an old carriage without any distinguishing marks. On the way a wheel broke. She found herself in the street in the middle of the night, masked and in her ball gown, reduced to knocking at the nearest door for help. A silk merchant hailed a fiacre and off she went to the Opera. What an adventure! Now that was a welcome bit of spice to enliven a monotonous existence! And she recounted to all and sundry, "Me! In a fiacre! Can you picture it?" The story was all over Paris, but with a variation: people concluded that she had come from an assignation with Coigny. No one thought enough about it to realize that if that had been the case, she certainly would have kept it quiet. It is certain on the other hand that a queen of France should never have exposed herself to such a mishap.

The empress' last disappointment

The young woman was clearly not in any hurry to resume marital relations. She realized of course that after the birth of a daughter she could not put it off forever, and she would have to do so sooner rather than later. But she was "put off by the birth" and wanted to wait a number of months before getting pregnant again. Her return to riding was evidence of that. There was a rumor that she wanted to nurse her baby herself, much to her mother's distress. It was fashionable at the time, but also a way of gaining eighteen carefree months. However, the discipline required for nursing would have been worse than a pregnancy. She wasn't really rejecting motherhood, but she did want to space her pregnancies and limit their number, as other women do. However, it was not acceptable in a queen of France at the end of the 18th century.

Pressure mounted. Although Mercy had a talk with her and claimed that he had convinced her, Maria Theresa saw fit in each of her letters to harp on her granddaughter's need of "a little brother to keep her company." Would it take another eight years? In the first days of spring a case of measles gave the young woman a reprieve; she had to be separated from the king, who had never had them. But what was she going to do without her dear Madame de Polignac,

---

* He lived at the Hôtel de Brionne on Petit Carroussel Place behind Marsan's villa.

who had also come down with them. She would die of boredom! Four men from her "little group" offered to entertain her. Coigny, Guines, Esterhazy and Besenval took up sick duty in her rooms and dished up the gossip. They declared themselves ready to spend the entire night! Decisive action was called for: they would arrive at seven in the morning and withdraw at eleven at night. But it was enough to get people muttering. Where were the ladies to look after the king when he fell ill? To cut short the rumors about their mutual indifference, Mercy suggested that the spouses write notes to each other, and then he set up a rendez-vous worthy of a novel or a play: from atop a balcony the queen exchanged words with the king that we are assured were most tender.

She spent the three weeks of convalescence ensconced with her four male nurses at Trianon. Louis XVI apparently did not worry about it. He had many other cares to occupy him, of a political order. What is more, his entourage decided the moment was right to again propose a mistress. Marie-Antoinette got wind of it. "Mortified and stung," she made up her mind to go back to Versailles and resume married life. Seeing her daughter again seemed to awaken her maternal feelings. At eight months the baby began walking quite well in her crib; she could say papa, and through her gums they could feel her first teeth starting to break through. "I hope soon to be able to announce to my dear mamma new hopes of expecting. She can rest assured about my conduct; I'm too aware of the need for more children to be negligent in that regard. If before I made mistakes, it was because I was a light-minded child, but at the present time I am much more settled, and she can count on my fulfilling my responsibilities. Besides, I owe it to the king because of his kindness, and I dare say his confidence in me, for which I can congratulate myself more and more." And in fact at the beginning of July a pregnancy was under way, but it ended in miscarriage. According to Madame Campan she "injured" herself by making too brusque a movement to push up the window of her carriage!

Time passed, and little Madame grew; she walked by herself, got up and down without help and was about to be weaned. But there was still no little brother in sight. The hopes that were so readily embraced faded with each passing month. 1780 came and went with no happy outcome. Without a dauphin the count d'Artois took to dreaming of the crown for his elder boy, whom he was grooming for future kingship. Marie-Antoinette was getting seriously worried, and in Vienna Maria Theresa was despondent.

At sixty-three the empress had had enough. Weighed down by excess pounds, she found it difficult to get about. Her hands deformed by rheumatism refused to hold a pen. Her old chronic catarrh was back with a vengeance and she was racked with a persistent cough. She had such difficulty breathing that she felt she was becoming "like a stone inside." That didn't stop her from getting so intensely hot that she kept her windows open day and night in all weather. At the end of 1780 she gave up, and asked to receive the last sacraments. Nights were unbearable; she was suffocating, but she struggled to stay awake: "How can I fall asleep when at any instant I can be called before my Maker? I fear falling asleep; I don't want to be taken by surprise. I want to see death arrive." Old fighter that she was, she wanted to look death in the face. On November 29th she refused a potion that would only have prolonged her suffering, and chased her daughters from her room so as to spare them the sight. In a final choking fit, she rose out of her armchair, collapsed on a sofa and as her son Joseph called out "You'll not be comfortable there," she replied, "Comfortable enough to die." She had the time to give her doctor her last instructions, "Light the mortuary candle and close my eyes; it would be too much to ask of the emperor." She expired a few minutes later.

Within two months she would have found out that her daughter was pregnant again, and this time she was carrying a dauphin.

When news of her death arrived in Versailles Louis XVI gave Vermond the task of telling the queen. Marie-Antoinette shed many wrenching, heartfelt tears. She was deeply attached to her mother, which was why their relationship was sometimes fraught with such difficulty. The umbilical cord was finally cut. With the fear gone, only admiration for her mother remained. Maria Theresa became a model, the ultimate reference when it came to courage, dignity and grandeur. It was about her that Marie-Antoinette would think when adversity struck. It was she who would help her face without flinching the horrible end that was in store for her. But until that time, she must achieve autonomy and become an adult. Given the state of dependence in which the empress had kept her, however, this would not be easy.

A dauphin

Marie-Antoinette's second pregnancy caused her as little discomfort as the first, and her uneventful delivery was quicker. On the 22nd of October 1781, "at exactly a quarter past one by my watch," wrote the king in his diary, "she most happily gave birth to a boy." The number of people admitted into her room was limited to a strict minimum, about ten. The others, relegated to the large study, were only allowed in at the last moment, and confined to the edge of the room so air could circulate. At the moment the child entered the world such a great silence reigned that, according to Madame Campan, "the queen believed it was only a girl again, but once the minister of justice noted the newborn's sex, the king approached her bed and said, 'Madame, you have fulfilled my wishes and those of France; you are the mother of a dauphin.' Louis XVI's joy was extreme, the tears were streaming down his face." Ordinarily so reserved, he shook everyone's hand and unleashed a flood of words, reveling in the frequent repetition of *my son* and *the dauphin*. The princess de Guéménée brought the washed and swaddled babe to his mother. Perhaps he didn't weigh thirteen pounds or measure twenty-two inches, but he did show promise of being vigorous. Marie-Antoinette proposed to the governess that she partially relieve her in what was now double duty by sharing supervision of her daughter's education with her.

Although court etiquette had been lightened for this second birth, it came back into full force to honor the boy. At three o'clock the baby was baptized by the cardinal de Rohan, the chief almoner. And then in his cradle he received "the customary homage and visits." In other words, anyone who was anyone in the kingdom came to pour out effusive praise and bow before the newborn babe who preferred suckling the milk of his wet nurse Madame Poitrine* – this was actually her name, but she was chosen for her buxom health. There was joy everywhere. Traditionally, the people saw in the birth of an heir to the throne "a guarantee of prosperity and public tranquility." The various workmen's guilds sent delegations to Versailles with gifts inspired by the occasion. There were a lot of dolphins made of different materials and dressed in various ways. In a thoughtful homage to the king, the locksmiths had forged a very complicated lock. When he figured out how to open it, out popped a dolphin. Even the gravediggers showed up, mercifully without any job-related trinkets, but they were not allowed admittance, as no shadow was to darken that fine day.

As was the custom, fifty ladies from Les Halles, the central food market, came dressed in black robes, the "great finery of their trade." Four of them were admitted into the bedchamber. One of them, who was pretty and blessed with a good voice, recited a speech composed especially for the occasion by the famous Academy member Monsieur de La Harpe. As she was afraid she'd

---

* *Translator's note: "poitrine" means "chest" or "bosom."*

make a mistake, she had written it out on the back of her fan, although she hardly needed it. But we mustn't confuse the ladies of Les Halles with the bawdy fishwives whose rhymes owed nothing to lofty academe. The king and queen took to one of those ditties, and it would be repeated in Versailles:

> *Do not fear, papa dear,*
> *To give more children to your bride.*
> *Of course you know God will provide.*
> *Make so many that Versailles will swarm,*
> *Even a hundred, where's the harm?*
> *With bread on the table and a fire warm.*

Marie-Antoinette's churching ceremony on January 21st brought the sovereigns to Notre-Dame and Sainte-Geneviève's to render thanks for the successful birth. They then went to the Hôtel de Ville where a wooden pavilion had been erected large enough to fit the seventy-eight guests invited for the feast. Service was so slow, it was later murmured, that the last ones were only just served when the king rose from the table, obliging everyone else to do likewise. As for the people, they could stuff themselves heedless of protocol on food distributed on the open thoroughfares; they could get drunk on the wine gushing from fountains, and dance till they dropped while awaiting the fireworks. Two days later the king and queen returned to the Hôtel de Ville for a formal ball, which marked the end of the festivities. Perhaps the monarchy was not all that unpopular after all. But it was clear that the homage was addressed, according to ancient tradition, to the fertile royal couple, who assured the continuity of the dynasty and the prosperity of the kingdom. There was sympathy for Marie-Antoinette only insofar as she fully carried out her functions.

She seemed to understand this. And if she had any doubts about how much this birth buttressed her position, the face on her brother-in-law Provence was enough to dispel them. For a long time he believed his older brother was sterile, and then the advent of a daughter had left him with some hope: he was still the number one heir to the throne. But now here he was demoted to second place. And there was no reason why the royal couple couldn't have more children. It was difficult for him to hide his dismay. His wife was able to put up a brave front; but as for him, already at the little girl's birth, he couldn't bring himself to show any joy, which would only, as he himself admitted, be seen as false. So he let his ill humor show. Did he help spread the rumors casting doubt on the dauphin's legitimacy? It's possible, even probable. Did he put together and later leave with the duke Fitz-James a complete dossier on all the royal children? There is no trace of such a document. What is sure is that injurious libels were circulating. Marie-Antoinette refused even more than previously to take any notice of them. She felt more secure than ever in her position.

There were no more pregnancies until 1783 when she had a miscarriage in November. Mercy showed his impatience, especially since the dauphin's health was not the best. In the spring of 1784 people noticed that he'd stopped growing. He was listless and growing thinner. A shaken Louis XVI wept. The doctors spoke of "a hint of scurvy." When he came down with a recurring fever, these puffed-up imbeciles claimed to see in the evolution of the disease "one of the most powerful means of fortifying the constitution of the young prince." Marie-Antoinette believed them and was reassured to see that he was doing better. She soon noticed she was pregnant. This was another smooth pregnancy. She had managed to deflect curiosity by hiding the imminence of the birth and on March 27th 1785 she gave birth to a son in the presence of a very sparse gathering of princes and princesses. The superb boy was quickly baptized and given the title duke de Normandie. There was less ado than for his older brother, but that was only natural. On the 24th of May the queen went to Paris to be churched, but was barely applauded. And she scandalously ended the day begun at Sainte-Geneviève's at the Opera – the theatre, not the ball. More insulting rhymes ensued.

Let's get a bit ahead of ourselves here. With two sons, she felt she had done enough for the dynasty. She took very badly what could only be the first signs of another pregnancy. For a long time she refused to believe it. She spoke of "upset and sickness" that she hoped would soon be over. The doctors let her go on. As the fifth month approached, she had to face the truth. She was very unhappy about it and didn't even bother trying to hide her annoyance from her brother[*]. As Joseph revealed to Mercy, "She wrote to me letting me know about the pregnancy; she says she is most unhappy about it, feeling that she has enough children... I am trying to show her what the disagreeable consequences would be of such conduct if ever she wished, either for convenience or precaution's sake, to separate herself from the king in order to have no more children... This idea inspires me to greater disquiet because it is the fashion

---

[*] In a letter and a response to it that were never found. We know their substance through Mercy's letter cited here.

these days among young ladies who believe it is the done thing to separate from their husbands, and that they've fulfilled their duty if they've had a child or two." And to frighten her he brought up the fate of so many queens of France who were shunned in favor of a mistress. But Marie-Antoinette knew she had no infidelity to fear from Louis XVI, as he was so little given to the pleasures of the flesh and so held back by powerful religious scruples.

On July 9th 1786 a very vigorous baby girl was born to her and given the name Sophie, but she was to die of convulsions less than a year later. Rumors abounded of further pregnancies. "If I were pregnant as often as they say in this country," she wrote to her brother, "I'd have had no rest and almost as many children as the grand duchess[*]." She had gained considerable weight, a fact she tried to hide by squeezing tightly into a corset, which enhanced the excessive opulence of her bosom. In short, she was no longer a young woman. Sophie's birth had taken its toll. She probably made that her pretext for getting her husband used to the loss of marital relations. She in any case had no more pregnancies, and she declared herself happy about that. She explained her refusal to keep on having children by her desire to take care of those she had. This was one of the rare points on which she dared to be critical of her mother, whose many duties had prevented her from supervising her daughters' education. She herself would have been much more useful, she confided in Madame Campan, had she been lucky enough to be directly tutored by such a wise sovereign. The spirit of the times dictated having fewer children and raising them better, but this was very foreign to tradition in princely families. And to Marie-Antoinette's credit, it wasn't all just talk. She took a far greater role in raising her children than most of her predecessors.

She wanted her daughter Marie-Thérèse to be happy. And her reaction to the marriage proposals that did not fail to be offered very early on tells us a lot about her own suffering. When in 1787 her sister Maria Carolina informally asked for the little girl's hand in marriage for her eldest son, heir to the throne of Naples, she declined in favor of the count d'Artois' son. According to Madame Campan, she claimed "that Madame, in being married to her cousin the duke d'Angoulême, would not lose her rank as daughter to the king, and that her position would be much preferable to that of queen in another country; that there was nothing comparable in Europe to the court of France; and that it would be necessary, if she

---

[*]   The wife of their brother Leopold, grand duke of Tuscany, who had at the time – 1788 – sixteen children.

were to be married off to a foreign prince, in order not to expose a French princess to the most cruel regrets, for them to oblige her at the age of seven to leave Versailles and go off to the court that would become her home; that at twelve it would be too late because by then she would remember and compare, which would harm her life forever." Madame Campan saw these reflections only as proof of the admiration and attachment Marie-Antoinette had for France. Yes, of course life in Versailles was more radiant than in Naples. But in refusing to tear her daughter away from her childhood world, we can also see a painful echo of herself being wrenched from her life in Vienna when an adolescent and transplanted into a foreign court far from the happy cocoon of her family. We can also see in this refusal the desire to leave politics out of the matchmaking. She would not do to her daughter what her mother had done to her – turn her into an agent of her country of origin. She wanted to spare her this double burden, and double suffering.

As a good educator she also tried to curb the pride of which the little girl showed signs early on. For "Mousseline," also called "Madame Serious," had an infrequent smile and an acid tongue. In order to rid her of her haughtiness, she was forced to treat little girls of modest rank with respect. She was raised with the daughter of a domestic* who got the same treatment, clothes and entertainments, to remind her that she was not an exceptional being; and since she was very jealous of her things, her mother forced her to share her toys with poor children. But these pedagogical efforts were resisted by the child, no doubt encouraged by Madame Adélaïde and Madame Élisabeth, who judged Marie-Antoinette too insouciant about safeguarding the superiority of their rank. The marquis de Bombelles told an anecdote according to which Vermond was appalled at the indifference the girl showed when her mother fell off a horse: if she had died she would have been glad for then she could have done whatever she liked. Whether the story is true or not we don't know, but we do know that the mother and daughter were not on the same wavelength as we would say nowadays, and didn't understand each other.

On the other hand, and this no doubt made the little girl jealous, Marie-Antoinette adored her two sons. First of all they were boys and therefore had been ardently desired. What's more, they both were very prepossessing, the first by his fragility, the second by his vivacity. As we shall see, they would each cause her terrible suffering.

---

* It has sometimes been wrongly believed that she was Louis XVI's natural daughter, but there isn't the least evidence of this.

For the moment, however, the birth of her children had metamorphosed Marie-Antoinette. They gave her life a meaning it hadn't had. They created a very strong bond between her and her husband. It was not love, but they would both feel just how intense it was when they fought together to protect them. They both loved them in their respective ways, she more demonstrably, he with more reserve, but just as deeply. Perhaps it's regrettable that it took them this long to finally come together in shared feeling. But it would not have been a tragedy had public opinion followed suit. Alas, as far as she was concerned, it was too late. The portraits of Marie-Antoinette as an attentive mother could not erase the image of the flighty scatterbrain gallivanting from party to party without her husband, gad up in feathers, not caring a fiddle for what anyone might think. For marrying her off before she was ready for it, France and Austria were the unwitting architects of this disaster.

CHAPTER 12

THE QUEEN OF TRIANON

In Marie-Antoinette's relationships with others there was that curious mix of puffed-up pride and charming simplicity so often found in sovereigns. But excessive as she was in everything, she carried it to an extreme. She could not bear haughtiness in others. She hated the fact that once Louis XVI was on the throne he allowed his brothers to continue treating him with the same easy manners as formerly and absolved them from paying daily court to him. She became indignant when her sister-in-law Marie-Joséphine got on her high horse and said to her "I may not be queen, but I am made of the same stuff as they." She detested Versailles' titled ladies with honorary positions who kept an eagle eye on their neighbors to make sure no infractions were made to the sacrosanct rules of rank and hierarchy. But her sweet nature returned with her subordinates, who were very attached to her. So that the heavily pregnant artist Madame Vigée-Lebrun need not bend over during a portrait sitting, she quickly picked up the paintbrush fallen from the artist's hand.

She craved simplicity, naturalness and intimacy. She was horrified by the hotel-lobby side of Versailles where everything one did was seen by anyone who happened to be around. Everything from meals to entertainments to promenades and dress were on display for prying eyes. In Vienna people were not so hemmed in by these things, and they especially didn't affect the empress-queen, who organized her life as she saw fit. The young woman shed bitter tears when the countess de Provence accompanied the king's sister Clotilde to the Savoy when she was about to wed the prince of Piedmont. Alas, unlike Marie-Joséphine, she would never again see the places she loved as a child, like the vast Hofburg halls, or Shönbrunn and its gardens. Her little escapes to Paris were more and more disappointing. She therefore attempted to flee the only way she could, by creating her own special haven on the palace grounds.

A deep, instinctive and vital need for privacy coexisted in her along with the fear of boredom that drove her to such foolish dissolute behavior. Even while she was indulging in a whirlwind of pleasures, she was having some very private retreats fitted out. She didn't like her apartments in the chateau, which were too dark and gloomy, and where she had to put up with her ladies-in-waiting. If at least there were a place where she could get away from everyone! She had some doors taken down and others put up. She built partitions and staircases to protect the rooms reserved for her. Everywhere there were keys, locks and bolts. In April 1781 when her Meridian Room was renovated, she had two bronze sash-bolts adorned with her monogram placed on the doors, and forbade access to the library through it, "desiring to be alone when she sees fit, without bothering her staff or being bothered by them." Seeking out greater light and tranquility, she gained a bit more space toward the upper floors, or when she couldn't find better, went deeper into the palace. Summoned one day by her for a private talk, Besenval, who knew the place quite well, was amazed to find her in a little room at roof level which he never even suspected existed. And the young d'Hézecques, wandering in the deserted chateau in 1789, discovered "a whole cluster of little apartments tributary to the queen's, looking out on somber little courtyards "simply furnished with mirrors and wood paneling."

What was she trying to hide? Nothing other than herself, undoubtedly. She remained for a long time the frightened little girl trembling with fear as she concealed the fact that she was writing to her mother, and tucking into her bed the letters she received in return. In this anything but cozy palace where all sorts of people roamed about, she wanted places that were cloistered, hidden, and protected. She increased the number of barriers and prohibitions, even in the reception rooms. A certain Mr. Young visiting France in 1787 wrote that he would have liked to see the queen's apartment, but did not get authorization:

"Is her majesty within?"

"No."

"Why can it not be visited then, as is the king's?"

"Ah, that's another matter, Sir..."

By withdrawing from the public, by slamming the door in its face so to speak, she alienated the immense number of admirers who came to worship the mighty French monarchy at the temple of Versailles. By cutting herself off, she openly defied the rule that a queen must never be alone. And the fact that Louis XV, who shared her fondness for little hideaways deep within the palace, had used them for his love affairs, added fuel to the fires of suspicion. If she wished, she could do the same. Besenval remarked cruelly, "I was astonished not by the queen's desire for so many accommodations, but by her daring to procure them." Thinking that she took advantage of them for dubious ends was just a step away – a step that the pamphleteers had no trouble taking.

But neither the little rooms buried in the bowels of the old chateau nor even the apartment she had furnished on the ground floor after her aunt Sophie's death could rival the amenities of the Petit Trianon, which had its own private gardens.

Trianon, or the great escape

This charming "country home" belonged to her personally. Here she was the mistress of her domain – here everything was "by order of the Queen" – she was free to have the guests she wanted, when she wanted. This was *her* home. She could remodel it according to her fancy and the kind of life she wished to lead there. We mustn't imagine that Trianon emerged full blown at the touch of a magic wand. It evolved and was transformed endlessly right up until the day when the Revolution fixed it forever. And in no other place was Marie-Antoinette's personal stamp so visible. She did not build for all eternity but for her immediate pleasure. Her fretfulness was innate; she didn't take easily to repetitiveness, immobility or monotony. She needed change. She didn't always know exactly what she wanted but she wanted it terribly. And right away. Hers was a lively imagination, less creative than quick to seize upon whatever vogue was in the air; she was of an imperious impatience that demanded instant gratification. She was so changeable that she was capable of stopping works as soon as they'd started or of turning her back on an idea that had enchanted her the day before. She had a royal disdain, at least in the beginning, for the cost and human effort involved. Nothing was too good for her, and little did it matter that the craftsmen worked round the clock at weaving their cloth or sculpting their wood to meet her deadlines. For the spoiled child that she had never ceased to be, Trianon was like one of her toys – a doll's house or a toy farm – whose bits and pieces could be changed and added to continually, a place fitted out just so, where little girls could create a world of their own and dream of being grown-ups.

At first Marie-Antoinette did not appreciate just how right Trianon was for fulfilling her desire for escape. In the beginning she used the elegant pavilion built for Madame de Pompadour as it was originally intended – as a nice place to stroll to, offering shelter from the sun or the rain; a stopping place for a little rest where you could find all the refreshments you needed for a little collation, perhaps even a supper. The young queen hardly went near the building. She was happy enough just to place around it a few *chinoiseries*, notably a sort of merry-go-round, with dragons to carry the gentlemen and peacocks for the ladies. Her efforts were initially devoted to the garden. She dared not dismantle Louis XV's work entirely, and kept an expanse of French gardens on the side leading to the Grand Trianon. But as fashion dictated, her preference went toward English gardens, reputed to reproduce nature's disorder but whose deficiencies one didn't hesitate to artfully disguise. The landscaping, conceived by the queen's favorite architect Richard Mique and carried out by the king's gardeners the Richard brothers, could not be more different from Le Nôtre's noble perspectives. He had all sorts of ideas and placed as many "picturesque" elements as possible in a confined space. They were organized in such a way that anyone strolling amongst them was led from one surprise to another. As the duke de Croÿ wrote, "I thought I was mad or dreaming when I found rather high mountains, a rocky outcropping and a brook where once had been the great heated greenhouse, which was the most scientific and expensive in Europe. Never have two acres of land changed as much, nor at so high a cost." And Croÿ didn't even know about the number of "follies" the queen had the good taste to discard from among those proposed to her. There was no hermitage. She made do with the little chapel put up by Louis XV, but she did have a clock added. No ruins either. Despite the fashionable paintings of Hubert Robert, she didn't like anything that suggested decrepitude. But one of the twin hills had at its summit an elegant belvedere, and on the little island placed in the middle of the brook, awash in a jumble of flowers, there was a Temple of Love for which Bouchardon sculpted the statue of the young god Cupid carving from Hercules' mace the bow he would use to pierce hearts.

In this landscape designed to be admired there was a telling detail that demonstrates Marie-Antoinette's striking need for seclusion – the famous Grotto nestled in a sort of depression between the rocky outcropping and Snail Mountain. Of course artificial grottos were nothing new. The park of Versailles itself had a famous one, the Thetis grotto, built in 1664-1666, but it was demolished during the construction of the north wing. This new grotto, however, aside from the fact that it was meant to seem like a natural crevice, was singularly protected from intruders. When you came from the terrace you went down a few steps cut into the rock and came upon an iron gate to which only the queen had the key. According to Hézecques, "The grotto was so dark that your eyes, at first blinded, needed time to adjust and make out what was in it. Entirely moss-covered, it was cooled by a stream of water that flowed through it. A bed, equally lined in moss, invited you to rest... A crevice that opened up at the head of the bed afforded a view of the whole plain and allowed you to detect in the distance anyone who might want to approach this mysterious hideaway." Another opening, looking out on the plain on the opposite side and closed by a trellised gate, allowed its occupants an emergency exit. Why such an arrangement? No, the grotto was not built to shelter the queen's supposed amours; it was included in the initial plans for the garden's refurbishment back when they ascended the throne. Never mind the fact that humidity made the place barely usable, even during the hottest weather, for someone so subject to catching the flu! So what purpose did this grotto serve? None, maybe. Perhaps it was a mere decoration, but how revealing it was of Marie-Antoinette's obsessions! Little did it matter if the young woman went there or not, the point was that the grotto was locked closed. At the heart of an area generally closed to the public but which must sometimes be opened of a Sunday or holiday, it was a concealed place, forbidden to all, symbol of a protected intimacy, of a preserved identity, a place where one could imagine returning to life's source, the significance of which psychoanalysis has no trouble deciphering.

From holiday decor to life setting

When Marie-Antoinette's priority was to build up the gardens, she was not thinking of using it for overnight stays. As queen she was supposed to live in the chateau where the king resided. She could little afford to risk deserting him, because at the time she and her husband were not on good terms; it was one thing to have separate beds, but separate dwellings quite another! She used her new domain for receiving guests. At Trianon it was she who personally invited her guests, not in the name of the king, but of her own accord: a subtle way of showing her power and demonstrating his trust in her. The parties she gave there remain famous to this day. The first, on September 3, 1777 held to honor Louis XVI for the inauguration of the garden, was inspired by one of Madame de Montespan's parties. They reproduced for it a fair in which the ladies of the court managed the stalls. Marie-

Antoinette quite enjoyed running a lemonade stand. There were others, one for Joseph II on his second visit in 1781; then in the years that followed for the Russian heirs the grand duke Paul and his wife; for the English ambassador; and the king of Sweden. All of them ended with a "nocturne." Torches in the gullies and little lanterns sprinkled through the woods gave off a gentle light, "like moonlight," said Grimm, "or the first glow of sunlight at dawn," a sort of luminous haze, surreal, magical, against which the silhouette of the Temple of Love could be discerned.

Unlike the parties given in the Versailles park, which were open to the public, Marie-Antoinette's were by invitation only. But gatecrashers managed to sneak in under the cover of darkness. At the gates preventing access to the grounds, the watchmen were not above having a gold coin slipped into their hand for the purpose. So it was that one evening Marie-Antoinette made out against the green grass the splash of red stocking, the owner of which the count d'Artois told her was the cardinal de Rohan – the first almoner whom she held in unyielding contempt, and of course had not invited. For one excluded individual whose name history has retained, how many others nursed their grievances, cursing the proud young woman who cast them out of her paradise?

But Trianon did not generally don its gala array. Big parties were expensive, very expensive, and the war in America was weighing heavily on finances. It is not sure either that Marie-Antoinette even wished to have more of these big showy events. She learned when the measles had forced her to stay away from her husband that the little chateau could be more fully lived in. Any excuse was good for almost daily trips there in whatever season. The smallest glimmer of sunshine placed on alert Bonnefoy du Plan, the concierge in charge of her house in the fields, because he knew that it took her no more than twelve minutes to get there on foot. And around one-thirty the dining services that prepared the meals at Versailles only had fifteen minutes to rush the food onto wagons, for they were dining today at Trianon, where the common rooms included a vast kitchen and reheating facilities. The table could be set, as Marie-Antoinette had ordered for Trianon a sumptuous dinner service bearing her monogram. But Bonnefoy du Plan had a big worry: he only had rectangular tablecloths whereas the tables there were round.

When financial difficulties forced the king to reduce the number of court displacements to his other chateaux, she took to living at Trianon throughout the warmest months. Far from opposing this, the king encouraged it. He had found a convenient *modus vivendi*. He never slept there, even though a bedroom had been furnished for him. But he came unannounced sometimes to his wife's bed when she woke up in the morning. During the day he went back and forth between the two chateaux as his activities permitted, happily showed up again in the evening for supper and went back to his usual bedchamber between eleven and midnight. He rather liked the gentle mood of the place and sometimes caught a little nap on a shaded bench. One day a prankster took advantage of his nap to replace the hunting treatise he was reading with a volume – illustrated! – of Aretino*. In fact, this to-and-fro between the chateau and Trianon suited him. The short distance between them was enough to keep the queen out of his hair. The more she got involved in the affairs of her little private kingdom, the less she bothered with the real one, making the king and his ministers' life a bit easier. Especially as for a few years she had been totally absorbed by her work organizing her little theatre.

Trianon's little theatre

Aside from the official theatrical performances given three evenings a week at court, Marie-Antoinette wanted her own private theatre. From 1776 to 1780 she used the *Orangerie de Trianon*, adapted with uneven success by the *Menus-Plaisirs* for shows by Parisian troops invited to perform before a select group of royal family members and friends. But she wanted a real theatre all her own, with a vast backstage area and above all machinery. The works, assigned to Richard Mique, lasted two years. The theatre was inaugurated on the first of June 1780. With its truncated oval layout and curved vault it looked like a smaller version of the great opera house of Versailles built by Gabriel. They saved money on the decor, sometimes using cardboard instead of wood for sculptures, and mixing copper with gold for the gilding, but they didn't skimp on the machinery or on the hangings, draperies or the trimmings of a blue and white color scheme. Care was taken to keep the sets the same size as those at Fontainebleau and Choisy so that they could be reused. In this charming little theatre, conceived by and for her, to her own tastes, she would seek the applause that Paris was refusing her. Not in her box, but on stage, as an actress, just like in the good old days of her childhood and adolescence.

In this too she wasn't original, happily following the vogue for

---

* *Translator's note: Pietro Aretino was a 16th century Italian playwright noted for his pornographic works.*

private theatres, called *théâtre de société*, that flourished throughout the century. She threw herself into it with ardor, the way she did everything. Mercy wrote in September of 1780, "For a month now, all her efforts have been devoted to the sole and unique purpose of preparing two little performances for the Trianon theatre... The time needed to learn the lines, and devoted to frequent rehearsals, plus other related details, was more than enough to fill her days." Marie-Antoinette liked comedy, particularly sweet comic operas with a sentimental love story in a pastoral setting. Their easy-to-sing arias suited her voice of modest range, whose limits she recognized. She was fond of the roles of young female leads like shepherdesses or ingénues, the other roles being distributed among the members of her little troop. She was Colette in Jean-Jacques Rousseau's "The Village Devine;" Rosine in Beaumarchais' "The Barber of Seville," just to mention the two best-known works. About her performing ability, reviews were mixed. Most people praised it, even if some stage-whispered that her performance was "a royal mess." For an amateur theatre, it seemed that their performances were estimable, even if they couldn't compare with the professional actors who also played there. Such as it was, this little entertainment was agreeable to the king, the principal and sometimes only spectator, who was obviously pleased at his wife's performances, and went backstage between acts to help her with her toilette. He much preferred watching her act or sing to seeing her waste vast sums of money at pharaoh. Was he aware of the ill effects of all this on public opinion?

It could be said that women everywhere act on stage. True, but a queen? Was it compatible with her image to be seen on stage, playing peasant girls or soubrettes that were so at odds with a queen's station in life? Was it seemly to seek the public's applause, even if the audience was made up of your family? Was something that could be tolerated in a young archduchess or perhaps even a dauphine acceptable in a sovereign? In running her little theatre, Marie-Antoinette emulated not Marie Leszczynska but Madame de Pompadour. What is more, in wanting to keep her theatre private, she prevented many important people from attending, even though their positions theoretically entitled them to. Such was the case of Madame de Lamballe, superintendent of her household, excluded because the queen found it hard to tolerate her evident inability to carry out her functions and her incessant recriminations against Madame de Polignac. Many others too were denied admittance to the performances. The few invitations extended made more people envious than happy. When it was noticed how disheartening it was for actors to play before a near-empty house, what did they think up to fill it? Rather than opening the doors to those who felt entitled to it, service personnel and their families were installed, like extras hired to fill up the audience rather than the stage, hardly more than mannequins. Anything just to keep things intimate, sheltered from the gaze of others. What is more, as Philippe Beaussant pointed out, the golden age of the queen's little theatre coincided with the years of penury produced by the American war. The autumnal visit to Fontainebleau was cancelled for economic reasons, thus putting a halt to the brilliant theatrical season that was one of its great attractions. Left at Versailles, the courtiers were deprived of the opera for want of an adequate theatre*. Trianon's theatre on the other hand was equipped to produce operas; but it was closed to them. Marie-Antoinette was bold enough, when she was not on stage herself, to offer *Iphigenia*, *Zémir and Azor* and *Dardanus*. How could they not feel doubly cheated?

The joys of private life

Marie-Antoinette's passion for acting hardly lasted five years, from 1780 to 1785. As with everything else, she got bored with it. Her stage appearances gradually petered out. She sought other ways to distract herself and escape.

For a long time her need for intimacy balanced out her desire to shine. The new art of living that she brought to Trianon owed much to the rage for a return to nature, of which *La Nouvelle Héloïse* was the purest expression – a trend that was none other than an avatar of the phenomenon that we know today as ecology. This striving for simplicity went hand in hand with her horror of all the pomp of Versailles, and it gave her the extra advantage of showing her good intention of keeping expenses down. Marie-Antoinette didn't go in for the grand scheme. She knew nothing about architecture; her taste went toward decorating. She kept the dining room decor that Gabriel designed for Madame du Barry: garlands of roses where little cupids romp, with pyramids of fruit, grape and olive branches. In the little salon that she made into a billiard room when she became enamored of the game, masks, reed pipes and trowels evoke the joys of country living. On the walls of the large salon, whose woodwork offered a harmonious blend of white and gold

---

* Using Gabriel's large theatre was so expensive that it was reserved for special occasions, and the little theatre in the Court of the Princes was not adapted for operatic productions.

against a pale-green background, humble wild flowers mingled with the royal lilies. The most private rooms that came next were on a mezzanine to which a lowered ceiling gave a more intimate feeling. In the bedroom the woodwork, delicately decorated with pastoral flora, remained much as she found it; all she did was cover the walls with muslin enhanced by vividly colored embroidery. There she kept sheltered from view, as a sort of *memento mori*, a few melancholy family portraits at odds with the gaiety of the rest of the decor: in them her brothers and sisters were depicted as members of religious orders digging their graves.

There were flowers everywhere: freshly cut in bouquets in vases, in porcelain on the park lanterns, and painted, sculpted or embroidered on the walls, furniture and quilts. The colors were subdued blues and greens. There was a lot of white, and a bit too many festoons, arabesques and ribbons for those of more sober tastes. The place was Marie-Antoinette's through and through, and perfectly reflected the life she strove to live there.

At Trianon the service personnel was reduced to a minimum, and was purely functional – two or three chambermaids, one or two guards. The Versailles ladies didn't sleep there. They came to supper only on Wednesdays and Saturdays, the "palace days." The only one the queen kept with her was Madame de Polignac, housed in the rooms on the third floor where she would soon furnish a space for her children. There was no one there to watch as she woke up, no ceremonial dressing. She required a minimum of help getting dressed. No visits, no friends; the mornings belonged to her alone. The guests arrived for dinner around one o'clock. Her young sister-in-law Madame Élisabeth often joined her usual little group, and now and again the countess de Provence. Her guests would spend the afternoon with her and stay for the evening meal before going back to their respective lodgings in the big chateau. Sartorial extravagance was out of place here. "Come dressed for the country, no fuss," she instructed her guests. She set the example in the hot weather by wearing a light dress of white batiste that had a large flounce at the neckline, just a simple belt to tuck in the waistline, and vast, flowing sleeves gathered in three places. She would tie a light muslin fichu over her robe when it was called for, and on her head she wore a straw hat with a ribbon.

To do away with the burdensome presence of domestics at mealtime, the dumbwaiter invented at the time of Louis XV was brought back. It would emerge laden with food from below and disappear into the depths when you wanted it to, at which point a daisy with silver petals would appear to cover it up. No rank, no protocol, no constraint. The queen left her friends free to come and go as they pleased and to choose how best to amuse themselves. "She had brought there some of the pastimes from the old chateau," Madame Campan tells us, but when "she entered the room the ladies didn't have to abandon their pianoforte or their tapestry frames and the men didn't interrupt their billiard game or backgammon." They chatted and gambled, in moderation, for she abandoned pharaoh a bit when she took up billiards. They played music, the queen on the clavichord, Polastron on the violin, and Vaudreuil on the flute. They strolled or played children's games like blind man's bluff. With a fondness for daredevil antics, the count d'Artois delighted his friends with a tightrope-walking act that he'd rehearsed under the guidance of a professional. In the evenings they would sit in a circle on the little island of the Temple of Love to enjoy the cool air and watch the darkness gather.

"You'd think you were a hundred leagues from the court," said the prince de Ligne, off in some part of the country inhabited by ordinary people. She herself liked to say, "Here, I am no longer the queen; I am *me*." But although she had rejected Versailles protocol, she imposed her own rules, which were less restrictive but comprised tacitly accepted limits. She played at no longer being the queen; but she would be very upset if *you* forgot the fact. There was a line that must not be crossed; a line that says there's a freedom here that looks genuine, but you'd better not overstep the bounds. When Madame de Polignac's friends, notably Vaudreuil, behaved with too much familiarity, the magic spell of the little group would be broken. A queen could never completely escape from her condition – unless she obliterated herself and was reborn as someone else, which at least at a symbolic level she tried to do.

Marie-Antoinette was heard to say, with an intensity that surprised people, "I am no longer queen; I am no longer anything." Perhaps it was in this attempt to be cut off from the world and become nothing, or someone else, or even several others, that she had an odd array of mirrors installed in the boudoir next to her bedroom. A pulley system allowed these mirrors to rise up along the walls to cover the windows, creating an environment completely closed off from the world, like the grotto, but where her image by shimmering candlelight was multiplied and metamorphosed as if she were herself in a kaleidoscope. She liked this phantasmagorical "room of moving mirrors" so much that she had an identical one made for Fontainebleau. It provided her with a little playhouse for herself alone, ever accessible, where she could play and watch herself play at the same time.

Given her deep-seated instability, it is not surprising that the life of a country chatelaine did not fulfill her. Trianon's interior didn't afford enough space to remodel and redecorate. And in any case, the little chateau was still a chateau – not simple enough, not rustic enough, and not natural enough.

Bucolic reverie

"Draw me a village," psychologists tell children when they want to sound them out. For Marie-Antoinette it was not enough to draw one, she made one rise out of the ground. It was not really a village but a hamlet; a place apart, an offshoot of the Petit Trianon, which took its principal attributes and consciously played them up to make the place feel more casual and folksy. In 1783 Richard Mique got back to work again. So that he was always on hand, Marie-Antoinette set him up on the second floor in the Billiards House. As one structure was added after another, the works were spread out over four years. As with the Petit Trianon, they would begin by remodeling the grounds. A brook was not enough, a pond had to be added, more aristocratically christened the *grand lac*. On a little promontory a watchtower was built, called Marleborough's Tower, because the signing of the peace with England had given new life to Anglo-mania, and the old folksong was back in fashion. The good Madame Poitrine, the dauphin's wet nurse, would rock him to sleep to the tune of "Marlborough Goes Off to War" and "The Lady to the Tower Mounts." The tower's exterior staircase was dotted with wallflowers and geraniums, giving it a look of an aerial flowerbed. At its bottom fishing gear was laid out, for the lake had been filled with carp, which would flourish, and pike, which wouldn't. There were two dairies, one for producing milk and cheese, and the other where visitors were treated to a buffet of selected dairy products. A bit farther on there was a barn that could double as a dance hall, just like in a real village. On the farm there were cattle-sheds that sheltered the livestock: cows, calves, goats and sheep. If a billy goat had to be replaced, Marie-Antoinette wanted it to be "pure white and sweet-natured." Her requirements concerning the bull have not come down to us. Nearby there were a chicken coop and a dovecote, a vast vegetable garden, the gardener's house and the linen closet; on the little river was a mill. The west side of the lake was taken up by buildings that the sovereign reserved for herself: a pavilion in two parts, one called Billiards House, and the other The Queen's House, linked on the ground and second floors by an openwork gallery. In the back there were a little garden and common rooms – a big kitchen, work areas and a drying room – and farther along a tiny, isolated salon, called the boudoir or the queen's little house.

Marie-Antoinette didn't consider the hamlet a place to live – it had no bedrooms – but a place to stroll and dine with her friends. Initially the farm, dairy, mill and chicken coop were to be just picturesque places that added a rustic note to the landscape, conceived for escapes into country living. Reed or thatched roofing, dovecotes, roughcast walls cleverly aged with artificial cracks; in short, the hamlet was in the "Norman village" style that passed for exotic. Here again, the young woman espoused the current fashions. There were other examples here and there, for instance the prince de Condé's park in Chantilly, where what appeared to be shacks surprisingly housed luxurious rooms, seen by no one except the prince's guests. At the Trianon, however, Marie-Antoinette very quickly got caught up in the fantasy, and went a step farther. To keep up a farm you must have a farmer, so in the summer of 1785, Valy Bussard was brought from the Touraine with his wife and two children. To help him with his work she hired a team of gardeners, two herdsmen, a mole-catcher and a rat-catcher, and a few other servants of both sexes. She did not dress up as a shepherdess, nor did she assign various village functions to her friends. She was happy enough just to see that the animals were fed, the cows milked, that the wheel on the mill was turning, perhaps even well enough to grind some grain. In other words, it should actually function like a real farm.

This was something quite new. The hamlet was a toy, but a living toy, where her need for activity could be continually satisfied. At the risk of complicating things, she oversaw the works, talked with the laborers, and corrected plans. In her efforts to manage her domain, she encountered nature's resistance in real problems: plants grew or festered, animals were born and died, the earth rendered its bounty to a greater or lesser degree, and sometimes men quarreled. During her morning visits she questioned the farmer, gauged results, dealt with requests, enquired about the health of this one or that one. This was much more captivating than giving orders to the *Menus-Plaisirs* for a stage set and having a fit when it was not ready in time. They presented their difficulties to her, and their quarrels, and she settled the matter, much like a country squire of old dispensing justice. In this period when the deficit cast a pall on everyone, she liked to think that she was doing her part in reducing it by living off what her farm produced. Anticipating our organic farming, she was very proud that at her table she served chickens from her coop, pigeons from her dovecotes, fish from her lake, cheese from her dairy, and fresh produce from her garden, reputed to be better than elsewhere; and everyone made a fuss over how delicious it all was, even if the carp smelled a bit of swamp bottom.

Was all this childish, make-believe, futile and laughable? Assuredly, but Marie-Antoinette at nearly thirty years of age was not entirely grown up yet. The child in her found here a kingdom to her own specifications, a kingdom in which men and things obeyed her, and of which she was the sole and unique sovereign. If she could not be a Maria Theresa reigning over Austria, Bohemia and Hungary, she could at least reign over her little hamlet. Why did they try to convince her that she was born to govern over France? She was never happier with Trianon than during those crucial years when she was becoming aware of her political ineptitude. What she was building was fragile, ephemeral? Yes, but she feared the future. In that she shared the anxiety of a whole generation, which pushed the art of living to extremes of refinement, even while beneath their feet rumbled the first tremors of the cataclysm that would destroy them.

The queen and the others

Marie-Antoinette's was not an isolated case. Other princesses and great ladies wanted their country retreat in which to revel in a supposed return to nature. But people were willing to accept in others – Mesdames aunts, the countess de Provence, and Madame Élisabeth for example – what they did not tolerate in the queen. Because they dared criticize his wife's misdeeds too sharply, the king rusticated his aunts to their Bellevue estates, where they fell in love with this charming home, especially the park, and where they too played at being gardeners and farmhands. Madame Victoire recounted, "I spent the entire night of Thursday to Friday in the garden. Oh, how beautiful the sun was as it rose, and how beautiful the weather! I finally went to bed at eight o'clock in the morning, having breakfasted on an excellent onion soup and a cup of coffee with cream... I really savored the lovely weather, the beautiful moon, the dawn and its beautiful sun, and then my cows, sheep and poultry." Madame Adélaïde roamed all over the estate with her big white griffon Vizir at her side, followed by two valets whose job it was to put the animal in a canvas bag each time they came across some mud in their path to prevent its getting dirty. Mesdames' affable but passé little court welcomed visitors. These fierce guardians of protocol at Versailles happily let things go a bit in their new home. People could expect an unaffected welcome. And since one could also expect fine dining at their table, nephews and nieces willingly came to dinner, according to Madame de Boigne, with hardly any prior warning. For the count de Provence they told the cook to improve the menu a bit. "For the others, no special instructions were given, not even for the king, who had a hearty appetite but was not at all as interested in fine dining as his brother." Since none of the sisters liked fish, they never served it, and sniffed at their male guests who sipped a barely tolerated glass of wine.

They went to court as little as decency allowed, making Bellevue something of a primary residence. Thus, they needed a second home, even more countrified than this one. This was the chateau of Louvois in the Champagne region. Their ladies-in-waiting did not want to be outdone. Madame Adélaïde never stopped arguing with hers, the imperious and tyrannical countess de Narbonne, but couldn't do without her. She had her granted in the canton of Craonne, near Laon, the La Bove estates. When Mesdames were staying at Louvois they would pay the countess de Narbonne regular neighborly visits, especially at grape-harvest time, so they could dabble in winemaking. In order to facilitate these visits the steward had a road built between Laon and La Bove and given the name *Chemin des Dames*, a name that remains to this day. Nowadays, do those who visit the scene of one of the greatest hecatombs of World War I know who these ladies were?

These three old maids, soon to be reduced to two by the death of Madame Sophie, were able to live their private lives as they pleased, planting their vegetables or feeding their foul, or spending the night in their garden to greet the first rays of the rising sun, without anyone finding fault with them. It might be objected that they were of a goodly age, and therefore more free to choose. This is true, but other younger princesses also enjoyed the pleasures of their own lands, without people questioning their cost or the use they made of them.

Abandoned by her husband who never consummated their marriage and on bad terms with the queen, the countess de Provence was bored and resentful at court. In 1781, she bought at the gates of Versailles in a parcel of land called Montreuil, a little property that she furnished lovingly, blending usefulness and comfort. There she had two vegetable plots near grounds landscaped in accordance with the tastes of the times. There was a stream branching out in many directions with little wooden bridges to cross its rivulets, two islands, one with a hermitage and the other a thatched cottage, a Chinese pavilion and a music kiosk. There would soon be added a hill, a tower, and of course a hamlet with farm, cowshed, sheep-pen, chicken coop, dairy and dovecote. Marie-Joséphine would spend her days feeding her animals, overseeing the gardeners and using nets to catch the little birds needed for her recipes. In the evening she would return to Versailles laden down with enormous bouquets and baskets full of vegetables and fragrant herbs.

The same year, the prince de Guéménée's bankruptcy enabled Louis XVI to acquire in the same area a domain for his young sister Élisabeth. He had Marie-Antoinette notify her of his decision: "You are mistress of the house here; this is your Trianon. The king, who takes great pleasure in giving it to you, has given me the pleasure of informing you." The narrowness of the garden was made up for by the view out over the neighbors' gardens. Even so, they found room to set up the inevitable farm, with cows to nourish needy children and old folks. Madame Élisabeth's charity inspired an original idea at odds with the usual frivolity of all these small-scale Trianons. She set up a dispensary where her neighbor the doctor and herbalist Le Monnier gave free care to all and sundry.

Why was Marie-Antoinette criticized for a lifestyle that was acceptable in her sisters-in-law? Purely because she was the queen, and all eyes turned toward her. The public knew virtually nothing about Bellevue or Montreuil, and they didn't care. Let princesses play at being farm lasses. But the queen must live up to the image the public has of her. She is not a private individual. Just because they weigh heavily on her, she cannot shake off the grandeur, the dignity and the splendor of her condition. How dare she imitate – and from such a lofty height – the life of the peasantry instead of doing her job as queen? This willingness to shirk the servitude of her state shocked those who could not escape their own. To have spent so much money on making the hamlet seem like a poor and lowly place was an insult to the poor and lowly. Since she had the wherewithal, she should have made a "ritzy" place. The polemics surrounding the cost of Trianon that would fill the dossiers against her during her trial reveal a certain frame of mind. Yes, redoing the gardens and building the hamlet were expensive, a lot more than the estimates foresaw; but they were infinitely less costly than other buildings the monarchy had erected over the centuries. They were an expensive indulgence, not a financial black hole. But that is precisely why they could not be forgiven: they were passing fancies, not enduring legacies. They entailed expenses that were "at once too visible and too private," according to P. Verlet, in a word "not monarchical enough." The people liked their kings to build prestigious edifices, not "follies."

What is more, they disapproved of the fact that the initiative was left to Marie-Antoinette for her personal ends. She thus inherited the animosity that had formerly been reserved for Louis XV's spoiled favorites, but with added resentment, because tradition dictated that the queen must possess nothing in her own right. Her obstinate insistence on putting her monogram on everything, on giving orders in her own name, on living a life of her own apart from her husband, or loudly voicing her claim that "this is *my* home here," made her suspect in the eyes of the people. Maria Theresa sensed this when she wrote to Mercy about Trianon, "I cannot approve of the queen sleeping there without the king," because she thus could sleep with someone else if she so desired, and above all because she seemed to be brazenly distancing herself from her husband. And since very few people knew that he joined her in her bedroom in the morning, their apparent separation opened the door to all sorts of calumny.

At Trianon it seemed that Marie-Antoinette was intentionally violating custom. A queen must be a queen, not a country chatelaine. She must dress in brilliant colors, not in white "like a chambermaid." She must dress in silk, to keep the Lyon silk manufacturers working, not in linen, which favored the Low Countries. She must hold court, not desert it; show herself to her people, not lock herself behind a gate. In short, a queen of France cannot and must not have an independent existence – at least during her husband's lifetime. Marie-Antoinette would pay a very high price for having preferred to be the queen of Trianon rather than the spouse of the king of France.

CHAPTER 13

AXEL VON FERSEN

"Oh, he's an old acquaintance," the queen exclaimed on August 25, 1778 when the Swedish ambassador to Paris Creutz introduced to her a young compatriot who had just returned from an extended visit to his family. She had not forgotten the handsome cavalier with whom, four and a half years earlier while she was still dauphine, she had bantered for a good quarter of an hour at the Opera ball from behind the safety of a mask. In marked contrast to the silence of the other members of the royal family, this flattering reception did not go unnoticed, and the young man, who was very proud, wrote about it the very next day in a letter to his father.

During the days that followed, favors came showering down on Axel von Fersen. The queen had him informed that he would be welcome in her apartments on gambling evenings. He would write again, "She is the prettiest and the most amiable princess I know. She was good enough to enquire about me often; she asked Creutz why I hadn't come to her session on Sunday, and having learned that I came on a day when there were no games, she rather excused herself for it." After a short absence – to go to Normandy to tour a military camp – he was back in Versailles, in regular attendance at Marie-Antoinette's table, where she always had time for a few kind words with him. In November she succumbed to a whim – she would like to see him in Swedish national dress. Even though he did his best not to arrive when there were many people about, he made quite a splash. The costume in question, the creation of the extravagant Gustav III, had many variations, none of them exactly inconspicuous. But everything looked good on Axel. A white tunic opening onto a blue doublet, form-fitting chamois breeches, silk stockings with blue garters, "Hungarian style" boots, a black shako with a blue and yellow aigrette, gold belt, ornamental short sword with a gilded hilt, all of it enhanced his tall and slender good looks. With his slightly tanned complexion and his big dark eyes under thick black eyebrows inherited from a distant maternal Gascon ancestor, he was the picture of a hero right out of a novel. But not a French novel, for according to the duke de Lévis, with his seriousness and reserve, he was different from France's fashionable young men, lacking as he did their impertinence and zest. "He was one of the handsomest men I've ever seen," said the count de Tilly, "although of a cold appearance that women don't detest, if there's hope of breathing warmth into it."

Son of a great Swedish lord

The young man was the scion of an ancient and powerful family of the highest Swedish nobility. His father, the worthy and respected Field Marshal and Senator Fersen, controlled a considerable fortune in which the family's traditional real-estate revenue was fleshed out by industrial and commercial income – iron mines in Finland and stocks in the East India Company. The elder Fersen was one of those men of great culture, a French speaker as they all were in the 18th century, very attached to his own country but very European too, free-thinking and above the common run of prejudice, recognizing no other morality than that of honor, a very exacting morality at that. The lukewarm Lutheran faith of his family veered in him toward deism. Imprisoned following the revolt against Gustav III, and believing he might be executed, he would write a farewell letter where he declared himself ready to justify his actions before "The Being of Beings." It would surprise no one therefore that for his son's journey abroad he would program a visit to the illustrious patriarch of Ferney, Voltaire himself, although we cannot ascribe to him any liberal sentiments for all that. His fondness for freedom did not go beyond the notion of it shared by others of his social class. If he had been king, he would have made a remarkable enlightened despot like Frederick II or Joseph II. But he wasn't king, and he had to deal with the erratic Gustav III, to whom his inviolable monarchic convictions obliged him to remain faithful.

A word about the political situation in Sweden is called for here, because it enables us to better understand Axel's reaction to the French Revolution. In reality the country was governed by a caste of nobles with a large majority in the Diet who held the king under tight rein. Senator Fersen was the heart and soul of this party, called the "Hats," a faction of noblemen and Francophiles who had always won out over their opponents, the "Bonnets," who were closer to the people and partial to an alliance with Russia. But in 1772 Gustav III satisfied neither faction when he carried out the equivalent of a "4th of August night," (when in 1789 the French nobles' privileges would be abolished), opening employment to everyone. In crushing the nobles' power the Swedish king ensured his own. However, he was careful not to get the senator's back up. The latter had lost the most from this coup d'état, but he was still dangerous. All the same, he fell prudently back into line. They each had to humor the other, but their entente was not smooth. At the time Fersen the younger, who thought of himself as more open than his father, applauded this bloodless coup that could make the people happy without tears or bloodshed being spilled. Nonetheless, with every fiber of his being he remained faithful to an aristocratic conception of society. We shall see later how much he was chained to the preconceived notions of his class of origin. For the time being, Gustav III deemed him useful and supported him in the conflict over his future that pitted him against his father.

His future consisted of a career and marriage to a handsomely endowed damsel. Nothing if not a realist, Axel enthusiastically subscribed to the idea. That is not where discord lay. The senator considered his eldest son to be his designated successor. He wanted him to settle down in Sweden and perpetuate the tradition that granted the Fersen heir an eminent role in his country's affairs. He didn't trifle with principles. He maintained patriarchal authority on his two sons and two daughters, at one point forcing Sophie into a distasteful marriage. Although he loved his second son Fabian very much, he felt that the first place must go to Axel. He noted with displeasure that the grand tour lasting four years gave his son a taste for countries where the climate was milder, the mood more lively, and the cultural life richer, and that he had absolutely no desire to return home. How could he get him to leave France for the frosty north? When appealing to his sentiments didn't work, he tightened the purse strings. But Axel held firm.

On the marriage front, he had hovered around a charming young widow, Madame de Matignon, daughter of the marquis de Breteuil, with whom he hoped to settle in France. But she refused to remarry. On his behalf, Senator Fersen asked the hand of a rich English woman of Swedish origins, Catherine Leyel. He obediently went off to see her in London, found in her every good quality, and forced himself to play the role of "the most passionate lover." He deplored the paternal miserliness that prevented him from buying the fashionable carriage indispensable for wooing her. Did the banker in Mr. Leyel find the Fersens too parsimonious? Did the young lady have doubts about the sincerity of the love he feigned for her? She asked concrete questions: where would the young couple live? Why in Sweden of course, in one of the family castles. So she declared that she did not wish to leave her family or country. He himself had understood that marriage would oblige him to return to the fold, and at twenty-three years of age wasn't really ready to settle down. His idea of married life did not of course include the necessity of being a faithful husband, but the burden of having a wife and children didn't appeal to him. He wasn't able to hide how happy he was at Miss Leyel's refusal: "I did everything I could to win her, more to please you, my dear father, than from any inclination on my part; I did not succeed, and I admit to you that I was rather glad of it as soon as I found out that you would consent to letting me go to war."

As far as careers go, he had only two choices: soldier or diplomat. He would certainly have liked to be an ambassador, as long as it was in Paris. Alas, the post occupied by Creutz was virtually promised to the baron de Staël, because of his age and experience. The young Fersen had to give up the idea, but he never gave up a deep resentment against poor de Staël. That left a military career, just the thing for a man of his station in life. Without ever even having seen a proper soldier or been under fire, he had already risen in his country's hierarchy. But Sweden, no longer basking in its past glories, was in no state to offer him an opportunity to carve out any legends on the battlefield. No one would blame him for dedicating his sword to the service of some foreign power. While traveling through Germany he had admired how the Prussians trained their military. But the king of Prussia wanted nothing to do with Swedes. So much the better; he'd offer his services to France. Hadn't his father shown the way? For ten years Fersen the elder had commanded a regiment bearing his name in the service of Louis XV. He therefore worked at getting a good position in a French unit. He seemed to choose his moment well: France was at war with England again. But he was unfortunately not the only one dreaming of glory; all the young men were doing the same. For want of better, he managed to get enlisted with troops that were to land on the British coast. But his stay in Le Havre did not last long, because the plan was aborted. Six months would be wiled away in hesitation and uncertainty before he could take the decisive step. At last he was able to join in with the cream of the French aristocracy, who were all vying for the honor of flying to the rescue of the American colonists in revolt. It would be across the Atlantic that he would first take up arms.

But the decision did not come from him alone; it was practically forced on him by Marie-Antoinette's imprudent behavior.

The heart leaps

When the queen had recognized Fersen as "an old acquaintance" at the end of August 1778, she was five months pregnant. "Her pregnancy is advanced and is quite noticeable," he observed. So many pleasures were denied her. It's hardly surprising that she jumped at anything that could break the monotony at Versailles just by being new. The Swedes were in fashion that autumn and Fersen was only one of them, the handsomest assuredly, but not the most prestigious. Soon court life was suspended by the birth of Madame Royale on December 20th. It was just when the young queen was rushing headlong into her pleasures again that she fell for Fersen. She invited him to all her parties, officially anointed him her dancing partner for the Opera balls, and – an unheard of privilege – introduced him to the suppers of the inner circle. For a whole year she dragged him along with her as her favorite. Playing on his foreignness, he avoided being sucked into her little group of intimates; he didn't like their cattiness and superficiality, and knew he would not fit in. The group at first was irritated, but made the best of it. They consoled themselves with the idea that since the Swede had no ambitious family to foster he would not be much of a threat to their pensions, gratifications and other hefty cash advantages. Besides, all the men who hovered around Marie-Antoinette were more or less in love with her, and relieved to see that an outsider won her heart rather than a member of her little set. But the tongues at court started to wag for good and earnest.

It's not the first time in French history that a queen fell in love with someone other than her husband. Fifty years before, the stillborn idyll between Anne of Austria and the duke of Buckingham was bandied from pillar to post. But in the present case, it was the queen who took the initiative. It is she who set her heart on the young Swede, spontaneously, impulsively, rashly, as she did everything when she obeyed her initial impulses. And clearly this too-sudden and unabashed favor embarrassed and worried Fersen more than it touched him. Marie-Antoinette was known to drop people as quickly as she got infatuated with them. If by chance this proved to be a lasting attachment, he knew perfectly well the risks he was running. Very wisely, he chose to flee. He had not let up requesting a military posting: he would take leave. Creutz felt he must tell Gustav III what everyone else was talking about:

> I must confide in Y.M. that the young count von Fersen was so well liked by the queen that it gave umbrage to a number of persons. I avow that I cannot help believing that she had a penchant for him; I saw signs of it that were too obvious to be doubted. The young count Fersen conducted himself admirably in all of this, with modesty and reserve and especially with the decision he made to go to America. In going away he precluded all the danger: but it clearly took a resolve beyond his years not to succumb to this temptation. The queen could not keep her eyes off him during the last days; in seeing him they filled with tears. I beg Y.M. to keep the secret for her sake and that of Senator Fersen. When they heard about the count's departure, all the favorites were delighted. The duchess Fitz-James said to him, 'What is this, Sir, you are abandoning your conquest?' – 'If I had made one, I would not have abandoned it,' he replied. 'I am going away a free man, and unfortunately, with no regrets.' Y.M. will admit that this reply was of a prudence and wisdom beyond his years[*].

By the end of March 1780 he had reached Brest where he was to join a naval squadron about to set sail for America. Should we believe an unverifiable anecdote? Sir Richard Barrington claimed in his memoirs to have seen a blushing Marie-Antoinette singing the air of the eponymous heroine of Piccinni's *Dido* in which the queen of Carthage declares how inspired she was when she welcomed Aeneas to her court. The queen's eyes apparently were drowned in tears and fixed on Fersen, who had lowered his. She was pale and shaken, overcome by the irrepressible feeling that this exquisite folly caused in her. But this account could well contain a large dose of novelistic afterthought. Fersen would stay away for three years, during which time he was not exactly eaten away by sorrow. He was

---

[*] This letter is generally thought to be dated 10 April 1779 but in April 1779 the queen's penchant for Axel von Fersen had not yet become a scandal. There was the birth of Madame Royale, then Lent, and von Fersen's departure for Le Havre at the end of March coinciding with queen's coming down with the measles. At the time their presumed romance had not yet hit the news. What is more, in Le Havre they were preparing for a landing in England whereas the letter mentions leaving for America. The most likely date therefore is that adopted by various historians of April 10, 1780.

finally able to make war on the American battlefields and qualify for the post he'd solicited while waiting to buy a regiment for himself. To rest the warriors' weary heads there was no want of friendly families to welcome them. "I'm doing marvelously here, I have lots to do, the women are pretty, friendly and flirtatious – everything I need," he wrote to his sister Sophie. It was not for Marie-Antoinette that he decided to settle in France upon his return, but because France for him was the most pleasant place to live and because what he had accomplished beyond the seas in the French army provided a stepping-stone to ascend the ranks.

Love was therefore initially one-sided. How can we explain the queen's passion? Their very first meeting in 1774 at the Opera ball does not seem to have made a deep impression on her. In the young man's journal, nothing indicates that she took any particular notice of him when he came to the balls in Versailles in the following days. But when she saw him again four years later, her feelings were immediately very powerful. Since their first meeting, there occurred in her a crystallization (in the sense Stendhal gives the term) around the memory of this encounter, associated with a certain quality of feeling. Fersen's undeniably superb looks played only a secondary role in this mysterious alchemy. Since first they met she had been to dozens of Opera balls where she played the same ambiguous game, knowing that she was recognized but pretending not to know, getting annoyed by the show of too much deference or too much familiarity. She never found again the enchantment of this brief flirtatious conversation innocent of any ulterior motives, because Fersen had no idea who she was. With him she was just a pretty woman like any other. She heard him utter the sweet things men say to pretty women all the time, except for the queen of course – words not without guile, like all words of love, but oh so different from those she was used to hearing. As time passed her entourage disappointed her more and more, and she was nostalgic for this experience that was unique in her life as queen: feeling herself on an equal footing with a man, freed from the yoke imposed by her condition.

Dangerous good looks

Who was this extraordinary young man, so handsome that it took your breath away, so endowed by fortune as to touch the heart of a queen, and so wise as to flee her advances? Actually, the man that history would turn into the prototype of the romantic hero was at heart much closer to the great libertine lords that populated 18th century novels, for whom love was merely sensual gratification. There was one major difference however: his exceptional beauty changed the rules of the game.

The fifteen-year-old student who launched his grand European tour under the debonair guidance of his Hungarian tutor was never exactly a choirboy; nor would his field-marshal father want him to be, knowing how important feminine support is in the trajectory of a man's career. Throughout the four years of his travels, the young man therefore not only studied the military arts and discovered Italian painting, he also began to be drawn to women, and very quickly noticed how attractive he was to them. His journal, which he started as soon as his travels began, at first listed the names of those who merely stuffed him with sandwiches, hazel nuts and prunes, or taught him dance steps. But by eighteen he was judging the ladies of Turin with the practiced eye of a connoisseur. He developed a taste for masked balls at Naples' San Carlo theatre and no sooner had he arrived in Paris than he made a bee-line for those at the Opera, where more daring partners than the dauphine made spicier advances: "I found a very pretty and welcoming mask who whispers that she was so upset that I was not her husband as then I could bed her. I told her that this was no obstacle. I wanted to convince her of it, but she fled. Another one that Plomenfeldt was pursuing to find out who she was did not prove so difficult. She sat down in a corridor and we had a long conversation with her; all she had over her face was a veil, which made it possible to kiss her at will, and she seemed to take to it quite nicely..." Resourceful as he was, however, he got no farther.

Did he always want to push his advantage? His good looks made the task so easy that he lost interest. He was not at all motivated by a desire for conquest. The competition for female attention so common in the male was absent in him. In this domain he had nothing to prove, either to himself or to anyone else: women flocked to him and offered themselves to him. Especially in the early years, this role reversal sometimes caused him to act rather like a woman; he backed away from advances. He became particularly wary of older or higher-ranking women who risked getting some sort of hold on him. In Stockholm the little duchess of Sudermania, the abandoned wife of the king's younger brother, literally threw herself at him, and he quickly fled. He knew how to remain aloof. To complete the picture we have to add that his seductive powers also attracted masculine attention. He would have to fend off Gustav III by making a big show of his resolute attraction for the opposite sex, and managed to dissuade him with the help of his official favorite, who was none too happy at the prospect of bowing out in favor of another. The young Axel's extreme prudence is therefore easily explained; and there was the unexpected result that his aloofness made him even more attractive, by casting an aura of melancholy and mystery about him.

Such was the young man, highly aware of his dangerous charms, who fled to America in the spring of 1780 because Marie-Antoinette had too blatant a crush on him. For three long years he made war in a far-away land. For her, life went on as usual, as she swung between self-indulgence and disgust. Then suddenly in June of 1783 he reappeared, "changed, older, having lost much of his former beauty" Madame de Boigne tells us, "but perhaps more touching and interesting because of the traces of suffering reflected in his features." Had he suffered greatly? Not necessarily. But he had certainly matured. Then so had Marie-Antoinette. No one knows what their first encounter was like upon his return, but it is clear that he stopped trying to evade her. From this time on he wanted more than ever to make his career in France, and said he was firmly resolved not to marry. "It's against my nature." So as not to clash with his father, he anemically wooed Mademoiselle Necker, whom he willingly ceded to his compatriot the baron de Staël. He admitted to his sister Sophie, "I cannot belong to the one person I want, the only one who really loves me, so I will belong to no one." It seems he was speaking about the queen. His misgivings had melted away, and he exalted: "I can hardly believe how happy I am, I have more than one reason for being so."

Peevish minds have of course pointed out that he got what he wanted out of this sudden favor: his career was assured. The senator did everything he possibly could to prevent him from settling in France, notably refusing him the money to buy the "Royal Swedish" regiment. But Gustav III realized that having a compatriot so well placed at court was quite an ace up his sleeve. He took it upon himself to convince the old man that his son could serve Sweden better in the corridors of Versailles than at home. He asked for Louis XVI's support of the regiment. Marie-Antoinette herself took the trouble to write to tell him of the success of the negotiations. All that remained to be done was to find the 100,000 pounds to pay the former title-holder. Axel borrowed the money and royal largesse soon put an end to his financial worries: he was granted a stipend of 20,000 pounds as the commander of a French regiment.

However, he was a battle-tested veteran of the American war, and did not settle into court life at the queen's side just to share her pleasures. That was neither possible nor attractive to him. He'd hardly been back in France three months when Gustav III asked him, in September 1783, to accompany him on a journey to Italy that lasted nine months. Sometimes his father asked him to come back to Sweden to help with family business. Militarily he was divided between two countries, and he had obligations to both. Service to the French often took him to Landrecies, then to Valenciennes on the Belgian border, where he ruled his regiment with a firm hand even while sighing over the boredom of garrison life. Duty to Sweden called him to Finland in 1788 during the war with Russia. He was forever on the road.

Contact with Marie-Antoinette was kept up through letters. We know that from November 1783 on he wrote to her regularly when he was away, and it is logical to assume that she answered him. Unfortunately we know nothing about their correspondence, or almost. None of their letters survives. Also, his journal for those crucial years of 1776-1791 is missing. We can only trace their correspondence through the *Brevdiarium*, a register where he kept a record of all the letters he sent, including the addressee, date and sometimes a brief summary of its contents. Marie-Antoinette appeared under the pseudonym of Joséphine*, which is similar to one of her middle names. Françoise Kermina, von Fersen's best biographer, who carefully sifted through the summaries in question, points out the great familiarity in their tone. He asked the queen to "do an errand for him, send him a sketch of a frock coat, or the score for a tune that, musicians both of them, they probably had sung together." He asked her what name to give a dog she's asked him to buy for her that he's about to send. They tell each other what's happening; he tells her about people he meets in his travels and she keeps him abreast of what's going on in Paris. As far as we can judge, this highly informal correspondence seemed to be carried on in a tone of friendship. But who knows?

One thing is sure: never would his feelings for Marie-Antoinette prevent him from carrying on the many simultaneous love affairs that came his way. As the years went by he refined his seductive skills in satisfying his lively libido. He had no religious or moral scruples when it came to women; he collected them according to his desires of the moment. Was he a cad? No, he did not seek

---

* The question of the two Joséphines included in the register cannot be dealt with here. In certain cases it is clear from the context that it can only refer to the queen; in others the same name obviously refers to someone else, apparently a servant. This was perhaps done on purpose to put busybodies off the scent.

to deceive his fleeting partners. He let himself be loved, without playing games. He offered women his expert skills at sharing pleasure, never forgetting that the first duty of a gallant man is to avoid putting them, or himself, in an embarrassing situation. He was known to have an impressive number of mistresses, but not a single child by any of them. It was out of the question for him to get sucked into a binding relationship. He did not wish to become attached. To those who seemed to expect more of him, he stopped them in their tracks: he "declares *everything*" – in other words they could not count on a heart that belonged exclusively to the queen. They made do with that, happy in the knowledge that they had a rival of such a lofty station, and even sometimes came round to sharing the cultish adoration he devoted to his idol. In his old age, the memory of the martyred queen cast a romantic glow on him that helped make up for his declining good looks. Not unselfishly, he got what he wanted out of this compartmentalizing of his life that preserved his freedom.

Friend or lover?

We can only surmise what his real relations were with Marie-Antoinette. Was he her lover? The biographers are divided on the issue. Some of them take the queen's honor as an article of faith, and defend it accordingly. Others seem inclined to smear her, and the monarchy along with her. Almost always, deep feelings are involved. Some want her chaste and pure, immaculate. Others, like Zweig, see in her a flesh-and-blood woman refusing to withhold the supreme gift from the man she loves. The historian must honestly admit that he or she hasn't a clue. But that shouldn't stop us from making a few inquiries.

There is little to learn from the Fersen Fund documents; too many of them are missing. The disappearance of ten crucial years from the journal seems to be the work of a secretary ordered, after Varennes, to eliminate all the compromising documents. However, there still existed in the family archives, it seems, all the letters between him and Marie-Antoinette. When in 1877 the baron von Klinckowström decided to make some of the correspondence public, he did what others were doing at the time: he selected what he wanted to go down in history. He only kept twenty-nine of the queen's letters and thirty-three of his grand-uncle's, which dated from the revolutionary period and dealt with politics; and he claimed to have destroyed the originals. Out of respect for the memory of their love, the other letters fell victim to an auto-da-fé in some sizeable Swedish stove. The ones he did publish were censured – whether by him or by someone else we don't know – but he was honest enough to mark with suspension marks the places where deletions were made in the body of the text. This naturally made people curious. So research was carried out and unearthed a few letters that were not completely expurgated, as well as some copies conserved by Mercy-Argenteau. They are tenderly written. We don't need them to know that Marie-Antoinette was in love with von Fersen, and they don't reveal whether or not they were lovers. But the censoring of their correspondence invites conjecture that they were.

For their contemporaries there was no doubt; everyone was convinced that they were lovers. But, one might object, how can we believe all the nonsense that was said of the queen? The patently outrageous nature of so many of the accusations against her discredits all of the tales told about her, and dispenses with the need to distinguish the false from the true. This permits those who want it that way to see her as lily-white once she's been cleansed of the filth heaped on her. This, however, requires ignoring measured testimony that, whatever one says, does not smack of ill will. This, for example, from the countess de Boigne: "The queen had only one great passion, and perhaps a failing. Her intimates hardly doubted that she had given in to her passion for Monsieur de Fersen. He justified this sacrifice by an infinite devotion, an affection that was as sincere as it was respectful and discreet; he breathed only for her, and the way he chose to live his life revolved around compromising her as little as possible. Thus, although this liaison was assumed, it never caused scandal." The marquis de Saint-Priest, less indulgent concerning this latter point, confirms the belief, adding a few details. The liaison was public knowledge in all the embassies, where von Fersen's principal title was that of "lover to the queen" – a designation he himself never sought to deny.

All this of course does not constitute irrefutable proof. So we are left with suppositions, buttressed when possible by other clues whose likelihood must be evaluated within their context. At this point we must continue the history of their relationship starting in the key year of 1783.

When Fersen came back from America we have seen how quickly he changed within the space of a few weeks, rejected any idea of marriage, and declared his happiness: the queen "truly loves him." He'd known for a long time that she was fond of him. But this was something altogether different. Once again, the initiative could only have come from her. What was the quality in him so rare that she could suddenly offer him another type of relationship? She had always needed a man or woman to confide in. She had been disappointed in turn by the likes of Besenval, Lauzun, Esterhazy and others who proved to be indiscreet, shallow and greedy. She was now distancing herself from the de Polignac clan; her friendship for the duchess was cooling and she felt terribly alone. Fersen showed up at a time when she was in disarray. He was aloof, reserved, sound – in short, different. She believed she could find in him sincere, judicious and disinterested affection. One can easily imagine – but it is really only a hypothesis – that she told him so and proposed, just like in the courtly novels, that he become her *chevalier servant*, her liege man. Only a pact of this kind can explain how they found themselves so quickly on the intimate terms that their correspondence hints at.

Unless, of course, they were overcome by human passion and thrust themselves into each other's arms. But at the time this was somewhat unlikely given Fersen's prudence and especially Marie-Antoinette's lack of experience. In these matters her mother had inculcated in her strong moral and religious scruples. Was she ready to throw them overboard without yet knowing what the consequences might be? Joseph II had noted that she had no taste for amorous matters, and clearly Louis XVI did not stun her with surprises in this domain. For her, sex remained a marital duty that she found taxing. For the moment, all she really strove for was genuine feeling. We can well imagine her dividing the two realms, the one – her body – for the husband that had been imposed on her, and the other – her heart – for the man of her election. What did he mean when he pointed out that she was the only one who truly loved him unless it's that she didn't see in him, as so many others did, a desirable lover or, like the young English woman in Florence, someone to turn into a husband?

There is another factor about which Françoise Kermina's analyses confirm our own. Belief in dynastic principles was very strong in Marie-Antoinette, like in all of Maria Theresa's daughters. As an heir of the Hapsburg line, she must not and could not bring into this world any other children than her husband the king's. In 1783 she still only had one son. She must have at least one more. She would take no risk of having doubt cast on the legitimacy of any future children; all the more so since she was terribly upset at seeing her public image tainted and knew that gossip had her unfaithful to her husband – she in no way wanted to add fuel to the fire. That didn't stop the gossip mill from cranking up when the duke de Normandie was born. His was the only birth whose timing could make it attributable to Fersen: he was born roughly nine months after the famous party under the stars where the Trianon woods could have afforded lovers a bit of complicit solitude. But the babe had his legitimate parents' blue eyes and his mother's golden, auburn-accented hair. Fersen himself expressed his indignation in the journal at the fact that the revolutionaries were toying with the idea of declaring him a bastard. His interest in the child, as compared to his interest in the boy's sister, merely reflected Marie-Antoinette's preference for him. The child was not his, but that of the king who never doubted his paternity, whatever has been said[*].

As long as the queen maintained conjugal relations with her husband, it is inconceivable that she could have been Fersen's mistress. In any case, he was often absent. They had to make do with a love affair by letter. However, it becomes conceivable once she decided that she wanted no more children and Louis XVI stopped demanding them of her. Her dynastic duties over with, why would she not take advantage of the freedom that so many couples in high society preached by example? Her Catholicism was too tepid to stop her committing a sin that seems absolved in advance by its depth of true feeling. And we know the state of Fersen's religious beliefs. At this point circumstances were ripe. When the Swede came back to France in April of 1787 he found the political climate hateful and the queen distraught, more isolated than ever, but also less monitored. He started to shuttle back and forth regularly between Flanders where his regiment was languishing for want of action and Versailles where she awaited him. All was set for them finally to abandon themselves to each other. Saint-Priest claimed that "Three or four times a week he would come on horseback to the park out by Trianon; the queen, unaccompanied, would do the same, and these rendez-vous caused a public scandal, despite the modesty and the rcstraint of the favorite, who always maintained a marble countenance and was, of all the queen's friends, the most discreet."

A pertinent clue has come to light proving that she wanted to have him as close to her as possible. In a letter to "Joséphine" before his 1787 return, a place "upstairs" for him to stay was mentioned, and in another at the beginning of October he asked to have an area set aside for a stove. People thought that this particular Josephine who was being asked to take care of a mundane matter could not be the queen, until the day when two researchers discovered in the

---

[*] Recent DNA tests on the child's heart have confirmed the king's paternity.

archives, a very explicit service note dated October 10th. It read, "The queen sought out the Swedish stove maker who made some stoves in Madame's apartments, and Her Majesty ordered another for one of her interior rooms, with pipes to heat a little room nearby..." She therefore had the means, both in Trianon and Versailles itself, to find intimate moments with the man she loved.

What they did with those moments no one knows. Did they actually become lovers? It's possible, but not certain. Marie-Antoinette's health, which was still suffering ill effects from her last pregnancy, and fear of an unwanted pregnancy, might have channeled their desires into less dangerous intimacies. With all due respect to Stefan Zweig, Marie-Antoinette, even in Fersen's most tender arms, must never have been a "divine lover." She was not, and would never be, gifted for it. Thus, they must have been, in Pierre Audiat's delicate phrase, repeated by André Castelot, "restrained lovers." It's an expression with a good pedigree as it comes from a manual written to train confessors. This hypothesis is given credence by Louis XVI's behavior. It is again Saint-Priest who tells us, "She found a way to get the king to agree to her relationship with the count von Fersen; repeating to her husband everything she heard about what was being said in public about their liaison, she offered to stop seeing him, which the king did not accept. No doubt she insinuated to him that with all the malign gossip unleashed against her, this foreigner was the only one they could count on... the monarch entirely concurred with this sentiment." The last statement can be disputed. The trust that Louis XVI did indeed put in Fersen was the consequence and not the cause of his agreeing to the relationship. There was only one thing that could have made him accept it, the assurance that the essentials were taken care of – as long as there was no procreation there was no infidelity. Thus our ancestors reasoned, and thus still do sometimes certain of our contemporaries.

The end of an idyll

Also, as events took on momentum, Fersen's place in Marie-Antoinette's life evolved. The idyll was inseparable from the place where it was born – in Versailles' little interior rooms and the shady groves of Trianon, where life was sweet. But all good things come to an end. Upon his return to Paris in October 1789, the royal couple was already in the Tuileries, and the nature of their relationship changed. Yes, Fersen had free access to the Tuileries thanks to a passkey.

Said La Fayette, "I left him the means to come in without being noticed by leaving a certain entrance to the apartment unguarded." Was this solidarity between two veterans of the American war, or as Saint-Priest perfidiously remarked, "another low trick to get her to compound her errors"? Whatever the case may be, in the Tuileries it was more difficult to find privacy because of the relative lack of space and the suspicion hanging over its inhabitants. Only the stay in Saint-Cloud during the summer of 1790 enabled the lovers to recover a bit of their old intimacy. But the heart was no longer in it, or the body either. The queen's health had deteriorated, her nerves were at breaking point, and she craved reassurance. Faced with the rumblings of revolution, she saw in Fersen a man of strength from whom she needed support and direction. And the king, who by then consulted her about everything, was present at many of their meetings. The queen's confidant thus became the secret political advisor to the royal couple, to whom he was also Gustav III's unofficial emissary. So the atmosphere of their meetings necessarily changed. Later on we'll talk about the very last of their meetings, in March 1792 – a high point in the romanticized biographies. But everything leads us to believe that at this time Fersen's love for the queen was largely sublimated into boundless admiration for the courage, and infinite compassion for the sufferings of her whom he henceforth evoked purely in ethereal terms: a perfect creation, an angel, a saint. And as we all know, angels have no sex, and saints very little...

As for Fersen, while taking his pleasure here, there and everywhere, and always careful not to get attached, he fell in the summer of 1789 under the spell of a mistress who could not be more different from the ill-fated sovereign. Eleonore Sullivan, née Franchi, was a little-known Italian actress who made a career for herself as a courtesan in high places. Going from the arms of the duke of Wurtemberg to those of Joseph II himself, she managed to marry an Irishman whose name she kept and whom she followed to India. But there she left him for Quentin Craufurd, a Scotsman who made a fabulous fortune in the East India Company, carried her off to Paris and set her up. Members of Paris' most glittery set made haste to their sumptuous *hôtel particulier* on the rue de Clichy, drawn by the host's outstanding refinement, (he collected paintings), and by the sensuous beauty of his companion, a stunning and curvaceous brunette. It is not known when she managed to ensnare the handsome Axel. He was already her lover when Craufurd invited him to live with them. He quickly smothered any scruples, if any scruples there were, and shamelessly settled into this little vaudeville-style *ménage à trois* where the lady's supposed protector took on the role of cuckolded husband. Distinction, it was murmured, was not Eleonore's finest quality, but she knew how to check herself when she felt that her noisy exuberance was beginning to grate. In any case, it didn't matter to Fersen. He was subjugated by her voluptuousness and captivated by her generosity. She was always ready to welcome and help him, joyful, warm-hearted and devoted. He could not do without her. He really loved her, alongside Marie-Antoinette, and so openly that his sister Sophie worried: what would poor *Elle* think if she found out that he was being unfaithful to her with *El?* – for such were the code names for the respective women in their letters to each other. In short, although he'd tried to keep his love affairs within the strict bounds of carnality, here was one that overpowered him, to the detriment of his more and more disincarnate love of Marie-Antoinette. She was no longer a woman to love, but a victim to tear away from the clutches of the revolutionary hydra, with all her family in tow. This was a cause to which Fersen would from then on devote all of his might.

At the end of this long incursion into psychological territory, in the realm of hypothesis bordering on the novelistic, the historian again takes the floor to conclude with two remarks, both of a political nature.

The first hardly seems to have been touched on up till now. What matters to the history of human behavior and modes of thought, and therefore to history full stop, it is not whether or not Fersen was Marie-Antoinette's lover in the full sense of the word. What matters is that all their contemporaries believed that he was, and that she did nothing to deny it. It is not important what the real nature was of the ties that bound her to the handsome Swede, or how intimate their relationship was. It is blindingly obvious that she broke one of the golden rules for the queen of France. She not only rejected outright the conventional pretense at being forever in love with her husband; she imposed the presence at her side of a man of her choosing, thus affirming her right to love where she pleased. She did so toward the end and relatively discreetly, but without the least feelings of guilt. And she even managed to get Louis XVI and part of the court to go along with it; and here too again, against tradition, against public pressure, she saw to it that her will prevailed. At her own risk and peril.

The other remark concerns her choice. Fersen was a foreigner. Since he was her advisor, his influence partly substituted that of

Mercy-Argenteau, another foreigner, who served Austria. Neither one of them helped in the difficult process of making her more French, and that was unfortunate. Fersen loved France, or rather the little he knew of it, not the French. Faced with the difficulties on the horizon, he reacted like a high and mighty Swedish lord. The dabbling in liberal notions that marked his American adventure was quickly shelved. Faced with the first stirrings of popular revolt, he fell back on his rigid aristocratic reflexes, and rejected the Revolution wholesale. Far from helping Marie-Antoinette understand what was going on, he set her in opposition to all those who were trying to get the king to take control of it. And after the Varennes fiasco, he would spew out curses against the French people, who deserved only to be enslaved, and against Paris, that he would like to see drown in blood. His political acumen was not on a par with his bravery. The same was true for Marie-Antoinette, and we can be forgiven for deploring the fact.

CHAPTER 14

"MY TWO COUNTRIES"

Louis XVI tried to keep Marie-Antoinette out of politics by indulging her every whim. He failed. Not that she had any passionate interest in politics; she could never be bothered making the effort it takes to master the details. For the eight years following Joseph II's visit and the commencement of normal relations with her husband, the young woman satisfied her appetite for authority by directing her little theatre and by getting Trianon the way she wanted it. But both her entourage and Mercy-Argenteau kept pushing her to take a political role. As we have seen in regard to internal affairs, she committed herself with muddle-headed fervor for or against ministers according to whether she liked them or not – the only result being to hasten their rise or fall that other factors made inevitable in any case.

We will take a quick step back here to take an overall look at foreign affairs, where again we will see her simplistic notions in action: there were the "good guys," the Austrians, and the "bad guys," at the top of the list Frederick II of Prussia. Only one thing counted for her: keeping alive the alliance between her two countries. However, Franco-Austrian relations kept deteriorating. While Louis XV and Maria Theresa had held each other in esteem despite their differences, Louis XVI and Joseph II had an instinctive dislike for each other, not to mention justified mistrust. It wasn't only out of love for his sister that Joseph II came to France in the spring of 1777. He was counting on forcing the king to support the big plans so dear to his heart. Disappointed when all he got were a few evasive polite replies, he consoled himself with the idea that he could rule this supposedly weak brother-in-law through his wife once the marital problems were sorted out. He found out, as early as the beginning of the next year, that Louis XVI was an unaccommodating ally, little disposed to falling into line with

Austria. With the excuse of "saving the alliance" therefore, more pressure was put on Marie-Antoinette through Mercy-Argenteau to offer her services in favor of Austria.

She threw herself into it with her usual impetuosity and blind stubbornness. But we mustn't be too harsh. This attitude had its roots in quite a natural feeling shared to some degree by all the queens of France who had to deal with the tensions between their father's country and their husband's. Marie-Antoinette was different from them in that she refused to suffer in silence the unhappy deterioration of the alliance of which she was the guarantee. More closely tied to her native land than were any of her forebears, she tried hard to bring her husband round to Vienna's point of view. While obstinately refusing for eight years to understand what her brother was trying to explain to her, she would be the conduit for his demands. And since she had no talent for diplomacy – lacking the necessary intelligence and flexibility – all her interventions were condemned to failure. But she would pay a high price indeed in French public opinion for this role of Austria's unconditional advocate that she so rashly got dragged into.

Mixed feelings, divergent interests

Years previously, circumstances had famously forced both countries to switch alliances, as enshrined by the 1756 treaty. However, no lasting common interests bound them together. They had quite distinct enemies. France held England as its number one enemy as conflict heightened over their colonial possessions. Austria's bête noire was Prussia, who'd grabbed Silesia from them and challenged their hegemony over Germany. But once upon a time the Prussians had been allied with France. It was their approaches to England that led Louis XV to respond to Maria Theresa's overtures. France committed itself to granting Austria financial and military aid against any aggression by Frederick II. In exchange, however, France could expect no support in its maritime and colonial war. But it was hoped that the Austrian threat would be enough to keep the Prussians and Hanovarians* at bay, and that a land war could thus be avoided. In Louis XV's mind therefore the aim of the alliance was to keep the status quo in Germany. In Maria Theresa's mind however the alliance should have enabled her to get back Silesia. Austria had finally managed to drag France

---

* Hanover belonged to the English king, whose family came from there.

into fighting on two fronts in the disastrous Seven Years War. The 1763 treaty of Paris left the two sides very unhappy with each other. Austria did not succeed in crushing Prussia, or even retaking Silesia – it got nothing out of it. France had to abandon to England most of her colonial empire. It was France that came out the worst.

It is easy to understand why the French were so indignant over the partition of Poland. First of all, France and Poland had been friends for centuries. Secondly and above all, Austria turned out to behave at least as cynically as Prussia. How? Without advising the French, Austria made a pact with the Prussians against whom it had just recently implored France's support, only to then go along with Prussia and attack a defenseless country at peace with France and blithely carve it up. Louis XV had preferred to hold his tongue rather than utter vain protests. But the episode left scars*.

Louis XVI chose well when at Maurepas' suggestion he took on the count de Vergennes as his secretary of state for foreign affairs. This career diplomat had been given "sensitive" postings, as we would say today. His fourteen years in Constantinople enabled him to measure the irreparable weakness of the France's ally the Ottoman Empire before the designs of Catherine the Great of Russia. Then sent to Stockholm, he brought France's support to Gustav III in his "coup d'état" to reestablish the monarchy's authority. He had a sound grasp of all the complexities of Eastern European politics. His great experience, his seriousness, and his steady approach all earned him the king's esteem and confidence. The two of them had the same moral rigor, disapproving of the "co-sharing system" that divided Poland among the three predators that had ganged up against it. They both hated this type of adventurism and preferred maintaining peace to territorial expansion. Learning from the Seven Years War and the partition of Poland, they resolved to interpret the treaty of 1756 as narrowly as possible: France would support Austria from foreign aggression, nothing more. But above all, it would do everything in its power to prevent any aggression and thus not tie its own hands vis-à-vis England. For despite their pacifist convictions, Louis XVI and Vergennes faced quite a temptation: revenge on England seemed within reach.

For more than ten years France had stood by and watched while relations between England and its American colonies soured. Until then the mother country exercised rather mild political control over the thirteen colonies, each of which enjoyed great autonomy in the management of its affairs through local councils and assemblies.

---

* See chapter 6.

Financially exhausted by the Seven Years War, England claimed the right to make the colonies pay for part of its costs, and peremptorily imposed various taxes in violation of the general rule according to which no British citizen need pay any tax without his consent or that of his representatives. So the Americans boycotted the taxed items. In 1773 Bostonians threw overboard an entire shipment of tea, setting off repressive measures, and tensions escalated. The following year, representatives from each colony met in the first Continental Congress and affirmed in a solemn declaration the right of all peoples to participate in framing any laws that concerned them. Two years after that, on the 4th of July 1776, the Declaration of Independence of the United States of America marked the colonies' break from the motherland. They had reached the point of no return. Should France seize the opportunity being offered of erasing the humiliation of the Treaty of Paris? Louis XVI could not make up his mind about the insurgents' call for help. True, for three years, while making a show of strict neutrality, he had been secretly helping them, getting money and supplies to them through a front company run by the one and only Beaumarchais. But from there to openly taking sides with them in the certainty that this would entail war with England, there was a step that he could not bring himself to take.

First of all for economic reasons: the royal coffers could not withstand another armed conflict. Since the tax reform put forward by Turgot had been squashed, his successors had to patch together one stopgap measure after another, which proved disastrous in the long run. There were other reasons to abstain as well. Louis XVI felt no sympathy whatsoever for the people who a few years earlier had led a violent guerrilla-type war against French forts in Canada and the Ohio Valley, thus contributing to France's defeat. Nor had he any desire, on principle, to support subjects in revolt against their sovereign, colonists who could set a bad example for the few "sugar islands" remaining in French control in the Caribbean, even if it could be objected that if the English won, they would not long remain so. He felt so assured of his power that he did not seem to fear that France itself might risk being contaminated. If he kept a prudent wait-and-see approach for as long as he did, it was because he wanted to gauge his chances of success before committing himself.

French public opinion on the other hand got all fired up about the insurgents. Not only was their national pride thirsting for revenge, they also had an instinctive sympathy for the underdog who dares to overthrow tyrannical power, and an ideological attraction for the laudable aspirations of the up-and-coming people: equal rights for all and participation in decision-making, especially as regards taxation. The fact that the new state was tending toward a republican form of government practically went unnoticed, because in order to get France's support the colonists took great care to keep the type of government out of the discussion. They were only claiming the same rights as their brethren in the mother country within the framework of a constitutional monarchy against which it would have no complaints if only it took their demands into account. It was without any difficulty therefore that the makers of French public opinion thoroughly identified with their cause. What is more, since young noblemen traditionally had no other career open to them except that of war, they were chafing at the bit and itching for a fight after years of peace and inaction.

The astuteness of the negotiators did the rest. In late 1776 the Americans dispatched to Europe a man of science of world renown, Benjamin Franklin, the man said to have tamed the heavens with his lightning rod. His reputation opened all doors for him, both to the salons and the academies. The Masonic network contributed to promoting him. He cleverly played on his own exotic foreignness. In those times people felt they should pit the authenticity of the noble savage or peasant against the vices of civilization; and he played his rustic simplicity to the hilt, with his long hair hanging from a thinning brow, his large spectacles, his brown velvet suit all shiny and threadbare, his shoes with no buckles, and his trapper's fur hat. His bonhomie and his cheerful mischievousness, even the awkward way he spoke French (which he wrote quite well by the way) all rendered him highly seductive. He navigated the shoals quite deftly, loudly proclaiming his liberalism with the progressives and his Anglophobia with the conservatives. In no time he was furiously fashionable and everyone swore by him. Against the king's orders, hordes of noble youth volunteered to fight alongside the Americans. In April 1777 the fiery marquis de La Fayette, a bare twenty-two years of age, set out at the head of an enthusiastic contingent, quite resolved to win glory in the battlefield. There he was to earn the moniker "hero of two worlds."

What did Marie-Antoinette make of all this? Not much apparently. She met Franklin and was fascinated, they say, by the strange musical instrument he was exhibiting, a glass armonica. It used a series of variously sized goblets that when rubbed produced musical tones. She would hardly have a political opinion, as Austria wasn't involved. Madame Campan states that she was against intervention not through fear of any ideological contamination but "because she saw too little generosity in the way France chose to attack English might." However, it was only after the fact, during the French Revolution, that her opinion changed. At the time she too got swept up in the general infatuation for it all. The countess Diane de Polignac, her favorite's sister-in-law, professed such a noisy admiration for Franklin that the king lost patience and gave her a chamber pot in Sèvres porcelaine, at the bottom of which he had engraved a medallion portrait of the savant very much in vogue at the time. It was wreathed in the proud legend *Eripuit coelo fulmen, septrumque tyrannis*⁎. A joke of such poor taste could only have pushed his wife toward the American camp, if indeed she hadn't already been won over.

Throughout 1777 Louis XVI and Vergennes continued to prevaricate. In Vienna Maria Theresa and Joseph II took the position of the despot – enlightened or not – that only sovereigns have what it takes to make the people happy, since nature has designed the people for obedience. If they were Louis XVI, they would abandon the rebels to their fate. Among other things, they feared an involvement that would exhaust French finances and thereby render their alliance useless. But since meeting Louis XVI, Joseph understood that he could not count on his good will. He therefore decided to take advantage of the diversion on the international scene caused by the Anglo-American conflict to take a bold and surprising step that would place the French before a fait accompli, and oblige them to respect the engagements they undertook in 1756 in the event of a European conflict. He planned to appropriate a large part of Bavaria. And his mother went into a panic, just as she had when Poland was partitioned, for both moral reasons – she disapproved of using force to despoil the weak – and for political reasons – she feared the Prussian response. But in the end-of-regime climate that prevailed in Vienna, the empress's word was no longer law. Kaunitz, her life-long accomplice and chancellor whose temperament could sometimes make things awkward but whose fidelity was unimpeachable, had gone over to Joseph's camp. For it was Joseph who represented the future, he was now calling the shots.

The changing of the generational guard was largely accomplished in 1777. Louis XVI had succeeded Louis XV, his twenty-three years happily buttressed by Vergennes' fifty-eight. Now in her sixties, Maria Theresa had to give way to her son and make do with playing Cassandra foretelling the disasters she saw on the

---

⁎ "He wrested the lightning from the heavens and the scepter from the tyrant," attributed to Turgot.

horizon. In France and Austria, two old political warhorses, Maurepas, seventy-six, and Kaunitz, sixty-six, survived by trying to make themselves indispensable. Age and the disappointments of the Seven Years War had chastened Frederick II, who at sixty-five wanted mainly to consolidate his gains and prevent others from capitalizing on theirs. He was not the troublemaker. Now at the age of thirty-six it was Joseph II whose appetite for conquering new territory threatened the peace. The famous alliance drawn up to defend Austria from Prussian imperialism lost its raison d'être once Joseph became the aggressor, leaving to Frederick the unfamiliar role of protector of the oppressed, while in the outer reaches of eastern Europe, the unpredictable Catherine the Great cynically moved her pawns west and southward, knowing that her back was covered by the desolate and immense Russian steppes. But France had no other options. Denouncing the alliance would mean throwing Austria into the arms of England without necessarily getting the support of Prussia, which could not be trusted despite its repeated advances. Vergennes therefore advocated saving appearances while secretly going back to what had been the golden rule of French politics in the 17th century: make sure Germany stays divided into a multitude of states of different sizes and strengths, none of which could dominate the others. This explained the reference to the 1648 treaty of Westphalia, which had consecrated this division. The policy implied maintaining an equal balance between Prussia and Austria so that they could cancel each other out.

Which clearly was not what Joseph had in mind.

The grab for Bavaria (1778-1779)

One needn't look too long at a map of the period to understand why Austria coveted Bavaria, embedded as it was in the middle of Austrian possessions. Lo and behold, in 1777, an excellent, unexpected opportunity seemed to be offered. Maximilian III, the Elector of Bavaria, was gravely ill and on his deathbed. He had no children; his heir was a distant cousin, the Palatine Elector Charles-Theodore von Wittelsbach-Sulzbach. This cousin, also childless, had no desire to leave the banks of the Rhine and his fair city of Mannheim to go live in Munich. Possessing two territories so far apart was not to his liking, and he understood that he would not be able to defend his new acquisition. It was better to accept with good grace what he couldn't prevent. When Austria unearthed old medieval charters that supposedly established Austria's claims on Lower Bavaria, he bowed to the inevitable in the hope of subsequently swapping the rest of the province for some districts of the Austrian Low Countries bordering on the Palatine. The Bavarian elector had barely rendered his spirit on December 30, 1777 when the following January 3rd Joseph II published the agreement signed by the elector's successor, and with all due haste dispatched his troops to Lower Bavaria.

"You won't like it much where you are," he wrote to Mercy, "but I can't see what there is to criticize in it, and the situation with the English seems very favorable." What with "the queen's ascendancy over her husband" and the risks involved in the latter's imminent recognition of the young American nation, he believed that France would be reduced to silence. The queen, at first surprised by the brouhaha raised in Paris over the invasion of Bavaria, made light of it, writing to her friend de Polignac that she feared her brother was "up to his old tricks." Fiddlesticks if political troubles were interfering with the carnival festivities. Mercy roundly scolded her: such flippancy could lead people to think that "far from adopting the views of her august house" she disapproved of them, thereby "failing" her mother and brother as well as herself, and "depriving herself of the means of employing her influence to maintain the unity of the two courts." From Vienna Maria Theresa sent the requisite warning: "A change in our alliance... would be the death of me." Mercy, who was present when she read the letter, saw the young woman "grow pale when reading that part." It would take nothing less to shake her out of her frivolity.

She consented therefore to intercede with her husband to plead the cause of "the alliance," in other words, the grab for Bavaria. She could not have chosen a worse moment. Joseph had believed he could outwit them all. While being careful not to inform his brother-in-law of what was in the January 3rd agreement, he spread the word in all the other courts of Europe that he had Louis XVI's backing. The latter, seeing that Joseph was trying to force his hand and compromise him, remained steadfast in his anger. He ordered Vergennes to send not only to Vienna but to Berlin as well, a note specifying that France was parting ways with the emperor on this issue, and that the treaty of 1756 did not oblige him "to share the ambitious and unjust views" of his allies. And when Marie-Antoinette took him to task "rather forcefully" over his "duties" to Austria, he spoke to her firmly and clearly for once:

> "It is your relations' ambitions that are going to turn every-thing upside down; they started with Poland, now Bavaria is volume two; it all makes me very unhappy with you."

"But you cannot deny, Sir, that you were informed and were in agreement with this Bavarian business."

"I was so little in agreement that orders have just been given to the French emissaries to let it be known in their respective courts that the dismemberment of Bavaria is being carried out against our will, and that we disapprove of it."

Did he hope to convince his wife? This fierce outburst could not overcome deep-seated convictions in her, nourished by her mother and Mercy. She resolved even more forcefully to fight for her country of origin, with a perfectly clear conscience, because they had convinced her that she was also fighting for France's real interests, which the king and his dim-witted ministers didn't understand.

However, for a while Joseph II could believe he had won the round. His brother-in-law's verbal protests didn't worry him. But he had underestimated the resentment against his incursion in the edgy little German states that felt threatened by it. The Palatine elector had heirs who were badly affected by the goings on. The duke de Deux-Ponts and his brother presented a complaint to the Imperial Diet. And Frederick soon took the lead in a movement that was forming to counter Joseph. Although Louis XVI and Vergennes were delighted, they kept prudently quiet about the whole business. The king pretended not to notice the blandishments coming out of Prussia, which was attempting to get him to break with Austria. He also resisted pressure from Joseph who was dangling the carrot and the stick, sometimes threatening to revert to the English alliance, sometimes hinting at offering the Low Countries in exchange for his support. He refused to give his brother-in-law any guarantees, which aside from the fact that this would have involved him in something unjust, would also have obliged him to take his side if a conflict ensued. Cut to the quick, Marie-Antoinette was proud to stand up stalwartly against what she took to be her husband's cowardice, without realizing that she was being manipulated by Mercy, who practically dictated what she was to say word for word. "The only person the king of Prussia fears is you," they said, to encourage her. But she couldn't prevent Louis XVI's "horrid dispatch" to Vienna of March 30th in which he reiterated his neutral stance in the event of Prussian aggression.

In mid-April an event of great importance seemed to change the whole deck of cards: finally, after so many years of fruitless waiting, Marie-Antoinette was expecting. Her family paraded the accomplishment, and the young woman would get from it a boost in recognition and prestige. Now she could be refused nothing. The pregnancy also lessened the dissent between her and her mother, making her more willing than ever to serve the empress. She went back on the offensive with Maurepas and Vergennes in a way that implied she'd have no truck with opposition: "I spoke to them with some force, and believe I made an impression, especially on the latter. I was not too happy with the reasoning of these gentlemen who seek only to take a different course and get the king used to it." Of course they did! They all did! Neither the ministers nor the king had any illusions about her. Even though the letters exchanged between her, her mother and Mercy were never tampered with, their content could easily be guessed: she acted as a spokesman for the whatever the Viennese court wanted. It would be useless to try to dissuade her from it because her mind was quite made up. Louis XVI was so indulgent that he found it "natural" that she should worry about her brother and try to help him. He pampered her, because of the child to be. Hence his compliance regarding the projects that distracted her from politics. When she did get involved, pushed to it by Mercy, they lulled her by telling her what she wanted to hear and granting her trivial concessions. For example, on April 26th she got what she took to be a great victory: in a new dispatch of a more conciliatory tone, the king committed himself to defending the Low Countries if the Prussians attacked. He was not risking much. Frederick II was no fool; he wouldn't attack the Low Countries and risk irritating France and Holland when it was so easy for him to invade Bohemia, as before.

For the most part, Marie-Antoinette came out empty-handed. But since they all avoided a head-on conflict with her, she persevered in her importuning ways. The king backed off because he hated pointless arguments, harsh words and tears. In June, for instance, she was not informed that there was a new dispatch being prepared for Berlin confirming French neutrality. Mercy was furious about this and explained to her that "if she let them get away with such behavior she would no longer be able to maintain her influence and credibility." So she went off to complain to her husband: "I could not hide from him the pain that his silence caused me; I even told him that I would be ashamed to admit to my dear mamma the way he was treating me..." His reply left her speechless. "You see I am so wrong that I can't even answer you," he told her, with some irony, to cut short the avalanche of reproofs, before turning his back on her. As for the ministers, they hadn't forgotten the price Turgot had to pay for his candor. They pretended they didn't know what was going on, shunted the responsibility from one to the other, and excused themselves for having to consult their colleagues or the king of Prussia. Their attempts to mollify her and their "talent for drowning everything in a flood of words" only exasperated her. She took their silence and evasiveness as insults and "failures" to perform their duties toward her. She said she'd get revenge or her "own justice," and vented her anger bordering on abusiveness.

Between Mercy who never gave her a moment's peace and the evasive ministers she couldn't get a handle on, she felt as if she were going around in circles, as if she were lost in a trap-strewn labyrinth with no exit. Would it not have been better to have the courage to put her in her place, and once and for all set limits on her political input? After all, what right had she to be kept in the know, to order the ministers around and impose her will on them? Hadn't Joseph informed her in the diatribe following the Rosenberg letter incident that it wasn't the custom among French monarchs to grant such prerogatives to the wives of its kings? By law she had no such rights. And she took high risks in trying to usurp them. Gentle persuasion was the only weapon in any queen's armory. Let her use it, for heaven's sake, instead of playing the outraged princess! Very aware of this, Maria Theresa tried to get her ambassador to lower the tone a bit: "However happy I am at the warmth with which my daughter is beginning to uphold the interests of her house, I cannot stop myself from repeating to you that I wish her to act with great circumspection so as not to compromise herself gratuitously for no good outcome." And she had distressing reasons to believe on this 30th of June that Austria would soon need a "good outcome."

Return to square one

Relations between Austria and Prussia were deteriorating rapidly. Frederick II was baring his fangs. Joseph wrote to his sister, "Since you do not want to prevent the war, we shall fight as brave men, and... you will have nothing to be ashamed of in a brother who will always merit your esteem." In other words, it was all the fault of the cowardly French who did not fulfill their obligations! And Marie-Antoinette was sick that she couldn't get the spineless ministers to understand how "just and reasonable" Vienna's demands were – and how much they were in France's higher interests too! The mutual misunderstanding was complete.

What had to happen happened. "Here we are at war," wrote the empress on July 7th, "it's what I've feared since January, and what a war it is!" The Prussian king's troops had just invaded

Bohemia. Maria Theresa always castigated her son's adventure as both dangerous and unjust. Her most pessimistic projections were coming true. And she shied away from seeking solace in her daughter, whose pregnancy might be jeopardized by too strong emotion. When Marie-Antoinette learned about the invasion, she wept bitter tears and wrote her mother a pathetic letter. The king tried to console her. "He came to see me; he found me so unhappy and alarmed that it moved him to tears." Does that mean that he'd decided to behave like a "good ally"? He told her he would go to the ends of the earth to lighten her sorrow, but he could not go against the advice of his ministers, "the good of his kingdom not permitting him to do more than he'd already done." Which only strengthened her illusion that the king was "subjugated" by Maurepas, mere putty in his hands. She therefore summoned the latter and made a terrible scene. "Here we are, Sir, the fourth or fifth time that we have spoken about matters, and you have never answered me sufficiently; I have been patient up till now, but things have become too serious, and I will no longer put up with such defeats." The old Mentor took it all in his stride, renewed his assurances of devotion, and left it at that. And to distract everyone's attention, the king urgently invited Madame de Polignac back from the countryside to keep her friend company.

Maria Theresa understood that Louis XVI would never accept seeing the king of Prussia as the aggressor – which would entail enacting the 1756 treaty – since the invasion of Bohemia was only in response to the Bavarian invasion, for which her son was responsible. Louis XVI would not take sides in the dispute, but he did offer to mediate, as long as the unjustly occupied territories were restored. The old empress, aware that Austria's cause was unjustifiable*, decided to take matters into her own hands, and unbeknownst to Joseph, tried to deal directly with Frederick. When Joseph found out, they had a terrible row. Frederick refused, countered with unacceptable demands, and pushed his troops on against the Austrians. In the end Joseph had to beat a retreat, but true to his old form, proceeded to methodically ravage the occupied country.

Faced with imminent disaster, Maria Theresa decided to throw caution to the winds and call upon Marie-Antoinette anyway. With each new letter her calls for help were more pressing and melodramatic. Bohemia was cruelly put to the sword, the emperor and his brother archduke Maximilian were sweating it out at the

---

* Most of the medieval documents on which Austrian pretensions were based were contradicted by others and seen as of questionable validity.

head of their troops; winter was not far off. Her daughter held in her hands the key to ending all their troubles: "You will save your utterly exhausted mother and two brothers who must succumb in the end, your fatherland, a whole nation that holds you so dear..." It would take so little for France, she added, to get the king of Prussia to back down. No, she was not talking about armed intervention; she knew there was no question of that; just a little show of force, a few "exercises" for all to see, some military build-up, just to dissuade them. But nothing would convince Louis XVI to abandon his neutrality.

While Marie-Antoinette didn't have many illusions left about her influence, she held out hope for mediation. But her idea of mediation was the Austrian one: pressure on Prussia alone, not on both parties. The abbé de Véri recounted that she tried to intervene in a meeting between the king, Maurepas and Vergennes to recite Mercy's litany. But the arrival of a courier from the French ambassador to Vienna obviated her speech. Unable to adapt what she had to say to the new information, "she limited herself to recommending her family's interests, saying that she was more French than Austrian, and asking the king to use his good offices to keep the king of Prussia from going too far." She could see that the three men, far from disagreeing with each other as she'd expected, spoke in one voice. Aware of her failure and nearing the birth, she stayed out of it from then on "so as not to put the king in an awkward position between his minister and his spouse," she told her mother. Privately, she too desired peace, which is understandable.

Peace? Frederick II had already won the round when he withdrew his troops to their winter quarters back home from a Bohemia that he'd bled dry. Had he been forewarned of the dramatic turn of events being planned behind their backs that was about to take place? It was the work of Catherine the Great, in her role of goddess *ex machina*. The czarina, who was tied to Prussia by a treaty of alliance and could congratulate herself on France's recent intervention in settling her conflict with the Turks, burst onto the political scene under the pretext of defending the interests of the German princes. She could apply the kind of diplomatic pressure that France couldn't: she would attack Austria if Joseph didn't give up Bavaria. Under French and Russian auspices, the negotiating was swift. The peace of Teschen, signed on May 13, 1779, enabled the emperor not to lose face altogether. He got a thin strip of Bavarian land bordered by the Danube, Inn and Salzach rivers in order to balance out what was granted to Frederick, who saw his rights confirmed on the principalities of Ansbach and Beyreuth*. The Palatine elector got back nearly all of Bavaria, which would go to the duke de Deux-Ponts after his death.

"Madame, my most dear mother," Marie-Antoinette wrote, "what happiness I feel upon learning that the peace we have yearned for has been sealed. We can thank my dear mother for that, and I would like to flatter myself that we here too had something to do with it. From now on my greatest concern will be maintaining unity between my two countries – if I may express myself thusly. I felt too keenly the need of it, and the unhappiness and the anguish I felt last year cannot be expressed. But I was born to owe everything to my dear mamma, and it is to her that I owe the tranquility that is being reborn in me through her goodness, her gentleness, and dare I say her patience toward this country here." Even if we make allowances for the maudlin sentimentality that the young woman felt she must indulge in when addressing her mother, her partiality for Austria was clear her. Her self-deception too.

Joseph II swallowed his tempestuous pride and put off till more propitious times his plans for Bavaria. As for Maria Theresa, she proved to be clear-sighted and fair enough to admit in a letter to Mercy that France would have seriously harmed its own interests if it had given in to Austrian demands, and that it had done everything Austria "could reasonably expect of their accord." The thanks she addressed to Louis XVI were therefore not devoid of sincerity. But her fundamental honesty did not stop her from taking every chance she got to push her advantage. She thought about getting her youngest son Maximilian elected coadjutor to the archbishop of Cologne, putting him in line for the post. This was more of a political position than an ecclesiastical one, for the archbishop was the undisputed sovereign of a rather large principality and was one of the eight electors who decided on how the empire was run. France cast a jaundiced eye on a territory so close to its borders falling under the umbrella of the Hapsburg-Lorraine family. So Austria kept the negotiations under wraps for as long as possible. Marie-Antoinette was not called upon to intercede with her husband until the thing was nearly settled. The king resigned himself to sending his congratulations on a success that he couldn't have prevented. The queen remained convinced that she had contributed to solidifying

---

* These two principalities, to which brothers of the elector of Brandenburg had been given exclusive rights at the beginning of the 16th century, fell into escheat with the extinction of their lines. They then were to revert quite legally to the older branch.

the union between her two families, without noticing the fact that her many interventions had alienated public opinion.

How to end the war in America

Across the Atlantic the tide seemed to be turning in favor of the insurgents. Their victory in Saratoga on October 31, 1777 swayed Louis XVI and Vergennes: there was a chance they could win this war. On February 6, 1778 France officially recognized the United States and signed a treaty of alliance and friendship with them. They did not have to wait long for the British response. As soon as the good weather set in, a surprise naval engagement marked the beginning of hostilities. Then on July 27th the two fleets confronted each other off the island of Ouessant. To everyone's surprise, the French routed the English. But the French victory would have been greater had the duke de Chartres, who apparently was ignorant of nautical signals, understood the orders he was getting from the flagship. Marie-Antoinette reacted like most of the French, and shared the widespread rejoicing. She applauded the victors, and laughed as much as everyone else at the jokes about her cousin's bungling of the signals. Once the Bavarian crisis was over and Fersen enlisted in the American cause, she would suddenly take an interest in the operations. Her letters to her mother show how much she shared the outlook of those around her. Like all women, she apprehended war and hoped it would be a short one. She feared the battles and the hazards of travel on the high seas. She rejoiced over the successes and lamented the setbacks – the loss of a convoy or the dysentery afflicting the troops. And not to break old habits, she went and preached to the ministers about how best to utilize the fleet: why didn't they direct their efforts against the English islands off America rather than intercepting their merchant vessels in the Channel? They listened politely, sure that these suggestions weren't coming from her Austrian relations but from her French friends. She didn't like the fact that her mother doubted France's ultimate victory; its superiority was so obvious to her.

It didn't even seem to occur to her that her native land might not be in favor of the budding republic of the United States, although she might have been tipped off by the fact that Austria refused to receive any of its envoys. In Vienna they were still smarting over the failure of the raid on Bavaria and held the French responsible for it. It would serve them right to be defeated after turning their back on them so sheepishly about Bavaria! The Austrians were still outraged about that, and their reactions to the course of the war were the opposite of those in Paris. They deplored French successes and applauded their defeats. The Austrians ardently hoped for an English victory. The French ambassador told Vergennes that the emperor and Kaunitz wished it too. Did Maria Theresa share in the general sentiment? We don't know. She made clear to her daughter in any case that she was more and more defeatist – the English were unbeatable, France was rushing headlong into disaster, a draw would be the best anyone could expect. She therefore made an unofficial offer to mediate – just to help out of course. But hurry! This couldn't wait! Everyone elbowed each other to try and get France and England to reconcile and to call the American rebels back to reason. They had to pull the rug out from under the Russians and Prussians who would also surely be offering their mediation services. The mere mention of Frederick II's name was enough to get Marie-Antoinette's back up. Convinced that Louis XVI "will make haste to take advantage of such a mark of good will," she advocated Austrian mediation, not realizing that this would be an admission of France's impotence.

The death of the empress at the end of 1780 only heightened the pressure. Since a good deal of the correspondence between Marie-Antoinette and her brother has disappeared, we only know about their content through what Joseph II, Kaunitz and Mercy-Argenteau said about it in theirs. The humanity that shone through in Maria Theresa' letters was replaced in these by a brutal cynicism. For them the queen was a mere puppet dangling between a timorous husband and incompetent ministers, and they prided themselves on pulling the strings. Maria Theresa's brand of manipulativeness was gone, replaced by appeals to her self-respect of the sort: how can you possibly tolerate being kept in the dark about everything and having your opinions laughed at? They didn't care if she was compromised as long as she served them. Kaunitz was fond of saying that from a bad debtor one is happy to extract whatever one can. He would try to extract the most out of Marie-Antoinette.

Joseph II and his chancellor hoped to humiliate France, as they had been humiliated over the whole Bavarian business. France wanted to maintain the balance between Prussia and Austria, did they? Okay, then they would see to it that France did not win out over England, and they didn't hide the fact either. As early as January 1781 they sent Versailles an official offer to mediate. Kaunitz knew perfectly well that the enemies would not give up until they were totally exhausted, which was still far from being the case, but he wanted to set the date for a peace conference anyway.

He could already see himself hosting at the emperor's side in Vienna the cream of European diplomacy. Vergennes sidestepped the offer with a number of excuses. While all this was happening, the queen discovered that she was expecting her second child. That would strengthen her "credibility." On his way to the Low Countries Joseph II popped down to Versailles to prop up his ambassador, whose powers of persuasion were always met with the young woman's shallowness or inertia. Yes, she did say to Mercy shortly after her mother's death, "Tell me what I have to do and I promise you I'll do it." But her show of good intentions was only matched by her inefficacity. Joseph's week with her between July 29th and August 5th was spent in leisurely conversation and parties, but it didn't turn his sister into a seasoned diplomat. The king and his ministers had become past masters at getting her off their backs; they let her say her piece and then promptly ignored it.

Soon it was learned that on October 19, 1781 – three days before the birth of the dauphin – the French and American troops won a decisive victory at Yorktown in the Chesapeake Bay, which forced England to grant independence to the United States. Not one to delude himself, Joseph II abandoned his hope of holding a congress that would make him Europe's arbiter. Even in defeat the English needed no one to negotiate for them. Despite the fact that a British emissary arrived in Versailles to broker a peace deal without any go-betweens, Marie-Antoinette was still trying to explain to her husband in April of 1782 "that the difficulties to be sorted out between the warring factions are too complicated to do without the intervention of intermediaries." The negotiations were indeed complicated, but they were sorted out without outside interference. On the 3rd of September 1783 the Treaty of Versailles put an end to the American war. Louis XVI triumphed, to the great dismay of Austria, because "the great power that until now had balanced out that of France" was "thoroughly and definitively defeated."

But Joseph II didn't wait for this added reason for bitterness towards his recalcitrant ally to launch into other enterprises for which he counted on his sister's support.

From carving up the Turkish Empire
to opening the Escaut estuaries

The new favor he was asking of the queen was right up her alley: organize a sumptuous reception for Catherine the Great's son Paul and his wife when they visited Versailles in the spring of 1782 under the pseudonym of the count and countess du Nord. Her instructions were to flatter their tastes and anticipate their wishes, to treat them like old friends. He sent her very precise information so she could prepare the visit properly, and suggested a few appropriate subjects of conversation like music and the education of children. The "Norths" were treated to performances of *Iphigenia in Aulide* in Versailles and *Zemir and Azor* at the Trianon, a formal ball in Gabriel's grand ballroom, and to banquets and illuminations in the park that left the ladies and their suite, and notably the baroness of Oberkirch, with memories worthy of *A Thousand And One Arabian Nights*. But Marie-Antoinette, obliged to watch her every word and terrified of making a false step, got thoroughly sick of it. She breathed a deep sigh of relief on seeing them off when the month was up: for her, having fun did not go hand in hand with politics. For once, however, she was not caught in a vise between her brother and her husband: Louis XVI wanted just as much as Joseph II to spoil his guests. But it all made her ill at ease, because neither one bothered to explain to her why.

Already in 1780 the czarina had wanted to add her two cents' worth to the Anglo-French conflict. She had joined in Austria's efforts to mediate. But unlike the Austrian emperor, she rendered France a great service. Many countries were put out by the arrogance of the British, who as true "masters of the seas" had assumed the right to board their ships to intercept any possible aid to the rebels. She had them all sign a neutrality pact. She did so because she needed Louis XVI's support for the big plans that she and Joseph II were hatching.

The Ottoman Empire was already the "sick man" of southeast Europe. No one suspected at the time that it would take it a century and a half to die. On paper, Austria and Russia had already partitioned it, but this is not the place to go into the plans in detail. Suffice it to say that Austria would keep the west while the Russians would set themselves up on the Black Sea and take Constantinople*. To hide how extensive the take-over would be, some parts of the Balkans would be set up as supposedly independent states but really either Austrian or Russian protectorates. Prussian opposition could be expected; having no borders with Turkey, Frederick II could hope for no territorial gain to counterbalance the increase in power of his two neighbors. Since France was Turkey's traditional ally, its opposition could also be expected. But Louis XVI, less bellicose

---

* In 1774 the treaty of Küçük Kaynarca had marked the beginning of Russia's grip on the Crimea, and in 1775, the Turks had to yield the Bukovine to Austria.

than his cousin in Berlin, had already encouraged the Turks many times to make concessions to the Russians in order to avoid a conflagration. If he were offered his piece of the pie, maybe he'd be a bit more understanding. They would set aside Egypt for him.

Such was the secret plan that the czarina's son came to Versailles to quietly divulge. Louis XVI's answer was a polite but categorical *no*. Russia was dangerous, however, so the sumptuousness of the Norths' reception was meant to soften the blow. Mercy confirmed to Vienna that it would be impossible to get the king "to agree, even passively, to the ruin of the Ottoman Empire." He wrote: "I am thoroughly convinced that no proposition, however advantageous it might be, could sway the king on this issue... Even the queen, notwithstanding the high degree of trust she commands with her august spouse, would not have enough of it to effectuate this complete turn-around in French political attitudes, and if she attempted it, she would only furnish the ministers with the means to deprive her of the king's confidence. With Maurepas gone, Vergennes was the strong man in the ministry, and thus Louis XVI's resolve was strengthened.

Unquestionably, these big plans could not be carried out against the expressed wishes of France and Prussia. Ever the realist, Catherine II did not belabor the issue. Falling back on her tactic of chipping away at the Ottoman lands by the Black Sea, she invaded and occupied the Crimea. And believing that he now was in a position of strength, Joseph II got Marie-Antoinette to make new overtures, which induced Vergennes to lecture her about the "monstrous system" of dividing up conquered territories. However, France, despite a feint show of military force in Toulon, had not the means to defend the Turks. As usual, Turkey was advised to cut its losses and surrender the Crimea to Catherine. She had won. But there was one consolation for Vergennes, "At least the emperor got nothing out of it."

The emperor still had two irons in the fire, however. The first concerned the Escaut estuaries. In order to get a picture of the issue, it is useful to look at a map from a century or so ago – even a present-day one will do. At the end of a long struggle against Spain by its Flemish provinces inherited from Charles V, only the Calvinist ones in the north gained their independence and became the "United Provinces" – now the Netherlands. The Catholic ones in the south remained within Madrid's orbit and were called the Low Countries (today's Belgium). The territorial partition guaranteed by the Münster and Westphalia treaties back in 1648 granted to the new state of the United Provinces maritime Flanders, the area that surrounds the estuary of the Escaut river. This meant that the traffic in and out of the great Belgian port of Antwerp depended on the good will of the Dutch. The latter hastened to close off the mouths of the river in order to kill Antwerp's competition with Rotterdam. This was a shocking situation, no doubt, but one that neither the Spanish nor the Austrians, who succeeded them in Brussels, had questioned.

But then Joseph did. He sent to the government of The Hague a *Summary Index* of his demands: opening the Escaut estuary, giving up Dutch Flanders, and the restitution of Maastricht, the fortified town that the Low Countries had been claiming for a century. But he had no hope of being heeded without French support. He therefore instructed his sister to convince her husband that he should be the one to send the United Provinces an ultimatum. Needless to say, Louis XVI hadn't the slightest intention of it, especially at that time – 1784 – when he was negotiating an alliance with them. Yet again, Marie-Antoinette had to take stock of the futility of her efforts.

Vienna decided therefore to resort to arms. In October a ship flying the imperial colors left Antwerp and started its descent up the river. Would the Dutch dare to intercept it? They dared. After the usual warnings, they fired. Struck by cannon blast in its lower decks, the *Louis** was forced back to its port of registry. Vienna blamed the Dutch for a scandalous act of aggression. We will spare the reader the details of the futile tongue-lashings the queen inflicted on the king, then on Vergennes. Neither of them hid their belief that the Dutch were within their rights, and that if the emperor carried out his threat to get vengeance through armed force, France would send troops to the border. As she threw in the minister's face the fact that she would hold him responsible should any breakdown of the precious alliance result from it all, he got exasperated and listed all the grievances that France was harboring against Austria. He had to be mighty sure of the king's support to abandon his customary reserve. Not a single word would be changed in the threatening message to be sent to Vienna. Marie-Antoinette would call it "unseemly." Would they at least consider delaying sending it for five days? Already Joseph II, seeing that fear of armed conflict was not making Louis XVI back down, had begun to retreat: no longer would he punish the Dutch, nor demand the reopening of the Escaut estuary, as long as they consented to cede back Maastricht.

Why? For the sake of it, no doubt, but also to improve the Low Countries' worth as a bargaining chip, for he had never given up the

---

* Was it by chance that the Austrians chose a ship of this name, or was it to imply that they had the French king's support?

old hope of exchanging them for Bavaria. Unfortunately for him, the rest of Europe was even less well disposed than before, now that he'd shown his fangs. And Marie-Antoinette nonetheless was set up to make an effort that was condemned in advance to failure. To get her off their backs, the king and ministers resorted to their usual temporizing and appeasement, while awaiting the Prussian king's predictable response. Sensing that she was being manipulated, and irritated by Mercy and his constant coaching, she lost her sang froid, progressed from criticism to hurtful accusations, causing Vergennes to offer his resignation, which the king immediately refused. In the meantime, the duke de Deux-Ponts, encouraged by Frederick II, had got most of the princes of the empire to rally to his objections. Joseph II had to back down.

But there was still the little Austro-Dutch tiff to deal with. Louis XVI got involved to convince him to agree to financial compensation. The emperor was resolved to play for high stakes with these "cheese merchants." He demanded twelve million florins for Maastricht, plus his "war costs." The Dutch protested loudly. Vienna wound up agreeing to lower the price. To be agreeable to his new Dutch allies, Louis XVI accepted to help with part of the payment, which they balked at making, two million florins, it appears*. In terms of any advantage in foreign affairs, this money was a pure waste. Soon, Holland would be brought into the Anglo-Prussian orbit anyway: for although Frederick II had died, his nephew and heir took advantage of the struggle between the opposing parties, and sent a military expedition into Holland to support his brother-in-law the stadholder against the big pro-French merchants. And as for French domestic affairs, the effects were even worse. It was said the queen extorted the king's financial support so that her brother could indulge his insatiable ambitions, and the sum kept getting higher. It was no longer two million but two hundred million that Marie-Antoinette was supposed to have wrung from the treasury to send to Vienna in a long convoy of wagons laden down with gold coin.

The jolt

Reading Mercy-Argenteau's terribly repetitive reports tends to give us the impression that Marie-Antoinette remained unchanged during the ten years between the ages of twenty-two and thirty-two,

---

* Depending on the source, the total of these sums varies. One florin was worth two and a half pounds.

from her state of semi-virginity to her stature as a full-fledged wife and mother of four children. From his point of view, she remained the frivolous and hare-brained young woman incapable of any "follow-through or energy in her undertakings" who had to be constantly badgered into understanding that it was purely up to her to dominate her dolt of a husband, to get control of ministers who were as "timorous" as they were "inept," and thereby govern France on behalf of the overarching house of Austria, from whose ambassador she got her orders. For instance, he wrote in September 1783, "In all justice I pay homage to her good intentions and her charming qualities, but she sometimes regrettably falls short of the mark because of her frivolity and little inconsistencies."

All the same, as one reads along, questions arise. Did her good intentions remain steady and unchanging as the years went by? Among "poor payers" there are those who can't pay, those who don't want to pay, and those who will no longer pay. Could Marie-Antoinette have gone from one category to another? In this regard, we can distinguish two periods: before and after the death of Maria Theresa. Before, we have the luxury of the letters the two exchanged. They leave no room for doubt about Marie-Antoinette's submission to her mother's will. But Maria Theresa knew not to go too far. It would take the Prussian troops' invasion and ravaging of Bohemia to get her to seek French help. She asked for what she thought was absolutely necessary, nothing more. With Joseph II alone at the helm, the tone changes. He makes demands. And as far as he's concerned, his sister never does enough. But it's one thing to fly to the aid of her country in danger, it is quite another to support the expansionist ambitions of her brother, who over and over again gets in over his head. Marie-Antoinette was sensitive and intuitive enough to see the difference.

Also, we mustn't forget that after the death of the empress our sources of information become less dependable. We only hear Marie-Antoinette's voice filtered through Mercy when he writes to Joseph II and Kaunitz. The ambassador would have us believe she speaks "the language of the alliance" with conviction, sure that her brother is in the right, passionate in his defense, and confronting the king and his ministers individually, or interfering in their meetings to show them how well-founded Austrian claims are, speaking loud and clear, causing scenes. He even sometimes transcribes the energetic arguments she was to have made. However, let's think about it a minute: he was reporting to the emperor and his chancellor what the queen *tells* him she said to the king and Vergennes. So much ricocheting, so much opportunity for misrepresentation. In order to avoid reprimands, did Marie-Antoinette not exaggerate the strength of her own arguments? Mercy's weakness was always trying to look good; was *he* not perhaps tempted to put his own slant on her remarks? Finally, since it was his custom to prepare word for word the arguments she had to put forward, to simplify matters did he merely rewrite the crib notes that he'd given her, instead of finding out what she actually said?

Why should we question Mercy's information when almost all historians have trusted his word? Because the picture he painted of Louis XVI and also of Vergennes completely runs counter to the reports he sent of what they actually got done politically. The history of these eight years makes it clear that Louis XVI, far from being an indecisive incompetent acquiescent to bungling ministers, showed proof, in full agreement with Vergennes, of the most steadfast continuity in his views, a man who having won the American war and checkmated all of the Austrian emperor's designs, emerged in 1784 and 1785 as Europe's arbiter. This being the case, to insist on affirming that the queen devoted herself to governing her husband if and when she bothered, stemmed either from self-deception or the desire to deceive others. Could Mercy admit to himself, or to his masters, that Marie-Antoinette's celebrated influence, upon which he rested all his hopes, only ever existed in his imagination? We will leave him the benefit of the doubt.

But Marie-Antoinette herself very quickly lost any belief in her own influence. Repeated failures convinced her of her powerlessness, and her pride suffered increasingly over time. She didn't dare refuse when Mercy pressed her into service, but she reacted with a heavy dose of inertia. As she had always done when faced with a disagreeable chore, she tried to wriggle out of it. He was annoyed when he found her chatting with friends or playing with her children when he came to talk business with her. She only half listened to him, making it obvious how tedious he was. When he importuned her too much, or she received threatening letters from Vienna, she grudgingly resolved to do what was required of her. And it was on the king and his ministers that she took out her anger at being forced to regurgitate the lessons that she knew to be inane. So much for the "energetic" interventions Mercy boasted of in Vienna. But she resented those who imposed them on her. She changes.

The changes came in stages, and we can glean traces of them here and there. On September 22, 1784, she made up her mind to come clean with her brother in a much-cited lengthy letter where she talked about the "few options" the king's temperament left her.

"By nature he is not much of a talker, and often he doesn't speak to me about important matters, even when he doesn't wish to hide them from me; he answers me when I talk about them, but he rarely brings them up first, and when I find out the quarter of something going on, I need to be clever in order to get the ministers to tell me the rest by letting on that the king has told me everything. When I reproach the king for not having told me certain things, he doesn't get angry, he seems a bit embarrassed, and sometimes he tells me quite naturally that he hadn't thought of it. I freely admit to you that political affairs* are the ones I have the least influence over... I'm not blind to my own credibility; I just know that when it comes to politics, I do not carry much weight in the king's mind. Would it be prudent of me to make scenes with his minister over things about which the king would almost certainly not support me? Without making a show of it or lying, I let the public believe that I have more credit than I actually have, because I would have even less if I didn't..."

These admissions, "hardly flattering to her self-esteem," show that she had not yet fully grasped matters, since she continued to hold to her brother's way of seeing things. But we see that they were above all an attempt to opt out: since I can't get anything done, for heaven's sake, leave me alone.

A year later, by August 8, 1785 she had already won a bit of independence. When her brother pressed her to get the king to make the Dutch do his bidding, she replied, "Since you are convinced that firm language from the king will suffice, why don't you ask him yourself to take up the cudgel with you when you write to him about it? ... I fear I shall not be able to obtain from the king what you yourself are not asking of him." Basically, she was telling him to do his own dirty work. And one is tempted to find a hint of irony in the sentence that ends the paragraph: "Whatever the case may be, my dear brother, my fear and skepticism about its outcome will not prevent me from working for it with all my soul, you must be sure of that." At this point Mercy worried at seeing her political sense develop: "She figures out a lot more than I would like," he admits.

Two years later, in February of 1787, she finally shook off the yoke. Vergennes was dying; Mercy, who was drawing up plans for his succession, was stunned to find that Marie-Antoinette was

---

* Unmodified "political affairs" referred at the time to foreign affairs.

going her own way. He wrote: "During Monsieur de Vergennes' illness, although she had the opportunity to speak emphatically in favor of Monsieur de Saint-Priest, *the queen suddenly was overcome with scruples about the court of Vienna's naming ministers to that of Versailles**." He adds: "I had to endure the strangest line of reasoning in support of this thesis; I countered it with my own reasons, if not to say with rather bald truths, and as a result the queen was more constrained than persuaded to put in a few half-hearted words on Monsieur Saint-Priest's behalf, as she informed me in a note of the 14th of which I enclose a copy. Your Highness will observe in it the phrase 'You know my principles...' – she is referring to the scruples about which I spoke above."

We unfortunately don't know what the note in question contained as Joseph II didn't keep it and Mercy said nothing more about the "strangest line of reasoning" that the queen served up to him to buttress her arguments. The only explanation the ambassador offered for such stupefying behavior was that the young woman "in ignorance of and distaste for all serious matters" was aware of "neither their importance nor their consequences," saw them all as a big bore, and made decisions "as the spirit moves her," according to her "bizarre reasoning."

We can be forgiven for being somewhat astonished by the fact that Mercy affected surprise here. After all, no one was in a better position to know that when she got mixed up in ministerial appointments she didn't follow Vienna's opinion, but that of her friends, as we saw during the years following her ascension to the throne**. The same applied in subsequent years. She backed Necker, who was confident he could finance the war in America without adding new taxes, and what is more was always at great pains to take her and her friends' wishes into account. She rejoiced when Sartine at the naval ministry and Montbarey at the ministry of war were fired for having tied up a lot of money for their departments without referring the matter to Necker. They were Maurepas' minions, and Maurepas was no friend of hers. The names she'd put forward to replace them were not suggested by Mercy but by her circle of friends. They were actually good choices. She got no opposition to Castries for the navy. For Ségur at the war ministry she clashed with the old Mentor, who was putting Puységur forward, and almost had to back down. At that point, Ségur's friend Madame de Polignac made a terrible tearful scene, with offers to resign and threats to retire to

---

*   The author's italics.

**   See chapter 7.

the country that ended with hugs and kisses. Her forcefulness was such that she got Ségur the post. No one at court had any illusions; this was a great victory for "the queen's party" over Maurepas'. But this "Austrian" party as it was called because it was made up of Choiseul's old friends, was not the least bit concerned about Joseph II or his interests. Its sights were set on power and the advantages to be reaped from it. This was clear when Necker was disgraced and it was his turn to be replaced; the new head of finance was Calonne, one hundred percent a product of this group.

What was capital – and new – in Marie-Antoinette's declaration to Mercy was not that she was distancing herself from Vienna's wishes – she had long since stopped taking them into account when it came to domestic affairs. It was that for the first time she came out and said so. And she didn't mince her words. For contrary to what the ambassador asserted, the few letters that have come down to us about it show that she had learned a lot, that she was thinking clearly, and that she spoke her mind with conviction. And she also knew how to mask her evasiveness with protestations of devotion that sounded as hollow as her brother's. She obviously did not feel guilty toward him. She had finally shaken off Austria's yoke. Her once pathological attachment to her native country had become no more than normal. In France she now had people whom she could admire and love: a friend, Madame de Polignac, and a *chevalier servant* and no doubt lover, Fersen, and above all children whose advent over the course of the years had given meaning to her life. Did Vergennes contribute to opening her eyes about her political duties to her son? One day, furious at his intractability she shouted at him "Do you not realize you are speaking to the sister of the emperor?" The minister replied, "I realize that I am speaking to the mother of the dauphin of France." The argument echoed deeply in her, since she would soon be using the phrase whenever she was criticized for her Austrian connections.

Throughout these years, Marie-Antoinette underwent extremely difficult psychological trials. As the alliance she was forced into representing crumbled, her mental universe cracked. To avoid this unbearable fracturing, her escape strategies merely masked the problem and were of little relief. Motherhood was the thing. With the birth of her children, a new woman emerges, freed from the ties that had enchained her to her family and her fatherland. At thirty, Marie-Antoinette was able to fend off a request from her brother and refuse an audience with Mercy. Her children embody the future and exorcise the past. She is finally an adult.

It was about time. She was now closer to her husband, tied to him by mutual interest. She thereby paradoxically gained the influence she'd sought in vain to extort from him. The illusory influence she prided herself on was replaced by genuine trust. He had lost his most trusted advisors, Maurepas in 1781, then Vergennes in 1787. He found no one capable of replacing them, just now when the regime was tottering. Also, Choiseul's death in 1785 put an end to the machinations over his reinstatement and changed the political landscape. Marie-Antoinette was no longer Austria's plaything; Louis XVI knew this, and besides, his brother-in-law's ambitions were the least of his worries. Faced with the dangers threatening both of them, united with her in adversity, he would consult his wife and include her in decision-making, letting her take the initiative when necessary. And politics would once again catch up with Marie-Antoinette, and impose on her a role that would be even more difficult because she'd become highly unpopular.

Had she become French? She was going in that direction, very slowly. But it was too late. Even if it wasn't officially abandoned, the famous Austro-French alliance was moribund. Marie-Antoinette had been its warranty. Her efforts to keep it alive, at the risk of involving France in a European conflict, completed the process of the public's alienation from her. Padding her interventions in the Bavarian and Escaut estuary affairs, the pamphleteers implicated her in a vast enterprise to subject France to Austria's dictates. Did the pressures Joseph II and Mercy put on her really amount to a conspiracy? To say so would be something of a stretch. And if there was a conspiracy, it was a total fiasco. It can be said that conspirators' failure does not exonerate them. However, Marie-Antoinette's intentions were pure; she sincerely believed that her two countries' interests were one. But if she persisted for so long in deceiving herself, it is because at heart she remained Austrian for want of finding in Versailles what her heart desired. It was unfortunate for her, and a sinister twist of fate, that just at the time when the lamentable wavering between her two countries was tipping resolutely in favor of France, public opinion belatedly and permanently labeled her otherwise. It was when she distanced herself from Austria that the injurious, indelible epithet of *Autrichienne** stuck to her.

This current of public opinion with its roots in national sentiment fed off other grievances arising from her imprudent behavior. Her

---

*   *Translator's note:* Autrichienne *means "Austrian woman" but contains the word* "chienne" *or female dog/bitch, a highly loaded connotation in Marie-Antoinette's case.*

unpopularity only grew. She didn't understand why she was no longer loved; she saw it as unjust. Gone were the days when she could laugh off the libels against her. Now they tormented her. She had the following conversation with her page, Tilly, in 1782:

> "Why did they hardly applaud at all? What have I done to them?"
> "I did not notice that the queen..."
> "How could you not have seen it? In any case, actually, too bad for the Parisians, it's not my fault."
> "H.M. attaches too much importance... (a few tears well up in his eyes) to something that can only be the result of chance."
> "Such fancy words coming from a scatterbrain! But still, when one has nothing with which to reproach oneself, it is very hurtful."

Two years later on May 24th when she went to Paris to be churched after the birth of the duke de Normandie, she received an icy welcome, "not a single exclamation, perfect silence," despite the fact that the crowd was huge. In such a case, silence is an insult. She was sobbing when she got back to the Tuileries, plunged into the same incomprehension: "But what have I done to them?"

She still didn't understand when the famous necklace scandal coincided with the signing of the treaty over the Escaut estuaries. It would open the floodgates to the torrents of contempt and hatred that she would never be able to wash away.

CHAPTER 15

THE NECKLACE AFFAIR

A fabulous gem, a gem that could have come out of *A Thousand And One Arabian Nights*, a gem so costly that no one in the whole world could afford to buy it – so it would have to be stolen. In the role of the adventuress with a fertile imagination, ready to do anything to grab the prize, there's a fake countess but a real descendant of the Valois dynasty, whose youthful beauty was matched by persuasive eloquence and outrageous audacity. In the role of the unsuspecting dupe, a cardinal archbishop of Strasburg, the king's chief almoner, scion of one of the most prominent families in the realm, devoured by ambition, with a high opinion of himself, and interested in the occult as professed by the "magician" Cagliostro. Among the other characters in the cast are the beauty's husband; her lover an expert forger; a pretty milliner a bit too susceptible to the compliments of the men on the prowl around the Palais-Royal gardens; and a monk of dubious dealings. In the role of a silent, invisible figure but central to the plot, is queen Marie-Antoinette of France. Everything was in place for what was not yet called a melodrama. With every outlandish twist in the plot, the affair kept the French and European public on tender hooks for an entire year. What should not have amounted to anything more than a sordid confidence trick very quickly took on a whole political life of its own thanks to a succession of silly mistakes. In the eyes of the public, not only was the queen on trial, but the monarchy itself. The affair would echo down the ensuing centuries. The public enquiry would show the fake countess to be the culprit and the cardinal her dupe. But there remained in the documents enough shady areas to incite the imagination around one major question – the only one the preliminary investigation refused to countenance because it was so sacrilegious: was the queen either directly or indirectly implicated in the affair? For two centuries historians, novelists and playwrights have hashed and rehashed this meaty material, concluding, in the absence of proof, whatever their innermost conviction has been.

Now it's our turn to speak up. We cannot go over it all again from A to Z. An entire book devoted to it would barely suffice. Some of the books about it go into great detail, reproducing the basic documentation. All of them tell the story by putting back into logical and chronological order what the enquiry uncovered haphazardly. At every stage of the story the reader knows what went before, so there is a tendency to think, instinctively, that the actors in this drama – notably the king and queen – also knew. But such was not the case. If we want to understand their reactions, which seem absurd to us, we must closely follow the different elements of the drama as they came to light. What did they know? On what did they base their reasoning? And above all, what feelings did each new development give rise to? The disadvantage of presenting the facts logically is that it renders practically incomprehensible the key role irrational passion played in their decisions. Few scandals are this replete with improbabilities and incredible errors. There are few other cases in which sensible people have behaved so unreasonably and have so vehemently refused to admit the obvious. To a great extent the necklace affair is a totally mad affair.

A fabulous necklace

Official jewelers to the crown, Mssrs. Charles-Auguste Boehmer and Paul Bassenge*, both originally from Saxony, were at the top of their profession and more than a little bit proud of it. Their boutique, "The Balcony," was the meeting point of all the elegant and moneyed set. Millions changed hands there. All that prestige went to their heads. In the beginning of the 1770s they decided to create the most beautiful necklace in the whole wide world, a masterpiece that would forever link their name to the splendors of the monarchy. Who would purchase this royal masterpiece? Louis XV of course, to adorn the fair bosom of his latest favorite. Why bother getting a purchasing agreement? All Madame du Barry had to do was look upon this marvel and the deal would be done; they were sure of it.

In order to realize their dream, they had to solve the practical problems their flights of fancy gave rise to. Bassenge was the

---

* Since Boehmer was the one who dealt with clients, there has been a tendency to call them the Boehmers.

designer, the technician; Boehmer was the businessman. But they were equally passionate about the enterprise. They went to great lengths, devoting much work and time to the effort. They were after all jewelers before artists: for them, the most beautiful creation was the most expensive. They searched among all of Europe's diamond dealers for the biggest and purest stones. They drew and redrew their sketches according to each new addition and then aligned the stones to fashion the bud, the cabochon or pear shape required to achieve the harmony they were seeking. The years passed, but there was always something not quite right. Finally, they had gathered together all the diamonds and were getting ready to set them when Louis XV's death forced them to change course. No catastrophe, they'd propose the necklace to the queen, who would lift even higher the renown of the house of Boehmer. They sought nothing less than perfection. Putting it all together took more time than they'd expected. They needed the right occasion, but the setting was not completed in time for the coronation in 1775. Soon afterward however they saw just how tempted Marie-Antoinette was by their earrings and bracelets*. Bursting with anticipation, they hastened to put the finishing touches on the masterpiece.

Was this most famous necklace of exceptional beauty? Certainly, if judged by the quality and brilliance of its stones. But it was over the top. A string of seventeen diamonds almost as large as hazel nuts each weighing between five and eight carats encircled the neck. Attached to this were piled interlacing rows of spirals, festoons and garlands. Between them there were clusters of pendants, the most noticeable ones pear shaped – from nine to eleven carats. The whole thing came together at a huge twelve-carat bud elongated by a trefoil, designed to nestle between the breasts. In the back, coming together at the clasp, were two rows of stones adorned with three layers of pendants to make the back of the neck sparkle. The Boehmers thought big, colossal, one might say. It was almost a breastplate. They called this type of necklace a "slave necklace," recalling the heavy iron collars that weighed down the shoulders of the black slaves. The 647 diamonds alone weighted 2,800 carats, or over a pound. Along with the setting, the necklace must have weighed close to four pounds. Would the queen's slender neck be able to carry it all? And would it not outshine the bosom it was supposed to enhance? It wasn't designed to blend in to the rest of one's apparel, or to highlight the beauty of the bearer, because it

---

*   See Chapter 8.

drew all the attention to itself. Marie-Antoinette was too feminine to overlook this shortcoming.

The price was exorbitant. The Boehmers at first put a price tag on it of 1,800,000 pounds. In order to buy the stones they had gone deep into debt, investing everything they had. There was interest to pay on the loans; they had to move things along. They came down to 1,600,000 pounds. Chastened by the troubles caused by the secret purchase of the famous bracelets a while back, Marie-Antoinette turned them down – the necklace was too dear. At the beginning of 1779 after the birth of Madame Royale, they changed tack and took their chances with the proud father, who found the necklace so beautiful that he desired "to see the queen adorned by it and had the jewelry case brought to her." If one can believe Madame Campan, at this point the queen made the famous remark that it would be better to spend the money on a battleship. For France was at war in America at the time and money was in short supply. They took up the charge again when the dauphin was born, and offered an installment plan. The queen apparently refused again, telling her husband that he could purchase it for his children, but as for her, she "would never wear it, not wishing people to blame her for wanting something so excessively expensive." Indeed, the necklace was beginning to take on a sulfurous reputation. Boehmer had offered it to a number of European courts, but all of them refused it. No one had the money to waste on such a costly object. They couldn't sell it.

Madame Campan reports the queen's rejection with too much studied insistence not to be suspect. She aimed to demonstrate that her mistress was not the unrepentant wastrel she was said to be*. But it is certain that by the beginning of the 1780s Marie-Antoinette was no longer quite the scatterbrain she had been when she acceded to the throne. She had learned how to count. Increased by the king's gifts at each birth, her personal fortune, previously in chronic deficit, now comprised a kitty of five to six hundred thousand pounds, half of which she distributed to the poor who had suffered the rigors of the terrible winter of 1783-1784. Wearing ostentatious jewelry clashed with her desire for simplicity and a

---

* Madame Campan, the queen's first lady of the bedchamber from 1774 to 1792, told her story rather late – at the time of the Restoration. Historians regard it with skepticism because it is tarnished by some factual errors, in the timing especially, and because of the good lady's care to show the queen in a favorable light and her desire to inflate her own role. However, this is not enough to completely reject her testimony and discard the anecdotes it supplies about the queen's daily life, even if the teller has obvious ulterior motives.

private, country life. Can we imagine the mind-boggling necklace gracing a white linen dress and straw hat? The accounts of the wise Madame d'Ossun, her new wardrobe mistress, show that she had not reduced her clothing expenses; but the jewelry chapter was closed. Less frivolous now, she was interested in weightier matters. The works on the Trianon and the hamlet were coming to an end; soon she would get the king to give her the Saint-Cloud chateau, whose renovation she would entrust to her favorite architect Richard Mique.

She therefore had other problems on her mind when one day Boehmer, at the end of his rope, came to throw himself at her feet in tears: "Madame, if you do not buy my necklace I am ruined, dishonored. I do not wish to survive such a disgrace. When I leave here I shall throw myself in the river." She scolded him sharply, called him insane, and set the matter straight: "Not only did I not order the object that is now causing you to despair, but every time that you proposed your lovely assortments I told you that I did not wish to add more diamonds to what I already had. I refused your necklace and when the king wished to give it to me, I equally refused him. Do not ever speak to me about them again. Try to take it apart and sell the diamonds piecemeal; and don't drown yourself..."

Boehmer didn't drown himself. But he couldn't get himself to take the necklace apart and sell off its parts. It would have been wisdom itself to do so, in spite of the losses this would incur. But the idea of destroying his masterpiece was unbearable. And since there were no other potential buyers, he did not give up hope that she would come around.

In which the necklace comes up again

"For a long time the queen had been avoiding Boehmer, fearing his exalted notions," when on 12 July 1785 he came to deliver to her some diamond buckles and a shoulder clasp from the king. He took advantage of the situation to hand her a note that, according to Madame Campan, completely mystified her:

> Madame, we are at the zenith of happiness to dare to think that the most recent arrangements that were proposed to us, and to which we devoted ourselves with respect and zeal, are a new proof of our submission and devotion to the orders of Your Majesty, and we have true satisfaction at the thought that

the most beautiful diamond necklace in existence will serve the greatest and best of queens.

It was too late to ask the jeweler to explain; he'd already left. She ordered Madame Campan to enquire about it when next she saw him, and burned the note with a candle, as was her custom with all letters she received. She added, "This man exists just to torment me; he's always got some mad scheme in his head; do not forget to tell him that I no longer like diamonds and I shall never again buy any for the rest of my life." Was the lady of the bedchamber to summon him to tell him so? No, better wait for the first opportunity to arise: "Whatever you do with such a man will be misconstrued."

If we credit Madame Campan's account, on August 3rd the jeweler arrived at her place in the country in a terrible state. She passed on the queen's message.

> "But, he said, to whom must I turn to obtain the reply to the letter I presented to her?"
>
> "To no one, I told him. Her Majesty burned your note, not having a clue what you meant."
>
> "But, Madame, that is not possible, he cried, the queen knows she has to give me money."
>
> "Money, Monsieur Boehmer? We settled the queen's last accounts long ago."
>
> "Madame, are you not in on this? I do not call it settled when a man is still owed more than fifteen hundred thousand francs, and when not being paid the sum is ruining him."
>
> "Have you lost your mind? I asked him. For what object can the queen owe you such an exorbitant sum?"
>
> "For my necklace, Madame", Boehmer replied coldly.
>
> "What! I replied. Not again – that necklace you've been uselessly tormenting the queen about for years now? But you told me that you'd sold it for Constantinople."
>
> "It is the queen who ordered me to say that to anyone who enquired about it, replied the hopeless imbecile. He then told me that the queen had wanted the necklace and had Monsignor the cardinal de Rohan buy it for her."
>
> "You are mistaken, I cried, the queen has spoken not a single word to the cardinal since his return from Vienna; no man is less in favor at court."
>
> "No, it is you who are mistaken, Madame, Boehmer tells me; she is so singularly well disposed to him that it is to His

Eminence that she handed over thirty thousand francs that were given to me as a down payment, and she took them, in his presence, out of the little secretary made of Sèvres porcelain near the fireplace in her boudoir."

"And is it the cardinal who told you this?"

"Yes, Madame, the cardinal himself."

"Oh, what odious trickery, I cried."

"Indeed, Madame, in truth I am beginning to be quite alarmed, since His Eminence had assured me that the queen would wear her necklace on the feast of Pentecost, and I didn't see it on her; that is what decided me to write to Her Majesty."

The conscientious lady of the bedchamber advised him at this point to go confide in the baron de Breteuil about the whole matter. As minister of king's household he was in charge of the police. But the jeweler went instead to see the cardinal, who encouraged him to go see the queen, who, it seems, refused to admit him. Why did Madame Campan not inform Marie-Antoinette right away? She claims her father-in-law talked her out of it. It was better to let the minister sort out this "infernal intrigue." She waited until her mistress brought it up incidentally on August 8th to tell her the upshot of the jeweler's visit. If her account can be trusted, Marie-Antoinette was flabbergasted, and it was only at that point that she summoned Boehmer the next day and found out that her name was being used in a confidence scheme of enormous proportions. Such is the account generally retained by Marie-Antoinette's biographers.

In fact, it seems that either Madame Campan was not aware of part of the truth or that she was hiding it. She herself actually implied in a passage of the *Clarifications* not included in the final version of her memoirs, that the queen had been advised somewhat earlier. This point of view was expanded upon by the abbé Georgel, cardinal de Rohan's secretary, in a memoir clearly favorable to his former boss, but often well documented. What earlier date exactly? And how did she find out? We don't know. But for certain the queen learned, undoubtedly during the second half of July, that the cardinal de Rohan was using her name to negotiate the purchase of the blighted necklace. She confided in abbé de Vermond and in Breteuil, and they decided together what strategy to follow. It would turn out to be an utterly disastrous one.

The cardinal de Rohan

All three of them saw red, so to speak, at the mere mention of the name cardinal de Rohan. All three of them hated him. The queen above all hated him with an old, unbending hatred, partly inherited from her mother.

The empress had been very cross when in 1771 she learned that Louis XV was about to name Prince Louis de Rohan as his representative in Vienna. She was hoping for the baron de Breteuil, whom Choiseul was planning to nominate to the post. But once Choiseul was disgraced, power was in the hands of his adversaries. Not only did the empress nurse certain misgivings about him as a member of the hostile clan, the candidate's character also worried her. Marie-Antoinette wrote to her, "He is of a very great house, but the life he has always led seems more like one of a soldier than one of a bishop." When she crossed the border at Strasburg and he held a reception for her, she couldn't help admiring his easy manners and eloquent suavity. But his ties to the du Barry clique very quickly rendered him suspect.

Louis de Rohan belonged to the very old and very powerful de Rohan family that harked back to the ancient sovereigns of Brittany. It could claim distant relations both with the Valois and the Bourbons. It had links with the Empire, which granted its members princely titles. At court it was represented among others by the prince de Soubise, a personal friend to the king; by the countess de Marsan, governess of the royal children who had raised the future Louis XVI and his brothers; and by the prince and princess de Guéménée. The prince Louis, as younger brother, was destined for the church, as was the custom, regardless of whether he had a vocation for it or not. He was cooling his heels in Strasburg, waiting to succeed his uncle, to whom he'd been assigned as coadjutor. He was still young, having been born in 1734, and was endowed with all he needed to be agreeable and succeed in the world: a good physique, a noble face brightened by blue eyes, a pride tempered by natural affability and the kind of "sensitive" heart that was so appealing at the time. At first glance it was clear that this was a great lord, an impression confirmed by his taste for pomp, his disdain for money, which he dispensed lavishly, and his refusal of any kind of servility – was not a Rohan the equal of any king? "He had a lot of intellectual gifts, and even some knowledge," said the sharp-tongued Besenval. Although his learning might have been superficial, he made the best of it thanks to his ability to speak glibly and animatedly, so he was not out of place in the French Academy, to which he was elected at the age of twenty-seven. His light and witty conversation was marveled at in the salons. Was he intelligent? Yes and no. "One couldn't say he lacked esprit," noted the duke de Lévis mischievously, "but as for judgment, he was totally lacking in it. Ambition that far outweighed his capacities made him covetous of the Vienna ambassadorship..." Fatuous as he was, he saw it as the first step in a brilliant career that would one day bring him a ministry, and his whole family backed him up.

Upon his arrival in Austria on January 10, 1772 at the head of a magnificent delegation, he set up house in grand style determined to conquer Viennese high society. He traded in his soutane for a green jerkin with gold braids to keep up with the best hunters in the country; he appeared at masked balls dressed to the nines; he gave suppers at his home at little tables where guests could sit where they liked, without having to deal with the bore of a neighbor imposed by protocol. And after supper there would be gambling, concerts or dancing. People were highly entertained in his company. To the noble gentleman mandated from on high to request that he give up these suppers, he had the temerity to reply that the invitations had been issued for the entire year and he could therefore not cancel them "without causing a lot of terrible gossip," and he thoroughly ignored the warning. The more the city went mad over him, the less the empress could bear the sight of him. He brought along with him the depravity that she felt infected the court of France. Her disapproval was contagious and both Joseph II and chancellor Kaunitz were ever ready to mock what she called his "gaffes, loose tongue and manias." As for the women, all of them, "young and old, beautiful and ugly, they're all bewitched by him," she moaned. "He is their idol; they are all drooling over him." In sum, he would corrupt her good, chaste Viennese ladies. He made her look like a cantankerous old religious zealot cramped in her prejudices from another era. He was a man of careless disregard, sarcasm, irony and impertinence – he lacked respect for the sovereign. Can he be accused of having scandalous morals, as was later claimed? If he had mistresses he did not flaunt them; but he was happy to cover up the peccadilloes of his entourage. He blew a lot of hot air; he took up too much room; he was a nuisance.

Did these grievances alone explain Maria Theresa's fervent animosity? Perhaps not, as it seems he personally offended her as well. Although seemingly frivolous, the prince did not shirk his tasks. He had set up, even within the chancellery itself, an intelligence network. But he was too loose-tongued and acerbic for a diplomat.

One of his letters contained such an apt remark about the partition of Poland that it made the rounds in Versailles. It had the empress making a show of hypocritical remorse: "In one hand she is holding a handkerchief to wipe her tears and in the other she's grabbing a sword to get her share." Maria Theresa did not forgive him, and neither did Marie-Antoinette. But there was worse. The empress had the right to think and speak ill of her daughter in her letters to Mercy, but would not tolerate it in others. But Rohan, whether on his own or at someone else's behest is not known, informed her of reservations inspired by the young dauphine's conduct: there were "certain difficulties" with regard to her, he informed her mother, and "she did not have around her people capable of advising her wisely." All over Vienna he spread "unfavorable rumors" about her flirtatiousness, which might inspire suitors to get their hopes up. He spoke of her with "his usual indiscretion," practically in the same wicked and libelous terms that Beaumarchais had used. "He even threatened, if we do not wish to go down the right road, that my daughter would feel the effects*."

All this was enough to explain the two women's violent anger. As long as Louis XV reigned, Maria Theresa didn't dare request the ambassador's recall, because such a severe sanction would have raised questions that could jeopardize Marie-Antoinette. But her letters to Mercy bore a long litany of complaints against this "abominable man" that she put up with "out of love of my daughter," but whom she would like to see "smoked out" of her home at the first opportunity. Her hatred became so intense that she made up her mind to have her daughter intervene in September 1773. She ordered her to tell Madame de Marsan in confidence that the court of Vienna, highly dissatisfied with Prince Louis' conduct, was about to demand his recall and that he would therefore be wise to prevent a scandal by asking to be discharged of his ambassadorship for personal reasons. But this ruse didn't fool anyone and alienated the entire de Rohan family from the dauphine. The ambassador stayed put in Vienna. It took Louis XV's death and Louis XVI's accession to the throne to force him out. Marie-Antoinette was queen. "You say that we no longer have anything to fear from that nasty clique of Soubises and Marsans," Maria Theresa wrote to Mercy, "so I have no need to humor them."

Marie-Antoinette was of the same opinion. She pursued Rohan

---

* These two last details appear in a letter to Mercy of August 28, 1774, after accession to the throne therefore, in which Maria Theresa recapitulates her prior grievances against Rohan.

with blatant vindictiveness. She wasn't able to prevent his being appointed grand almoner in 1777, because Louis XVI didn't dare go back on a promise made to his governess Madame de Marsan. They refused to put him forward for a cardinal's hat, but he got one anyway through the king of Poland. Neither could they prevent his succeeding to his uncle's bishropric of Strasburg, and he was therefore one of the highest-ranking dignitaries of the Church of France. And Maria Theresa shared her obsessive fears with her daughter. "He is a cruel enemy, as much for you as for his principles, which could not be more perverse. He puts on an affable, agreeable and considerate face, but he has done a lot of damage here, and now I must see him at your side with the king! He will hardly bring honor to his post as bishop either." In short, it was as if she were depicting the devil himself to Marie-Antoinette, this man who was to officiate at all of the grandest events at Versailles and baptize her newborn children. Just as she was steely-eyed and closed-mouthed with Madame du Barry, so she would be with Rohan. She would not address one single word to him after his return to France, and she eluded all of his requests for an audience. She would be beside herself at the mere mention of his name.

It goes without saying that Vermond shared the animosity of the two sovereigns who employed him, but he had his own reasons as well. Rohan was targeting him when he denounced the dauphine's bad advisors. As for Breteuil, he had two reasons for resenting the cardinal. In 1771, the Viennese Embassy was to go to him, but Rohan had whisked it away it from him. And when he finally got the post in 1774, he had to face the contempt of all Viennese high society who missed the splendorous affairs his predecessor invited them to. He hadn't the means to compete with Rohan the Magnificent; he was taken for what he was: a lackluster functionary.

Now that it appeared that the cardinal was implicated in some funny business about a necklace smacking of fraud, Marie-Antoinette was extremely angry. It wasn't the first time something like this had happened. A few years earlier a certain lady Cahuet de Villers had been convicted of extorting money from someone using notes falsely attributed to the sovereign. But this time, the offense seemed much more serious, because it involved such a highly placed person and an object people could suspect her of coveting. How could this prelate whom she detested have dared to use her name in such sordid business? She demanded immediate punishment. Vermond and Breteuil joined the chorus. Everyone criticized Rohan. He led such a lavish lifestyle that his vast revenues were not enough to maintain it. Everyone knew he was up to his eyes in debt, especially since his Saverne castle burnt down to the ground along with all its treasures. It was also known that he'd dipped into the Quinze-Vingts fund, which he administered, taking from it a temporary loan that he had not yet paid back*. Infatuated with spiritualism, he swore by Cagliostro, the famous magician who could pull out of his hat as much gold and as many diamonds as you please, and who prophesized a brilliant career for him after reading his future in a carafe of water. Rohan was the ideal bad guy. The queen and her two confidants needn't bother to give it another thought. They were utterly convinced he had bought the necklace so as to make money on it and pay off his most pressing debts before paying the jewelers' drafts. They entertained not the tiniest doubt about this, not even about the enormous loss such an operation would have caused him.

They concerted their efforts. The honest thing to do would have been to speak to the king about it immediately, the wise thing too. But they were set on getting their revenge, and Marie-Antoinette wanted hers right away. Breteuil pointed out, however, that for the moment a confidence trick had not been proven. If the cardinal paid for it, the only thing they could criticize him for was using the queen's name without her permission – but could they prove that? He had a good chance of getting away with it. They therefore had to prove that he was not able to honor the debt. And for that all they need do was wait for the first due date, which was coming up. Most probably Marie-Antoinette left it up to Breteuil to follow through. And Breteuil, as the abbé Georgel stated, merely assured the Boehmers of his support and invited them to remain in close contact with him, without sharing his suspicions with them, so as not to alert the prey to the trap they wanted to set.

What the jewelers revealed

Questioned, the jewelers recounted the story of how the necklace was sold. They were beginning to think that the necklace would be left on their hands when mutual acquaintances put them in contact with a certain countess de La Motte-Valois, who led them to believe that she could perhaps intervene on their behalf with her cousin the

---

* Founded by Saint Louis to house destitute blind people, the Quinze-Vingts hospice was an independent establishment under Church control. In 1779 the cardinal de Rohan had undertaken to transfer it from the rue Saint-Honoré quarter to the Hotel of the Black Musketeers on the rue de Charenton so as to start a profitable building operation on the ex-hospice grounds. This is when he was accused of having helped himself to some of the funds.

queen. She soon told them that a very great lord would take over the negotiations, but this had to remain a secret. As she was a lady of standing, she refused any payment or gift. They were to make arrangements directly with the cardinal de Rohan, leaving her name out of it. The cardinal went to see the necklace at the Boehmers' shop on the 24th of January and on the 29th summoned the jewelers to the Strasburg Palace* to work out the conditions and sign an agreement. Delivery would take place immediately. The exorbitant price – 1,600,000 pounds – was accepted without argument. But the sum could be paid over two years, one quarter every six months, the first payment being due on Austust 1st. Interest would be levied on the sums involved. The cardinal did not hide the fact that he was not acting on his own account, but the contract he himself wrote offered the Boehmers enough of a guarantee: the Rohans had the wherewithal. On February 1st therefore they handed over to the cardinal the huge case containing the precious necklace. At that point he could no longer resist the temptation of confiding in them, under the seal of secrecy, that he was negotiating on behalf of the queen and showed them the contract now approved by her and bearing her signature *Marie-Antoinette of France*. All's well that ends well: the masterpiece finally belonged to the only woman worthy of it.

The Boehmers were a bit taken aback that she was not wearing her necklace on the feast of the Purification, the second of February, as expected. That's because she hadn't the time to warn the king, Rohan explained to them. They were so happy to have concluded the deal they had stopped believing in that they thought nothing more about it. The months passed. The queen, heavy with child and then housebound by the birth, was not seen in public. When she appeared on May 24th not wearing the necklace at her churching ceremony, they started to wonder what was going on. They were informed that she thought the price was too high and was threatening to send the necklace back. On July 10th she apparently demanded a discount of 200,000 pounds and asked for the due date of August 1st to be pushed back a few days. In return, they would receive a payment of 700,000 pounds. They accepted. What else could they do? Rohan then advised them to thank the queen in a letter that he helped them write: the very one Marie-Antoinette was to burn in front of Madame Campan.

The jewelers' account mentioned a newcomer to the plot. The

---

* The Rohan residence in Paris was called the Strasburg Palace. Today it holds the National Archives.

countess de La Motte, of course, made only very brief appearances. But Breteuil ran a quick police check on her. Although she was indeed a distant descendent of King Henry II on an illegitimate line, Jeanne de Saint-Rémy was an adventuress living as best she could off her husband, an ex-gendarme who passed himself off as a count, and her lover, a certain Rétaux de Villette, best known for scratching out a tune on the guitar and belting out a song or two. The police enquiry revealed that the couple had recently begun to wallow in opulence, living the high life in their Parisian home on the rue Neuve-Saint-Gilles, not far from Rohan's palace, and that they had just bought and lavishly furnished a splendid home in the young woman's native city of Bar-sur-Aube. It also appeared that Villette had sold off to some Paris jewelers precious stones whose origins were so suspect that the buyers felt it wise to alert the police; but since no jewelry theft had been reported, there was no follow-up. It was clear what was going on: the dismantled necklace explained the sudden wealth of the La Mottes. But Breteuil saw them as mere pawns who had the job of selling the diamonds and were being rewarded for their services. How could such nobodies even conceive of, let alone set up, such a swindle, and above all drag Rohan into it? For him, the mastermind of the whole thing was the cardinal.

The fateful day of August 1st was approaching. At the end of July, Rohan asked the jewelers for another delay – the promised 700,000 pounds would be paid in October, but they were brought 30,000 in interest. They accepted this money as a down payment. It was clear that Rohan was up against the wall. This was confirmed by the treasurer of the naval ministry, the financier Saint-James, from whom he'd been trying for weeks to borrow some money – 300,000 at first and then 700,000 – for the purchase of the famous necklace. The financier, from whom the Boehmers had borrowed 800,000 pounds for the same necklace, proved reticent. So Rohan showed him the contract approved and signed by Marie-Antoinette, and since he still hemmed and hawed, Rohan told him, "I saw the queen who authorized me to do business in her name." But Saint-James declined and went straight away to tell all to Vermond. A delighted Breteuil welcomed his statement in due form. Now he had a witness who confirmed what the jewelers were saying.

On the 3rd of August while a worried Boehmer went to ask Madame Campan what the queen had thought of his letter, Madame de La Motte sent for Boehmer's partner Bassenge and delivered a shock that made him reel. Marie-Antoinette's signature on the agreement in Rohan's hands was a forgery! How would the prelate manage to wriggle his way out of this one? That was his problem; he alone had dealt with the jewelers. All they had to do was demand the money he owed them – he was rich enough. He obviously would have paid on the quiet to avoid a scandal had not Boehmer alerted the queen.

This time there was really more than enough evidence to undo the culprit. All they had to do was tighten the noose. On August 9th the queen, Vermond and minister Breteuil invited the Boehmers to recapitulate all they knew about the affair and helped them hone the version they would submit to the king. They had them collect all their revelations in a single dossier dated August 12th accompanied by supporting documents – notably a copy of the contract. And since the three were aware that they were at serious fault for undertaking this enquiry without the sovereign's knowledge, they asked the jewelers to make no mention of their previous encounters*. On August 14th Breteuil informed Louis XVI of the matter. The king became furiously indignant, and subscribed to the scenario the minister set out before him. The word "scenario" is not misplaced here: everything was done to set the stage for the fall from grace of the highest dignitary of the Church of France.

Was this a reasonable thing to do? Reason, as we said, had clearly deserted the protagonists in the whole affair.

The cardinal is arrested

August 15th is a High Holy Day. Versailles was full to the brim with visitors. Gathered together in the Œil-de-Bœuf and the Hall of Mirrors, the over-packed court awaited the king and queen to accompany them to the chapel where the grand almoner de Rohan was to celebrate the mass of the Assumption. It was nearly mid-day. They watched as the cardinal arrived in his pontifical robes, dressed from head to toe in purple. He showed nothing of the anxiety that had been eating away at him for the last fortnight. Soon the door to the royal family's quarters opened, but instead of the sovereigns, out came a bailiff who called the prelate.

Proceedings behind closed doors followed. Madame Campan and

---

* Boehmer entrusted Georgel with this information a number of years later. Marie-Antoinette's awkward persistence in denying the fact implicitly confirms it. "Everything had been devised between the king and me," she wrote to Joseph II, "the ministers knew nothing about it until the king sent for the cardinal and questioned him."

the abbé Georgel (neither of whom attended them) reported them somewhat differently, but the whole thing is easy to reconstitute. The cardinal suddenly found himself before a sort of impromptu court. Aside from the king, the queen and Breteuil, there was the minister of justice Miromesnil, because he was the head of the judiciary, and perhaps Vergennes – the testimony differs on this point. Did the king begin by subjecting him to the humiliation of having the incriminating documents read to him, as Georgel suggests? It is more likely that he got straight to the point, as Madame Campan attests.

> "Did you buy diamonds from Boehmer?"
> "Yes, Sire."
> "What did you do with them?"
> "I believed they had been delivered to the queen."
> "Upon whose authority were you acting?"
> "A lady by the name of the countess de La Motte-Valois, who presented me with a letter from the queen, and I thought that I was paying due court to Her Majesty by carrying out this mission."

At this point the queen burst out, "How, Sir, could you possibly believe – you, to whom I have not addressed a single word in eight years – that I would have chosen you to conduct these negotiations, and through the intermediary of such a woman?"

"I see that I was cruelly deceived; I will pay for the necklace; my desire to please Your Majesty blurred my vision; I did not perceive the deception; and I am aggrieved."

From here on accounts get muddled. Did the cardinal exhibit the letter in which the countess entrusted the commission to him or did he simply reply that he had it in Paris? It matters little. The king knew from the Boehmers that the contract was signed *Marie-Antoinette of France*. How could a prince of the Church ignore the fact that queens only sign by their baptismal name*? Rohan grew visibly pale in front of them, almost fainting. Taking pity on him, the king invited him to withdraw to the next room where he would find implements to commit a summary of the facts to paper. The queen, in tears she was so enraged, demanded his immediate arrest. "Hideous vice must be unmasked. When a mere wretch and crook

---

* The error was even more gross because like all queens of foreign origin, Marie-Antoinette kept her patronymic "of Austria" or rather "of Lorraine-Hapsburg" despite her marriage. The name "of France" was reserved for the sons and daughters of the king of France.

hides behind the Roman purple and the title of prince, all of France and Europe must know about it." Her nerves had been bad for a month or so, and now they gave out altogether. She could no longer reason properly. As she later confided to Madame Campan, a terrifying idea occurred to her. If the hidden agenda of this whole business was "a plan to completely discredit her in the eyes of the king and France, perhaps the cardinal was going to say that she had the necklace in her possession; that she had honored him by trusting him to acquire it without the king's knowledge, and that he could have got a traitor in her midst to put it in a secret hiding place in her apartment." The only ones who kept their heads were the two ministers, who were only just learning about it all. The minister of justice favored a further enquiry. Such was also the opinion of Vergennes, whom the king had consulted the day before, but he knew that the queen hated him too much for him to be effective. At this point Rohan reappeared after jotting down a few lines that were as muddled as his original statements. The sovereign couldn't make up his mind. The queen's tears and Breteuil's vehemence won out.

The prelate was allowed to leave the room. But Breteuil immediately appeared at the door shouting, "Someone arrest Monsieur le cardinal!" In front of the whole stupefied court, an ashen Rohan made his way towards the Œil-de-Bœuf where the duke de Villeroy, who could well have done without this chore, informed him of his arrest. He gradually regained his composure, and taking advantage of the guards' momentary inattention, he managed to slip one of his valets a note ordering the abbé Georgel in Paris to burn the contents of a little red portfolio he had been careful not to mention, but that will come up again later. He was allowed to confer with his intimates and spend the night at home, where a search didn't turn up much. After that, he was imprisoned in the Bastille; although imprisoned is not exactly the right term. The prison director, respectful of the greats of this world, assigned him a very comfortable apartment where he was allowed to receive as many visitors as he liked and even offer them meals prepared by an excellent caterer. Backed by his family, he prepared his defense.

The authorities were so convinced that the countess de La Motte was a mere stooge that they waited three days before going to collect her in Bar-sur-Aube. Marie-Antoinette clung to her conviction that Rohan had engineered the whole thing. She expressed – or merely affected – relief about the 15th of August interrogation of the cardinal in the letter to her brother. "I was really touched by the reasoning and resolve of the king during this dreadful event. When the cardinal begged not to be sent to prison, the king replied he could not grant this, neither as king nor as husband." But she remained profoundly hurt.

It is worth lingering for a moment on why she was so angry. She had not felt the same way at all a few years earlier when the lady de Villers used her name to swindle some money. This time it was not about money but about diamonds. The fraud cleverly played upon the image she projected of a woman chronically debt-ridden and enamored of jewelry, who bought it behind her husband's back. It was this image she wanted to destroy by crushing the culprit. But that's not all. This time the presumed culprit was not a woman but a man, and not just any man either: a man of his quality, rank and charm could easily have been admitted into her circle. In presenting himself as an intermediary mandated by her to negotiate a secret deal, he invited questions about the nature of their relationship. After all, the accusation of questionable morals that weighed on the dauphine with regard to the count d'Artois was grounded in the notorious "dissipations" of the beginning of the reign. The pamphlets found all sorts of fathers for her children – except the king. Could the cardinal de Rohan be the queen's lover? This was a sacrilegious question that no one dared entertain for the moment. But while waiting for it to be asked – as well it would be – it festered vaguely in the mind not only of Marie-Antoinette, who was sickened by the mere sight of the man, but also in Louis XVI's. The affair dealt him a hard blow as king, but also as husband, for he could not bear anyone to criticize the mother of his children, and through her himself [*].

The haste and self-deception that paralyzed all reflection on both sides is thus explicable. "I hope this business will be over with shortly," Marie-Antoinette wrote to her brother on August 22nd. She was wrong. It was just beginning. As concerns public opinion, the scandal was exactly what she wanted, enormous. But it would not play out as she wanted, and would not produce the results she expected. The bearishness of the arrest, at the very moment the grand almoner was about to celebrate Assumption Day mass, outraged the nobility and the Church: a prince and prelate is not manhandled this way – even if he is guilty – and of what, no one was even sure. As for the monarchy's enemies, they were delighted at a scandal that muddied both "the crosier and the crown."

---

[*] According to Georgel, during the August 15 interrogation Rohan had a "rather disrespectful" look, either out of anger or collusion, which made the queen blush.

The cardinal's story

The cardinal's official interrogation took place on August 19th. It was held not by Breteuil, whom he recused, but by Vergennes and marshal de Castries. Rohan was reluctant to speak "for fear of compromising anyone." Castries insisted: "You cannot and must not, when your honor is at stake, hide the truth." What the two men were about to hear and Castries to record was downright stupefying.

Back in the autumn of 1781 in Saverne, the marquise de Boulainvilliers introduced the prelate to one of her long-standing protégés. At the age of seven the little girl in question had been found in rags begging along the roads whimpering "Take pity on a poor orphan girl of Valois blood." Intrigued, the marquise made enquiries and discovered that the baron de Saint-Rémy, latest offshoot of a Henry II illegitimate line, had married the concierge of his estate in Fontette, near Bar-sur-Aube, and managed to eat and drink what was left of his fortune before dying in a hospital, leaving his wife and children in penury. She took the little beggar in, raised her and had her trained as a seamstress. Thanks to her origins the marquise managed to obtain a modest pension for her. Pretty and saucy, the adolescent threw caution to the winds along with her sewing basket, and married a nasty specimen, Nicolas de La Motte, an equerry and gendarme of the king, who gave her a set of twins who had the good taste to die as soon as they were born. Whereupon, the couple set out to seek their fortune. In search of benefactors, they showed up in Saverne where their patroness advocated for them. Generously, the prince de Rohan opened his doors to them, and when the marquise died, promised to help them – which he did. Did Jeanne's beauty have anything to do with this good deed? If so, Rohan was careful not to mention it.

He saw her again in Paris in 1784. She told him that she'd gained the friendship of her "cousin" Marie-Antoinette, showed him the letters she said she got from her, and since he was so troubled by the queen's contemptuous treatment of him, she offered to help remedy the situation. For a few months she kept him abreast of the "progress" she was making in winning over the sovereign. Then he solicited an audience. The queen, he was told, could only grant him one secretly, because the king and his ministers mistrusted him so. Time was needed to prepare his return to her good graces and advancement to high functions. In August a rendez-vous was set up one evening at midnight in Versailles' terraced gardens. "At the appointed hour," he stated, "I saw appear a woman in a black hat, holding a fan in her hand with which she raised her hat, which had been over her face; I believed I could clearly recognize the queen by the light of the stars; I told her I was happy to find in her goodness proof that she had got over the reservations she had held against me; she answered me with a few words; and just as I was about to explain my actions, someone came to tell her that Madame and the count d'Artois were a few steps away. She left me precipitously and I did not see her again."

The defendant, aware that this episode was highly damaging, cleaned up the story, leaving some aspects out. It would later be discovered that the rendez-vous did indeed take place, but not in the gardens, where Marie-Antoinette often took an evening stroll, but in one of the darkest corners of the park, the so-called Venus Wood, at the foot of the hundred steps. For the moment, however, Vergennes and Castries were not dwelling on topographical details. Their stupefaction was boundless. Was Rohan a diabolical liar? A tale-spinning megalomaniac? Or the dupe of God knows what kind of machinations?

The rest of his story did nothing to reassure them. Two days after the August rendez-vous, he went, on the countess' orders, to pay court to the queen. He placed himself where she would have to pass him in the great gallery and thought he could make out in a gesture, an expression on her face, a sign of good will. This seems less surprising if we recall that Marie-Antoinette always had the knack of dispensing smiles all around by directing them to ten people at once.

It wasn't long before requests for money started coming in. Her "cousin" Marie-Antoinette's fund for charity emergencies was in trouble. He handed over 50,000 pounds, then 100,000. Then in January negotiations over the necklace began. The cardinal's account matched that of the jewelers in every detail, and added that Madame de La Motte took it upon herself to get the contract to the queen and return it with her signature. She urged him not to let it out of his sight under any circumstances and to show it to no one – but with that he failed to comply. On the first of February, bearing the precious jewelry case, he went to the apartment where she was lodging in the town of Versailles. Any minute now the queen's servant would come there to pick it up and bring it back to her in the chateau. Hidden in a glassed-in alcove in her apartment, he did not let his eyes stray from the case. Then he watched as the countess handed it over to a man dressed all in black who hastily withdrew. He had absolutely no doubt that the necklace was now in the sovereign's hands.

We know the rest of the story. Even the difficulties the queen was supposed to be having meeting the payments didn't clue him in. The more skeptical Boehmer and Saint-James became, the more he assured them that she was giving him guarantees. Did he go so far as to maintain, in his attempt to extort a loan from Saint-James, "I saw the queen, who authorized me..."? Saint-James said he did. Or did the cardinal merely state, as he asserted under interrogation, "You have seen the queen's order..." in other words, some piece of paper? It is impossible to know, because Saint-James wound up stating that he could no longer say for sure. At his wit's end, Rohan denied the obvious. He bowed to the evidence only after comparing the handwriting of the letters in his possession to an example of the queen's. The signature on the contract was a forgery, as Madame de La Motte confirmed to him. Now all he could do was pay up. It took him the first two weeks of July to absorb the annihilation of his dreams, but he still didn't fully grasp the extent of the confidence trick of which he had been the dupe. For he vehemently demanded to be interviewed with the countess, who, he was sure, would back up his story. He knew they'd brought her to the Bastille the night before, and he was impatient for them to interrogate her. He appeared genuinely stupefied to learn that she denied everything. And what was her relationship to him? Why she was his mistress, of course. That's why he showered her with gifts.

Rohan's interrogation greatly disturbed Vergennes and Castries. His story, although – or perhaps because – it was so outlandish, had the hallmark of authenticity. If he were the mastermind of such a complex plot, why would he be furnishing such absurd explanations? The swindle, hatched with care over a whole year, just did not make sense as the work of this great and glamorous lord accustomed to spending lavishly without blinking an eye. Even Joseph II, who had been well acquainted with him in Vienna, conveyed his doubts to Marie-Antoinette. On the other hand, was it conceivable that an educated, cultivated and witty fifty-year-old man invested with the Church's highest functions could be so utterly silly as to be hoodwinked? The two ministers could not make up their mind which unlikely possibility to believe, but Rohan's disarray pleaded in his favor. If he wasn't the mastermind, who was? Maybe the false countess would give them a clue. A pity they hadn't called her in for questioning before, and especially that they hadn't thought more carefully about it before making a highly embarrassing public arrest. But the harm was already done; they had to decide what course to take. But they first had to deal with the queen's anger when she found out about the rendez-vous scene.

Procedural debates

Rohan's case now appeared more serious. Now there was another crime aside from swindling. To believe or lead others to believe that the queen had accorded him a midnight rendez-vous was an attack on her sacred person. He had only spoken of a very brief meeting, but the idea of a possible romantic entanglement could not be dismissed. Marie-Antoinette was all the more indignant because in the pamphlets she'd already been accused of cavorting in the gardens with her lovers. It got so bad that she had to give up taking the evening air in the gardens. She quickly understood the implications of it all. Her pointed and public hatred of the man made it unthinkable that Rohan could have bought her the necklace out of disinterested good will. But what if she were secretly on the best of terms with him? Then it made all the sense in the world that she should entrust such a mission to him. That way, she was an accomplice; in fact, she was the silent partner in the whole swindle! "I've been incriminated!" she cried. "People think that I've got the necklace and haven't paid for it. I want to know the truth of a matter in which my name has been used." She demanded swift and public justice.

There were two possible procedures for judging and punishing a culprit. The first consisted in trying him in the ordinary court of jurisdiction, in this case the Parliament. But the king, chief justice at the top of the pyramid of judiciary institutions, could also keep the case for himself and pass judgment on his own authority, without having to furnish grounds for his decision. For a simple case of fraud the king generally delegated his power to the court of jurisdiction, but cases of lèse-majesté were normally his responsibility. Louis XVI was greatly criticized later on for allowing Rohan to be tried before Parliament, which at the time was populated by malcontents, instead of trying him himself – a major political blunder. It was a mistake, but it wasn't in choosing the jurisdiction that he commit his worst blunder. What was unforgivable was the cardinal's messy arrest. That was the point at which he lost control of events.

A vindictive Marie-Antoinette wanted the "horrible" man whom she'd hated for so long to be sent before an ordinary court as a "vile and maladroit counterfeiter." Now that she herself was implicated because of the alleged meeting in the garden, she wanted more than ever for him to be tried in public so as to show that she had nothing to do with the whole business. The ministers would have preferred the king's more discreet extra-judiciary solution. But the time for discretion was over. Details of the interrogation had leaked out. In the public's eye, the queen and the cardinal were in it together, and the worst rumors were circulating. Fersen wrote to the king of Sweden, "All the stories that they are spewing about the cardinal are perfectly outlandish, and especially in the provinces; people are saying that the necklace and the queen's forged signature are not the real reason for his detention. They assume there's a political reason for it, which there certainly is not. Even in Paris, they are saying it was only a game the queen was playing with the cardinal, that they were on the best of terms, and that in effect she had put him up to buying the necklace… that the queen was pretending she couldn't bear the sight of him so as better to hide her game; that the king had found out, that he had criticized her for it; that she was feeling bad and made believe she was pregnant." In such a climate the king couldn't exercise his authority severely, as this would have looked as if he were burying the whole business because his wife was in the wrong.

The queen was impatient for the trial to begin, and to stop all the talk she suggested leaving the cardinal the choice of jurisdiction. It seemed a good idea; if he chose his own procedure, no one could accuse the king of being partial. Rohan, they were sure, would rather throw himself at the king's mercy than deal with the "severe and humiliating procedures of the criminal justice system." In that way, they could just pack him off to some nameless prison and throw away the key, without causing a scandal. They took it for granted that he would shrink from seeing his wicked ways exposed to public scrutiny.

Yes, but what wicked ways? The king, the queen and Breteuil did not believe a word of his bizarre story and remained convinced he was guilty of fraud. They refused to investigate further and notably to have him confront the countess, whose denials they accepted as gospel. Rohan for his part was willing to admit and take the consequences for the crime of lèse-majesté, but he refused to be condemned as a crook. Getting good advice from the lawyers supplied by his family, he wrote an extremely clever reply.

> Sire,
>
> I hoped by the confrontation to acquire the proof that would have convinced Your Majesty of the certitude of the fraud of which I was the plaything, in which case I would have wished no other judge than your justice and goodness. The refusal to grant such a confrontation having deprived me of that hope, I accept with the most respectful gratitude the permission Your Majesty has given me to prove my innocence in a court

of law, and consequently, I beg Your Majesty to give the orders needed for my case to be sent and attributed to the assembled chambers of the Paris parliament.

However, if I had hope that clarifications that might have come to light of which I am not aware have led Your Majesty to conclude that I am guilty of nothing other than having been duped, I would dare to beg, Sire, that you pass judgment on me according to your justice and goodness.

This letter surprised and consternated the king and queen. Although the last paragraph gave them an escape hatch, they were too blinded by anger to take advantage of it. And in any case, it was too late. So the cardinal's case was sent to Parliament. The whole thing was absurd, because the Parliament would have the task of weighing all the evidence and would thus have to hand down a verdict on a matter of lèse-majesté! This meant that the king, the holder of supreme judiciary power, was submitting for trial a case in which he appeared as the plaintiff against one of his subjects. He was giving the Parliament the task of defending his wife's honor!

Marie-Antoinette thought she was out of the woods. "I'm delighted that we'll hear no more about this horror," she wrote to her brother. Confident in her innocence, she chose to brave the hostility of Paris. In the beginning of October, to get from Versailles to Fontainebleau, she took a barge at Issy that was glittering with gold leaf and dragged along the banks by fifteen horses. She paraded on deck scoffing at the inquisitive onlookers – an ill-advised provocation. As for the public, it couldn't wait for the show trial.

The enquiry and the trial

The Parliament lived up to its legendary reputation for dragging its feet. First, the calendar announced that it was time to go on vacation. At the Bastille, since the cardinal was now under regular jurisdiction, he had to make do with an ordinary cell and could only communicate with his people by notes written in invisible ink entrusted to his physician. He had to cool his heels. His friends and family took advantage of the delays to lead their own enquiry, because the public prosecutor and his assistant clearly considered the investigation closed. They began with the people close to La Motte. Wasn't it suspicious that the countess' husband and lover had both vanished into thin air? A cleric from the Place Royale monks minor, who was in the de La Mottes' employ as steward, was able to get some peripheral information, and gave them a few leads. This cleric, Father Loth, had heard some vague mention of the necklace, and had seen Villette forge signatures. Could there be any truth to the story about the Venus Wood? He recalled a certain young lady d'Oliva whose employers had congratulated her on the role she'd played so well at Versailles. They tracked down the driver of the coach who'd driven her there. The young woman, alerted by Madame de La Motte, fled to Brussels with her lover du jour. They were hunted down and talked into returning to Paris with the promise of clemency.

The young lady in question, whose real name was Nicole Leguay, was a tall, slender and pretty milliner, who looked rather like Marie-Antoinette. According to the police reports, she was "more stupid than bad or roguish," and plied an evening trade in the gardens of the Palais-Royal. The "count" spotted her, flirted with her a bit and promised her 15,000 pounds – quite a gold mine – if she agreed to performing an amusing little masquerade organized by the queen herself. Dressed in clothing similar to what she was wearing in a famous portrait by Madame Vigée-Lebrun – a reproduction of it was found at the La Mottes' home on a snuff-box cover – she was packed off at midnight to the Venus Wood, which was quite dark on that moonless night of August 11, 1784. She held a rose in her hand and a letter in her pocket, and her job was to deliver them to a great lord who would approach her. She was to murmur to him, "You know what this means." The man threw himself at her feet. Terrified, she mumbled something, dropped the rose, forgot all about the letter, and was very relieved when the organizers of the little drama got her out of there by shouting that someone was approaching. Of the money promised, all she got was 4,000 pounds, and she had to make do with that. She clearly hadn't a clue about the role they'd got her to play. In November they threw her into the Bastille just on principle, but her testimony shed no light whatsoever on the purchase of the necklace.

Vergennes' collaboration was indispensable in the enquiries abroad. He lent his support gladly, convinced that the cardinal had been the dupe of the whole farce. His sleuths were the ones who hunted down the young d'Oliva, and they came quite close to finding La Motte in England. But from some London jewelers they got really damning statements: among the numerous stones that the so-called count had sold them were the necklace's most beautiful diamonds, easily identifiable from drawings they were shown. And in Geneva they pulled off a master coup. Villette, recognized under an assumed name, broke down. He confirmed

– undoubtedly with the promise that his head would be spared – everything they already knew. Not only did he authenticate Rohan's story from top to bottom, he also added some important new information. He himself was the forger – a pretty poor one at that, who cared little for accuracy, he told them in an attempt to vindicate himself! He was also a busy forger. It wasn't enough just to write in the contract's margin *approved* and to sign *Marie-Antoinette of France*. He actually wrote a number of letters supposedly from the queen dealing with the purchase of the necklace. For over a year, at Madame de La Motte's dictation, he wrote love letters to the cardinal on pretty white paper edged in blue with the lily of France in the corner. They ranged from expressions of friendly concern to passionate attachment. Rohan, a man attractive to women, was fatuous enough to believe wholeheartedly in the letters' authenticity, and he replied in the same tone. What had become of these letters? Villette had no idea. But we have. Those from the "queen" were in the little red portfolio that the abbé Georgel was ordered to burn when Rohan was arrested. And only this thunderbolt could have forced Rohan to give them up, so powerful was his certainty of being loved by the sovereign and destined to high places thanks to her. Madame de La Motte would later say that the letters were so affectionate that Marie-Antoinette used the familiar *tu* with him. The cardinal's replies – those real ones – were kept by the countess in Bar-sur-Aube in case she needed to blackmail him. She too burned them just before being arrested, but first she let her former lover, the young lawyer Beugnot, read some of them so that he could testify to having seen them if necessary. For the moment he kept quiet. But he referred to them in his memoirs written after an illustrious career during the Empire: "What was this century then in which a prince of the Church did not hesitate to write, sign and address to a women he knew so little and so ill, letters that today any self-respecting man could perhaps begin to read, but would not be able to finish!"

We cannot report here all the twists and turns of this amazing trial. Madame de La Motte denounced the magician Cagliostro not only to get revenge on this rival (he had been fighting for some of the loot ensuing from the prelate's gullibility), but also to put the authorities off the scent. A number of other minor players were also mixed up in the affair. All of them had lawyers who drew up articles of defense for them, which at the time could be published. What novel could have rivaled this trial whose twists and turns were so astounding and whose political implications were so subversive? *The Marriage of Figaro* had been banned and Beaumarchais harassed for this rather bold tirade against social inequality. And here the public was being served up fresh slices of real-life fare that even Beaumarchais could not have imagined! The printers couldn't keep up with demand; each new installment was grabbed hot off the press; and copies were resold at exorbitant prices. The frenzy that was gripping France spread all over Europe. And with each new installment, Marie-Antoinette was splattered with a bit more mud.

Time for the verdict finally came. Each defendant appeared in turn before the assembled magistrates. Cagliostro came out a winner and made a splash by evoking, in a hodge-podge he invented from all and sundry languages, his adventures in the Egypt of the pharaohs and the Holy Land at the time of the Apostles. They couldn't get him on anything and he was acquitted. The sweet young thing d'Oliva melted the judges' hearts by asking for a few minutes' delay to finish nursing her baby son born in the Bastille. She was released as the court declared there were no grounds for prosecution and imposed a reprimand. Villette, keeping a low profile, humbly pleaded guilty and was much relieved to get off with being banished. Despite her vehement denials, there was no doubt about Madame de La Motte's overwhelming guilt. The court handed down a unanimous decision to pass the heaviest sentence aside from death: she was to be whipped and branded with hot irons before being shut up in a women's prison for life. Her husband was condemned *in absentia* to the galley ships.

The only case left was the thorniest one, the cardinal's. All the evidence pointed to his being the dupe rather than the organizer of the confidence trick. The measures the abbé Georgel took on his behalf to pay the jewelers helped a lot. The royals' flawed maneuvers insisting loudly on his guilt, and their refusal to pursue the enquiry, also played in his favor. He had public opinion on his side, and this weighed on the judges. The public prosecutor, who was planning to base his indictment on two counts, had to abandon the first. As for passing judgment on the second count, the Parliament was ill at ease and preferred to speak of an "offense" to the queen rather than lèse-majesté. Contrary to widespread belief, not all the magistrates were determined to turn the case into a war machine against the monarchy. Some of them regretted having to touch upon such a delicate matter that shouldn't even have come under their jurisdiction. It was unpleasant for them to have to come down on the side either of the queen or the highest-ranking prelate in the realm. Why had the king left this horrible chore to them? The judges had come under a lot of pressure from people in favor of the cardinal, but also from those against him. For instance, with the assent of Marie-Antoinette, Mercy-Argenteau had sent the chief magistrate d'Aligre a summary of the steps he was to take to get the cardinal convicted. But it is always easier to implore compassion than preach severity. Seventeen members of the Rohan family, dressed in high mourning, stood on either side of the entrance to the Great Chamber and greeted the judges in a silence more moving than words. Above all, the royals' arrogance in predicting the outcome of the trial was shocking. "How singular," wrote Joseph II to Mercy, "that ten or twelve days before the verdict, everyone agreed what the sentence would be. That shows that in France even justice is dealt politically." If such was the opinion of Marie-Antoinette's own brother, we can imagine what the Parisians must have thought!

The court in the meantime was discussing punishment. A reprimand was impossible, much less banishment in perpetuity, which would have entailed a loss of all civil rights and his ecclesiastic benefits – in other words his entire income. The prosecutor suggested no grounds for prosecution, together with a relatively moderate sanction; that is, the defendant should publicly and solemnly make honorable amends to the king and queen by reading a declaration from which Marie-Antoinette made sure any mention of the Venus Wood was deleted. After which, he would be banished from Versailles and give up his grand almoner post. But even this was too much for the cardinal's friends, and especially for Marie-Antoinette's enemies. A vehement altercation pitted the prosecutor against one of his colleagues, the one calling the other a sell-out and a debauchee. Sickened by it all, the chief magistrate d'Aligre remained neutral. In an extremely tense atmosphere, by a majority of three votes, the decision between no grounds for prosecution and a plain and simple acquittal was made. At ten o'clock at night on May 31, 1786, Rohan walked out a free man, exonerated by the Great Chamber, cleared of all charges by twenty-six votes to twenty-three. A jubilant crowd greeted him with shouts of joy and escorted him to the Bastille, where he would spend the night for the last time. "Long Live the Parliament!" "Long Live the Innocent Cardinal!"

Thanks to much faulty reasoning fed by extremely virulent feelings, what should have been a simple court case over the swindling of a necklace through a foolish dupe became a gigantic political show-trial for which the queen, and through her the entire monarchy, would pay the price.

Political fall-out

Marie-Antoinette's surprise was total and her indignation boundless. "Come pity your outraged queen, the victim of cabals and injustice," she groaned to Madame Campan. And all of a sudden she resented this France where she had "not found fair judges" to defend her honor. "A people is indeed unfortunate to have for its highest court a bunch of men who only consult their passions...!" Coming on the scene at this point, the king tried to console her. "All they wanted to see in this case was a prince of the Church and the prince de Rohan, but he's nothing but a wretch in need of money; and all of this was just a ploy to feather his nest, in which the cardinal then got swindled too... He thought he could give Boehmer big enough payments to pay the necklace off in time, but he was too familiar with the ways of the court, and is not enough of an imbecile to believe that Madame de La Motte would ever be admitted to the queen's presence and entrusted with such an errand... Nothing is easier to judge and one needn't be Alexander to cut this Gordian knot." Blinded to the bitter end by their prejudices, and deaf to anything they didn't want to hear, they seem to have been tragically cut off from reality, on which they no longer had a handle.

All the same, Louis XVI still had one more card to play. After Parliament's verdict he could still if he chose be the final arbiter in the case. Once again, he made a hasty mistake and gave in to his anger. As acquitted as he might be of all charges, the cardinal had not come out unharmed from the whole mess. He would have welcomed being forgotten about for a while, especially as he was feeling some remorse. ("Is the queen still gloomy?" he had written from prison to his lawyer on a little wrinkled piece of paper.) But the king had him dismissed from his grand almoner post even though he had seen it coming and tended his resignation. He sent him into exile at La Chaise-Dieu in the Auvergne region, in other words in the middle of nowhere. In doing so he overturned Parliament's decision, causing cries of injustice and tyranny to rain down on him. Would he not have been better advised to invite him to remain in the Alsace where his functions required his presence anyway? Rohan would have to keep his belt firmly tightened for another eight years during which the lion's share of his income would be devoted to paying off Boehmer, capital plus interest. In brief, it would have been better to put him to the test and offer him the chance of redeeming himself, while keeping the option of punishing him should he make a false move. But this would have required a bit of leniency, and Marie-Antoinette had none whatsoever. She haughtily received Madame de Marsan who had come to implore granting her relative a more salubrious place to live than in the biting frosts of Auvergne. She insisted on official, public punishment. Inevitably, it backfired on her.

The one who lost the most in this trial was Marie-Antoinette. Too much care had been taken to avoid calling her into question or indeed even pronouncing her name. As a result, her role in the whole affair was never made completely clear. The countess de La Motte had done everything possible to compromise her. Claiming to do nothing more than carry out her wishes, she accused her of having set the whole thing up to get hold of the necklace while bringing shame on the cardinal, whom she detested. There was no lack of people who believed her. The queen could not make a move without being suspected. Some people felt, for example, that she could save the countess de La Motte from being branded. If she had done so, she would have been accused of protecting her accomplice. She didn't and was accused of being cruel. While she was being branded, the witnesses were horrified by the convict's screams. All the charitable souls of Paris – including the princess de Lamballe! – visited her in her cell at la Salpêtrière. When in short order she escaped – with whose complicity it is not known – word went around that the queen was paying her off for keeping quiet. That particular rumor was quickly squashed. She had hardly arrived in London when the lady started writing the story of her life, where she told her version of the necklace affair, replete with extracts from those famous little love letters, trotting out all the most abominable calumnies against Marie-Antoinette that had been spewed in the gazettes for years. This had all the greater impact because she was claiming to have been in close contact with the queen – very close contact. Nothing could stop this mud-slinging fest, which would be used during the Revolution to fill up the dossiers of the public prosecutor, Fouquier-Tinville.

Napoléon would remark, "The queen was innocent, and to give greater publicity to her innocence she wanted Parliament to try the case. The result was that people believed the queen to be guilty, and that cast discredit on the king's court." Discredit is hardly the word: it was the beginning of the end.

It remains true, however, that Marie-Antoinette, even if involuntarily, was partly to blame. The fraud had its roots in her reputation as a woman who 1) was willing to do anything to get her hands on the jewels she coveted; 2) was susceptible to amorous advances that could prove successful; and 3) whose position brought along political responsibilities. We thus recognize the three ingredients exploited by the shrewd de La Motte in setting up the swindle, and which also explained the cardinal's mind-boggling gullibility. For it cannot be denied that in these three areas Marie-Antoinette had behaved recklessly enough to make the accusations seem believable. She was conscious of this, and that is why she felt great grief – so great that Mercy saw it as excessive. The affair acted like a fairground's hall of mirrors, brutally bringing her face to face with the fattened and twisted image of herself that so many others saw – a truly deplorable image.

She wanted to live the life of an ordinary woman but still preserve her queenly prerogatives. But by playing at being a private individual, by casting overboard the pageantry that surrounded her sacred person, she lost what distinguished her from the ordinary run of mortals. In asking Parliament "the just satisfaction due to the queen of whom one has dared to compromise the illustrious name," she expected to be treated like a sovereign. But Parliament let her know that in its eyes she was nothing more than a woman like any other. This inversion was illustrated to perfection by a quatrain in dialogue form that was making the rounds in Paris:

> *Marie-Antoinette:*
> *– You tart, it becomes you, it would seem*
> *To play so well my role of queen.*
> *Mademoiselle d'Oliva:*
> *– And wherefore not, dear queen of mine,*
> *When you play my role all the time?*

Marie-Antoinette was never comfortable on her pedestal, and wanted to descend from it whenever it suited her. Now she was brutally dragged off it, once and for all. As François Furet pointed out, could there still be lèse-majesté when there was no longer any majesté?

The blow thus inflicted on her was unfair in a way, but it wasn't inexplicable. In her career the necklace affair was not an accident that somehow suddenly changed her trajectory. It was a culminating point at which converged a multitude of thoughtless, careless, light-minded and clumsy acts. It was a punishment for her blindness and inability to see beyond her feelings, or question her preconceived notions, to understand others – or to forgive.

Ere long, she would have to pay a high price for her errors.

CHAPTER 16

ENTERING POLITICS

Worked up into a white heat by incendiary libels, public opinion was ruthless. The Escaut estuary affair made of Marie-Antoinette "l'Autrichienne," but the necklace affair made her out to be a new Messalina, the Roman empress wantonly given over to all the furies of the flesh. And for her "cruelty" – towards that poor Rohan and that poor de La Motte! – you could add to the list Agrippina and Catherine de Médicis. There would be no end to the name-calling – for the habit was now well ingrained, and popular imagination knew no bounds.

After doing some painful soul-searching, she finally took stock of the danger she and the whole monarchy were in when it was learned that the royal treasury, riddled with chronic debt, was on the verge of collapse. The king was paralyzed by stress and vacillated. Having no one better to fall back on, the ministers turned to her for support. For the first time in her life, backed into a corner and torn from the pleasures in which she was still trying to find relief, she got involved in the real business of the court, and made decisions. Was another Marie-Antoinette emerging from the crucible? Although she was the same person, with the same passion, energy, vehemence and refusal to bend, she began to reflect, something she had never done before in her whole life. She made the effort to learn about the serious matters that had hitherto repelled her. And above all, she learned to be prudent. It was with trepidation that she made her first hesitant steps into a real political role.

The specter of bankruptcy

At the headquarters of the finance ministry, Maurepas was fond of saying, "only an idiot or a felon would want this post," but that was underestimating the lure of power. The building in which the headquarters was located was nicknamed the "movers" because its directors came and went with such frequency. From 1774 to 1790 there were ten of them, the longest serving for four years and the shortest for four days. Four of them were no strangers to headlines: Turgot, Necker, Calonne and Brienne, alternating or in tandem with various experts for expediting everyday matters[*].

The financial problems could not be solved, and the French monarchy died as a result. We must take a brief step back in order to understand the causes of the disaster. Slowly extending administrative control over entire swathes of the country's business, the king had long been reduced to struggling to make ends meet, because he lacked the needed tax revenue. They couldn't go on increasing the existing taxes, which in effect were levied only on the poorest people – the most numerous, but still. The only recourse would have been to get everyone without exception to share the burden by taxing either income or property through an estate tax. But all attempts at reform came up against opposition from the kingdom's first and second estates, whose privileges exempted them from direct taxation. The clergy in particular, who controlled considerable wealth and managed it competently and efficiently, refused to submit to any obligatory contribution, but did accept to periodically give the sovereign a voluntary donation, which was derisory in comparison with its actual revenues. In 1750 Louis XV's minister Machault d'Arnouville had tried and failed. And of course, the clergy's resistance encouraged that of the other privileged classes, the nobles of the sword and the nobles of the robe, who had powerful spokesmen in the parliaments.

Of all of them, Turgot, who had a coherent economic doctrine, was the only one who might have had a chance of getting some tax reform; but he was in too much of a hurry to push his plans through, and did not get the king's support. Those who came after him weren't asked to reform the kingdom's tax codes, but instead to furnish the state the means to pay the bills. Severe belt-tightening measures might perhaps have helped to balance the budget, as long as no extra expenses were added. But taking up the cause of the American insurgents prevented that from happening. Statistics at the ready, today's historians are able to prove that the war in America dug a

---

[*]   For various reasons, the real head of the finance ministry did not always occupy the post of controller general, which was sometimes filled by a mere figurehead. Such was the case when it was necessary to make it seem that Necker, because he was a foreigner, only had subordinate functions.

hole in the royal finances from which it was impossible to climb out. Over five years, it cost more than a billion pounds. The situation was aggravated by the fact that instead of facing the problem head on, the authorities felt they could solve the problem with no pain, all the while merrily wasting what resources there were.

It was a sign of the times – when modern capitalism was being born – that the magician who pulled this particular rabbit out of his hat was a Swiss banker, Jacques Necker, the representative to Paris of the Calvinist republic of Geneva. Having conjured a colossal fortune out of thin air through lucrative speculating, he had the highest regard for his own talents. After money, what he wanted most was power. He realized that as a foreigner, a commoner and a heretic, he would find the ordinary circuits closed to him, so he aimed to get public opinion on his side. He cultivated intellectuals and scholars, artists and philosophers – especially if they had made names for themselves. To promote himself he had two incomparable helpers. The first was his wife Suzanne, who had but one aim in life: the worldly success of husband, whom she made the object of a veritable cult. "She had transformed her house," said the duke de Lévis, "into a temple of which she was the priestess, and their friends, no matter their rank, were reduced to the humble role of worshippers." Every Friday she drew to her celebrated salon all that Paris had to offer by way of distinguished minds and influential people. The other helper, their daughter Germaine, married to Sweden's ambassador to Paris, the baron de Staël, brought to the altar of paternal glory her considerable talents and her vast network of connections. Devoid of elegance, grave rather than noble, and taking himself very seriously, Necker was the object of some ridicule at court, with his toupee of hair lying at a curious angle to his head, and on either side "those two big rolls of hair that sweep up, like the rest of his face." But the Paris bourgeoisie liked him; he was a kindred spirit. The opposite of the much despised tax and customs officials, who got rich from their cut of the revenue they collected from the taxpayers, Necker offered the reassuring image of a man who had simply got rich at the stock market or in commerce – a dream come true! And besides, his money had not gone to his head, because he readily opened his pockets to those in need. Genuinely openhanded, Suzanne Necker contributed a portion of her husband's gains to a few judiciously chosen charitable causes. But she made sure everyone knew about it.

There is no point in wondering if France should have left England to deplete itself in the struggle against the rebellious colonies and thereby become stronger vis-à-vis its exhausted rival, whatever the outcome of their colonial war. We can't remake history. But once

France opted for war, it had to find the means to wage it. Since the ministry's financial experts despaired of pushing any new taxes through Parliament, the only recourse left was loans. Alas, no one was breaking down doors to invest in government bonds, because everyone knew that dividends were slow in materializing. Money is only lent to the wealthy; everyone knows that. So the king resigned himself to asking the rich Necker to find the loans to foot the bill for the American war.

The clever man at first succeeded beyond all expectations. The mere mention of his name inspired confidence. The loans he set up were made more attractive by a few ploys like lotteries or previously unheard of lifetime guaranties. People stampeded with such fervor to get these certificates that the ensuing speculation sent the prices skyrocketing to way over their initial value. All of France fell into line singing the praises of this "magician," who like Cagliostro, could pump out all the gold he wanted. He knew full well that he was mortgaging the future. The few savings gained by the cleanup in the financial services did not go far; he didn't have the political clout to institute the indispensable tax reform, which could only happen if he took on the tax-exempt. He tried to get around the problem by proposing, like Turgot before him, to bring the wealthy categories into the management of financial and economic matters in every province through local assemblies, where all the three estates would be represented*. But even this very timid measure was enough to alienate those concerned. He hoped to get the public behind him by publishing a *Report to the King,* which was one of the booksellers' hottest items of the day. "It is the work of a man who shows great zeal for the glory of the king and the welfare of his people," exclaimed Marie-Antoinette naively. But people who knew their stuff soon noticed that he had cheated when it came to the numbers, quite simply omitting, during the height of the American conflict, any mention of the costs involved, as they were "extraordinary." Since the little publication's jacket was blue, Maurepas punned that it was nothing but a *"conte bleu,"* or "blue tale" instead of blue report. In fact, the government was in the red to the tune of eighty million. Vulnerable, Necker wanted to have a greater political say than his technocrat position afforded. He thought he was indispensable and demanded admission to the King's Council. When Maurepas refused, he sent the king a curt letter of resignation, and was stunned when it was accepted. Louis XVI couldn't forgive him for this kind of blackmail and swore he could never employ him again.

---

* Appointed, not elected, and chosen only from property owners.

Necker had been aware that the queen was dangerous. He'd always been careful not to get her back up, so she got everything she wanted out of him. Receiving a writ for 150,000 pounds that she asked him to pay, he replied, "The state of the treasury absolutely forbids my granting Y.M. this request, but my personal fortune enables me to offer the same sum from my own pocket and I will have the honor of delivering it to her this evening." She must have shed a tear or two over the departure of "that charming man." When, after an interregnum of two years, Calonne was appointed to the finance ministry at the end of 1783, she accepted his appointment with bad grace, not sharing in the joy of her Polignac friends. The new controller was not incompetent, as has often been said; he was just faced with an impossible situation. In the year to come, revenue of 600 million was expected, of which already 176 had been spent. There were also 390 in arrears to come up with, and servicing the public debt swallowed up 250. There was no choice but to borrow, and in order to obtain loans they had to hide the dreadful state of the treasury. Calonne was forced to go into financial contortions with the hope that the sums invested in major public works would finally produce results and bring in some tax revenue.

He quickly understood that it would be nothing but suicide to try to impose belt-tightening on the court. He poured lavish sums on it. If Necker was the "magician," Calonne was the "enchanter." In 1785 Marie-Antoinette got it into her head that she had to buy Saint-Cloud, which would be a most charming and agreeable residence "since it brought her closer to the theatres in Paris," according to her secretary Augeard. The duke d'Orléans, who owned the chateau, refused to exchange it for either Choisy or La Muette, as had been suggested, and demanded six million in cash for it. The bill seemed high to Calonne, and he balked. Augeard reported that he was treated to a violent outburst:

> I know all about what you have said to the king, Sir, to dissuade him of my purchase. If this business were not public, I would happily desist, despite its attractiveness to me, but since you have used the state of the royal treasury as an excuse, I shall remit to him a highly detailed account of everything you have squandered and misused, and of the vast sums you have handed over to the princes of the blood and my brothers-in-law to bolster your standing before the king, and of all the other sums you have poured into the purses of the court grandees so as to get closer to the king and surround him with favor-seekers

and cheat him on a daily basis. Do as you please, but if I do not get Saint-Cloud, I forbid you from appearing before me, and especially from being present at Madame de Polignac's home when I am there.

So Calonne bought his peace of mind for a borrowed six million, to which he added an equivalent sum for improvements. And Marie-Antoinette continued to delude herself over the state of the royal treasury. "If it's possible, it's done; if it's impossible, it will be done," he would reply to her requests. She would later say, "How could I have guessed the terrible state of financial affairs? When I asked for 50,000 pounds they would bring me 100,000." She ordered for Saint-Cloud the most expensive furnishings and the most refined of decors. What is more, she had her boudoir in Fontainebleau redecorated. (Although she only enjoyed this exquisite room for a single year, it has remained unchanged through the centuries.) Aristocratic society lived off borrowing, and as if it sensed that its days were numbered, it giddily indulged in the twilight delights of a dying civilization. Talleyrand would say that never was "life's sweetness" so intense as it was in that summer of 1786, when the monarchy's disintegration seemed to be suspended for a few months. But even at this time serious people realized that no conjuring tricks would prevent bankruptcy. In fact, Necker took it upon himself to tell the public so, in his *Administration des Finances*, which only hastened its dismantling. In terms of numbers, the deficit got deeper by 100 million a year.

Profoundly honest, the king refused to suspend payments and despoil the lenders who trusted him. He very often helped his near and dear ones pay their debts and saved them from bankruptcy, but he would not erase at the stroke of a pen sums that he himself owed. He therefore backed Calonne when he again undertook the never-ending attempts at tax reform – this time by way of a "territorial tax" proportional to income and paid by everyone without exception – but with the indispensable corollary of creating elected consultative assemblies. And as he knew perfectly well that the Parliament would never consent to such measures, Calonne proposed gathering together some carefully selected "notables" whose approval he could count on to get Parliament to fall into line. The tactic wasn't new; both Henry IV and Richelieu had used it successfully. But times had changed, and so had the people.

From fiscal equality to social equality

The first two estates had not only tax privileges but societal ones as well. In former times these had been justified by the functions that the kingdom's three orders fulfilled within the state. The clergy, aside from its spiritual mission, was responsible for education and public assistance; the nobility, the military professionals, protected the kingdom from aggression by shedding "the blood tax," and the third estate furnished the labor to sustain society as a whole. The system could only function if it remained somewhat flexible: it had to be possible to climb the social ladder. In the 18ᵗʰ century, this system faltered. Unlike Louis XIV who was careful not to close the wealthier bourgeoisie off from access to positions of responsibility, Louis XV and Louis XVI allowed a situation to develop in which the nobility kept the most prestigious and lucrative jobs for those who could prove they had a certain number of "heraldic quarterings." All court appointments were held by the nobility. In the same way, the Ségur decree reserved for them the officer ranks in the army so as to offer an outlet for insolvent gentlemen who were excluded from other professions because of the rule of *non-dérogeance**. This, however, removed all hope any commoner might have of ascending to the highest military ranks. The disastrous effects of this would be seen when the army, deprived of its commanders through emigration, was won over to the Revolution by its non-commissioned officers. And in the Church, too, the gulf widened between the prelates of noble extraction, as a rule handsomely endowed, and the simple curates, who had to live off their meager salaries and felt more and more alienated from their superiors.

At the same time, the advantages granted to the privileged classes were called into question by the public debate over taxation. Necker's *Report to the King* owed its success to the fact that it put a chink in the armor of secrecy that had hitherto surrounded the state budget: "The king renders account to his people..." it had claimed. But Louis XVI felt that the king had to render account to God alone. Vergennes considered this text "just an appeal to the people, whose pernicious effects on the monarchy" would soon be felt. And in fact, nothing like this had ever existed before. The people got to see the inner workings of royal finances. They were told how and why the royal treasury was going dry. Necker saw to it that his actions would be judged by public onion, not the king.

---

* *Translator's note: aristocrats could not abandon a military career without risking the loss of their noble status.*

All of his successors would have to do the same, if they didn't want to be accused of hiding thefts. Thus details of expenditures were poured out onto the public thoroughfare for all to see.

The only ones paid any heed were the court's expenditures. Actually, they represented only six percent of the total, but that did nothing to attenuate the scandal over them because, unlike warships, they seemed completely unwarranted. The salaries of the crown's highest officeholders were out of proportion to the work involved. There was no check at all on the vast number of cash payments that the king signed over to God knows whom. People were scandalized by the pensions and gifts the queen lavished on her favorites, by the number of useless posts, and the chronic waste in all departments. What good were all these nobles at court who got rich at the expense of the treasury? What good were all these dubious and often penniless little country nobles who were so attached to their outdated feudal rights, when the monarchy had stripped them of their age-old policing and judicial functions? So the king was calling for the removal of their tax advantages? While he was at it, why didn't he follow his own good example and get rid of the nobles' other privileges, like the monopoly on jobs for example? The demand for equality quickly went beyond just the question of taxation and took issue with the rigid social order of three distinct estates. It started to instill in the people an animosity towards the nobility that would soon take on fearful proportions.

In 1783-1784, when life's sweetness still pervaded court life, a hint of things to come could be sensed all the same. The incorrigible Beaumarchais was once more at the center of a highly controversial affair. He ran ragged trying to get his *Marriage of Figaro* staged. The play was excellent, but subversive: two good reasons to be talked about. It made the rounds clandestinely; it was read in the salons. The intellectual set supported it, and with the help of the Polignacs, the Comédie-Française accepted it and started rehearsals. Marie-Antoinette was delighted to give it a big hand before it even opened. The count d'Artois talked about it enthusiastically, the count de Provence indignantly. The king wanted to have a clean conscience about it, so he took a look at the text and called in Madame Campan to read it to the queen. She recounted, "At Figaro's monologue in which he attacks various sections of the administration, but more particularly at the tirade against the State's prisons, the king rose heatedly and said, 'This is detestable, it will never be put on stage; the Bastille would have to be leveled for this play not to be dangerously at odds with our rule... This man wants to thwart everything that must be respected in a government...' 'So the play will not be produced?' asked the queen. 'Certainly not,' replied the king, 'you can be sure of that.'"

The king was a bit late. The royal ban fell *in extremis* when the theatre was already half filled. People complained that this was an attack on public freedom; they called it oppressive and tyrannical. Beaumarchais took up the challenge, swearing that his comedy would be produced, and implied that he had taken out the parts offensive to the government – but in fact, he cut very little. The play, finally put on at the *Théâtre-Français* on April 27, 1784, was greeted with wild enthusiasm. Beaumarchais won that match.

Whatever Madame Campan said, Marie-Antoinette supported Beaumarchais and didn't understand at all why her husband found fault with him, for the following year she would have no scruples about putting on another of his plays at Trianon. She was in the middle of rehearsals as Rosine in *The Barber of Seville* when the necklace affair broke out. But actually, did Louis XVI himself really understand the true import of *The Marriage of Figaro*? Did he hear its compelling cry of the common man against the nobility?

> Because you are a great lord, you think you are a great genius! ... Nobility, wealth, rank, position... they all make you feel so proud! What have you done to deserve so much? You went to the trouble of being born – nothing more! As for the rest – a rather ordinary man! And as for me, heavens! Lost among the obscure masses, I have had to use more knowledge and be more calculating just to survive than all the rulers of Spain have needed over the last hundred years!

Less than five years later, the sentiment would be echoed in the writings of the abbé Sieyès – in the *Essai sur les privilèges* and then *Qu'est-ce que le Tiers État?* – where he posited a brilliant theoretical formulation: the nobles form a caste of men who have neither function nor utility, and therefore by their mere existence, enjoy the privileges attached to their person. The caste of nobles has usurped all the good positions; it has turned them into a sort of hereditary right exploited purely for its exclusive advantage. "What is the third estate? It is everything. What has it been until now within the political order? Nothing. What does it seek? To become something."

Marie-Antoinette's misfortune was that for the public she embodied this parasitical nobility, and especially that of the court, the most tightly knit and visible, on which all the people's rancor was concentrated. Victim of her own predilection for a tiny group of favorites who within the noble class monopolized the most lucrative positions, she was the figurehead and epitome of this selfish and rapacious group. The king's bourgeois simplicity by contrast rendered her more detestable, without for all that earning him any particular sympathy, because people saw in him a husband, perhaps cuckolded, and certainly unable to control his wife.

Learning how to be alone

The best portrait of Marie-Antoinette, the one in which we get a glimpse of her soul, is by the sculptor Houdon. It dates from the period of the necklace affair*. In it, the queen, beautiful but imperious, holds her head up high and casts it back, in a familiar attitude inspired by her keen sense of her own dignity. One day Madame Vigée-Lebrun complimented her on it and got the reply, "If I were not the queen, they would say I had an insolent air, is that not so?" Houdon didn't render her as insolent, he showed her as defiant. The disdainful mouth, given emphasis by the lower "Austrian" lip, observed Pierre de Nolhac, seems to lend itself equally to anger or amusement. She responds with bravado and contempt to the insult of the necklace-affair verdict. The outrageous calumnies against her person only serve to reinforce her sense of self-righteousness and thus her lack of self-awareness. She has nothing to be ashamed of; there are good people and there are bad people. She's one of the good ones; the bad ones have got it all wrong, not she. She could not admit that her behavior might have had something to do with creating her current predicament. She decided to change not an iota of her ways. But she found that her ways no longer afforded the same pleasures.

At the time of Rohan's acquittal, her brother Ferdinand, the duke of Modena and governor of Lombardy along with his wife Beatrice of Este, had been her guests for three weeks under an assumed name. Although she felt no pleasure at all in seeing him after sixteen years, she did her best to honor his presence in Versailles. But she would have preferred he not be there for the verdict. As her heart wasn't in it, she cancelled an evening party planned for the Trianon, citing poor health. She was reaching the end of her fourth pregnancy; this one was undesired. Unhappy at having gained so much weight during the previous one – so much so that she was thought to be expecting twins – she anxiously watched her waist thicken, and even insisted on keeping her corset to help keep her svelte silhouette. She

---

* She posed for Houdon in 1786, perhaps before the dénouement of the affair, but when public opinion was already rabidly against her.

was past thirty now, and as much as she was fond of saying that she was no longer a young woman, she did everything possible to make it appear otherwise.

No sooner had her guests departed than Louis XVI left on an official visit to Normandy. She would have liked for the trip to be postponed so that she could accompany him, just for the change of scenery, but he had refused to put it off. She had to sit in bored anticipation of the birth while he toured the Cherbourg and Le Havre arsenals, where the naval engineers and crews were impressed with his technical knowledge. He was greeted everywhere with shouts of joy and other marks of respect and affection. He replied with unaffected kindness to the population's enthusiasm, finding just the right word for each of his hosts to show that he had made the effort to find out about their function and service record. He returned home thrilled with his visit. As he approached, the queen took up position on the balcony overlooking the marble courtyard with her three children, and when the little ones could make him out, they started to shout "Papa! Papa!" at the top of their lungs. The courtyard was bursting with people, and "satisfaction was painted on every face." Her husband's clear popularity showed Marie-Antoinette that love of the monarchy was alive and well, but that made it all the more painful for her to contrast it with the discredit into which she had sunk.

Little Sophie was born ten days later. The queen returned to her functions very quickly, too quickly perhaps, for she remained fatigued. She had to play host to more family members, this time her sister Maria Christina and brother-in-law Prince Albert of Saxony-Teschen, the governors of the Low Countries. But she had never liked this older sister, a woman of intelligence and strong will, her mother's favorite, who tried to impose her humorless authority on her siblings. She feared her sister would subject her to interrogation and ask indiscreet questions, and seemed to think, according to Mercy, that her sister would try to "win over minds and dominate them." Frankly, after the necklace scandal, she was expecting a good scolding, in the purest Joseph II style, which in fact he had suggested. If her visit had been inspired simply by affection, she would have come a lot sooner, given the relative proximity of the Low Countries. Her timing was no accident. Maria Christina's mission was to get a picture of the untoward events in France and to set her sister back on the right track.

Despite Mercy's attempts to disperse the "clouds" and Louis XVI's thoughtfulness – he treated his brother-in-law to a number of hunting parties – the sisters' reunion was singularly chilly. Maria Christina insisted on being "often and for long periods at Versailles." Marie-Antoinette worked at keeping her at a distance, proposing a heavy schedule of excursions to Paris, and wound up telling her in no uncertain terms that her presence was not welcome on those days when she had things to take care of, when she wanted to be left alone. She kept the Saxony-Teschens within the solemn walls of Versailles, and did not invite them to Trianon. She was greatly relieved when they left. Although appearances were saved, the ambassador had to admit that the reunion had been a failure. The emperor could see that his sister's usual unconditional support was faltering, and his hope was to strengthen family ties; but the visits with both Ferdinand and Maria Christina had the opposite effect. Marie-Antoinette had never felt so estranged from her country of origin and from those she had until then considered her own. As we have seen, it was from this moment on that she began to rebel openly against Joseph II's demands.

Trianon offered a month's respite. But she was deprived of Fersen's company, because he would be away for nearly a year. Autumn brought the usual stay in Fontainebleau with its attendant amusements. But she didn't enjoy it as much as before. She distanced herself from the Polignacs. Mercy's warnings about the cupidity of those who made up what he called her "rapacious surroundings" would not have been enough to put her off them without the tarnishing of their friendship over the years and their taking unseemly liberties – thanks to the relaxing of courtly etiquette. She no longer got much respect. With the countess she maintained a somewhat stormy friendship, but she couldn't bear the rest of the clan. She abhorred the arrogance of Vaudreuil, the countess' acknowledged lover. She was so fearful of meeting at her friend's home people she didn't want to see that she found out beforehand who'd be there and often stayed away. The countess did not like this one bit: how could the queen expect her to exclude some of her friends from her own salon just because she was there? The queen still showered lots of attention on Madame de Polignac, Besenval notes, "but now only informs her of what has happened, no longer consulting her on what's ahead." She didn't dare break off relations with her, Madame Campan explains, fearing that the loss of constancy in such a lasting and well-known friendship could have "very serious drawbacks." The fact is she was hostage to all the confidences she had so imprudently shared with her through the years.

It's not good to be the one who triggers scandal. At court, the atmosphere around Marie-Antoinette subtly deteriorated. No one could be entirely natural around her. Between the humiliating pity of the most indulgent towards her and the insulting, barely hidden glee of those she had offended by her mockery or wounded by her indifference – and they were legion! – she found no one whose company she truly enjoyed. Within the family, the aunts did not forgive her for the harm she'd done to the monarchy. Madame Adélaïde railed against her insouciance about the libels, and played the prophet of doom: "She says the Parisians are mere croaking frogs, but I fear the frogs will turn into snakes." From within her cloister walls in Saint-Denis, Madame Louise could only pray and get others to do so, but she made sure people knew about it. The king's sister Madame Élisabeth distanced herself, and the two Savoyard sisters-in-law broadened the already existing gulf. Neither of them had much influence but their husbands were dangerous, and so were the cousins.

Provence was to be feared the most. His hatred of Marie-Antoinette stemmed from unrequited attraction and frustrated ambition. When they were young he had tried to get on her good side. Not that he was in love with her, but he was sensitive to the spell she cast on men – let's not forget Rohan – and the brilliance of her queenly majesty coupled with that of her all-conquering femininity. He wanted her to recognize his superior intelligence. But instead of the appreciation he expected, she treated him with mistrust and derision. He had never forgiven her. At least he had the consolation during the long years of the royal couple's infertility, of thinking he might one day succeed his brother to the throne. The birth of one son and then another dashed those hopes. But the recent scandal rekindled them. If these children were the fruit of illegitimate dalliances, he would again be first in line to the throne. He thus took pleasure in feeding the rumor mill on the subject, at the very time when the difficulties overwhelming his brother offered him a pretext for slipping into the government.

The queen had another adversary within the bosom of the family, this one fiercer and less coy about it, and that was the king's cousin the duke d'Orléans, the future Philippe-Égalité, a muddle-headed troublemaker who for years had been entrenched in an opposition inspired less by ambition than by a desire for revenge. Solidly implanted in the heart of Paris at the Palais-Royal, he was better able to take the pulse of public opinion than those in Versailles, and to orchestrate it through the gutter press that flourished around him.

In the beginning of 1787, Marie-Antoinette was crushed by the vile press that held her responsible for all the ills of the realm. She no longer dared show her face at the theatre in Paris. At the

Opera she had been hissed at. At the Comédie-Française, during a performance of *Athalie*, there was great applause at the point where the high priest implored God to cast on the cruel queen, "the spirit of vanity and falsehood/Fatal forerunner of the fall of kings!" Faced with the hostility directed at her from all sides, she tried to push against the current. For the year's salon at the end of August, it had been cleverly decided to display a portrait of her that showed her at her best, surrounded by her children – and wearing pendant earrings but no necklace. The artist Madame Vigée-Lebrun was late in handing in the work. Until it arrived its spot remained empty, which inspired a jokester to paste a sign to it reading "Madame Déficit." The finished work showed an entirely different Marie-Antoinette from Houdon's bust. For once the official portrait painter abandoned her usual blandness. It is of course a flattering image. But what we see in her frozen features, in her vacant look, is no longer defiance but anguish.

From then on her husband was the only one she could depend on. But he was now in the state of collapse, and thoroughly depended on her.

Transfer of power

The decision to convene an Assembly of Notables was a dangerous gamble. From Vienna, an ironic Kaunitz called it a sideshow, and more crudely, a "load of crap." Hardly had it commenced at the end of February 1787, when the men whose obedience was counted on rebelled and declared themselves incompetent. It would have been surprising otherwise. Mostly from the ranks of the nobility – for it was hardly imaginable finding notables anywhere else – they were being asked to support a single and proportional tax, from which they would be the first to suffer. According to François Furet's clever phrase, it was as if Calonne were a company director calling together his biggest stockholders to ask them to give up their dividends. Paris public opinion held him responsible for the financial collapse, and Louis XVI, after trying to support him, sent him packing in the beginning of April. The well-informed Calonne had a better sense of which way the wind was blowing than most. He took himself off to Holland and then to England, where he became the first of the émigrés.

Deeply saddened by his foreign minister Vergennes' death in February, the king found neither his experience nor his energy in the faithful but mediocre childhood companion Montmorin, with whom he replaced him. He appeared to be losing his ground. He had fired Calonne without finding a successor. As far as the public was concerned, there were only two men capable of resolving the financial crisis: the much-regretted Necker, whose work was familiar, and the archbishop of Toulouse Loménie de Brienne, who as a member of the Assembly of Notables led the attack on Calonne, putting himself forward as an alternative. The king wanted nothing to do with either of them: "Neither Necker nor nasty priests!" He couldn't bear the arrogance of the bourgeois gentleman from Geneva. As for Brienne, the man was repulsive to him for his libertine ways and *philosophe* connections. When he'd been suggested for the Paris episcopal seat, the king vociferated, "The least we can ask of the archbishop of Paris is that he believe in God!" Alas, the trustworthy counselor of state he finally picked lasted only three weeks. There was nothing to do but choose one of the other two.

The king was in a state of inertia about it, so Montmorin called on the queen. She couldn't make up her mind. Her old confidant the abbé de Vermond had for a long time been singing Brienne's praises; they had once been students together. She had begun to help the king choose by sending him the document in which Brienne set out his plans. On the other hand, Necker had already proven himself and was very popular, so she and Montmorin agreed on putting him forward instead. Louis XVI used up his last reserves of energy to brush him off. Whereupon he accepted Brienne with unseemly haste, even agreeing to grant him the title of chief minister, something he'd never wanted to give anyone. For the first time in her life, Marie-Antoinette had had a real role in making a major appointment.

It can be said of course that she wasn't the only one making the decision, and above all that there wasn't exactly a host of candidates. So this wasn't a victory like the one she and Ségur had once won against Maurepas. But this is precisely what was new. This was different from the days when she saw her political interventions as power struggles against the dominant minister – Maurepas or Vergennes – to get her protégés positions or favors. There weren't any favors or positions to grant any more; in fact, they were considering doing away with some. And even if Brienne had the title, there was no chief minister any more either. The situation was so serious that everyone was now in a precarious position, especially in the absence of support from the king. Now resistance to the queen's will was not restricted to the government within the microcosm of Versailles; it was in Parliament and the

Assembly of Notables as well. What was at stake now was not some friend's promotion but royal authority itself. This she understood. Her combativeness was of a different order now, as were the ends to which she asserted it. In this new challenge, she chose solidarity with her husband. When it came to finding the man who could providentially bring the finance ministry back from the brink and at the same time bend Parliament to his will, the presumed talents of the candidate took precedence over her personal feelings. She was no doubt wrong about Brienne; she didn't develop a political brain overnight – she never would. But she started to think like a queen and not like the head of a clique. What mattered now was the good of the kingdom. She entered politics for good and earnest.

Brienne helped her make progress, letting her in on debates and decisions, something all previous ministers were careful to avoid. Not only because he was grateful to her, although Mercy was shouting far and wide that Brienne owed his post to him, but because he found her receptive – which was new – and especially because he desperately needed her support, for Louis XVI was in a state of utter disarray.

Today we'd call it depression, and if in the 18th century there was no such diagnosis, the symptoms were at least recognized. Mercy noticed them as soon as Brienne was chosen. In an official dispatch in German, on May 19th he wrote: "The king came every day to see the queen and he was so shaken and disconsolate over the critical state of his kingdom that he shed tears." In a letter to Joseph II of August 14th: "The state of the king's mood offers... few resources, and his physical habits are more and more taking their toll; he is growing heavier, and after the hunt he eats so immoderately that he has lapses in reasoning capacity and a sort of brusque disregard which is very hard on those who must put up with it." Panic attacks, crying fits, and apathy alternated with exhausting bursts of activity, eating binges, disconnected thinking, refusal to speak, along with an irresistible urge to sleep at inappropriate times: "During the two years I was a member of the Council of State," wrote Saint-Priest, "I never heard him utter an opinion. It wasn't rare to see him sleep there." Perhaps the indifference and apparent ennui masked an effort to flee from an intolerable situation. Upon his return from the extremely taxing hunting expeditions and little suppers, the valets helping him get out of his coach saw him stagger and concluded that he was drunk. This was probably from fatigue rather than wine. But there is no doubt that throughout Europe and even as far away as America, he had the reputation of a drunkard, which Fersen did his best to deny to Gustave III of Sweden. That he overate cannot be denied, however. He put on an enormous amount of weight, which hindered his ability to move – he would soon need help mounting his horse – and his image was severely tarnished. People sang:

> *That in what he takes delight*
> *Is eatin' and drinkin' through the night*

In the following years he would swing between periods of feeling better and suffering relapses, sometimes aggravated by real diseases that confined him to bed, like the dermatitis he had in the autumn of 1787. And convulsive crying fits or entire days spent without uttering a word would punctuate the crucial stages in the collapse of his kingdom.

The king's limitations placed a heavy burden on Marie-Antoinette, because he instinctively recognized and depended on her strength. He now put his trust in her. His failures weakened her position as well, however, because they roused the hopes of the pretenders to the throne. The king could die. Or he could be declared incompetent, taken into protective custody, or deposed. If any of these were to happen, her lot would be nothing but tears. A revealing couplet was making the rounds in Paris:

> *Louis XVI barred, Marie-Antoinette in the convent,*
> *D'Artois at Saint-Lazare, and Provence regent.*

Already presiding over the main office at the Assembly of Notables, the cunning Provence was moving his pawns. Marie-Antoinette faced the situation with a force born of desperation. She subjected her household to economic stringency: "Need has shut the door on pillaging." Her former friends criticized her bitterly for doing away with some of their posts. How could it be that in France one could be robbed of one's status overnight? Besenval had the nerve to tell her, "That only happens in Turkey." In any case, a lot more than that would be needed to fill the budget gap.

She had greater success in supporting Brienne. She was discreet about it, having learned one thing at least – how to be cautious. The king's somewhat illusory confidence in her that she used to boast about, came back to haunt her. From now on she would avoid the limelight and remain in the background, like an obedient wife. But her participation in the select committees at Brienne's invitation contributed to getting strong measures passed. Convinced that the only viable form of government was absolutist monarchy of the kind the king inherited from his forefathers and she saw practiced in Austria, she pushed the minister to do everything possible to bring the malcontents back into line, ignorant of the fact that they had the whole country behind them.

Brienne fails

When Brienne came on the scene, Marie-Antoinette was optimistic. "We have given the king a good minister; all we need do now is let him get on with it." They let him get on with it, and as a result, as Saint-Priest points out, there were some bad moves. His first one was to send away the recalcitrant notables. But he might as well have jumped from the frying pan into the fire, because he then had to deal with the Paris Parliament, furious at the government's attempt to short-circuit them. His efforts to get Calonne's territorial tax project passed came up against the magistrates' resistance. They declared that any reform in tax law required representation at a national level and demanded a meeting of the Estates General. So he went for a showdown, and the whole thing followed a predictable pattern. The conflict resulted in a *lit de justice* to impose registering the edict; then some of the magistrates were exiled to Troyes. Then came nationwide unrest; the government backed down, recalled the exiled magistrates and withdrew the edict. And since the treasury's coffers were more depleted than ever, Brienne had to resort to borrowing.

On November 19th the king went to Parliament to present a series of technical measures, appending an edict outlining the modalities of a new loan. None of this was supposed to pose any particular problems. The *lit de justice* had been avoided to satisfy the magistrates, who hated it because it prohibited any discussion and suspended "voting rights." So a simple *séance royale* was called, to which the sovereign's presence merely added a layer of solemnity, and where everyone could speak for as long as he wished. The king was obliged to promise to convene the Estates General in 1792 – when, hopefully, the finance ministry would be back on its feet. Some found the proposed date too far off, demanding it be convened immediately. In the end, however, a large majority emerged in favor of a loan. But then there was a misstep. They thought they could save time by putting an end to the interminable speeches justifying the magistrates' votes. "Having heard your opinions, I find it is necessary to set up the loans referred to in my edict," declared the king. "I have promised a meeting of the Estates General before 1792: my word must suffice. I hereby order my edict to be enacted." At that point the duke d'Orléans stood up and protested that this was illegal. "It is legal because I wish it," replied the king, barely controlling his anger. Strictly speaking, d'Orléans wasn't wrong, there should have been an official count of the votes. But his ill intent was all too obvious, because no law had been violated, just a custom, and it didn't affect the outcome of the vote. He was using a technicality to be provocative. The king was correct when he said he was the sole source of the law. But it wasn't very smart of him to state so bluntly the first article of the absolute monarchy's creed in front of an assembly that was calling its very fundaments into question. Furious, Louis XVI banished his cousin to his Villers-Cotterêts lands, and had two of his most zealous advisers arrested. Marie-Antoinette couldn't find words strong enough to criticize the duke d'Orléans. Convinced her husband was in the right, she believed naively in the efficacy of strong-arm tactics. "It pains me to be obliged to use authoritarian methods," she wrote to her brother, "but unfortunately they have become necessary, and I hope they will have the desired results."

However, between the court and Parliament, war had been declared. All winter long skirmishes multiplied and were amplified through the echo chambers of the salons, clubs, cafés, Masonic lodges and the press. When spring came Brienne resolved to nip the problem in its parliamentary bud. Emulating a plan enacted by Maupeou at the end of Louis XV's reign, he tried to deprive the magistrates of the power to ratify laws by conferring it on a group especially created for the purpose. "We are contemplating limiting them to their judiciary functions," Marie-Antoinette wrote again, "and setting up a new assembly with the power to ratify the kingdom's general laws and taxes. I believe we took all the measures and precautions compatible with the greatest secrecy." But as a result, she added, they weren't able to evaluate how strong the opposition was. All the same, she seemed to harbor no doubts about the success of her show of force. Unfortunately, the secret leaked out, and Parliament was girding for a fight. When guards were sent to arrest two leaders of the opposition, d'Éprémesnil and Montsabert, they were met with a mass of people sheilding them, and were unable to hand over the culprits until the following day.

At this point the revolt spread like wildfire to the provincial parliaments, with Grenoble taking the lead. The queen still chose to believe that things would sort themselves out: "It is sad to be obliged to resort to rigorous means whose ramifications we cannot calculate, but they have become necessary and the king is determined to maintain his laws and his authority." In fact, this was a case of wishful thinking, and already showed the discrepancy between her point of view and her husband's. She was for repressive measures, at whatever the risk. But as for the king, even if he said he had decided to safeguard his authority, he was not willing to use the means necessary to maintain it.

The financial situation in the meantime was dangerously deteriorating. In the beginning of August, the treasury was empty; there were only 200,000 francs left in the till while there were several millions to be paid out at the end of the month. Brienne suspended some payments and talked about compulsory loans, which sent stockholders into a panic. Then something entirely novel took place. It was clear that the king was in a state of complete paralysis. It was the queen who, for the first time, took the initiative in a ministerial shake-up. At the same time there was something of a revolution in her relationship with Mercy-Argenteau. For years on end she had been the more or less compliant recipient of the lectures the ambassador transmitted to her from her mother or brother. Now she gave him, in her own name, responsibility for a mission concerning France's domestic affairs. She would of course listen to his opinion, but it was she who commanded, and she who made the decision. Marie-Antoinette's metamorphosis was so surprising to him that he sent his master Joseph II a complete dossier regarding the delicate negotiations she had been conducting to bring Necker back to power.

Necker's return

Only one man seemed able to re-establish government credit, and that was Necker. However, there were a number of obstacles in the way of his return. First of all the king had to be talked into allowing him to return; after all, he'd sworn he never would. And Necker himself would have to be talked into getting mixed up in a risky undertaking that could tarnish his image. It would also be necessary to rigorously differentiate the respective areas of responsibility between the banker Necker and the archbishop Brienne. Marie-Antoinette did not want to get rid of the archbishop altogether. She had been leaning on him for a year; he was seen as her man; the opposition would interpret dismissing him as a victory against her. On August 19th she summoned Mercy, who found her in a bit of a predicament. She had convinced Brienne of the wisdom of recalling Necker, but she needed an intermediary to sound the latter out. She confided the task to Mercy, with strict instructions that her name not be mentioned.

Negotiations got off to a bad start. The archbishop agreed that Necker should come back to the finance ministry as long as he himself as chief minister remained the boss. Necker was delighted to find himself in a position of strength again after the humiliation he had suffered a few years back and milked the situation for all it was worth. If they wanted him, they would have to work for it. He told them that by getting mixed up with such an unpopular minister as Brienne, he risked losing public confidence and failing to get the job done, thus sacrificing his good name without any advantage to the state. The queen, advised of his reply by Mercy, had to agree that it was necessary to come down in favor of either one or the other. All right, she was willing to let Brienne go, but would not give Necker carte blanche either. "He will need to be kept in check. The person above me," she added, "cannot perform his functions, and whatever they say and whatever might happen, I am and ever will be only in second place, and despite the trust the first has in me, he doesn't let me forget it." She had come a long way since the day when she tricked "the poor man" into letting her receive a visit from Choiseul. Her roundabout way of referring to Louis XVI was not pejorative; she was simply acknowledging the facts: her husband's mood swings and lack of resolve left her to face responsibilities that terrified her, but she could not take his place for all that.

Confident that time was on his side Necker kept them waiting. He set out his conditions. For one, he refused to get involved without the king's expressed agreement, which is understandable. But Brienne, sent to sound out the king at the queen's behest, met initially with his "great abhorrence." He said he could only try to overcome his loathing once he knew what Monsieur Necker had in mind. But Necker, despite guessing that Mercy was speaking for the queen, waited to find out what the king himself thought of it all. Time was running short; Marie-Antoinette tried to persuade her husband: Necker should be put on the Council and should have "absolutely a free hand in his department." This position implied getting rid of the archbishop. To avoid having to fire him, would he not just leave of his own accord? It again fell to Mercy to perform the delicate mission of getting him to resign. He was happily surprised to find Brienne "tormented by the same preoccupations" and quite willing to put the ministerial hornets' nest behind him. He immediately handed in his resignation. On August 26, the king and queen together granted Necker a royal audience, whereupon he immediately took up his functions. This too was a first; Marie-Antoinette had never before had a role in such a ceremony.

However, she was in no mood for feeling triumphant. She knew Necker would keep her at a greater distance, so she would miss Brienne. Insensitive enough to lavish great attention on the departing Brienne, she offended Necker and irritated the public. But above all, she realized that this changing of the ministerial guard was seen as yet another defeat for the king. She was terribly fearful of the future. She wrote to Mercy on August 25th, "The archbishop is gone. I cannot tell you how much this day has affected me. I believe this move was necessary, but I fear all the same that it will cause much trouble in the parliaments." The sooner Necker got down to work, the better it would be. But would he succeed? "I tremble, may I be forgiven for this weakness, to think that it is I who have brought him back. It is my fate to spread misfortune. If he fails again because of all the infernal machinations, or if it leads to the weakening of the king's authority, I will be detested all the more."

During these two years and under the most trying conditions, Marie-Antoinette underwent something of a political apprenticeship, but it was not nearly enough. Although she did not gain an overview of what was happening, she at least gained a sense of responsibility. Besides, she won her husband's confidence. From now on he would do nothing without consulting her. At the very end of the year he would even invite her to sit on the King's Council, to which for as long as anyone could remember no women except regents had ever had access.

On the other hand, it was Necker who now in effect held power. He fulfilled the functions of chief minister even if he didn't hold the title. Once he succeeded in getting the bank loans crucial to filling the treasury's financial gap, he had to face the underlying problem, which was a political one. Always good at guessing which way the wind is blowing, he didn't need to recall the frustrations of Brienne's tenure to know that coercive measures couldn't succeed. The first thing he did was to restore to the Paris Parliament its full functions. He felt that the king had to take the lead in the great events that were unfolding, whatever changes they might bring. He was sure that the queen, who had supported Brienne's attempt to get Parliament under control, was opposed to it. But the weight of events had already forced Louis XVI to bend, to make concessions that started him down a slippery slope. On the 8th of August, having in vain tried to put off a meeting of the Estates General for as long as possible, he was forced to promise to call one for the first of May 1789. Necker made sure he confirmed it.

Electing its members was now a matter of urgency. During the most recent Estates General – which was back in 1614! – society's basic divisions had been respected. Each of the three estates, the clergy, the nobility and the third estate, had the same number of representatives and each deliberated separately. Since the first two together were mathematically assured of a majority against the third, the king was protected from the people's demands. But in 1788, by blocking any fiscal reform, the clergy and the nobles were the major obstacle to royal will. That was also made clear by the recent Assembly of Notables who, called back, proved just as recalcitrant as the first time and had to be dismissed. Necker therefore suggested doubling the number of representatives of the third estate to counterbalance the power of the privileged classes. Since the king was so exasperated by the latter's resistance, he went along with it.

Doubling the third estate's representation was decided on during a special meeting of the King's Council on December 27th, to which he invited his wife and brothers. Provence and d'Artois could not agree, the one approving and the other criticizing the measure. The queen, who was attending for the first time, did not open her mouth. What did she really think, if indeed she had an opinion? She was very ill at ease. Her "disapproval ratings" were reaching their highest point. The vicious personal invective directed against her only increased when Brienne failed to subdue Parliament. She was seen as the ringleader against all reform. Mercy wrote to Joseph II, "At such a critical juncture, the queen was careful to take the wise and necessary decision to remain aloof and keep her opinions to herself, so as to avoid any show of leaning toward one side or the other." Like her husband, she voted for double representation. In that she was the soul of discretion.

An era was ending. The countdown had begun, although the world was as yet unaware of it. In the two-year period that was coming to an end, Marie-Antoinette had been given some latitude, and played an effective role in French internal affairs. She worked sincerely for what she believed was the good of the State. But that period was now over. The king was losing his decision-making powers, and as a result so was the queen, for she could only work through him. Marie-Antoinette's ability to accomplish anything was shrinking – when it had only just begun to grow. From now on, all her efforts would be directed toward loosening the ever-tightening stranglehold on the royal family. They would only succeed in increasing her isolation.

Marie-Antoinette shortly after ascending to the throne.
Terra cotta medallion by Jean-Baptiste Nini, 1774.
Nini didn't try to flatter his model;
we can see most of the features noticed by her contemporaries:
the high and protruding forehead, the slightly hooked nose,
the "Hapsburg" lip and a tendency toward fleshiness.
But this profile startlingly captures her strength of character.
Chateau de Chaumont.

The marriage of the dauphin Louis Auguste and Marie-Antoinette
in the Versailles chapel, 16 May 1770.
Engraving after Desrais.
BnF (Bibliothèque nationale de France), Prints.

The official ball.
A difficult ordeal for the young couples
called to take their turn on the dance floor one at a time
under the gaze of the king and the entire court.
Engraving by P. Rameau.
BnF, Prints.

The masked ball, during the festivities offered by the City of Paris
on 23 January 1782, in honor of the queen's churching
after the birth of the dauphin.
Engraving on silk by J.-M. Moreau the younger.
BnF, Prints.

The empress Maria Theresa on horseback,
subduing the Hungarian nobles,
an image of her mother
that left an indelible mark on Marie-Antoinette. Engraving.
Vienna, Schönbrun Castle.

At the age of twenty,
a young man of fragile beauty.
Private collection.

In 1785,
having proven himself
in the American campaign,
a mature man
of more virile charm.
Portrait by Pasch.
Private collection.

AXEL DE FERSEN

Count Mercy-Argenteau,
after a miniature by Vestier.
Private collection.

Cardinal de Rohan,
BnF, Prints.

Mirabeau, by Joseph Boze,
Versailles Museum.

Barnave.

LA POULLE D'AUTRYCHE,

Je digere lór largent avec facilitée | mais la constitution je ne puis lavaler

One of the numerous satirical
engravings taking aim at Marie-Antoinette.
The ostrich is holding in its mouth a copy of the Constitution.
The caption reads: "I gobble down gold and dough with ease.
But swallow the Constitution, never, please!"
Louvre Museum.

Louis XVI's arrest in Varennes.
Seated at a table at the home of the grocer Sauce,
the royal family is accosted by a raging mob.
Engraving by Prieur.
BnF, Prints.

"Liberty Cap presented to the king
by the French people, 20 June 1792."
Revolutionary engraving.
Under the title LOUIS THE SIXTEENTH,
the wording KING OF FRANCE
is corrected to KING OF THE FRENCH.
BnF, Prints.

Meeting of the Convention at the *Manège* on 10 August 1792.
Sepia drawing by the baron F. Gérard.
To the right behind the grating we see the royal family
watching helplessly as the monarchy collapses.
Louvre Museum, Drawings Section.

The royal family at the Temple.
To the left of the keep is the little tower.
In the foreground the family strolls in the garden
under the surveillance of a guard (left).
The dauphin is playing ball with Cléry.
BnF Prints.

Louis XVI bids farewell to his family on the eve of his execution,
after a sketch made at the time
by J.-B. Mallet, an officer on duty.
However, the scene was doctored,
since two guards are pictured. 1798 engraving.
Private collection.

The young Louis Charles is taken from his mother
at the Temple, 13 July 1793.
1798 engraving.
BnF, Prints.

Marie-Antoinette before the revolutionary court
(royalist engraving).
Disgusted by the accusation of incest made against her,
the queen called on "all mothers" to reject the charge.
Seated on the left is Hébert; behind the table, Fouquier-Tinville.
The image has been doctored. Here Marie-Antoinette is in white,
whereas she wore black to the trial.
We can barely make out the black ribbons of her widow's bonnet.
Engraving after a painting by Bouillon, 1794.
BnF, Prints.

Execution of Marie-Antoinette, 16 October 1793
at the Place de la Révolution (today Place de la Concorde).
To the right the entrance to the Tuileries Gardens.
On the left on its pedestal is the Statue of Liberty,
which replaced one of Louis XV.
In the forefront the rough tumbril that carried the condemned woman.
As was customary, the executioner showed the people the bloodied head.
Louvre Museum.

Part III

The Prisoner

CHAPTER 17

"THIS IS A REVOLUTION"

"We are entering a year that will be remarkable for the history of France," the marquis de Bombelles noted in his diary on January 1, 1789. He had no idea how right he was. For the first four months, however, all was quiet on the political front. The groundwork was being laid. A great wave of hope had overtaken the country. The Estates General would be the miracle cure that would put an end to all of the country's ills. In a mood of great anticipation, its representatives were being elected and the list of grievances was being drawn up. This would be brought to the king so that he could learn the wishes of his loyal subjects. Meanwhile, in Versailles, court life followed its usual rhythms, even if they had lost some of their luster.

But for Marie-Antoinette, 1789 first brought a terrible blow that would keep her far removed from any political concerns, for the older of her sons was dying.

The dauphin lies dying

Little Louis Joseph's health had given cause for concern for some time. Already in the spring of 1784, when he was two and a half, Mercy referred to "scurvy-like humors that require great care" and, what was worse, he noted recurring fevers, and that instead of growing, he was wasting away. At first Marie-Antoinette got some reassurance. Staying at La Muette where the air was considered better, he seemed to get stronger every day. Everyone was astonished to see him in such good form when he got back to Versailles. "My son is doing splendidly," she repeated like a leitmotif in her letters to Joseph II over the next two years. That remained to be seen. At the beginning of September 1785 he was inoculated and had a violent reaction. "Aside from the spots from the injections and on various parts of the body, a second outbreak appeared that brought him great suffering; but medicine given him in time warded off the ill effects..." Is it that the inoculation was performed on an already contaminated organism or did it introduce another contamination? Whatever the case, his health deteriorated throughout the spring of 1786.

During the autumn Fontainebleau visit, Calonne, feeling the weight of the queen's hostility towards him, made a very sensitive gesture to win over her mother's heart. He had a miniature coach built, imported tiny three-foot-high dwarf horses from Siberia, and recruited a team of children to drive it. The dauphin's coat of arms decorated the sides. Coachman, postilion, equerry and footman all wore his livery. Marie-Antoinette was moved to tears when he asked her permission to give her son the gift. Alas, the poor little patient could only admire it from a distance. The royal children's governess the duchess de Polignac, who could see him wasting away day by day, began to greatly fear for his younger brother also. He was in fine fettle, but then who can ever know for sure? She took it upon herself to find him a physician without consulting the queen. They had a violent clash over it, and later came to a less than cordial reconciliation. Any doubt about her children's health tortured Marie-Antoinette.

The illness was in remission during 1787, but by February of the following year, the fact could no longer be ignored: the dauphin was devoured by fever and was developing a hunchback. "Although he's always been frail and delicate," his mother said, "I wasn't expecting the crisis he's going through. His shape has changed because one of his hips is higher than the other, and his backbone has also shifted and is sticking out." She believed it was the fault of growing teeth. "For a few days now, they have grown a lot. One has even entirely pushed through, which is somewhat hopeful." But Mercy told Joseph II the truth: "The physicians are hiding what they can; attributing to tooth formation what appears rather to be more similar to scurvy and vapors. The young prince's spine is deviated, and he is so depleted that he is in great peril."

They brought him to Meudon[*], whose salubrious air had once done his father the world of good. He showed improvement briefly; cheerfulness and appetite returned as the large molars emerged: "There is one tooth entirely out and two others whose tops we can

---

[*] Not to Bellevue, home of Mesdames aunts, but to the vast chateau that had housed the Grand Dauphin, son of Louis XIV.

see." But wearing a metal brace tortured the poor child without properly realigning his spine. Dissention broke out among his caregivers. Should they, as the doctors wished, forbid him sweets and take away the ones his mother gave him? Should they allow him, when his condition permitted, to attend court festivities? Marie-Antoinette hated the idea of putting his deformities on display; she was somewhat ashamed of them, as if she herself were to blame. His heart was already set on going to the August reception for the sultan of Mysore's envoys. She asked his tutor, the duke d'Harcourt, to talk him out of it. But he couldn't stop the child from writing to his mother to ask her permission. She refused, not without a guilty conscience, and took her anger out on the duke.

By the beginning of 1789, he was in dire straits. "For the last three weeks, the dauphin's state has not ceased to worsen," Mercy wrote to Joseph II on the 22nd of February; "the joints of his hands and feet are losing their flexibility, and we see signs of growths that surely indicate an onset of rickets." The doctors threw up their hands, and the queen, even though they were still lying to her, lost all hope. In the weeks leading up to the opening of the Estates General, the deathly pale child looked like a little old man. He could no longer stand; he had to be carried or moved about in a wheel chair. It was now only a matter of days.

"Although the queen is resigned to the inevitable," Mercy said, "the long wait only makes it more bitter..." She had arrived at that terrible stage where one wishes for it all to be over with. She spent most of her time in Meudon trying to get him to eat something, while herself swallowing "more tears than bread," and attempting to distract him, even though he already had that lost look of those who no longer are entirely of this world. There are few accounts of his last days. No edifying or historic last words were attributed to him, as there were in the case of Louis XVI's older brother. If he got testy with his governess or even his mother, we must recall, as did Madame Campan, that his little body was a mass of pain. For his parents his last weeks were a time of pure suffering – naked, mute and deep.

Little Sophie's death at the age of eleven months had not so deeply affected them; people were accustomed to losing babies, and besides, she was only a girl. But the loss of this son, whom they had desired so deeply, cut them to the quick. Marie-Antoinette spoke little, Louis XVI not at all. But from his journal we know that he rushed to Meudon nearly every day throughout the month of May. His sorrow was accentuated by memories of another loss. The same tragedy was repeating itself in this new generation: his older brother too had died, leaving him heir to the throne. Although he was quite young at the time, he could not have forgotten his brother's slow decline, which he was forced to witness on a daily basis. As deeply religious as he was, was he tempted to see in the death of his son a sign of God's wrath, when the power he had vowed to transmit intact to him was slipping from his hands? We don't know. All we know is that this ordeal left him less able to confront the vital political conflict that was brewing.

An Estates General not like any other

During the discussions that led to doubling third estate representation, they intentionally left out a very thorny related issue: would each estate's representatives vote as a block or individually? The archives had furnished no rules on the matter. As a general rule, the three estates, divided into three blocks of equal number, deliberated separately and each issued a single overall vote. But the kings had sometimes exercised the right to call them together to vote on some particular business at hand. This was a convenient way of getting the majority vote they wanted. In the present instance, one man-one vote seemed to go without saying; otherwise, what was the point of doubling the third estate's representation? Needless to say, the clergy and nobility were violently opposed to the idea. As for the king, he did not think for a moment that one man-one vote should become the norm. He probably would be willing to use it on a case-by-case basis, however. Necker must have shown him that this would be the only way to get enough votes for the territorial tax, but he certainly didn't inform him of all his ulterior motives. Convinced that the French monarchy would not survive unless it accepted big changes, the gentleman from Geneva was hoping, he would later say, for an English-style constitutional monarchy with two houses, the clergy and the nobility together in the upper house, with the third estate making up the lower house. But for the moment, he was counting on the third estate to give him the support that the privileged estates were refusing him. In short, the king and the minister were both hoping to divide and conquer, one intending thereby to return to a *status quo ante*, and the other to be carried forward on the wave of populist reform that was sweeping the country. And Necker was hoping to force the king's hand. There was therefore at the highest level of government a misunderstanding rife with danger, aggravated by the fact that among the king's family members there were those who advocated strong resistance. As ever prey to his chronic inability to decide, Louis XVI would be caught in the middle of the conflict between his chief minister and his family.

Elsewhere, another conflict was brewing, this one between the two first estates and the third, for control of the Assembly.

No one with a head on his shoulders thought at this point that the clock could be turned back. Not that the monarchy itself was at issue; the vast majority of the French population remained deeply attached to their king. Amongst the most humble, there was a deeply ingrained emotional attachment to the monarch, conceived as benevolent and paternal in his protection of the people. Amongst the better educated, an intellectual acceptance either reinforced or replaced sentimental attachment. The political theorists of the day never tired of repeating that although small states could practice direct democracy, republican government did not suit vast, highly populated countries. France, therefore, had to remain a monarchy. For years the debate had been over precisely what type of monarchy, absolute or constitutional. Louis XVI still thought he could maintain uncontested royal authority. But the mere fact that he had been forced to convene the Estates General proved that that this was no longer possible. So-called absolute monarchy was virtually dead. The king had to abandon some of his sovereignty, at least as concerned the economy. Sharing power was inevitable. It remained to be seen how extensive it would be, and to whose benefit.

By stridently demanding a meeting of the Estates General, the Paris Parliament, made up mainly of nobles, was not working for the benefit of the third estate; that was absolutely clear. They thought they could get the Estates General granted control of the financial sector, but were speculating on the fact that the Estates could not exercise control by themselves, as they were not a properly constituted government assembly. During the intervals between sessions – and people assumed they would be long ones as no schedule had been imposed – they would set up a permanent commission for the purpose, composed of members of Parliament. The latter thought that they could thus keep power in their own hands, and wield it to promote their own interests and those of the nobility of the sword, with whom they had close ties. What they were aiming for, therefore, was the aristocracy's gaining ascendancy over the king. How would they get the deficit under control? They would worry about that later.

Even before the elections, the view of the second Assembly of Notables – block voting and no doubling of third estate representation – gave an indication of the machinations to come.

The partisans of the new ideas, who now demanded to be called "patriots," had no intention of missing an opportunity the likes of which had not come along in a 150 years, and probably would not come again any time soon. They organized. They had contacts pretty much throughout the country thanks to intellectual circles and clubs. The king, partly through naivety and partly through honesty, refused to "prepare" for the elections, unlike his less scrupulous ancestors. Necker flaunted his confidence about the whole thing: "Let them come; once they're here, we'll do with them what we like." The election, which took place without any pressure from the government, brought into the third estate's ambit a large number of innovators. They showed up quite determined not to let victory be wrested from their grasp.

There was, however, one big unknown: the people. For the third estate, a catchall order grouping together everyone who wasn't in either of the others, was anything but homogenous. Its representatives all belonged to the wealthy and cultivated bourgeoisie. The poor could hardly have helped draw up the preparatory documents; they could neither read nor write, nor speak in a public forum. But they made up the vast majority of the population. And because of their numbers, they would soon play a role that the armchair theoreticians had not anticipated.

The meeting of the Estates General took place during a period of great economic and social upheaval. Even the weather had its part to play. The dreadful summer of 1787 was followed in 1788 by a drought and devastating hailstorms in the west of the country. The harvest was a disaster. At the end of the particularly bitter winter of 1788-1789, prices skyrocketed, filling the highways and byways with beggars and tramps, while a depression in the textile industry, which was suffering stiff competition from the English, left thousands of unemployed workers to fend for themselves on the city streets. These were nothing like the deadly famines of 1692 and 1709; no one was dying of hunger in France at the end of the 18th century. But the primeval fear of hunger deep-seated in the human heart rose to the surface as soon as the price of wheat went up. And since the government kept switching back and forth between trying to control prices and letting the market dictate them, people were quick to panic. Throughout the country, granaries were ransacked and deliveries halted. Wheat riots were not new, but this time they were accompanied by new disorders. People were refusing to pay taxes. Why bother, when the Estates would soon change everything? And the poor began to attack the rich; the sacking of the Réveillon wallpaper factory was a prime example.

The fact that the owner had "a social conscience," as we would say today, did nothing to prevent the pillage. The troops fired, leaving some hundred dead and many wounded.

The king and queen, enclosed in the fairyland bubble that was Versailles, had a rather abstract notion of the poor. For the monarchs, the only way of treating them was through charity, dispensed through subsidies in case of catastrophic situations, or through donations to individuals, which of course implied that they were somewhat rare. This doesn't mean they were heartless, however. Saint-Priest noted that "Marie-Antoinette, without being overly sensitive, something quite rare in princes, did not suffer from the yawning indifference that is so common among them." She could show great pity for a footman fallen from his coach, or for a wretched peasant family. Louis XVI could find just the right memorable word of kindness for a field hand whose plough he took up momentarily; and while hunting he avoided riding roughshod with his huntsmen and hounds over lands under cultivation. But this compassion for the people did not encompass any ability to understand their joys, their resentments or their fears; nor did it enable the sovereigns to comprehend their desire to shake off the endless restrictions on their autonomy that burdened their daily existence. In their eyes, the people enjoying leisurely outings were little more than a rabble. The king in distaste called the masses who crowded each Sunday into the Saint-Cloud gardens "bumpkins and trollops." The people in revolt were mere beasts. But these were the exception to the rule. The sovereigns' basic assumption was that the people were decent folk, both by nature and by vocation.

They would soon have to get to know them better.

The Estates General meet

More intuitive than Louis XVI, Marie-Antoinette had been dreading the Estates General. As the date approached, her apprehension would only deepen, and it was shared by those around her. Provence, throwing off his thin veneer of liberalism, joined d'Artois in trying to get the king to fire Necker, rightly suspected of organizing reforms deadly to absolute monarchy. She approved a report his brothers addressed to the king, but he rejected it, as it contained measures that would have delivered him bound and gagged to the aristocratic faction. He was still clinging to hope. He shared his opinion with his wife, who mistrusted her brothers-in-law as much as Necker. But she was not sure he had the energy it took to play the sides off against each other and act as referee.

The Estates General opening ceremonies in Versailles did nothing to reassure her. Her dear Léonard, come to do her hair for the occasion, found her listless. Her breasts sagged and her arms were thin. But she was stately and proud on May 4th, the day the dying monarchy attempted, in one last desperate burst of vigor, to deploy its pomp and glory. There would be a solemn procession followed by mass at the church of Notre-Dame. The deputies had been cooling their heels since early morning in anticipation of the sovereigns' arrival. Behind mounted pages and falconers, their brilliantly gilded coaches finally pulled up, in the first the king, his brothers and nephews, in the second the queen and the princesses. Already, the public gave them a very different welcome, for the king there was applause, but a hostile silence greeted the queen. Toward eleven o'clock, the cortege was formed and wound its way slowly, on foot, to the church of Saint-Louis through packed and festooned streets. The deputies came first, each carrying a candle and wearing the attire dictated by protocol. Only the sovereigns and the highest levels of the clergy were allowed color. Most of the deputies had to make do with black and white. Then came the third estate deputies, dressed in black redingotes and white ties; but these did not make them look any more cheerful – they all looked as if they were going to a funeral. Then came the deputies from the nobility, also dressed in black, but sporting white breeches, lace ties and lavishly feathered hats. And their proudly displayed swords distinguished them from the common run of humanity. In black too were the curates who followed. Behind them, cardinals and bishops in either red or purple gave the cortege its first splash of color. Then came the palanquin sheltering the archbishop of Paris holding aloft the Blessed Sacrament, and only then the sovereigns. The king was dressed in gold cloth studded with diamonds and on his head for all to see was the famous Regent diamond, the same one he had worn for his coronation. The Sancy diamond shone brightly in the queen's hair, and her gown of silver thread was resplendent with precious stones. Again, she abstained from wearing a necklace.

The journey, although quite short, was a terrible ordeal for her. Dense, palpable hatred oozed from the pores of the gathered masses. The customary acclamations were no more. Anyone brave enough to call out in her praise was quickly hushed. There was little hostile murmuring, just silence everywhere, made uglier by sullen looks. All of a sudden, like a slap in the face, came the cry *Long Live the Duke d'Orléans!* – Orléans, her cousin, who had deserted his class and was marching in the ranks of the third estate. She stumbled under the weight of the insult. People rushed to help her up. She quickly recovered her composure and adopted a pose of haughty defiance. Elsewhere, an ordeal of an entirely different order brought her to tears. On the balcony of the *Petite Écurie*, she perceived the little ravaged face of the dauphin who had been carried on a stretcher from Meudon for this one last celebration. How could she not in her heart of hearts link the child's dying days with those of royal authority?

At the religious ceremony another insult was in store for her. Bishop de La Fare of Nancy was the deputy from his province, and by no means a liberal, but in expounding on the commonplace theme of the contrast between the luxury of some and the wretchedness of others, he thought he could slip in a few allusions to the wastefulness of the court. And when he denounced the idle rich "who sought enjoyment in the childish imitation of nature," there was no mistake about it: he was referring to the queen and her Trianon. Marie-Antoinette didn't flinch, but she couldn't help pursing her lips. The king hadn't heard any of it; he was asleep. Awakened by the clapping – something unheard of in a church – at the end of the sermon, he smiled, which could be taken as a sign of his approval. When he left the church to go back to his coach, a few shouts of "Long Live the King" were heard. The queen awaited something similar, but hearing no acclamations, scurried into hers. Only silence accompanied her.

The opening session the next day caused her less pain. Looking very elegant in her mauve cape over a white satin dress, wearing one simple diamond plume in her hair and holding a large fan, she took her seat a bit below the throne to the left, where she neither moved nor uttered a word. Despite her less than warm reception, she managed to be forgotten about. She had four long hours to contemplate the deputies. Were they all just one big blur because of her nearsightedness, or had she hidden in her fan a spyglass with which to put a name to a face here and there? There were nearly twelve hundred of them*, grouped according to their estate in the great hall of the *Menus-Plaisirs*. Deputies from the third estate, who were constantly reminded of their inferior status, sat in front of the

---

* What with defections and errors, historians are still arguing over the exact number. The following count comes from Jean Tulard's *Dictionnaire de la Révolution*: 291 clergy, of whom 206 were curates; 285 noblemen, together numbering 576; 578 from the third estate. Total: 1,154. But sometimes a total of 1,196 is given.

throne as a compact block, cut off from the rest. They were clearly distrustful of the whole business.

The king was the first to take the floor. He had weighed every single word and rehearsed his speech over and over so as to hit the right tone. The staccato beating of the queen's fan betrayed the agitation she tried to hide. The king managed quite well, saying nothing to which anyone could take offense. He only spoke of the financial crisis, which he not unreasonably put down to the war in America, declared he was his people's best friend, and ended his speech by warning the deputies against "innovations." He did not breathe a word about the burning question: would the deputies vote in one group or as three distinct blocks? But he had been straightforward and kindly; he was applauded. Up next was the maddeningly dull chancellor, who said more or less the same thing. A lot was expected of Necker; but he turned out to be the day's big disappointment. In a monotone voice, he launched into an interminable technical account of the kingdom's finances, went hoarse after a half an hour and had to have his secretary read the rest of his speech, which took up three hours. Nothing was settled. The deputies, especially those of the third estate, left as disgruntled as they had arrived.

Departing, the king was greeted with cheers. He turned gallantly towards his spouse to have her recognized as well. To the few cries of *"Long Live the Queen!"* that ensued, she made a slight bow. It would have taken a lot more to convince her that she'd regained any popularity.

The third estate gathers steam

For about six weeks time seemed to stand still. All the royal couple could think about was their dying son. The queen no longer slept, abandoning herself to sinister premonitions. One evening at the end of May she watched as one after the other, three candles on her table went out. Madame Campan recounts that she cried out, "Misfortune can make us superstitious; if the fourth candle goes out like the rest, nothing will stop me from seeing it as a baleful omen," whereupon the candle went out. Between visits to his dying little boy the king deadened his sorrows in feverish hunting. What was it to him if the Estates voted in blocks or not? Left to their own devices, they managed only to chase their own tails. Deputies from the third estate took advantage of the situation to explore Versailles. They asked to see at the Petit Trianon "the diamond-studded room with the twisted columns laced with sapphires and rubies" that they'd heard about back home in their little rural villages. They were incredulous when they were told that no such thing existed. They also used the time to get to know each other and develop a common strategy.

Nothing had been decided about officially stating the deputies' powers. Had the task been entrusted to royal officials before the Estates General got started, things would have been simpler. But there had been no directives, so the nobility and the clergy began to deal with the matter of powers separately. Already on the 6th of May, however, the third estate refused to discuss it unless they all worked together. It was obvious they were aiming to impose deliberating and voting in one group. They met the king with passive resistance, and began to work on their colleagues from the other two estates, whom they called upon to join forces with them. Even though there were more than a few high-ranking lords of liberal persuasion amongst them, the vast majority of the nobility refused. But within the clergy the margin was smaller. The clear line of demarcation between noble and commoner that ran so deep in French society cut right through the Estates' proceedings as well. The parish priests, generally commoners themselves, were much closer to the third estate than to the first estate's opulent hierarchy. They were the weak link in the chain.

The king was called upon to decide. He couldn't. He certainly had excuses. The dauphin was on his deathbed. He died at one o'clock in the morning on June 4th. As was customary, Marie-Antoinette was torn from his bedside and Louis XVI, who only found out at six o'clock, could not see him. The autopsy revealed he had "decayed, enlarged and deviated vertebrae, arched ribs and adherent lungs." In an effort to economize, they decided not to give him a state funeral, to which he had the right, having just reached the age of reason. As was the tradition, his body was buried in Saint-Denis and his heart delivered to Val-de-Grâce. On June 7th the devastated parents had to go through with the receiving line of mourners. The queen, choking down her grief, had to lean against the balustrade of her bedchamber to avoid falling down. And since there wasn't a penny left in the till to pay for the thousand masses the king wanted to offer up in memory of his poor innocent child, he ordered them paid for through the household budget.

When he was informed that the Estates were getting impatient with his lethargy, Louis XVI, who usually held a tight lid on his feelings, burst out, "Are there no fathers among them?" Indeed, there weren't many. Only the nobility had an average number of children. By definition, the clergy hadn't any to speak of. And the most troublesome deputies from the third estate, often young and ambitious, had put off the responsibilities of fatherhood, as tended to be the rule among the bourgeoisie. What was the death of a seven-year-old to these hotheads when the fate of the country was at stake? And besides, there was a dauphin to spare; the little duke de Normandie had sobbed his heart out when he was addressed by the name. The exhausted king and queen decided to take refuge for a few days at Marly to mourn in private. They left Versailles on June 14th.

In the building housing the *Menus-Plaisirs*, meanwhile, in which the third estate occupied the vast ground floor and the other two shared the second floor, things were moving fast. On June 13th three curates answered their colleagues' call. Six others followed suit on June 14th, and ten more on the 16th. On the 17th at the suggestion of Sieyès, the third estate, "considering the fact that it represented 96 percent of the nation," declared itself the National Assembly. On the 19th, unable to cope, the hierarchy could not prevent their ranks from voting by a slim majority to join them. This drew the king out of his lethargy, and he summoned his ministers to Marly for an extraordinary meeting of his Council, of which Saint-Priest left an account.

Necker had sent the king a document outlining how powers would be ascertained, and itemizing the cases in which the estates should deliberate separately or together. What he was proposing came down to authorizing whatever they couldn't prevent. But Louis XVI was more indecisive than ever. He showed the document to his entourage and they prepared a counteroffensive. This was the point at which the queen chose her side; the third estate's latest initiatives sent her into the arms of the reactionaries. Summoned by her as soon as he arrived in Marly, Necker found her irritated in the extreme. With the help of her two brothers-in-law, she tried to get him to abandon his plan. He refused. During the Council meeting that ensued, with only the ministers present, he had just enough time to read his proposal when an usher arrived to advise the king that the queen requested he go see her. To interrupt a meeting of the King's Council was unheard of! None of her predecessors would have dared do such a thing. By the time the king reappeared about an hour later, the king returned in a different frame of mind, and put the decision off to a later date. They were going back to Versailles; they could deal with the matter there.

While awaiting the *séance royale* of June 23rd, at which he was to inform the Estates General of his decision, he tried to suspend the whole thing by closing off their rooms in the *Menus-Plaisirs* under the pretext that preparations were called for. What happened next is well known. Finding the doors closed on the morning of June 20th, the deputies retreated to the *Jeu de Paume,* where they swore the famous oath "not to separate... until the constitution of the kingdom is established and consolidated upon firm foundations." The subsequent meeting of the King's Council in Versailles was a stormy one. Pressure from the queen and the king's brothers forced such modifications on Necker's text that he decided not to show up at the *séance royale.* Clearly, the king's family was about to send him packing.

Power struggle

There were in fact two intimately linked power struggles going on. One, within the government, pitted the chief minister against the royal clan and the aristocratic faction; the other, outside the government, pitted royal power against the National Assembly.

The outcome of the first seemed to be settled on June 23rd, when Louis XVI finally disclosed his decision to the deputies. He restricted his concessions to a bare minimum: he granted individual freedom and freedom of the press, and promised to ask for the Estates General's agreement on taxing and borrowing. He expressed his wish that the privileged estates accept to share the tax burden more equally, which did nothing to solve the problem. He authorized the three orders to vote together only in very limited cases, and only for the current session. In future, they would remain separate. He didn't breathe a word about free access to employment. In short, he reiterated his support for a society based on the three estates, and ended his speech by threatening to dissolve the Assembly if they resisted. The traditionalists were getting the upper hand, as the queen had wished.

In the chateau gardens, however, a turbulent and dense crowd, alerted by Necker's absence, gathered to defend the Assembly. It was not necessary. When the sovereign left, followed by the noblemen and the church hierarchy, the marquis de Dreux-Brézé, the master of ceremonies, very cordially invited the third estate deputies to leave the hall: "Gentlemen, you are aware of the king's intentions." The answer he got has been handed down to us: "The assembled nation cannot receive any order," said Bailly. Mirabeau cried, "We stand here by the will of the people and we will leave only by the force of bayonets." Powerless to do anything about it, Louis XVI watched as the hostile crowd grew ever thicker. He shrugged his shoulders and cursed, "They want to stay? Well, then, fuck! Let them stay!" They stayed, and held their ground.

At first Marie-Antoinette was delighted that Necker handed in his resignation, but she quickly backtracked. She brought him to see the king and joined the latter in pleading with him to take up his functions again at once. He tried to make it appear that he would do so only out of interest in the public good. Modesty in victory did not come naturally to him. The next day, the 24th, most of the clergy joined the Assembly, and on the 25th forty-seven deputies from the nobility followed them, among them some of the most notable names in the kingdom. On the 27th the king surrendered to the inevitable; he approved the fait accompli in pretending to be responsible for it. He ordered "his clergy and his faithful nobility" to join with the third estate. The latter had won the second round. On the 7th of July the National Assembly declared itself the National Constituent Assembly. The "absolute" monarchy was no longer.

What role did the queen play during this crucial period? While the count d'Artois was still preaching a hard line, she was wise enough, according to Mercy, to encourage the king to give in to avoid "worse calamities." For those four days, "everyone was out of their mind." If they had arrested Necker, as some of the royal family wanted, "the people would have risen up in revolt, quite likely massacring members of the clergy and nobility." Mercy was by no means a liberal, but he was a realist. He was in a position to know, thanks to the recent revolt in the Low Countries against Austrian domination, that it was not a good idea to take popular uprisings lightly. As to what stance to adopt toward it, he advised the queen to remain firm – meaning that she should develop a clear and coherent line of conduct – and above all to be cautious. But he didn't have any illusions about his chances of being heeded.

For her part, Marie-Antoinette sought nothing but revenge. As always when she encountered resistance, she took it as a personal affront, and passion overcame reflection. She could not accept defeat. During the two years in which she worked hand in hand with Brienne, she believed it was she who held power, and worked hard for "the good of the State." Now facing a more powerful force, she took umbrage. Compromise was out of the question; every concession had to be unmade, the rebellious Assembly and that traitor from Geneva had to be sent packing, and everything returned to its previous state. Louis XVI on the other hand would not have been adverse to granting the Estates General some control over taxes or to giving the provincial assemblies some say in local

affairs, provided the social hierarchy was left intact. Not Marie-
Antoinette; for her it was all or nothing. It is beyond doubt that she
and her brothers-in-law pushed the king to go for a showdown.

On May 23rd, they realized that Versailles could not be defended,
especially since the king's guard had been trimmed down to save
money. The court briefly thought of taking refuge in a safer place.
But how could they leave? They had seen soldiers from the French
Guard fraternizing with demonstrators. A better solution seemed
to be to send for more dependable troops from the provinces. The
marquis de Bombelles noted in his journal July 8th that the Royal-
Allemand was camped out in the Boulogne wood and that four
Swiss regiments were in the Champ-de-Mars, that the Provence
Infantry was in Saint-Denis and there was artillery at the Invalides.
The Assembly got nervous. The king gave evasive answers to
delegates come to ask him to send the troops away. He now had
about thirty thousand men at his disposal. His wife and brothers
put pressure on him to get rid of the minister who instigated all
this trouble; they had the right hard-liner on hand to replace him,
Breteuil. When Saint-Priest attempted to impress on the queen
that "any violent measures would be dangerous," he could see that
she did not appreciate his advice. On July 11th the king dismissed
Necker and asked him to leave France as quietly as possible. On the
12th, Marie-Antoinette appeared in all her splendor in the Œil-de-
Bœuf before the visitors who had come to be presented to her.
On the 13th she attended the parties given in honor of the foreign
troops billeted in the Orangerie. A ministry was set up specifically
to combat the revolt and re-establish the monarchy to its original
purity and was, according to François Furet, "a declaration of
counter-Revolution." A "committee" inspired by the queen and the
count d'Artois wanted the Assembly abolished, it was not known
through what means. How far would they go if, as was likely, an
uprising took place? They counted no doubt on the troops' ability
to calm things down and keep the peace. They were wrong. Scuffles
broke out here and there. The prince of Lambesc, commander of
the Royal-Allemands, struck out with his saber when rocks were
thrown. In the Assembly he was accused of brutality. Marie-
Antoinette didn't even try to defend him; she knew it would only
make matters worse.

In contrast, all was quiet in Versailles on July 14th. The king,
who did not go hunting that day, wrote in his diary "nothing." He
was in bed sleeping the sleep of the just when his chief steward of
the wardrobe, the duke de Liancourt, made bold to awaken him.
The Bastille had been stormed; the people were marching through

the streets of Paris with its governor's head at the end of a pike. Here again, another historic phrase was uttered, and if it cannot be authenticated, it at least has the merit of being plausible: "Is this then a revolt?" the king asked. "No, Sire, this is a revolution." In truth, the main cause of the attack on the Bastille was fear, a fear amplified by rumors spread by agitators. They proclaimed that Paris would be starved and put to the sword. To defend themselves, the Paris poor went looking for weapons. They first went to the Invalides storerooms, which they pillaged. In search of more, they went to the Bastille. The battle that ensued was the result of a misunderstanding, or perhaps provocation. Cannon fire killed about a hundred people. It was only after the fact that the patriots understood its symbolic value. The prisoners they brought out, only seven in number – two lunatics, four counterfeiters and one son of a good family gone astray - were hailed as victims of tyranny, and the clever entrepreneur hired to demolish it made a fortune selling it off stone by stone by way of souvenirs.

At the Hôtel de Ville, the provost of commerce had been slain. The city government over which he had presided was replaced by the "Commune de Paris" and a member of the Academy, Bailly, was elected its mayor. The job of keeping order was confided to the newly formed middle-class militia given the name of National Guard and placed under the command of La Fayette. A new cockade was created with the Paris colors of blue and red encircling the monarchical white. It would evolve into the tricolor flag of France. One more step had been taken in the dismantlement of royal authority. But there was something entirely novel here: there was now a new player on the scene: the people had entered the conflict. And in the Assembly, many deputies began to fear them at least as much as they feared the court; which says a lot.

When the details of this memorable day's events became known the next day, the court panicked. The troops had been useless, for two reasons. One was that their leaders had not received orders, and the other because they knew that some of the troops would not obey them. The French Guards were crossing over to the side of the Revolution. Would it not be better to leave Versailles, which was too close to the capital, and seek refuge in a safer place under the protection of as yet uncontaminated regiments? Metz was a possibility. They asked the opinion of the old marshal de Broglie, commander-in-chief of all the troops and for the last three days minister of war. "Yes," he said, "we can go to Metz. But what will we do when we get there?" A very good question, which the supporters of flight refused to ask because – as the history of the Fronde and

The League proved – that would require admitting the possibility of a civil war. And if d'Artois was ready to wage one, Louis XVI was absolutely not, on principle. On this point the queen and Provence agreed with him, for the risks were too great. The decision was taken; they would stay. Three years later Louis XVI would confide in Fersen, who was putting pressure on him to flee, that it was in the aftermath of July 14th that they should have left. He had missed his chance. What he meant by that was merely that at that date an escape would have succeeded. But there were so many missed opportunities that one is tempted to believe that in his heart of hearts he did not want to leave.

So he went the next day to the Assembly, who were not free from anxiety either. He announced the withdrawal of the troops and the recall of Necker and the other ministers who had been dismissed four days previously. He was brought back to the chateau by cheering crowds who had gathered on the palace grounds. A relieved Marie-Antoinette appeared on the balcony holding the new dauphin in her arms and her daughter Madame Royale by the hand, offering the public the image of motherhood she thenceforth hoped would prevail. She shed a few tears and was applauded. But it quickly became clear that she and the count d'Artois were held responsible for the show of force that had just failed. In the courtyard of the chateau, a woman brusquely grabbed Madame Campan's arm with a warning: "Tell your queen to stop meddling with governing us; she should leave it up to her husband and our good Estates General to work for the people's welfare." In Paris the atmosphere gave great cause for concern. At the Palais-Royal, a price was put on the head of the queen and the count d'Artois. Louis XVI insisted that those most in danger should leave France, at least for a while. D'Artois didn't have to be asked twice. Although he had been separated for a long time from his wife, who sought consolation in the arms of her bodyguards, he recalled that she was from the Piedmont, and made haste to Turin with his children, abandoning her to Versailles, where her insignificance sheltered her from any danger. For her part, Madame de Polignac at first refused to leave. The king joined forces with his tearful queen to convince her to go. She ran the risk of being killed. It was not mentioned, but she no doubt understood that they had to remove from the queen's presence all those who were seen as her partners in turpitude and treason. For the same reason the abbé de Vermond too, despised as Austria's henchman, had to go into exile. With them disappeared Marie-Antoinette's entire entourage;

she was abandoned to the solitude she so greatly feared. All the misunderstandings, quarrels and periods when the queen and the duchess did not speak to each other were forgotten. When they parted ways what came to the surface, most painfully, was the memory of fourteen years of friendship. She prudently didn't see her off. "Farewell, most tender of friends," she scribbled at midnight, "the word is atrocious; here is the order for the horses! Farewell, I have only enough strength to embrace you."

The next day, July 17th, at the request of the Assembly and the Commune, Louis XVI agreed to go to his "good city" of Paris to assure the people of his affection. Terrified, Marie-Antoinette begged him not to go, or at least to let her accompany him. He refused. She was convinced he would not survive the journey. Anxious himself, he took the precaution of appointing his brother regent. In former times when kings went to war they took the same precaution, but in those days it was the king's wife who was given this responsibility. But under the present circumstances distrust of Marie-Antoinette was such that any delegation of power to her would have been contested immediately. She understood the implications for the future: should her husband cease to exist, she would not be made regent and she would lose custody of her son. Her fate would be quickly sealed, and she steeled herself against the eventuality. If worse came to worst, she would seek the protection of the Assembly, to which she would read a proclamation she had carefully written. The first sentence has come down to us thanks to Madame Campan: "Gentlemen, I place in your hands the spouse and family of your sovereign; do not allow to be separated on earth what has been joined in heaven."

She did not have to resort to this measure. The king returned safe and sound. She flew weeping into his arms. "Fortunately," he cried, "no blood was shed, and I swear that never a drop of French blood will be shed by my order." He returned reinvigorated. The people loved him; he had no doubt of that. He was cheered when he pinned to his hat the new tricolor cockade "distinguishing emblem of the French nation," guarantee of the "august and eternal alliance between the monarch and his people." But he had caved in on every point, ratifying everything that had been done so far, not only by the Assembly, but by the Commune too. In the streets sporadic hostilities continued to break out all the same. On July 22nd a crowd massacred the Paris controller Bertier de Sauvigny and is father-in-law Foulon, whom they accused of starving out the city. Yes, according to all of the foreign observers, this was definitely a revolution.

Last summer in Versailles

Marie-Antoinette was afraid. Hatred of her was coming to a crescendo. The Bastille casualties were but a foretaste of what the bloodthirsty tigress would get up to if she weren't put out of action. So she tried to disappear from the scene. She spent the rest of the summer not daring to venture beyond the palace gardens. She felt quite alone, a prisoner in her own home. The flight of the Polignacs instigated something of a stampede, leaving many vacated apartments sounding hollow, with padlocks hanging from their doors. She no longer had any faith in the troops; more and more of them were defecting. She believed, and she wasn't wrong, that her service personnel was riddled with enemies. Sure that she was being spied upon, she hid when writing to Madame de Polignac, and advised her to avoid the regular post when replying. "What is more," she added, "don't write anything that cannot be read by others, because they search everyone and nothing is safe."

Daily life continued its usual course. The king went hunting. The queen, erect and proud, presided over what was left of the court between walks to her dear Trianon. On August 15ᵗʰ, the feast of the Assumption, which was also her name day, she took part in the procession commemorating Louis XIII's vow to the Blessed Virgin. August 25ᵗʰ was the feast of Saint Louis. When Bailly arrived to pay homage to her, according to the marquise de La Tour du Pin, she thanked him peremptorily with "a little nod of the head that wasn't pleasant enough," because she noticed with irritation that he had not genuflected. When La Fayette introduced her to the delegates from the National Guard she was so flushed with rage that she could hardly manage to utter a few tremulous words in reply. She was as yet unable to hide her feelings. People found her disagreeable. The market women's famous cheerfulness only exasperated her, and she took them to task. Every now and then the grip of fear loosened a bit. "Things seem to be going better," she wrote to Madame de Polignac at the end of the month; "… we can't be too complacent… But there are fewer wicked minds about, or at least the good ones are coming together, from every class and social order. It's the best that can be hoped for." Some whom she'd considered friends had abandoned her in adversity, but she found in others unexpected loyalty. She was learning how to understand people better. And her strength and courage remained intact.

Fortunately, she had her children. They were her joy and

consolation. Most often, they were with her. With Madame de Polignac gone, she had to find another governess. This time not friendship but worthiness determined her choice. Madame de Tourzel, six years her senior, had a stainless reputation. Her husband had died in a hunting accident in the presence of Louis XVI, leaving her with five children. She was an educator who took her job very seriously, but Marie-Antoinette had no intention of letting her take the lead, especially as concerns the new dauphin, who had to be prepared for his royal calling.

Between her two remaining children, her affections were more unevenly divided than ever. She seemed to be disappointed in her daughter. Curt and unapproachable, Maria Theresa at nearly eleven shrank from any show of tenderness. Had she been taught to mistrust her mother? It does seem that Mesdames aunts had sought Madame Élisabeth's help in removing her from what they saw as her mother's pernicious influence. Whatever the truth of the matter, hers was not a likable disposition.

On the other hand, Marie-Antoinette was crazy about her son. At nearly four and a half, he was bursting with health and joie de vivre – he was "quite the little peasant." For his new governess, she painted a picture of him that was also a course of study designed specifically for him. Did she have her own childhood in mind? The empress-queen's instructions and general precepts with which she was raised were from another world. In her respect for the nature of the child, we can detect Rousseau's influence, even if she hadn't read *Émile*. But above all they radiated profound maternal love.

Although he was healthy and had survived the dangers of teething, Louis Charles was a high-strung little fellow. He jumped at the slightest noise. "For example, he is afraid of dogs because he has heard them barking nearby. I have never forced him to approach them because I feel that as he grows more mature his fears will disappear." Why oblige him to go walking with the grown-ups? Better to leave him free "to play and work in the dirt in the gardens." (His father had a garden made for him to grow things in.) What was he like? He was tenderhearted and physically affectionate; he loved his sister and wanted to share everything with her. He was "very absent-minded, very light-hearted, and prone to lose his temper." By appealing to his pride, which was "excessive," he was easily led "to get a hold of himself, and even to overcome his impatience and anger, regaining his sweetness and amiability." On the other hand, he found it terribly difficult to say he was sorry, even though he was not the least bit arrogant. "He has no concept of haughtiness, and I very much want for that to continue: our children always learn soon enough who they are," she noted, thinking of her daughter perhaps. "He is very true to his word when he promises something; but he is terribly indiscreet, he thinks nothing of repeating whatever he hears; and often, not that he is lying, he just says what his fancy dictates." She emphasized the fact that this was "his greatest fault, and it must be corrected." By handling him gently but firmly and avoiding severity, which would only rub him the wrong way, "we will always get him to do what we want." His was a liberal education, therefore, based on respect for children's nature.

But the most striking aspect of his education was its emphasis on the mother-child relationship. "We have always accustomed my children to have great trust in me and to tell me themselves when they have made a mistake. That way, when I scold them I look as if I'm less angry than pained and upset at what they've done. And I have got them used to the fact that my word is law, but I always give them an explanation they can understand, so that they can see I'm not being bad-tempered." This passage is remarkable for its modernity; any mother today could have said the exact same thing. It is also remarkable for its time because of what it did not say. Here maternal love became the basis of the child's moral education, without any reference to religion. The abbé hired to teach him how to read, unsuccessfully it must be said, was exhorted to stick to the job at hand. Not that Marie-Antoinette was a non-believer, she just felt that religious practice would come in due time when he reached the age of reason. Louis XVI, a very pious man, agreed with her that he should not be subjected too early to priestly power.

Mother and son grew together and changed each other. We can't help wondering what they would have become if the course of history had had a different fate in store for them.

"The tomb of royal authority"

In this summer of 1789, while Marie-Antoinette lulled herself into a deceptive calm and Louis XVI withdrew behind a wall of silence, the Great Fear was overtaking the countryside, nourished by unverifiable rumors that got more frightening as they were repeated, causing panic everywhere. Villages built barricades, self-defense militia brandished scythes and pitchforks against "brigands" – that is, anyone from anywhere else – and commerce was paralyzed, making daily life even more difficult. Soon, rumors (whether orchestrated or not is still a matter of dispute) spread about counter-revolutionaries trying to stop the Assembly from doing away with feudal rights. The peasants rushed to attack their chateaux to take away and burn the legal documents justifying the feudal taxes. Sometimes they burned the chateau too.

The financial situation was dire. Back in France and terribly arrogant – did he not insolently refuse to thank the queen for recalling him? – Necker clearly had lost his magic wand on his way from Basel. His loans were no longer paying dividends, and the deficit remained as entrenched as ever. The Assembly dithered; it recoiled before the risks involved in trying to quell the uprising, which in any case it was in no position to do, and came down on the side of meeting the peasants' demands. From that decision flowed the very well-known session of August 4th, a strange night in which the nobility completely lost its bearings and in a contagious fit of madness threw overboard everything that for centuries had marked its difference and brought in a good part of its revenue. Although the event was not as spontaneous as has been said, its organizers soon lost control of it. The clergy had to follow suit, much to its regret. The "abolition of privileges" was enthusiastically voted in. Equality was hailed, as was access to employment for all. And the king, whose opinion had not been sought, was declared "the restorer of French freedom." Another essential part of what was beginning to be called the "Ancien Régime" was collapsing. French society was no longer divided into three orders.

While they were at it, the Assembly, with the help of a number of excellent legal minds from the third estate familiar with political theory, drew up the Declaration of the Rights of Man, inspired by the American model. It's a pity that a handful of deputies who suggested adding a mention of man's responsibilities were ignored. There was fierce debate on the future constitution, which was to be based on the separation of powers. Mercy said of it that it would be "the tomb of royal authority." What place would the king hold? After all, he was the head of the executive. The right of absolute veto would have enabled him to paralyze the legislative branch; they therefore tended toward a suspensive veto. For the present, however, all measures adopted by the Assembly required his approval.

Louis XVI had to come out of the silence in which he'd barricaded himself without any fixed ideas. Mercy said he was "leaving it all up to fate." He no doubt consulted his wife, but nothing of their conversations has come down to us. They probably agreed that it was necessary to bide their time, but his subsequent behavior bore his stamp rather than hers. As was his wont, he tried to be all things to all people. He claimed that he approved of the August 4th decrees and the Declaration of the Rights of Man. They were excellent texts, full of the best intentions. But had people given enough thought to their consequences, which could lead to other injustices? He thought it was his duty therefore to put off signing his approval. If only he had initiated an open and incisive debate on the possible consequences! But his intervention was vague and lacked coherency. He annoyed everyone, including his supporters, many of whom still sat in the Assembly.

At this point, new rumors were spreading. People said he was letting things slide because he was getting ready to leave and once he did, the capital would be put to the sword and drowned in its own blood. At the time he was not yet considering departure as an option, but others were. Montmorin got wind of a plot to compel him to leave Versailles through the ruse of a riot fomented especially for the purpose. Paris was on edge again. La Fayette let it be known that Versailles was in danger. In the King's Council the question of the chateau's inability to defend itself was raised again. Saint-Priest therefore found an excuse for bringing the Flanders Regiment from Douai, whose arrival brought on the same protests as the July troop movements. With things as they were, a mere spark was all that was needed to ignite the powder keg.

On October first, as was the custom, officers from the king's bodyguards held a banquet for those of the Flanders Regiment. The court had gone all out. There were 210 guests around the horseshoe-shaped table that had been set up in Gabriel's great hall. The menu was chosen with care; the wine flowed freely. Deputies and courtiers observed the proceedings from the balconies, sometimes joining in the cheers for His Majesty. The king and queen had taken the wise decision not to attend, but a lady-in-waiting came to inform Marie-Antoinette that her company was resoundingly requested. She gave in to her love of the theatrical moment, to her nostalgia for the time so near yet so far when she reigned in this very hall over operas, balls and banquets. Louis XVI gave his consent. Together with the dauphin, they made a triumphal appearance in their box. The officers sang out the ministrel Blondel's famous tune in Grétry's[*] *Richard The Lionhearted*, which had become something of a royal anthem:

---

[*] A composer fashionable at the time, Grétry had a big hit in 1784 with his comic opera *Richard The Lionhearted*, the story of this famous English king's trials and tribulations. Richard was imprisoned but his faithful minstrel traveled in search of him, eventually finding and freeing him.

Oh Richard, oh my king!
The universe now thee forsakes,
On this earth it is only I
Who interest in thy person takes.

With the queen's consent, a Swiss officer took the little boy in his arms and placed him on the vast table. Madame Campan recalled that "smiling and very boldly" he walked up and down the table, much less frightened by the uproar than his mother, who hugged him lovingly upon his return. The free-flowing wine helped bring enthusiasm to a feverish pitch. Years later, the young Pauline de Tourzel, now the countess de Béarn, could still recall the stunning queen in her blue and white gown on the verge of tears, such was her joy. For a long time after the sovereigns departed, the most spirited of the soldiers were still shouting to them from beneath their windows, trying to climb onto their balcony. Marie-Antoinette was intoxicated by it all, very touched to see that there were still those who loved and defended her. She felt reinvigorated, ready for battle.

In the capital where bread was becoming scarce, the newspapers and clubs were raising a big fuss over these "orgies," causing great indignation. This banquet was an insult to the hungry people. And if the court was fussing so over the troops from Flanders, it was unquestionably to get them ready for an assault on the Revolution. Had the soldiers trampled on a few tricolor cockades or merely, as Madame Campan reported, turned them around to show the (monarchical) white side? It hardly mattered, for the personal loyalty to the king and queen that the Flanders officers displayed had the unmistakable whiff of reaction. This banquet was a provocation.

The Flanders regiment had been called back with the sole purpose of bolstering the king's security. Because of their rashly ostentatious show of loyalty, however, this purely defensive measure led to just the opposite: it triggered a catastrophe. While the "prodigiously blinded" court took comfort in the idea that it was no longer in danger, Paris worked up into a white heat, prepared to fight back.

The 5th of October

Monday, October 5th promised to be a quiet day. About ten in the morning the king set out on his hunt. Despite the threatening weather, the queen went to spend the day at the Trianon. Fersen, billeted in Valenciennes since mid-June, had arrived ten days earlier and taken up lodgings in Versailles. His presence was reassuring. As much as having the Flanders Regiment around, it no doubt contributed to her false sense of security. Was he with her that morning in the Trianon? We don't know[*]. But it is quite possible. About eleven o'clock a valet arrived with a hastily scribbled note from Saint-Priest: hordes of angry women were marching on Versailles; it was imperative to get back to the chateau as quickly as possible[**]. Other messengers went searching for the king in the surrounding woods. They had difficulty finding him, but when they did he immediately galloped back, finally arriving at the chateau about one o'clock.

In the meantime they learned that the National Guard was marching behind the women demanding bread. A council was hastily called. Was there still enough time to send troops to close off the bridges over the Seine? Saint-Priest proposed that the king himself lead his bodyguards to head off the rioters with a solemn summons to call off their protest[***]. If this failed, he could make his way to Rambouillet where his family could have already been sent to take refuge. But not only was Necker against this; so was the queen. Necker claimed that the crowd had only peaceful intentions. He raised the specter of a civil war if violence were used to repel them. Marie-Antoinette categorically refused to leave for Rambouillet without her husband; her place was at his side, whatever might happen. Marie-Antoinette's admirers have seen this decision as an act of great heroism on her part. Saint-Priest, who did not like her, gave a less exalted interpretation of her behavior: knowing that the people hated her, "she was convinced that her only safety lay in

---

[*] In her *Memories*, Madame d'Adhémar, alias the baron de La Mothe-Langon, gives him an entirely fanciful role. According to her, in Paris, he "took part in the revolt, so as better to understand it," then rushed to Versailles to warn her of the arrival of the insurrectionary women. It was also supposedly on his advice that the queen then sent a servant in search of the king. Historians consistently confront contradictions concerning numerous details of the events of these two dramatic days, making it difficult to come down in favor of one or another.

[**] Here we follow Saint-Priest's account. At that time he was the "chargé de la Maison du roi," the equivalent of the French Minister of the Interior today. It is preferable to that of Madame Royale who wrote hers long after the event and under the supervision of Louis XVIII. She claimed that Madame Élisabeth was the first to receive the news, but gave no details of how. Madame Élisabeth was to have informed her brother the count de Provence and they both then went in person to Trianon to warn the queen.

[***] In 1775 during the Flour Wars, Louis XVI had already successfully done something similar. He was not a coward; he did not lack physical courage.

not separating herself from the person of the king." It is quite true that she could not have had a better shield against the rioters than the king, who still inspired a certain amount of respect; but that does not allow us to doubt her courage; attested to by all of those present.

The decision was therefore taken to stay at Versailles. They gave up the idea of blocking off the bridges, and now it was a waiting game. Rain was beating down. A first contingent of women – three or four hundred of them – arrived and headed for the Assembly, who tried to contain them before being completely overwhelmed. They demanded bread and the withdrawal of the troops. The Assembly president Mounier, a moderate supporter of a constitutional monarchy with a strong executive branch, quickly realized the import of what was happening. The apparent aim of this women's march – we could call it the pretext if it were not for the fact that there really was no bread to be found in Paris at all – was to get inexpensive wheat to the capital's bakeries. But the women were being led by a hero of the Bastille called Maillard, and there were men with them, some disguised, who had other designs in mind. Among the crowd there were those who started calling for moving the king to Paris. And if the king went, so would the Assembly. How could it remain in a deserted Versailles in any case? The hidden motive was therefore to keep the king and the Assembly deputies under the watchful and menacing eye of the Paris populace. We see here the first instance of what was to become a constant recurrence in the history of the French Revolution: attempts by the left to overpower the moderates.

There was nothing spontaneous about this women's march; it was organized and orchestrated by the most radical wing of the Assembly so as to drown out the more moderate elements. Because of his chronic indecisiveness, the king does not appear to have been the primary target in the day's events. The queen on the other hand was still feared, because she was believed to have the energy he lacked, and the ability to influence him. If she perished in the confrontation, so much the better. So the hatred of the crowd was worked up against the Austrian whore who was ruining France for her brother's sake, and who was wallowing in luxury while the people were starving to death and craving revenge. The rioters were encouraged to target her in particular. And among the rabble armed with broom handles, larding pins and kitchen knives, there were those who wanted nothing better than to batter her to death, rip out her heart, and pull out her bowels to make cockades out of them.

Mounier, who had every reason to be worried, chose a handful of women to go as a delegation into the chateau. Louis XVI, as expected, received them kindly and saw to it that the one fainting from hunger and exhaustion was taken care of. He listened patiently as a pretty and saucy young working lass gave her speech, then sent them off to the kitchens for some nourishment. When they reappeared delighted with their mission, they were booed by the others who had been traipsing in the mud since the morning, drenched, dirty and at the end of their rope, their feet bloodied and their bellies empty.

At this point, hoping to disarm his most virulent colleagues, Mounier came to plead with the king to sign the contentious decrees on the abolition of privileges and the Declaration of the Rights of Man. He advised him also to leave Versailles and take refuge in Rouen, where the Assembly would join him. His carriages were waiting outside. Yet again the King's Council deliberated. "Sire, if tomorrow you are brought to Paris, your crown is lost," Saint-Priest insisted. And given the dire situation, the possibility of taking refuge in Rambouillet was again brought up. This time the queen agreed, as the king would be going as well. But it was too late. The crowd had managed to make its way into the chateau courtyards and unhitched the coaches, making departure impossible. The king caved in and fixed his signature to the bottom of the notorious decrees. In vain, Mounier went to show it to the assembled crowd that looked more like a gypsy camp than anything: "Will that put bread into the mouths of the poor people of Paris, Mister President?" they jeered.

At this juncture, La Fayette's imminent arrival was announced. He was at the head, or rather being headed by, the National Guard that he was supposed to command. They wanted to march with the protesters. He arrived around eleven o'clock at night, drenched and collapsing from exhaustion like everyone else, protesting his devotion to the monarch, and above all guaranteeing the loyalty of his troops and therefore the safety of the palace. At this late hour, the raiders, refreshed after being given some food, retired to inns or whatever bivouac they could find, totally worn out by the day's exertions. Back from reviewing his troops, La Fayette made one last visit, and managed to set the king's mind at ease somewhat. The latter told his first *valet de chambre*, "Go to the queen. Tell her I say she should rest assured about the situation at present and go to bed. I am going to do the same." Should she have, as she had been advised, shared her husband's bed that night? She apparently said to Madame de Tourzel, "If there should be danger, I would rather expose myself to it, and keep the king and my children out of harm's way." But the women protesters seemed more to be pitied than feared. Madame Royale, used to dispensing charity among the more presentable poor, would long recall the shock she received that night, when seeing these poor, frantic wretches dressed in dirty rags, she discovered what utter destitution meant. No, there was no need to worry.

The 6ᵗʰ of October

An exhausted Marie-Antoinette finally fell asleep around two o'clock in the morning. Four of her ladies watched over her. At daybreak a noise roused her from her sleep. It was nothing, she was told, it was just the wretched women who were camping outside the palace and stretching their legs a bit. She had just fallen back to sleep when she was abruptly awoken by Madame Auguié* and Madame Thibault; people were hearing horrible screeches and rifle fire. Responding to the news, Madame Auguié rushed out of the antechamber, opened the door that led to the guardroom and was met by a bodyguard covered in blood who was trying to hold back a screaming mob. He shouted to her, "Madame, save the queen; they've come to murder her!" She closed the door, bolted it, ran through the antechamber again to reach the queen's bedchamber, and bolted that door too. "You must get out of bed, Madame, don't get dressed, just hurry and get to the king." They gave her some stockings and a petticoat they forgot to tie, and pushed her into the dressing room from which another door led to the Œil-de-Bœuf. There was a moment of panic: the door was locked, which was unheard of. They had to bang frantically to get a valet's attention. He recognized their voices and let them out. More terror: the king's bedchamber was empty. Alerted by the tumult, he too had gone in search of his wife via the secret inner passageway. All he found in her room were bodyguards who had sought refuge there. They all managed to regroup in his bedchamber, where Madame de Tourzel had just brought the dauphin and Madame Royale. They were safe, for now**.

---

* Madame Campan's sister, who recounted the events to her, and she in turn recorded them at length.

** It has often been said that the rioters got as far as the queen's bedchamber and in a disappointed rage at not finding her, tore her bed to shreds. Madame Campan states that this is not true.

Then the count and countess de Provence, along with Madame Élisabeth, joined them there. Since they slept in the princes' wing, they had heard nothing. Necker, who had taken the time to don his magnificent embroidered suit, arrived along with Mesdames aunts, whose ground-floor windows in the main building had been smashed when the riot started. Within yards of their apartment, under the vault, two guards had been killed and decapitated. Subsequent accounts have lent to the actors in this drama heroic deeds and words worthy of Plutarch, the authenticity of which we may be permitted to doubt. Madame Campan is the only one to relate, honestly, that the queen left her bed in a panic. Who could presume to criticize her for that?

What happened next is a matter of confusion. La Fayette, who committed the foolish error of sleeping through this most perilous of nights, redeemed his culpable insouciance by stemming the flow of the carnage: the king's guards and the National Guard who had been about to cut each others' throats, were now fraternizing with shouts of *Long Live the King! Long Live the Nation!* With some difficulty, he managed to make his way to the king, pulled him onto the balcony with his family, and tried over the din to calm the mob with a pacifying speech. Soon a tumult of a thousand voices rose up repeating in unison "To Paris! To Paris!" Struck dumb with stupefaction, the king and queen withdrew, leaving La Fayette the impossible task of dispersing the crowd. In the midst of the uproar shots were fired into the air. Suddenly, the mob demanded to see the queen, and as she seemed to be advancing with her children, they shouted "No! No children!" She took up the challenge and walked forward alone, her head held high, a perfect target for any would-be assassins. The masses were subdued by her dignity and courage. No one dared to fire. She was applauded. But the cry soon rang out again: "To Paris!"

The king was going round in circles, unable to make a decision. Saint-Priest convinced him that he had no choice, "that he had to regard himself as a prisoner and suffer whatever was being imposed on him." "Why didn't we leave yesterday?" the queen groaned to the minister. "It's not my fault," he replied. "Of course, I know that," she said. There's no point trying to pin the blame on any of the ministers; the blame is entirely Louis XVI's. He did not think politically; he obeyed his moral and religious imperatives. His education taught him that the place of the king, the father of the people, was always with them, come what may. In his eyes, fleeing meant deserting them. And as things stood, he did not want to run the risk of setting off a civil war, which according to his concept of the monarchy would not only be a crime, but a most wicked sin.

The cortege set out for Paris shortly after mid-day. The king, the queen, their children, the Provences and Madame Élisabeth all squeezed into one coach. Other carriages followed with the rest of the court. Fersen was in one of them*. "Great God, what a cortege! The haggard women were in front of Their Majesties' coach and swarming all around it. 'We'll go without bread no longer! We've got the baker, his wife and their little baker's boy!' they cried." In the middle of this throng, the hacked-off heads of the king's guards were swaying on top of pikes. Riding on either side of the vehicle, La Fayette and the count d'Estaing tried in vain to protect the queen from threats and insults. And seated on her lap, the dauphin whimpered, "Mamma, I'm hungry." It took over six hours to get to Paris, whose streets were packed with onlookers. Leaning out of his window, the future Louis-Philippe, son of the duke d'Orléans, asked for a spyglass to see better what was going on, and nearly vomited at the sight of the severed heads. His father was not at his side. Had he, as it was whispered, taken on a disguise and joined the rioters? It cannot be proven. But it is certain that he took an active role in the campaign of vilification and the incitement to murder Marie-Antoinette.

Before being sent to the Tuileries, the sovereigns were obliged to make a detour around the Hôtel de Ville. *Le Moniteur* reported that the queen "was much affected by finding herself at this place, near the Lantern." This was where Foulon and Bertier had been hanged before being decapitated**. Mayor Bailly welcomed them as if they were paying an informal visit. The king played along; "he replied that he always came with pleasure and confidence among the inhabitants of his good city of Paris." In quoting this phrase to the Commune representatives there to greet them, Bailly left

---

* Where was he on the night of 5 – 6 October? With the queen, it was claimed. At least Madame Campan is supposed to have entrusted this information to Talleyrand who related it in confidence to Lord Holland, who in turn recorded it in his *Memories*. The relevant passage of Madame Campan's memoirs did not make it into print and was destroyed after her death. It is highly unlikely that Marie-Antoinette admitted Fersen that night into her official residence. Under the circumstances it is of little consequence whether he was in his rented house or some remote corner of the chateau that night.

** Located at the corner of the now-vanished rue de la Vannerie and the place de l'Hôtel de Ville facing the main entrance (at the beginning of what is now Avenue Victoria) stood a Lantern from which a well-known song promised to have every last aristocrat hanged.

out the word "confidence." The queen had the presence of mind to notice the error and quickly corrected him in a very loud voice.

The night was already advanced when they were finally allowed to retire to their new dwelling. Fersen thought he could await them there, but Montmorin and Saint-Priest felt his presence could jeopardize the queen, who certainly had no need of that, and he withdrew. Marie-Antoinette barely touched the food they were served, but Louis XVI had an appetite and declared himself "happy." This word, however, in the classical sense, didn't carry the connotation of being delighted, as it is too often repeated in criticism of the king, but simply meant that he had eaten enough and was no longer hungry.

Beds had to be found. They had to make do with whatever they could muster in this inhospitable place. Only the king and queen found a welcome refuge, the charming pied-à-terre that the queen had furnished for her nights at the opera. But it must have brought back wistful memories of happier times that no doubt made sleep that night even more elusive.

CHAPTER 18

HOUSE ARREST

Events of the past few months had dampened certain enthusiasms. The bloody parading of severed heads did not sit well with the ideal of a free and fraternal society. Among the nobles who had been temporarily seduced by the new ideas, many shared the view of the young viscount de Chateaubriand: "Those heads, and others which I encountered soon after, altered my political tendencies; I was horrified by those cannibal feasts, and the idea of leaving France for some distant country took root in my mind." A second wave of émigrés left the country, and the royal family, now under house arrest in the capital, became even more isolated.

The Revolution, however, seemed to be abating. Was the situation returning to normal or was this just the calm before the storm? No one could say.

Settling in

"Is it today or still yesterday?" asked the dauphin when he woke up on a camping bed in an unfamiliar bedroom whose dilapidated door had to be barricaded by a piece of furniture. But no, today is not yesterday. On the morning of the 7th of October, a raucous although not hostile crowd poured into the Tuileries gardens. They just wanted to see the king and queen and make sure they were still there and hadn't escaped. The queen made an appearance. A woman spoke up and "tells her that now she had to get rid of all those courtiers who are the ruin of kings and that she should love the people of her good city." Marie-Antoinette protested that she had always loved them. Someone else piped up, "That may be, but on July 14th you wanted to lay siege to the city and have it bombarded, and on October 6th you were about to flee the country." The queen replied that it was not so, they had been lied to. When someone said a few words in German to her, she pretended not to understand; "she had become so French that she had even forgotten her mother tongue." They suggested making a pact with her, but she said there was no need for that as her queenly duties were as good as a pact. As they requested, she took the ribbons and flowers off her hat and distributed them amidst cries of joy: *Long Live Marie-Antoinette, Long Live Our Good Queen!*

Madame Campan no doubt embellished this episode. She neglected to mention, for instance, that a flustered Marie-Antoinette, to her detriment, made an awkward mistake. She told the women that she would underwrite the redemption of any items they had pawned up to the value of one louis. But since she then forgot to inform the pawnbrokers, the poor women at first met with refusal, and when the sums involved were later tallied, they were found to be so high that restrictions had to be placed on the offer. As a result, the frustrated beneficiaries, who had been let down, resented the queen for having deceived them.

In a letter to Mercy of the same day, Marie-Antoinette wrote with measured optimism: "If we forget where we are and how we got here, we can be contented with the people's actions, especially this morning. I hope that if there is no lack of bread, many things will be righted. I am in touch with the people; militiamen, market women; they all hold out their hand to me, and I hold out mine to them... The people, this morning, asked us to stay. I told them on behalf of the king, who was at my side, that it depended on them whether we stayed or not; that we asked for nothing better; that all hatred must cease; that we would flee in horror from any bloodshed whatsoever. Those closest to me swore that it was all over. I told the market women to go tell others what we had just said to each other." Three days later she was brought down to earth. There was no let-up in the spiteful behavior towards her. It would take a lot of patience and kindness to destroy "the horrible mistrust" that had infected everyone. In the meantime, daily life had to be organized.

"It's so ugly here, mamma" the dauphin is supposed to have said when he woke up. It was certainly less beautiful than Versailles. The old Tuileries chateau, left in disuse by the kings over the last sixty-five years*, was in need of repair, but it wasn't, as has been too often charged, entirely taken over by spiders and mice. Quite the contrary, it was overpopulated. With royal consent, it had been colonized by

---

* Louis XIV started gradually abandoning the Tuileries in 1665, but Louis XV spent part of his adolescence there.

numerous courtiers, some of whom had made comfortable lodgings for themselves. They were asked to clear the premises. The queen chose a ground-floor garden apartment in the south wing that had recently been renovated by the countess de La Marck, for which she wanted to compensate her. Above there was a mezzanine at her disposal and on the second floor were rooms for the dauphin and Madame Royale. It was also on the second floor that the king fitted out his ceremonial rooms, which contained a salon, a formal bedchamber, a billiard room and antechambers. For his daily life he set aside a private apartment next to the children's, and he set up his map room on the mezzanine. Little staircases were built to facilitate access to each other's rooms. It was important for the king and queen to reproduce a livable environment that was not too far beneath their royal dignity.

They found the Assembly very cooperative. It had lost no time moving to Paris as expected, and got set up in the great hall of the *Manège*, very close to the Tuileries*. The vast majority of deputies remained faithful to the idea of some sort of monarchy. No effort was spared in making the sovereigns comfortable. Not only did the king have at his disposal twenty-five million worth of household expenses, he also still received revenue from his private domains and was no longer responsible for his public expenses, which were now included in the national budget. Louis XVI was feeling richer than he had in a long time. A caravan of wagons was sent to Versailles for the necessary furniture, and new orders were placed with Riesener and the most renowned cabinetmakers. The irreplaceable Léonard came to do the queen's hair, and Mademoiselle Bertin reappeared. Both were instructed to keep things simple, as this was now the new catchword. Marie-Antoinette continued to have delivered from Ville-d'Avray the spring water over which she had exclusive rights, and every day a gardener brought Madame Élisabeth milk from her own cows in Montreuil, along with news of their health. In short, life was bearable as long as they forgot about the humiliations they had suffered and set aside their fears of the future.

Deeply traumatized by the events of October 5th and 6th, the king and queen were in need of a bit of peace and quiet. But they had to put up with visits from all sorts of deputies who came to call on them as if nothing were out of the ordinary. Stiff and on edge, Marie-Antoinette found it hard to hide her anger with the delegates

---

* It was along the northern side of the gardens, where the rue de Rivoli was later built. Home to the royal equestrian academy, it contained the city's largest indoor space.

from Parliament and the municipality. When foreign ambassadors came calling, she displayed more sorrow than anger; she could hardly get a word out without choking down tears. Louis XVI's face betrayed no emotion. He played to perfection a role that didn't seem to concern him in the least.

In the days that followed, the royal family wavered between total withdrawal and the reestablishment of some sort of court life. They wound up opting for a combination of the two. Some of their attendants had accompanied them to Paris. The princess de Lamballe, who had been absent due to ill health during the recent riots, took up her supervisory functions again. The most important monarchical rituals were reinstated: ceremonial rising and retiring for the night, and daily mass. Twice a week the queen held court before mass, which was followed by dinner in public. No concerts, no balls, no parties. Only Madame de Lamballe, as per her functions, held a few receptions, and all the Paris smart set flocked to them. It was an odd smart set, where the old guard rubbed shoulders with those aspiring to be the new guard. Just as in Versailles, there was public access to the Tuileries. The gardens were packed with people delighted to see the happy little dauphin with his fretful mother hovering over him.

On the days not reserved for her public functions, Marie-Antoinette preferred to "be left to her own devices in her private quarters" so as to avoid being spoken about by anyone, unless it was to praise her courage. There she "makes conversation while working." Highly dexterous, she had always liked needlework. She made large tapestries, which helped calm her nerves. And she kept harping on the recent events with her ladies. Why do they hate her so? She put it all down to their "partisan spirit," to the duke d'Orléans' intrigues, or the insanity of the French. Her one true consolation was her children, who were almost always with her. She attended their lessons, and was thrilled at her son's every achievement. He gave her the best Christmas present possible by fulfilling his promise to learn how to read. He was only five! She wrote to her friend Madame de Polignac, "My *love pet** has such charm; I'm mad about him. In his own way he loves me very much, and is quite easy with me... He is in good health and is no longer irritable." When someone asked him if he missed Versailles, he answered, "I like Paris better because I see Papa and Mamma more."

Louis XVI was a stick-in-the-mud; he hated change. He regained

---

* A nickname Marie-Josèphe of Saxony had already given to her oldest son.

his balance when life returned to normal. But he couldn't bear being cooped up in the city, where he did not have the physical release of hunting. More taciturn than ever, he spent days on end in the depths of silence, as if wandering in some inner abyss. During those periods, his was merely an animal existence: he ate, drank and slept. He consumed a lot of food, which would be normal in an active man; but his daily game of billiards with his wife was not enough to burn off the calories he was absorbing, and he grew fatter. That and his lethargy caused concern for his health. Although Marie-Antoinette was not overly worried, she understood that she could not remain aloof from affairs of state as she had hoped, and that she would have to take an active role as soon as there were decisions to be made.

Family tensions

The king's family was of no help whatsoever. Dining together in the evening as before afforded a veneer of good relations. The suppers no longer took place in the countess de Provence's apartments but in the queen's, and of course the d'Artois were no longer there. Every evening the Provences arrived around eight-thirty and went back to their Palais du Luxembourg shortly after eleven, whereas Madame Élisabeth had only a few steps to go to get back to her bedchamber in the *pavillon de Flore*. But relations were chilly.

Like her aunts, Élisabeth refused to marry because, she said, she preferred to remain French "at the foot of my brother's throne" rather than ascend another. If truth be told, she would only have a future king, and there were not many of those to be had. She therefore showered on her much-admired brothers all her unspent love and affection. At first very close to Marie-Antoinette, she began to harbor that unconscious envy that unmarried sisters can have toward their brother's wives. With the advent of all the scandals and public disapproval, she resented her sister-in-law for damaging the king – ah, how different things would be if she were queen! Neither one could admit it, but each woman competed for Louis XVI's affection, and would soon vie with each other for influence over him as well. Élisabeth did not hide the fact that she was a true-blue conservative, and her position only hardened as the king's authority collapsed. She started to compare him unfavorably with their brother d'Artois, the white knight of the crusade against political heresies. Instead of the concessions the queen seemed to be encouraging, she preached radical resistance, and would not even be adverse to violence, given the grandeur of the cause. She and d'Artois, now in Turin, exchanged ardent letters that would have gravely compromised everyone's position had they fallen into the hands of the Assembly. She also was in close contact with "men with plans" in Paris who were cooking up dangerous schemes.

With the count and countess de Provence relations were downright hostile. Old enmities nourished by years of hurt feelings and frustrated ambitions were now deepened by the reactions of this incurable troublemaker to the recent upheavals, whose effects would be felt during the months to follow. As for his wife Marie-Joséphine of Savoy, she had lost neither her acid tongue nor her taste for amateur psychology, but she played her own game. There was now open warfare between her and her husband. It must be admitted that she had reason to be bitter toward him. Having lost hope that her marriage would ever be consummated, she had followed the fashion of the day and developed a special friendship with her mistress of the wardrobe, the petulant Madame de Balbi. She had led a pleasant life at her home in Montreuil while her husband, living in Brunoy, held notoriously wanton bachelor nights. That he was impotent there was no doubt, but he was careful to hide the fact and went so far as swiping Madame de Balbi from her and flaunting her as his supposed mistress. Doubly betrayed and hurt, she withdrew into her shell, seeking comfort in alcohol; to such an extent that Mercy-Argenteau wrote to his superior that some ghastly scenes had resulted. What is more, around 1785 she fell into the clutches of an ambitious and money-hungry reader, a certain Marguerite Gourbillon, with whom she fell insanely and scandalously in love. The outraged husband had the woman sent into exile in Lille in February of 1789, breaking Marie-Joséphine's heart. "For you alone I want to live, to love you alone," she wrote to her beloved Marguerite. People got wind of the princely soap opera, and Marguerite had to be recalled from exile; but she did not get her job back. Condemned to hiding their continuing relationship, Marie-Joséphine developed a penchant for revolution, despite the prejudices her education had instilled in her. She applauded the events of August 4th; her bitterness towards her husband was only matched by her contempt for him.

The family circle afforded Marie-Antoinette little opportunity for companionship. Fersen was the only one she could count on. Given her isolation, he was even more eager to remain at her side.

He wrote to his sister, "On the 24ᵗʰ [of November*] I spent the whole day with her; it was the first time. You can imagine my joy; you are the only one with whom I can share it." She counted on him for comfort and advice.

Prisoners

When on October 7ᵗʰ the Madrid ambassador Nuñez asked Marie-Antoinette how the king was doing, he received the forceful answer "like a king in captivity." The next day when Bailly came to ask her on behalf of the city of Paris to attend a performance, she rebuffed him. According to Madame Campan, "Time was needed to forget the last few terrible days that had made her heart bleed... Having arrived in Paris behind the heads of two faithful guards slain at their sovereign's door, she couldn't find it in her heart to take part in festivities after such an entrance into the capital." Saint-Priest's more somber memoirs confirm what Madame Campan recalled: the king and queen for months on end walled themselves up in the Tuileries, obstinately refusing to go out.

This refusal can be explained first of all by the shock they had undergone, which they would never quite get over. If pushed to it, Marie-Antoinette could bring herself to have a talk on her doorstep with some women of the people; at least her back was covered. However, she refused to expose herself to danger in public places. Under the circumstances, a degree of agoraphobia was understandable, especially when underpinned by fears of being insulted or even assaulted. Aside from the physical danger – potentially aimed at her in particular – both of them dreaded the many occasions on which calculated infractions of the old rules of etiquette would hurtfully remind them that they no longer enjoyed their old status, and that sovereignty was now in the hands of the nation, as represented by the Assembly. A decree on October 10ᵗʰ declared that Louis XVI had ceased to be "Louis by the grace of God king of France and of Navarre," to become "Louis by the grace of God and the constitutional law of the State, king of the French." Within the walls of the Tuileries, the remnants of the court mimed

---

* Since this letter was dated 27 December, it is generally thought that the day referred to here is the 24ᵗʰ of December. But it is very unlikely that Fersen would have spent Christmas Eve alone with the queen. A few lines farther down he alludes to his sister's letter of 20 November, thus the supposition that he was referring here to the 24ᵗʰ of November.

the ancient rituals and permitted the illusion that they still reigned. But as soon as they ventured forth, everything reminded them that the king was not free, since he had lost his power to decide: he was a political prisoner.

One can therefore understand their self-imposed confinement as a reaction to the ordeal they were subjected to, and their lamentations as the ambiguous moral comfort they took in seeing themselves as innocent victims. Marie-Antoinette wrote to her sister, "I challenge the universe to find any real fault with me; in fact, I can only gain from being investigated and carefully watched…" But that was not the whole story. Behind the king's "captivity," there were forces taking shape that had major political implications. During the months following his forced return to Paris, the Assembly worked relentlessly to draw up a constitution and administer national affairs according to new criteria altogether. Without waiting for the constitution to be finalized, the Assembly began to vote on its first articles. And since the king remained the head of the executive, he was invited to support them. However, as everyone knew at the time, an ancient ruling going back to Roman law had it that only a free man was responsible for his actions. A prisoner therefore had the right to lie, and he could subsequently take back his word if it had been given under restraint. That is why Louis XVI and Marie-Antoinette put so much emphasis on the violence they had been subjected to: it would exonerate the king of all responsibility as regards the decrees he was forced to sign.

That was the thrust of the letter he addressed on October 12th to Charles IV of Spain. In it he registered a solemn protest against the measures they had exacted from him since the 14th of July and those they would exact in the months to come. He did not solicit any aid. He looked forward to the day when he could declare null and void everything he was forced under threat to accept. His cousin in Madrid, head of the house of Bourbon, would be his witness and guarantor. That Marie-Antoinette on her own initiative instructed the messenger to enquire about any possible assistance is another matter. The king's letter, the purpose of which was to protect him from being accused of perjury, was a legal document[*], written according to accepted norms, undoubtedly with the help

---

[*] It is similar to the document that François Ier, prisoner of Charles V in Madrid, registered before two jurists stating that the oaths he was about to take under threat of force would be invalid. Rather surprisingly but logically, these legal precautions had to be taken *before* lying about subsequent commitments rather than *afterwards*, so as to avoid *ex post facto* retractions of commitments.

and advice of legal experts or priests. The rule of law also raised a moral issue: could a prisoner make promises he had no intention of keeping without committing a sin? The answer, nuanced because everything depended on the degree of constraint, was yes all the same. Louis XVI took comfort in a clear conscience. However, he was wrong to do so. The argument, according to which a private individual could be exonerated for a particular act before judges or in the privacy of a confessional, held no weight among the common run of man when it came to a Head of State proliferating commitments he did not intend to fulfill. With Marie-Antoinette's strong backing, he got involved in a political double game that would severely tarnish his image and wind up being their downfall.

However, the Assembly, made up largely of lawyers, didn't need to know of his letter to the king of Spain to sense the danger. They tried to preempt it, which brought about a paradoxical situation: while the king and queen were doing everything they could to prove to the world that they were being held prisoner, the Assembly never missed an opportunity to show that the sovereigns were free to do whatever they pleased, and to pressure them into saying that they were delighted to be living in the fair city of Paris. It partially succeeded. Over the winter, they realized that their self-imposed seclusion in the Tuileries had its risks. With every passing day, the gulf that separated them from their people widened, and gave credence to the suspicions that they were plotting against them. They decided therefore to come down from their ivory tower. On February 4th, after the session in which the king declared himself in complete agreement with the Assembly, some deputies accompanied him back home, and Marie-Antoinette, hiding her bitter rage, managed to address a few polite words to them. The Assembly accepted at face value what seemed to be signs of the sovereigns' good will, and relaxed their hold on them a bit. Not only were they perfectly free to move about within Paris; they were also authorized to spend the summer of 1790 in Saint-Cloud. How could they not succumb to the temptation and take advantage of the milder treatment? They remained from the 11th of June until the 30th of October in Saint-Cloud's lovely country setting, far from the pressures brewing in the city streets.

If we can believe Marie-Antoinette's complaints to Saint-Priest, they were under constant surveillance there. La Fayette included a few of his aides-de-camp among their guards. Those assigned to protect the queen never let her out of their sight. "When I look around in the flower garden I notice this man on the hillside above; if I go where I saw him, I see him on the other hill." Whether on foot or on horseback, he invariably followed her, and he slept in her antechamber at night. In fact the surveillance was not as close as she said, and in the end a certain familiarity grew between the sovereigns and their guards, who were chosen from among good bourgeois families. Those who accompanied her to Bellevue to visit her aunts spent the afternoon playing with the dauphin and the future Madame de Boigne's little brother. As for the king, he came back to life now that he could gallop for all his might after his favorite prey. There were no restrictions on visitors. Fersen, who stayed with friends nearby, stopped by as freely as he had in Paris, and sometimes left at unseemly hours. At one point a guard noticed him at three o'clock in the morning and nearly arrested him. He mentioned it to Saint-Priest, who thought he ought to warn the queen of the risks he was taking, and received the reply, "Tell him yourself if you believe it appropriate. As for me, I take no notice."

Had they wished to escape, it would have been very easy – so easy that one wonders whether or not their degree of resignation was being tested. On the other hand, perhaps the lack of security was meant to show that they were indeed quite free. In any case they were allowed to take long walks in the afternoon from which they didn't return until about nine o'clock at night. For each one there was only one aide-de-camp guarding them, whereas they kept their own pages and equerries with them. All they would have to do was gather a few miles from Saint-Cloud in some wooded area where accomplices would be waiting to help them escape. If they had the willing or imposed help of a few aides-de-camp, the whole family could be carried off in a big coach led by a team of steaming horses. The escape would not be noticed for quite a while, giving the fugitives a good six or seven hours lead. Where would they go? The faithful Madame Campan doesn't say. It is possible that the question was never raised because Louis XVI refused to envisage the possibility. The sovereigns believed that time was on their side.

Hopes and illusions

In May of 1790 Marie-Antoinette wrote, "We must inspire confidence in our wretched people; they have been made to fear and dislike us so! Only an overabundance of patience and pure motives on our part can bring them back to us; sooner or later they will understand how much, for their own good, they must cling to one sole leader, and such a leader! One who is too good, who for the peace and wellbeing of his people, has sacrificed his convictions, his safety and even his freedom! No, I cannot bring myself to believe that such virtue and self-sacrifice will not be repaid one day."

The royal couple's self-deception was extreme. Nothing illustrates better than this letter – chosen from among other similar ones – how much they lulled themselves into an illusory sense of security. It's all quite clear. To begin with, there was the unshakable conviction that the only regime suitable for France was absolute monarchy, because it alone could assure the country's wellbeing, for the simple reason that it alone conformed to the world order imposed by God for all eternity. There was no explicit religious reference, but it was implicit in the idea that their suffering was a test, and that they would later be compensated for their virtue and merit. A naïve sense of self-righteousness enabled her to transform concessions wrung from the king by mob violence into voluntary self-sacrifice. Present also was the conspiracy theory that enabled her to ignore the social and political reasons for the crisis. Men of evil intent had led the "good" people astray and turned them against their "good" king, but they would not remain blind forever. They would get over it; it was enough to wait, "to be on the look-out for the moment when they have regained enough sense to be granted the right and just amount of freedom, such as the king has always desired for them." Marie-Antoinette confused politics with morality, which for her took the form of a wishy-washy sentimentality.

Although Louis XVI never confided in anyone, it can be hoped that his opinions were a bit less simplistic. But his faith prevented him from questioning the concept of the monarchy according to which he was God's representative on earth and the embodiment of undivided sovereignty. Besides, the education he received from Bossuet and Fénelon taught him to take the king's traditional role of "father" of his subjects very seriously. He saw the final wreckage into which his reign was sinking as a failure. This was psychologically destabilizing, but it did not destroy his faith in the dogmas that justified his existence. Was he able to measure the depth of the upheaval in French society? Did he realize that when he was cheered at the Hôtel de Ville or the Assembly, what they were actually applauding was his capitulation? Did he have any inkling that with every passing day the feelings of personal loyalty that had kept the people bound to their king were being transferred more and more to the nation? If he had any doubts about the matter, the public celebration of the Federation should have been enough to destroy them.

It was no plot, no spur-of-the-moment impulse, no mass manipulation that caused 25,000 federated troops or *fédérés* to march to Paris in July of 1790 from their distant country villages to commemorate the storming of the Bastille the year before. Likewise, Parisians of both sexes, workers and bourgeois class alike, worked with their shovels, pick axes and wheelbarrows to set up the speakers platform in the Champ-de-Mars in time for the event. The people were drunk on the bitter wine of freedom and equality. Come what may, they would never forget its taste. We don't know when Louis XVI understood that the movement was irreversible and that nothing would ever be the same again. But as always when he faced difficulties, notably his marital problems, he took refuge in a wait-and-see attitude, counting on time, or a miracle, to improve matters. If he didn't entirely share Marie-Antoinette's faith in the people's change of heart, he at least agreed with her on how to proceed: wait, hold on, even if they had to make concessions that their "captivity" cancelled in advance.

Any counter-revolutionary maneuvers would only compromise their efforts to win back the hearts of the French people. They were terribly dismayed, therefore, when right after the October events, d'Artois in Turin launched a misguided appeal to Joseph II to come to the aid of his outraged sister and brother-in-law and to stop the spread of the revolutionary "venom" that was threatening to infect all of Europe. But the emperor and the Russians were fighting a war against the Turks, in which French support was sorely lacking. He did not have the means to intervene. He was certainly not unaware of the risks of contagion; his own states were rising up against the radical reforms he had prematurely imposed on them. First Bohemia, and now Hungary were on the move. In both they would soon be singing the *Marseillaise* and *Ça ira*. And the Low Countries were in the middle of an insurrection to depose him and declare their independence. Struggling to restore order in his own lands, how could he restore it elsewhere? He understood that d'Artois' saber rattling could only hurt the king and queen. He invited him very firmly to give up any notions of going on the offensive and return to France to work with his brother for the good of the state while they waited for passions to cool. Racked with fever, spitting blood, in the last stages of pulmonary tuberculosis, he was at death's door. Joseph II died on February 20, 1790, haunted by the idea that he had failed. "Why am I not loved by my people?" he groaned, echoing Marie-Antoinette's own lament. Hard experience had finally taught him the virtues of moderation and patience. His brother Leopold II, who succeeded him to the throne, was wiser; he had always understood their importance. He worked toward pacifying his states and expelled the émigrés, who alas, continued nonetheless to spread their inflammatory proclamations, causing the greatest harm to the French sovereigns.

Plans to escape carried a similar risk for them; if they were suspected of trying to flee, the regained popularity they were hoping for would be lost. But on this point Marie-Antoinette was less adamant than about the émigrés. Ever since the day when she was dragged to Paris in the grip of the triumphalist Revolution, she had not stopped mulling over the possibility of escape. She had remained true to the rebellious little dauphine revolted by the mere idea of constraint, only now she had better reason to throw off the yoke. Her very freedom was at stake. It is obvious that she could not resist the desire. Therefore, anyone with any plan, however hazardous, turned to her.

As soon as she arrived at the Tuileries, her principal secretary Augeard suggested she go to Vienna with her children to plead her cause with the emperor. Would it endanger the king? No, Augeard answered, "They would wrap him in cotton to avoid doing him the least bit of harm. Those people know that in France you can't get rid of the king." Not terribly convinced, she thought about it and then refused, fearing perhaps, he added, "that they would have forced the king, whose weakness she is only too familiar with, to sacrifice her." She would not leave without him.

Louis XVI's apathy and chronic inability to make a decision inspired a lot of far-fetched ideas on the part of would-be plotters. They would save him whether he liked it or not. They would abduct him. Such was the proposition that a certain count d'Inisdal and a handful of aristocrats tried to get the queen to agree to in March of 1790. Everything was ready: the national guardsmen on duty that day had been won over and the relay stations organized. As they could hardly force him physically to decamp, they were counting on his wife to get him to commit himself at the last minute. He was playing whist with her when Campan, according to his daughter-in-law, passed the message. He continued playing his hand as if he hadn't heard a thing, and finally gave his reply, "Tell Monsieur d'Inisdal that I cannot consent to be abducted." All the same, recounted Madame Campan, the queen continued getting her jewelry boxes ready for her departure. "She thought the king's answer would be interpreted as tacit consent, as long as he was not seen as taking an active part." Did she really think her husband had become so spineless that he wanted to be forced into fleeing? Did she really think this would prevent his being held to account should the escape attempt fail? We know that Madame Campan's memoirs must be read with some degree of skepticism. There is no guarantee that this episode happened exactly as she said. But it is clear that the idea of abducting the king was in the air. And it is just as clear that the queen wanted to flee.

In the summer of 1790, the temptation was too great; the possibilities offered in Saint-Cloud incited the imagination. Marie-Antoinette wrote so many letters and was so feverishly active that suspicions were raised. Was she going riding again with an eye towards an escape attempt? People already pictured her on horseback holding on to the dauphin, galvanizing the troops in some fortified town in the provinces, as her mother once did to face down the Hungarians. But the king would hear none of it. In the 9th of October issue of the *Correspondance secrète*[*] we read:

> At all costs, the queen wanted the king out of the capital. We can say that with all the plots that proliferate on a daily basis, there isn't a single one that is well thought out, or a single leader directing them. Lately, the king has forcefully demonstrated his way of thinking as concerns all these counter-revolutionary plans. Angry over the position he's been put in by the endless, obsessive intrigues, he says, "The next b[astard]… who talks to me about plots or leaving will get my f… foot in his belly."

He would have to have been really exasperated to use this kind of language! But, the fiction writer adds mischievously, he did not say "The next b[itch] – and that's exactly how the good king will meet his downfall."

Mirabeau, or mutual deception

There was indeed a leader with a well thought-out plan who offered to save them. But he was one of the top members of the National Assembly, and his plan was not counter-revolutionary.

Honoré-Gabriel Riquetti, the count de Mirabeau, seemed to take pleasure in missing the opportunities that his high birth afforded him when the Revolution handed him a theatre of operations commensurate with his ambitions. His scandalous private life, his debauchery and fondness for dueling had made him *persona non grata* amongst the nobility of Provence and earned him more than one stay in France's prisons, which he would subsequently decry

---

[*]   *Translator's note:* La Correspondance secrète, politique et littéraire *was a French périodical that existed from 1787 to 1790.*

with so much vehemence. Rejected by his family and disowned by his peers, he was elected to the Estates General as a commoner by the districts of Aix and Marseille. He quickly came to dominate the Assembly. At the time he was 40 years old. He was of average height, corpulent, with a low forehead topped by a massive head of hair. He himself admitted to having a powerfully ugly "face of a wild boar." It reminded Chateaubriand of the tortured faces of Michelangelo's "Last Judgment." He was so pockmarked from small pox that he looked like a burn victim. "When he shook his mane as he eyed the assembled masses, he stopped them dead in their tracks. All he had to do was lift his little finger for the proles to go berserk." When he let loose torrents of inflamed rhetoric, no one would dare interrupt him. He was behind all the major blows inflicted by the deputies on the absolute monarchy: the oath at the *Jeu de paume*, the conversion of the Estates General into the National Assembly, and the night of August 4th. But he did not get mixed up in any of the popular uprisings. He was anything but a demagogue. According to the duke de Lévis, "liberty appealed to his feelings, the monarchy to his reason, and the nobility to his vanity." He tended toward a constitutional monarchy with a strong executive, in which he himself would not be adverse to the post of prime minister. And in October of 1789, he felt that it was necessary to put a brake on the Revolution to save the country from collapsing into a state of anarchy.

There had to be a king in the regime he dreamed of setting up. He therefore let the sovereigns know that he was there to help. They were horrified and roundly rejected his advances. For Marie-Antoinette he was no better then a cut-throat: "I do not think we shall ever be so unfortunate as to be reduced to the painful extremity of turning to Mirabeau for assistance." So he thought of an alternative solution – get the king to abdicate in favor of his son, and appoint a regent. But he very quickly realized that the duke d'Orléans did not have what it takes, and the count de Provence, to whom he sent out feelers, remained wary. He therefore had to do business with Louis XVI, and win his wife's favor. When in February of 1790 she took the initiative to reopen negotiations, he jumped at the opportunity.

Since the monarchist ranks in the Assembly were thinning out due to emigration, and in any case their support was ineffectual, the king and queen were contemplating rallying to their cause the two men calling the shots: La Fayette, who led the National Guard, and Mirabeau, who headed the Assembly. But as far as La Fayette was concerned, an insurmountable abhorrence born of the October events held them back. On the other hand, they had heard that Mirabeau's backing could be very useful. Mercy was undoubtedly the source of this opinion, as he had very close ties with his compatriot, the count de La Marck*, a friend of the silver-tongued Mirabeau. In any case, it was La Marck and Mercy who were given the task of contacting him. Beforehand, however, they had to make sure that Mirabeau "had no part in the horrors of October." Marie-Antoinette was not reassured for all that. Out of pure necessity, the sovereigns were obliged "to sacrifice their personal feelings" toward a man whose existence "was nothing but treachery, trickery and lies." They resigned themselves to "employing" him, as long as they never had to meet him face to face. If you dine with the devil, you need a long spoon; so two intermediaries were not too many to protect them from his unclean presence. Although Marie-Antoinette never stopped complaining about their "dreadful situation," neither she nor her husband seemed to have any idea of the danger they were in, or that the great orator held their fate in his hands. They paid him a salary "to be of use," that is, to do whatever they wanted. He should start by "putting his thoughts on paper." La Marck would show them to the queen, who would communicate them to the king. Above all, he had to keep things top secret, with the paltry excuse that Necker would not put up with seeing his prerogatives trampled upon. His venality was such that they believed they could control and outwit him. They could not have been more mistaken.

An appalled La Marck quickly caught on. He couldn't understand how the king would even dream of employing a man like Mirabeau without informing his ministers. His advice and activities would be diametrically opposed to theirs. Mirabeau on the other hand had absolutely no scruples about being given the means to pay his debts and win over a few allies – after all, Louis XVI had paid back a lot of other debts and remunerated courtiers for much less crucial services – he in no way betrayed his principles in working for the king. He promised "loyalty, zeal, action, energy and courage," but made it clear that his intention was "to reestablish order, but not the old order." He thought he could talk the king into leading the movement instead of opposing it. That way he would be able to win

---

* The count de La Marck, prince of Arenberg, was one of the great lords of the Austrian Low Countries, who, like Mercy, made a career for themselves wherever their fancy, sympathies or interests led them. At the time he was a deputy in the Estates General from a northern district where his properties got him elected. He would end his life in the service of Austria.

back, as the head of the weakened nation, the authority of which he had been robbed by years of aristocratic revolt. The idea wasn't new. Malesherbes had vigorously articulated the same notion a few years previously, and in 1790 all enlightened minds thought the same way.

Mirabeau had brilliant ideas on the strategy to follow, and set them out in a series of "notes" that have survived. The problem is, they were not easy to carry out. Very roughly speaking, they were as follows. First of all the Assembly must be allowed to discredit itself through misguided measures, causing it to lose popular support. The king and queen could help matters by venturing out more frequently in public, by chatting with people and winning back their esteem. They had already begun doing so in any case. But it was a minutely detailed task, requiring the backup of a whole department of propaganda capable of opposing the adverse effects of the libels that continued to rain down. It isn't possible to go into detail about all the different "*ateliers d'influence*" that would carry it out. Suffice it to say that it was quite advanced for its time. Then, once the king had regained some of his popularity, he could leave Paris to get some relief from the pressure he was under from all the agitators. But this by no means implied that he would be fleeing. "A king goes forth only in broad daylight, and to perform his kingly functions." He would advise the Assembly of his departure. Were he to "withdraw to Metz or any other border area" he would run the risk "of being unable to return to his States unless he had armed support, and of being reduced to begging for foreign support." He could go to Normandy, for instance, or at least Fontainebleau or Compiègne, and surrounded by loyal troops, he could address a solemn appeal to the entire country, inviting his people to rally to him as the leader of his and their "national party."

It was a superb plan, and Mirabeau was ecstatic over it. But how could he convey his ardor with a few little hand-written notes, and delivered by an intermediary at that? He knew his own power to fascinate those who saw him in person and heard him speak. He wanted an audience. It was the queen he had to win over; he realized that. He thought that the grandeur and audacity of his plan would find an echo with this daughter of Maria Theresa. "The king has only one man: his wife. She can only find safety in the restitution of royal authority. I rather think she would prefer not to live without her crown; but I know for a fact that she *cannot* live without it." Much to everyone's surprise, Mercy had no trouble at all persuading Marie-Antoinette. She accepted to meet him, not without ulterior motives. She suspected how vainglorious he was, and felt she could get the upper hand. Were it not for her revulsion at his "immorality", she confided to an Alsatian correspondent in April, she would already have agreed to meet him, believing that her "womanly nature" above all would give her "more power and deftness in dealing with him." Once she made up her mind to meet him, she would call into play the inexhaustible resources of her charm – he was a lady's man after all. Their meeting promised to be, beyond any political discussion, a confrontation between two strong personalities, each intent on seducing the other.

The top-secret interview took place in Saint-Cloud on July 3, 1790. The accounts that have survived, second-hand or third-hand and written much later, are fanciful. There is a question about where exactly it took place. But there was no tête-à-tête in a little wooded corner of the estate; that tale is just a daylight version of the famous scene with Rohan. The count de La Marck was categorical about it: Mirabeau "arrived at the appointed hour at the queen's apartment, where the king had joined her." Does this contradict a letter to Mercy she had written a few days earlier in which she states, "I have found a place to see him that is not exactly practical, but it avoids all the disadvantages of the gardens or the chateau." It has been suggested that this neutral and discreet place could have been the house that Breteuil had once occupied as the superintendent but was now in private hands.

Regarding the interview itself, however, the only reliable account is that of La Marck. The queen had to suppress "a show of horror and fright" on seeing the man she considered a monster, and that she was so agitated that she later suffered a malaise. It seems she hid her feelings, because Mirabeau was full of enthusiasm when he left Saint-Cloud: "All he could talk about was how pleasant the interview was." Since one cannot put his fervor down to the king's eloquence (we can imagine that Louis XVI remained silent, as was his wont), the queen was no doubt pouring on the charm. In her presence, Mirabeau virtually took flight, fancying himself her knight in shining armor. He undoubtedly did not declaim, as the count de Vieil-Castel stated, "How great she is, and noble and unhappy, but I will save her." What La Marck quoted sounds more believable: "I will stop at nothing; I will perish rather than fail to fulfill my promises" – which more prosaically speaking, came down to more or less the same thing. Mirabeau was infatuated with Marie-Antoinette, but the feeling was not mutual. Her confidant and adviser Fersen was watching over her, and he advised caution.

Disillusion set in early on both sides. Mirabeau's plan was unrealistic. The *ateliers d'influence* got no farther than the drawing board, because there was no way to fund them and no one to man them. The sovereigns' efforts to win back their people did not really pay off. During important events like the feast of the Federation where they were applauded, they were able to rise to the occasion and play the part, but left to their own devices, they very quickly reverted to character. The little court around them now was of a highly reactionary bent, and acted as a barrier between them and the people, just as the court of Versailles had done. They were ill at ease outside of it, and people could see that in public – out and about or visiting hospitals – their amiability was forced. According to La Fayette, the queen "has everything it takes to win the hearts of the Parisians, but the ancestral haughtiness and temper that she cannot sufficiently hide, alienate them more often than not." As for the king, he hasn't got what it takes at all, and withdraws into a gloomy silence. And as their adversaries had a large audience thanks to the press, it was clear that things would never get back to normal. Under the circumstances, it was vain even to consider leaving Paris. Perhaps it would be feasible if La Fayette cooperated, but it would be too much to ask of the queen to curry favor with this man who was the very symbol of the 5th and 6th of October, especially as there was no guarantee of success. Besides, she was disappointed with the meager results Mirabeau obtained at the Assembly; he had not been able to retain the king's exclusive power over war and peace.

Conflict quickly broke out between them. Wanting to shake the king out of his lethargy and get him to take a firm stand, Mirabeau took it upon himself on August 13th to strike out and declare, "Four enemies are galloping towards us: taxes, bankruptcy, the army and winter. A decision must be made... prepare for events by leading them. In short, civil war is certain and perhaps even necessary." Marie-Antoinette was indignant. "This is madness from top to bottom... How can he possibly believe that we could ever, but especially now, provoke a civil war?" This was not quite what Mirabeau meant. In the autumn he still harbored the belief that another audience would enable him to clear the air. But his position in the Assembly was rocky. The spectacular improvement in his standard of living raised suspicions. He was accused of betraying the Revolution. He tried to redeem himself by attacking the Assembly's royalist right wing, all the more fiercely because the latter, not knowing that he was working for the king, kept countering his efforts. The queen in turn accused him of betrayal. How could he get her to understand that this was just a tactical maneuver? Their trust in each other died, the victim of secretiveness, pretence and ambiguity. La Marck was very upset when the queen told him to inform Mirabeau, and not gently, that "the best way to serve people is to serve them the way they wish to be served." She added, "He is smart enough, and I would like to think zealous enough, to take the road I have just mapped out."

Mirabeau understood that it was all over. He would not awaken them from their impenetrable slumber while their house burned down around them. His great dream was dead. He himself had only six months to live. Having burnt the candle at both ends, he would die on the 2nd of April 1791 telling his friends, "Don't cry for me. Cry for the monarchy; it goes to the grave with me." Not yet, the fruit was not quite ripe. For now, it was only the queen who was in jeopardy.

Marie-Antoinette in great danger

As far as the new regime was concerned, the queen didn't officially exist. There were unmistakable signs that the Assembly was trying to dissociate her from her husband. The first article of the upcoming constitution granted inviolability to the king, but not to her. On Federation Day she was not beside him on the speakers platform set up in front of the military academy. She was relegated to a nearby balcony. In March of 1791 the Assembly proposed excluding women from the regency. Clearly, she was in the way. Her covert influence on the government was shocking to a largely misogynistic public. Those who had the king's best interests at heart were unhappy to see him suffer from guilt by association. Supporters of a constitutional monarchy saw her as the soul of resistance to reform, and believed that without her, the king would be more conciliatory. She was advised to leave; she refused, and according to Madame Campan, made to the duchess de Luynes one of those heroic remarks that hide a more trivial reality: if she is the only one people are angry at, she will "sacrifice her life to the people's hatred," but since the throne itself is the object of opprobrium, it would be cowardly on her part to abandon the king in peril. In reality, she knew that if she left she would never come back, but she was not entirely wrong in thinking that her husband would gain nothing by it. For there were plenty of people in France who wanted to remove her purely to deprive him of the little bit of energy she infused in him. Without her it would be easy to get rid of this nonentity of a king who seemed to have no more interest in his own affairs than he had in those of the emperor of China.

What good was Louis XVI anyway? His passivity inspired two

kinds of speculation. On the one hand, those who were nostalgic for the days of a strong monarchy thought that things would be a lot better if there were a different monarch on the throne. At one point Mirabeau shared that opinion. On the other hand, the left wing of the Assembly and a section of public opinion were beginning to think that they could well do without the king altogether. In either case, the queen was the first obstacle to overcome. Even though once or twice an assassination attempt or a poisoning had been averted, she was not in real fear for her life. She recalled the lesson of the *Marriage of Figaro*: calumny is the thing to fear.

What follows are only two examples of the machinations whose aim was either to dislodge her, or through her the king.

The first was the Favras plot of Christmas 1789. It was kept so secret that little is known about it; however, we know enough to get a glimpse of its objectives. The count de Provence was behind it, and the leading role was played by one of those bighearted, bold and muddle-headed fanatics that troubled periods tend to produce. He was busy getting the funds for his enterprise when he was caught. The plot soon became public knowledge thanks to a bulletin that was distributed at the end of midnight mass. "The marquis de Favras was arrested with the marquise his wife on the night of the 24th for his plan to have Monsieur de La Fayette and the mayor assassinated and subsequently to cut off our food supplies. The king's brother was the ringleader." It was signed mysteriously by one Barrauz, but he was never identified and the so-called assassination plot could never be confirmed. But there was something fishy going on. The count de Provence parried the blow brilliantly by personally going to the Paris city hall to explain that Favras as far as he knew was just a financial middleman who was negotiating a loan needed to pay off some debts. Provence's eloquence and sang froid were superb, and he was cleared. But the poor Favras was indicted for a widespread conspiracy. He had to be silenced. He sacrificed himself, or rather was pushed to sacrifice himself, by being told he would be pardoned at the last minute if he held his tongue. At the foot of the scaffold, he knew that he could get his revenge if he spoke up, but that it wouldn't save his head. He held his tongue. He was hanged on February 19th and Marie-Antoinette, along with the rest of the royal family, breathed a deep sigh of relief.

She was much vexed when a few days later his widow and son were brought to her. "Had I been free to choose," she told Madame Campan, "I should have taken the child of the man who sacrificed himself for us and placed him at the table between the king and me;

but surrounded as I was by the butchers who had just executed his father, I didn't even dare to look at him. The royalists will blame me for not taking care of him; and the revolutionaries will be furious, believing that some people thought they would give me a nice opportunity to gloat by meeting the poor child." In fact, no one was seeking to make her gloat, they were trying to compromise her by making it seem she had been in on the plot. Compared to what would have been in store for her had the plot succeeded, this was minor indeed. She never did find out what she had narrowly escaped. Apparently, the plotters were planning to abduct her along with her husband and children, isolate them somewhere in the countryside, supposedly for their own safety, and take advantage of the situation to depose Louis XVI for incompetence in favor of his younger brother, who would become regent and then perhaps king of France.

Soon thereafter another attack was being planned against the queen, quite openly this time, but from the opposite side of the political divide. "They want to bring up the question of the regency and the king's divorce," La Marck wrote to Mercy on the 9th of November 1790. La Fayette, forever being dragged along by whoever was the strongest, had the temerity to put pressure on the queen, even going so far as to tell her that "they would go after her for adultery to get a divorce." And there was talk of bringing Jeanne de La Motte back to Paris to reopen her trial. A brief rumor even had it that she was living it up as bold as brass in a superb townhouse in the Place Vendôme at the duke d'Orléans' expense. Let's hear what Mirabeau had to say about it. In a note dated November 12th, he clearly set out the devious inner workings of the plan:

> They would use Madame de La Motte's trial to further poison the queen's reputation and turn the most absurd calumnies into legal proofs capable of duping the king. This in turn would raise questions about divorce, the regency, the nature of royal marriages, and the dauphin's education. What with all this contention, it would be easy to fill the king with dread, and render the burden of the crown ever more unbearable. Thus, they could weaken his authority so much that he would abdicate or consent to put his power in the hands of others for the rest of his reign.

The plan was enough to throw Marie-Antoinette into a panic. She could be imprisoned for life in some convent; or worse, a trial for adultery could result in declaring the dauphin illegitimate and depriving him of his rights. She no longer held out any hope except for flight and rescue by foreign powers. But how Louis XVI viewed the matter remained to be seen. It is surprising that during these two crucial years, all eyes are fixed on the queen. She was credited with a level of energy and influence that she probably didn't actually have. Her husband was considered "a hopeless case;" a wet rag with which people could do whatever they wanted. But Louis XVI was not a wet rag. It is highly unlikely that he would ever have abdicated or agreed to divorce. Unquestionably, he did not know how to impose his will on others, and put up with things that others would have found intolerable. However, even if he was infinitely patient, he was not soft. When it came to brass tacks, he did not bend. He was able to say no, even if it could lead to his own downfall.

The schism

The Assembly churned out decrees by the bucketful. Louis XVI signed them, whether he liked them or not. He surely didn't appreciate, for example, the fact that his kingdom had been carved up into 83 departments replacing the old provinces that had pulsed for centuries to the rhythms of his ancestors' reign. But he signed it. (At least Mirabeau had prevented the imposition of a worse grid system of equally proportioned squares!) All administrative reforms could be overturned – or at least that's what he thought. On July 14, 1790 he agreed, with a heavy heart surely, to take the oath of allegiance to the nation. It had been demanded of everyone in the wave of passion raised by of the Federation Day celebrations. There were, however, things he balked at. Even though theoretically his imprisonment cleared him of responsibility, he had some scruples. To his credit, he did not like to couch his promises in mental reservations. One's word is one's word. On this point he was more conscientious than Marie-Antoinette; one should not make a promise lightly.

For months now, the repeated attacks on the Church of France had been bothering him. As concerns finance, now the shoe was on the other foot. Since he was sent to Paris, it had been the Assembly's turn to grapple with the deficit. How could they plug up that gaping hole? Well, for a long time there had been a source of treasure that was right there staring everyone in the face. Rich, too rich, the Church displayed its wealth for all to see. They justified their tax-exempt status by claiming they didn't own their wealth but merely administered it in fulfillment of their functions, some of them spiritual, some of them temporal, education and public assistance, for instance. There was a simple solution: by appropriating the clergy's wealth, the nation would be doing nothing more than taking back what belonged to it. It would replace the church in fulfilling its temporal mission, and remunerate the priests for their religious services. The plan, supported by the bishop of Autun Talleyrand, raised the hackles of the hierarchy, but got the backing of the lowly curates, who were promised unheard of improvements in their living standards. The plan had been adopted on the 2nd of November 1789. How could the Church's wealth be turned into currency? It would be sold. This would kill two birds with one stone: it would erase the public debt and at the same time win the useful support of the new owners of the church's former property. This wasn't a new phenomenon. It had been highly successful in the 16th century for all of the rulers who went over to the Reform. A whiff of schism surrounded it. Every new enactment of the law brought the country closer to the brink of schism, much to the despair of Louis XVI, whose conscience rebelled against such measures.

For two and a half centuries, the monarchy had held the French clergy in check, thanks to what became known as the Concordat of Bologna, which enabled the king to choose the bishops, limiting the pope's role to conferring investiture. Now that the nation had taken on the king's powers, it took on the right to assume those of the Church as well. The Assembly claimed that its role was purely to deal with the Church's temporal functions, that it was not encroaching on the Church's spiritual functions, but how was it possible to distinguish the two? It began by abolishing monastic vows because they were contrary to freedom, and by closing convents. Soon, on April 21, 1790, the civil constitution of the clergy revised the ecclesiastical circumscription map, and more drastically, decided that bishops and priests would be elected by the entire electorate, including non-Catholics. In July Louis XVI had to pledge his assent, but managed to drag its ratification out until August 24th, even though he knew that the pope would be opposed to it. He still hoped that his ambassador to Rome, the cardinal de Bernis, would come to some sort of accommodation with Pius VI. The Assembly on the other hand had not lost its stride. On the 27th of November it ruled that priests had to take an oath of fidelity to the nation, the law and the king, and thus implicitly to the civil constitution, or risked being declared resistors and lose their rights. A month later, just after Christmas, "with an aching heart," the king signed it. There was no need to await the pope's condemnation to understand that the schism was complete.

The line had been crossed. The consequences of these measures were too vast to examine closely here. To put it simply, only four bishops obeyed, and the rest of the clergy was divided into those who took the oath and those who did not, commonly known as the "jurors" and "non-jurors." They had to decide who got which church, and one can imagine the squabbles that produced. France was shaken to its core. Louis XVI could not forgive himself for giving in. Yes, he had done so to avoid bloodshed, under threat from the mobs growling just outside the Tuileries gates. But to spare the lives of his subjects here below, must one jeopardize their immortal souls? It was all well and good to tell himself that his captivity spared him the responsibility of measures he promised he would revoke once he was free; he still trembled at the idea that until then his subjects, delivered into the hands of unworthy priests, were being deprived of the true sacraments for months, perhaps years, without proper spiritual guidance. There was no making up for that.

He sank into a depression again, and in the spring of 1791 his health bore the brunt of it. He fell gravely ill. He was confined to bed for a whole week suffering from a high fever and spitting up blood. It took him a good month to recover. Again, Marie-Antoinette had to take the helm. At this point all of her energies were devoted to readying their escape. It is not known how she reacted to the trauma the Church was undergoing; her letters we have from this period hardly refer to it at all. Her religious faith was not as deep as her husband's; she surely did not suffer the same pangs of conscience. But as concerns religious practices, she remained faithful to the church's teaching. And besides, she hated the Assembly too much to submit to decrees that after all concerned one's soul. For her, communion taken from the hands of a schismatic priest would never be valid.

As Easter approached, the public was looking forward to seeing the king make a misstep. His Easter duty would force him to make a public choice. If he refused to take the sacraments with a priest who had taken the oath, his double-dealing would be exposed and people would conclude that he was planning his escape and thereupon reverse all of his decisions. And more than ever fear of invasion was in the air.

Suspicion prevails

Jacobin surveillance of the Tuileries increased noticeably after the February departure of Mesdames aunts, which seemed to prefigure that of the royal family.

The elderly ladies themselves were of no particular interest to anyone, and would have been completely forgotten about had they not been the king's aunts. At the very beginning of the troubles they had left their Bellevue property, believing that at Versailles they would be better protected. They were deluding themselves. On the 6th of October they were greatly relieved when their carriage was authorized to leave the sinister cortege and turn off to the Meudon estate, where they barricaded themselves in. Since no one was paying any homage to them as they had in bygone days, they didn't feel safe anywhere so they spent the winter at the Tuileries. But horrified by the atmosphere in the capital, they went back to their cherished Bellevue in the spring, entrusting themselves to God's grace.

There were only two of them now, Adélaïde and Victoire. The Good Lord had kindly granted Madame Louise eternal rest before the advent of all the horrors. She had breathed her last at the Carmelite convent in Saint-Denis on the 23rd of December 1787, coming out of her semi-coma to utter the astonishing words, "To heaven! Quickly! Gallop!" Surely she was better off where she was. What would she have thought, learning that the nation had "liberated" her from her vows and chased her from her convent? Secularizing the clergy struck a mortal blow to the two survivors; their universe collapsed around them entirely. The only thing that kept them in France was the king. He told them he thought it better that they leave. He could neither add another two people to his escape plans nor expose them to danger by leaving them where they were. They therefore had to leave before him. They would go to Rome, where their old friend the cardinal de Bernis would find a home for them. To clear Louis XVI of any suspicion, Madame Adélaïde wrote him a letter in which she claimed the initiative had been hers, "You can be sure, my dear nephew, that it is with great regret that we have made our decision and take leave of you. It required the strongest reasons, those of my religion about which I have already spoken to you, for me to make this decision, which weighs so cruelly on my heart."

However secret the aunts' plans were, they hadn't escaped the notice of the spies in their midst. The Assembly put forward a motion about it and the newspapers took up the affair. Camille Desmoulins stormed, "Sire, your aunts have no right to go gobble up our millions in papal lands." Marat echoed him, "We must keep these nuns as hostages, and treble the rest of the family's guards." Called upon to forbid them to leave, the king blew up: "When you show me an Assembly decree that forbids travel I shall prohibit my aunts from leaving; until such time they are as free to leave the kingdom as any other citizen." Their departure was fixed for the 20th of February at four in the morning, but at about six o'clock on the previous evening a messenger came to advise them that they hadn't a minute to lose: Meudon was about to be attacked.

No sooner had the carriages exited their property on one side than the raiders burst into the other. In the darkness of night, however, the two sisters had no trouble leaving Paris, but their trials were not over for all that. In Moret-sur-Loing, a menacing, jeering crowd stopped them. Soldiers from the Fontainebleau garrison came to their rescue, but at Arnay-le-Duc, things went wrong altogether. They had to get down from their coach and go to an inn to wait for the Assembly to confirm the validity of their passports. They waited a long time, all the while exposed to the insults of a hostile population. One of their biographers said they passed the time playing cards with the curate – although history has failed to note whether he was a juror or not. The torrents of verbiage spilled about them at the Assembly were beyond grotesque. Why, the people's safety was in jeopardy! Fortunately for them, France had not entirely lost its sense of the ridiculous, not yet. The baron de Menou finally put an end to the debate when he exclaimed, "I do believe that Europe will be quite astonished to learn that the National Assembly spent four hours debating the departure of two ladies who prefer to hear mass in Rome rather than Paris."

Despite some rear-guard maneuvering, the Jacobins lost that round. After a couple of weeks, Arnay-le-Duc had to give up its prey. This time Mesdames reached Pont-de-Beauvoisin without a hitch; from there they crossed into the Savoy. Forced to let them go, their Burgundy jailers had seen fit to remind them that "liberty exists for the people, not for princes," a highly inauspicious phrase as far as the royal family was concerned.

Louis XVI was unable to hide his aversion for the priests who had taken the infamous oath. He dismissed those in his service and changed his confessor. Consumed by remorse, he hesitated to make his Easter duty, feeling that he was in a state of mortal sin for having supported the secularizing of the clergy. On Palm Sunday, 17 April 1791, he and his family went to the Tuileries chapel to attend mass with the famously non-juror cardinal Montmorency; it is not known whether or not he received communion. The next day the entire family was embarking upon its journey to Saint-Cloud when the coaches it had just entered were surrounded by a hostile crowd who were clearly receiving orders from somewhere. Cabanis testified that the crowd was made up of middle-class people, not the populace, and – this was a first – the National Guard was on their side. Under the circumstances, it seemed likely that the Assembly was wreaking its revenge for its failure to retain the king's aunts. The king was criticized for reneging on his support for a secular constitution and accused of double-dealing. He was suspected of readying his escape. La Fayette strove to calm his troops down – to no avail.

After two hours stuck in their coach surrounded by insults and threats, the rulers gave up. The Assembly's cherished fiction that the king supported its decrees of his own free will was exposed for what it was. "You must admit that we are no longer free," exclaimed the queen. Never had she appeared more proud than on that day when she lectured her weeping lady-in-waiting about the meaning of courage, and mounting the Tuileries steps with the dauphin in her arms, proclaimed that she preferred death to acts of violence. La Fayette thus had another occasion to attest that the queen "was more concerned with looking good when faced with danger than with trying to deflect it." Illness had confined her to her bedchamber for a number of days and the strain was showing. For six months now Fersen had been working out his secret plans, and as the date approached, her nerves were stretched to their limit and were at the point of breaking down altogether. To deflect suspicion, she forced herself to attend mass with her husband in Saint-Germain-l'Auxerrois where the priest, the king's ex-confessor, had taken the oath. For both of them, tension was reaching the limits of endurance.

It was high time to get out of there. But suspicion about their doings had never been more intense.

CHAPTER 19

THE LONGEST DAY

Throughout the winter of 1790-1791, Marie-Antoinette worked relentlessly with Fersen's help to fine-tune a precise and coherent escape plan with some chance of success. Although Louis XVI was less and less hostile to the idea of leaving Paris, she knew he couldn't be counted on to take part in organizing the matter. She'd be lucky if he didn't pull out at the last minute. The only way to get him to agree would be to present him with a well worked out plan to which he could have no objection. He didn't want to be abducted? His wife would be the one to abduct him, but she would give him the impression that he was still the master of the ship with his family in tow.

The escape took place on the 21st of June 1791, the summer solstice, the longest day of the year. It got very close to succeeding. As we know, it all fell apart in a little village called Varennes. Thanks to a good deal of scholarly research, we know about its detailed planning, the ups and downs as it was carried out, and the immediate causes of its failure. We are much less well informed about how it all ended, because the available documents are remarkable for their ambiguity and leave much unsaid, in part deliberately. What would Louis XVI have done had the attempt succeeded? What would have become of him? No one can tell, despite the claims that are sometimes made that the Revolution would have been checked. We do know for sure, however, that the failure hastened the end of the monarchy and sealed the king's fate. Clear-sightedly, Mercy warned Marie-Antoinette that she was going for all or nothing. She had to "succeed or perish." But nothing at this point would have dissuaded her from clutching at this chance of freedom.

Help from abroad?

All the escape plans had a common goal: the king had to reach a safe haven where he would be protected by loyal troops. From there he could launch an appeal and rally to his side all those Frenchmen who remained true to the monarchy and those frightened by the mounting disorder. The moment was not ill chosen. Enthusiasm for the new ideas was diminishing as the troubles increased. The collapse of the ancient structures was paralyzing economic activity, and the secularization of the clergy was bringing religious strife to the countryside. In short, the king was hoping he would be heeded if he promised to maintain a few concessions.

The baron de Breteuil, who had sought refuge in Switzerland and then Brussels, worked out a plan that Fersen transmitted to Marie-Antoinette. Among the high-ranking officers who had not emigrated, a certain one stood out as the ideal candidate to receive the royal family. At the age of 52, the marquis de Bouillé had acquired a great deal of military experience on the battlefields of the Seven Years War, then in the West Indies during the American expedition. He had recently proven himself to be a man of few scruples when it came to imposing order. In September he had ruthlessly put down the popularly supported revolt of the Nancy garrison. As commander-in-chief of the Lorraine, the Alsace and the Franche-Comté, he offered the king a wide choice of fortified towns to flee to. The troops, however, could not be counted on. Many of the top echelons of the officer class had emigrated, leaving the troops in the hands of the non-commissioned officers who were closer to the people and drawn to the new ideas. No, the troops were not willing to fight for the king. A sign of the times: even the Swiss auxiliaries in the Châteauvieux regiment took part in the 1790 mutiny in Nancy. Even the mercenaries were contaminated. All of these troops needed to be contained and bolstered up by foreign ones if they were to succeed.

To carry out Breteuil's plan therefore, help was needed from the outside. Naturally, Marie-Antoinette looked to her family. Had not her brother Leopold when he succeeded Joseph II confirmed his "friendship, interest, true and sincere attachment" for her? She had no trouble at all convincing him to reject the émigrés' schemes. But when she asked for solid support, she came up against a brick wall. The new emperor did not lack reasons or excuses for disappointing her. By canceling Joseph II's hasty centralizing measures, he managed to calm things down in Bohemia and Hungary, and then to restore his authority over the Low Countries. But his victories were still fragile. His armies managed to get back to Brussels only in the beginning of December 1790, while throughout the Brabant the embers of revolution were still smoldering. With the Russians he was engaged in a grueling war against the Turks. Since he had no support from the French on that score, the Prussians could be tempted, with England's blessing, to take advantage of the situation and grab some of his lands, so he busied himself trying to patch things up with them. He had neither the desire nor the means to undertake a risky military venture just to make his little sister happy. Even just deploying some troops to intimidate the "factious elements" was too risky. As the English couldn't disguise their pleasure at France's sufferings, could he orchestrate a diplomatic effort in favor of Louis XVI without getting on their wrong side? If the current tenuous balance of power were upset in Europe, he would be the first to have to pick up the pieces. He didn't need to study for twenty years at the school of Florence to see that his interests did not lie there. Leopold was a clear-headed realist. Besides, was he that unhappy to see the humbling of this ally who so recently fought Austria for European dominance and refused to back Joseph II up despite their much-touted alliance?

If truth be told, the foreign powers witnessed with surprise but not excessive regret the swift disintegration of the most prosperous and powerful country in Europe. None of them wanted to take the risk of coming to France's aid except for Sweden, which lacked the means. Marie-Antoinette's pathetic appeals to Spain were greeted with silence. She tried to wave the red flag of contagion in front of the other European rulers. If they didn't intervene, they too would be infected with the revolutionary virus. Exasperated, she would go so far as to say that she wished it on them! But it all fell on deaf ears because they did not believe they were in danger – for the moment. They thought they could keep order at home; for them the French disaster was merely the result of Louis XVI's weakness. Not one of them harbored any illusions about the poor man's chances of regaining power. Mercy confided to Kaunitz:

> Rather than remedying the real sources of the conflict, which are poverty and discontent in the provinces, all they ever talk about are the supposed plans of the foreign powers to overturn the new French constitution. Always on the lookout for what they take to be outside movements to rescue them, always without insight about the very real movements inside the country, they have not seen the growing anarchy. It has become

so rampant that we can be excused for thinking that we have arrived at that terrible point of *every man for himself.*

This harsh judgment, shared by all the rulers of Europe, kept them from intervening. Why embark on this hellish ship that was taking on water on all sides for the sake of two incompetents who understood nothing about what was happening to them? Nuñez, Madrid's ambassador, could barely hide the contempt behind the commiseration in his reports. He relayed to his superiors the desperate supplications of the queen screaming that she had "a knife at her throat." "The poor lady... it is such a pity to see her clutching at the thinnest branches within reach to keep from sinking straight to the bottom."

But if the distant Spanish cousin could turn a cold shoulder, Leopold, as Marie-Antoinette's brother, had to at least appear to be concerned about her fate. He called upon the indefatigable Mercy-Argenteau to transmit messages to his ex-pupil. Although now settled in Brussels where he was carrying out the less perilous and more gratifying functions of provisional governor, he was still in contact with her. Together, he and Leopold tried at all costs to prevent an escape, emphasizing the risks involved. But at the same time, Mercy wrote to Marie-Antoinette, "As long as one* is not in a safe place, no foreign intervention can be effective, the least appearance of one would even become frightfully dangerous." In other words, what they should do first was secure their own safety; help would follow! It was up to them to figure out how to leave Paris, find a safe haven, and secure for themselves "sufficient support, a few loyal troops, and enough to live on for two or three months." Then they would get help. But they had to realize that the king would still be jeopardizing his throne and perhaps even his life. Because, Mercy added, a decisive change in favor of the royalty can only be won by a civil war in which England would be happy to support the opposing side. Last argument: foreign powers "do nothing for nothing." Their aid comes at a price. The king of Spain coveted a piece of Navarre, and the king of the Piedmont a strip of the Var coast plus a few districts in the vicinity of Geneva. Leopold would ask for nothing, but he was willing to entertain the whims of the empire's princes in the Alsace for independence, reduced as they were by the abolition of feudal rights. In other words, it was better to temporize and wait for better times.

The letter dated 19 February 1791 in which Mercy brought up

---

* That is "you" – the king and queen.

the necessity of abandoning territories was intercepted. But the Assembly did nothing with it. Its intention was not to bring down the king; he was a passive but central figure in the constitution it was writing. It did, however, find confirmation of what it already knew: Marie-Antoinette was seeking help from Vienna. But the letter made it reassuringly clear that Austria would not budge without British approval. The deputies could carry on with their work unmolested as long as the king stayed put in Paris, and all indications were that no one had the means to help him leave. In any case, the Parisian masses' constant and obsessive fear of his fleeing was such that they became his volunteer jailers.

Marie-Antoinette understood what was going on: the Pontius Pilates of Madrid and Vienna were washing their hands of her. But she didn't respond as they'd expected. She refused to bend. It was blatantly obvious that the advice they kept hammering home was dictated by Austria's interests, not hers. Neither Leopold nor Mercy wanted to admit the torture she was going through in Paris, where with every passing day another shred of her raison d'être was torn from her. Any danger was preferable to this slow death punctuated by mob violence that directly threatened her life. She took up the challenge therefore and put their feet to the fire: if we manage to escape, what help will you give us? She was hoping that Madrid and Vienna would send troops to the borders to bolster the efforts of those French who rallied to the king. Were they willing, "*yes or no?*" she underlined with a furious stroke of the pen. Once again, all she got in reply were stalling tactics, for neither Leopold nor Charles IV wanted to risk a military intervention. Never, not even in the case of "pressing events" would Austrians cross the border to come to the aid of Louis XVI's troops. So be it, she would leave anyway. The preparations were already well under way. Nothing in the world would stop her now. She begged her brother for financial support – which would never come – and she asked him at least to deploy a few regiments to the Luxembourg border, thereby giving Bouillé an excuse to gather the troops on the French side in order to counter a supposed threat from Austria.

The emperor had to face the fact: the escape attempt would happen come what may. To justify it, Marie-Antoinette found the right tone of pathos. She wrote to Mercy on May 6th:

> Our situation is ghastly... we have only one alternative left here, especially since the 18th of April[*]; either we blindly do

___
[*]   The day when the crowds prevented the rulers from going to Saint-Cloud.

whatever the rebels demand or perish by the sword that is perpetually hanging over our heads. Trust that I in no way exaggerate the dangers. You know that as much as possible I was for a mild approach, patient and attentive to public opinion, but now everything has changed: either we perish or take the only course left to us. We are far from deluding ourselves into thinking that this course presents no danger; but if perish we must, it will at least be gloriously, and we will have done what we could to fulfill our duty, and preserve our honor and our religion... Everything requires us to leave and flee a place where by our silence and our impotence we are giving tacit support to such horrors*.

And Mercy's efforts to redirect the coming storm from the Austrian Low Countries toward the Alsace and Switzerland were to no avail. The fugitives were counting on going for the Luxembourg border**. At the beginning of June, baron de Breteuil, to whom Louis XVI had given complete control as his secret foreign representative, advised the emperor of their approach. He would have to deal with the situation as best he could. He said all the right things while waiting to fly to their aid in the improbable event that they succeeded. As for actually doing anything, that was another matter. Mercy wrote to him, "If they carry this plan out and we are notified in time, we can always send a few divisions of hussars to gallop around." In other words, the French rulers could count on no one but themselves.

Laying the groundwork

In December, shortly after having affixed his signature to the decree ordering the clergy to take the oath of allegiance to the secular constitution, Louis XVI agreed in principle to the escape. Without involving him in the preparations, they needed his input in making decisions, but just to be safe, he acted through intermediaries. When the marquis' son Louis de Bouillé, came to Paris shortly after Christmas to explain his father's plan, he was put in touch with Fersen, who transmitted his proposals to the queen, who in turn brought them to the king and reported back his responses. This was

---

* Allusion to the annexation in 1791 of the region around Avignon until then under papal control, and to the ensuing massacres.

** Luxembourg was then part of the Austrian Low Countries.

not the best way to weigh the pros and cons, but it was the only way they had.

First of all a destination had to be chosen. The king would have preferred Metz, a big city that could pass for a provisional capital if need be. But Bouillé, who knew the city well because he lived there, was against the idea; its inhabitants had largely been won over to the new way of thinking. He proposed Besançon, but it was considered too far away. The nearest possible town to Paris, Valenciennes, remained loyal and would have offered an ideal solution except for the fact that it was not under Bouillé's control but that of Rochambeau. A hero of the American war, he could not be counted on. They finally settled on the little citadel of Montmédy, which had no civilian population, was heavily fortified, and close to the Luxembourg border.

Bouillé's idea was for the king to travel separately from the queen and her children, going in light carriages by two different routes, but they did not want to be separated. Marie-Antoinette hoped that her sister-in-law Élisabeth would leave with the count de Provence who was also preparing to flee, but she refused to leave the king's side. Since they were planning to have the energetic and experienced officer the count d'Agoult join them, there was a total of six people, four adults and two children. Such a heavy load of passengers could not travel unnoticed. The itinerary had to be worked out. The most direct route went via Reims, but the king feared he would be recognized in the region where his coronation had taken place. To bypass the dangerous area they could take a little detour through the Low Countries, but Louis XVI did not want to contravene an Assembly decree threatening to depose him if he fled. They therefore decided to avoid Reims altogether by taking the more southern Metz road which passing through Meaux, La Ferté-sous-Jouarre, Montmirail, Châlons and Sainte-Menehould would lead them to Clermont-en-Argonne, from which point they would turn north.

The choice of route was tied to other important factors. Louis XVI agreed that it was necessary to leave Paris and the Ile-de-France secretly. The fugitives would get out of the capital in disguise and with false papers. But for safety's sake as well as his prestige, he wanted then to find military detachments to escort them along the way – starting from Montmirail, he specified. In order to avoid having to depend on the ordinary relay stations*, he wanted private ones to be prepared. Bouillé knew that such lavish

---

*   Horses had to be replaced about every four leagues, or 15-16 kilometers.

precautions would arouse peasant suspicions, and advised against it. It would be better to travel as ordinary people did. True to form, Louis XVI opted for half-measures that had the disadvantages of both alternatives. Fersen pleaded in vain for complete anonymity, which would allow them to pass "quite simply" without drawing any attention to themselves, at least until they got to the border zone where the presence of troops would surprise no one. But the king insisted, and Bouillé had to promise that cavalry detachments would intervene as soon as they'd passed Châlons. The first one, under the duke de Choiseul*, would await them at Pont-de-Somme-Vesle. However, private relay stations were out of the question. That would have appeared too suspect – except at Varennes, a little town off the beaten track that didn't have a relay station but where they would have to change horses all the same. But there, a hussar regiment would meet them. The baron Goguelat, an officer who served as the queen's secretary, was given the task of figuring out the itinerary and calculating the time involved. He took into account the fact that the heavily laden coach would move slowly. If they left Paris about midnight and made no unnecessary stops, the travelers could reach their destination within twenty-four hours. In Metz, all the marquis de Bouillé had to do was wait to find out when they had left Paris to put the plan into operation. At his end everything seemed to be in place. As long as the royal family left Paris safe and sound, all would go well.

That first part of the enterprise, by far the most hazardous, was the sole responsibility of Marie-Antoinette and Fersen. The Swede worked like the devil to get what was needed and fine-tune the details. He threw every penny he had into the undertaking and borrowed the rest. He got a few trusted friends on his side. Like himself, they were foreigners, to whom he imparted his passion for the royal cause, among them Eleonore Sullivan and her acknowledged lover the wealthy Craufurd, as well as the Franco-Russian baroness Madame de Korff. She was supposed to be returning to Moscow with her children and domestics, and it was in her name that he had a vast "berlin" coach custom made to take six people on a long journey.

Should the rulers be blamed, as they have often been, for not knowing how to make do with a simpler means of transport? Yes and no. Its size drew attention, but its exterior appearance was not out of the ordinary. The coach was of a dark green color; only the wheels and springs added a splash of yellow. The inside was a bit

---

* The former minister's nephew.

lavish, upholstered as it was all in white velvet, but it was built mostly with comfort in mind. It was to be their only home for twenty-four hours, for unlike ordinary travelers, they were not allowed to set foot on the ground. Thus the colorful details, like a whole battery of cookware, a folding table for dining, a stove for reheating the dishes, a set of toiletries that included tortoise-shell hairpins and a mirror, and of course the indispensable chamber pots. There was nothing particularly unusual about such a house on wheels for a lady going back to her far-off Russia, quite the contrary. But it did attract attention.

They have been much criticized for excessive insistence on decorum, judged inappropriate in fugitives. But if they were leaving as outlaws, they intended to arrive as sovereigns. They needed formalwear, spare undergarments, children's clothes – all of which Marie-Antoinette gathered together at some risk and in spite of Madame de Campan's observation that "the queen of France would find chemises and gowns everywhere she went." She filled up an entire trunk that she sent to one of her former servants living in Arras with the instructions that she was to send it on to an address she would be given. She would carry with her only the strict necessities, making do with only a few jewels, as most of her privy purse had been sent off to Brussels as a reserve fund. But she could not do without a hairdresser. The duke de Choiseul would bring one of the Léonard brothers to Montmédy with him in his carriage, along with the king's ceremonial robes and Madame Élisabeth's jewelry. Was it all a bit of a ridiculous and pathetic effort? Undoubtedly, since it failed. But it was touching also, as it bore witness to how desperately they wanted to regain their ruling status, which could not be separated from a show of wealth and prestige.

Who exactly would make up the group was not settled until rather late. The officer who was supposed to accompany them – either d'Agoult or another – gave his place to the marquise de Tourzel. She apparently asserted "the *rights of her position* never to leave Monsieur le dauphin." This insistence on form was inappropriate, according to Madame de Boigne, because it deprived the royal family of a military man, the only person capable of handling an unforeseen snag. The catastrophe, we are told, was the fault of that silly woman de Tourzel. But isn't it perfectly clear that there was a simple solution to the problem? The gentleman, a good horseman like all officers, could follow the berlin on horseback. Actually, it was the king who evicted him; he never liked being "governed." And God knows he had been for the last two years! His bondage was about to end. He still had to put his fate in Fersen's hands until they got to Bondy. But seeing freedom within reach revived his old impulses – for the rest of the journey he would be the master. This is clear from the fact that he chose as bodyguards, according to Louis de Bouillé, men who were "more loyal and devoted than vigorous or intelligent," in other words obedient followers. Fersen would call them "good for nothings." A certain Valory, the sharpest of the three, was chosen to run ahead of the coach from relay to relay to get the fresh horses harnessed. The other two, of impressive appearance, would ride at the doors of the berlin so as to frighten off any highway robbers, but they were unarmed, and one of them was so nearsighted that he lived in a perpetual fog. Not being familiar with the road and having received few instructions, they did not risk taking any initiatives. To the team was added, God knows why, two *femmes de chambre* for the royal children. They preceded their young masters in a cabriolet. There would be a lot to do during the relays – ten or eleven horses had to be changed each time*, so they were not exactly inconspicuous.

For the departure, they would take on false identities and be in disguise. Madame de Tourzel would be the baroness de Korff, accompanied by her two daughters, Aglaé and Amélie; to play the part the dauphin was fitted out in a dress. The king and queen, respectively the children's steward and governess, would have the very French and plebian names of Monsieur Durant and Madame Rochet. Madame Élisabeth, now Rosalie, was supposed to be a traveling companion. The three bodyguards dressed as valets were to be called Saint-Jean, Melchior and François. Marie-Antoinette chose clothing appropriate to each one's new station. Fersen got them passports with false names but otherwise in order. He would run all day long from pillar to post to acquire the necessary paraphernalia. And since he was the point man between Paris and Metz, he spent his nights ciphering and deciphering the letters to and from Louis de Bouillé, which were relayed by ordinary post but via friends. Everything was ready. The berlin, completely fitted out by March 12th, was awaiting its guests. In order to stock the provisions of food and drink, the Swede needed only to know the departure date.

The suspense lasted three and a half months. Although he agreed in principle, Louis XVI could not make up his mind to act. In March he was ill. Then they awaited the emperor's help, which finally in May Marie-Antoinette had to admit would not be forthcoming. Money was not to be had; it was deemed opportune

---

* Six for the berlin, two for the cabriolet and two or three for the bodyguards, depending on whether one of them was riding or seated atop the berlin.

to postpone departure until after early June when the two million due from the king's civil list were due to be paid. Then they found out that the woman in charge of the dauphin's commode was an informer, so no one could leave as long as she was in place. Then came the Pentecost celebrations, which would bring the peasants out in the villages they would pass through. In Brussels Mercy was calling on them to hang on, but in Metz Bouillé was getting impatient. Twice a week the agreed-upon program changed; there were orders, counter-orders and disorder. They became more and more liable to wagging tongues. The officers implicated in the plot risked their careers for sure, and perhaps their lives too. A thinly veiled ultimatum was submitted to the Tuileries: it would be the 20th of June or never; after that, "everything would be put an end to." Because of that "awful chambermaid" who had just left their service on the morning of June 20th, wrote Fersen, they could only leave that same night, a Monday, around midnight. Bouillé received this information as definitive, and on that basis adjusted his instructions of the previous evening, and sent out orders to the detachments that were to collect the fugitives. But it was clear that everyone involved had the greatest doubts about the success of such a dubious enterprise, which was no longer all that secret.

A successful exit

Some of his partners were skeptical about Fersen's confidence in his ability to get his charges out of Paris. But in an odd way, he was able to take advantage of the mass hysteria over a possible escape that had gripped the population for months. No one paid any attention to the chamber-pot servant's warnings about suspicious activities. So many had cried wolf so often that people stopped getting alarmed. The main thing was therefore to keep the actual date of departure top secret.

On the 20th of June 1791 all seemed quite normal at the Tuileries. Madame Royale applied herself to her lessons, the dauphin played. The king was shut up in his office, working. Only after dinner was Madame Élisabeth informed. In the afternoon Fersen came to bring the latest directives, receive Louis XVI's thanks, and try to console a weeping Marie-Antoinette. Afterwards she would show exemplary sang froid. About four o'clock in the afternoon she appeared with her children at a fashionable amusement park, la Folie-Boutin, and upon their return, she gave her orders for the following day. The king's brother and sister-in-law came to supper as usual, and were told that departure was set for that very evening. They were requested to immediately carry out their own escape plans, which were to bring them to the Low Countries via Valenciennes in separate vehicles and by different roads. And since circumstances required that the count make peace with his wife, he lifted the sanction against Marguerite Gourbillon and personally called upon the former reader to bring Marie-Joséphine to a safe place. At their end too, all was going well.

At about ten o'clock, Marie-Antoinette quietly left her card table to go wake up the children and get them dressed. The little boy, who was told that they were going to a safe place, asked for his sword, and was not happy when he was dressed in a long flowery dress. But since it was all just a game, he was quickly won over. Her mother had warned Madame Royale not to be surprised by anything, and she walled herself into an anxious silence. Marie-Antoinette went back to the gaming room just to be seen, and left quickly. Holding her daughter's hand and followed by Madame de Tourzel carrying the dauphin, she passed through the apartments of the marquis de Villequier, which had been deserted since their occupant's emigration, went down a private little inner stairway and landed in front of a closed and disused windowed door that led out to the Court of Princes*. She could see through the window that the door was not guarded, so she took the key out of her pocket and opened it. Everything went smoothly as they proceeded to the Royal Court where Fersen, disguised as a coachman, awaited them in a hired fiacre. She confided the governess and children to him and hastily went back upstairs by the same route to finish the card game. The Provences left about ten forty-five, as usual.

The spot where they would rendez-vous was a bit off the beaten track, Ladder Street, which was one of a warren of little streets bordering the north side of the chateau. Fersen went there after making a long detour along the embankment so as to avoid having to park for too long. The three adults had to see to their own exit. Élisabeth, who was never paid much notice, managed it easily. The king and queen could not do so until they pretended to go to bed for the night. Louis XVI had to endure the usual official bedding down ritual, which all the riots had not managed to kill off. He couldn't

---

* There were three courtyards on the east side of the Tuileries. The largest one, in the center, was called the Royal Court and led to the formal entrance. As a result, it was a very busy place; that's where carriages awaited and the guards were stationed. Two smaller courtyards surrounded it; to the north was the one containing the stables, and to the south the Court of Princes, which was infrequently used and little monitored.

wait for La Fayette to stop his endless chatter. Finally, he was able to slip out of bed, don a brown waistcoat, a fitted gray coat, and a wig that he topped off with a round hat. At that hour of the night, the Tuileries teamed with people; there was a constant coming and going. He blended easily into the crowds of service personnel just off their shifts. Taken in hand by his bodyguard Malden, he found his way to Ladder Street where his sister and children were waiting for him. Once the queen arrived, Fersen would drive them in the fiacre to meet the awaiting berlin.

Midnight struck, but there was no queen. She wanted to stay behind until she was sure everyone else had left. She knew she was late. She got undressed with her ladies' help, dismissed them, quickly got up again, put on a very simple dress, and hid her features under a large veiled hat. Carefully, she opened her apartment door. Catastrophe: a sentinel was perfunctorily pacing up and down the corridor. She waited for the man's back to be turned to slip out through an exit, hoping the sounds of his feet would cover her own. Mission accomplished. With no trouble she reached Villequier's apartment. At the door to the Court of Princes, an accomplice was waiting*. He gallantly offered her his arm; they were a couple out taking the air. A carriage rolled toward them preceded by torchbearers – it was Monsieur de La Fayette, commander of the National Guard! The two runaways got nothing more than a fright; they passed for a couple of nameless shadows. But what was frightening was that they lost their way. What to do but ask a Horse Guards orderly the way! They finally reached the fiacre just as the anxious king was about to go in search of her. It was half past midnight.

Fersen wanted to be sure that the berlin had left Craufurd's rented house on the rue de Clichy before going to the Saint-Martin tollgate where they were all to rendez-vous. Deliberately therefore, not through lack of familiarity with Paris, he made a detour, which alarmed the king and wasted a bit of time. There had been a wedding and the toll keepers were busy celebrating; they got through the gate without a hitch. However, the berlin was nowhere to be found. Fersen plunged into the darkness in search of it, and the king, his nerves on edge, pretended to do the same. They finally found the thing a bit further on, away from the lights and merrymaking of the wedding. Everyone was quickly bundled into it. The rented fiacre was ditched, and they galloped off towards the Bondy relay station. They had to hurry, for Valory, who was

---

* According to Fersen's *Journal* it was "M. d'A." (Monsieur d'Agoult?)

waiting for them there, had been instructed to set off a general alert if they were not there by three-thirty in the morning. In that case, one by one, having been advised that the attempt had failed, the military detachments would withdraw. Thank God, it was only three when the travelers reached Bondy. This was where Fersen had to take leave of them. He pleaded on bended knee to be allowed to follow them. Marie-Antoinette was crying. But Louis XVI would not budge. He thanked him profusely, but refused. People said that he did not want to arrive in Montmédy chaperoned by the man everyone assumed was his wife's lover. That's possible. But his refusal can also be explained by his determination to let no one else lead the operation once he thought he had escaped from his prison. "Farewell, Madame de Korff" Fersen shouted loudly for the sake of the coach drivers. He watched the heavy coach lumber off into the distance against the horizon that was glimmering with the first colors of dawn. The melancholy of leaving her was mixed with his pride at having accomplished his duty: the part of the enterprise that he had directed was a complete success. All he could do now was hope that the travelers remained vigilant. "Everything depends on speed and secrecy," he kept repeating. And Bouillé insisted that under no circumstances was the king to show himself.

We're free!

In the berlin, everyone began to breathe easy. Things were going according to plan; the road was straight, flat and dusty. It extended as far as the eye could see through the quiet Champagne region. Meaux was still slumbering when they relayed there. The Ferté-sous-Jouarre stop went off perfectly too. It was seven-thirty in the morning, broad daylight. They were hungry. The savory victuals provided by Fersen put the party in an excellent mood. Back in Paris, the valets who were supposed to awaken their master at seven must around then be alerting La Fayette, in charge of the chateau's surveillance. "Just now he must be feeling a right fool," declared the king with a hearty laugh, and the queen echoed his mirth. Reinvigorated, he cried, "You can rest assured that once my behind is back in the saddle, I will be a different man from the one you have seen up till now." They got through a succession of isolated relay stations, big farmhouses surrounded by open fields. The king ventured outside the vehicle to "relieve himself of a bit of water" and engage in a brief conversation about the harvest. Keeping secrecy? What harm was there in talking to an honest peasant who did not recognize him? And what about speed? They were seven hours ahead of any search party, for heaven's sake. If it occurred to him that his pursuers on horseback could go twice as fast as his berlin, he could take comfort in the idea that he would shortly be under the protection of Bouillé's hussars.

They came to a rather steep hill. They had to proceed on foot for a bit, just like ordinary people, to spare the horses. The fields were aflame with scarlet poppies; the children ran to pick some. They lingered a bit. At the top of the hill the berlin awaited them. Another relay station brought more conversation. One of the guards, Moustier, took the liberty of advising caution. "I don't think that's necessary any longer," said the king, "I feel my journey will be shielded from any incident." He could not conceive of himself as a fugitive. As soon as he felt out of harm's way, he instinctively reverted to the behavior of a ruler visiting his provinces. A bit before Châlons in Chantrix, where three houses on the side of the road made up the relay station, he showed himself again. Recognized this time by the son-in-law of the local postmaster, he was delighted to receive the man's respectful homage, and since it was dinner hour, he accepted to take some rest and refreshment at the inn with his whole family. The escape was becoming a family outing! When it came time to leave, the postmaster's son-in-law wanted to take the reins himself, and in his excitement he bumped into a bridge post. The horses faltered; harness leads were broken and had to be repaired. In all, a good hour was lost. As far as any secrecy was concerned, it is hard to believe that the coachmen would not pass along to their colleagues at each stop the amazing news: they were carrying the royal family!

They arrived in Châlons, which was considered the last dangerous stop. The king could not resist appearing at his carriage door. He was identified, but thanks to the support of the postmaster and the mayor, the big coach got away before some vigilant local patriot could rile up the citizenry. "We are saved!" sighed the queen, for there remained only 18 kilometers of open countryside to go before they would be welcomed into the arms of the duke de Choiseul and his forty hussars. Yes, they were four hours late, but in the good old days, soldiers were trained to wait a lot longer than that.

When the berlin arrived at the isolated Pont-de-Somme-Vesle stop, the king received a blow; he thought that "the earth had forsaken him." There was no sign of the promised horsemen. Having looked for them in vain, Valory ventured to ask the postmaster if he had seen any hussars in the vicinity. He replied, "Yes, I have, but they left about an hour ago!" The rendez-vous had been set for around one o'clock in the afternoon, by the latest two-thirty. It was now well past six o'clock. Choiseul, gnawed by anxiety, without news of any sort – not even the possible message of cancellation from Fersen – cannot be blamed for thinking either that the messenger had been caught, or that all those involved had been arrested. In either case, the king would not materialize. He therefore sent Goguelat and Léonard to his colleagues farther up the line to advise them that in all likelihood the "treasure" they were expecting would not arrive. He waited for another good while, then at about five-fifteen decided to lead his men back to their billets in Varennes by the quickest route. Of course, he should have left someone behind just in case. But he had never really believed in the success of this mission, which had so often been postponed and was in the hands of a sovereign considered to be the very personification of indecision. Since the whole business seemed a lost cause, and was being bruited about, he had to consider his own safety.

At Pont-de-Somme-Vesle, in the meantime, although they did not find their horsemen they did find horses, and no one prevented them from leaving. The same calm reigned in the humble Orbéval relay station, where no military detachment had been planned. But Sainte-Menehould, the following stop, was on tender hooks. The hussars had just passed through this big town, and they behaved arrogantly enough to get people's backs up. They were gone now, but replaced by dragoons, whose commander, the baron d'Andoins, was careful to treat them with more respect. Alas, the local National Guard was on the alert, and insisted on helping him get the "treasure" through. While waiting, the two groups of soldiers fraternized. Valory then showed up, and d'Andoins was just telling him that he could do nothing for him and that they must get the relay over with as soon as possible when the berlin finally rolled up. Forgetting all about her false identity, Madame de Tourzel leaned out the window and called out to d'Andoins in front of the curious onlookers. He whispered to her, "Things have gone wrong; I'm getting out of here; otherwise it will look suspicious. Leave! Hurry!" Oblivious to the danger, the king was having a chat with Valory at the window on the left side of the coach facing the relay station, watched by the postmaster Jean-Baptiste Drouet. When the horses were hitched up, they departed.

Drouet had no need to compare the face he could make out at the coach window with any coin or banknote to recognize the king; the coachmen had without any doubt already transmitted the news. It is of no use wondering what pushed him subsequently to intervene. We do not know whether he was motivated by revolutionary zeal or fear of getting grief for not denouncing the fugitives. For the moment he didn't make a move, however, and the passengers were able to leave Sainte-Menehould safe and sound. But it should be pointed out that, as Fersen feared, the presence of soldiers did more harm than good, because it threw the population into turmoil. The trials of the last two years had put them on edge. Louis XVI harbored deep illusions about the feelings of his good people; and they were only revived by the warm welcome the inhabitants of Chantrix had given him. What is more, not having had a military education, he had no idea of the problems involved in moving even small numbers of troops around, or of the difficulties their presence raised among country folk. He had even less of a clue about the dangers incurred by their extended stay, which inevitably entailed gossip and drinking, if not fraternization with the locals. He therefore underestimated the danger they were in.

The same scenario was repeated at Clermont-en-Argonne, where the count de Damas at first ignored Madame de Tourzel's beckoning but then approached the berlin with his finger to his lips. He heard the king declare, in a voice so loud that the queen asked him to lower his tone, that he had no need of an escort and learned from the governess that the children were getting impatient. No matter, he thought, for the horses were harnessed, and the royal family was departing without a hitch; they were only an hour from Varennes, where they would be at a private relay station under the protection of Louis de Bouillé with his two squadrons of hussars. But after their departure, a little argument degenerated into a riot, and the dragoons disbanded. Oblivious of it all, ensconced in their great big coach, the weary travelers fell asleep.

Varennes

It was eleven fifteen; the night was dark when the two coaches arrived at the entrance to Varennes. The town was not in ferment; it was asleep. But there was no relay station at the appointed place, and no sign of Valory, who had gone ahead as usual to get the horses ready. There wasn't a soul about. They stopped in front of the first house; the two bodyguards beat on the door, but there was no reply. The king came to assist them but was rebuffed. They could not go on. The coachmen's boss had asked them to return to Clermont as quickly as possible, and they refused to go any further. In any case, where would they go? A good half hour went by. Still nothing. No, that's not quite true, they did see a cavalryman stop to have a few words with the coachmen. Inside the berlin, they began to get jittery. When Valory came back empty-handed a bit later, having found neither the promised horses nor Bouillé's son and his hussars, Louis XVI explained the situation, "We have been double-crossed. A courier has just come by and has forbidden the coachmen to go any further; he has ordered them in the nation's name to unhitch the horses, adding that they were carrying the king."

Suddenly they heard the beating of drums. The city was roused from its sleep. The party could not linger there any longer. They managed to persuade the coachmen to take them down the principal thoroughfare towards the river. Valory on horseback took the lead; behind him was the cabriolet with the chambermaids, and the berlin took up the rear. Half way down the street, the convoy had to stop. The road went through a vaulted passage under the chateau's church with a closed gate blocking it. Two National Guardsmen carrying rifles were on duty. At this point an individual appeared who said he was the local district magistrate and demanded to see their passports. He went to examine them in a nearby inn and returned in a conciliatory mood. Their papers were in order. But around the passageway thick crowds were gathering, worked up by a man on horseback who had sounded the alarm. They knew him well; it was Drouet, the Sainte-Menehould postmaster. For an order had gone out from Paris to seek the fugitives along all possible routes. Bayon, the captain in charge of the Châlons road, quickly caught on that this was the one. Tired out, he stopped in Châlons, and had the bright idea to pass on the orders via the postmasters along the way. So it was that Drouet could declare, "This is the king, this his family. If you let them go, you will be guilty of treason."

At this point the tocsin sounded and the crowd grew restless. At a loss to know what to do, the authorities hesitated. In the absence of the mayor, who was a deputy in the National Assembly, the district magistrate named Sauce, a simple grocer and candle-maker, trembled at having to make a decision. Louis XVI got impatient and ordered the coachmen to proceed, but the guards at the gate threatened to fire, arguing that the city officials had to meet and discuss the matter. Louis XVI thought that by the time they did so, Bouillé's hussars would surely have arrived. He therefore accepted the Sauce family's offer of hospitality. Marie-Antoinette and her husband climbed the spiral staircase leading to the second floor, where the grocer hastily had a bedroom made up. For the children, there was a bed, where they were soon sound asleep; for the adults a table, some chairs and a bite to eat. An engraving of the king hanging on the bedroom wall invited comparison, but without his ermine-lined mantle or the diamond-studded hat, the stranger in a gray coat could continue to hide his identity. Marie-Antoinette, still pretending to be in the service of Madame de Korff, seconded her protests against their unjust arrest.

Wanting to do the right thing, Sauce called upon a local judge for some legal guidance. He arrived in the middle of a discussion that a group of puzzled men were having in the next room. Now this judge, whose parents-in-law worked in the queen's culinary service, had often seen the sovereigns at Versailles. "Oh, Sire!" he exclaimed, bending over and making an awkward bow. At this point, Louis XVI, relieved at being able to throw off a tiresome disguise, burst out, "Yes, that is right. I am your king. Sent to the capital amidst daggers and bayonets, I have come here amongst my faithful subjects in search of the peace you all enjoy; I can no longer stay in Paris without dying there along with my family." He spoke well, with such frank kindness that his listeners were moved. According to the town's official account, "In an outburst from his tender and paternal soul, he embraced everyone around him." Marie-Antoinette said nothing – at least nothing deemed worthy of being recorded by the local scribes.

The king in Varennes! What!? The news spread like wildfire and reached the nearby villages. Everyone wanted to come get a glimpse of him. They were all armed, as in the middle of the night in times like these no peasant would risk going out without his pitchfork or scythe, or at least a good strong club. Soon, keyed up by all the shouting, the tocsin that kept sounding and the beating of the drums, two to three thousand people were in the streets of the town, all of whose routes suitable for vehicular traffic had been closed off by the militia, notably the bridge over the Aire leading to the lower districts and the road to Stenay. It was impossible either to enter or leave by that route. It was not a hostile crowd, just curious, ready to shout out a hearty *Long Live the King!* As for sacrificing their lives for him, that was another matter. But what on earth was he doing in this obscure little village? He was emigrating, of course; people had been talking about it for a long time now. And everyone feared his departure. The patriots' dread was easily explained; they believed that without its hostage, the new regime would leave itself open to a merciless deployment of Austrian troops come to reestablish "despotism." But patriots were in a minority here; most of the inhabitants of rural France remained deeply attached to their king, whom they considered to be the living incarnation of their country's spirit. The thing is, the king's symbolic link to his kingdom was also a physical one, and implied his presence in the country. He was the father of all his subjects. If he went away, if he left the country, he was abandoning his people, he betrayed them, and thereby exposed them to the worst calamities. Louis XVI knew this, because he too felt the same visceral link – unlike Marie-Antoinette, who remained an outsider. Had he the right to violently disperse these people, as he actually could have done?

For the strangest thing on this strangest of all nights is that soldiers were there, and their leaders too, ready to serve. Not all of them. Bouillé had made the mistake of replacing his son Louis with another son François for what seemed an easy task. But François panicked when he realized all the errors that had accumulated, and took flight rather than try to repair them. However, at one o'clock in the morning Choiseul arrived, and Damas too, and Goguelat. Fresh hussars were billeted nearby. The officers were politely conducted to Sauce's house to get the king's orders. "All right then, Goguelat, when do we leave?" he asked. "Sire, when Your Majesty so desires," he was told. The city officials seemed to agree, and even offered an escort, provided the king only went as far as Montmédy; but they must wait till dawn. In the meantime the crowd had swollen. The berlin was hopelessly trapped. Damas and Choiseul suggested getting the royal family out of there, either on foot or horseback, between two rows of hussars. "Can you assure me that the queen, my son, my daughter or my sister will not be shot dead?" No, of course Choiseul could not assure him of that. Other solutions might be found. Goguelat proposed one to the queen, who was visibly ready to go all out. But she could only sigh, "It is up to the king to give the orders." He didn't. He was waiting for the marquis de Bouillé's army, which would surely show up at any minute, as his son must have alerted him by now. But did he really still believe that everything would be settled "without violence"?

While the king gladly accepted refreshment, the local councilors got more and more worried. Whatever they decided would be held against them. When Marie-Antoinette implored aid from Madame Sauce, the latter shot back as quick as a wink, "My God, Madame, I'm fond of my king; but indeed I like my husband too! He's the one in charge. I don't want anyone to pick a quarrel with him." What a difference between her and her mother-in-law, who fell on her knees in prayer before the royal children's bed, covering their hands in tears. From one generation to another the egalitarian way of thinking had seeped in. For the younger of the two women, the king was only a man like any other.

About half past five in the morning, the fretful Sauce was relieved of his anxieties: two important gentlemen arrived from Paris to take charge. Two messengers from the Assembly, Bayon and Romeuf, appeared in front of the king bearing decrees. "What, sir, is that you? I would never have believed it of you!" cried Marie-Antoinette to the second one, who had once been her equerry and could not hide his sorrow at having succeeded in catching up with them, as he had really hoped not to. The king read the decree enjoining all public officials, National Guardsmen and any troops on the scene to put a stop to his "abduction" and prevent his continuing. "France no longer has a king," he said simply as he placed the paper on the bed where his son and daughter were sleeping. Marie-Antoinette rushed at it in a rage and threw it on the floor screaming, "I do not want that thing to sully my children!" Amidst scandalized murmuring, Choiseul hastened to pick it up. At this point other friendly officers arrived, ready for action. Marie-Antoinette exchanged a few words with them in German, and learned that Bouillé had finally got word: "But will he ever get here in time?" She seemed to take favorably to the officers' plan to get them out of there by force. The king intimated to them that they should keep quiet and replied, "I am a prisoner; I have no more orders to give."

Word had gotten out however that he was waiting for Bouillé's troops to arrive. The latter's suppression of the Nancy uprising was so infamous that his name was enough to sew terror in every heart. No doubt about it: he would put Varennes to fire and the sword unless the king was got out of there immediately. Outside the slogan was given; the crowd chanted "Back to Paris! Back to Paris!" Having exhausted all their excuses for gaining time – breakfast, feeling unwell, digestive problems – the royal family resigned itself to departing. At eight o'clock they got into the berlin surrounded by cheers, escorted by a mass of two to three thousand armed men who wanted to make sure they took the right road home. When about nine the marquis de Bouillé finally arrived on the high ground above the town at the head of the Royal-Germans, the cortege was already far away. Should he catch up with them and attack? That was out of the question; the whole country had gone haywire. All he could do was turn around and gallop at top speed to Luxembourg to escape the warrant for his arrest. But the rumor that he was on the march to reach the king would continue for a long time and stir up the villagers and peasants along the way.

The return

It had taken them twenty-four hours to get there. It would take them four days to get back. Four hellish days. The first part of the trip, as far as Châlons, was sluggish but soon over with. The two vehicles trundled very slowly along in a cloud of dust, surrounded by hordes of people on foot. They were vigilant but devoid of hatred, which was lucky, for the royal family was without any protection. The heat rose along with the sun, making the stiflingly hot air inside the berlin hard to breathe. Along the way, one group of marchers was replaced by another, and the word was passed on: Stop the king from emigrating! Get him back to Paris, fast! Bouillé was on his way to rescue him! As a result, the unfortunate passengers were not allowed a pause. However, in Sainte-Menehould a lunch awaited them at the Golden Sun inn. They had not slept in two days. Could they not spend the night? The cheers that at first greeted the king's appearance on the balcony quickly turned into hostile cries: "Back to Paris!" They were obliged to leave again under a beastly hot sun. The pervasive jitteriness among the crowds turned their coach into a rolling bomb that the tiniest spark could set off. On the way, therefore, the local authorities, whatever their political stripe, endeavored with good grace or bad to avoid chaos. Châlons officials kindly sent ahead some National Guardsmen to escort them. They were not able, however, to stop the crowd from massacring the count de Dampierre as he was helping one of the chambermaids get back into her carriage after a stop, or from having them exhibit the victim's remains to the passengers.

They reached Châlons around midnight. The city officials gave them a warm welcome, with testimonials and flowers for the queen, as well as an excellent supper and comfortable bedrooms. But the next day, the feast of Corpus Christi, mass was interrupted by protests. The royal party had to make a quick getaway. A man spat in the king's face. The queen and Madame Élisabeth were jostled, and their skirts torn; they wept while the dauphin screamed in terror.

Épernay was hostile, and offered them only the strict minimum. They had to slice through a furious crowd calling for their blood in order to get to the Hôtel de Rohan, where they were served a nasty lunch. The closer they got to the capital, the more the atmosphere degenerated; insults and threats were repeated. The Assembly was notified and got nervous. The majority of the deputies were moderates, and they in no way wanted to see the party massacred by a mob. Three of them were chosen to go take control of the situation and ensure their safety. A mix of delegates was carefully chosen: one royalist, the marquis de Latour-Maubourg; one veteran revolutionary who had been converted to the constitutional monarchy, the Grenoble lawyer Barnave; and another lawyer, Pétion, an extreme leftist who didn't try hard to hide his ardent egalitarian convictions. They were accompanied by a modest escort led by the National Guard officer Mathieu Dumas.

A military courier announced the delegates' arrival to the passengers. Help at last! The two groups met in front of the Split Oak farm on the banks of the Marne, near the village of Boursault, as crowds of onlookers watched. The three delegates had a keen sense of their own importance and wanted to observe protocol scrupulously. They were completely taken aback by the queen and her sister-in-law, who rushed to their coach doors with anguished cries. They entreated them, "Oh, gentlemen, gentlemen!" Marie-Antoinette grabbed the hand of Latour-Maubourg whom she knew well, and called him by his name. After a moment's hesitation, she also extended her hand to Barnave, but barely brushed that of Pétion. Madame Élisabeth immediately declared that the king had no intention of leaving France. He quickly confirmed what she said. The queen grasped that their three bodyguards were in danger of falling prey to the crowd's fury and added: "No misfortune must come of this. The people who accompanied us must not be victimized, let no one try to take their life!"

The deputies would join the royal family for the rest of the way back to Paris, but this brought up a novel little problem of protocol: what about seating arrangements? The Assembly's delegates, who had been given full authority on such an important mission, did not want to be upstaged. However, Latour-Maubourg obligingly consented to join the chambermaids in their fiacre. The other two would ride in the royal coach. But the king insisted that they not take the place of any of his party. They would all just have to pile in together. Barnave slipped into the forward-facing seat between the king and queen, and she took the dauphin on her lap. Facing them, Pétion sat between Madame Élisabeth and Madame de Tourzel, with Madame Royale awkwardly perched on her knees. In such tight quarters tension ran very high. The two deputies, who had very set ideas about the "tyrant" and his arrogant wife, were completely disarmed by the helplessness of these poor, dirty people who were exhausted and terrified, and what is more, welcomed them as their saviors. They were all the more uneasy as they were from two opposing parties, the Republican Pétion keeping a close eye on Barnave, whom he suspected of treason. The two sisters-in-law noticed that if they joined together and played their hand right, they could make the best of a bad situation.

The silence was getting hard to bear. Madame Élisabeth broke it by standing up bravely for her brother, and Marie-Antoinette concurred. Their political views did not win over the two lawyers, who came back with a defense of the Assembly's actions. Pétion found the queen's remarks quite superficial: "no idea she came out with was well thought out or of any substance." She would have liked them to believe her to be of some substance, and courageously defended her position, but her excessive insistence did not convince them. It was not the group's courage that touched them, but their ordinariness. They seemed for all the world like any middle-class family. "I found an air of simplicity about them that I liked," Pétion testified, "They were no longer playing their royal roles; there was a domestic ease and affability about them... The queen let the prince dance on her lap. Madame, although more reserved, played with her little brother; the king seemed rather to enjoy it all." The dauphin's playfulness put the finishing touches to the miracle. He went from one deputy's lap to the other, and settled into Barnave's. He played with his shirt ruffles and belt, asking him a thousand questions, and proudly showed off his new-found knowledge in deciphering the Jacobin motto on his buttons: *Live free or die*. Barnave's most recent biographer, Pierre d'Amarzit, states that the young lawyer thought he could see tears in the queen's eyes.

Pétion's obvious boorishness, aggravated by his political prejudices, threw into marked contrast the attractive, elegant and delicate appearance of Barnave, who was from an excellent bourgeois family in the Dauphiné region. It was clear to Marie-Antoinette from the beginning that he was the more accessible of the two. So it was with him that she deployed her famous charm, whose power she had so often exercised. Seeing that he was trying to figure out who their bodyguards were, she enjoyed the impish pleasure of naming them. It was he who blushed for having dared look for Fersen among them. At one point he blurted out, "Was Monsieur de La Fayette in on the secret of Their Majesties' departure?" "Certainly not," she shot back with a laugh, "I even joked with Madame de Tourzel about what a face little Mister Blondie Boy would pull once he found out we were gone." On the defensive, Pétion played up his importance, pretending to know it all. He stated that when leaving the Tuileries the fugitives had got into a hired carriage driven by a Swede. What was his name? But the queen answered deftly with a spirited: "It is not my custom to know the names of hired coachmen." The king took part in the conversation by pouring rounds of orangeade for everyone. The deputies kept an eye on the road, ready to take action if necessary, and thus Barnave was able to intervene forcefully to stop some hotheads from attacking the bodyguards. A bit farther on, seeing that a priest who was blessing the berlin was about to be lynched, he leaned so far out that Madame Élisabeth had to hold on to him by his coattails. "Are you not Frenchmen?" he cried, "Nation of honest men, have you become a bunch of murderers?" They stopped in their tracks. "I thank you, sir," the queen said simply. From then on there was nothing he wouldn't do to protect her.

Lulled by the swaying of the coach, they eventually fell asleep. Pétion, noticing that Élisabeth's head had slipped onto his shoulder, indulged in the gratifying fantasy that if by some wizardry the entire world disappeared around them, she would abandon herself to him "as nature intended." This of course was a crude projection of his own feelings, which he could not admit to. At the Dormans stop, where a carefully prepared reception was awaiting them, Louis XVI thought he could win back some of his lost dignity at his expense. The sovereign found that Pétion had helped himself to a seat at a table he thought should be for everyone, to the right of what was meant to be the queen's seat. He roundly reproached him, sending him back to the adjoining room where the two others had the good taste to take their places. He would have done better to use him more gently: the boor was less influential than Barnave at the moment, but his day would come.

They slept badly because of what Madame Royale would later call the din of the mobs, and Pétion the joy of the masses. It's also probable that Marie-Antoinette's sleep was troubled by the burning disappointment of yet another missed opportunity. For when they were about to retire for the night, on behalf of his family, the innkeeper's son-in-law proposed an escape plan. All of them could leave through the back yard, from which a staircase led down to the river. By boat and then harvest cart, going from brother-in-law to cousin and farmhouse to farmhouse, they could reach the border in complete safety. The queen was very tempted, but Louis XVI said no: "He was counting on his good city of Paris, which he had left despite himself and because of false insinuations." Here we can begin to see the outline of the person he was to become.

In La Ferté-sous-Jouarre, it seemed like the good old days. At the mayor's residence Marie-Antoinette asked where the mistress of the house was, and the lady in question, Madame Reynard de l'Isle, who wanted to do the honors of the house, was very moved. She replied, "Wherever Her Majesty goes, there is no other mistress than she." On the other hand, in Meaux the new bishop, who had taken the oath, was not terribly welcoming. But the idyll between the fugitives and the deputies continued. Since this was after all now an egalitarian society, they switched places in the coach. Marie-Antoinette never missed a chance to have a little tête-à-tête with Barnave, while Élisabeth monopolized Pétion, who forgot all about spying on his colleague. As they got nearer to Paris, however, they were recalled to harsh reality. The crowd that had become ever denser was now downright menacing. The memory of October 6th haunted the sovereigns. They did not want to make another entrance into Paris like that one, with the heads of their bodyguards waving over them like standards. Dumas suggested letting the three men escape or be disguised as National Guardsmen, but standing on her dignity, the queen protested, "The king must come back to Paris the way he left: with his family and his people." So three National Guardsmen were sent to join them on top of the coach to help save their lives.

In point of fact, the convoy bypassed central Paris altogether. To be on the safe side, they circumvented the city along the outer boulevards so as to avoid the narrow little streets of the center, and reached the Tuileries through its western gardens. From Bondy to the Pantin gates the abuse, insults, threats and the calls for their death hurled at them were a foretaste of the ferocity of popular outrage that was to come. At times Dumas could hardly extricate the berlin from the tide of humanity beating on its doors. La Fayette was waiting at the tollgate, flanked by his entire military staff. His troops were lined along the boulevards to contain the crowd with their guns facing down at their sides – something of a dishonor guard. As the cortege passed, no one doffed his hat; a deadly silence had replaced the booing, for dozens of signs had been posted on the city's walls that promised, "Whoever applauds the king shall be beaten; whoever insults him shall be hanged." And this almost unearthly silence was more striking than any howling.

They re-entered Paris via Étoile, the Champs-Élysées and Louis XV Square, all teaming with people. At the Feuillants Terrace in the Tuileries where the rulers had to leave the coach, a scuffle broke out, and Dumas had to get reinforcements to clear the way for the three bodyguards. The baron de Menou carried the screaming dauphin to safety, and Marie-Antoinette was being lifted along rather than walking to the chateau. Once they were safely inside the king's apartments, it took all her strength to smother the rage that was devouring her, but she managed one last quip with Barnave, "I must confess that I never expected we would spend thirteen hours in a coach together." Louis XVI received dispassionately the flowery phrases intoned by La Fayette, who had all the same removed his hat. But when the latter asked "Has Your Majesty any orders to give me?" he shot back a stinging reply, "It seems to me that I am more at your orders than you are at mine." Were these words actually stated, or were they adapted for the purpose? At least all of these "historic remarks" have the merit of perfectly conveying the atmosphere that produced them.

To Pétion's stupefaction, court rituals were automatically resumed. Louis XVI was taken in hand by his bedchamber valets for the bath he badly needed. The deputy wrote, "Seeing the king, one could not have guessed what he had just been through; he was as phlegmatic and calm as if nothing had happened. All of a sudden, he was in his kingly mode again." The queen had disappeared. When Assembly delegates arrived the next day to get the sovereigns' version of the journey, she had the message relayed that she was in her bath. Thus, the following day she was able to declare without fear of contradicting her husband: "The king desiring to depart, nothing would have prevented me from following. And what made up my mind was his positive assurance that he had no intention of leaving his kingdom." The little Varennes junket had to be forgotten about, and quickly.

What would they have done at Montmédy?

For more than two centuries now people have been desperately seeking the one little detail responsible for toppling an enterprise that was so close to succeeding. The protagonists themselves did so, with the primary purpose of placing the blame on others. It would seem an easy task, given that among the numerous errors that piled up and contributed to the disaster, no one has any trouble finding those that buttress their version of events. At every stage of the journey, it is easy to show that if they had done or not done this or that, then everything would have gone quite smoothly. Certainly, there were people more culpable than others: Fersen, who ordered a vehicle that was too flashy; Goguelat who perhaps underestimated how slowly it would move when he was calculating the time needed; Choiseul, surely, who left no one behind in Pont-de-Somme-Vesle; and above all the young François de Bouillé, who thinking that the trip had been cancelled, neglected to have a relay station at the entrance to Varennes then lost his head and warned his father too late. But none of them lacked excuses. The reason for the failure resides above all in the three months of wavering before the departure, which robbed the participants of faith in its success. This wavering was the king's doing, just like the errors of judgment he haplessly repeated along the way, and his subsequent refusal to use force to pry open the trap they fell into at Varennes. It was Louis XVI himself who was responsible for the failure. It's worth asking why.

The entire problem resided in the ambiguity over the enterprise's final outcome. We recall that on July 14th marshal de Broglie when asked about a possible flight to Metz had replied, "Yes, but what will we do there?" The question was now in sharper focus: what would they have done at Montmédy? And it appears that each participant had a different answer to that question.

Louis XVI's answer is well known. He drew up a long statement about it before leaving Paris. We find it again in a memorandum Marie-Antoinette sent a bit later on to her brother. The marquise de Bombelles summed it up very well: "He wanted to hark back to the June 23rd 1789 declaration by which he fulfilled the nation's wish expressed in its mandates during the Estates General; it restricted his power but at the same time assured it, and reassured the people; for despotism could never return to France, and in all fairness, it is not desirable. The king therefore did not want to conquer his kingdom with the help of armed forces from abroad; he wanted to make an impact on his people and deal with them." In order to do that, he had to free himself from the pressure of the Parisian people's committees and recover his freedom. He was hoping for massive support.

However, none of the conspirators who helped get him out of Paris gave this plan the least credibility. How could a plan that had seemed less than sufficient on 23 June 1789 find any credibility two years later? There was a lot of wishful thinking involved. "I don't have a clear notion of what His Majesty is proposing," said Breteuil. Later Bouillé would write: "I never understood what measures the king would have taken in Montmédy." Everyone shared Fersen's conviction that the king would only regain his authority at the cost of a civil or foreign war, or both. What would they do at Montmédy? For the military man Bouillé, the answer was *nothing*, because nothing could be done there. The place hadn't the means to provide for royalty. Even if the local gentry, as the abbé de Courville planned, could welcome the royal family in the border town of Thonnelle, it couldn't house all the personnel necessary for governing and diplomatic negotiating. Besides, the army could not be counted on; Bouillé knew that better than anyone. As we have seen, the French troops had largely been won over to the Revolution. As for foreign mercenaries, if they were not paid, they simply up and left. There wasn't the financial wherewithal to hold the place. In his eyes, Montmédy was just a steppingstone via Longwy or Virton to Luxembourg, for which he had already laid the groundwork. For their part, the politicians Fersen and Breteuil had understood that Leopold II would never let Austrian troops set foot in France. How could his soldiers ever help Louis XVI if he didn't leave France?

The truth is that everything was in place for the Austrians to receive the French rulers for a brief time. This is clear from the fact that, having received some prematurely optimistic news, Leopold II for a few weeks thought that the escape had been successful and sent his sister letters that leave no doubt about where they planned to go. July 2nd: "I first received the post with the news of your happy flight from Paris, then that of your arrest at Vannières [*sic*] and lastly of your deliverance. I now await with the greatest impatience news of your arrival in Luxembourg." And in a *post-scriptum*: "As soon as I am sure of your arrival either in Brussels or at my home, and I know what your intentions are, I will provide whatever you need to execute them." And again on July 5th: "Finally, thanks be to God, I have received news of your happy arrival in Luxembourg, and that the king is safe in Metz." He felt he must make offers of help, but they were too broad and vague to be believable given his prior reticence. "Everything I have is yours, money, troops, everything," he said, and promised to get all of Europe interested in their fate. What would he have really done if the reports had been true? It's hard to see how his view of European stability would have changed for all that. Without the support of Austrian troops, Metz would quickly have become untenable. The fugitives would have wound up in Luxembourg. The emperor would undoubtedly have given them a meager pension allowing them to lead the sad existence of exiled rulers. But at least they would have been safe.

All of this raises two questions.

The first one has often been asked, "Did Marie-Antoinette consciously orchestrate, unbeknownst to her husband, a plan aiming to get him to go abroad with or without his consent? The answer to this question generally depends on the biographer's sympathy or lack of it, the result of which is to show her as either entirely innocent or entirely guilty. There are even those who have gone so far as to claim despite all plausibility that she considered abandoning her husband and declaring herself regent in the name of her son. We can conclude nothing from the fact that she sent jewelry, funds and luggage to her sister, Fersen and Mercy in Brussels. It was the only way to safeguard them. More worthy of note is Goguelat's testimony, although it came later on: "It is true that at the hour of his furtive departure, the king did not suppose that his journey would end beyond the border. But the queen would have certainly brought him to where she deemed it appropriate." However, that does not prove that she was already at their departure determined to leave the country.

A more nuanced hypothesis seems plausible. In all probability, the escape organizers believed that Louis XVI could not on his own, through a simple appeal to the country, regain the authority of which he had been gradually stripped over the previous two years. But they needed Marie-Antoinette to believe he could, for she, they knew, was the only one who could convince him to leave. Why would they show her how pessimistic they were and thereby make the task more difficult? She was no more keen than her husband to join the pack of émigrés whom she detested. What she wanted more than anything was a plan that satisfied her taste for actions of some panache. In letters whose sincerity cannot be doubted she said she was confident; she expressed her faith in Louis XVI's ability to gather together those of good will. To the duchess Fitz-James: "To get out of this crisis, he must dazzle people with the force and courage of his enterprise." To Mercy: "Our safety and our grandeur will stem from removing ourselves from this situation; I hope not to leave the credit for it entirely to others." For her, Montmédy was a mere stopgap measure. Luxembourg, very close by, would be a solution if need be. But, she wrote to Mercy on April 14th, it was in the Alsace that they would envisage settling if their faithful did not manage to win the capital back for them. In short, it seems that far from trying to force her husband into exile, she generally shared his illusions about their alternatives.

The second question on the other hand is rarely posed. It concerns Louis XVI's attitude before and during the journey. People speak of irresolution, weakness or apathy, and leave it at that. One thing is incontestable, however; he was telling the truth when he said that he did not want to leave France. He had poured over Hume's *The History of England*, which he read in English. As has often been pointed out, he had been struck by the fate of Charles I who was beheaded in 1649 during the English civil war. He also read in it that during the second revolution of 1688, James II lost his throne when he fled. He therefore also surely had thought a lot about the saying that a sovereign who leaves his kingdom loses it.

His supposed lack of resolution in the months preceding the escape attempt was above all a reflection of his malaise. We have seen that he often refused to leave. It was only in December that he agreed to the plan Marie-Antoinette had been working on for several months. All right, he would go to Montmédy to organize his rapprochement with his people. He consented to it after the decree forcing the priests to take the oath, but he did so with a heavy and despairing heart. At the end of February with his aunts' misadventures in Arnay-le-Duc, he saw that Paris had no monopoly on revolutionary unrest. He began to have doubts. Would the French countryside rally to him as quickly as he hoped? In other words, could not such an initiative spark a civil war? It was in March, let's not forget, that he fell seriously ill, perhaps in response to his woes. But it was no longer possible to retreat without jeopardizing all those who had taken enormous risks to ready his flight, from whence came all the terrible pressure on him to finally set a date.

Once they fixed a date, his composure and self-mastery were exemplary. He left the Tuileries behind with no difficulty. And the farther they got from the capital, the more he was infused with the elation they were all feeling, which is understandable: they were safe; they were free. This euphoria led to some careless mistakes in timing and their anonymity. The favorable welcome of those who saw and recognized him gave him the hope that his appeal would be heard. After Châlons, he wanted to travel openly as the king, despite the advice to the contrary. He was no doubt preparing to do so as soon as he had the escort that was supposed to be waiting for him at Pont-de-Somme-Vesle. But from there on, everything went to pieces. He learned in Sainte-Menehould and then in Clermont that neither the people nor the troops were necessarily on his side. Yes, his vehicle passed unmolested. But he suspected that the rallying of the masses he was counting on might not materialize. Now the journey had become what it really had always been: an attempt to get his family to safety.

In Varennes he saw his last hopes compromised, and he had, tragically, to face his conscience. He could, as each of his officers proposed, get the hussars to clear the road before the berlin or force his passage through on horseback under their protection. Each time he refused, preferring to wait, more on principle than through fear of not being successful. He acted upon his moral and religious convictions – he would not give the order to shed blood. There was no doubt some casuistry on his part in passing the burden onto Bouillé, who did not share the same scruples. He played that last card through love of his family. But people's behavior once the messengers arrived from the Assembly removed any remaining political illusions he might have had: it was not by some proclamation launched from Montmédy or anywhere else that he would regain the love of his subjects. He had the choice of either going abroad or letting himself be brought back to Paris, for better or worse – and he knew now what the worse would be.

What would he have done if Bouillé had arrived in time to deliver him? The question cannot be answered of course, but witnesses attest to two possible outcomes. Perhaps, having taken the full measure of his impotence, he might have let himself be brought to Luxembourg by Marie-Antoinette and her rescuers, as Goguelat supposed. But perhaps on the other hand, having sent his wife and children to safety there, he would have gone back to Paris to take his place among his people. That was in any case what he claimed after his forced return – excuse with the benefit of hindsight, one might protest. But with this king, who did not reason the way other people did, it is not impossible that he was telling the truth.

CHAPTER 20

SPIRALING DOWNWARD

"We are alive, that's all I can say," Marie-Antoinette is to have remarked to Madame Campan from deep within her bath where she endeavored to wash away the stains of Varennes. On June 28th she managed to send a note to Fersen, "Be reassured: we are alive." She added: "The Assembly chiefs seem to want to go easy. Speak to my relations about possible steps from abroad; if they are afraid, come to terms with them." In a similar vein on June 29th she wrote in a second note, "I am alive... How worried I am about you, and how heavy-hearted I am for all you must have suffered, having no news of us! Will the heavens allow this to reach you? Do not write to me; it would expose us, and above all do not come back here under any circumstances. They know it was you who got us out of here; everything would be lost if you were to reappear. We are under surveillance night and day, but I give it no notice... Put your mind at rest; nothing will happen to me. The Assembly wants to treat us gently. Adieu... I shall no longer be able to write to you...*"

She was correct about the Assembly: they very much wanted to help them out of a tight spot. Compared to what the hostile reentry into Paris seemed to promise, they were not doing too badly. At least it appeared that way. They would get a year's reprieve, but it came at a high price. They were dragged into a downward spiral that would bring them from resistance to capitulation and finally crush them. And all Marie-Antoinette's efforts to hold back the tide would only lead to hastening their ruin.

---

* The suspension marks in this extract represent lines that were crossed out. And she would manage to write to him quite a lot subsequently, as we'll see.

Forget Varennes?

What was to be done with the king, deserter from the new regime? For the Assembly, his flight was a bad blow. The deputies were putting the finishing touches on the definitive text of the constitution before distributing it. They had already set up electoral procedures to designate those who were to exercise legislative power alongside the monarch's executive power. If he left them in the lurch, they would have to start from square one.

Up until then no one, or nearly no one, dared envisage a republic for France. Republics were for small states where each citizen could participate directly in the management of public affairs. The recent example of the United States did not contradict this dogma, since they were only a grouping of autonomous little republics. Among French revolutionaries, therefore, there was a consensus for a constitutional monarchy. In point of fact, so limited were Louis XVI's powers that what they called by this name was nearly a republic in any case. But by keeping him in place in his role as figurehead, the regime was able to unite the French, the immense majority of whom were very attached to the person of the king, who had since time immemorial been the living incarnation of the country and guarantor of its unity. They wanted to build something like the monarchies that have survived in Europe today. But for Louis XVI and Marie-Antoinette, such a system was downright inconceivable; it was intellectually unfathomable and morally reprehensible. The Assembly believed however that it had brought them to heel. Their defection obliged the deputies to face the political problem that they were trying to avoid. The desire for a republic was in the air. Demands for one were rising virtually everywhere.

However, the idea of doing without a king was heavy with potential conflicts. In two years the make-up of the Assembly had greatly changed, and the members' positioning in what was not yet called the semicircle* but where already a right and left wing were emerging, had shifted somewhat. Emigration had already trimmed the ranks of the Ancien Régime as well as the supporters of an English-style monarchy. Those who remained took to abstaining, as

---

* The hall in the *Manège* where the Assembly met was a very long rectangle, but the president's office had been placed in the middle of one of its long sides, with the speakers platform facing it.

they were being paid no heed in any case. Political power was in the hands of the constitutionalists, then led by a triumvirate composed of Alexandre de Lameth, Adrien Duport and Barnave, the best orator around since the death of Mirabeau. Liberal noblemen or men of the well-to-do bourgeoisie, they had thrown themselves into the Revolution with the ardor and idealism of youth. Barnave was one of the pioneers who in the Dauphiné region advocated the fusion of the three estates. During the troubles following July 14th, he had silenced those who were indignant about the Bertier and Foulon murders instead of crying over the people's blood being shed: "Was their blood as pure as all that?" he had asked. He had changed his tune. Now, whatever blood was shed filled him with dread.

For even if they still held the Assembly, the constitutionalists were under heavy pressure from their left wing. Since the spring, war was raging between them and the more or less open advocates of more social equality. This opinion had strong backing in the clubs. The most powerful of them, the Jacobins, had branches all over France, which spread their slogans. The triumvirs were Jacobins, but they did not hold sway over the clubs. It was not difficult for the little group surreptitiously led by Robespierre to condemn the bourgeois nature of a constitution that restricted the right to vote to those wealthy enough to pay certain taxes. This extreme left wing got support from another more popular club called the Cordeliers that had newspapers – amongst them Marat's sadly famous *Ami du Peuple* – and above all, from soldiers. The Revolution won over the peasantry by doing away with feudal rights and the tithe. But it had done nothing for those who had never paid taxes because they had never had a penny to their name. With the economy falling apart, the Parisian streets were filling up with workers without work and craftsmen without customers who were open to any call to action. Because they had nothing to lose, they were ready to go blow off steam on the *Manège* speakers platform or scream for blood at the Tuileries windows. The triumvirs feared that this radical egalitarian ideology verging on anarchy would lead to trouble and strife, and on a more prosaic scale, to a power struggle that could jeopardize their position. They tried therefore to curb this movement that could so easily get out of hand, sweeping not only them away but also their precious constitution, which for them was the culmination of the Revolution. They had got what they wanted; it was now time to "terminate the revolution" and solidify its gains. This point of view was shared by La Fayette who, as the head of the National Guard*, held military power in the capital.

They therefore greatly needed the king. La Fayette's first concern on learning of the escape was to fetch him back. He had an added reason for wanting to do so: since he was in charge of surveillance at the Tuileries, he could be accused of being an accomplice. Once they were back, the Assembly tried to gloss over the whole episode. However preposterous the idea, they claimed with a straight face that Louis XVI had been "abducted." The king had had nothing to do with it, the guilty parties where the conspirators who had grabbed him from the Tuileries to bring him to Montmédy against his will. The term abduction had been used with regard to various escape plans that were proposed to him, but it was known that he had always refused. Despite the protests from the left – or perhaps because of them – a great number of deputies were willing to rally around this absurd fiction, because it avoided the necessity of posing the redoubtable issue of a republic. But then something amazing happened: on the president's desk someone placed a longwinded manifesto containing a declaration from the king that he had decided to leave because he could no longer tolerate the abuses of power to which he was subjected, and that all of the acts "emanating from him during his captivity" – that is, since October 1789! – were null and void. He had been mulling over this text for months; Marie-Antoinette in the beginning of February had already outlined its main themes to Mercy.

There is no better indication than this of just how misguided Louis XVI's reactions were. It was simply foolish to leave such a document where it could be found, rather than keep it under wraps and wait to issue it from a safe place. And such inappropriate language! Much too long and dry, too technical in its criticism of the Assembly's reforms, the text was sadly lacking in energy, passion or hope. It was so boring that historians don't quote it *in extenso*. It was above all an exercise in self-justification, pitiable and pathetic given the circumstances. Instead of launching a vigorous appeal to the country capable of galvanizing energies and winning over the undecided, he fiercely tried to justify his flight. Was it a good idea to list all the attacks on his authority and the insults he received, from the most serious to the most ludicrous – like having to stay in a chateau that did not provide all the necessary comforts?

---

* The National Guard was a bourgeois militia, recruited from among the "active" citizens, that is, those paying a minimum of taxes. Very favorable to a constitutional government, it disapproved of street violence.

Everyone knew he had been humiliated. To remind everyone of all he had suffered in silence was simply to broadcast his weakness. The document had nothing of a political manifesto about it; it sprang from the author's religious convictions. It revealed on the one hand his hope that the wrongs he had heroically suffered would be counted as meritorious when he went to meet his Maker, but also his guilt for not measuring up, and for fleeing his situation.

The Assembly's first reaction to the document was one of consternation, but the deputies breathed more easily at the end. It concluded by expressing how much the king would like to forget the wrongs done to him and take his place among his people again once a constitution he could freely accept reestablished order and security. They had to admit that he had addressed the main issues: he was not about to join the émigrés in counter-revolution, and was not dismissing out of hand the idea of a constitutional monarchy. They decided to remain silent about this declaration – after all it was just a harmless draft, not countersigned by any minister! And they pretended to believe that an accommodation could be reached. As for Louis XVI, he no longer had any choice. It was clear from the conversations in the berlin on the way back to Paris that he had to play along with the moderates. The officials sent afterwards to question him had purposely asked him vague questions, which he had answered just as evasively. Marie-Antoinette stuck to her line about just being the wife. According to the texts voted in, the person of the king was inviolable. Besides, what had he done wrong? Why should he not have the right, like everyone else, to go about freely within his country? The left's vigorous protests could not undo him. But beyond the question of his kingly inviolability, the ideological implications of the debate were brought out into the open. On the Assembly floor Robespierre strongly attacked Barnave, who replied that everything that could be torn down had been torn down, and it was time to stop. "If the Revolution goes a step further," he said, "it cannot do so without danger; as regards liberty, the first danger it could lead to would be the annihilation of the monarchy; as regards equality the first thing it could bring about would be an attack on property." His remark was met with thunderous applause. Fear of violence, coupled with the keen desire on the part of the provincial deputies to return home after two years in the capital, won the day. The king was absolved. This constitution had to be written with all possible haste and everything returned to normal!

But this fleeting consensus barely disguised the deep party antagonisms. The Jacobin club was too heterogeneous and therefore broke up. The moderates left en masse and set up a new club in the former convent of the Feuillants, from which they took their name. Among the remaining Jacobins, republican convictions were openly declared. Vanquished in the political arena, the patriots sought their revenge in the streets. The citizens were called to the Altar of the Country on the Champ-de-Mars to sign a petition calling for the king to be deposed. On Sunday the 17th of July the operation started out calmly, but in the evening strife broke out – apparently unexpectedly*. Called in to restore order, the National Guards were jeered by the demonstrators and fired into the crowd, leavings dozens of dead on the paving stones. The leaders of the Assembly approved of the National Guards' and the authorities' behavior, blaming the tragedy on the demonstration's organizers, against whom they initiated legal proceedings. But they realized they were in danger. The conflict between the constitutionalists and the republicans had received its baptism of blood and it would be resolved in blood. And the king's fate would be the ball they knocked back and forth to mark points against each other.

Louis XVI's image was hardly burnished by this adventure. Who needed a king who would have it that he consented to his own abduction? A king who got arrested by some obscure villagers? A king who used his own impotence to argue against commitments he let himself be browbeaten into? A king who caved in at the first obstacle? As Lamartine so cruelly wrote, after Varennes "Europe would see in him nothing but an escapee from the throne dragged back to his torment; the people would see in him nothing but a traitor, and the Revolution nothing but a toy." He was safe for now, but at what price? He remained unable to fulfill his functions until such time as he subscribed to the revolution – willingly; they would make sure of that! In the meantime, he was confined to the Tuileries with his spouse, under close surveillance.

The queen strikes back

The failure of the escape attempt was all the more painful for Marie-Antoinette because it was her doing and she had invested so much hope in it. At first she seemed terribly affected by it. No doubt Madame Campan was succumbing to her taste for drama when she stated that Marie-Antoinette upon removing her nightcap one

---

*   Apparently, two hapless voyeurs were hiding under the altar to have a look up ladies' skirts. Mistaken for bombers about to set off a blast, they were taken out and lynched, and the event quickly degenerated.

morning found her hair had turned gray overnight, making her look sixty years old. She had been "whitened by misfortune." In fact, she had begun to go gray quite young, and her hair would remain salt-and-pepper all her life. It is certain, however, that undermined by nervous tension, she suddenly lost her most beautiful features, her luminous skin and her sparkling eyes. She grew thin and frail. But being restricted energized her, and she didn't weaken.

Wanting to make sure they could not make another escape attempt, La Fayette had the Tuileries searched from top to bottom. Chimneysweeps checked the chimney shafts to be sure they were not hiding any secret escape routes. They eliminated most of the inside staircases that made a labyrinth of the chateau. They arranged for the apartments of the king, queen and their son to have but one entrance point, guarded round the clock. They double-locked the doors and saw to it that the keys remained firmly in the jailors' pockets. The gardens were studded with sentinels just in case the captives got it into their heads to jump out a window. At first two guards were permanently stationed in the bedroom to which Marie-Antoinette was confined with orders not to let her out of sight at any time, day or night. She had to rise, get dressed and go to bed in front of them. One was even so bold as to rest his elbows on her pillow and chat with her one evening when illness had kept her in bed. La Fayette gave in to the king's protestations and granted that when she was in bed the guards would withdraw to a little space between the two doors leading to the room as long as the second remained ajar, allowing them to see whatever was going on inside. She could go visit her son only if accompanied by numerous guards who locked and unlocked all the doors along the way. Although the heat was suffocating, she was not allowed outside, although she would not have wanted to go out in any case, for fear of insults. A relentless stream of foul libels made her a target for mob violence. Of course there were among her guards decent people who tried to ease her lot. But the suspicious atmosphere put everyone's nerves on edge. Madame Élisabeth told the story of a sentinel in the garden who set off a shooting spree when he mistook some chestnuts falling on his head for rocks being thrown at him. Another one crying out in his sleep sent his mates into a panic.

The queen was kept under this kind of custody until the end of August 1791 when the king let it be known that he would agree to the constitution. But tying her down like this had the opposite of its intended effect. Rather than defeating her, it whipped up her energy, for despite the close surveillance, she managed to set up an exchange of letters with Fersen, Mercy-Argenteau, Leopold II and

Barnave. On July 4ᵗʰ, just five days after she told Fersen she would no longer be able to write to him, she found a way to send him, in as tender terms as ever issued from her pen*, instructions on how to proceed with the correspondence: "... I can tell you that I love you, indeed at every moment. I am well. You need not worry on my account. I would like to know that you are well too. Write to me in code through the post, use Monsieur de Browne's address... inside put another envelope addressed to Monsieur de Gougens. Have your valet de chambre write out the addresses. Let me know to whom I should send my replies, for I cannot live without this. Adieu, the most loved and loving of men. I embrace you with all my heart."

The letters came and went inside a servant's pocket or down a chambermaid's bodice. Since special couriers were costly and risked attracting attention, the accomplices saw to it that the correspondence was exchanged via the ordinary mails, and often had the address written out by another hand. They would be sent along with packages, inserted into journals, glued into book bindings, slipped into biscuit boxes, or sewn into the lining of hats. Sometimes they were written in code, other times not, depending on the carrier's trustworthiness and the sensitivity of the content. The code required their each having an identical copy of *Paul et Virginie*. They also needed lemon juice that when heated brought out the invisible ink, which in turn required another substance to give it color, but this wasn't always available. With rare exceptions, the originals of the letters to Fersen were destroyed by his heirs. But the Vienna archives still contain some of Marie-Antoinette's letters to Mercy from this period. In her own hand on various small bits of paper, she wrote with no margins in a tight and tiny handwriting so as to say as much as possible in the least amount of space. Very touchingly, some of the letters still show signs of having been folded to fit into very small envelopes – 8 by 10 centimeters – some of which can still be found with the letters**.

This correspondence was of vital necessity for the prisoner, and served various purposes. It was an antidote to her loneliness, a form of escape, an emotional release; it kept alive the flame of a love made problematic by separation. But it was first and foremost a means to act, for most of her letters, including those to Fersen, included plans. As the days went by, politics invaded them and their number

---

* This is no doubt why the first one to publish this correspondence left this particular letter out.

** Envelopes came into common use in the second half of the 18ᵗʰ century. Before that letters were merely folded, sealed and addressed on the back.

increased. The writing was difficult for her; she worked hard to make it as clear as possible. It used up a lot of time and energy, and caused her "prodigious mental fatigue." We are sometimes tempted to see her letter writing as pointless, given the results it obtained. But by simultaneously giving her the pleasure of outwitting her jailers and the illusion that she was doing something about her fate, this substitute for action became as indispensable to her as a drug. If it didn't give her an escape hatch, at least it gave her moral sustenance. Marie-Antoinette could never bear to be still. When she got worked up and fought back she felt alive.

Madame Élisabeth shared her combativeness, but was of no help whatsoever. Hyperconscious of her honor, rectitude and heroism, and of a strong religious bent, she disapproved of the ambivalent political line being followed. She regretted that her brother had not abstained from or resisted the latest criminal developments. Clearheaded enough to understand that they would not get out of this situation without outside help, she placed all her hope in the émigrés. She admired the count d'Artois, who had been trying to get Europe agitated about their cause, and who had just got some reinforcement. The count de Provence crossed the border without a hitch and joined him on the banks of the Rhine in Koblenz, where their maternal uncle, the bishop prince of Trier, had offered them hospitality. She expected her brothers to save them with a military intervention that would sweep away all these troublemakers and re-render onto Caesar the things that were Caesar's and to God the things that were God's.

Her intransigence was an endless source of family tension. "It's hell here," groaned Marie-Antoinette; "even with the best intentions, you can't say anything. My sister is so indiscreet, surrounded by schemers and above all dominated by her brothers abroad, that there's no way to talk to her; or else we'd be quarreling all day long." The two women agreed on the end – a return to life the way it was – but not on the means. The queen was hostile to the activism of her brothers-in-law, not only because she detested them, but for perfectly legitimate reasons that Louis XVI shared. If they came armed into French territory loftily brandishing the standards of hardcore counter-Revolution, they would concentrate the forces of all those – and they were very numerous – who feared a return to the "old abuses," in other words, the nobles' privileges. Civil war would be unavoidable and the king put in the terrible position of having to do battle either with them or the majority of his people. Besides, should they be victorious, they promised each other to place the monarch under the supervision of a council that would leave him barely more power than did the much-hated constitution. And who could say they wouldn't take advantage of the situation to depose him in favor of his son, with the count de Provence as regent?

It was therefore from her brother Leopold II that Marie-Antoinette sought help. She would like him to call an "Armed Congress" bringing the main powers together to demand that France fulfill its international commitments and grant the king his freedom. There would be no question of interfering in France's internal affairs. They would simply point out how France's recent unilateral decisions such as the annexation of Avignon and the despoiling of the German princes in the Alsace* had destabilized Europe. If such a congress were held in a border town like Aix-la-Chapelle and accompanied by an impressive military presence, it would terrify "the most rabid of the seditious elements," while giving "reasonable" people the feeling that they were being supported. It would be a dissuasive measure, not unlike those practiced in previous decades.

Let us refrain from mocking her. Marie-Antoinette had worked very hard to educate herself; she had thought things out, and worked relentlessly. Her plan was not absurd, merely unrealistic. Her inadequate education, as well as the fact that she had been kept out of the political loop for twenty-five years, caused her to have quite a simplistic and naive notion of international affairs. Two things at the moment escaped her. To her mind, solidarity among sovereigns, cemented by treaties and marriages, was a given. She therefore based her plans on a belief that the foreign powers were united in a common cause by good will toward one another. However, there was manifestly neither good will nor common cause. Secondly, she had abolutely no doubt about the efficacy of intimidation. Wasn't it used to good effect against Joseph II in Bavaria and the Low Countries? How was she to know that a threat that was apt to make a seasoned ruler stop and think could explode like a bombshell among revolutionary fanatics? An aristocratic contempt for all that is not of the nobility reinforced her self-confidence. The "scoundrels" who were running France were by their very nature cowards who would flee in terror as soon as the emperor bat an eyelash. One thing should have clued her in, however. Not wanting to appear like a disgraceful brother, Leopold II made an empty gesture. On August 24th he cosigned with the king of Prussia the so-called Pillnitz Declaration stating their desire to "enable

---

* Revolutionary France had extended its new policies to the Empire's princes who held fiefdoms in the Alsace, thereby jeopardizing their seigniorial rights.

the king of France to strengthen the foundations of a monarchic government," but their "prompt" intervention was subject to the agreement of the other powers. In other words, the king of France could wait until doomsday for their prompt intervention! All the same, the Jacobins took these remarks as a slap in the face. They replied with violent, bellicose rhetoric.

It would take more than that to discourage Marie-Antoinette. She was sure that the French would finally get fed up with a regime that brought them nothing but poverty and strife. The European rulers would finally fly to the aid of one of their own. Until such time, they just had to hold on, and as always, dissemble. So she simultaneously pursued two different strategies. First of all she appointed Fersen and Mercy-Argenteau as her spokesmen with the emperor. Their job was to fight the Revolution. Secondly, through Barnave, she tried to get the moderates to include in the definitive version of the constitution clauses that were more favorable to the king.

The king? Who cared what he thought? There was a good reason for that: he said nothing. While the queen poured forth her soul in writing, the king got lost in his inner meditations and encased himself in silence. Can we conclude from this, as some historians do, that the queen, behind his back and against his will, was running things for her own ends? Nothing allows us to think so. He agreed with her that they must temporize and dissemble. Madame de Boigne clearly stated that he was aware of her correspondence with the two men in Brussels. The letters and memoranda she sent to Vienna, the messengers she dispatched there, often got a brief written go-ahead from him. But between them there was a psychological abyss. In her heart of hearts, Marie-Antoinette knew that he was largely responsible for the failure of the escape attempt; she could not help but resent him for all the missed opportunities. The old contempt for this wishy-washy and inept husband, which she never quite smothered, welled up in her again. There was also the rankling fact that, unlike her mother, she was not a real queen. Madame Campan attributed to her these apocryphal but convincing remarks: "I could well take the reins if necessary. But if I were to act, I would only be giving weapons to the king's enemies; all over France they would vociferate against that dreadful Austrian, against the domination of a woman; and besides, by putting myself forward, I would destroy the king. A queen who is not regent must under circumstances like these do nothing save prepare herself for death."

Really, she was wrong at this point to see nothing but weakness in her husband. Since Varennes they had been living in two separate universes. To her, any means at all seemed legitimate in facing down the "monsters." More scrupulous, he took ill to being duplicitous. She wanted to fight. He thought they had already lost the battle. Not that he believed the new regime would last – France would get tired of it – but first it must go through a lot of turbulence of which he would necessarily be the victim. Already at this time he was acting like a man preparing to die. People noticed a change in his behavior; while he was still trying to protect his family, his son in particular, and to spare his subjects the horrors of civil war, he no longer did anything that violated his conscience. Marie-Antoinette struggled to save her life, her throne, and her salvation here on earth. Louis thought about his heavenly salvation, and sacrificed his life to it. They were therefore out of step with each other. He escaped from the queen. He did not disown her activities; he sometimes supported them. He was perhaps glad that she had something to occupy her time, as "dissipations" had formerly, but he didn't get involved in her activities really, because he did not believe they would do any good – and because in his eyes what really mattered lay elsewhere.

Barnave, or a double game

The death of Mirabeau deprived the king of one of the rare men capable of applying the brakes to the Assembly's dismantling of the monarchy. After the coach-ride conversations on the road back from Varennes, Barnave seemed just the right man to replace him. Marie-Antoinette felt him out for the role of secret advisor. She wrote to the colonel de Jarjayes, who was to contact him:

> Having thought a lot since my return about the strength, manner and mind of the man with whom I had chatted, I thought I could only profit from setting up some sort of correspondence with him, under the condition of course, that I would always frankly state my way of thinking... Tell him that struck by the character and forthrightness he demonstrated during the two days we spent together, I greatly desire for him to tell me what we are to do in our current situation... He must have seen for himself during our discussions that I am of good faith, and that I will always be; it is the last thing remaining to me, and no one shall ever take it from me. I believe he wants to do the right thing; so do we, and despite what they say, we

always have… It is therefore the man who loves the people and his country the most, and who I believe is the best equipped, whom I call upon to save both.

Her adroit flattery was not in the least needed to make up the young deputy's mind to take under his wing a woman, and a queen at that, whose misfortune had only enhanced her seductiveness. With all due honesty, he told his friends and colleagues Duport and Alexandre de Lameth about the proposal. Although they mistrusted Marie-Antoinette's capriciousness, they thought it was worth a try. In the greatest secrecy and through de Jarjayes, husband of one of the queen's ladies, an exchange of letters was arranged. He would often rewrite the letters in his own hand in order to disguise their source.

Like Mirabeau before him, the young man from Grenoble did not betray his convictions in accepting to serve as a liaison between the Revolution and the throne. Like him, he tried to convert the royal couple to the virtues of a constitutional monarchy and convince them that only by sincerely joining their cause would they win back the love and trust of their people. There was one slight difference, however. He did it for free, although he did get something out of it. His commitment was chivalrous, but it can't be forgotten that he had at all costs to get the king on his side, because his own political survival depended on the success or failure of the constitutional monarchy being set up. His pact with Marie-Antoinette therefore seemed like a good idea. What made it morally dubious is that one of them was acting sincerely but the other not. The whims of fate that either annihilate historical documents or save them from oblivion have preserved for us all of the texts involved*. The letters from Marie-Antoinette to Mercy, Fersen and her brother offer quite a contrast to those she sent Barnave. Her so-called good faith was purely a disguise; she never had any intention of subscribing to his ideas; she only wanted to put him off guard and get all she could out of him in order to gain time while she waited for the foreign powers to come to her rescue. Not a pretty picture. But how can we criticize her under such stressful circumstances for using any means at her disposal and lying to people who until only yesterday were her opponents? One would have preferred her not to use her feminine wiles toward political ends, or, accomplished flirt that she was, play on the sentiments of the poor Barnave, who found "a sweet and pure delight in consoling and serving her." But rather than dwelling

---

* In an ironic twist, this is thanks to Marie-Antoinette herself, who kept the letters she exchanged with Barnave and entrusted them to Fersen.

on unanswerable moral questions, it is better to investigate how this skewed alliance developed and what it produced.

It was hard for Marie-Antoinette to get used to a relationship where her counterpart forgot the infinite distance between a little provincial lawyer and a queen, and had the temerity to behave like the boss. She did not like getting advice that seemed like an order. She was offended by his trenchant tone when right from the start he lay down that she could "neither adopt other ideas nor move away from this course without destroying herself." He did try to understand her, however, and help her overcome her bitterness. And he did more than just give his opinion; he took action, so it was worth it for her to overlook a few liberties of speech. After the Champ-de-Mars shootings, she applauded his resolve before the mob ringleaders. She noted with pleasure that he dominated the debates about the constitution, which the nation was obsessed with. All along Louis XVI had given his support to a good number of decrees, but the final revisions left the door open to possible changes. Barnave worked at getting rid of some measures that were harmful to the king: the right to reprieve was restored to him; the secular status of the clergy, now answerable to ordinary legal channels, became more easily revisable; the king's ministers, although chosen from outside the Assembly, had the right to attend its sessions. As the king had the prerogative of declaring and ending war, and the right of veto allowed him to suspend the application of any law for up to two legislative sessions, Barnave found the text "quite monarchical." But it wasn't enough for the queen. She argued, enquired, and called for explanations. Suddenly, on August 4th, after a page of awkward circumlocutions, her real opinion starkly erupted: "Words are not what we need; it is upholding the monarch's true rights, granting him his due dignity, in a word, restoring to him the influence and means to govern by the law and in concert with it." Clearly put, she was asking the triumvirate to restore most of his powers. If they didn't, she would break with them, leaving them responsible for the resulting disasters. This was the first hiccup, which led them to suspect that Marie-Antoinette, although she claimed to be cut off from everyone and everything, was getting advice from people other than themselves. And in fact from Brussels, Fersen was constantly placing her on guard against them.

She was beginning to suffer from the perverse effects of the double game she was playing. The triumvirs were requiring her to take steps she disapproved of. Here's a typical example: Since they were very fearful of possible outside aggression, they dictated a letter to her brother in which she invites him to calm the ardor of the émigrés – something she was quite happy to do – but where she also explains that the Revolution is over and in the interests of peace, she and the king have both decided to rally to the new regime, which is not perfect but can be improved. She immediately justified herself to Mercy: "On the 29th I wrote you a letter that you can easily see is not in my stlye*. I believed I had to accede to the desires of the party chieftains here, who were the ones who drew up the letter. I wrote another one like it to the emperor yesterday, the 30th. I would be humiliated by it all if I did not trust that my brother deemed that in my position I am obliged to do and write all they require of me." She also asked that her brother reply "in a nuanced letter that could be shown to others."

Let's get ahead of ourselves a bit here. As we shall see, until the new Assembly was set up, the king and queen followed Barnave's advice. They knew he was irreplaceable. The king's ministers were all cabinet men, ill prepared for public debate; not one of them was capable of writing the speeches he had to give. It was Barnave who secretly wrote them, and they were a success. But once they were reassured, the sovereigns thought they could do without him. By then he was no longer a deputy; his audience was abandoning him. What good was it to keep up a relationship that was no longer serving its purpose while remaining a liability? For everyone knew about it by now and from abroad came loud protests against the queen's collusion with the revolutionaries, even moderate ones. Troubled, and perhaps a bit jealous, Fersen asked, "Do you really intend to join the Revolution; do you believe there is no other way? She replied, "You needn't worry; I am not fooled by the firebrands; and if I see or have contact with a few of them, it is merely to use them; I am too horrified by them ever to let myself be won over to them." But the Swede cautioned her to be more careful: "You will be vilified by all of Europe." This didn't prevent him from writing in his journal, without further comment, "They say the queen is sleeping with Barnave and lets him rule her." She had compromised herself in vain, and compromised her benefactors as well; they were seen as having betrayed their side.

They pretty quickly were convinced she was toying with them. As Mirabeau had, Barnave thought that a meeting would sort out their misunderstandings. He obtained a first audience with the queen on October 5th, which he attended with his friend de Lameth, then a second on the 12th. No one knows what they said to each other.

---

*   This letter has not been found.

But a letter of his dated the 19ᵗʰ is bitter. The sovereigns were no longer listening to him. Without telling him, they were following someone else's advice, someone else's policies. They had changed, not he. Why carry on a relationship from which trust has fled? His bitterness was justified. We know that the same day, October 19ᵗʰ, the queen wrote Fersen the letter cited above – which did not stop her from replying to Barnave on the 20ᵗʰ flaunting her "good faith" and playing the offended princess. Her will to survive, whatever the outcome of the coming conflict, was what dictated her successive stances, which now outright contradicted each other. Perhaps this can be explained by the terrible trials she was undergoing. What is more, every day she had to grapple with the king, whom she tried to dominate but did not understand. At her wit's end, devoured by anxiety, she was no longer mistress of what she said, or of what she wrote. "Sometimes I don't even understand myself," she admitted to Fersen, "and I am obliged to think hard to see if it is indeed myself who is speaking." We get the impression that each series of letters, to Barnave, Mercy, Leopold II and even Fersen, obeyed its own internal logic; that she wrote to each correspondent what she thought they expected from her; it seems she carried on with each of them an autonomous dialogue irrespective of the others. It is possible that when a contradiction was pointed out to her, she was sincerely surprised and indignant, so much she compartmentalized the various facets of her mental universe, because she simply could not make them come together.

By autumn Barnave harbored no more illusions about her. Hoping to salvage both his political influence and the constitution for which he felt an artist's tenderness towards his masterpiece, he drew out for two whole months a correspondence that clearly irritated its recipient. At the end of the year he decided to go back to the Dauphiné. He still hoped that moderation would prevail, and professed some optimism. Before going, however, he went to the Tuileries, alone, according to Lameth, to take leave of the queen. To the histrionic speech and kiss he reverently placed on the weeping queen's hand that Madame Campan tells us about, we prefer the last words in his last letter, dated 5 January 1792: "I will always recall that in our last conversation, the queen assured me that her trust was sincere and her intentions unchangeable. This memory shall govern my opinions and motivate all of my public conduct." It would have been hard to say more in fewer words. But upon his death they found on him a piece of embroidered silk that had come off Marie-Antoinette's dress on the way back from Varennes, kept today at the Carnavalet museum.

A *"monstrous work"?*

Barnave deserved better than the frosty brush-off he got. His advice was wiser than Fersen's, and while the constitution was being drawn up, he was of quite remarkable service to the sovereigns.

It came time to inaugurate the new constitution. In truth, Marie-Antoinette never saw in this constitution anything but a "monstrous work," a "tissue of impracticable absurdities" that would only lead to disaster and the loss of the kingdom. But subscribe to it she must. The end of August 1791 found the royal family in a trancelike state, still hoping there would be foreign intervention. But she had to admit the obvious: there would be no miracle. If Louis XVI wanted them to lift the suspension of his powers under which he labored since Varennes, if he wanted to regain some freedom of movement and get an amnesty for all those who took part in his escape attempt, he would have to comply with it. At the end of August he made his agreement known, and the vice-grip around the Tuileries began to loosen. The queen and Barnave had long debated over the wording of his speech at the inauguration of the Constitution. She complained to Mercy, "You will see in it a few strong features, but nothing of the language of a king who keenly feels how he has been outraged." Time was running out, and besides, Louis XVI, who had just come within an inch of being indicted, was in no position to speak his mind. His speech, written by the triumvirate, was moderate and dignified, and made an excellent impression.

No one can think of everything. They believed they had ironed out the tiniest details of the ceremony to inaugurate the Constitution. However, an incident occurred that would have been termed burlesque were it not for the seriousness of the occasion. The king was to take the president's podium to pronounce his agreement and his oath. Upon his arrival Louis XVI went ashen. He saw at the same level two identical armchairs decorated in *fleurs de lis*. He learned that he would occupy the one on the right. From the box fitted out for her above some steps, Marie-Antoinette watched stone-faced as the proceedings progressed. When the king got up to speak, all the deputies, who had risen to welcome him, remained seated, including the chairman, Thouret, next to him. Momentarily disconcerted by this unimaginable slight, he decided to continue, but from a seated position. When Thouret rose to answer him, he didn't budge, causing the other to sit back down too. He could hardly control his anger. He got up again, as was obligatory, to take the oath, and could not suppress an abrupt show of indignation when he saw that everyone remained riveted to their seats. The queen could not bear it any longer, and had herself brought back to the Tuileries. When he returned home he threw himself into an armchair and wept, "All is lost! Oh, Madame! And you had to witness this humiliation!"

The following Sunday the acclamations of the people should have lightened their spirits. A volley of one hundred and one cannon shots was fired over the Champ-de-Mars. Copies of the Constitution wafted down over the city from beribboned hot-air balloons. The Champs-Élysées was all lit up and alive with open-air dance floors. Everywhere people sang and danced for joy. "How sad it is that something so beautiful leaves in our hearts only a feeling of sadness and apprehension," sighed the queen in the open carriage from which she was admiring the spectacle. The king's supposed reconciliation with his people left her with a bitter taste.

In bidding farewell to the Constituent Assembly and greeting the new Legislative Assembly, the triumvirs took precautions, and etiquette was less botched. But they had shot their last bolt in trying to no avail to outlaw the clubs, which the republicans used for keeping up popular pressure. By all appearances the new Legislative Assembly would be farther to the left than the previous one. The moderate Feuillants had lost power to another group that came out of the Jacobins led by another republican orator, Brissot. They would soon become known as the Girondins.

What would be the attitude of the king, a constitutionalist in spite of himself? Marie-Antoinette advocated trying to make things worse in order to make them better: they must do everything to prove that the new regime was not viable, and therefore made an all-out push for it. She wrote to Fersen at the end of September, "I believe that the best way to get people disgusted with it all is to seem to be all for it. That would show them soon enough that it can't work." Madame Élisabeth on the other hand advised systematic obstruction. Louis XVI didn't agree with either one. He knew that this latest oath of allegiance to all the new institutions tied him down much more than the decrees he was forced to agree to before renouncing them once he fled. If he broke his word a second time, he would bring irremediable shame upon himself. The marquis d'Osmond, seeing that his entourage was trying to get him to put every possible obstacle in the way of the constitution's success, put him on guard:

"Since you have sworn allegiance to it, Sire, it is necessary to follow it loyally, openly, and carry out everything it requires of you."

"But it cannot work."

"Well then, it will fall apart, but it must not be through your fault."

What is more, the least infringement of the law, the least instance of perjury, would cause his ruin, for it would entail the immediate loss of his inviolability. Prudence as well as moral obligation therefore required him to keep his oath. He chose to respect the Constitution to the letter, but to use every means it left him to impose his will.

It wasn't his fault that it fell apart, at least not entirely. His entourage had something to do with it, the émigrés a lot to do with it, and the Legislative Assembly the most of all; for the Jacobins, furious at not being able to dethrone him, stopped at nothing to sabotage it. No constitution in the world can be put into operation if one of its creators only supports it half-heartedly and the other provokes mayhem to torpedo it.

After two years of upheaval, everything had to be done all over again. Barnave encouraged the sovereigns to take advantage of the slight improvement in the post-Constitution atmosphere to "popularize" themselves. They had to go out in public more, show up at the theatre; resume their old ways. If they cooped themselves up in the Tuileries, it would be seen as a rejection of the new regime. So Marie-Antoinette was seen at the Opera and *les Italiens*, where her presence brought some applause, but also caused a few incidents. Was it a good idea to choose *Richard the Lion-Hearted*, whose most famous tune had become the royalist anthem since the famous bodyguard banquet? She was asked to pick her events more carefully. And once when she was dragged to a performance of *Castor and Pollux*, Madame Élisabeth snubbed the audience by turning her back while they were giving them an ovation.

But the queen's compliance had its limits. That was clear when it came to reconstituting the "households" that traditionally surrounded her person and that of the king. The less real power he had, the more his new masters wanted Louis XVI to show himself in his role as figurehead: this concession to tradition would facilitate the country's acceptance of the transfer of sovereignty. He was therefore given, under the name of the Constitutional Guard, a pale imitation of his former household military service. Barnave repeatedly warned them: the new guards could not be chosen solely from among the known royalists. This would be taken as an attempt to prepare a coup against the current regime. They had to offer this kind of social promotion to National Guardsmen from the bourgeoisie so as to win their support. Instead of which, the king put in charge a very high-ranking lord, the duke de Brissac, and recruited the officers from among the nobility in opposition; he wanted to be surrounded by troops "upon whom he could rely." For a whole month, Marie-Antoinette fiercely haggled over the color of the uniforms. She rejected the three national colors, proposing instead a light blue with daffodil yellow lining. She gave up when she was told that yellow was the municipal color of Koblenz.

Sickened, she refused a non-aristocratic household. Not to be jeopardized by the new regime, some of her ladies of quality resigned. Would she replace them with bourgeois ladies? How could they force her to keep courtly company with Madame Bailly and Madame Pétion!? Besides, appointing new position holders would only complicate matters when the time came for them to hand back their prerogatives to their predecessors as soon as the Ancien Régime was restored – which event she believed would not be long in coming. She recalled Madame de Lamballe, whom she'd sent away before going to Varennes. Barnave made it clear that if Madame de Lamballe went out in public, her return would be seen as a patriotic act and a guarantee of the queen's intentions; but if she stayed shut off inside the Tuileries, the people would see it as part of a conspiracy. But Marie-Antoinette's ill will was patently obvious. With all her might she fought the abolition of the three estates, which had equalized society's ranks. She for one would not be the agent of the vast mixing of the social orders that the constitutionalists were aiming at so as to blend the old nobility into the bourgeois elites. As a result, the attempt to win back public opinion ended in failure.

In the meantime, the make-up of the new ministries gave rise to bitter debates that showed that the king was not being above board in his dealings with the constitutionalists. The Assembly very quickly took up the cudgel.

How to use the veto

The veto, which allowed the king to suspend ratifying decrees for two legislative sessions, in other words for four years, was a double-edged sword. Sieyès said that the veto was nothing other than the king's *lettre de cachet* against the will of the people. Faced with a measure he disapproved of, the king had only two choices: either he complied or was seen as an enemy of the people. It would be wise, therefore, to apply his veto as seldom as possible. But everyone knew the sensitive areas in which he could be provoked into using it, especially two of them: emigration and the non-compliant priests.

The Assembly first went on the offensive about the émigrés. Admittedly, they were itching for a fight. The issue of the king's dethronement after Varennes planted the seed of ambition in the count de Provence's soul. His dream was to be proclaimed regent, replace his imprisoned brother, and to set up a French government in exile in Koblenz, the only one recognized by the foreign powers. As soon as he learned of the escape attempt's failure, he gave Fersen the task of getting from the captive king a letter granting him full powers; he even took the trouble of furnishing the text of the letter himself. His refusal, conveyed by Marie-Antoinette, irritated him. When he learned that Louis XVI was going to take the oath to the Constitution, he was utterly furious. He didn't even wait for the Constitution's inauguration ceremony to publish, on October 10th, a manifesto co-signed by his brother d'Artois, where he in turn declared the king dethroned for breaking his coronation oath, which forbade his giving up even the least of his royal prerogatives. For all royalists, disobedience became a duty. Upon reading this manifesto, it is said the queen uttered one terrible word, "Cain." Amongst the émigrés, hatred of the king, and especially of the queen, who was blamed for his capitulation, flamed out of control.

Little aware of dissentions in the royal family and seeing only subterfuge, the Assembly undertook to force Louis XVI's hand. It feared, and rightly so, a fresh wave of emigration. At this stage it was a point of honor among many noblemen to go join the princes who were refusing to make a pact with the devil. It watched as the country was emptied of some of its vital resources and began to fear an offensive from Koblenz. On October 31st it issued a decree directing the count de Provence to return to France or lose his right to the regency. Nothing could have pleased the king more, who hastened to write his brother a letter couched in moralistic terms beseeching him to return. For her part, Marie-Antoinette tried hard to convince Mercy-Argenteau to get the emperor to cool down the émigrés' zeal, and she called for the famous "Armed Congress" to convene. To get the king of Prussia involved, she had Louis XVI write him a letter, one that Fersen outlined for him.

In the meantime, the Assembly, flush with what it considered a victory, went further. On November 9th it threatened with death any émigré who had sought refuge abroad and not returned by January 1st. Barnave agreed that Louis XVI could not sanction without losing face a decree against his brother and former supporters. He approved resorting to the veto, which was applied on

November 11th, but at the same time he advised sending a strongly worded appeal both to the émigrés enjoining them to return, and to the foreign powers hosting them to invite them to leave. The appeal only caused contemptuous irony among the émigrés, but they stopped laughing when their hosts asked them to clear off. The bishop prince of Trier, tired of hosting their arrogant and rowdy court, gladly caved in to the emperor's pressure, at his sister's behest, to send them packing. In the end, this first application of the veto, thanks to the measures that accompanied it, did not cause a break between Louis XVI and the Assembly. What came close was the decree of the 29th. It forced non-juror priests to take a fidelity oath "to the nation, to the law, and to the king" or risk being considered suspect[*]. The king slapped an abrupt and irreversible veto on it. But since religious conflict was still smoldering, stoked by the strife spreading in the provinces, the Assembly looked for another line of attack that was more likely to get general approval. It again took up the charge against the émigrés, decreeing on the 9th of February 1792 that their wealth would be sequestered. Would this be the breaking point? No. The king did not oppose the measure: sequestration would keep these goods from being sold or stolen.

Disappointed by his unexpected moderation – "if this devil of a man caves in on everything, how can we depose him?" – the left wing of the Assembly began to think that only a war would sweep away the monarchy. It therefore sought to provoke the German princes and the emperor into the vigorous reaction they couldn't get from the king. But Leopold worked to calm things down, less through solidarity with his brother-in-law than for keeping his hands free vis-à-vis Eastern Europe. He would not be dragged into a dubious conflict at his western doorstep while Russia and Prussia were busy carving up Poland again and maybe excluding him from the process! Since the French had threatened to invade his Electorates if their princes did not send back the émigrés, he was reduced to promising them his support in case of attack. Since he was secretly encouraging the princes to expel them anyway, he didn't have much to lose. But in France the warmongers saw this as a hostile act and decided to up the ante. Betting on the people's abhorrence of their kings, the republicans wanted war. They thought they were sure to win it. Both inside and outside the country, the royalists wanted war as well, but for their own reasons. They saw France as so ill

---

[*] The word was not defined precisely and left the door open to fruitless debate and persecution. The famous *Law of the Suspects* came later on 17 September 1793.

prepared that it could only lose against the war-hardened Austrian and Prussian troops. Marie-Antoinette caressed this hope and tried to get her hesitant husband to share it.

It was in this supercharged atmosphere that Fersen decided to go to Paris himself for a secret meeting with the royal couple.

Fersen's visit

The romantic aspects of the relationship between Marie-Antoinette and the highly seductive Swede often completely overshadow its political dimension; so much so that the main concern of the commentators has been whether she did or did not spend that night in his arms. The encounter has been hallowed by history with an aura of tragedy, but at the time, they didn't think it would be their last. Although she was exasperated with her brother for taking so long in coming to her rescue, she didn't doubt that she would soon be liberated. Fersen therefore was not coming to see her one last time, but to clear up some misunderstandings and try to develop some sort of strategy.

Misunderstandings? God knows plenty of them had been building up between them over the six preceding months. The last letter she got from him, which had crossed in the mails with the three loving notes she had penned to him upon her return from Varennes, must have put a terrible damper on her spirits: "The awful disaster that has just taken place must entirely change the course of action," he said, before asking for full powers to be granted to Provence. Let's not lend too much credence to the chilly tone; it is possible that the baron von Klinckowström censored a few affectionate words at the beginning or the end of the letter. But Fersen could not have known that relying on the émigrés was her worst option. She had to inform him that the king was placing his bets solely on the foreign powers, without the émigrés. Then he got wind of the king's acceptance of the constitution. Living in Brussels in an environment violently hostile to revolutionary France, he could not figure out why the royal couple was complying with the constitutionalists. He was surprised and indignant about Barnave's role as the queen's adviser. He felt betrayed by her. He was so hurt that he put off deciphering one of her letters for four days. Then he was scandalized by the routing of the émigrés. What did the king and queen actually want? He asked for precise instructions. And as she brought up the Armed Congress again, he drafted letters for her to the kings of Spain, Sweden and Prussia as well as to the czarina. But he was highly critical of the double game they were playing. The king would never win over the factious elements; they were too intent on keeping him under their thumb. By dealing with them he was alienating the French aristocracy, lowering himself in the eyes of the other sovereigns and demobilizing those who were willing to support him.

The problem was that the king's supporters couldn't agree amongst themselves. The zeal of Gustav III of Sweden in wanting to lead an expeditionary force without delay was only matched by Leopold II's inertia. The latter used the fact that Louis XVI had rallied to the constitution to argue against interfering in France's "internal affairs." Fersen took it upon himself to warn the queen both against the emperor's duplicity and Mercy-Argenteau's guidance. The old ambassador was pretending to serve her still, but all he was doing was preaching resignation.

He needed a meeting to get everyone updated. He had a few points he wanted to straighten out, a few suggestions to make, and above all some solutions to propose. He knew that before any military action could be taken, the sovereigns had to be saved from Parisian mob violence. Marie-Antoinette was not overjoyed by the prospect of his visit, and twice asked him to put it off. Not that she didn't want to see him – she missed him terribly. Her only comfort in life was looking after her children. She had written to him: "This latter occupation, not the humblest, is my sole happiness [when far from you*], and when I am really sad I take my little boy in my arms and I embrace him with all my heart, and that consoles me for a little while." But she was apprehensive about a visit that she felt was futile and dangerous – futile because she knew the king would only sit and wait, and dangerous because "fermentation" was on the rise in Paris. Fersen was certainly taking risks, for the amnesty that applied to those who took part in the failed escape did not cover those who were judged *in absentia*. However, since he was a foreigner and friend of the king of Sweden, a person of note despite his lack of official diplomatic status, perhaps they would think twice about going after him. And the inauguration of the Constitution had restored a minimum of order and freedom in France; there was less surveillance of travelers. The most dangerous part would be his visit to the Tuileries – especially for the queen; for her enemies would only be too happy to catch her in *flagrant délit* colluding with a militant counter-revolutionary.

---

* This handwritten letter of the 7th, 8th and 9th of December 1791 is kept in the French National Archives, serial number 440 AP 01/2. Beneath the looped crossing out of the words after "happiness" it is possible to make out "when far from you."

She finally gave him the green light. Even though the Assembly had decided against obligatory passports, just to be on the safe side, he had a false one made, as well as a mission statement sprinkled with equally false stamps and signatures for a supposed courier from the king of Sweden to the king of Portugal. No one would ask him for them and no one bothered to look under the wig he donned. Having left Brussels on Saturday morning, February 11, 1792 in a light carriage, he took his time so as not to attract attention to himself, and arrived in Paris the following Monday evening. He got confirmation from Goguelat that he was expected and arrived at the Tuileries shortly after seven. He noted in his *Private Journal*, "Went to *her* place, took the usual route, fear of the National Guards; her apartment well suited*." Something has been crossed out after this, but there seem to be the two words: "stayed there."

Few words have caused so much ink to flow or given rise to so much conjecture. We can leave aside all the technical discussions about the exact wording, for it is quite clear that he did not leave the Tuileries that night. He could not take the chance twice in one night of being stopped by the National Guard. Yes, we are told, but he always used the term "stayed there" to refer to the occasions when he spent the night in the bed of one of his mistresses. But why must one necessarily interpret them this way**? In writing about his journey, he obsessively jotted down what the weather was like, where he stopped, where he dined and where he slept. In fact, if the erasure hadn't drawn attention to this detail, it might have passed unnoticed – except for the fact that there is another element that does make us wonder. The journal leaves no doubt but that he only met Louis XVI the next evening at six o'clock. This raises two key questions: why did he wait twenty-four hours and what did he do in the meantime? He had reasons for seeing the queen by herself. Yes, but what were they? "We can guess!" insists jubilantly Madame Söderhjelm, Fersen's highly learned biographer, convinced that this proves they were lovers.

It is certainly quite possible that he wanted to carve out a few hours of intimacy, in which case he could just as well have spent time alone with her between seeing the king and taking leave of her.

---

*   Contrary to what Zweig claims, the queen's apartment consisted not just of her bedroom and a miniscule *cabinet de toilette*. Above them on a mezzanine she had rooms inconspicuous enough to hide someone for a night.

**   Françoise Kermina notes that when he spent the night with one of his mistresses, the two words were always written in Swedish, but in this instance it would seem they are in French.

On the other hand, very pressing political reasons required that he see her first. He couldn't propose anything to Louis XVI until he'd got some things clear first. What was the king's state of mind? He needed to get information from the queen, and to agree with her on what to say to him. Picking up the threads, he had her tell him everything that transpired since they had bid each other adieu at the Bondy relay station eight months previously. His journal gives a concise summary, sprinkled with a few dialogues and some concrete details, of the long account she gave him. She spoke of the trying journey home and the captivity that followed. Then she mentioned the Feuillants, the recent services they had rendered, and the dissentions that caused their being at loggerheads with the new Assembly. She painted him a portrait of the ministers, nearly all of them "traitors." He was able to get a better handle on the situation and found again that they were like-minded. Together they prepared the interview with Louis XVI.

Fersen met with him the next evening at six. He proposed a number of different escape plans, all of which were discarded, as they'd expected. "I lost my chance," Louis XVI objected, "on the 14th of July, and since then I have not had another. The whole world has abandoned me." He used the close surveillance he was under as an excuse, "but actually, he is too scrupulous to flee, having so often promised to stay, for he is an honest man." He was still counting on the Armed Congress to liberate him. If that failed, "he consents to the foreign powers' intervention, and submits to all its potential dangers." But his dream was still to become the mediator between his subjects in revolt and the foreign governments, whom he could only imagine victorious. Until such time, he asked Fersen to invite those governments to be surprised at nothing, for whatever he did would be the result of *force majeure*: "They must leave me alone to do what I have to do." In other words, his choice, as usual, was to bide his time and avoid doing anything that might further aggravate the situation.

Fersen left the Tuileries about nine-thirty the same evening, carrying with him a precious document: the queen's correspondence with Barnave. He went to his friend Craufurd's house, where he lay low for the week he was supposed to be on the imaginary mission in Spain. Without scruple, he took advantage of his stay to abundantly cheat on his host with the beautiful Eleonore Sullivan. Did he feel he was also cheating on Marie-Antoinette? Clearly not. He certainly loved her, but he was not bewitched. He was yet another who could keep things quite compartmentalized. Back in Brussels on the night of 23–24 February, he concluded his journal prosaically with the words, "My joy was great to have succeeded so well and to be home again." He brought back with him a small glimmer of hope. He explained to the king of Sweden that far from standing firmly with the Revolution, the French sovereigns were convinced that having any truck with the rebels was a waste of time; they knew that if they were to regain power, it would only be with outside help. Although he didn't admit it, he hoped he would be the intermediary of choice in the negotiations to follow, and make a career for himself at their side once they took back the throne.

It's easy to understand why he also refrained from revealing that he had a long tête-à-tête with Marie-Antoinette the night before. As a result, we cannot know anything more about his relationship with her. That way, each of us can indulge our own imagination about this last night together, on which they had the freedom to do whatever they wanted, but no one can say for sure what they did with it.

"A little war with no future"

If he couldn't convince the king, at least he strengthened Marie-Antoinette's resolve: war was the only solution. For some months now, she had been hoping and praying for one. If the emperor didn't agree, they would just have to force his hand. The best thing would be for France to declare war on Austria, for once they start, "all the governments will have to get involved to defend their rights." Constantly humiliated, the queen became passionately bellicose. She was counting on a French defeat not only to restore royal authority, but to punish the fanatics as well. She went so far as hoping that the last-ditch negotiations would fail so that they could "finally get revenge for all the outrages this country has inflicted on us!" And to her mind, everyone was guilty; France was nothing but a pack of scoundrels and madmen, imbeciles and cowards. Pride in having been born German swelled in her again, bolstered by hatred of a people that had never quite accepted her: "On whatever side, the French are horrible..." and "Oh, this cursed nation, how awful it is to have to live amongst them!" She would get no contradiction on that score from Fersen. Having erstwhile preferred France to his native Sweden, he now harbored toward the country the feelings of a spurned lover.

At the Assembly, passions were running just as high. The Girondins were now the dominant faction, and they were hoping for a war to distract people from the economic crisis, fire up revolutionary fervor, and get rid of the king. The only one to protest was Robespierre, because he knew the country was not prepared for it and because he feared that a war, by giving military leaders so much power, could lead to a dictatorship*. But he was no more able than were the Feuillants to hold back the great tidal wave raised by Brissot's inflamed speeches. According to him, this would be a just war, a people's crusade against the kings; it would export throughout Europe the dream of liberty, equality and fraternity. There were also those out to seek their own fortunes. The possibility of war quickened personal ambitions in men who felt or were told they had a talent for war. La Fayette, for instance, was hoping that at the head of an army he would regain his former glory. Dumouriez, whom the Assembly had just imposed on Louix XVI as a minister, calculated that he could come up smelling like a rose if France went to war, whether or not it won it. As Jean Tulard wrote, "a defeat, by sweeping away the throne, would make him dictator; a victory, in consolidating the monarchy, would make him supreme military commander." All the apprentice sorcerers expected different results from the war, but they all shared the belief that, in the words of count de Narbonne, this would be "a little war with no future." It was to last twenty-three years, and very few of those who bet on its outcome would be around to see the end of it.

When everyone wants a war, it is very rare that it doesn't break out. In the spring of 1792, destiny saw to it that it did. Europe had just been rocked by two major events. First, the most resolute of the doves, Leopold II, beginning to worry about the plan to "liberate" the Low Countries, died suddenly on March 1st, having just turned forty-five. His son and successor Francis II was much more combative than his father, and all the more determined to take up the French challenge as his back was covered thanks to Austria's recent reconciliation with Prussia. Secondly, at the end of the same month, the king of Sweden, a passionate hawk, succumbed to the wounds he received when assassins attacked him at a masked ball. Gustav III had been the only one of the sovereigns who saw the war in chivalrous terms as having to be waged above all to save the French rulers. Francis II on the other hand could not care less about an aunt he had never met and an uncle through marriage of whom he was contemptuous. Therefore, the nature of the upcoming conflict changed. Now more than ever, Leopold's words were bandied about: "The French want a war? They'll get it then; but they'll pay the price." The European rulers would not be

---

* He was a good prophet, for that is exactly what happened with Bonaparte.

going to war to put Louis XVI back on the throne. If they gathered the troops, it would be to have France at their mercy. And since Poland had whetted their appetites, why shouldn't France also fall prey to the carving knife? Marie-Antoinette refused to confront this reality, despite Mercy's repeated warnings. She preferred to believe in the rulers' disinterested solidarity.

Francis II deliberately provoked France by demanding the reinstatement of the king and calling the Assembly a "furious blood-soaked faction." On March 25th the latter replied with an ultimatum. In the name of the 1756 alliance treaty, it called upon Austria to recognize the new French regime and cease all military preparations against it; a negative reply would constitute a *casus belli*. The queen sent Goguelat to Vienna to assure her nephew that as soon as war was declared, "a large part of the nation would rally around the throne and aid the liberators." The Assembly labored under similar but opposite delusions that they could look forward to the French army leading the peoples of Europe in overthrowing their tyrants. According to the constitution it was incumbent upon poor Louis XVI to formulate the declaration of war, but in fact on this point he could only follow the advice of his ministers. He was in a most invidious position: he was going to push his country into a war it was sure to lose – and what is worse – he wanted it to lose. Certainly he saw a foreign war as the lesser of two evils, preferable to a civil war, but he went into it with despair in his heart. Deathly pale and with tears in his eyes, he went to the speakers platform at the *Manège* on April 20th to propose opening hostilities against the king of Bohemia and Hungary[*]. He spoke in a flat monotone, spokesman of a course of action he did not believe in. The deputies voted almost unanimously for war, despite the fact that the French armed forces were obviously not prepared for it.

The queen's reaction was unqualified joy. Even before war was officially declared, she tried to contribute to the Austro-Prussian victory by transmitting information to Brussels. On the 26th of March she had written to Mercy: "Monsieur Dumouriez... plans to begin here first by an attack on the Savoy and another around Liège. La Fayette's army is to be used in the second attack. Here is the outcome of yesterday's Cabinet meeting: it is good to be familiar with this plan so as to be on guard and take all suitable measures." And to Fersen on the 30th of March, "The plan is to attack via the Savoy and the Liège country... I notified Turin three

---

[*]   Such was Francis of Hapsburg-Lorraine's official title, as he had not yet had enough time to be elected emperor.

weeks ago." Could anyone find the semblance of a strategy in these little bits of information? Surely not; but it was not for want of trying. Before we accuse her of treason, however, let us recall that she was not the first queen to be caught in a conflict between her native land and her country of adoption. In 1637, under far less tragic circumstances, Anne of Austria had reacted in the same way. And the revolutionaries gave Marie-Antoinette an excuse that Anne of Austria did not have. In going beyond nationwide antagonisms and turning this war outside France's national boundaries into a clash between two opposing visions of the world, they enabled her to choose her side without any scruples or qualms of conscience. Together with her nephew, she was fighting for her husband, her son, her very universe.

It took little over a week for the French offensive in Flanders to turn into a fiasco, and the public to point the finger. Only some internal conspiracy could explain their defeat. And the heart of the plot, although it had many arteries, could only be in the Tuileries among the queen's entourage. Even though they knew nothing of her Brussels correspondence, the triumvirate vituperated with built-up fury against the "Austrian committee" lying in ambush in the chateau, leading the king around by the nose. Of course, there was never any plot, or even an organized "committee" pursuing any particular policy. But it cannot be denied that Marie-Antoinette tried for as long as she could to coordinate her husband's activities with those of Vienna. And public opinion was not entirely wrong in denouncing her, in a new rash of pamphlets, as that Austrian woman who could not be assimilated, the enemy's Trojan horse in the very heart of France.

For his part, the king was riddled with aching remorse. Grief, coupled with the lack of exercise and perhaps an undiagnosed malady, prematurely aged him. At thirty-eight years of age, weighed down by excess fat, he looked like an old man. In the spring of 1792 he fell into one of his habitual depressions. Madame Campan said, "He remained ten days in a row without uttering a word, not even to his family... the queen drew him out of this baneful state... by throwing herself at his feet, finding terms designed either to frighten him or express her tenderness for him... She went so far as telling him that if they must perish, it had to be with honor and without waiting to be snuffed out together on the floor of their home."

In the meantime, the Assembly tried to placate the extremists while backing further into a corner this submissive king who had so easily been pushed into declaring war on his own nephew. One after the other, three redoubtable decrees were issued on the 27th and

29th of May and the 8th of June. The first called for non-juror priests to be deported, the second did away with the Constitutional Guard, and the third proposed raising 20,000 *fédérés* from all over France to maintain order in the capital. Although he risked losing all his protection, the king agreed to the one that was the most provocative but concerned only him, and allowed his guards to be dismissed. But he vetoed the other two. He opposed the first because it profoundly offended his personal convictions, and besides, violated the Constitution. The third he opposed because it would provide cover for the riots that were to come. Madame Campan claimed that he wanted to approve all of them so as to avoid a general insurrection, but Marie-Antoinette talked him out of it. As regards the *fédérés* it's possible; but it is inconceivable that he would agree to the deportation of non-compliant priests. Popular condemnation was swift: they were given another nickname: Monsieur and Madame Veto.

This time Louis XVI stood up to all the clamor denouncing him for opposing the two decrees. When his minister of the interior Roland called upon him insolently to withdraw his veto from the decrees, he fired him, together with all of his colleagues except for Dumouriez, who chose to resign. He called upon some moderates to take their place. The Assembly did nothing more than protest. The Jacobins then took to the streets to get rid of this monarchy they could not bring down legally. The first time they didn't succeed, the second time they did.

CHAPTER 21

THE FINAL ASSAULT

Unlike the "days of revolution" in 1789, which had something of a spontaneous and improvised nature, those of 1792 were organized by the clubs, which were represented on the ground by the most active members in the various Parisian "sections*."The war whipped up an obsessive fear that was easily exploited. It was a time of suspicion, informing and witch hunts against "the enemy within" who were responsible for the defeat. Conflict raged in the Assembly between the constitutionalists and the republicans. To combat the former, who got their support from the well-to-do bourgeoisie, the latter appealed to the less well-heeled masses, whom they undertook to indoctrinate, making them aware of their power. It was at this point that appeared for the first time in the imagery of the French Revolution the emblematic figure of the sans-culotte brandishing a pike and sporting a Phrygian cap. His striped trousers cut from coarse homespun – which up until then had been a symbol of social inferiority compared to the britches tightened at the knee over silk stockings – became a badge of glory. His red cap – the very same one that still graces the head of Marianne, the national symbol of France – was meant to represent emancipation**. He was refused entrance into the National Guard because he was only a "passive citizen***," but was invited to enlist to go get slaughtered on the

---

* Administrative and electoral divisions that roughly correspond to the present-day arrondissements.

** It claimed to recall the bonnet that the ancient Romans placed on the heads of slaves during their emancipation ritual. It was actually quite different because the top fell forward. It seems to have been inspired by certain eastern deities (Attis or Mithra) depicted in Greco-Roman art.

*** As opposed to "active citizens," "passive citizens" were those who were too poor to pay taxes, and thus excluded from the electoral rolls.

border. It wasn't on the border but in Paris, right away, that he demanded weapons, to defend the Revolution against the enemies the clubs would identify. Since the clubs could not furnish him with a rifle, they would supply him with a long or a short pike, especially produced for the purpose. Provoked by rumors and worked up into a rage by slogans, taken in hand by agitators, the most fearsome of the rioters that were sent to storm the Tuileries were not the wretched and the destitute, or drunken and bribed vagrants, but the people of modest means, the craftsmen and shopkeepers who felt betrayed by the new regime, the fanaticized petite bourgeoisie. They were swamped in hatred, and for lack of the better life they had been promised, they were offered aristocrats to slaughter.

June 20th, the rioters miss their mark

Great denigrators of religious holidays, the revolutionaries had tried to get them replaced by secular ones. Each 14th of July, the storming of the Bastille was celebrated. But in June of 1792, with the fury over Louis XVI's two vetoes and the sacking of the Jacobin ministers, the patriots were looking for an immediate riposte; they weren't going to wait for a whole month. One date seemed like a good one, as it was that of a double anniversary. On the 20th of June 1789 the taking of the oath at the *Jeu de paume* signaled the start of the revolt, and on the night of June 20th 1791, the king attempted to make the get-away that ended so piteously. There was a lot to celebrate. A pleasant holiday was announced. The people would go plant a tree in the Tuileries' Feuillants Terrace and drop off a petition calling for a repeal of the vetoes and the reinstatement of the sacked ministers. Nothing special, just liberty trees; there were loads of them being planted at the time. As for petitions, the Assembly was drowning in them. But there were numerous indications that the festivities were to serve as a pretext, because the organizers had called upon the advisory board of the Paris mayor's office to authorize the demonstrators to come "dressed in the clothing they were wearing in 1789 and with their arms," and totally ignored the anti-crowd measures in effect. It appeared that the working-class districts of Saint-Antoine and Saint-Martin were gearing up for action.

Having been informed about it three days earlier, Louis XVI was on edge. The Tuileries was too close to the *Manège* not to offer a tempting target. He knew the chateau could not be defended. His Constitutional Guards had just been dissolved, so he had to count on the unreliable National Guard. What was there to do but wait and try to deal with the situation when it came? All Wednesday morning he was on the alert for news. At the head of the demonstration coming from Saint-Antoine, the boys and girls surrounding the liberty tree couldn't hide the scowling masses bristling with pikes that followed them. The crowds from Saint-Martin brought two cannon. In order to reach the *Manège* from the more accessible west side, the two groups of demonstrators made a wide detour via the Place Vendôme. On the way they abandoned the pretext of the tree, dumping it in the Capuchin Court, and waved banners hostile to the king. They descended en masse on the *Manège*, demanding to march through the great room where the Assembly was in session. Outnumbered, the Assembly was taken over, while demonstrators who had not been able to get in knocked down the metal gates to the Tuileries gardens and swarmed in. Louis XVI, who had given orders to channel the crowds, watched from his bedroom window, surrounded by his family. They marched along the chateau towards the river but did not attack the three rows of National Guardsmen there to defend it. It was hoped they would just disperse along the riverside.

The drama gathered steam at about three o'clock in the afternoon at the east side of the main facade; it happened so quickly that it took everyone by surprise. Four to five thousand men suddenly flooded back under an archway by the river and invaded the Cour du Carrousel. The brewer Santerre, who reigned supreme over the Saint-Antoine district, arrived from the *Manège*. He shouted to his gunners, "Why haven't you gone into the chateau? Get into the chateau; that's what we're here for!" They met no resistance. They got through the central gate and then through the metal grill of the royal gate, rushed up the grand staircase, hauled the cannon to the second floor, and pointed it toward the king's quarters. They had already started to chop down the door of the Œil-de-Bœuf when Louis XVI was finally alerted and went to confront them, ordering the door to be opened. His wife and sister hastened to join him. Clinging to his jacket and managing to keep up with him, Madame Élisabeth kept insisting, "You will have to kill me first!" But a servant held back Marie-Antoinette. According to the *Gazette de Paris* of June 26th, she cried, "Let me go, my place is with the king; I want to join him. If I must I will perish in his defense!" It took two of them to restrain her. They had heard the mob spewing "a thousand horrors" against her and calling for her head. Gently, they got her to understand that her presence, far from protecting the king, could quite well be his undoing. In any case, how could she push through a crowd of 400 brigands to get to his side? "Even if she weren't massacred, she'd have been trampled underfoot before she got there, and her efforts would only have harmed the king who... would have braved the pikes to get to her." They told her that her place was with her son, and she let herself be brought to the dauphin's room. She had a moment of panic; the child, who had been swept off when the attack started, was not there. He was brought back quickly however and after that she didn't leave his side.

She was therefore not present to see her husband, hoisted on a bench at a window, holding sway over the mob at his feet. She did not witness the much touted but perhaps apocryphal conversation said to have taken place between him and one of his faithful who were surrounding him: "Sire, have no fear." Placing his hand on his heart, he answered, "Fear? Give me your hand. Touch and see if it is trembling." She could only faintly make out that they were calling for her blood, but Élisabeth heard them all right, and pretended to the mob to be the queen so as to give her time to escape. Slipping through the familiar passageways, servants brought her reassuring news. The king had endured insults, but was not physically attacked, although he had been threatened with a pike and sword, which were quickly deflected. Rejecting any kind of violence, which would have certainly backfired, he faced the mob armed only with moral courage. He bravely donned the red cap handed to him and drank a glass of wine to the health of the nation, but invoking respect for the law, he refused to cancel his veto under the threat of violence. His impressive calm and resolve kept the most violent among them at bay for three hours, while the few city officials and deputies who managed to get to him tried in vain to restore order.

As the crowd ceaselessly thickened around him, those who had arrived first swarmed into their living quarters in search of the queen. Up until now she had escaped the mob; this time they caught up with her. Fleeing from room to room as each door was hatcheted down; she went from the dauphin's room to the king's; and then since there was no other choice, she and her children took refuge in the Council room, protected by a few loyal guards from the Daughters of Saint-Thomas. In the meantime, the Paris mayor Pétion had finally shown up and was playing a duplicitous game of peacemaker. Since Louis XVI had successfully resisted the rioters, there was nothing left to do but evacuate the premises. To avoid clogging up the grand stairway someone came up with the idea of herding the crowd in a single direction toward another exit. The king himself invited the invaders to "visit" his ceremonial reception rooms and he was then able to get away from them and back to his private bedchamber. The route they were invited to take brought them to the Council room from the ceremonial bedchamber, where they scoffed at the sight of "that fat Mr. Veto's bed." It was there that the queen, for whom they'd been looking everywhere, came suddenly face to face with them. The good old grenadiers got her behind the great Council table with her daughter and a few of her ladies-in-waiting. They sat the dauphin on the table, with his hand firmly clasped in his mother's. They stood in front of them in three rows to form a rampart against the aggressors.

It was late; the king had won this round. The leaders tried to put a brave face on it: his people had merely paid him a "courtesy call." As they were unable to hurt Marie-Antoinette physically, Santerre, who was directing the operation, wanted to throw the crowd a sop by publicly humiliating her. Cutting a path through the guards, he cried, "Make way for the people to come in and see the queen." Pretending to protect her, he stood to her right, reassuring her she had nothing to fear, saying "You have been misinformed; the people wish you no harm." She loudly refused his protection: "I am not misinformed, nor have I lost my way; and I am not afraid. One has nothing to fear when one is with good people." A red cap was handed to her. She couldn't help shuddering, or gasping in indignation when she had to put it on her son's head. It covered half his face. Their progress was blocked, they didn't know why. Annoyed at seeing the women's tender feelings being aroused by the dauphin, Santerre ordered, "Take the boy's cap off; he's too hot." When one of the women burst into tears before the queen, he sent her packing: "Get her out of here, she's drunk." Marie-Antoinette, like her husband, acquitted herself honorably, through sheer willpower.

She was very lucky they caught up with her at the last minute, when the invaders' violence had been largely spent and the leaders were back in control of their men. She was personally targeted from the beginning. Had she been felled by a knock on the head by some anonymous rioter in the heat of the initial assault, it would have been all that the event's organizers could have wished for. But they would surely be held responsible if they allowed her to be murdered in cold blood once calm had been restored. She'd had a narrow escape, and she knew it. When she and her children were finally able to get to his bedroom, where the exhausted king had thrown himself into an armchair, she collapsed at his feet in tears. They had one last trial to get through; they had to welcome a delegation from the Assembly who had come to reassure them – a bit belatedly! – of their support. They showed the delegates the damage. Aside from the shattered doors, damage to the property was relatively limited. The Tuileries remained inhabitable. Marie-Antoinette's personal apartment on the ground floor escaped the hordes that had rushed upstairs. But throughout the chateau, the surge of rioters left in its wake a trail of filth that could not be erased. The comparison with October 1789, which she could not fail to make, must have made her realize how much things had degenerated. At Versailles, they were able to keep the rioters outside the chateau. This time they had swarmed over the inner sanctum of the sovereigns' home, their refuge. And as everyone knows, this kind of intrusion feels like a rape. It is unbearable to the psyche. From now on, the royal family would not feel safe anywhere.

Time stands still

"It's a miracle I am still alive," Marie-Antoinette wrote to Fersen shortly thereafter. "The 20th was an atrocious day. I am no longer their principal target; it's my husband's very life they are after, and they no longer hide the fact. He showed a strength and resolve that held them in check for the time being, but at any moment the danger can reappear..." She showed no desperation, however, in the other notes she managed to get to him, or in the letter she sent to Mercy about it. The events of June 20th occasioned a period of reprieve for the king. There was a powerful wave of indignation against them not only abroad but in France as well, where moderates of every stripe were terrified to see the collapse of the institutions that had been so painstakingly set up. Were they going to start the Revolution all over again, against the constitution, against the king, against the duly elected Assembly? The provinces rose up against the dictatorship of Paris, of the Parisian streets. If at this point Louis XVI had clearly denounced the attack and predicted the dangers ahead in a brief and resolute proclamation, he would have won over a large majority of the population. He had a good hand to play here, as long as he acted quickly. Quick-wittedness, however, was not in his nature. And Marie-Antoinette, for whom all revolutionaries were alike whether they were moderates or extremists, shuffled the cards in such a way as to preclude any compromise. Thus, yet again, opportunities would be missed.

La Fayette was scandalized by the June 20th outrages against royal majesty and left the Ardennes where he was heading one of the French armies to hasten to the Assembly and demand sanctions. Despite some grumbling, he was generally applauded, and Pétion was suspended from his mayoral duties. A review of the National Guard was scheduled for the next day, the 29th of June. He wanted very much to use the occasion to rally his veteran soldiers and march with them to the Jacobin club to arrest its leaders. He was no doubt harboring some illusions about his own charisma, which had melted like snow in the sun. He didn't get the chance; the review was cancelled. It was claimed that the queen herself had alerted the city government, but there is no proof of this. But it is true that the sovereigns had a jaundiced view of the whole business. The queen waxed ironic: "Yes, I understand that Monsieur de La Fayette wants to save us; but who will save us from Monsieur de La Fayette?"

The "hero of two worlds" got a better reception a few days later, however, when he proposed an escape plan. He was confident that during the July 14th festivities, with the help of marshal Luckner, he could get the king and his family out in broad daylight surrounded by devoted cavalrymen and Swiss Guards. He thought he could get them as far as Compiègne where he would then be able to act as mediator. If the Assembly resisted, he and Luckner would march on Paris at the head of their troops. Even though this plan smacked of civil war, since he was in imminent danger, the king was "willing to lend himself to it." But this time the queen was against it, not only because she hated La Fayette and feared the perils involved; she also thought she had a better alternative. Why risk fleeing when all they had to do was wait? Why be indebted to the constitutional party to whom they would have to pay allegiance, when the advance of the coalition forces against France would soon restore the old regime?

Marie-Antoinette placed all of her hope in the foreign armies. Since the war began, she had been counting the days till her deliverance. They should be able to hold on until then. "I feel courageous, and something tells me that we shall soon be safe and happy," she wrote to Fersen on July 3rd. Unlike Mercy, who exhorted them to get out of Paris if they possibly could, the Swede admonished the king and queen not to leave the capital under any circumstances. He believed they were safer holed up in the Tuileries than out on the roads. That way at least they could not be eliminated without people knowing about it. She wouldn't even think of fleeing on her own, as prince George of Hesse suggested, leaving her husband and children behind to fend for themselves. Nor would she countenance adventuring abroad with them. But for pity's sake, their liberators must hurry! Either explicitly or through coded medical metaphors, a sense of urgency permeated her missives to Fersen. Every week and soon every day counted, for the Jacobins were on the counter-attack.

The movement in support of Louis XVI had momentarily neutralized the hotheads, but it eventually got their backs up. Repeatedly frustrated, they pushed for more and more radical action. It was now or never that they must do what could not be undone; it was a race for time between them and the European armies. They instigated street demonstrations again and kept petitioning for the king to be deposed. On June 11th, the balance of power saw the beginning of a brief period of stabilization when, having proclaimed "the country in danger," the deputies of every persuasion embraced each other at the behest of one of them, the aptly named Lamourette. Then in early July power seemed to be wavering between the constitutionalists and the republicans. But by Federation Day the die was cast. In effect, the clubs got around the veto against setting up camps of federated troops to defend Paris. They invited the best *fédérés* from all over the country to come to Paris to celebrate the 14th of July and paid their travel expenses. The atmosphere was very tense as the ceremonies commenced. Louis XVI had supported the suspension of Pétion, and the Federation Day ceremonies became a showdown between the two of them. The "good Pétion" was given an ovation; the king was booed. Madame de Staël noted: "The armed men who had gathered on the Champ-de-Mars looked more ready for a riot than a commemoration." The queen in her most stately attire, terribly dignified but "her eyes lost in tears," watched through a looking glass while her husband approached the Altar of the Country looking like a sacrificial lamb. Although she got him to wear the bullet- and dagger-proof vest that she had custom-made for him, the only attack he suffered was silence as he swore allegiance. But he came out the loser on this grand occasion, for the next day Pétion was reinstated as mayor. And soon the queen received an unexpected rebuff; on July 20th the sentence imposed on Jeanne de La Motte of necklace fame was overturned. The lady had died in London in the meantime, a ruined woman, in conditions as suspect as the rest of her life. It was said she jumped out of a third floor window to escape some creditors. But her reputation was rehabilitated in order yet again to smear Marie-Antoinette with the affair.

Week after week, from all over France, federated troops converged on Paris. Thus on the 30th of July six hundred men from Marseille, worked up into a fury, arrived in the capital singing a tune that a young musician named Rouget de l'Isle had just composed for the army of the Rhine*. Everything was ready for the kill. The only question that remained was when.

Living with fear

Although they had repaired and double-locked the doors, the inhabitants of the Tuileries were in constant fear. They were imprisoned, living in a state of siege. They couldn't leave the chateau grounds. The garden, closed to the public since June 20th, was the only place for them to get some fresh air. But a deputy proposed opening the adjoining Feuillants grounds to the public, arguing that this section of the chateau lands belonged to the Assembly. So a mere tricolor ribbon separated it from the rest of the gardens. It was seen as a symbolic border – on the one side national land and on the other that of Koblenz – over which people outdid each other hurling insults at the royal family, who were denounced as the enemy. The king and queen had to give up their breath of fresh air. Since the dauphin needed to get some exercise, Madame de Tourzel brought him outside but hurried him back to his room where his tutor told him stories to try to dispel the ringing in his ears from the abusive shouting. The windows that faced the gardens had to be kept firmly shut in this torrid July weather to drown out the insults or the last verses of *Ça ira*.

Trepidation crept in through the doors, although the fear of being poisoned, which had been very strong at the beginning of the year, was alleviated. For a few months the presence of a rabid Jacobin on the kitchen staff required them to be as sly as cats so as not to be seen avoiding the bread, wine, sugar and pastries they were served. They abandoned the pretense when Louis XVI realized that his fate would not be that of Henry III but of Charles I of England. He would be put to death legally, along with the monarchy.

But Marie-Antoinette still felt targeted. She imagined that all around the chateau there were assassins on the prowl, sharpening their daggers. Above all, she was terrified of the dark. One night she heard footsteps in the corridor outside her apartment, which was closed at both ends. Madame Campan called a manservant. Soon the women heard a struggle: "Madame, I know this scoundrel; I've got him," he cried. "Let him go," the queen replied; "open the door for him; he's come to assassinate me; tomorrow he'll be hailed as a hero by the Jacobins." Her bedroom was on the ground floor

---

* *Translator's note: It would become the French national anthem,* La Marseillaise.

and therefore easily accessible. Madame de Tourzel pressed her to sleep on the second floor with the dauphin, but she did not want to be accused of being cowardly. The marquise protested that no one would find out if she went via the little inner stairway. But it was in her own eyes that she didn't want to be seen as a weakling. She finally relented, "only on those days when Paris is agitated." By doing so, she experienced one of the rare joys that brightened these sinister days. Her son, "delighted to have her sleeping in his room, ran to her bed as soon as she was awake, hugged her in his little arms and said the sweetest, most adorable things to her." On the nights she slept in her own room downstairs, she kept a little dog by her bed to warn her of any intrusion. Hardly sleeping, jumping at the slightest noise, she was overcome with nervous spasms and crying fits.

No doubt her fear of assassination was excessive. But a very real and far more terrible threat weighed on them all. The Jacobin papers were openly calling for insurrection. It had fallen short on June 20th, but a lesson was learned – they would be back, and this time, they would not miss their mark. The recluses in the Tuileries therefore were ever on the lookout for the least spike in fever in the poor districts. The threats multiplied, stretching their nerves to the limit. One night at the end of July around four o'clock in the morning, disturbing noises alerted the guards; the Saint-Antoine neighborhood was on the move. The king was warned. "Now what do they want of me? Are they looking for another June 20th? Bring them on! I'm ready for anything at this point." Madame Élisabeth had also heard the warning and joined him, but Marie-Antoinette slept through it. The king did not want her disturbed. The crowd finally dispersed and everyone got back to bed, but poor Madame Campan was bitterly reproached by her mistress for not having awakened her. "It was no use telling her over and over that it had all been a false alarm, that she needed to rebuild her lost strength. 'It hasn't been lost,' she replied, 'misfortune makes one very strong. Élisabeth was with the king while I was sleeping, I who want to die at his side; I am his wife, and I do not want him to run the smallest risk without me.'" Behind these noble sentiments, however improved in the telling, we can sense the unspoken competition that again erupted between the king's wife and sister – which goes some way in authenticating the anecdote. They rivaled each other in courage. Just as in the old days when Marie-Antoinette had to be the most beautiful, she now had to be the most heroic.

Five weeks of this were enough to undermine her psychic resistance. She wanted it all over with one way or another; it didn't matter how. Death – a quick death – was better than this endless waiting. Alas, she realized that the foreign troops might arrive too late. Fersen kept her informed of their progress, which was maddeningly slow. Yes, the duke of Brunswick, a German prince working for the king of Prussia, the best general around, had been chosen to lead the coalition forces. He was a mature, experienced man, who knew his profession inside out. But he hated to hurry. He would arrive in Koblenz on July 5th, soon followed by the Prussian front lines. The rest of the troops would not be operational until about August 4th. At that point he would "advance, neutralize their defenses, and with 30,000 elite troops march straight to Paris." In other words, his idea was not to make a lightening strike on the capital to free the prisoners, but to wage a conventional war where you didn't venture into enemy territory until your back was covered. If he waited to neutralize all the towns on the border, he wouldn't be in Paris any time soon. The king would be long lost by then. A rumor was spreading that the Jacobins planned to take him and his family hostage and withdraw to the southern provinces where they could create an impregnable stronghold.

That is why Marie-Antoinette called for a manifesto to be issued urgently, without delay, threatening the ringleaders with terrifying reprisals if another attempt was made on the safety of the royal family. She was extremely impatient to get it, for it would "rally a lot of people to the king and surround him in safety." But hurry! Every day counted, and with every one that passed the assassins were growing bolder.

The duke of Brunswick signed the manifesto on July 25th and Paris found out about it at the end of the month. Contrary to what Marie-Antoinette had hoped, it exploded like a huge incendiary bomb on the city.

A most counter-productive manifesto

Already at the start of the war, the coalition forces had planned to address a proclamation to the people of France designed to rally the moderates. Louis XVI had even sent a Swiss journalist, Mallet du Pan, to Vienna with the express purpose of explaining his viewpoint. In an April 30th letter to Fersen, Marie-Antoinette had specified what a manifesto should and shouldn't say: they were not waging war on the nation, only on the troublemakers; their intention was merely to secure the king's freedom. He would then thrash out with his people what kind of government to set up. Above all, they had to stay clear of French internal affairs! "The French will always repel political interference in their business from foreigners," she noted sensibly, "and national pride is so attached to this idea that it is impossible for the king to depart from it if he wants to reestablish his kingdom." Getting what she wanted would have been tantamount to squaring a circle, so at odds was her desire for them to wage a war to free the king with her pretense that they should not meddle in the dispute between the king and the duly elected Assembly. But with a bit of tinkering, a good diplomat could have packaged the thing properly. Unfortunately, in coalition headquarters, there was a decided lack of good diplomats.

The eight-part manifesto that they gave the duke of Brunswick to sign would have roused the fury of the most peaceable people. Only the first two corresponded to Marie-Antoinette's wishes. The rest, in the form of an ultimatum, called on civilians and soldiers to submit to the foreign armies or be subjected to "the rigors of the rules of war." Very harsh words referred to the Assembly as "a faction" that was subjugating and oppressing the nation. Between the lines a promise to return to the old order could be read, and at that point all the decrees forced on the king would be abolished. The last paragraph was meant to terrorize the capital. It promised to put to death all the Assembly members and city officials, and threatened the entire population. The least violence, the least insult to the royal family would incur "exemplary and unforgettable retribution." The city of Paris would be subjected to "military rule and total ruin." This unbearably arrogant document was presumptuous as well, for the coalition members were speaking as if they had already occupied and defeated the country, whereas they had not yet set foot in it. This was selling the revolutionary bear's skin before it was killed.

An obscure émigré, a certain marquis de Limon, has come down in history as the author of this monument of stupidity. But all he did really was to state openly in legalese the substance of a text supplied by Fersen. Of course it expressed the émigrés' rancor and prejudices about the supposed cowardice of the "rogues" who, they expected, would flee as soon as the emperor bat an eyelash. But the vehemence of the language bore Fersen's mark. Not that he underestimated the danger Marie-Antoinette was in. On the contrary, he was frantic about her anguished appeals. But he knew that help would be long in coming. It was to try to stem the inexorable tide of revolution that he had Brunswick let loose this ill-considered bolt of lightening. And the revenge promised on the guilty city was commensurate with the hate he felt for it. Had he paid any attention to the queen's warnings? Had he given a single thought to how such imprecations would be perceived? Not at all! To the contrary; he was quite proud of it all. On July 28th he wrote to Marie-Antoinette, "The declaration is quite good; it is by Monsieur de Limon, and he is the one who sent it to me." And on August 3rd, "You already have the manifesto and you must be happy with it." He was so sure of its miraculous effects that, like the milkmaid of the fable, he had already decided which ministers would carry it out under the iron fist of the marquis de Breteuil.

Happy? The sovereigns were not happy at all when they read this incendiary document. It is never a wise thing to insult and challenge a nation. Brunswick's manifesto managed to do what the fiercest republicans would not even have dared to hope for. It roused the hatred of the entire French population against the invaders. They were ready to take up the challenge. It reawakened the centuries' old hostility against Austria, which the recent alliance had not entirely smothered. The manifesto overcame the partisan undercurrents in national feeling, which until then tended toward defending the Revolution. Now the people came together in the new objective of defending France's threatened territorial integrity. It created a sacred union to serve the country in danger. And it ricocheted against the king and queen, guilty of solidarity with the enemy. The tragic and fateful irony is that the proclamation so loudly called for by Marie-Antoinette and so passionately elaborated by Fersen in order to save her, served only to trigger the catastrophe.

Knightly vigil

While the despondent Louis XVI was making a doomed attempt to distinguish himself from his dodgy allies in a solemn appeal to the Assembly, Robespierre was calling for his dethronement and the election by universal suffrage of a national convention to set the framework for a republican constitution. Before a mass of deputies paralyzed by fear, the power struggle raged among the leaders. This time it was the Girondins who were overwhelmed from the left. Ever combative, Marie-Antoinette tried to play one side off against the other to forestall the inevitable. We don't know the details of the secret dealings with the Girondin leaders, but we do know that they gave the sovereigns advice and that some of them, including Pétion, got paid for it, as well as for promising to protect the Tuileries. That explains the sovereigns' misguided confidence in the first days of August despite the ever-increasing number of hostile street actions.

To be on the safe side, however, they did a bit of housekeeping in their papers; the king especially had "a prodigious quantity" of them. They sorted them, burnt many, and grouped the most important ones in some portfolios that they confided to trustworthy aids like the marquis de Jarjayes and Madame Campan. In a corridor wall of his private quarters, Louis XVI had the locksmith Gamain build a hiding place whose door was opened by a rather simple key. That was security enough as the safe blended so nicely into the stone wall. In it he left a plethora of documents concerning, it seems, his dealings with a whole range of successive members of the two assemblies, more compromising for them than for him.

A new escape plan was submitted to them *in extremis* by the most faithful of the faithful, Montmorin and Bertrand de Moleville: they could take refuge in Gaillon under the protection of the Normandy commander, the duke de Liancourt. The king informed the queen, thought about it for a few days, approved it, and sent out a scout to reconnoiter. A favorable report came back. Departure was scheduled for the night of August 7th. Moleville waited for the final okay all afternoon on the 6th. That evening he found out that the king and queen had put it off, "not wishing to leave except under the most extreme circumstances." He was enraged. If these weren't "extreme circumstances" what were? They hadn't a moment to lose. The king sent his letter back with a note scribbled in the margin, "I have it on good authority that the insurrection is not so imminent as you imagine; it still can be stopped; we just have to bide our time. I have reason to believe that there is less danger in staying than in fleeing." What reason? Montmorin imputed the refusal to the queen, who just kept repeating her favorite argument: by trusting Liancourt, they would be throwing themselves "at the mercy of the constitutionalists." But it is more likely that she recoiled from the disastrous effects of a new failure. As for Louis XVI, he was already convinced that his cause was lost, and prepared himself for the supreme sacrifice, hoping that his family would be spared.

By this time the face-off was imminent. It was no secret that the clubs were gearing up for it. It was a matter of days if not hours. The countdown was on, and Marie-Antoinette was putting all her hopes in the coalition forces. Tragically for her, it was clear that they had lost the race for time against the revolutionary forces. If they didn't arrive – and we know they never would – then "only Providence" could save the king and his family.

The situation before the events of August 10th, however, showed a stark contrast to that of June 20th. Preparations were made to defend the Tuileries, with the help of what remained of the Feuillants and the tacit agreement of the Girondins squaring off against

Robespierre. Some National Guardsmen were involved, under the command of the marquis de Mandat*, but how many is not known. They were known, however, to be unreliable, especially the gunners. There were also apparently nine hundred Swiss Guards, called up again from their base in Courbevoie, an elite troop, known for their unqualified loyalty. Two to three hundred aristocrats volunteered to rally round the king, but they were more liable to sacrifice their lives than to be useful in any organized maneuvers. They were nicknamed the "Knights of the Dagger," although their weapons were an ill-assorted lot; two who showed up empty-handed had to share a pair of fireplace tongs! In the hands of an expert, this could have sufficed to face down a mob. Marie-Antoinette, for once agreeing with Élisabeth, was in favor of resisting the rioters. But the king had given strict orders; they must not fire first; they may only respond in case of attack. But what did he mean by attack? If a furious mob broke down grates and doors for instance, even if they didn't fire, did that warrant a response? This ambiguity would have dramatic consequences, but it sprang from his obstinate refusal to shed blood. If he were alone he might have taken the risk of leaving the Tuileries unguarded; but there was his family to consider. Thus the course he adopted was neither fish nor fowl: he called together those willing to defend the chateau but he tied their hands behind their back: their only hope was that the attackers would turn around and go home when they saw the chateau was guarded. He was really deluding himself, as Mercy-Argenteau's informer Pellenc testified: "Will the Wednesday [June 20th] miracle be reproduced? They seem to think resisting the rioters will do the trick; I find that almost inconceivable. And if they give in after having resisted, all is lost."

The 10th of August

August 9th was a beautiful, quiet, warm day. But everyone knew that the assault would happen the next day. No one could sleep that night. There was no nightly bedding down ritual, and there was a good reason for that, for the king stayed up all night. So did the queen and Élisabeth, only the children went to bed. There was no more courtly etiquette at all: various individuals who wandered

---

* Since La Fayette's resignation the previous year, the National Guard was led on a rotating basis. Every two weeks command was given to a different battalion head. Mandat had been in the French Guards and was a moderate with constitutional-monarchist leanings.

through the building that night, who wound up slumped over any handy bench or balustrade, rubbed shoulders with princesses, much to the horror of the old servants, who were witnessing the dying embers of a glorious past. Everyone was waiting, their nerves stretched to breaking point, trying to catch a breath of fresh air at an open window, jumping at the slightest noise. They comforted themselves with the idea that the authorities were on their side. They would soon find out what that was worth.

At the king's request the local *procureur-syndic*[*] Roederer arrived about eleven at night to give him an update of the security situation. Tall, terse and somber, this ambitious lawman from the Lorraine was a cautious individual who knew which way the wind was blowing. A lukewarm Jacobin, he was greedy for honors, but not for responsibilities. On the evening of August 9th, his main concern was to find a superior to work under, so he wanted to get the mayor involved. Sure enough, Pétion showed up to save the day: "I have come to personally oversee the safety of the king and his family." At this point a furious marquis de Mandat also arrived to complain that the mayor's office had refused to give him ammunition for the National Guard. To protect himself, he demanded that the mayor give him a signed document to the effect that he had to "repel force with force." But Pétion was made of no sterner stuff than Roederer. Very grudgingly, he signed the paper and went off to the gardens outside, supposedly to take some fresh air. Really not keen to be trapped in a situation he knew to be doomed, he took advantage of his stroll to ask the Assembly to summon him on a most urgent matter of business. He would not be seen again. He went home to lie low until it all blew over. Clearly, no one wanted to take responsibility.

About half past midnight, Roederer told the king, the queen and Élisabeth that they had received word that the Saint-Antoine district was about to march. A quarter of an hour later they heard the distant chimes of a church bell, and then another, and still others. They made out the sound: it was the ringing of the tocsin, rallying cry for the rioters, death knell for the designated victims. Drums were beating a call to arms. Would Roederer not declare marshal law so that they could fire on the assailants? Élisabeth saw him

---

[*] The 1791 Constitution had set up institutions to govern the various administrative districts. Paris was administered by an elected city government. The Seine department was governed by a department-wide council, also elected, where the *procureur-syndic* fulfilled similar functions to those of a police chief.

leafing busily through a little book marked in three colors. "What have you there?" she asked him. "Madame, it's a police manual. I was looking to see if it true that the department has the power to declare marshal law." He concluded, of course, that it did not.

Were they approaching or not? They were taking a long time. For two hours nothing happened. Someone murmured, "The tocsin hasn't had any effect." The king took advantage of the situation to sleep a bit, fully clothed. Too nervous to sleep, the two women kept watch side by side, stretched out on a sofa in a little room on the mezzanine overlooking the gardens. The days of rivalry were over; they huddled close in an attempt to reassure one another. At four o'clock day was beginning to break. Élisabeth went to the window and looked at the vivid red sky. She said to the queen, "My sister, come see the dawn breaking." It was blood red. Just then Louis XVI emerged from his chamber. The marquis de Mandat was waiting for him with a question: should he comply with the city authorities' repeated calls for him to go to the Hôtel de Ville? He feared it was a trap. Roederer insisted, and reluctantly he went. The *procureur syndic* was already playing a defeatist role and advised the king to abandon the struggle and take refuge in the Assembly. "You are proposing to deliver him to his enemies!" the naval minister cried out. "Not exactly his enemies," Roederer replied, "… Besides, I'm proposing it because it is the least dangerous solution." But the queen intervened sharply, "Sir, we have forces protecting us here; it is time to see who will win out, the king and the Constitution, or factionalism." She hit the mark, and spoke valiantly, but could they count on the forces protecting them?

To galvanize their support, Marie-Antoinette prevailed upon her husband to review the troops. He was not lacking in courage; he had refused to put on the padded vest his wife had insisted he wear on July 14th; he intended to confront the danger on an equal footing with his faithful. But as usual, neglectful of his appearance he reviewed the troops as he was, with his clothes all wrinkled and his hair sticking out on one side but all flattened on the other, the side he'd slept on. The slept-on side had lost its powder as well. He was ungainly as he timidly walked along, and his lackluster words had nothing of the ardent proclamation the troops were expecting. The disciplined Swiss Guards said nothing; they didn't need to be encouraged to do their job. Some National Guardsmen shouted out *Long Live the King! Long Live the Nation!* But in some sections, others were turning hostile. He was greeted with insults as he approached the gunners: *Down with the Veto! Down with the Fat Pig!* The shouts were heard on the second floor where the queen was parleying with the ministers. "Great God," she cried, "it is the king they are booing! We must go find him immediately." And while they ran to his rescue, Marie-Antoinette, her red eyes filled with tears running "down to the middle of her cheeks," had to admit that this review of the troops had done more harm than good. Some of the National Guardsmen had gone over to the opposition; others refused to "fire on their brothers." Ingloriously, many of their discouraged ranks just left. Only four or five hundred remained faithfully at their posts.

Terrible news arrived. During the night, the duly elected city council was ousted by a self-proclaimed insurrectional Commune that had taken control of the government. Having gone as directed to see the city officials, the marquis de Mandat was stripped of his functions by the Commune, handed over to the crowd, and slaughtered. They were carrying his head at the end of a pike, a warning to all those who might be contemplating defending the Tuileries. It was now eight o'clock in the morning. The insurgents were getting closer; they had already reached the Carrousel. With a colleague on either side of him, Roederer asked to speak to the king – alone, with only his family as witnesses. "Sire, Your Majesty has barely five minutes left; your only safety is in the National Assembly... You do not have sufficient men here to defend the chateau. Nor is their will strong enough..." When the king replied that he did not see big crowds at the Carrousel, he was told, "Sire, there are twelve cannon, and a huge crowd is descending from the poorer districts." Marie-Antoinette tried to intervene: "But, Sir, we have our protection;" and Roederer replied, "Madame, all of Paris is on the march." He added, "If you oppose this measure, you could have the blood of your husband and children on your hands." This silenced her, but she was so overcome that Madame de Tourzel saw her face and bosom become instantly lined with deep creases. Louis XVI stared fixedly at the official for a moment, then turned and said simply, "Let's move." Madame Élisabeth spoke up, "Monsieur Roederer, do you take responsibility for the king's life?" "Upon my own, I do, Madame. I will walk immediately in front of him."

Only his family members, his ministers, the princess de Lamballe and the dauphin's governess Madame de Tourzel were allowed to accompany him. "What will become of all the people who remain upstairs?" he asked when he got to the bottom of the staircase. Roederer avoided the question by saying they could just exit via the garden. That was more easily said than done, if the royal family's difficulty reaching the *Manège* was any indication. All went smoothly as long as they kept to the reserved sections. The king and Roederer headed the group, then came the queen holding her children by the hand, after them Madame Élisabeth, Madame de Lamballe, and Madame de Tourzel, who was heartsick because her daughter Pauline was left behind in the chateau. The ministers helped the women along. A row of guards flanked them on either side. The dauphin in his boyish innocence had fun kicking the huge piles of dry leaves the gardeners had amassed. "They are falling early this year," remarked the king. And Roederer thought of a recently published article in a rabble-rousing newssheet prophesizing that the king would only last until the leaves fell. Things went haywire when they reached the Feuillants Terrace – Assembly territory. It was swarming with a bloodthirsty, menacing crowd. They had to parley; there was a scuffle. The queen either dropped or was robbed of her purse and watch. When they finally arrived at the *Manège*, she thought for a moment that they had taken her son, but he was in the arms of a guard, and everyone safely met up in the Assembly's meeting hall. The king declared, "Gentlemen, I have come so as to prevent terrible violence, believing that I can be in no safer hands than yours;" to which the Assembly chairman Vergniaud replied bombastically, "You can count, Sire, on the constancy of the National Assembly; its members have sworn to die upholding the rights of the people and their constitutional authorities."

It is pointless here to enter into the unsolvable debate that is still dividing historians: was it possible to defend the Tuileries or not? It is beyond doubt that Roederer was terrorized by Mandat's murder, thought only of getting out of there, and put pressure on the royal family to decamp immediately. But he can't be blamed for that. To be sure, if the one in control had been the inquisitive young Corsican artillery lieutenant who was present taking it all in, instead of Louis XVI, the Carrousel esplanade would have been swept clear of the demonstrators in no time. But Louis XVI was no Napoléon, and given his character, the die had already been cast. He had no alternative but to be massacred on the spot with his family or to save them by capitulating. Faced with this appalling choice, Marie-Antoinette finally caved in. No one could blame her husband for having done what he did. Believing that it was his fate alone that was in the balance, he thought he had defused the riot by taking refuge in the Assembly. And Vergniaud wasn't lying when he said that the Assembly would maintain order; he just hadn't yet understood that it would not be able to. For the most radical of the Jacobins were taking aim not only at the king, but at others as well: the Assembly, which was too timorous for their tastes; the institutions set up the previous year, which were too conservative; and the constitutional monarchy, which even gutted was still holding on to some shreds of its old prestige. They wanted nothing less than to set up, on a slate finally wiped clean, a new regime, a new society, a new man.

All it took them was a bloodbath and three days – three days during which, parked in a little corner of the *Manège* and reduced to silence, the king and queen had nothing to do but watch as the radicals brought down their world.

In the logographs' office

Within the Assembly's hall there was no place for them. They were briefly seated at the ministers' benches, but a deputy pointed out that the rules forbade deliberations in the presence of the king. So they put them in a sort of recess behind the president's desk reserved in general for "logographers[*]." The heat was suffocating in this cramped little room with a low ceiling, whitewashed walls, one table and some benches, and separated off by a grate. To give them some breathable air and also to prevent their being trapped like rats if they were attacked, the grate was taken down. But an invisible barrier continued to isolate them. They were an unacknowledged presence, there and not there at the same time, mute spectators of a game they had no part in but in which their fate was at stake.

They didn't have much time to mull over their uncomfortable and humiliating situation. About nine o'clock, shots were heard and soon covered by the rumble of cannon. The twenty commissioners sent by the Assembly to explain to the rioters still at the Tuileries that the king was no longer there had to beat a hasty retreat. What else could they have done? You can't stop a raging river. Muddled reports got back to the *Manège*, but one thing was certain: there was a struggle between the insurgents and the Swiss Guards. The king realized that before he left he should have had the chateau evacuated or at least have given clear instructions to those defending it; but at the time he hadn't imagined it would need defending. Now it was too late. Obeying the initial instructions, the Knights of the Dagger and the Swiss Guards were resisting the invasion. Who struck first? The endlessly debated question remains unanswerable because all the witnesses' accounts were partial and contradicted each other. In any case, when it comes to a riot, the question is irrelevant, because

---

[*]   Roughly the equivalent of stenographers who published verbatim accounts of the Assembly's proceedings in a publication called *The Logograph*, hence the name.

a massive surge of enraged humanity obviously constitutes an act of aggression, and under such circumstances it is pointless to wonder who fired the first shot.

More precise news was arriving. They were beginning to realize what had happened. Those left in the chateau had no way out. They had to fight for their lives. For a while, entrenched inside, they fought off with cannon fire the Marseille *fédérés* crammed into the Carrousel area. The *fédérés* fell back in panic but were able to regroup. They got reinforcements and went on the offensive. They broke into the chateau and started a fire. There must have been hundreds of dead by now, from both sides. The defending forces were now trying to escape through the gardens, clashing swords with the rioters. Prisoners in their cage, the royal family listened. They were deathly pale; their hearts were broken. Marie-Antoinette found it hard to fight back the tears. The dauphin was crying, asking for Pauline de Tourzel, who had been left behind. Soon a flow of all sorts of people came piling in: the wounded, the fleeing, military men, rioters, and Swiss Guards. Then the inevitable petitioners arrived, incriminating the king and demanding he be dethroned. Meanwhile, the insurrectional Commune took care to let the Assembly know that it was now the sole master of Paris, sending a list of its new leaders.

Seeing the dreadful scope of the massacre, Louis XVI, who had been able neither to foresee nor forestall it, tried to stop it under pressure from the Assembly when the beaten Swiss Guards came straggling back to the *Manège*. He bade them give up their weapons, as a note to that effect testifies. This absurd order, arriving too late, could only worsen the refugees' fate. But he did not cause the death of the great number of people who had already paid with their lives and perished defending the Tuileries. The fight, too unequal, was lost from the start. Not having a fortified keep at their disposal, nine hundred seasoned Swiss Guards helped by a few hundred disparate combatants, could not stand up to the advance of 20,000 desperate men who would stop at nothing. But that night more than ever before, the monarch proved himself incapable of managing a crisis, of taking a decision, or of cutting his losses. Like his wife, he lacked political acumen. Both were victims of tragic self-deception. Thanks to Marie-Antoinette's rash ploy to get foreign support, the people she was hoping to crush rose up against them; and Louis XVI's naïve assumption that everything would work out for the best as long as he didn't cause a drop of blood to be spilled had the opposite effect: it flowed in torrents.

Another terrible blow was in store for him: he was accused of having willfully sought the bloodletting. This was a perfect excuse for dethroning a king whose legitimacy resided in a constitution. He was blamed for the massacre. It was claimed that he ordered the Swiss Guards to parley with the insurgents to get them within range of their cannon. Once they were victorious, they would have marched on the Assembly, routed the deputies, arrested or killed the Jacobins and got the king out of Paris. Weren't Swiss Guards seen running toward the *Manège*? Yes, they were bloodied and begging for asylum, but this was no time to quibble over details. This version of events, adopted by Michelet, was popular for a long time among historians keen to whitewash the Republic's founders of any crime. Needless to say, the assertion is completely incompatible with what we know of Louis XVI's character and convictions.

*Is fecit cui prodest**. Who else profited from the bloodbath but the Jacobins? We are a bit better informed than our antecedents about the techniques of revolutionary war. The evidence was clear: the taking of the chateau was meticulously organized and led, not by hordes of raving mad protesters but by trained and directed assault troops. The following example bears witness to the fact. In the chateau under siege, a few terrified women had gathered in the queen's apartment where all the candelabra were lit so that they would not be mistaken for combatants. Among them were Pauline de Tourzel and Madame Campan, both of whom recounted the episode in entirely different styles, but basically saying the same thing. When the door opened and blood-spattered men came pouring in, the women believed they were about to be killed. But more than by their courage under pressure, they were saved by the orders their assailants had been given: "Don't kill any women." Not only were they not raped or butchered, but the men took care to deliver them from the hell they were in, stepping over the corpses in their way. Another clue: as the day wore on, more and more people arrived at the *Manège* laden down with things taken from the Tuileries – gold, jewelry, documents, letters and banknotes – that they deposited on the president's desk, as property of the nation. The orders had been explicit: thievery would be punishable by death. And it is clear that the rioters' plundering was selective. They were allowed to pillage the wine cellars and the kitchen, and they took full advantage of that. The Swiss Guards on the other hand were delivered up to their ferocity: they were tortured, disemboweled, castrated and

---

* *Translator's note: "Done by the one who profits from it."*

dismembered to serve as a warning; those were their instructions. The Terror had just made its political debut.

The effects were immediate. At seven o'clock the deputies had been prepared to open their arms to the king "with the honors duly set forth in the Constitution." Vergniaud had promised him help and protection. But by ten o'clock the same Vergniaud, without daring to pronounce the word dethronement, was calling for "the revocation of the authority that had been delegated to him" and the establishment of a provisional executive council until a "National Convention" could be elected at the earliest possibility to work out the details of new institutions. The king and his family would remain inside the Assembly's walls until such time as peace was restored in Paris, after which he proposed they be lodged at the Palais du Luxembourg, which was under strict surveillance and poorly provisioned. Was there cowardice on Vergniaud's part? Of course, but mostly he was powerless. By this time he realized that the Commune was in control of the *fédérés* and the National Guard, in other words, all of the armed forces. The organizers of the insurrection had calculated correctly; they could kill two birds with one stone. They were forcing the Assembly to abandon the king and thus to scuttle itself as well. Power had changed hands. The Girondins had lost. The winners were Danton, the mastermind of the day's events, and Robespierre, chief theoretician of the new order.

For hours on end the king and queen listened while one enraged demonstrator after another took the floor to enumerate their crimes and demand they be dethroned. Overwhelmed by the heat, terribly thirsty and thoroughly exhausted, they saw torn from them, one by one, every last shred they possessed, not of power – they no longer had any – but of autonomy. With each succeeding decree, the king's few remaining rights were stripped from him and shared among the citizens. Throughout the proceedings Louis XVI retained an impenetrable silence. In her sweat-drenched dress that was sticking to her shoulders, Marie-Antoinette fidgeted, looked for her handkerchief, found it dripping with tears, and asked the count de La Rochefoucauld who was sitting near her, to lend her one. In the nick of time, he recalled that his own was drenched in the old viscount de Maillé's blood. He had been swabbing his wounds. He found her another one, which she quickly moistened. She must hold on, however; she must not collapse. She barely listened to the avalanche of words that was inundating the speakers platform. At this point, nothing mattered to them. No, that's not quite true; they were again discussing the dauphin's education! He was over seven years old. Wasn't it about time he was removed from his parents' pernicious influence and placed in the hands of someone won over to the new way of thinking? They were sickened. Mercifully, the Assembly had more urgent matters to deal with and didn't appoint the royal prince a new tutor. It was, according to Madame de Tourzel, the one moment of consolation during this entire horrifying day.

That evening they were housed in the Feuillants convent adjoining the *Manège*. They had to crowd into three hastily prepared cells. The king had one to himself, the queen shared one with her daughter, and the ladies Élisabeth, de Tourzel and de Lamballe all shared the third with the little boy. A fourth one was placed at the disposal of a few gentlemen who insisted on following their master. They all slept badly. The corridor outside their cells was closed by a mere grate, which the sentinels had a hard time defending from the screaming rioters who kept a keen eye on their prey. They had eaten nothing all day. The next day a sympathetic official had an excellent meal catered for them, which the king honored with a lusty appetite that exasperated his wife. They had been able to take nothing with them when they left the Tuileries. A few lady friends arranged a change of clothing for them. Seeing that they had no money – the queen had to borrow twenty-five louis from a chamber maid – a few faithful friends offered to give them everything they had on them, but the king refused, saying they would have no use for it. Did Marie-Antoinette make a grandiloquent speech against all those responsible for their misfortune? Perhaps Madame Campan was exaggerating, as this seems unlikely. We can believe one thing, however, that she was convulsed with sobbing.

They would endure the same torture another two days and nights between their tight quarters at the *Manège* and the equally cramped Feuillants cells, now minus the gentlemen. At the *Manège*, they heard the endless rehashing of the same insults and grievances. Their future was rapidly darkening. While waiting for the Convention to decide their fate, they would be held hostage under the city authorities' surveillance. The deputies planned for them to be housed at the Luxembourg, which had been vacated by the count de Provence. This vast palace with its gardens would have afforded them a residence that was comfortable and in conformity with their rank. But it was not considered secure enough; there were subterranean passageways that could provide an exit. The minister of justice's home in the Place Vendôme was then suggested, but there were too many houses around it, which also could have facilitated an escape. The Commune proposed, or rather imposed, the Temple, because it was "out of the way and surrounded by high walls."

From the Tuileries to the Temple

A relic from the time when the Knights Templar formed something of a state within a state, the Temple was a vast enclosure situated in the northern part of the Marais*. At the end of the 13th century they had built a fortress there that was surrounded by high, crenellated walls and dominated by a massive quadrangular keep. Subsequently the lodgings of the Grand Prior of the Knights of Malta, it was still at the time of the Revolution an independent domain beyond local jurisdiction. Its buildings were a hodge-podge of different types. The Grand Prior's luxurious palace, recently deserted by the count d'Artois, was next to the dilapidated keep. There were vast gardens, a hospital, a cemetery, and outbuildings. The rest of the space was occupied by dwellings ranging from the most extravagant to the most humble. The old medieval ramparts had been replaced by perimeter walls that were not as high as the ramparts but quite solid, through which there was only one entrance gate, which is the reason the Commune chose it.

In the Grand Prior's Palace the royal family could have lodgings that were certainly more fortress-like than the Luxembourg, but comfortable as well. The Assembly in their haste to get rid of the king didn't ask questions, and perhaps didn't even think about it. But when Marie-Antoinette heard of their decision, she could not suppress a shudder. "You'll see; they'll put us in the tower, and they'll turn it into a veritable prison for us," she murmured in Madame de Tourzel's ear. "I've always held that tower in such horror that I begged the count d'Artois a thousand times to have it torn down, and it was surely a premonition of what we are going to suffer there." The governess protested but she carried on, "You'll see whether I'm wrong or not." Her apprehensions must have been confirmed by the measures taken for their household service. They were provided with only one domestic per person: a *valet de chambre* for the king and four chambermaids shared among the queen, Madame Élisabeth, Madame Royale and the dauphin**; not exactly enough to maintain their grand style of life.

The day of the 13th was spent making arrangements. What was to

---

* Roughly, it was bounded on its four sides by what are now the rue du Temple, rue de Bretagne, rue de Picardie and rue Beranger.

** François Hue, affected to the dauphin's service, also received authorization to follow him, but was soon dismissed.

be done with Madame de Lamballe and Madame de Tourzel, who had been accompanying the sovereigns since they left the Tuileries? It was decided that for the moment they would remain with the group. Louis insisted on sending away the gentlemen who remained desirous of following him, as he did not want them to be uselessly victimized on his account. "Leave me, I pray you... This is perhaps the last order you will ever receive from me." The unthinking Marie-Antoinette on the other hand believed she was doing Madame de Tourzel a favor by suggesting her daughter Pauline be brought to keep her company! The tears and supplications of the dauphin and his sister forced the poor woman to give in, dreading it terribly, and Pétion was delighted to oblige.

At six o'clock in the evening everyone piled in to one of the court carriages guarded by three city officials, among them Pétion and Manuel. Only two horses were used. There was no hurry, and besides, they had to parade the imprisoned royal family through the streets so they could savor their own debasement. The carriage went at a snail's pace as insults were hurled at them. At the Place Vendôme the equestrian statue of Louis XIV lay upended on the ground. Manuel stopped the carriage so that it seemed momentarily ensnared in the horse's legs. He upbraided Louis XVI: "You see, Sire, how the people deals with its kings." To which the king replied calmly, "Please God they unleash their fury only on inanimate objects." *Sire*? Was Manuel momentarily distracted? As a rule, the Jacobins merely called him Monsieur. Or perhaps the narrator, the good Madame de Tourzel, corrected his manners.

Along the boulevards there was such a press of seething masses that the two city officials had to summon them in the name of the law to let the carriage through. Punctuated by stops demanded by this "horrifying escort," the wretched journey took two and a half hours. Marie-Antoinette was so on edge that she actually looked forward to getting to the Temple as soon as possible to escape the grip of the rabble and to find behind its walls some silence and solitude. But a surprise awaited them. "The Temple was festively festooned in lights, even in the crenellations of the garden wall." In the salon, "lit up by an infinity of candles," members of the Commune were waiting for the royal family to have a supper that promised to be carefully prepared. But really, not all of them were properly attired, nor were their manners anything like those of Versailles. "What is your profession?" asked the king of one of them, who was waxing eloquent about equality. "Cobbler" he replied. Louis XVI and Marie-Antoinette suffered these liberties with grace. But chin up! Surely they would soon be lodged in the palace.

CHAPTER 22

THE TEMPLE KEEP

The dauphin could hardly stand he was so tired. Madame de Tourzel enquired about his room. She was told it wasn't ready. He fell asleep over his soup. He was sleeping on her lap when a guard finally arrived to fetch him. According to the governess:

> He took him in his arms and carried him off with such haste that Madame de Saint-Brice and I had a terribly difficult time keeping up with him. A deadly fear overcame us as we crossed the underground passageway*; and it only increased when he brought the young prince into a tower and deposited him in the room they had waiting for him. Terrified of being separated from him yet not wanting to irritate the city officials, I asked no questions. Without uttering a word, I put him to bed, and then sat down in a chair, given over to the most somber of reflections. I was trembling at the idea of his being separated from the king and queen, and was greatly relieved to see the princess enter the room. She held my hand in hers saying, "Didn't I tell you so?" And then as she approached the bed where her sweet child lay sleeping soundly, her eyes filled with tears...

It was thus that Marie-Antoinette learned what lodgings the Commune had chosen for them.

---

* Madame de Saint-Brice was the *femme de chambre* assigned to the dauphin. What Madame de Tourzel took for an underground passageway was actually a covered walkway connecting the palace to the small tower where the library was housed.

Model prisoners

The keep itself was uninhabitable. But on its north face was attached a markedly lower rectangular building with two small corner turrets. They called it the little tower. The Order of Malta's archivist used it, but he was summarily evicted. The royal family was squeezed into its third and fourth floors. According to Madame de Tourzel, "There were only two rooms on each floor, with a little one serving as a passageway between the two. The princess de Lamballe was placed in the small central room, and the queen occupied one of the larger ones, facing that of milord the dauphin. The king lodged above the queen, and they set up a guardroom in the room next to his. Madame Élisabeth was assigned to a kitchen that adjoined the guardroom, which was filthy dirty." The industrious Élisabeth lost no time in organizing their life there; both male and female servants worked at making the place presentable.

They didn't have much time to do so. During the night of August 19th-20th, they were awakened by a commotion. They had come to arrest Madame de Lamballe. Then all of the members of their staff were invited to don their street clothes and follow the officials to the Commune to be questioned. They would return shortly, they were told. Their pleas and entreaties were of no avail. The queen bid Madame de Lamballe a tearful farewell, and knowing her friend to be greatly lacking in strength of mind, she entrusted her to Madame de Tourzel. She managed to whisper to her that should her friend be interrogated, she was to try to speak for her, so that she could avoid answering any difficult questions. She had the feeling none of them would come back. She was right; the Commune was behaving with the same hypocritical circumspection about their household staff as they had about their dwelling place. Fearing the Assembly deputies' reaction, the city officials led them to believe that the royal family would be treated with due respect for custom and allowed to keep their staff. Just as they had not made it clear whether the family would be housed in the Grand Prior's Palace or the keep, they let them retain their staff for five days, after which who would even wonder about it? They were correct.

Refusing the personnel they were offered, the two sisters-in-law chose to do some of the household tasks themselves. Marie-Antoinette took care of her son and Élisabeth took charge of Madame Royale. Propriety required that the king have a manservant. The next day therefore François Hue returned. In the meantime another candidate volunteered for the position. Jean-Baptiste Cléry was a farmer's son from the vicinity of Versailles, who had occupied the position of *valet de chambre* for the second dauphin. His mother had been a nursery attendant at the chateau. He offered his services to the little boy. In 1789 he had shown proof of his revolutionary sentiments. On Pétion's recommendation, he was hired on the 26th of August. He was to replace Hue, who was arrested a week later. Thanks to his journal we are able to know something of the royal family's life in captivity.

The ground floor of the building contained disused kitchens. One of the little corner turrets had a spiral staircase. On the second floor there were an antechamber and a dining room, and in the turret was the archivist's library with from twelve to fifteen hundred volumes – a true godsend! On the third floor the queen shared the largest room with the dauphin, which the dark little antechamber separated from the room assigned to Élisabeth and her niece. "It was necessary to cross this room to get to the toilet in the turret, and this toilet was used by the entire building, royal family, city officials and soldiers alike." On the fourth floor, the king slept in the large room and used the turret as a reading room; next to it there was a little kitchen. The top floor above him remained empty. The whole place bristled with warders. At all times there were two municipal guards keeping the prisoners under close surveillance except when the doors closed on their bedrooms at night, but then the guards' camping beds were arranged so as to obstruct them.

The prisoners could no longer even dream of escaping, but they did try to reestablish some semblance of normalcy. The monotony of their life helped, as did the obligation to keep a brave face. The king rose at six and shaved himself, but Cléry dressed and coiffed him. He then withdrew to his reading room for a short prayer, on his knees; after which he read until nine. The valet tidied his room and set the table for breakfast then proceeded to look after the queen, who awaited his arrival before opening her door. He did his best to arrange the three ladies' and little boy's hair. At nine o'clock all four joined the king for breakfast while the valet cleaned their rooms. At ten o'clock they all went down to the queen's room, which was the most pleasant of them, to spend the better part of the day. Until eleven it served as a classroom. The king had his son recite monologues from Corneille and Racine, and gave him geography lessons by showing him how to find rivers, cities and even departments – since departments there were – on a map of France. At the same time the queen helped her daughter with her lessons. Then the women would sew, knit or read. At noon, to maintain a bit of decorum, the women would change out of their morning dresses.

If it was a good day, at one they asked the Temple administrators' permission to walk in the gardens, under the vigilant eyes of five guards. The dauphin, who needed to work off some of his boyish energy, would run or play ball or quoits with Cléry.

At two o'clock dinner was served in the second-floor dining room. The fearsome Santerre, now the commander of the National Guard, then arrived to do a thorough inspection of the apartments. Unlike her husband, Marie-Antoinette could never get herself to speak a word to him. At about four in the afternoon, the king napped in his armchair surrounded by the princesses, each with her book. When he awoke, they resumed their conversation. The dauphin wrote out pages of his writing lessons so as to gain the right to go play for a few moments in his aunt's room. The queen and her sister-in-law then took turns reading educational materials out loud. The king amused the children by asking them to solve "enigmas" – we would say riddles or word puzzles – taken from old issues of the *Mercure* found in the archivist's library. At eight o'clock the little boy had his supper; his mother listened as he said his prayers and put him to bed. Mother or aunt would stay with him as he nibbled on something brought to him in bed, while the other took a meal in the dining room with the king. After supper, he would stop on the third floor to shake the hand of his wife and his sister by way of good night and to kiss his daughter. The queen and the princesses retired to their rooms for the night and closed their doors. He took himself off to his room upstairs and read until about midnight.

In the beginning the Commune gave the captives some leeway. They had no spare clothing so they were given credit. The king remained sober in his attire, but the princesses were allowed to order from their usual suppliers the latest fashions in clothing and accessories: dresses, shoes, stockings, shawls and hats – even some cosmetics. The list would hardly be believed had not André Castelot found all the invoices in the archives. The table was likewise splendidly arrayed. Just as Cléry had done, other former food-service staff members from Versailles days found a way to get hired; after all, they had already earned their credentials. And when it came to buying food, their credit was always good, even when they would subsequently have to haggle over their clothing. The head of the service personnel, Turgy, knew how to win over the jailers; he fed them, and fed them well, sharing the fruits of his culinary talents with them. Life would almost have been bearable, materially speaking, if it were not for the constant and obsessive surveillance. The only dignified response was to show the most inalterable patience. Louis XVI had a natural talent for it; the two proud women followed suit. So it was that the three of them offered their persecutors the very image of model prisoners.

Most of the municipal workers assigned to the Temple came from the ranks of the rioters. Many of them rivaled each other in insolence, either because they were naturally crude or because they wanted to prove themselves. They tried to outdo each other. Aside from anything else, the family knew that they were being spied upon by a husband and wife team named Tison, two domestics who were hired to help Cléry with the heavier work but whose main task was to spy on everyone. Prying, harassment, groundless suspicions, reprimands and snitching were their stock in trade. One of them thought he saw in the multiplication tables being used to teach the dauphin arithmetic an initiation into coded language; another interpreted his mother's embroidered tapestries as some sort of hieroglyphics she was using to communicate with the outside. One of the jailers took to rattling his keys before letting the prisoners exit their rooms only to blow pipe smoke in their faces when they crossed the threshold. They would find their walls covered with threats and insults. Republican virtues were flaunted in their presence; they were threatened with the guillotine[*]. In front of the Austrian "she-wolf" they spoke of cutting the throats of the wolverines. The walks in the garden were particularly trying. Their arrival would bring on a riot of insults and revolutionary songs. The words of the most recent one, the *Carmagnole*, rehashed the accusations of August 10th.

> *Madame Veto had promised.*
> *To cut everyone's throat in Paris.*
> *But her attempt was aborted,*
> *By our cannons retorted.*
> *So let's dance the Carmagnole,*
> *Long live the roar of the cannon.*

---

[*] Under the Ancien Régime, noblemen were generally beheaded with an axe and commoners were hanged. Recourse to the guillotine was inspired both by an egalitarian impulse ("All who are condemned to death shall have their head severed,") and by humanitarian concern: the machine was fast and dependable, thus avoiding needless suffering. This mechanism, whose conception was attributed to a Doctor Guillotin, and fabrication to the surgeon Louis, was first used on a thief on April 25, 1792 at the Place de Grève. Later it was principally used for political executions at the Place du Carrousel from August 21, 1792 to May 10, 1793. An exception was made for the king, who was brought to the Place de la Révolution, (now Place de la Concorde). It remained in use there from May 10, 1793 until June 8, 1794.

The recipients of the abuse didn't show any dismay or offer any protest; they simply ignored the provocations. Their apparent serenity exasperated their most ferocious warders, but it troubled many others, who refused to vie with their colleagues to be unkind. It isn't easy to gratuitously insult defenseless people. The same ones who were shouting for Mr. Fat Veto's blood in the heat of a riot, were disarmed by the ordinary, decent family man before them. Why not raise your hat to him, as just plain common courtesy would require? Despite instructions, the Commune's delegate, the city official Goret, offered him his arm and spoke politely to him. At one point, the king and his sister were playing chess by the window in their low-ceilinged, ill-lit room, as the rest of the family looked on. Goret felt out of place and was at a loss to know what to do, so he took a book to read. Marie-Antoinette gently called him, "Come over with us, Monsieur, you'll see better." For a moment the roles were reversed: he had become his prisoners' guest.

This was not a unique occurrence. Sometimes the guards behaved with delicacy. A little later on, one of them saw that the queen was disappointed that a harpsichord at their disposal could not be used as it was out of tune. He intervened to get it repaired, and that very evening she was able to give her daughter a lesson. Others found it hard to hide their sympathy, and risked being compromised as a result. The city authorities were warned, and never let anyone work there too long. Thus they saw a constant turnover of guards, with its concomitant renewed efforts to get acquainted and peacefully coexist. These were sometimes more successful than others. They never knew if the new guards would be insolent or humane, reproachful or kind, so they had to be constantly on guard. Who knows what tomorrow might bring? The prisoners knew that their fate depended on the mood of their jailers.

They soon found out that it depended also on events happening elsewhere.

Red September

As August waned into September, they sensed that the atmosphere was worsening. They had hardly gone down into the garden on September 2nd, when a city official said to a colleague, "It was a bad idea to let them out this afternoon." They were sent right back upstairs. Then suddenly two officials who were not on duty that day entered the queen's room. One of them, a man by the name of Mathieu, addressed the king gruffly: "You don't know, Monsieur, what is happening. The country is in the greatest danger. The enemy is in the Champagne region; the king of Prussia is marching on Châlons: you will answer for any harm that results. We know that we, our women and our children will perish, but the people will be avenged. You will go to your death before we do. However, there is still time and you can..." But the king interrupted: "I have done everything I could for my people; I have nothing for which to blame myself."

What was happening? On 19 August 1792, the duke of Brunswick's army had crossed the border. That same day, La Fayette, having despaired of turning his troops against the Paris insurgents, had surrendered to the Austrians. Longwy surrendered on the 23rd, after three days under siege. On the 30th they learned that Verdun was overrun and about to surrender, which would open the enemy's way to Paris. Some ministers wanted to flee to the Val-de-Loire. Danton opposed this, in a speech that has remained famous: "We need audacity, and yet more audacity, and always audacity, and France is saved!" An army of 30,000 volunteers was raised to defend Paris in danger. The coalition forces had fulfilled Marie-Antoinette's wishes. And by a baleful historical irony, the Commune under threat handed Louis XVI the role he had often dreamed of: there is still time and you can... Alas, the poor man knew perfectly well that he could not, that he had no power to stop the coalition's offensive. And the war he and his wife had hoped would be their salvation closed in on them like a trap.

The next day, September 3rd, the captives were not allowed to go out for their walk. They dined and returned upstairs to the queen's room on the third floor. Shouts and drum rolls were heard. All of a sudden there was a terrible screech, and Cléry appeared, his face twisted in terror. "Why are you not going to dine?" the queen asked him. "Madame, I am indisposed." Around them, the officials were quietly and anxiously conferring. They had lowered the blinds. The king asked them if his family was safe. "There is a rumor about that you and your family are no longer here in the tower;" he replied, "they are demanding you appear at the window, but we will have none of it: the people must show greater trust in its city councilors." They could hear the queen being insulted. At that point four men showed up saying they were the people's deputies come to force them to the window. One of the four finally blurted out to the queen, "These people are just trying to spare you the sight of Lamballe's head that has been brought here to show you how the people take revenge on tyrants. I advise you to go to the window if you don't want the people to come up here." For a moment frozen in horror, Marie-Antoinette fainted. The four men left. Through a slit in the blind, Cléry saw for the second time the poor woman's bloody but not at all disfigured head with its still curly blond locks dangling around the pike on which it was displayed.

He found out what had happened. Roughly grabbing her from the La Force prison, the band of cutthroats who had been dealing death in the prisons since the night before knocked her senseless, decapitated her and proceeded to hack away at different parts of her body, inflicting particular savagery on her vagina – after all, wasn't she Marie-Antoinette's partner in Sapphic crime? They then dragged it all to the Temple shouting that they would make the queen kiss the dead lips of her lover, in the hope, no doubt, of subjecting her to the same fate. Not without difficulty, the guards succeeded in preventing the rabble from entering the Temple grounds, but not the pike bearers who had managed to get to the foot of the little tower. Blocking access to the stairs, a city official had let in the four "deputies," and in order to disperse the others made quite a peculiar speech: "Antoinette's head does not belong to you; the departments have some claim to it; France has entrusted the guard of these evildoers to the city of Paris: it is up to you to help us in this effort until national justice will have avenged the people." But saying this, he did manage to save them.

All night long Madame Royale heard her mother sobbing while drums continued their sinister beat, calling the masses to arms. This incident marked Marie-Antoinette deeply; she never got over it. But Louis XVI immediately grasped the double lesson. The prison walls had protected them; the tower's narrow spiral staircase afforded greater protection than the Tuileries' grand stairway. As long as the guards continued to do their job, they were relatively safe. They had actually done more than required in trying to save the queen from the hideous spectacle. Among the Commune members, revolutionaries from the start and staunch republicans, there were many who were sickened, and the royal family found with some of them, not salvation, which was out of the question, but at least a bit of human warmth.

On the lookout for news

To isolate the prisoners even further, an inner wall was built around the little tower and the part of the garden allotted to them. Cut off from the outside world, they only knew what people were willing to tell them. And what they were told was censored. They were given only reading materials insulting to them. Sometimes news would reach them unexpectedly thanks to the ingenuity of some of their faithful. One day Élisabeth saw a large sign held up behind the window of a neighboring house that read: *Verdun has fallen.* But after the massacres, they felt an urgent need to know more. Cléry was able to reassure them about the fate of Pauline and Madame de Tourzel. They had managed to escape unharmed from the La Force prison along with the four chambermaids.

They soon set about creating their own information network. Cléry was its lynchpin. He was not allowed to leave their compound, but as he was watchful and clever, he circulated freely within it and was good at getting the guards to talk. But he also had to communicate with the outside world, so his wife acted as his go-between. It was she who quite early on had the shrewd idea of hiring a newspaper seller to come punctually every evening at seven to shout very loud a summary of everything that had gone on at the Assembly, the Commune and the army. What is more, she visited him once a week supposedly to deliver laundry, and since she arrived while the guards were on dinner break, she was able to chat with him or even exchange notes. But the main source of news was Turgy, whose culinary functions included shopping for food two or three times a week at city markets. If an urgent matter arose, the two assistants played out a little ruse. Cléry would declare loudly that he had to get something that was needed urgently, and Turgy would reply, "Not today, you won't." Cléry would shrug and say, "Then I guess the king will just have to wait," whereupon some official could generally be counted on to let him go do his errand. But they had to be careful not to pull the trick twice with the same guard.

Next they had the problem of circulating the information within the tower. Turgy was only allowed to speak to Cléry about business and then only in the presence of warders. In the same way, the prisoners were only supposed to speak audibly to each other or a third party and that in the presence of witnesses, so they had to resort to trickery. Hairdressing lent itself to private conversations as heads necessarily came into close contact. Turgy did Cléry's hair and Cléry did the royal family's while one of the women distracted the guards, and the children's noisy games lent background noise. Morning and evening routines afforded Cléry other good opportunities. He took advantage of the times he dressed the king behind his bed curtains and when the queen had the dauphin recite his prayers before going to sleep.

When surveillance got stricter, they got more inventive. As the two women did a lot of needlework, Turgy would slip notes into balls of twine or cotton that he scattered about in odd places, discreetly signaling the women where they were. He even had the audacity to roll up some notes into bottle stoppers. Élisabeth, more gifted than her sister-in-law for practical matters, actually invented a complex system of coded gestures somewhat resembling modern-day sign language. "For the English, bring your right thumb to your right eye; if they land by way of Nantes, bring it to your right ear; if by way of Calais to the left ear. If the Austrians prevail up by Belgium, the second finger of the right hand on your right eye. If they arrive by way of Lille or Mayence, the third finger as above. The king of Sardinia's troops, the fourth finger as above. – *Nota bene*: care must be taken to keep the finger lifted a length of time commensurate with the importance of the battle." Similar tricks must have allowed them to describe precisely enough the various workings of the Convention.

The king was content merely to listen to the news, and once in a while ask a question. Buried in the archivist's library, he spent his time reading – 250 volumes in five months, they say. Religious books, but also Montesquieu, Buffon, Torquato Tasso, classics of the French theater, travelogues, Hume's *History of England,* and even Horace's *Odes* to refresh his Latin so as to impart the basics to his son. Most of the message transmission he left to his wife and sister. They got caught up in the game, as it occupied their minds and fulfilled their need to do something. Their successful efforts to trick the warders were so many minor victories that in their eyes prefigured the big one, the real one, that of the coalition forces who were sure to come. Unlike the king, they never ceased to hope.

Alas, Élisabeth's code was not put into much use, at least not by the end of September 1792. For news, official this time, came pouring down on the prisoners, and it was not good.

The moribund Legislative Assembly had caved in to all the pressure from the Commune, consenting to the creation of a "people's court" elected by the Paris sections, reinforcing religious persecution, supporting the hunting down of the "enemies from within," and not daring to condemn the September massacres. Taking place in a climate of civil war, the elections brought to power a more radical assembly than the preceding one, in which the influence of Paris and the most agitated provinces risked tipping the balance. The Girondins were still in a majority, but since those who would come to be known as the Montagnards were in control of the city, there was little doubt that a clash was ahead. Between them, the king's fate would become an apple of discord.

The Convention met on September 21st and its first act was to abolish the monarchy. The same day, at four o'clock in the afternoon, an envoy from the city surrounded by mounted gendarmes and a mass of people stopped at the foot of the tower, ordered the trumpets to sound, and read a proclamation in a stentorian voice: royal rule was abolished and replaced by a republic. Hébert, editor of the famous *Père Duchesne**, whose specialty was insulting the royal family, had volunteered to mount the guard around them that day, and "stared smirking at the king." Neither he nor the queen batted an eyelash, said Cléry. But Hébert treated his readers to his own brand of reporting: "The big fat jackass... puts up a brave show of it but he is suffocating with rage; to hide her chagrin the Austrian bitch says she has the vapors; the tub o'lard Élisabeth goes weeping into her corner. This farce lasted until supper time when the fat jackass did not miss the chance to bolt down some food; but Madame Veto had already taken herself off to bed, her only soup having been a glass of water." But the government's official language could not indulge in this kind of invective; they gave the former monarchs the commoner's name of Capet, borrowed from the distance founder of the dynasty.

It got a lot worse a few days later. They learned that the Austro-Prussian troops were beating a retreat. At first they did not want to believe it; it could only be disinformation meant to demoralize them. But they were soon disabused of the notion. On the 20th of September the duke of Brunswick, cornered in the Argonne gorges by Dumouriez and Kellermann, gave up trying to take the knoll where the Valmy mill was, from which gunners were firing at his troops. He turned back. Militarily speaking it was not a decisive battle; the enemy forces remained intact. But psychologically, it was a shock. This victory gave the lie to all the prognosticating about the war's outcome. It was a veritable consecration of the revolutionary army, and caused the coalition forces to rethink their strategy. At first they were convinced Paris would fall like a ripe apple; now they realized that it would be ferociously defended. They had already seen, whatever Marie-Antoinette might have promised, that the people were not welcoming them with open arms. And their rear was not well protected. The supply corps was not following them. It was better now that winter was coming not to tempt the devil. Revolutionary France started accruing a series of victories that Manuel gleefully reported to Louis XVI: "You are no doubt aware of the success of our armies, about the taking of Spire and of Nice, and of the conquest of the Savoy?" He instructed the city officials, "to give monsieur all the newspapers; it will be good for him to be educated about all our successes."

---

* *Translator's note: An extremely radical and rabble-rousing newspaper during the French Revolution published from September 1790 to March 1794, when Hébert was guillotined.*

The desperate royal family felt well and truly abandoned. Immediately following Valmy, however, Dumouriez tried for a settlement. Brunswick was not adverse to a separate peace, as long as Louis XVI's fate was decided honorably. But the king of Prussia insisted that a re-empowered French king be restored to his throne at the very time when the Convention was declaring the Republic. The negotiations failed and as a result the fallen king was put in great danger. Because for the new Assembly, his only use was as a hostage whose release and expulsion could be bartered for substantial gains; there would be no question of his being restored to the throne. Deprived therefore of any value on the international political market, he had value only at home, where his life was the mere plaything of two rivals, both of whom hated him equally.

A tight prison

Only a muffled echo of what was happening reached the prisoners, but they soon felt its effects. The keep was being fitted out in order to house them, and this became an excuse for tightening restrictions.

There would be no more clandestine correspondence hidden in the folds of clothing or anywhere else. Through the windows at night warders had seen "those ladies busy reading and writing letters." On the morning of 29 September messengers came from the Paris Commune to deliver an order: "paper, ink, quills and pencils" were to be taken from them and their valet. Louis XVI and his sister handed them all over, but Marie-Antoinette and her daughter managed to hide their pencils. That evening the same envoys returned with an order to transfer the king to the large tower, the keep. His bedroom, still smelling of paint, had no furniture but a bed. The next morning Cléry, who had followed his master to his new lodgings and slept on a chair, was getting ready to go look after the dauphin when he was stopped. "You will have no more communications with the prisoners, nor with your master; he must not even see his children." When the king wanted to go join his family for lunch, and then intervened on Cléry's behalf, he got the reply, "We have no orders to that effect," and, "This is not our doing."

In fact, there were no orders; the men were applying their own zealous rules. Cléry found a way to get to the queen. She pleaded with the guards to let her see her husband for a few hours a day, at least at mealtime. She was past protest or even tears; these were cries of sheer, wrenching heartache. Said one official, "Oh well, then, today they may eat together, but we take orders from the

Commune; in future we'll do what it rules." The joy of the women and children was such that it brought tears to the jailers' eyes. Simon the cobbler grumbled, "I do believe these hussies will make me cry." He added, addressing the queen, "You weren't weeping when you slew the people on August the 10th." She gave her usual reply: "The people are quite misled about our sentiments." The Commune in fact had laid down no rules, and the king was allowed to join the rest of the royal family for meals on the condition that they spoke in French and in loud and intelligible voices.

A month later, they were all reunited in the keep. As was the case with the little tower, they occupied the third and fourth floors, but occupancy was reversed; the king had the third floor and the women the fourth. Each floor consisted of one vast hall with a vaulted ogival ceiling held up by a central pillar dividing the room in four. Since it was more spacious than the little tower, they put the dining room on the third floor, which freed the two lower floors for the guards, whose number was increased. Some pains had been taken to furnish it; a dropped ceiling was put in and wallpaper applied, although not always of exquisite taste. The king's antechamber for instance was decorated like the inside of a prison, with the Declaration of the Rights of Man posted in big letters on one of its panels. But a few bits of well-made furniture were brought from the Grand Prior's Palace and on each floor fairly decent English toilets were installed in one of the three available turrets (the fourth being taken up by the staircase). Alas, they were so keen to completely cut the prisoners off from world that they had built seven consecutive staging posts into the staircase in the fourth turret. Each one had a lowered ceiling and a block built into the floor so that all those entering or leaving had to lower their head while simultaneously straddling the block. They could enter their apartments only after two doors had been opened, one a nail-studded wooden door and the other an iron one. The windows were barred and splayed so that the sky could barely be seen and little air circulated. Since the walls were nine feet thick, the prisoners had to go to the embrasures to see anything clearly. To top it all off, the roof over the unoccupied fifth floor was now used for their walks, but slats were fitted between the parapets to prevent the royal family from seeing or being seen from outside.

It was within these medieval surroundings that the family gradually resumed its daily life. But there was one major change: the dauphin was taken from Marie-Antoinette and sent to his father's quarters. Was this a way for perverse jailers to punish a mother who too clearly adored her child? Was it to spare Cléry a lot of coming and going between the floors and thereby hamper his liaison activities? Or – who knows? – was it through respect for the tradition dictating that a little boy "went over to the men" at the age of seven? We don't know. At first the queen complained bitterly, then made her peace with it once life returned to a semblance of order with its meals, lessons, walks, and games. But the atmosphere remained tense. Goret the city official saw them again at this point and was struck by how much they had changed. Their former composure was gone. The king, normally so even-tempered, paced up and down in his room, as did his sister, whereas Marie-Antoinette locked herself into hers. They spoke less with each other, "fearful of aggravating the others' pain by referring to their own." And the children had lost their playfulness. "Everything had absorbed the gloomy atmosphere they had given to this place by allowing light to enter only from atop the windows."

The weeks that followed did nothing to alleviate the situation. The month of November brought its harvest of setbacks. On the 6th, Dumouriez beat the Austrians at Jemappes, causing panic among their representatives in Brussels. On the 14th, he made a triumphal entrance into the city. At the end of the month, all of Belgium was conquered and Savoy reunited with France. With the republican French victorious, it became a perfect waste of time to keep a worthless hostage. The humiliations increased. Goodbye to all the credit liberally allotted for their wardrobe. With the start of winter in November they asked for suitable clothing, but their request remained unanswered. The badly heated keep oozed an unwholesome dampness. The king was the first to fall ill. It wasn't until his fever caused alarm that they agreed to send for a doctor. Everyone else fell ill in turn, including the valet, and they nursed one another back to health. In December a change in the city government brought new vexations. "Knives, razors, scissors, penknives, and all other sharp instruments of which reputed criminals in prison are deprived" were taken away from them. Their pockets, beds and other furniture were rummaged through. At one point Marie-Antoinette gave vent to her irritation and blurted out imprudently: "If that's the way it is, why don't you take our needles too? They could give you a good prick all right." Élisabeth nudged her with her elbow to get her to quiet down. Even the king, summoned to show what remained in his little tool kit, turned over his flint and steel plus his screwdriver and remarked, pointing to the fireplace tongs, "Aren't they sharp instruments as well?" A concession was made only for their silverware, which they were allowed to keep during meals. But for want of scissors Élisabeth, who mended her brother's clothes, had to cut the thread with her teeth.

Clearly, something untoward was about to happen. Understanding that uncertainty was the worst kind of torture, Cléry tried to find out what was brewing, and warned the captives of any measures about to be taken against them. Forewarned, they braced themselves for the blows and were able to accept them with more equanimity when official word arrived. They prepared their reactions in advance, and when official word did arrive, they could feign a surprise that would quickly settle into outward signs of the most serene indifference. They could also attempt to protect themselves against some of the consequences. Thus it was that on a certain Thursday in December, a visit from his wife furnished Cléry with the news that the following Tuesday the king would be brought for trial before the Convention. The king was informed the same night, along with the news that they were planning to separate him from his family. He only had four hours to arrange with them how they would stay in contact.

The separation

At five o'clock in the morning on December 11th, the prisoners heard the drums beat a call to arms. This sound bode ill: would his trip to the Convention provide the excuse for another riot, during which Louis XVI might well be slaughtered? The guards' silence in response to all their questions only increased their anxiety. After breakfast the king brought his son back downstairs. The wait was agonizing. The little boy insisted on playing a game of siam*. He kept losing and complained that the number sixteen repeatedly caused him to lose the match. The king said nothing but Cléry thought he saw that this number made "a certain impression on him." At eleven o'clock a guard announced that the mayor was coming and that the child was to be removed, so he was brought upstairs to his mother. A city official who went up to see the princesses found them "in paroxysms of fear." Marie-Antoinette already knew from her son that the mayor had been to see the king. "But where is the king now?" she asked him anxiously. He reassured her that a large force was protecting him on his way to the Convention. "We are not at all anxious, just saddened," Élisabeth replied, and unintentionally contradicted herself by adding, "If you had told us so before, you would have put our minds at rest."

The king returned in one piece that night only to learn that he was about to be separated from his family. "At least leave him his son," Marie-Antoinette implored. The guard replied, "Madame... I believe

---

* A game played with little pucks instead of marbles.

it falls to the one who is supposed to have the most courage to deal with this separation; besides a boy of his age has more need of his mother than of his father." All her supplications fell on deaf ears. The dauphin spent the night in her room, and since he hadn't his own bed, she took him into hers. She did not get permission to see her husband. The next day she asked to see the newspapers to read accounts of his appearance before the Assembly. And if she couldn't see him, could her children at least do so? The king made the same request. They didn't get an answer. The Convention kept them in suspense until the 15th, when they seemingly made a concession, but it was one of subtle cruelty. "Louis Capet will be able to see his children, but until his verdict is determined they will not be allowed to communicate either with their mother or their aunt." So their father made a heroic sacrifice: "You see the cruel alternative they have just given me; I cannot get myself to keep my children with me; for my daughter it is out of the question, and as regards my son, I feel all the heartache the queen would have to endure." He even had the delicacy to ascribe a different motive to his decision, claiming that he needed time to prepare his defense, so as to spare his wife any scruples his sacrifice might cause her. The little boy's bed was therefore put in his mother's room and the king remained alone on the third floor. He spent his time in prayer, reading and examining his defense file, which grew bigger each day, in the company of advisers supplied by the Convention: Tronchet, de Sèze and Malesherbes.

The two princesses hadn't given up trying to communicate with him. No guard was heartless enough to refuse passing on a modest birthday gift to his daughter – the "Almanac of the Republic" – or conveying New Year's greetings back and forth on January 1st. But this wasn't enough to satisfy the longing of the prisoners, who yet again had the ingenuity to overcome the obstacles. As soon as they were separated, Élisabeth got Turgy to transmit to her brother a piece of paper with a message written with pin pricks inviting him to reply to her. He did so, by the same system. They soon improved on the method. He succeeded in sending his sister a few pencils and some of the copious paper he'd been provided for preparing his defense. Cléry had collected bits of string used to wrap packets of candles and tied them together until he had a little rope long enough to reach from one floor to the next. At the end he placed a hooked pin and weighed it down with a piece of wood. He was able each night around eight o'clock to set up an exchange of correspondence through superposed windows in a little tower that was not closely watched. Thanks to the windows' slope, the notes were in no danger of falling to the ground, except once, the dauphin would later say, but it went unnoticed. Family ties were thus maintained. Rather than about the trial, whose outcome was still pending, the messages seem to have dealt more than anything with everyone's health. But it could not make up for being together.

Why this decision to remove the king from his family? Some believe that it was purely a strict interpretation of the law that required isolating the accused during trial. But even before the trial began, when they were being transferred to the keep, they had tried to cut him off. And the emotional blackmail over his children betrayed their deliberate, unremitting vindictiveness. The Commune leaders in charge of the Temple, above all the redoubtable Hébert, perceived that their strength lay in their deep family ties. There were unforeseen effects of cooping up in such close proximity people they considered, thanks to the pamphlets, riddled with family strife. Far from tearing one another apart with mutual recriminations, the family formed a united and closely knit front. They remained impervious to pressure, and each one's ability to resist increased exponentially. The authorities could not get a handle on them. By cutting them off from each other after having cut them off from the outside world, and by leaving them hanging in perpetual uncertainty over each one's fate, they were trying a different tack: they played on their feelings and their nerves in the hope of breaking their spirit. But this underhanded psychological torture, inflicted particularly on the king and queen, did not have the desired outcome. And it brought Marie-Antoinette slowly but surely to realize the depth of the ties that bound her to her husband.

Marie-Antoinette's soul searching

Let's be forthright about it: the documents from this period of the queen's life are few and far between. She didn't write any longer; she hardly even spoke. Cléry, having followed the king into his confinement, no longer saw her. Aside from a few pages written later by her daughter and some depositions by municipal officials, we know very little about the crucial weeks leading up to the king's execution. But we can sense that Marie-Antoinette had changed, and profoundly. Or rather, her relationship with her husband had changed. There was by no means any sudden revelation or conversion. It was the result of a long, slow process caused by imprisonment, which led to self-knowledge. Perhaps she wasn't even quite aware that the change was happening; perhaps she didn't articulate it to herself. But it was clear from her behavior. She was attached to her husband in a way she hadn't been in twenty-two years of married life. And the idea of losing him was wrenching to her.

All her life, cheered on by sycophants, she believed she was superior to him, more intelligent, seductive and energetic, more apt to personify royal majesty than this unassuming, chubby, accommodating man of too simple tastes. His least little failings would irritate her, as would his hearty appetite and cumbersome gait. She despaired at his inertia in dealing with the revolution: he was nothing but a weakling who could not be counted on because of his ever wavering will, a dead weight she had to prop up, with only retractions and failures to show for it. For many years the two had led separate lives, coming together only as etiquette and political necessity dictated. Except when she was in danger – and this was already a sign – she sought him out as her natural protector.

Prison cut her off from her usual circle. Her ladies-in-waiting were all gone now. There was no contact with Fersen. Was she self-aware enough to gauge the harm caused by her heedlessness? We don't know. But the lifesaving lift afforded by their epistolary exchange was no longer there. For adult company all she had left were her husband and Élisabeth, with neither of whom she had ever felt very close – an understatement as far as her sister-in-law was concerned. Now in the Temple, she took the measure of her own weakness. Of the three prisoners she was the most vulnerable. Of more delicate nerves than the others, she found it harder to recover from the successive shocks, especially as they proliferated. Her sister-in-law and daughter had an easier time of it. But she was the queen, so surveillance over her was tighter, her freedom of movement and speech more restricted. Lively and impatient as she was, getting a grip on herself required greater effort. But above all, the crushing, suffocating hatred of which virtually she alone was the recipient, poisoned the very air she breathed and the bread she ate. She slept very badly, hardly touched her food and withdrew from the world, as she visibly grew thin and feeble. Whereas before she insisted so exactingly on her prerogatives and guarded so jealously her power, she now increasingly left the initiative to Élisabeth, who reigned supreme over the women's quarters. For the first time in her family life, she was in retreat, hovering in the background.

In prison, however, it was a metamorphosed Louis XVI who took her place in the forefront of the family. It is said that he told Malesherbes one day, "You are more fortunate than I am, Monsieur, you can hand in your notice." But here he was, having been handed his "notice," or more precisely dethroned. He was not happy about it, of course not; but in a sense he felt relieved, freed from the anguish that was eating away at him. His lack of resolution sprang from his inability to choose between solutions that were all equally abhorrent to him. With all political responsibility removed from him, no longer being called upon to make any decisions, at peace with himself, he achieved some sort of serenity. He no longer had to act; all he need do was submit to fate. Already on June 20th, he showed himself capable of meeting insults with undeniable magnanimity. Without being absolutely sure of it – can one ever totally kill hope? – he believed he was going to die, and he was ready. This does not mean he wasn't suffering, not at all. But death was a passage, a deliverance, the way to eternal life. Until then, in the eyes of God his suffering was meaningful. His duties were clear. In everything he did he aimed to apply the teachings of the gospel: selflessness, charity and forgiveness. Seeing his destiny in these familiar terms, this wavering, chronically depressed man was suddenly the embodiment of serenity, equilibrium and strength. And the radiance he gave off struck even the thickest and most obtuse of his jailers.

The truest martyrs are not those who pose as martyrs. Louis XVI's principal virtue was simplicity. He had no trouble applying it; it had always come naturally to him. But now Marie-Antoinette saw it in an unfamiliar framework, in their family life. Now their life was organized around him, not her. He knew how to deal with the situation, she didn't. The fact that the family ran smoothly was his doing. It was not only because he needed to follow strict schedules; he realized that a degree of normalcy would allow his family to retain some balance, despite a situation that was anything but normal. His unshakeable appetite and snore-filled sleep, far from being signs of a life deeply rooted in animal-like physicality, became signs of an independent spirit that relegated to insignificance the constraints they lived under. His steady nerves had a reassuring and calming influence. It was an antidote to anguish. They gave the illusion of security, which *is* security of a sort. What if tomorrow the sky fell on them in the shape of a rabble of assassins? In the meantime he taught them how to live as if nothing were amiss. The children needed their Latin, geography and mathematics lessons. They could always play a game of backgammon after dinner, or solve the *Mercure* riddles. To fill the void there was also reading or needlework. Above all he was wonderfully willing to play with his little son and surround him with the gaiety and good humor so needed at his age. He was an admirable father.

This aspect of him was new to Marie-Antoinette, whom he included in his child-caring activities out of fear for his own future. He reminisced about the little archduchess who came all the way from Vienna to become queen of France, and expressed his sorrow to Malesherbes at having failed his marriage contract in dragging her down into such a disaster. "Unfortunate princess, by marrying me she was promised a throne. Now what can she look forward to?" As if wishing to make up for it, he showered her with attention. He gradually became irreplaceable to her. She only realized it when they wanted to separate them; the vehemence of her protests and the violence of her grief showed that he had become indispensable to her. No, she had not fallen in love with him. It's not that their marriage suddenly became a vibrant one. He was content to shake her hand by way of good night, just as he did with Élisabeth, and that was fine with her. What she looked for and found in him now was the same protectiveness she got as a child from her father, whom she adored. And that was what she needed most at the moment. Throughout their marriage, he had never found his place in her life. Now *in extremis*, he found it as a father figure; now he had the substance that he lacked as a husband. Just like her mother, he would become a role model; she would be his as well as her mother's worthy successor when it came time to die.

So they were both very close and very far from each other. She could not enter into her husband's spiritual universe. For her, a solid but superficial faith had never fostered an inner life. Although her daughter noted a new interest on her part in pious readings, the spiritual source of her husband's way of thinking remained foreign to her. But her attachment to him did not depend on understanding him. Now she saw and respected his generosity of spirit, and that is what was important. He expected no counsel or support from her; he felt he was responsible for her. As long as he was alive, he would shield her. If he died, he realized that she would be defenseless against the hatred of which she was the target. And if she died, their son would be targeted in turn. He knew that his imminent trial jeopardized his own life and that of his family, who would share the same tragic fate. And she knew it too.

A political trial

What to do with a fallen king in a country prey to revolutionary torment and facing a war that could spread throughout Europe? The Legislature shunted the decision on to the Convention. The Paris subdivisions and the clubs were screaming for blood. But the Temple's captives were wrong to fear being assassinated in cold blood.

What the Jacobin activists wanted was a trial leading to conviction;

but that's not what the Girondins wanted. Not that they had become royalists: horrified by the September massacres, they dreaded the dictatorship of the streets. Now it was their turn to try to "stop the revolution." But that only added fuel to the Jacobin fire, and they demanded a trial all the more strenuously. Not all of them, however. For some, there was no need of a trial. He was guilty and deserved to die because he was the king, Saint-Just peremptorily declared from the speakers platform. Danton agreed. Chateaubriand quoted him as saying, "We'll not try him; we'll kill him." He added, "These priests, these noblemen, they're not guilty, but they must die because there is no place for them, they hamper progress, and jeopardize the future." Robespierre took it upon himself to clothe this viewpoint in legal jargon. With superb sophism he stated, "Louis denounced the people as rebellious; the Revolution and the people have shown that he alone was the rebellious one. Louis cannot therefore be tried; he has already been tried, and convicted. Either that or the Revolution cannot be absolved." An excellent tactician, the deputy from Arras was loath to grant the king a trial, as it might lead the people to take pity on him, not to mention give his political adversaries an excuse to use juridical chicanery to open a wide-ranging debate about the legitimacy of the new regime.

But how could they kill Louis XVI without a trial? Just killing him wouldn't do; it might appear to have been an accident. No, the Temple captives had nothing to fear from that: no accused man was ever better protected on his way between prison and court. He had to be put to death collectively, officially, legally. A trial was therefore necessary, which would serve, proclaimed Marat, "to educate the people." But he had to be charged with something. In no way did they want to enter into a thorough debate about the Ancien Régime. Who knows where that could lead? They decided to try the man who became constitutional monarch as of 1791. But Louis XVI's scrupulous care to respect the constitution to the letter of the law did not facilitate the task. Everyone knew that in reality he was opposed to it and was merely waiting for the opportunity to denounce it. But the judges lacked proof – until the corridor-wall hiding place at the Tuileries was discovered. Gone down in history by the name of *armoire de fer* this iron coffer gave them a veritable harvest of evidence[*]. Most of the documents Louis XVI kept there

---

[*] There is no doubt that Roland, in charge of registering the contents of the coffer, removed a certain number of documents, especially those concerning his friends. But he did not fabricate the ones he produced, and got them from nowhere else. Where else would he have found them?

– undoubtedly in order to hold something over them – concerned his relationships with the various revolutionary leaders whose services he had paid for. The documents of course compromised them; they showed how widespread corruption was among the new political chiefs. But it also compromised him, as it proved the double game he was playing. Mirabeau was already dead; all they could do was expel him from the Panthéon. But Louis XVI was still alive, and the guillotine was well oiled.

Once the iron coffer was found, a trial became inevitable. Just as the king had done in former times, the Convention held the reins on the three branches of government: legislative, executive and judicial. It called for a trial. It isn't possible here to explore the meanderings of the ensuing debates, which were terribly disconnected from reality. What was the point of spending hours and hours pouring over the constitutional inviolability of a deposed and imprisoned king? Louis XVI knew that he would be convicted even before the trial began. They were not going to weigh his merits and demerits; they were doing what they had to do to kill him, and with him the monarchy. He appeared before the court twice, the first time on December 11th and then on the 26th. The day before, Christmas Day, with no illusions, he made out his last will and testament. Before the judges, he denied everything. He didn't use the opportunity to explain his actions – what good would that have done? He did not try to defend himself, except on one sole point, an essential one for him: he refused to accept responsibility for the bloodshed of August 10th. But one fact could not be denied; in his soul he was a counter-revolutionary; he only pretended to subscribe to the Legislative Assembly's decrees in the hopes of gaining the time it took to abolish them. In his eyes this was far from being a crime; it was his duty. But from the deputies' point of view it was treason. No half measures were possible, because they were dealing with irreconcilable differences: they had diametrically opposed notions of good and evil. It is therefore no surprise that during the final vote the first question – was he innocent or guilty? – got the quasi-unanimous vote of *guilty*.

On the other hand, the Assembly was divided on what his punishment should be. The international situation precluded banishment. The Girondins wanted to keep him in prison until peace was restored. They tried to save him by proposing to submit the idea to a popular vote via electoral commissions throughout France. This direct appeal to the people was rejected during the second vote; it would have been a long, complicated and impracticable operation. The third question, "What sentence has Louis, formerly king of

France, incurred?" set the scene for one of the most dramatic episodes in all of history. Between imprisonment and death, his fate hung in the balance for thirty-six hours. In the Tuileries' great hall, where the Convention was seated, the public galleries were filled with club members who punctuated proceedings with applause or booing. In this extremely tense atmosphere, the rules required that the deputy from each department cast his vote one by one. They had to declare themselves publicly, justifying their vote if necessary. Louis XVI's lawyers checked off each one. They counted the votes and recounted them. And on January 18th, immediate death won out, by a single vote. The duke d'Orléans, Philippe-Égalité, caused a scandal by voting for his cousin's death. One last effort was made to save the condemned man through a stay of execution, but it was refused the next day.

The Jacobins got what they wanted – a ritualistic murder that would found the very Republic and bind to it all those who soaked their hands in the blood they had spilled together. From then on none of them could turn back without being destroyed. Together they would build a new world. But the vote had been an extremely close one. The other, hidden side of the coin was that this murder risked dragging all of them into the bloody abyss.

The immediate result was that this Jacobin victory sealed the fate of the Girondins and accelerated the revolutionary impulse. Louis XVI knew only what his lawyers told him about the final vote. It was enough for him to know that unless there was a reversal of fortune, the queen would be the next designated victim.

Torn from one another

Marie-Antoinette, who only got distant echoes of what was happening, was frantic. Her informants tried to calm her down by implying that a sentence of banishment might well prevail. Since the 17th of January Louis XVI knew he was doomed, but he awaited the final verdict before telling his family. On the 20th an official delegation brought him word. He asked for a three-day reprieve to prepare for death. The Convention was consulted and refused. He would be executed, therefore, the next day. He was granted permission to be attended by a priest of his choosing. At his sister Élisabeth's recommendation, he chose a non-juror Irish abbé by the name of Edgeworth de Firmont, who accepted immediately.

He was finally allowed to see his family. But the meeting was put off when a grotesque argument developed between the Convention and the Commune. The official wording required him to see them "*en particulier*," that is, without witnesses. But the guards produced a municipal order specifying that they were not to let the prisoners out of their sight, either day or night. A hybrid solution was therefore found; they would meet in the dining room with the doors closed; but since the doors had windows, the guards would be able to see them, although not hear them. The abbé de Firmont discreetly retired to one of the little towers, where he didn't hear anything, or at least claimed he didn't. Cléry reported an astonishing silent scene that was serendipitously captured by one of the city officials on duty who had a gift for sketching.

At eight-thirty in the evening, the queen appeared holding her son by the hand and followed by Madame Élisabeth and the young girl. In a mournful hush they embraced; there was sobbing. "Let's go into the room, I am only permitted to see you there," the king told them. The door closed behind them. He sat down; his wife was to his left, his sister to his right, his daughter almost directly in front of him, his son standing between his legs. They were all bending towards him, holding him in their arms. For an hour and forty-five minutes he spoke to them, sobs greeting his every pause. "It was easy to see from how they reacted that he himself had informed them of the death sentence," Cléry noted. Actually, they had heard it from the newspaper criers, the young Madame would later relate in her rather dry rendering of the meeting. But her account is better than nothing. It contains the only details that have come down to us about what the king said to them: "He cried over our pain, not for fear of dying; he told my mother about the trial, forgiving the blackguards who were putting him to death... He then gave my brother religious instructions, telling him above all to forgive those who were putting him to death, and he gave us both his blessing." At a quarter past ten, he was the first to get up. It was he who began the process of separation, and they all left the room, hanging on to him and "emitting the most painful cries." He told them:

"Be assured, I will see you tomorrow morning at eight o'clock."

"Do you promise?"

"Yes, I promise."

"Why not at seven o'clock?" asks the queen.

"Oh, yes, at seven then," he replies. "Farewell..."

And he tore himself away from them, leaving his daughter nearly fainting in a fit of convulsions. Going back up to her own quarters,

Marie-Antoinette could not help screaming at the city officials, "You are nothing but blackguards, all of you!"

The king didn't keep his promise. The abbé de Firmont, who had said mass at six in the morning and given him communion, advised against it, as much for them as for him. He therefore gave Cléry the task of bidding them his goodbyes. To his son he left a silver seal and to his wife his wedding band, engraved with her initials *M.A.A.A.* and the date *19 Aprilis 1770*. "Tell her I take leave of it* with difficulty..." He also left them a little packet containing locks of hair from each family member.

Marie-Antoinette, unable to sleep, threw herself onto her bed fully dressed, and all night long her daughter heard her tossing and turning in anguish, trembling with cold. At six, she was startled when the heavy door was opened. But no, they had not come to summon her to her husband's side; they came to borrow Élisabeth's missal. She watched the hands of her watch turn, exhausting herself in fruitless waiting. Her sister-in-law asked a guard if he knew anything, and he of course replied in the negative. About eight-thirty, they heard trumpets sounding, footsteps in the courtyard, different noises in the staircase and in the room beneath them, then the roll of drums growing faint. This was it then; the king had gone. Towards ten, Turgy brought breakfast, which no one touched. Suddenly, at exactly ten twenty-two, a powerful artillery salvo went off in the distance, the Temple guards beat their drums and there were shouts of "*Long Live the Republic!*" The head of Louis XVI had just been severed.

The king is dead; long live the king. The tears, laments and sobs were hardly subdued when one tradition has it that the three women knelt in front of the little Louis Charles to salute him with the title Louis XVII, but many biographers contest this version of events, alleging it would not have been possible given the surveillance they were under. But to this one could reply that there were more inconspicuous ways of enthroning him as king. One thing is for sure in any case. The officials noticed, and later testified to the fact, that from then on the women gave him precedence in the one area for ceremonial deference left to them, at the table. They reserved for him the place of honor at the head of the table, and they had him served first, enough to show that in their eyes, he was the king of France.

One more word about Louis XVI before we leave him. Since Varennes, insult after insult had been heaped on him. But in

---

* Cléry's text says "it" and not 'her,' as is sometimes claimed. He is therefore talking about his wedding ring. This phrase is like a renewal of his betrothal promises. M.A.A.A. stands for Maria Antonia Archduchess of Austria, and the date is that of their wedding by proxy.

his final moments no one sought to humiliate him. He was not subjected to the ordinary courts; he had the right to be tried before the Convention, representing the entire nation. He was granted the defense team he wanted and a non-juror confessor of his own choosing. For his final journey, he was allowed a handsome closed carriage where he was given the place of honor on the seat facing forward. The abbé de Firmont was allowed to accompany him to the bitter end. All along the route they were permitted to quietly intone the prayer for the dying.

Every available man in Paris was mobilized, and not only to forestall any attempts to deliver him – although many feared this, it would prove impossible. The men were armed because this was imperative if they were to be associated symbolically with the ritualistic murder. And if anything were ever a serious matter, ritualistic murder is. No women were allowed. Doors and windows remained firmly closed. Not a sound was to be heard. No one spoke. The drummers in front of the cortege did not beat their drums; they were there to cover any shouts that might arise. At the foot of the scaffold they wanted to bind the king's hands but he protested that this was humiliating. In fact, it was no doubt a technical necessity. He only gave in when the abbé de Firmont invoked the example of Jesus Christ. At the last moment, he wanted to address his people and cried out in a powerful voice, "I die innocent of all the crimes laid to my charge; I pardon those who have occasioned my death..." But the drum rolls covered his last words. The ceremony that the revolutionaries had in mind did not include a speech.

But there was a sense of the sacred as well as showmanship in the revolutionaries' putting to death of the king. They staged the death of the monarchy, not of a man. Just as in days gone by when they used to richly attire sacrificial victims being led to the altar, they showed consideration to the man who embodied the repudiated regime, so as to immolate him with solemnity on the baptismal font of the Republic. By doing so they forgot that such consecration worked both ways. Everything was in place to transform the victim into a martyr.

CHAPTER 23

WIDOW CAPET

Among Louis XVI's last requests there was one that revealed his greatest fear: "I would desire for the National Convention to deal immediately with the matter of my family's fate and leave them free to retire to a suitable place of their choosing." The reply was pompous and vague. "The French nation, as lofty in its benevolence as it is rigorous in its justice, will take care of his family and will insure they meet a fitting destiny." He pressed upon them the urgency of the matter; "immediately" he had said, hoping that his death would staunch for a while plebian Paris' thirst for blood. And in fact, for a few weeks, street violence was suspended, as if the flames were smoldering before flaring up again. The Revolution had to deal with the horrified protests from the European sovereigns over the execution of one of their own. The struggle against kings, now won in France, turned abroad; it was time to concentrate on the war. Heartened by its successes of the previous autumn, the Convention went on the offensive, declaring war on England and Holland on February 1st, and Spain on March 7th. They had more important things to do than busy themselves with the late Citizen Capet's family. They were in the Temple; let them stay there. They were not completely forgotten, however; in the coming conflict, they could prove useful as a bargaining chip.

This explains the relative improvements in their comfort, which helped Marie-Antoinette emerge from the despondency into which her husband's death had cast her*.

---

* Most of the concrete details and anecdotes in this chapter and the next come from accounts of a later period whose authors were clearly trying to emphasize the services they had rendered. What is more, many of them were illiterate so the accounts attributed to them were the work of professionals, and how they handled the confidences entrusted to them is open to question. But if we discard

In mourning

Since the separation from her husband during the trial, Marie-Antoinette was but the shadow of her former self. No longer sleeping and barely eating, she had grown extremely thin. His execution left her mute, prostrate, at times regarding her children "with such pity that it sent a shiver down your spine." She sank deeper and deeper into a torpor that worried her sister-in-law and daughter. To help her get over it, they thought it a good idea – and psychologists today would not disagree – to bring Cléry to her: "We wanted to see her jolted like this to help her vent her baleful grief, which might release her from the suffocating despondency she was in." Cléry didn't get permission to visit, but the sympathetic city official Goret had taken the precaution of volunteering his services for guard duty, allowing him access. He addressed the weeping queen in a shaky voice, "Madame, you must keep yourself going for your family." He was the first to give her an account of Louis XVI's death; no one had even bothered to officially notify her of it. She asked him, therefore, between two outpourings of grief, to request mourning clothes for her and her family – the "simplest available," she added. He promised to do so and went to the antechamber to write out the request. While he was writing, she reappeared before him; she had come to give him the name and address of a seamstress familiar with her tastes and measurements. And thus life began to flow more freely in her again.

Goret noticed that the whole family was languishing for want of fresh air. The queen had given up her walks in the garden since the beginning of the trial, because the king could no longer accompany them. She remained obstinate in her refusal. "We do not wish," she said, "to pass in front of the door from which my husband issued only to go to his death." In any case, she hated the garden, where she was exposed to insults. So the considerate Goret had an idea. Since she refused to go downstairs, why not go upstairs? At the top of the tower, there was a narrow, circular and crenellated gallery where they could walk, and the turrets at the corners had enough

them all, there is nothing left to help us imagine what Marie-Antoinette's life was like during this period. We have therefore included here elements taken from these questionable sources when they appear convincing, especially when they are confirmed for example by cross-references in interrogation statements or official Commune documents.

space for chairs. The princesses sat there as the boy ran and played around them. He was too short to see above the parapet, which was four feet high. He wanted the guard to pick him up, but since the little group could be seen from below and was attracting attention, he advised against it. That is when the alerted Temple authorities sealed the space between the battlements. They couldn't see the street but they could at least contemplate the sky and breathe some outdoor air.

The Commune proved generous about the clothing. Right away Marie-Antoinette got "a black taffeta mantle, a black scarf and skirt, a pair of black silk gloves, two pairs of leather gloves, and two black taffeta hair bands. Dresses and shoes were also provided. They were even allowed measuring sessions, under the guards' watchful surveillance. When her high mourning garments were ready, she wanted to have her portrait painted. We should not be shocked by this. It was not through vanity; just as with her desire to wear mourning clothes, she was merely following tradition. Widowhood required that a queen furnish her people with a new image of herself corresponding to her new state – no matter that she was no longer queen and no longer had a people! She called on the services of the Polish artist Kucharski, who had already started a portrait of her at the Tuileries that remained unfinished. It isn't known how or when he went into the Temple tower, but he no doubt got authorization, since during her trial the queen was merely asked if he had passed information on to her. Quite likely he took brief sketches that he later fleshed out in his studio*.

Surveillance became noticeably more lax. Guarding the Temple had lost its novelty; the warders were dying of boredom there and what's more, felt rather useless because word was the prisoners would soon be released. Most of the Commune guards took pity on the royal family. Among them was a particular true-blue republican by the name of Toulan, one of the August 10th rioters. But he converted – the word is appropriate – when he saw the family's sufferings, and certainly earned his nickname of "Fidel." Intelligent, energetic, with no axe to grind, he was as passionate about the queen's wellbeing as he was about the Revolution's success. He showed singular and rare audacity in treating the prisoners with a compassion that was full of delicacy. His first concern was to convey to Marie-Antoinette her husband's last wishes in the form of a copy of his last will and

---

* As was the custom, he produced a number of portraits from his original sketches. After Marie-Antoinette's death, many copies were made that either idealized the model or not; thus, not all of them are reliable likenesses.

testament written out by Cléry, because she was not allowed to see the original. Some sections of it dealt directly with her:

> I recommend my children to my wife; I have never had any doubt about her motherly love; I especially recommend that she make good Christians out of them, and upright individuals, and make them see that greatness in the eyes of this world here below – if they are condemned to experience it – is a dangerous and perishable thing, and that they must rather turn their gaze toward the only true and lasting glory of eternity. I beseech my sister to continue treating my children tenderly, and to be as a mother to them should they suffer the misfortune of losing their own. I beg my wife to forgive me for all the wrongs she has suffered for my sake and the sorrows I might have caused her during the course of our union, as she can be assured that I hold nothing against her if ever she believed she had any cause to reproach herself.

We should resist the temptation to look for particular grievances in these last words. No one knows exactly how each of the spouses interpreted them. It doesn't really matter, since Louis XVI speaks hypothetically of reciprocal wrongs only to sweep them away in reciprocal forgiveness. Bathed in anguish and hope, radiating ardent faith, this text is above all a message of love and peace. Which is what Marie-Antoinette was in greatest need of at the moment.

Another message was soon added. We recall that when leaving for the scaffold, Louis XVI handed Cléry his seal, his wedding ring and a packet of hair locks. Immediately confiscated, these things were sealed up and locked in an armoire on the tower's ground floor. Toulan broke open the armoire and the seals, took them away, and passed the incident off as a robbery. Thanks to him, Marie-Antoinette was able to take possession of the relics, and these things also helped her to mourn.

"A beautiful dream…"

Soon there were more communications with the outside world than there had ever been. And the idea of another escape attempt took root in the minds of those who worked with the prisoners. How could they ever leave such a well-guarded place? In fact, the Temple was both well guarded and not. Few people had full-time posts there – only the Tison couple who were in the immediate service of the royal family, and the Simons who did odd jobs. The others were all municipal workers who did no more than 48 hours in a row. It added up to a lot of people. But these people were in a hurry to get their jobs over with, and had no interest in their work; except, of course, those who wanted to save the queen. Sorting out all the comings and goings became increasingly difficult. The more new guards that came in, the easier it was to pass through unnoticed, if you had the right kind of disguise. Because of this, Toulan thought he could get all the royal family out of the Temple*. Once they were out, he would need outside help. Marie-Antoinette therefore sent him to a very close former attendant who was still in Paris. The chevalier Jarjayes must have broken out into a cold sweat when a Commune official landed at his door. The visitor handed him a letter of introduction. "You can trust this man, who will speak to you on my behalf when he gives you this note. His sentiments are known to me; they have remained unchanged for five months." Yes, it was the queen's handwriting, but the chevalier refused to go into this blindfolded and demanded to be brought to her. Not to worry; Toulan would get him in. Duly compensated, the lamplighter who made his rounds in the Temple every evening consented to lend his work clothes and implements to this odd fellow curious to see the place; and didn't Jarjayes get in to see Marie-Antoinette face to face! She started to believe escape was possible.

The plan took shape. The Tisons would be incapacitated with sedatives. The two women, dressed as municipal guards, would leave during a change of shifts, surrounded by a patrol made up of sympathizers. The children would be gotten out another way. The lamplighter's sons, who almost always accompanied their father, were familiar figures in the enclosure. Dressed like a ragamuffin, the little Madame would pretend to be one of them. The boy king would be slipped among the dirty washing into the laundry wagon. No more big flashy berlins, three modest-looking carriages would pick them up once they left the Temple and whisk them away to Dieppe, where they would embark for England. Jarjayes took charge of setting up the relays. But they needed an accomplice who could get them false passports from the Commune. A certain Lepître, enticed by the expectation of a hefty reward, promised to provide them.

Was this plan unrealistic? There is no lack of evidence for successful

---

* We have details of this plan only through the subsequent account by one of the surviving participants, Lepître, but his story is consistent with that of Goguelat, who reproduced some notes written by Marie-Antoinette. It is also consistent with her long letter to Jarjayes, cited a bit further on.

outlandish escapes. March 8ᵗʰ was the projected date. But the whole thing dragged on until it was aborted, for lack of money, it appears. Lepître still hadn't come up with the passports when the Convention suddenly took a harder line. It was now out of the question to get four people out at one time. They proposed to the queen, the one in the greatest danger, that she should go alone. She refused. "It was a beautiful dream, that's all," she wrote to Jarjayes when she informed him she was desisting; "but we got a lot out of it, finding again on this occasion another proof of your entire devotion to me. My trust in you knows no bounds; you will always and on every occasion find courage and strength of character in me; but my son's welfare is my only guide, and however happy I would have been at being out of this place, I could not consent to being separated from him..."

Now the "beautiful dream" was nothing more than a memory. But she didn't sink into despair for all that. Her energy and spirits returned, for she took advantage of Jarjayes' journey abroad to give him a twofold mission.

The first concerned her brothers-in-law and displayed inveterate hope and unbroken political will. Her long-standing opinion of them had not changed and the count de Provence's recent actions had done nothing to render him more congenial. As soon as news of Louis XVI's death reached him, the count recognized his nephew as the king of France and proclaimed himself regent according to "the fundamental laws of the kingdom*." It is not certain whether Marie-Antoinette ever found out about this proclamation, which circulated widely but clandestinely in Paris. Regardless however, she knew that he would fight her for the regency. Not having the upper hand at present, she decided to reconcile with him, by the same token conferring obligations on him towards her. Jarjayes would therefore bring him the seal that Louis XVI bequeathed to his son along with a letter: "Having a faithful being on whom we can depend, I take this opportunity to send my friend and brother this object, which can be entrusted to his hands alone... Because of the impossibility until now of giving you any news of us, and the excess of tribulations we have been subjected to, we feel all the more cruelly our separation. May it end before long. Until such time, I embrace you, as I love you, and you know it is with all my heart." In a postscript Élisabeth and the little Madame also assure him, with greater sincerity no doubt, of their affection. Since it was just as necessary to mollify the count d'Artois, Marie-Antoinette sacrificed Louis XVI's wedding band: "I thought you would like to

---

* Which in fact never clearly stipulated to whom the regency should fall.

have something of his; keep it as a sign of the most tender friendship with which I embrace you with all my heart."

Jarjayes' other mission was entirely private: "When you arrive in a safe place, I hope that you can give news of me to my great friend who came to see me last year; I do not know where he is... I dare not write, but here is an imprint of my device. Convey to the person to whom you send it that the one to whom the device belongs has never felt its truth more keenly." Having copied to his journal this part of the letter that the messenger had delivered to him, Fersen explained what it meant. The imprint was stamped from a seal she had made for herself of the coat of arms of her "great friend." It showed an open-winged dove because the flying fish on his arms had been mistaken for a bird. The motto read *Tutto a te mi guida*. Alas, with the heat, almost everything had disappeared from the piece of paper on which the seal was stamped – except for the motto: *All leads me to you*. It was truer now than it ever had been. Louis XVI's death freed Marie-Antoinette legally; his testament freed her morally. At this point she had not yet despaired of escaping from the grip of the Revolution. Could she dare to dream, for the first time, of a future at Fersen's side, as Napoléon's second wife the empress Marie-Louise would one day have with Neipperg? Or was it perhaps a promise that were she never to see him again her soul would fly to him? Or why not simply a straightforward and spontaneous outpouring to the man she loved? Readers are free to interpret her message as they wish. Fersen, however, was not. By the time it finally got to him, in the beginning of the next year, it could only be a message of farewell: Marie-Antoinette had already died.

Dumouriez's endeavor

While the escape attempt was being plotted at the Temple, Dumouriez, at that time lieutenant general of the Armies of the Republic, was dreaming of taking charge of the counter-revolutionary forces and putting little Louis XVII on the throne of his fathers. He had of course not deemed it necessary to notify Marie-Antoinette of the fact. He didn't trust her. When he had met her at the beginning of the previous year upon his entry into the ministry, she had treated him very high-handedly. Like Mirabeau and Barnave before him, he tried to convince her to play along with the constitutionalists. She cut him down to size: "You must believe that neither the king nor I can suffer all these novelties, the constitution either... You must come to terms with it." He replied,

"This is no momentary popular uprising... it is a nearly unanimous insurrection of a great nation against age-old abuses," and added that if the king were to cut himself off from the nation, both he and the nation would go to their "mutual ruination."

A year later, it had come to pass. The king was dead and the nation was sinking into uncontrollable violence. Dumouriez was an ambitious man who had faith in his own great destiny. It is certainly not for love of Marie-Antoinette or sympathy for her little king that he undertook to overthrow the new regime. Not only was he disgusted by the anarchy reigning in France, he was also furious to see his victories ruined by the ideologues in the Convention. The battle for Jemappes had delivered Belgium* to him in the fall of 1792. His intention was to leave the liberated Belgians to manage their own future democratic state. But at the Convention, Danton was leading a movement to annex Belgium, and his was the dominant faction. They sent Dumouriez political emissaries who only managed to exasperate him. They insisted on imposing all French laws on the Belgians, including those on religion. At the same time, since armies had to be supplied and fed, Belgium was treated like a conquered province. It didn't take Belgian patriots long to figure out that mild domination by faraway Vienna was preferable to the iron fist of the Parisian Jacobins. When the first fine days of spring brought good weather, the coalition forces went back on the offensive and the Belgian population abandoned the French. After a disastrous defeat at Neerwinden, Dumouriez had to evacuate Belgium. He was furious at the waste, which he attributed to the foolishness of the politicians. It is at this point that he adopted as his own La Fayette's old cherished hope of marching on the capital at the head of his army to reestablish order. To get a free hand, he concluded an armistice with the Austrians, and handed over to them the four emissaries sent from the Convention to make him see reason. In Brussels, Fersen was exultant; he could already see the royal family "being carried in triumph through Paris." But when Dumouriez tried to get his troops to follow him, he failed. His only alternative now was to pass over to the enemy, which he did on April 4th.

A few months earlier France had been victorious on all fronts. Now it was on the defensive everywhere, with the Vendée insurrection bleeding its western flank. It had been brewing all winter and triumphed that spring of 1793. The hunt for the "enemies within" intensified in a climate of widespread suspicion, and new organs of

---

* With the 1790 revolt against Austria, the name Belgium replaced the former one of Austrian Low Countries.

state were set up. To the recently created Revolutionary Tribunal was added the Committee of Public Safety, which functioned as the executive branch of government, in reality holding all powers. Attention was paid again to the Temple captives, implicated even if they didn't know it, in all the counter-revolutionary tumult. Surveillance over them was tightened.

Over the last two months Marie-Antoinette and Élisabeth had taken to corresponding freely with the outside; their guard was down. Tison was hoping to catch them in the act, and thanks to his wife, found a drop of sealing wax on a candlestick. This proved that some city officials, Toulan, Lepître and a few others, had been providing them pencils and paper and bars of sealing wax, aiding and abetting them in their secret correspondence. Twice their quarters were searched; their furniture was rifled, their pockets were emptied, without much to show for it but a bit of sealing wax, a religious tract and a picture of the Sacred Heart of Jesus, which they took for a sign of political allegiance. Actually, the second time, they did come up with some damning evidence: a man's hat, which instigated a lengthy enquiry and caused a lot of ink to flow in the minutes of the Tower Council. Was this part of a disguise to be used in an escape attempt? Or was it, as Élisabeth contended, a hat that had belonged to her brother and she cherished as a keepsake? But in that case, how did it get there? Louis XVI had only one hat, which was handed over to the people along with his coat at the foot of the scaffold. Unless – but they could not admit this – the faithful Toulan had managed to exchange his own hat for the king's when he was about to leave the Temple! We'll never know the truth of the matter. But the incident was indicative of the harassment the prisoners would again be subjected to, obliging them to resort once again to using coded signs in need of an update.

Of the two household spies, Tison's wife bowed out; the job her husband imposed on her drove her crazy. But the cobbler Simon, until then very solicitous of the princesses, providing them with all they asked for, saw that the wind was changing, and started to spy on them. It is he who gave away the escape plan of another city official, Michonis, who was acting for baron de Batz, an intrepid loyalist who cooked up a scheme to abduct Louis XVI on his way to the scaffold*. The conspirators narrowly escaped punishment,

---

* The baron Jean-Pierre de Batz, a daring and enterprising Gascon, was the ringleader of a number of attempts to free the king. On the day of the execution, the mass of armed men defending the route was so dense that his group of nobles, who wanted to grab the condemned man on his way to the scaffold, could get no where near him.

thanks to their insistence that Simon was insane and had dreamt the whole thing up. But from then on there was no longer any hope of the royal family's escaping.

The price of a hostage

Abroad, Louis XVI's execution had raised a host of indignant protests. The real feelings of those objecting were mixed, however. The count de Provence made a show of his chagrin; he could not do otherwise. But in Koblenz the émigrés had a hard time hiding their satisfaction: the "traitor" had finally paid the price for his compromises with the constitutionalists. As for the reigning monarchs, they had despised his weakness for too long to really mourn his loss. But their conviction was only strengthened that the spread of the revolutionary venom must be stopped immediately. That is why they again took up the military offensive, with the results we have seen. Would they act to save the royal family held hostage in Paris? In theory, the fate of Louis XVI's sister and children was none of their business. But Austria was concerned about the queen, whose marriage contract stipulated that upon widowhood she could regain her status as archduchess and come back to her native land. Everyone knew that this sort of argument was out of step with reality. But could the court of Vienna really afford to abandon her to her fate? On the other hand, could they intervene on her behalf? And if so, how – by fighting or bargaining?

In April 1793 there were some preliminary negotiations that were aborted as soon as they began. By handing over the Convention emissaries to Austria at the time of his plan to march on Paris at the head of a counter-revolutionary force, Dumouriez furnished the Austrians with a bargaining chip that could protect the queen until he reached the French capital. When he failed, the revolutionaries wanted to use the hostages as international currency. The Convention valued its emissaries, but not enough to get them back at any price. If the foreign powers wanted the Temple prisoner to be liberated, they would have to come up with more than that – they would have to declare an "unlimited armistice," something the victorious coalition had no intention of doing.

In desperation, Fersen pleaded for violent intervention, and hounded Mercy to that effect. What he wanted was a new manifesto, threatening even more dire consequences than the previous one, and accompanied this time with a military advance to lend it credence. The wily old diplomat tempered his zeal. The queen, he told him, would be the first to suffer from any rash move. Although he didn't say so, he knew that the coalition's march on Paris was not just around the corner. He pushed for a return to negotiations. Ransom a prisoner? Classical warfare afforded numerous examples of it. Everything depended on market conditions. The asking price, just like the offering price, varies according to the vicissitudes of war. But in this particular case, it also varied with the infighting raging within the Convention among its different factions. For the Girondins were more willing to let the queen go than the Montagnard extremists, who had other plans for her: she must be immolated to insure their hold on Paris through sheer terror. Marie-Antoinette's fate remained in the balance throughout the summer of 1793.

In July the war took a bad turn for France. The coalition forces had crossed the border, the Austrians took Condé-sur-Escaut at the beginning of the month, and the Anglo-Dutch forces were marching on Valenciennes, which would fall to them on the 27th. The Convention dispatched an ambassador to Naples and another to Constantinople to solicit the intervention of Austria's Italian client states that had remained neutral – Venice, Florence and Naples – in a quest to declare a truce or even initiate peace talks, in exchange for the queen. But Austria intercepted the two emissaries and incarcerated them in Mantua. They thus had two more hostages to bargain with[*].

So naturally, the queen's friends thought of bribery; they sought to buy off Danton through a financier called Ribes. But that would take money, a lot of money; and Francis II was not willing to pay a penny. In any case it was too late. By then, the fearsome orator Danton, mastermind of August 10th, had to give up control of the Assembly to Robespierre. As Mercy pointed out, "public opinion changes in Paris with the rapidity of the winds in a storm." Where could a foreign diplomat find a reliable counterpart to turn to in any case? "How can you influence unknown, nameless men, men of no property and no substance, guilty today of every crime and assured tomorrow of sinking back into the multitude to remain there unnoticed and unpunished?" – or sentenced tomorrow, as we shall soon see, to take their turn under the guillotine's blade. No sooner did they deal with one than he was swept away by another. As for the sums devoted to bribing them, they would be drained, as Louis XVI had learned the previous year, into the Danaides' bottomless jar.

---

[*]   In 1795 they were exchanged for Madame Royale.

There would be no ransom, and no politico-military concessions. Mercy wound up agreeing with Fersen that only a raid on the capital could save Marie-Antoinette. But his anguished letters to Vienna produced no results. He lamented: "it seems that anything that breathes in the Viennese air is immediately paralyzed." He soon found out why. Instead of marching on the capital, the coalition forces were disbanding. The war was showing its true face. When the warring nations' chiefs had met at a conference in Antwerp on April 8th, the British representative had dotted his *i*'s and crossed his *t*'s, saying "Each of the coalition powers must seek to make conquests and guard them." In this way, they could cover their expenses and at the same time crush France's predominance in Europe. This was actually what was happening on the ground. The Prussian king called back his troops; they had nothing to gain from it all but his two partners' consent to break up Poland. The English went off to lay siege to Dunkirk; they had never reconciled themselves to its restitution to France. The Austrians tried to seize all the key spots along the Belgian border while waiting for the right moment to get their hands on the Alsace. The far-off Russians sent their approval; they had already got what they wanted, at Warsaw's expense.

Marie-Antoinette was the least of their worries. The Convention would not let her go unless the coalition suspended hostilities. But the foreign powers were not going to stop their well-greased war machine just to liberate her. Free her by taking Paris by force? It would be too costly and in any case useless; none of them wanted to annex the Paris region. Even worse, it would be a political blunder. If they marched on Paris and managed to reestablish the monarchy, they would then have to settle the conflict between her and her brother-in-law over the regency. Whoever came out on top of that particular contest, they would still have to defer to the winner. Knowing Marie-Antoinette, they realized she would probably be the more troublesome of the two. What good did it do for Mercy to warn her "the powers do nothing for nothing" – she still obstinately believed in her Austrian family's selfless support. She had proclaimed loud and clear that she would defend the inviolability of her son's inheritance. Who knows how she would respond to the demands of her liberators? If on the other hand republican France continued to sink into anarchy, it would be a lot easier to get together and crush the whole country. Vienna's diplomatic correspondence during that summer left no doubt whatsoever: Marie-Antoinette was cold-bloodedly sacrificed to Austria's broader interests.

On the hostage exchange, how much was she worth at a time when the people were calling for her head? Nothing.

An eight-year-old prisoner

The failure of the escape attempts had consequences for her son that Marie-Antoinette could not have imagined. On July 3rd the Convention decided to take him from her. This would help them put a stop to any further flight plans, and detach his fate from his mother's, thus making him useful as a separate hostage in the on-going negotiations. The Commune added an initiative of their own stamp: why not take advantage of the situation to give him a good "republican education"? On this last point it succeeded, and within just a few weeks, beyond their wildest expectations. Her son's betrayal was an excruciating ordeal for Marie-Antoinette and a source of great scandal for the royalists. The historiography of the Restoration period put forward an explanation for it that was accepted for a long time: the child had been subjected to harsh treatment to get him to testify against his mother. The documents that are available today show that this was not the case. Only by looking into the story of this orphaned, imprisoned and very unhappy little boy can we find the key to his role in this drama.

We must go back a ways. Born on the 27th of March 1785, he was four and a half when the riots tore him away from his charmed existence in Versailles and sent him to the Tuileries where he too had to suffer the insults and strident hostility. The good Madame de Tourzel did her best to protect him from the harrowing atmosphere. But between the return from Varennes and the "days of revolution," a lot went on that would destabilize the most well adjusted of children. The regularity of life at the Temple did him good. He was an attractive little blond blue-eyed boy, unruly, out-going and cheerful. To please his father, he didn't balk too much at having to do his lessons, as long as he could also run and play and use up his energy that way. Louis XVI understood him. He made sure to play with him whenever he could, leaving Cléry to play the more physically challenging games from which his corpulence excluded him. They would play *siam* together, but it was the valet who ran after the ball with the boy. He was a remarkable educator, very attentive to whatever interested his son. Cléry told the story of finding Louis XVI one day enjoying handling the tools of a mason who had come to install bolts on some doors. He took the hammer and scissors and showed the little boy how to use them. Perhaps he had lost his propensity for bursting out laughing at schoolboy pranks that had so irritated

Marie-Antoinette, but it would be nice to think that he was still capable of having a laugh with his son.

When they were moved to the keep, we recall that the dauphin had to leave his mother to live with his father. For Marie-Antoinette, this was harassment; but the little Louis Charles apparently took it as an honor. He was crossing over "to the men" and was becoming one of them. For six weeks he lived in a close relationship with his father. No one knows what they had to say to each other during this time, but the king was so obviously devastated when he was taken away during the trial, that we can be sure they had developed a very strong bond. What is more, the family took the child seriously, including him in their daily activities and little ruses to trick the guards; he had figured out who were the nice ones and who were not, and was on the lookout at shift-change time to warn his relations of who was where. When Cléry fell ill, he looked after him and took it upon himself to secretly get some medicine to him. He felt important; he counted.

On December 11th he was suddenly cut off from the king, brought back to the women to live out the weeks of anguish leading up to the wrenching goodbyes of January 20th. The next day he found out that his father was dead. Throughout the trial and then in mourning, Marie-Antoinette, prostrate with grief, does not seem to have paid a lot of attention to him. It would take her daughter's illness to draw her out of her stupor. The young Madame, having reached puberty, had various ailments, including an infected scab on her leg. It took a lot of doing to get the family doctor admitted; he had her over it within a month. The little boy, however, was doing well. That he was heartsick, that he needed to be listened to, pampered and consoled does not seem to have occurred to his mother or aunt, who were too absorbed in their own grief to notice. Madame Royale, Élisabeth's favorite and now considered an adult, was closer to the two women than to her little brother with whom she had still been playing just the year before. And just when his father was cruelly taken from him, the child was neglected by the others, left to his own devices, deprived of activity. There were no more walks; the tower's roof was no substitute for the garden. There was no more playing ball either, for Cléry had also been taken from him. No doubt his secret accession to the throne earned him a few more lessons in proper behavior; the atmosphere suffocated him; it was depressing and debilitating.

The clandestine return to correspondence with the outside world and then the escape attempt entirely absorbed his mother's attention, and this added to his isolation. In the picture she had painted of him for his future governess when he was four, she called him very indiscreet, merrily repeating whatever he heard and adding to it, without meaning to lie, anything his imagination dictated. She was a bit mistrustful of him therefore, and kept him out of whatever was going on. When Toulan and his accomplices came to discuss the escape with her, she sent him and his sister off into one of the lesser towers, where it was freezing; young Madame would later say that it was to get them used to the cold. But he wasn't stupid; he figured out what was going on – his sister had been told to keep an eye on him and he was angry at his exclusion. He was eight years old now. Would it not have been better to treat him like a grown-up, explain things to him in a way he could understand, and trust him to keep quiet? Surely, the way he was being dealt with had catastrophic consequences. Having got so close to the king, he could not bear being excluded.

And there were aggravating circumstances. He couldn't sit still. Playing at riding a horse on a broom handle he strained a testicle, which became herniated. At least someone paid attention to him; the doctor was brought in and had it bandaged. But he was scolded for his rowdiness – there would be no more running and jumping! At the same time, Marie-Antoinette found out, much to her horror, that he was playing with himself, a most commonplace and harmless occurrence, really. Her sister-in-law, who was even more prudish than she was, joined her in making a terrible fuss: he was reprimanded and watched carefully for signs of recidivism. He blamed his mother and aunt for all the changes in his life since his father's death, and he resented them. His health was badly affected by being cooped up, and his spirits suffered from being so neglected.

Had he already fallen ill, as his sister would state? Only normal childhood illnesses seem to have bothered him; in May he had a high fever accompanied by convulsions, which he got over quickly. In June he came down with bronchitis. He was just recovering from it when they took him away from his mother on July 13th, on a double order from the Convention: 1) "The young Louis, son of Capet, will be separated from his mother and placed in separate quarters, the best defended of all the Temple," in fact, the room his father occupied on the third floor, and 2) "He will be placed in the care of a teacher chosen by the Commune's General Council."

According to the official minutes, "the separation was effected with all the sensitivity required by the circumstances, where the people's magistrates showed all the consideration compatible with the severity of their functions." Madame Royale told quite a different story; she said her mother fought fiercely for a whole hour at her son's bedside. She defended him like a tigress against the city officials trying to tear him away from her, and only gave up when they threatened to kill him and his sister. No doubt the truth lies somewhere in between. But the one sure thing is that Marie-Antoinette's pain was excruciating. She passionately loved her little boy, even if she didn't always understand him. The three women, now deprived of servants, lived behind bolted doors day and night, except for brief periods when they were permitted to take short walks behind the parapets at the top of the tower. They were to have no contact with the boy. But Marie-Antoinette found a spot from where she could see him when he went outside. She stayed for hours longing to get a distant glimpse of him through a small crack in the shutters. Élisabeth did not pass on the news she was getting from Tison; it was simply "horrific." In what way was it horrific? At this point the documents we have contradict the usual version of events transmitted by Madame Royale, that of a child who was mistreated, beaten, plied with alcohol and terrorized into telling outlandish tales.

"A republican education"

Every now and then the Legislative Assembly had turned to the question of the dauphin's education. If he was to become a constitutional monarch, shouldn't he be given a tutor capable of instilling in him the new worldview? But each time, much to the monarchs' relief, more urgent matters eclipsed the issue. Now that there was no longer a king, the Commune opted for a "republican education." What this really meant was that they wanted to cut the child off from his environment altogether and prepare him for life as an ordinary citizen who would be absorbed into the masses. That way, he would not be up to the task should there ever be question of his restoration to the throne. That is why Simon the cobbler was chosen as his "teacher." Simon was a staunch republican, a member of the Cordeliers club, a faithful *Père Duchesne* reader, coarse, vulgar and barely literate. Marie-Antoinette was understandably terribly upset. All the same, Simon and his wife were not brutish. At fifty-seven years of age, they were still unhappy about never having had children of their own. They wanted very much to fulfill as best they could a task for which they were very well paid.

We can well imagine, as his sister claimed, that the little Louis Charles let out heart-wrenching screams when he was torn from his mother, and that he spent the next two nights sobbing in his bed on the floor beneath them. But he soon calmed down, comforted by people who were kind to him. He became easier to deal with. The Convention delegates who arrived on July 6th to make sure he was still in the Temple, found him playing cards with his "mentor." The Simons took good care of his physical needs. The wife helped him get over his bronchitis and noticed that he was suffering from intestinal parasites, so gave him some anti-worm medicine; the husband got him out of mourning clothes and into cheerier attire. Then he had the king's old tailor fit him out from head to toe with two new silk-lined outfits, one of nankeen cotton for the very hot weather, the other of Louviers broadcloth for cooler days. The child, who liked to be liked – in that he took after his mother – was delighted that people were paying attention to him. The Simons had nothing else to do. No more school lessons; the "teacher" was in no position to teach anything to a little boy who already knew more than he did. Except for one thing: he taught him all the songs in the revolutionary repertoire. They did not discipline him in any way; he could run around and play to his heart's content. His new guardians couldn't do enough to entertain him; they got him a little dog, some birds and chickens. Soon Simon found a fabulous toy in the old Prior's Palace; it was a big cage with a bird-organ inside, that is, one of those little devices used in training songbirds. The thingamabob didn't work? Not a problem: The Commune would pay out 300 pounds to a watchmaker to get the little mechanical bird up and running again, shaking its head, flapping its wings, and whistling the "King's March." No, the little boy was not abused; he was not beaten or mistreated. Was he given wine to drink? That's possible; not to debauch him but to treat him like a man, as was all too common among the masses. Heedless and enjoying his relative freedom, not to mention outrageously spoiled, the boy was having a great time.

His way of speaking necessarily changed with his new environment, which scandalized his sister and Élisabeth: "We would hear him and Simon sing *La Carmagnole*, *La Marseillaise*, and a thousand other horrors... he made him sing at the windows so the guards could hear him and taught him to repeat terrible swear words against God, his family and the aristocrats." Young Madame was not the only one to be horrified. The child repeated everything they said around him. Some city officials felt that Simon was going too far and didn't shrink from telling him that he was wrong to sing obscene songs in front of the "little Capet," who should be receiving an education "more in conformity with good morals." One day when noise was heard coming from his relatives' apartment above, one of them was shocked to hear the boy shout, "Aren't those whores up there supposed to be guillotined soon?" Their protests led to nothing: it was the Commune's intention to make of him a good little sans-culotte.

All of this was atrocious; but a lot worse was to come. It didn't take the child long, unfortunately, to chatter with his caretakers freely once they gained his trust. It had been a long time since anyone really listened to him or took him seriously. Did he realize he was betraying secrets? His mother never exacted a promise from him not to say anything to his captors because she didn't tell him anything. But he had figured certain things out, and was not a little proud of it. What is more, he hadn't forgotten having to spend an hour and a half in the freezing tower. And he shared what he had learned. He revealed that some of the Tower staff whom he named – Toulan, Lepître, Bruneau and Le Bœuf – had had many long conversations and were on familiar terms with the prisoners.

Soon what he said took an infinitely more horrid turn. What he said about the staff was true. But he was about to tell lies. Just as his mother had done, Simon and his wife happened upon his nocturnal amusements. What!? For the first time, they were angry with him. What was he to do? He still was smarting from the scoldings he'd received previously. To tough it out, he replied that it was his mother who taught him the practice. We can imagine the effect this had on the Simons, steeped as they were in filthy propaganda against this lecherous Messalina who had wallowed in every vice. It didn't even occur to them to doubt what the little boy, caught in the act, told them. Imbued with a sense of his own importance, the cobbler went off to report it all to the Commune, who called the boy in for questioning.

On the 6th of October the "little Capet" appeared before the mayor, the deputy public prosecutor Hébert, and a handful of municipal dignitaries. Questioned by Chaumette, he willingly repeated everything he'd said about the guards. Luckily, he didn't talk about the escape plan, because he hadn't heard it discussed, but the sympathy they showed for the captives was enough to get them fired. It seems that it was his interrogators who suggested a few names to add to the list, for it was physically impossible for Pétion, Manuel, Bailly and La Fayette to have been implicated in the affair. As for the other matter, this is what was recorded in the minutes: "Declares amongst other things that having been discovered a number of times by Simon and his wife in bed committing indecent acts harmful to his health, he admitted to them that he had been instructed in these pernicious habits by his mother and his aunt;

and that at various times they had been amused watching him repeat these practices before them and that this often happened when they had him lying between them." The rest only appears in the margin, by way of commentary: "That from the way the child spoke to us, we understood that at one point his mother had him come to her and that copulation ensued, and that from this resulted a swelling in one of his testicles, known to Citizen Simon's wife, over which he was still wearing a bandage, that his mother had told him never to mention this, and that this act has been repeated many times since."

However, the depths of ignominy had not yet been plumbed. The little boy was placed before his aunt and sister, to whom he obstinately repeated his allegations. The investigators had already cleverly pitted him against them over the confabulations with the guards. It exasperated the boy to hear them deny what he knew to be true. Once he was set on this path, he could not tolerate being contradicted, he dug his heels in and held to his other statements. Was he able, given the conditions he was living under, to distinguish the truth from falsity? Above all, was he able to understand the implications of what they were getting him to say? We can easily understand that his horrified sister and aunt wanted to clear the young boy of wrongdoing by blaming it all on Simon's ill treatment. Today we would hardly blame the child any more than they did. He had, over the last four years, been the victim of repeated traumas, shunted from pillar to post, sensitive to the extreme stress and anxiety of his parents. And worst of all, he was not over the loss of his much-loved father. Poor, poor child. One wonders, had he lived, how he would have coped with such memories!

As yet, Marie-Antoinette knew nothing of all this. All she knew was that her son was now singing popular revolutionary songs. When the revelations burst upon a scandalized public and her interrogation was under way, she had already been gone from the Temple for two months; she was in the Conciergerie, awaiting the outcome of her trial.

CHAPTER 24

THE FUNERAL MARCH

At two o'clock during the night of the 1st to 2nd of August 1793, the Temple prisoners were noisily roused from their sleep by four commissioners from the Commune led by Michonis, rigid in the strict fulfillment of his functions*. They read to Marie-Antoinette the decision taken by the Convention at the behest of the Committee of Public Safety requiring her to appear before a special criminal court and ordering her immediate transfer to the Conciergerie. "She listened to the reading of this decree without any sign of emotion," said Madame Royale, "and without uttering a word to them. While she packed her clothing, the guards did not let her out of their sight; she was even obliged to dress in front of them. They asked for her pockets**, which she gave them. They went through them and took possession of everything there was inside, even though they contained nothing at all of any importance. They wrapped it all up and sent it to the special criminal court where the package would be opened in front of her. All they left her was a handkerchief and a flask, for fear she might feel faint." She told her daughter to obey her aunt as if she were her second mother and Élisabeth to take care of her children; then she kissed them both. There were no lamentations and no tears as during the previous separations. She went to meet her destiny without looking back, "fearing no doubt that her steadfastness would give out." At the bottom of the staircase as she passed the last step barrier, she forgot to bend and bumped her head.

---

* A leading member of the Commune, he was then its *administrateur de police* in charge of prisons.

** Women's pockets at the time were separate from their clothing, hanging from strings tied around the waist. The flask mentioned later was for holding smelling salts.

Michonis asked her if she had hurt herself. "No," she replied, "nothing can hurt me now."

Escorted by her guards, she passed through the garden, crossed the Grand Prior's Palace, went into one of the three waiting carriages surrounded by mounted gendarmes, and was swiftly transported to the Palace of Justice. Mission accomplished. Fearing an abduction attempt, they took decisive action as soon as the decree had been signed. The moment was well chosen. In the middle of the night the escort met no resistance. No one was aware of it; there wasn't a soul about.

So she was to be tried. But she received less consideration than had her husband. Louis XVI was tried by the Convention, which declared itself a court for the occasion. He had been separated from his family, but he was allowed to return to his own apartment, where he could see his lawyers whenever he wished. Marie-Antoinette was sent before a court for common criminals*, and she was taken from the relative comfort of her Temple prison and sent to a commoners' jail. This treatment sprang from the egalitarianism that was growing greater every day: "Citizen Capet" was just an ordinary defendant. But it also shows the kind of odium she had long been subjected to. From the very start, the revolutionaries took great pains to disassociate her from her husband. They saw in her a determined adversary; she was removed from her place at his side during ceremonies; the 1791 constitution specified that he alone enjoyed inviolability, not she. The war was doing nothing to improve matters either; by humiliating the proud "Autrichienne," sister of the emperor, they were taking revenge on the enemy. What a pleasure to see her getting a taste of her own bitter medicine!

A prisoner (not quite) like any other

It was barely three o'clock in the morning when the deposed queen's convoy reached the Cour du Mai at the Palace of Justice. To the right of the grand staircase there was a corridor leading to the prison. At the sound of the soldiers' rifle butts banging on the door, the gatekeeper on duty, a man called Larivière, still all disheveled from sleep, saw before him a woman the waxen whiteness of whose skin was in stark contrast to her long black robe. He

---

* The court was called "special" because it had not been set up through regular legislative procedures; it was considered temporary and adapted to the gravity of the circumstances.

hardly recognized the woman he had seen in all the splendor of her beauty at Versailles when he was a little apprentice pastry boy. The concierge Richard arrived with his prison register to take care of the usual formalities. Yes, she must undergo them too, but Michonis, either through compassion or wariness, immediately escorted her to her cell for the registration procedures. To the routine question about her name, she is said to have answered simply, "Look at me." In her presence they emptied the contents of the little pack of things confiscated from her at the Temple. An inventory was made, and everything was put under lock and key. She had been duly registered as prisoner number 280.

As much as they wanted to humble her, it was out of the question to let her mix with the other prisoners. An individual cell had been prepared for her where in theory she would be cut off from the outside world. The room chosen was the former council hall, the previous occupant, the general Custine, having been hastily ousted. It was dark and stuffy, situated on a lower ground floor somewhat below an inner courtyard that could be glimpsed from a window. Because of the close proximity of the Seine, the leprous walls oozed a stream of dampness that was ill masked by a hanging sheet of painted cloth. With all the humidity, the brick tiles glistened. The only furnishings were a table and two chairs, a trestle bed with two mattresses, a cane chair that could be used as a commode, and a bidet. Madame Richard, the concierge's wife, took some pains trying to make the place less off-putting; she provided clean, finely woven sheets and a pillow bordered with lace. The young servant, Rosalie Lamorlière[*], brought from her home a little fabric-covered stool. She was there to greet the prisoner, and offered to help her undress. "Thank you, child, but since they took away all my help, I quite make do myself," she was told. The terse reply is understandable. Thrown into a dreadful, alien environment, Marie-Antoinette intended to rely on herself alone. Withdrawing is an act of defiance. She would say nothing and ask for nothing; she would owe nothing to anyone – especially not to the people posted there to spy on her.

She was already used to living within sight of guards, but they had never before been in such close proximity. So little space was afforded to her that she could never be alone. There was no

---

[*] Most of the details from which we can piece together Marie-Antoinette's life at the Conciergerie come from Rosalie Lamorlière's account. Of course, the young girl did not write out her memories herself; she was practically illiterate. They were written by a trained writer in a more elevated style, but that is no reason to dismiss the precise and concrete details that he gleaned from his conversations with her.

little tower to hold her wardrobe. The two gendarmes responsible for guarding her day and night shared her very cell, a room that measured twelve feet by twelve feet. The four-foot high partition, which was all there was to separate her from them, was barely high enough to shield her from their gaze when she dressed or did her grooming. She just had to put up with their male presence and hope they remained discreet.

She soon discovered however that the staff was not hostile to her at all. Unlike the municipal guards who reigned over the Temple, the lower-echelon prison staff had not been chosen according to political criteria. They were people left out in the cold when the Ancien Régime fell who found whatever work they could. These simple folk had retained for the monarchy, or what was left of it, an instinctive respect, not to mention the compassion that the fall of the mighty naturally inspires. Had Michonis given them instructions? Had he set an example of leniency that the others were following? Whatever the case may be, the prisoner was treated well. The Richards tried to lighten her burden. The black robe that she was wearing when she arrived was worn thin under the arms and threadbare at the hem from dragging along the Temple's stone floors. Right away they sent her the gatekeeper's aged mother who brought fabric to mend it. Soon they found for her either from the Temple or elsewhere a white dress, some underwear, handkerchiefs, black stockings, a calico petticoat, shoulder scarves and some shoes to replace her slippers that had fallen apart from the humidity.

Two women assisted her. The little Rosalie, whose job it was to bring her meals, was too lowly a character to be part of her surveillance staff. Her heart went out to the poor unfortunate woman, and she was won over. As she was allowed to come and go, she did a few errands when necessary, brought her back an item or two, even bought with her own money a little red-rimmed mirror for her. Madame Harel on the other hand, despite her talent for tying the queen's hair in a white ribbon and drawing it back into a chignon, was much less kind. She was something of a martinet whose "job" consisted mainly in keeping an eye on the prisoner. The food was well prepared; Madame Richard always managed to find a greengrocer ready to provide her with the best of everything "for the queen." And the gendarmes – as they confirmed during their subsequent interrogation – took turns bringing her flowers: mostly carnations, but also rocket and tuberose. So the Jacobin newspapers, fearful that people might be moved to pity for her, put an idyllic slant on her daily life: "Antoinette rises every day at seven and retires at ten... She has a hearty appetite; in the morning there is chocolate and a bun, and she dines on soup and a lot of meat: chicken, veal cutlets and lamb; she drinks nothing but water, just like her mother, she tells us, who never drank wine. She has stopped reading about the English revolutions and is now reading *The Journey of the Young Anarcharsis*; she does her own grooming, in fact with stylishness, which doesn't even abandon a woman breathing her last." And if we add that the water in question was not from the Seine but from her own Ville-d'Avray spring, forwarded from the Temple, it seems that friends and enemies alike have passed the word down to us that Marie-Antoinette wound up in the best of all possible prisons.

A lot could be said about this slant on things. But the various improvements in her lot did not compensate for the anxiety about the future, the solitude, intensified by the absence of all loved ones, the boredom and the forced immobility. Unlike the other prisoners, she was not even allowed outside; she was condemned to go stir-crazy in a few square feet. She had been given books to read, but she was allowed no embroidery or knitting because she could "hurt herself with the needles." So to occupy her hands, she removed the threads from the worn-out wall hanging and braided them – quite smoothly and regularly – into something like the "knots" that to kill time Louis XV's daughters used to make from gold thread, but in much rougher materials. During the day there was some life around her. Michonis took advantage of his rounds to visit and give her news of her children. From her window she could see faces in the women's yard; when time really dragged she watched the two guards play backgammon. But some of the kindness only rubbed salt into the wounds. Thinking it would be nice for her, Madame Richard brought her little seven- or eight-year old son for a visit, but seeing the woman's little fair-haired boy broke her heart. Nightfall brought her back to herself with only her destiny for company.

Perhaps the food was what it should be, at least in the beginning, but that's not to say she did it justice. Rosalie often had to insist to get her to eat anything at all. As a matter of fact, she was very ill. At thirty-seven years of age, she had "changed prodigiously." Nothing remained of her former beauty. She was unrecognizable, an old, used-up woman, visibly sapped from within. Even before the Revolution, her health was not the best; there was some sort of problem with one of her legs, and above all, she had never completely recovered from her last pregnancy. The previous May, the Temple doctor had treated her for convulsions. Now suffering from chronic hemorrhaging, perhaps as a result of fibroids or a tumor, she was gradually losing flesh and blood. Overwhelming lassitude took away her appetite for life.

Others, however, were looking after her interests, and did not despair of coming to her rescue.

The carnation plot

Surprising as it might seem, the Conciergerie offered better opportunities for escape than did the Temple. First of all, it was only a matter of one person and not four. And secondly, surveillance was much less strict.

The Conciergerie, which housed both political prisoners and common criminals, was a veritable camping ground where suspects from all over the spectrum mingled: there were refractory priests, prostitutes, pickpockets and burnt-out former revolutionaries, and there was a constant to and fro. Everyone had to be fed, however badly, which required a lot of service staff with links to the outside. Prisoners gathered during outdoor recreation and lost no time in sharing news. It didn't take long to find out that the queen was among them; she was an immediate sensation. Although the women detainees soon got tired of sticking their nose against her cell window to have a peek, the guards found a way to make a handy profit, which was convenient, seeing as it was getting more and more difficult to pay the bills. For an adequate sum, they let themselves be talked into bringing visitors to the illustrious captive. Fersen wrote in his journal, "An Englishman, arrived in Switzerland, says he paid twenty-five louis to enter the queen's prison. He brought in a jug of water; it is under ground and there is only a nasty bed and a table and chair. He found the queen seated, her face lying in her hands, her head wrapped in two handkerchiefs and extremely badly dressed; she didn't even look up at him and he didn't speak either, as had been agreed." The poor wretch on exhibit like some sort of strange beast protected herself as best she could against these insensitive intrusions by shutting tight her eyes and ears. To her the visitors were mere nameless, fleeting shadows. How could she acknowledge them? "There were so many of them," she would tell the prosecutors.

But not all of them were driven by simple curiosity. Some historians are skeptical about the testimony – given very much after the fact – of a certain young woman called Fouché who stated that she saw the queen receiving the consolation of the true religion. Among the Conciergerie's prisoners were non-juror priests who, along with colleagues who were still free, had perfected a system whereby the items needed to say mass were smuggled into the prison, even previously consecrated hosts. This pious trafficking was made possible by the collusion of a number of staff members who had not yet been completely converted to the cult of the goddess Reason, and could not in good conscience refuse the condemned prisoners the comfort of this last viaticum. Over three successive visits Mademoiselle Fouché apparently won Marie-Antoinette's confidence. From then on the concierge turned a blind eye to a certain abbé Magnin who came "twice to hear the queen's confession and bring her Holy Communion." At least that is what he would later state under oath. Did he actually have the time, as the young lady claimed, to say a full mass of a whole hour and a half? That is less likely. And yet, all it would have taken was for her two guards to still be believers*.

Another intrusion in any case is very widely attested to, although we only know a part of the story**.

Michonis was the only visitor who could draw Marie-Antoinette out of her torpor, thanks to the news he brought. So it is that she stood up to greet him on Wednesday the 28th of August. With him that day was a short man just an inch over five-feet tall, as the gendarmes would describe him, pale, fair-complexioned, with something of a round face pitted with pockmarks, his auburn hair hanging down in curls, dressed in striped clothing of a "Paris mud" color. As soon as she set eyes on him her whole body "twitched." Her face was "on fire" as tears flowed from her eyes. She recognized him as one of the Knights of Saint-Louis who were at the Tuileries on June 20th. He was among those who prevented her from following the king on

---

* This could perhaps be a pious legend to make it appear that the queen had "a good death." One of the main arguments for questioning this version of events is the fact that in her last will it specified that she was going to her death "without any spiritual consolation... not knowing if there are still here priests of that religion," (Roman Catholics) and not wanting to expose them to danger by summoning them to her. But the abbé did testify that his ministrations occurred "in the days of concierge Richard," that is, before Marie-Antoinette was transferred into a more closely guarded cell where she would spend a month, a long enough time for her to wonder if there were still refractory priests at the Conciergerie, and for her to deplore not getting from any of their number the succor generally given to the dying.

** This affair, which caused much ink to flow, was the inspiration for Alexandre Dumas' "The Knight of Maison-Rouge." All we know is what is related in the minutes of the interrogation of the main characters, who were more anxious to protect themselves than to tell the truth. Was there only one carnation, or two? The minutes only mention one. But Rougeville would claim that there was a second that contained an escape plan. Unable to verify all the later claims, we will stick here to what appears in the minutes.

his way to face the rioters. Perhaps she didn't know his name, as she would assert during her interrogation; but she certainly knew why he had come. The chevalier de Rougeville may have invented his military and aristocratic rank, but there was nothing fake about either his fearlessness or his pro-monarchy sentiments. Taking a carnation from his buttonhole, he threw it across the floor where it landed near the stove, all the time trying to get and fix the queen's attention. Then seeing that she was not following him, he bent towards her and murmured something in her ear. This time she got it. The two men went outside; she saw them in the courtyard and then distracted gendarme Gilbert's attention by sending him after them to ask them to deal with the authorities about some complaints she had concerning the food. What was the other gendarme doing? He had observed the unknown visitor and saw the queen's discomfiture, but didn't hear their conversation, and didn't notice anything out of the ordinary. And what was the Harel woman doing? No, she wasn't playing cards with the gendarmes that day, she was just "doing her job," and neither saw nor heard anything.

Marie-Antoinette quickly slipped behind the partition to pick up the carnation. Inside, she found a note. What was written on this piece of paper that she destroyed once she'd read it? "It was all rather vague," she would claim when a second interrogation obliged her to go back on her initial denials. However, there were two precise details: there was an offer of money as well as a promise to come back the following Friday. It all pointed to an escape plan. Rougeville reappeared, along with Michonis, within a quarter of an hour. The carnation was no longer on the floor near the stove, but had she been able to read it in the meantime? It doesn't appear so.

What happened next, as told by the gendarme Gilbert before the tribunal, is perfectly unbelievable. He reported that once the men had departed she said, "Look how I'm trembling! The individual that you just saw is a former Knight of Saint-Louis... You will never guess how he managed to get that little note to me..." After which, he said, she told him what had just transpired. As if that were not enough, she showed him "a piece of paper she had perforated to form a few lines of writing," and she said to him proudly, "You see, I can do without a quill." She added that what she was writing was an answer to the man with the carnation. A woman on duty, who had gone to get some water, came back at this point, and the gendarme precipitously pocketed the perforated paper shown to him. He hastened to bring it to Madame Richard with instructions that she was to inform Michonis about it.

Madame Richard ran straight off to bring the dangerous object to Michonis, who first tried to reassure the good woman by saying it was a trifling matter, and quickly countermanded any follow-up operation. Just to make sure, he perforated the paper with more pinpricks to render it illegible. The notorious missive was placed in the file and still exists today. A specialist who tried to decipher it thought he could make out "I am under constant guard. I speak to no one. I place myself in your hands. I will come." Twice interrogated about this, Marie-Antoinette would admit, "With a pin I tried to mark that I was under constant guard, that it was too dangerous to come back here, and that I could neither speak nor write." And "I tried with my pin, not to respond to him, but to get him to agree not to return, should he be thinking of it."

She obviously would not have confided anything to the gendarme Gilbert unless she was convinced he was on her side, as were no doubt the other gendarme and Madame Harel. Her network of sympathizers must have extended to the Richards. But the risks were so great and informers so common, that each one remained extremely cagey. Marie-Antoinette, having neither the presence of mind nor the means to answer her potential rescuers right then and there, most probably asked Gilbert for an exceptional favor. If the escape was to take place in two days' time, more than just turning a blind eye; she needed him to let them know that she agreed. She was counting on Gilbert therefore to warn Michonis immediately. So he pocketed the note, not to hide it from the woman warder's eyes, but to bring it to Michonis. And if she talked to him about it the next day, it was not, as he would claim, to gain him to her cause, but to ask him if her note had arrived at its destination. Not free to come and go as he pleased, Gilbert had left the note with Madame Richard, who quite naturally handed it over to Michonis. At this point the interrogation minutes go silent, and we can understand why. Were the conspirators really trying to abduct Marie-Antoinette, as Rougeville would report, and were they then arrested on the doorstep by a gendarme who had not been forewarned? Or did the would-be abductors get instructions to desist? The only thing we know for sure is that six days later, on September 3rd, Gilbert decided to report the carnation incident to his superior. This six-day delay in itself is enough to prove that he was involved.

Why did Marie-Antoinette feel the need to reply when all that was needed was for the plot's instigators to know that she knew about it so as not to show surprise when they came to spirit her away? She had always displayed the need to intervene, to act, to take things in hand. Since her days in the Temple, she had developed a taste for clandestine communication; it became part of her way of life. And we also have to admit her fundamental inability to think clearly, which led her to underestimate the dangers she was incurring to herself and those around her.

The Committee of General Security soon got wind of the whole affair. Rougeville managed to escape the dragnet. The minor actors were acquitted. The Richards lost their post and got off with a six-month prison sentence. Michonis, the most suspect of all, guilty at very least of gross negligence, was imprisoned, and little Louis Charles' revelations would soon prove his undoing: he met his fate on the scaffold. Confronted with the confessions of the others, Marie-Antoinette, who at first denied everything, decided to speak, but said as little as possible. She explained that her initial silence was due to her not wanting to compromise her visitor; but "seeing the thing discovered, she didn't shrink from declaring what she knew." The investigators used these two interrogations to question her on her political role in general, something of a foretaste and a dress rehearsal for her coming trial. It would leave her with some tips on how to deal with them.

But for the time being, all she got from it was a tightening of the screws. They searched her cell from top to bottom; they took away the last personal effects remaining to her: a gold ring – undoubtedly her wedding band – four little rings, a number of gold seals one of which bore the legend *Amour et Fidelité*, a medallion containing a lock of hair, and a gold watch*. It was said that her mother had given it to her, but it was actually a gift from Louis XVI to replace the one that was stolen from her on August 10th on their way to the Assembly. It bore the name of Bréguet, 46 quai de l'Horloge in Paris. Then they changed her cell. No rooms were secure enough, so they furnished what had been the pharmacist's workplace, which he was asked to empty of all its contents, even its glass cases. Aside from the door there were three possible entry points. They sealed off the window to the infirmary with a thick sheet of metal. Another little window onto the corridor was filled in with masonry, and lastly, the large grated window that looked out on the women's courtyard was covered to mid-height with sheet metal, and from there to the top by a dense iron mesh. They went so far as to cement over a water-spouting gargoyle. And just to be doubly sure, the place was turned into a fortress by the installation of a second, very thick

---

* It indicated the day of the month and could be set to chime every quarter of an hour.

studded door. Each was fitted out with security locks and bolts. Marie-Antoinette was in solitary confinement.

Except for the insignificant Rosalie, all of the personnel were replaced. New gendarmes settled into her cell. Two more were added outside. One would keep guard in the corridor outside her door, the other in the courtyard. He had orders to prevent the curious from getting within ten paces of her window and was positioned in such a way that he could look above the metal barrier to see her entire cell inside. She had no candles. The captive had no other light than that which the day provided, or rather, the little bit that filtered in. At night she lived in total darkness. The new concierges, Monsieur and Madame Bault, who were allowed in her presence only if accompanied by an officer of the gendarmerie, kept to a strict application of the rules. Farewell the bouquets of flowers; farewell the treats to eat. Marie-Antoinette was subjected to the same fare as the other prisoners. But since they wanted to keep her alive, she was given calming potions and refreshing broths. She could not bear the isolation, the emptiness, the deprivation of all activity, the absence of any life around her, the dreariness of each hour and day that dragged on, of which she finally lost count. There was also the nerve-racking probability of impending death, which is worse torture than death itself.

The suspense is over

As soon as the king was executed, the Assembly started demanding the queen's head as well. On March 27th, Robespierre clamored from the speakers platform "Will the punishment of a tyrant... be the only homage that we have rendered to liberty and equality? Will we suffer that a being who is no less culpable, who is no less accused by the nation, and who has until now been cosseted through some sort of residual superstition about royalty, will we suffer, I say, that she calmly await the fruits of her evil deeds?" Throughout the months that followed, the theme of "that Austrian woman's crimes" peppered the speeches of the Montagnard orators and continued to inspire Hébert's smutty verve in *Le Père Duchesne*. But Marie-Antoinette's fate was left dangling, to keep up the suspense. They held her in reserve for the right moment.

Actually, during this dramatic summer of 1793, the Convention had more pressing matters to consider than the fate of the deposed queen. On every front, the enemy coalition forces were victorious. In Paris, the masses were grumbling: as the value of the revolutionary banknotes fell, bread prices rose. Although the grain harvest was excellent, tax policy forced wheat to disappear from the market. The people waiting on the ever-longer bread lines outside bakeries were vituperating against the government. On June 2nd it was the deputies' turn to be attacked by the rioters in the Tuileries, to which the Assembly had moved to replace the defunct monarchy. In desperation, the Assembly sacrificed the Girondins: arrest warrants were issued for twenty-nine of them. The luckiest of them fled, the others would face the guillotine. The fall of the Girondins caused a violent reaction in the provinces, where many of them came from. Big cities like Lyon, Caen, Bordeaux, Marseille, Toulon and Bayonne demanded their autonomy within a federation that would free them from the capital's dictatorship – to say nothing of Corsica, where the pro-independence movement was born again. On July 13th Charlotte Corday came from Normandy with the express purpose of stabbing Marat to death. Peasants who were called on to leave their fields in the middle of the busy summer season rebelled against conscription into the army, which was highly resented in those regions not threatened with invasion. In the very Catholic Vendée, royalists and refractory priests had no trouble recruiting them to the cause of the counter-Revolution. Besieged on all sides, the Republic, now entirely in the hands of the Montagnards, seemed lost; as a result, it hardened. On September 5th it put "The Reign of Terror" on the agenda against the enemies within[*]. Soon, on the 17th, the law regarding suspects allowed trying "all those who, by their conduct, relations, speech or writings show themselves to be partisans of federalism and the enemies of liberty" – a definition so vague that it allowed for the incrimination of just about any undesirable.

According to these criteria, Marie-Antoinette was most certainly a "suspect." Now that the Girondin wing had been amputated, the Convention had a big enough majority to send her before the Revolutionary Tribunal, and the legislative clout to condemn her

---

[*] Juridically speaking, the Terror was the suspension of the laws in place in order to confront a situation of great crisis. Historians sometimes call the period beginning with the post-August 10, 1792 repression and ending with the September massacres the first Reign of Terror. But the true, great Reign of Terror, which actually began with the arrest of the Girondins on 2 June 1793, was officially instituted and accorded the necessary means the following September. The serial executions began in October, and the queen was one of its first victims. The Terror would end with the fall of Robespierre, after Thermidor (July 1794). It would contribute to the success of the war abroad by fiercely crushing all internal opposition.

618 *The Indomitable Marie-Antoinette*

to death. However, despite the vociferations of what would soon be known as *les Enragés*, she was kept for two whole months in the Conciergerie without being sent to trial. This situation was too grave and this hostage too valuable to waste on small stakes. The Convention was waiting for Austria to make a move. While it sent agents to Brussels to negotiate, it also pumped up the pressure by raising the specter of the guillotine poised over the captive's head, hoping that all of Europe would be pushed to make a deal with France for her. But Europe didn't budge. Just as the threat to level Paris had no other effect than to galvanize the spirit of resistance in France, so too the treatment inflicted on the queen incited only vengeful indignation. The European powers vowed to punish the murderers, but in the meantime, none of them lifted a finger for her. It is sometimes said that it was all a misunderstanding. Perhaps the emperor hadn't figured out that they were offering him a deal? No, the truth of the matter is, as we saw earlier, that the coalition forces were not willing to save the queen and thereby jeopardize the fruitful victory they believed was at their fingertips.

The Convention finally got the message. Keeping her as a hostage wasn't worth the trouble. And besides, as far as hostages go, "Capet's boy" would do just as well. Marie-Antoinette would thus be immolated on the pyre of the people's rage. But they had better hurry; she seemed on the brink of collapse. What a shame it would be if a natural death snatched from Paris a spectacle it had been promised a hundred times – the sight of that Austrian tart's head falling into the bag! That way they would also put a stop to all the shenanigans that constantly went on around her. For however ravaged her former beauty, she still had the power to seduce. The contrast between her past splendor and her present debasement melted the heart of all those who met her. The Committee of Public Safety was obsessed with the possibility of her escaping. What a slap in the face that would be if she managed to be set free! The matter was settled: Marie-Antoinette would die. Not in punishment for her "crimes," but with an eye on the expected political advantages, which were many.

As concerns domestic affairs, her death would put the finishing touches on the Commune's control of the Convention. Hébert screamed to the deputies, "I have promised Marie-Antoinette's head, I will go cut it off myself if you don't hand it to me soon. I have promised it on your behalf to the sans-culottes who are crying out for it, and without whom you are finished." A word to the wise! As for the outside world, her death would be seen as a gauntlet thrown down by revolutionary France to the European coalition. Given the queen's origins, her execution would have a resonance beyond that of Louis XVI's. They would throw in the face of that arrogant Austria the head of one of its archduchesses. It was a well-calculated move. Mercy would see in it an outrage against the court of Vienna, an insult to "the illustrious blood of Maria Theresa." Finally, at a moment when the counter-Revolution seemed about to triumph, her death would serve to kill off any possibility of restoring the monarchy by associating the sans-culottes with an "expiatory sacrifice" that solidified their allegiance to the Republic. The regicides in the Convention would not be the only ones to burn bridges behind them; the people itself would be bound by this new blood sacrifice. We shall perish, Hébert said of the leaders, but we will leave behind us millions of nameless avengers who are saved by their anonymity and who will safeguard the inheritance. Thus can be explained the "popular" slant given to the trial that would conduct Marie-Antoinette to the scaffold.

An empty file

The court that gathered to hear her case was presided over by a certain Herman, who was one of Robespierre's right-hand men; he was assisted by three judges and a court clerk. The redoubtable Fouquier-Tinville acted as public prosecutor. The final decision was in the hands of twelve jurors. Aside from a couple of notable figures, they were for the most part commoners, chosen precisely for that reason. There were a printer, a wig-maker, a tailor, a surgeon, a joiner, and a bailiff. It was not only to humiliate her that the queen's fate was put in the hands of men some of whom could barely read or write. They were there, as today's market researchers would say, to offer a "representative sample" of the French people, who would collectively and anonymously be responsible for the sentence inflicted. The same principle is still in use today to choose jury members – with one essential difference, however. They were not chosen randomly but because of their political convictions. They would play their role by the script in a theatrical production whose end was a foregone conclusion.

But the production needed a veneer of authenticity. It had to look like a real trial. At first glance, nothing is more astonishing than the pains the revolutionaries took always and everywhere to lend an air of legality to the most arbitrary decisions – thus the plethora of political trials fixed in advance. They understood that the people thirst for justice but abhor its arbitrary application. The 1789 revolutionaries who claimed to be the sons of the Enlightenment, and many of whom were either lawyers or magistrates, made obsessive efforts to surround their proceedings with an aura of legality. But Marie-Antoinette's file was practically empty. Although numerous suspicions weighed on her, proof was lacking. Perhaps there was some in the voluminous dossier collected for Louis XVI's trial and deposited in the Archives. But neither Herman nor Fouquier-Tinville wanted to waste time picking through this mountain of paper. They therefore referred to it as a block, postulating that because she exercised such influence over her husband, she was an accomplice in his "crimes." All the same, being good men of the law, they would like to get something like a confession out of her. They managed to back her against a wall over the carnation affair. They hoped to do the same in the October 12th pre-trial "secret interrogation" she would be subjected to. Thanks are due to Louis XVI for the fact that defendants were no longer tortured into confessing, but there were psychological methods for undermining them.

That evening at six o'clock she was shivering and drowned in darkness in her cell when they came for her. She was led through inner corridors to the Great Hall of the Palace of Justice, the very same hall where the kings of old held their *lit de justice*, from which the fleur-de-lis wall covering and the large Crucifixion scene had been removed. She was made to sit on a bench in front of Fouquier-Tinville. The only light issued from the two candles on the clerk's table. Close to the light, she couldn't hide her facial expressions. She could barely make out Herman who was presiding, and could not see at all the other shadowy figures whose threatening presence unnerved her. Who were they? She didn't know, but in any case, no members of the public were present.

Age, profession, country and place of residence? "Marie-Antoinette [of] Lorraine of Austria, aged thirty-eight, widow of the king of France." Nothing in the world would force her to give up her name and title; she refused to call herself "widow Capet." Her interrogators were careful not to challenge her on this: at the trial, it would be a proof that she had not been converted to the Republic. The well-conducted interrogation got right to the point: her relationship with her brother, to whom she formerly sent millions and with whom she never stopped corresponding in her efforts to get the foreign powers to help overthrow the Revolution. Faced with her denials, they went from Louis XVI's vetoes against the émigré and the non-juror priest decrees to the duplicity she showed in the Varennes misadventure. But she adroitly took shelter behind her duties as an obedient wife, while entirely exonerating her husband from any blame, denying that he deceived the French people or intended to flee the country. At every chance she got she tried to turn the tables: yes, the people had been deceived, and cruelly so, but it was not by her husband or by herself. By whom then? By those whose interests it served. If she didn't name them it was because she didn't know their names.

They thought she had tripped up when she incidentally mentioned that it was she who opened the door for the fugitives that night in Varennes. In this they saw proof that she "directed Louis Capet in all his actions," and that she had convinced him to flee. At this point she made bold to state ironically, "she did not believe that opening a door meant directing all actions." In the trial by insinuation that they subsequently subjected her to – "You never ceased for a moment to destroy liberty; you wanted to reign at whatever cost and get back to the throne by trampling on the cadavers of the patriots" – she resorted to her usual tack, noting "that they had no need to get back to the throne as they had never left it." Questioned about the war, into which they accused her of pushing the foreign powers to "annihilate freedom," she shot back that it was France who declared the war. About the October 1789 bodyguards' banquet and the August 10th resistance at the Tuileries, the discouraged investigators gave up. But there was still that carnation, to which they returned at length, with nothing to show for it but what they already knew: it wasn't enough to warrant a death sentence! She cleverly sidestepped all their trick questions without stooping to a profession of faith in the Republic.

"What interest have you in the Republic's arms?"

"Replied France's good fortune was her greatest desire."

"Do you think kings are necessary for the people's happiness'"

"Replied that one individual alone could not be responsible for such a thing."

"You no doubt regret your son lost the throne to which he would have ascended had the people, at last enlightened as to its rights, not toppled it."

"Replied that she would regret nothing as concerns her son as long as the country was blessed with good fortune."

Exhausted by months of torment, Marie-Antoinette managed to call up from within herself the strength to cope and battle on. All alone, with no help whatsoever, she found the words and arguments that would disarm expert interrogators without violating her inner being. When it was all over she was asked, as required, if she had legal counsel. Having learned from her husband's experience, she didn't want to put anyone in danger by representing her, and therefore consented to being assigned two legal advisers, like the lowliest of detainees. As accustomed as they were to the ways of the Revolution, Chauveau-Lagarde (who had just defended Charlotte Corday and the Girondins), and his colleague Tronson-Ducoudray, were all the same most alarmed when they learned on October 13th about their new defendant and found out that she would appear before the court the very next day! They therefore suggested that Marie-Antoinette request a three-day deferral to study the "evidence in the trial" – which actually consisted solely of an eight-page indictment. At first she vehemently refused; she would ask for nothing at all. But she finally consented, not for herself, as she emphasized at the end of her letter: "I owe it to my children to omit no necessary means whereby their mother can be exonerated. My defense requests a three-day delay; I hope the Convention will grant it them." But the Committee of General Security seemed to have intercepted the letter, which remained unanswered. The defense team would have to make it up as they went along; they had no illusions about the trial's outcome.

A strange trial

The first inkling as to the nature of the trial was its ungodly schedule. The revolutionaries in the Assembly often used the ploy of laying siege for hours and days at a time to wear down the adversary and go for the jugular when their guard was down. Marie-Antoinette came out unscathed from her secret interrogation. They hoped this time that her debilitated state would erode her resistance. The trial began on October 14th at eight o'clock in the morning and went on until eleven o'clock that night with only a brief pause at midday. It resumed the next day at the same time and it ended only with the verdict at four-thirty in the morning of the following day. It was a most peculiar trial. As much as the questions during the October 12th interrogation were straightforward, precise and targeted, these issues were insubstantial. The reason for the difference is clear: this trial was open to the public and called witnesses. Sundry sans-culottes and fishwives crowded onto the reserved benches to finally see with their own eyes this she-monster whose crimes they'd heard all about, and to assist at her humiliation. They had come for a good show, and the court wanted to give them their money's worth so to speak, since entrance was free. The pleasure had to be drawn out for as long as possible so that all those who wanted to could get their turn on the bench. The line-up of forty witnesses had the double advantage of fleshing out the skimpy file and including the people in the proceedings. For most of the witnesses were from the lower ranks of society, and they were invited to testify to what they saw or thought they saw when on such and such a day they happened to be at the right place and time to cross paths with the queen. Knowing the witnesses to be of similar background to theirs, the members of the public should feel the pulse of fellow feeling, and their approval of the jury's verdict should burnish the popular gloss her accusers wanted to give to the conviction.

Marie-Antoinette, walking very erect in her black widow's robe, reached the brightly lit place that had been reserved for her on a little platform. Her pallid, waxen face did not move an iota. The only sign of nerves she betrayed was tapping her fingers on the arms of her chair, "as if on a keyboard," while the court clerk read Fouquier-Tinville's indictment. It read like a summing up for the prosecution. She was accused among other things of squandering the people's money and supporting Austria's interests throughout her reign. She was then accused of having been the heartbeat of the counter-Revolution, having hosted the October 1, 1789 bodyguards' banquet, having colluded with the émigrés and enemies of France, having masterminded the flight to Varennes, and inspired the Swiss Guards' resistance on August 10th. Just for good measure, they threw in that she organized the famine to starve the people and that she caused royalist brochures to be distributed, even libels against the royals "to put people off the scent" and get the foreign powers worked up against the French by making them think that the people were mistreating them! There was no proof of any of this, of course. "This is what you are accused of," concluded the presiding judge, "lend an attentive ear; you are going to hear the charges that will be brought against you." The charges in question were the witnesses' depositions. Herman seemed to be counting on them to throw the defendant off balance.

But things didn't quite go according to plan. The organizers took a big risk in letting the witnesses testify, thereby allowing contradictory claims to be aired. Firstly, although all those called to testify were presumed to be witnesses for the prosecution, there were those who claimed to know nothing, and even a few, like the former minister of war Jean-Frédéric de La Tour du Pin, who did justice to the queen. Many others blew out of all proportion laughably insignificant facts or expressed themselves so poorly that they appeared ridiculous, which the defendant had no trouble pointing out – as if, for example, the empty bottles found under her bed after the sacking of the Tuileries proved that she had tried to get the Swiss Guards drunk beforehand! Groundless accusations based on gossip were brought against her: "the deponent got this fact from a citizen, a woman of excellent patriotism, who served at Versailles under the Ancien Régime and to whom a gentleman, favorite of the above-named court, confided the information." Fouquier-Tinville had trouble getting all these people to stick to the point. There was the additional problem that some of the witnesses, themselves suspects or under indictment, said as little as possible or tried to exculpate themselves by pointing the finger at others. In short, reading the minutes of the trial would be comical if it were not for the fact that its outcome was so tragic.

Fouquier managed to slip into this mess a few dangerous questions, those of the secret interrogation, to which Marie-Antoinette replied with the same evasiveness or denial. The only thing he caught her on was the painter Kucharski's presence in the Temple, which implied that contrary to her claims, she did have ways of communicating with the outside. She also slipped up perhaps by trying to justify the Trianon works going over budget instead of pointing out that it had not been built for her but for la Pompadour. On the whole, however, she defended herself intelligently and even pointedly, with the same vigor that she displayed during the preceding interrogations. And the inquisitors very quickly realized that this public trial afforded her a platform that she took full advantage of.

Already on the first morning, Hébert drew attention to a serious accusation in the deposition. He was the fourth witness to testify, as the official in charge of surveillance at the Temple. To the usual charge that the prisoner won over the cooperation of a certain number of her guards, he added the crime of incest drawn from little Louis Charles' "confidences." Hébert, who was not uneducated and knew how to speak in a highly polished way when necessary, built his journalistic business on smutty anecdotes and trashy language. He worked on the theory that the spiciest allegations were what the people enjoyed, since his paper sold well – which, parenthetically, shows a certain level of cynical disdain on his part. So he decided to go for broke. Not satisfied with merely repeating what the boy had said and what they thought they could deduce from his remarks, he laid it on thick. According to him, the two women often had the child sleep between them where "acts of the most unbridled debauchery" took place. There was no doubt but that there had been "an incestuous act between the mother and the son." And as if that were not enough, he claimed that Marie-Antoinette did it for selfish reasons: "There is reason to believe that this criminal gratification was not dictated by the desire for pleasure, but with the political intention to overexcite the body of this child, whom they still fondly believed was destined for the throne, and over whom they wanted through this maneuver to gain the right to reign over his mind." The proof: he got a hernia from it, which had to be bandaged. Fortunately, since his removal from his mother, the poor child was recovering.

Too much is too much. Marie-Antoinette, horrified to see spelled out what the indictment only vaguely hinted at, had the strength of character not to flinch. She replied only to the initial charges about the guards. Did the presiding judge get the impression that the crowd would not fall for the incest allegations? He seemed disposed to dropping the subject. But one of the jurors intervened, astutely beating around the bush: "Citizen Presiding Judge, I invite you to point out to the accused that she has not replied to the point raised by Citizen Hébert with regard to what took place between her and her son." Marie-Antoinette was standing as if ready to pounce; her words gushed forth in a stinging blow. And there was nothing false about her "violent emotion:" "If I have not replied, it is because nature refuses to reply to such a charge made against a mother. I appeal to every mother that might be present here today." There were indeed mothers in the hall, and some of them were visibly indignant at such charges. Because having stuffed the public to the gills with pumped-up rhetoric comparing Marie-Antoinette to history's other infamous queens – Messalina, Brunehilda, Fredegund, Catherine de Médicis and Agrippina – as the prosecutor had just done, they robbed certain words of their meaning. Those words therefore lost their power to affect people. And when things are said bluntly and brutally, viciously stinging a living person in front of your very eyes, reality wins the day, and clear thinking returns. This outpouring of her maternal fiber erased the image of the lustful she-wolf that had been so carefully polished by misogynistic pamphleteers. Madame de Staël would call on "women of every country and of every social class" to try to save the queen, and it was on her son's lips that she would place the last prayer for her. Herman got the message; he rapidly moved on. And when Robespierre found out about the incident he had a raging fit against "that imbecile Hébert," who had found a way to present Marie-Antoinette with one final public triumph.

She held up remarkably well under this grueling ordeal, which she faced on an empty stomach, her nerves stretched to breaking point. Exhausted, she sat down. People were shoving each other and crowding around to get a look at her. They demanded that she stand up: get up, the people want a better look! Rising, she exclaimed, "Will the people ever tire of my travails?" But the people did not tire of watching her struggle, alone against the world, scoring points. In the show produced to bring her down, she seemed about to conquer her audience. Around four o'clock in the afternoon of the second day, the trail of witnesses came to an end. She had replied to each one of them, down to the most trivial detail; she had got round the prosecutor's most cunning questions; she had said nothing to compromise herself. When the presiding judge asked her if she had anything more to say in her defense, she declared boldly: "Yesterday, I had no idea who the witnesses were; I did not know what they would say: well, not one of them has articulated against me a single positive fact. I will end by pointing out that I was only the wife of Louis XVI, and as such was obliged to conform to his wishes."

At this point her role was over, she could only await the defense arguments and the verdict. Had this been a genuine trial, an acquittal would have been beyond doubt. Her lawyers, who knew from the beginning the case was not winnable, almost believed she would get off with imprisonment or banishment. Swept up by the momentum of it all, she herself got carried away by her own arguments. Once the deliberations were over she asked Chauveau-Lagarde, "Did I deliver my answers with too much dignity?" Why such a question? She had noticed that the people were shocked by her dignified bearing and had heard a woman say, "You see how proud she is?" But pride is also the mark of courage, and courage is always impressive.

After a pause in the proceedings, Fouquier-Tinville delivered the prosecution's closing arguments, which did not deviate from his initial topics; he merely reduced them to their essentials. It was as if all the witnesses' testimony had just been whistling down the wind. One could draw from some of the depositions, he said, a few facts supporting the principal indictment, but "all the other details... vanish before the accusation of high treason weighing on Marie-Antoinette, widow of the aforesaid king." Nothing could have expressed better the fact that the so-called trial was a travesty of justice, conducted for the benefit of the masses. It was getting time to come down to brass tacks. Her two solicitors, by now cured of their fleeting optimism, each delivered a lackluster defense, one regarding foreign and the other domestic affairs. The presiding judge then asked the jury members the following questions:

1) Is it consistent that there existed maneuvering and intelligence with the foreign powers and other external enemies of the Republic, the said maneuvering and intelligence tending to furnish them with monetary aid, grant them access to French soil, and facilitate the advance of their armies?

2) Is Marie-Antoinette of Austria, widow of Louis Capet, proven guilty of having collaborated in the maneuvers and having entertained contact with the enemy?

3) Is it consistent that there existed a plot and a conspiracy tending to set off civil war within the Republic?

4) Is Marie-Antoinette of Austria, widow of Louis Capet, proven guilty of having taken part in this plot and this conspiracy?

The jury retired to deliberate and an hour later came back to report their findings. That's more than enough time for a show trial. Did some among them really debate the issues? It's more likely that they hung around in an attempt to show that they took the job seriously. Whatever the case may be, each question was answered with a unanimous yes. The sentence, according to the pertinent articles of the civil code, which Fouquier hastened to read, was death. It was four o'clock in the morning. Execution was scheduled for the same day. Did the accused have anything to say? She shook her head no. The minutes recorded that her face was "in no way altered." According to one of her lawyers, "she was stunned. She descended the steps without a word or a gesture, crossed the hall as if in a trance, and when she arrived at the barrier separating her from the spectators, she raised her head with majesty. Is it not evident that until this terrible moment the queen had held out hope?" With all due respect to Monsieur Chauveau-Lagarde, it is impossible to know. He had only met her two days previously and admitted that she was always "negative" with him, refusing him any trust, which is understandable since he had been imposed on her. What is more, it is very difficult to interpret the silence of someone who has just been dealt a brutal shock. Twelve hours had elapsed since the end of her interrogation. Born of the excitement of defending herself, hope – if hope there was – had had plenty of time to fade. The summing up of the prosecution showed that the grievances against her remained intact. Most probably, she was so crushed under the weight of utter weariness that she was anesthetized. It was over with; she held up right to the bitter end; she did not weaken. Her torment was almost over. There was only one more ordeal to face before she could find peace.

Will the historian be forgiven for abandoning for a moment the pathos of the situation to comment on the trial and verdict? The trial was scandalously conducted: botched procedures, absence of proof, contempt for the defendant's rights, conviction a foregone conclusion. The apparent respect for legal form only highlights the violation of its spirit. But – and this is not the least of the paradoxes of this strange trial – today we know that the chief accusation was well founded. What the revolutionary court lacked we now have at our disposal in the Archives in Vienna and in Stockholm's Fersen Collection. Marie-Antoinette was certainly not guilty of everything she was accused of, far from it. For instance, she had nothing to do with the uprisings rocking France. But the fuss over baseless accusations must not hide the essence of the matter: she never ceased her correspondence abroad until her imprisonment in the Temple; she did call her brothers and then her nephew to her aid; she did desire the war and she did hope the French forces would be defeated, and even sent Brussels their plans for the first military campaigns. The fact that her hopes were dashed and her efforts fruitless does not absolve her, for her intentions were quite clear. Her iniquitous trial led therefore to a verdict that in a war-torn France according to the laws then in effect was not unjustified.

Of course Marie-Antoinette refused to accept its legality. She was sure she was in the right, the indisputable right of sovereigns, and she could invoke legitimate self-defense. She fought against the Revolution that insulted, dispossessed and imprisoned her, with all the might she could muster. Unlike Louis XVI, she never had a moment's doubt or remorse. That is why she lied so naturally and convincingly. We can easily understand her. In her situation, she could not but lie. All the same, her obviously clear conscience is a bit surprising; for if we examine her conduct throughout the year 1792, we cannot avoid the crucial question – one that is more pertinent than ever: to save one's life, or even to win what one believes to be the good of one's country, are any and all means permissible when the price to pay could involve a heavy loss of human life and ravages of every kind? Marie-Antoinette never asked herself that question. Louis XVI did. United in the same tragic destiny, the couple did not inhabit the same moral universe. On the other hand, she had an excuse that he did not share. Louis XVI was derided, but not hated; she had to face the masses' hatred. What is more, he was French, she wasn't. Her country of adoption had repudiated her. By killing off whatever attachment she was beginning to have for France, the stream of loathing heaped on her for years on end deadened her scruples. How can she be blamed for a betrayal for which the responsibility was so widely shared?

Last will

Descending the Bonbec tower's stairs to go back to her cell, Marie-Antoinette could no longer stand up. She feared falling in the dark on the damp steps. "I can hardly see where I'm going," she said. Lieutenant of the gendarmerie de Busne held out his hand to her. He had already offered her a glass of water, and here he was having doffed his hat, helping her down the stairs. Such "scandalous" consideration, reported by one of his colleagues, would earn him an appearance before the public prosecutor! In her cell, she was alone again. For this her last pre-dawn hour, they would deign to grant her some light, paper, a pen and ink. She wrote to Élisabeth, as if to echo Louis XVI's testament. It is an admirable letter, glowing with maternal love, a hymn to the family and a profession of spiritual faith:

> This 16th of October, 4:30 in the morning
> It is to you, my sister, that I write for the last time. I have just been condemned, not to a shameful death, for such is only for criminals, but to go rejoin your brother. Innocent like him, I hope to show the same firmness in these last moments. I am calm, as one is when one's conscience reproaches one with nothing. I feel profound regret at leaving my poor children: you know that I lived only for them and for you, my good and tender sister. You who out of love have sacrificed everything to be with us, in what a state do I leave you! I have learned from the proceedings at my trial that my daughter was separated from you*. Alas! poor child; I do not venture to write to her; the letter would not reach her. I do not even know whether this will reach you. Receive my blessing for both of them. I hope that one day when they are older they may be able to rejoin you again, and enjoy to the full your tender care. May they both recall what I have never ceased to impress upon them, that the principles and the exact performance of their duties are life's first rule; and that affection and trust in one another will constitute its happiness. May my daughter feel that at her age, she ought always to help her brother by the advice that her greater experience and her affection for him may inspire

---

* This was an error due to the fact that the two women were interrogated separately.

her to give. And may my son in his turn render to his sister all the care and services that affection can inspire. May they both feel that, in whatever situations they might face, it is only their union that will make them truly happy. In that may they follow our example. In our own misfortunes how much comfort has our affection for one another afforded us! And in good times we enjoy happiness doubly from being able to share it with a friend; and where can one find closer or more tender friends than in one's own family? May my son never forget his father's last words: he must never seek to avenge our deaths.

I must speak to you of one thing that weighs heavily on my heart. I know how much pain the child must have caused you. Forgive him, my dear sister; remember his age, and how easy it is to make a child say whatever one wishes, even what he does not understand. The day will come, I hope, when he will better feel the value of your kindness and of your tender affection for both of them.

It remains to confide my last thoughts to you. I should have wished to write them at the beginning of my trial; but aside from the fact that they did not allow me to write, it all happened so quickly that I really would not have had time.

I die in the Roman, Catholic and Apostolic Faith, that of my fathers, that in which I was brought up, and that I have always professed. Unable to expect any spiritual consolation, not knowing whether there are still in this place any priests of that religion, and indeed the place where I am would expose them to too much danger if they were to enter it but once, I sincerely implore God's forgiveness for all the faults I may have committed during my life. I trust that, in his goodness, He will hear my last prayers, like those that I have for a long time addressed to Him, to receive my soul into His mercy and goodness.

I beg the pardon of all those I know, and especially yours, my sister, for all the sorrows that, without intending it, I may have caused you. I pardon all my enemies for the evils that they have done me. I bid farewell to my aunts and to all my brothers and sisters. I had friends. The idea of being forever separated from them and their troubles is one of the greatest sorrows that I carry to my death. May they at least know that to my last moment I thought of them.

Farewell, my good and tender sister. I hope this letter reaches you. Think always of me; I embrace you with all my heart, as I do my poor dear children. My God, what a heartache it is to leave them forever! Farewell! Farewell! Only my spiritual duties await me now. Since I am not free to choose, they perhaps will bring me a priest; but I hereby declare that I will not say a word to him, and that I will treat him as a total stranger.

After writing "Farewell!" twice, which might have ended the letter, she continues, as if tearing herself away is too painful. The letter has an unfinished feel about it, but everything was said. It is unsigned, as were most of Marie-Antoinette's letters. It did not reach its destination. The concierge, Madame Bault, handed it over to Fouquier-Tinville who sent it to Robespierre. An obscure Convention member called Courtois was assigned the task of going through Robespierre's papers after his death, and found the letter among them. He kept it in his possession in anticipation of better times, and tried to barter it in 1816 with Louis XVIII in exchange for a pardon. Thus it arrived at the Royal Archives, today the National Archives, where it still can be seen today[*].

The execution

Marie-Antoinette lay down fully dressed on her bed; but she didn't sleep. She was crying, but silently. About seven o'clock a shattered Rosalie slipped in to see her, saying, "Madame, you took nothing to eat last night and hardly anything during the day either. What would you like to have this morning?" only to get the answer, "My child, I no longer have need of anything, my life is over." As the young girl insisted, she accepted a bit of broth, which she had difficulty swallowing. Soon it would be time to change her clothing. She had been forbidden to go to her execution wearing her black widow's weeds with the excuse that this might aggravate the people – one wonders how. She therefore donned her modest morning attire, more like a dressing gown than a robe, two skirts, a white one over a black one, and on top a sort of nighttime camisole, also white; for her head a little white bonnet bound by a black ribbon. What matter if this outfit was inappropriate to the occasion and out of season, for the cold had already begun to bite. But she wanted to change her shift as she had lost a lot of blood. No sooner did she try to find a bit of privacy between the wall and her bed than she

---

[*] The archivists do not doubt its authenticity, which certain historians have contested. It carries Fouquier-Tinville's signature as it had been entrusted to him, and those of the commissioners who then inventoried it.

saw approaching the new gendarme who had replaced lieutenant de Busne, under arrest for having shown too much compassion. "In the name of decency, sir, permit me some privacy to change my clothing." The callous guard replied: "I cannot consent to that; my orders stipulate that I must watch your every movement." She dealt with the situation as best she could, the maid acting as a shield. She hastened to roll up the soiled shift and slip it into a crevice in the wall behind the stove. This was only the first of the humiliations awaiting her in her last hours of this life.

At about ten o'clock the turnkey arrived, sent by the concierge who was devoured by curiosity. He found her kneeling by her bed in prayer. "Do you know, Larivière, that they are about to put me to death? Tell your good mother that I thank her for her assistance [she had mended her black dress] and that I enjoin her to pray God for me." Already the door was opening to reveal the judges and the court clerk. She hastened to rise.

"Pay attention; we are about to read you your sentence."
"You needn't bother. I know full well what the sentence is."
"No matter, it must be read to you a second time."

She remained so impassive that Larivière felt he could truthfully declare: "the judges are struck by her majestic and estimable spirit," for although it was generally not done, all four of them removed their hats.

When the reading of her sentence was almost over, a young man "of enormous size" arrived. He was the high executioner. The profession was one that was handed down from generation to generation. Henri Sanson had just taken the job over from his father, who retired after executing the king. He approached her saying, "Present your hands." She was startled and protested: "You are going to tie my hands? They did not tie Louis XVI's hands*!" The judges told Sanson, "Do your job." So he tied her hands behind her back, very tightly, while she tried to rein in the tears. Then he took off her bonnet and cut her hair, which he pocketed. It would later be burned so as not to become a relic.

She was ready. There was one last formality to go through at the clerk's office. Release from prison required a heap of paper to be duly certified by the bailiff. A tumbrel drew up in the Cour du Mai. It was the same tumbrel used for carting common criminals to their

---

*   More exactly, they were only tied at the last minute, at the foot of the scaffold. But his hands were free all along the way to the place of execution.

deaths. The king was granted a proper coach, the one belonging to the mayor of Paris. The queen would be subjected to what *Le Père Duchesne* called the "cart of countless exits," meaning it had none. It was a simple, flat wagon made of rough wood placed on axles without the benefit of springs, drawn by two rustic percheron horses. Holding her by a leash, the executioner helped her climb the rickety stepladder leading up to it. Between the slatted sides there was a bench in the middle that she was about to step over so as to sit down facing forward, but Sanson stopped her. In a throwback to medieval practices, she had to proceed to the place of execution facing backwards, as a sign of her shame. The executioner was just following orders. But since their orders stipulated nothing about hats, he and his assistant had removed theirs.

Louis XVI had been granted a priest of his own choosing, one notorious for not having taken the oath. Marie-Antoinette had not wanted to ask for anything, knowing she would be rebuffed. A "juror" priest called Girard in civilian clothing, who was also hoisted into the tumbrel with her, tried to press his services on her but she obstinately refused; "she was not of his religion; she would die professing that of her august spouse." All the same, he was polite enough not to sit next to her but on the bench behind her.

They had taken colossal precautions to avoid any attempt to rescue her, just as they had done for the king. Starting at five o'clock in the morning the call went out to the poor sections of Paris. At seven o'clock all the armed forces were at the ready. Along the entire route the cortege would follow to the Place de la Révolution, all traffic had been prohibited, and cannons had been placed at the bridges, in the squares and the crossroads. An impressive armed contingent of 30,000 men it is said had been summoned to line the entire route. The wretched "wig-makers" – in fact a collection of craftsmen and shopkeepers – who fantasized about saving her, managed to muster a mere handful of plotters only good for getting themselves arrested.

About eleven o'clock a shiver rippled through the crowd that had gathered in the rue de la Barillerie along the iron gate of the Palace of Justice. The doomed woman was approaching. It was a hushed rather than a noisy crowd. But soon the atmosphere changed. The death of Louis XVI was a ritual sacrifice imbued with a sense of gravity, of contemplation even. They tried to turn Marie-Antoinette's into a farce. The guillotine, however, did not lend itself to farce; it was certainly imposing, but too quick. Its inventor, the good doctor Guillotin, intended it to be swift. He wasn't wrong in seeing it as a humane improvement over the good old-fashioned way of lopping off heads with an axe, which was difficult to do cleanly. So if you wanted a show, it had to take place before you got there. They dragged out the trip to about an hour and a half, and put on a good show. In front of her cart, a mounted escort led by the former actor Grammont was whipping up the crowd as if it were all some sort of circus act, inciting them to hoot and jeer, "Here she is, my friends, the infamous Marie-Antoinette! She is fucked, so she is!" They made planned stops along the way where old cronies were gathered. In front of Saint-Roch the fishwives on the steps of the church chanted in chorus, "Death to the Austrian bitch!" or "Messalina! Messalina!" They made what jest they could of it. At one point, when a more jolting bump than usual almost knocked her off her bench, a spectator sniggered "Where are your cushy Trianon pillows now?" The endless rue Saint-Honoré was hell, only brightened for the time it took to smile at the sight of a child held up in his mother's arms.

Her cheeks red, her bloodshot eyes stiffened by eyelashes salt-caked from her tears, her arms twisted behind her by the rope that was too tight, Marie-Antoinette soldiered on, erect, dignified, impassive, meeting insult with disdain. More expressive than any words is the rough sketch in profile, jotted down hastily by the painter David, even though he was a fanatic supporter of the Montagnards. Stephan Zweig would call it "a sketch of horrifying grandeur, of a sinister power, an old woman without beauty... her mouth proudly closed, as if uttering an inward cry, her eyes indifferent and alien, there she is in the tumbrel with her hands tied behind her back, as straight and as proud as if she were on her throne... Hatred itself could not deny seeing in this image the nobility with which Marie-Antoinette by her sublime stance, triumphs over the humiliation of the tumbrel."

Finally she reached the old rue Royale that opened onto the Place de la Révolution. The sight of the Tuileries gardens with the chateau's facade behind it brought her back to earth for a moment in a brief flush of emotion, but she quickly recovered her composure. She saw the guillotine standing between the swing bridge and the statue of Liberty that had replaced that of Louis XV. She was in a hurry to get it all over with. She descended from the tumbrel "with promptitude and a light step," said the journalist for the *Republican Magician*, "without needing to be held, although her hands were still tied." She likewise went up the few steps to the scaffold "with bravado, seeming calmer and more at peace even than when she left the prison." She lost one of her slippers en route, stepped on the executioner's foot with the other, and with the supreme good manners of the sovereign said to him, "I beg your pardon, sir." Those were her last words. She would not try to address the people, to whom Louis XVI wanted to proclaim his innocence. She had nothing to say to them. She regarded them with superb indifference and had nothing but scorn for what they might think. Throwing off her bonnet with a sudden thrust of her head, she calmly allowed them to attach her, standing face forward, to the plank, which then swung to a horizontal position. The wooden collar was clasped around her neck. The guillotine cord was let go; the blade dropped. Sanson picked up her bloodied head and brandished it before the people, who shouted *Long Live the Republic! Long Live Freedom!* It was exactly twelve fifteen in the afternoon of October 16th, 1793.

The revolutionary press was not wrong in its unanimous desire, whether seriously or trivially, to emphasize her pride. But by doing so they admitted defeat. The best political or religious trials are designed for repentance. Terror, tears, supplications, confessions, contrition and final conversion lead the victims to subscribe to their own execution. They are thus reconciled with the society that puts them to death, in recognition of their common values, of their shared idea of good and evil. True to herself, Marie-Antoinette refused to be drawn into this perverse game. Right up until her death she remained steadfast in her rejection of the new regime. The Revolution was able to kill her; it never succeeded in defeating her. She was indomitable to the end.

Marie-Antoinette, by David, 16 October 1793.

EPILOGUE

When the winds of history whip up a storm

"I have brought misfortune to you all," Marie-Antoinette wrote to Madame de Polignac shortly after Christmas 1789. It was just a figure of speech, surely; but it cannot be denied that fate wreaked havoc on those around the woman Barbey d'Aurevilly called "The Dame of Death." Around her, not because of her. We'll say a word here about what became of the principal figures among them.

Marie-Antoinette was one of the first victims of "The Reign of Terror" created by the Montagnards to maintain their grip on the country. She died in plentiful company. Even though the military situation had eased somewhat both at home and abroad, the tempest whipped up a torrent where the cadavers of friends and enemies who played a part in her story were swept along indiscriminately. In the autumn of 1793, in chronological order, the guillotine dispatched: on the 31st of October, the Girondins, who wanted to spare the king after having defeated him; on the 6th of November, Philippe-Égalité, who thought he could save his own skin by voting for his cousin's death; on the 29th, Barnave, who paid the price for helping the sovereigns after Varennes; the 8th of December, Madame du Barry, guilty of having served as a liaison with the royalists, and who was not forgiven for having betrayed her class of origin. In 1794, on May the 10th, Madame Élisabeth, condemned to death for having corresponded with the émigrés, confronted her final torment with heroic simplicity. If fortune had been on her side and given her three more months, she could have escaped this fate.

Already the Revolution had begun to devour its own children: after the Girondins, Hébert, then Danton and their friends fell under the blade. Once Robespierre met the same fate, Thermidor sent those responsible for the Terror to their deaths as well: Fouquier-Tinville would in turn take the same road down which he had sent Marie-Antoinette. As for the duchess de Polignac, saved from the clutches of the Revolution by emigrating, she died of natural causes in Vienna a few weeks after her friend's execution.

Thermidor would come too late for the little captive king. The Convention in victory had no need of hostages. It dare not kill him, but it created the conditions that would. In January of 1794, the Simon couple was dismissed. Claiming that they were merely withdrawing any special privileges, the authorities left him to rot for six months in disgusting, filthy conditions, walled up in what had been his father's unheated, unventilated and sparsely lit fourth-floor apartment in the Temple, his only company the guards who passed him food through a window. When Barras found him at the end of July 1794, it was too late; he did not respond to medical care. He was mentally and physically destroyed. Tuberculosis, against which his father struggled all his life and which had killed his brother, would take his life in turn. The doctors were powerless against the disease that was eating away at all of his joints. He would die less than a year later, on the 8th of June 1795. There is no need to go into the theory about his having been replaced by another little boy; recent genetic tests have refuted this legend.

His sister, older and more mature, was less horribly treated. She would be imprisoned in the company of Madame Élisabeth. So cut off from the world that they didn't even know about Marie-Antoinette's execution, they supported each other, imposing a certain salutary order on their lives. After her aunt left for a destination she was not informed of, the young lady would spend only two and a half months in solitary confinement. The Thermidorians treated her more gently and then, on December 19th, 1795, negotiated her freedom in exchange for the hostages that Austria was holding. Three and a half years later she married her cousin the count d'Artois' son, the duke d'Angoulême, as her mother had wished. It was not a happy marriage and since there were no children, Marie-Antoinette's direct line ended with her.

In the years that followed, other members of the royal family played at hide-and-seek across Europe with the republican and then the imperial armies. Twice the countess d'Artois was hunted out of Turin. Soon the king's two aged aunts, Mesdames Adélaïde and Victoire, who had thought they were safe in Rome, were forced to flee before Bonaparte's lightning advance. No sooner had they reached Caserta, where the queen of Naples Maria-Carolina offered them asylum, than they had to flee again; the conqueror was on his way there too! They hurried south, got stuck in Bari, and managed to embark on a boat going up the Adriatic. The ship dropped them off in Trieste, at the end of their resources and their strength. They had just enough left to survive briefly, dying within six months of each other, the irrepressible Adélaïde fittingly the last to go.

It was in Turin as well that the count de Provence's wife Marie-Joséphine of Savoy learned of the death of the little Louis XVII, which made her queen. She too had to flee Italy. Having fallen out with her husband over her beloved lady reader, she wandered from one place of exile to another, dragging her poverty with her, used up and in poor health. She died in England on 13 November 1810, five years after her sister. Thus, neither of the two Savoyard sisters was at her husband's side to see the Restoration. Marie-Joséphine was officially the last queen of France*, but she never functioned as such. She would never dethrone Marie-Antoinette.

What became of Fersen affords a look into the mysteries of life's coincidences. His beloved's execution broke not only his heart, but his chances of a successful career as well. For him it was a personal failure, and was seen as such in all the courts of Europe. After Louis XVI's death, he believed the Jacobin revolution was lost. He already pictured himself as the special adviser to the regent Marie-Antoinette. The dream didn't last. At the age of thirty-eight, he was relegated to a moment in history that everyone preferred to forget. In Vienna, which did not have a very good conscience, no one wanted to hear any more about the unfortunate woman. He tried in vain to get Madame Royale, who had inherited her mother's jewels, to reimburse him for the expenses he incurred preparing for the Varennes adventure. He had to fall back on his native country, which appointed him to the Congress of Rastadt. Burning with hatred for France, he appeared to be a man from a distant epoch, unfit for any diplomatic post. He became embittered. Eleonore Sullivan refused to go bury herself in icy Sweden to nurse his declining health and worship with him at the altar of his fallen heroine. She was better off marrying Craufurd instead. Fersen inherited an immense fortune from his parents, received his father's titles and functions, and lived in Stockholm with his sister Sophie at his side, leading the life of an extravagant and arrogant lord. More rigidly conservative than ever, he was widely detested. He

---

* Strictly speaking, the last queen of France was the duchess d'Angoulême, Marie-Antoinette's daughter, who held this title for a few hours in 1830, before the crown passed to the Orléans family. Marie-Amélie and her husband Louis-Philippe would bear the titles of the queen and king *of the French*, not *of France*.

disapproved of the ousting of King Gustav-Adolph, although he was quite mad, and that of his son who was too young and replaced by a Danish prince. When this prince died suddenly in 1810, the rumor spread, although there wasn't an iota of proof, that Fersen had had him poisoned. Despite warnings not to attend his funeral, Fersen set out dressed to the nines in his Marshal of the Kingdom uniform. The crowd, worked up into a frenzy, dragged him from his coach and lynched him. He perished as he had so often feared to see Marie-Antoinette perish, torn from limb to limb by a furious mob. The drama took place on June 20th, the double anniversary of the departure for Varennes and the first invasion of the Tuileries. A tragic and ironic twist of fate joined him in death with the women to whom he had devoted his life.

An attempt to sum up

We will not tarry here with the polemical texts that dotted the 19th century; they were all written to exploit the queen's role in the political debate for or against the Revolution. Today, passions have died down somewhat. Having arrived at the end of this account, perhaps we can try to draw some conclusions.

No, Marie-Antoinette was not responsible for the French Revolution. It had been brewing for a long time in the widening gap between the ossified state institutions and great changes in social realities. But because of her light-mindedness, she helped hasten the monarchy's disrepute. The waving of her fan whipped up the flames of revolution that would engulf the fragile court edifice, which Louis XV had already begun to fracture, causing it to fall apart and come crumbling down. Her marital difficulties, widely known and commented upon, set a slightly ridiculous cast on Louis XVI's very real virtues; and his tendency to accommodate her put the finishing touches on his reputation as a weakling. Toppled from their pedestal and deprived of their sacred status, they were just like anyone else.

No, she did not bring financial ruin on France. Bankruptcy was the price of France's support for the American war. The treasury did not have the means to finance it without profound fiscal change. But her spendthrift ways were shocking because they served such frivolity; her largesse scandalized people, because it was capricious, and without regard for merit.

No, she did not subjugate France to the dictates of Austria. But it was not for want of trying. She consented to being a conduit for her mother and her brother Joseph II, although without appreciable results. Louis XVI always resisted her efforts. She never took part in any "Austrian conspiracy" before the Revolution; and later, while in prison, she appealed for help, but the little bit of information she did get through to Belgium did not change the course of events. It is true, however, that she never became completely French; that was the doing of the empress and Louis XV, who agreed that the umbilical cord with her native country should not be severed, unlike for queens in the past. This incurred an indelible mark against her in the eyes of an anti-Austrian public.

No, she did not make and unmake ministers at will. With regard to both domestic and foreign affairs, her influence was negligible. But she was seen as having influence, and liked people to believe she did. She hardly ever really weighed in on the decision-making process. She wasn't able to, lacking the education required for that. Everyone, however, was at a loss when confronted with her willpower. So her mother laid down the law: she must simply obey; she needn't understand anything other than the need for the Franco-Austrian alliance. Louis XVI and his ministers took the easy way out; rather than try to reason with her, they chose to sidetrack her into trivial pursuits, encouraging her self-indulgence. No doubt it would have been better to educate her, as Turgot briefly suggested. Saint-Priest, who could not be accused of liking her, said all the same, "We must render justice to the queen; as soon as we had the courage to resist her by citing the good of the State, she stopped trying." But they cited nothing; they fed her with delusions. Her real role only began on the eve of the Revolution; too late for her to have acquired any genuine political ability. That she pushed the king to resist is undeniable; that she encouraged him to play a double game is certain. But no one can say for sure that without her he would have rallied in good faith to a constitutional monarchy that was so foreign to his deepest convictions. But she was so unsuccessful at hiding her feelings that each successive Assembly could not help considering her an enemy. She was seen in fact as the most active proponent of the counter-Revolution.

It is clear therefore that she never did anything terribly harmful, but because of her continued imprudence, provocation and defiance, she indirectly caused the monarchy considerable damage. But all of this is not enough to explain the extraordinary outpouring of hatred she inspired. In effect, all the criticism leveled against her comes down to one alone: she did not do what was expected of her. The spouse of the king of France must submit to two duties, that of queen and that of wife. Infinitely more was expected of her because at the time, in the collective imagination, the queen, out

642   *The Indomitable Marie-Antoinette*

of step with evolving ways of thinking, remained the repository of traditional values; even if there was only one left, the queen had to be it. Marie-Antoinette did not understand this; vehemently, insolently, she rejected the model. She thought she was free; she refused the burdens and constraints of her condition. She wanted to live life on her own terms, outside the family orbit. And she wished to take part in the affairs of state, in power, the exclusive domain of the male.

The court nobility would not forgive her for preferring her unaffected pleasures at the Trianon to their stiff "apartment" evenings in Versailles, or for having scorned the rules governing rank. The bourgeoisie and the common people, who were as misogynistic as they were moralistic, criticized her for not being a good wife, a homemaker given over to specifically feminine tasks. Royal mistresses were given the prerogative to dictate fashion, even to have something of a say in politics; people knew that, they complained about them and gibed at them, but that's how it was; it was accepted. But the queen was another matter altogether; she must show nothing but gentleness, discretion and acceptance of her role. And her role was limited to making her husband happy, educating her children, and bestowing charity on her people. By bucking tradition, the indomitable and flamboyant Marie-Antoinette struck a blow against the world order. For this crime no punishment was too harsh.

Unlike her husband, she was partly to blame for her fate. Louis XVI was executed less for what he did than for what he was: through him the monarchy was put to death. Marie-Antoinette on the other hand was personally targeted. She perhaps would have escaped the guillotine – although it is not certain – had she been a retiring, self-effacing queen, like so many of her predecessors. She herself, with her own hands, day after day, blindly wove together the rope with which the executioner bound her and led her to the scaffold. "My daughter will be her own undoing," Maria Theresa had groaned when learning of her girlish, rebellious escapades. In effect, her mother was right; she paid a ghastly price for refusing programmed obedience, because she wasn't able to carve out her own niche within the confines of the space accorded to her. Ill prepared for her role and married too young, the pawn of an alliance rejected by the French people, she was more a victim than a perpetrator, and the ordeals she was subjected to, especially as regards her son, seem to far outweigh her faults. She made the mistake of not being what was needed, when it was needed, where it was needed. And her intransigent character in the long run made everything worse, for she was not one of those who stoop to compromise.

Posthumous comeback

When we reflect on Marie-Antoinette's life, we are struck by a paradox. For in the end, what she is criticized for is striving for what all of her contemporaries dreamed of. She was very much in step with the times. Her desire for freedom, her appetite for life, her will to be herself, were all typical of a generation that was challenging the values of yesteryear. In a society where the Tridentine Church was losing its grip, the obsession with eternal salvation was being replaced by the pursuit of happiness here on earth. It was a time when the individual, refusing to be a mere link in the generational chain, aspired to personal fulfillment. Infinitely receptive to the whims of fashion, Marie-Antoinette enjoyed the soppy sentimentality of contemporary theatre; she shared with the emulators of Jean-Jacques Rousseau the cult of nature, studied and corrected by English gardeners. She languished in the moonlight and exalted in the sunrise. She complained of *ennui* and gave in to *spleen*; she proclaimed the rights of the heart over the duties of marriage. She also shared the feverish enthusiasms so typical of the last years of the Ancien Régime, when people were turning a deaf ear to the coming storm and savoring the last sweet fruits of the dying season. Romanticism was sewing its first seeds, with its obsessive preoccupation with the passage of time, its inability to capture the moment that offers itself without ruining it with the idea that it was going to end. More generally, Marie-Antoinette can be described as modern, provided we attach no moral judgment to the word. She was infinitely closer to us than to her immediate predecessors, Marie Leszczynska or Marie-Josèphe of Saxony for example. In the history of ideas, of tastes, of sensibility, she shared little with the classical centuries; she was on the other side, the one that has led to today's world.

But this modernity, which would prove her downfall, contributed to the fascination she has never ceased to exercise over us. As ChantalThomas pointed out, "Her charm reaches beyond the grave, amplified if not rendered sacred by the tragic story of her death." To a supreme degree both woman and queen, strong-willed and fragile at the same time, arrogant in her rebellious intransigence, true to herself right to the end of her torment, she arouses passion. The rational beings who rightly list her errors and reckless doings are powerless against the heart's fascination for her. Why? Above all because her fate fits in to a tried and true literary tradition that in turn affords comparisons that shed light on it. She offers to the dramatist a perfect example of Aristotle's tragic personage, neither entirely good nor entirely bad, who descends into disgrace both through her own fault and through the force of circumstances. It is easy to discern the tragic sequence of events that brought her from the rapturous applause to the jeering, from the gilded trappings of Versailles to the leprous walls of the Conciergerie. The novelist is handed on a silver platter the scenes of a doomed passion – whether consummated or not – to mull over to his or her heart's content. What is more, history, if wrapped in a time warp, offers an improbable and superb denouement by uniting in the same death the lovers who were sacrificed to the hatred of the masses. Thus, thanks to combined associations of thought and memory, Marie-Antoinette joins the cohort of the great literary heroines, and shares in their immortality.

Her survival is due as well to her own qualities. She embodied one of the imagination's archetypes. It is useless for historians to keep on repeating, documents in hand, that the job of queen is a tough job, we only half believe them. When an adolescent or even a more mature woman becomes queen, she does not see herself as a docile wife enslaved to the duties of her position. The queen is the most beautiful, the most admired, the most loved; her life takes place in a universe of festivities. She has the world at her feet and her wishes become others' command. In our world today, queens are celebrities and celebrities are queens. During her three years of "folly" Marie-Antoinette was a bit of both. We get a hint of this in the portraits painted of her at the time where she stands proudly, beribboned and plumed, her bust swelling in her iridescent silk and gold-speckled gowns.

But this image of the most queenly of queens is enhanced, dare we say, by its incomparable setting. This image cannot be found among the icy marbles of the Expiatory Chapel or Saint-Denis. The image is reflected in the places where she lived, in the objects she touched, and which we can still see today. When she left Versailles on the 6th of October 1789 never to see it again, she left behind the decor of her daily life. Miraculously, this decor still survives. None of those who have since tried to make a home of Versailles has succeeded in taming its spirit or making it their own. What is more – and this is not the least paradox of the story – the Third Republic, for which the Revolution provided its founding myth, finished the task of converting the royal chateau into a museum, repository of the Ancien Régime, opened up for all the world to admire. Along with the Sun King, Louis XIV, it is Marie-Antoinette almost exclusively who shares ownership of it. The Hall of Mirrors is his, as are the reception halls, the Grand Canal and the French gardens. Hers are the living quarters, the Petit Trianon and the Hamlet. Of a summer's evening, when the doors have closed on the last departing tourists, it is pleasing to imagine that the shade of the Sun King in his most resplendent attire retakes possession of the palace over which he officiated so long ago; while the light spirit of Marie-Antoinette in her white dress ambles with her airy step over the lawns bathed in moonlight beside the little lake, between the mill and the Temple of Love. They are figures forever reborn, an eternal link between the past and the present, who live a life that outlives our own, because it has been entrusted to humanity's collective memory.

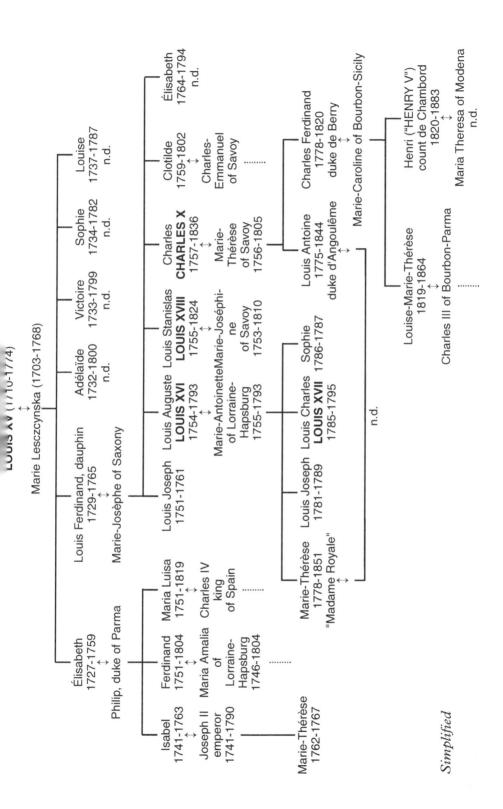

LOUIS XV (1710-1774)
↕
Marie Leszczynska (1703-1768)

Élisabeth 1727-1759
Philip, duke of Parma

Louis Ferdinand, dauphin 1729-1765
↕
Marie-Josèphe of Saxony

Adélaïde 1732-1800 n.d.

Victoire 1733-1799 n.d.

Sophie 1734-1782 n.d.

Louise 1737-1787 n.d.

Isabel 1741-1763
↕
Joseph II emperor 1741-1790

Ferdinand 1751-1804
↕
Maria Amalia of Lorraine-Hapsburg 1746-1804

Maria Luisa 1751-1819
↕
Charles IV king of Spain
⋯⋯⋯

Louis Joseph 1751-1761

Louis Auguste LOUIS XVI 1754-1793
↕
Marie-Antoinette of Lorraine-Hapsburg 1755-1793

Louis Stanislas LOUIS XVIII 1755-1824
↕
Marie-Joséphine of Savoy 1753-1810

Charles CHARLES X 1757-1836
↕
Marie-Thérèse of Savoy 1756-1805

Clotilde 1759-1802
↕
Charles-Emmanuel of Savoy
⋯⋯⋯

Élisabeth 1764-1794 n.d.

Marie-Thérèse 1762-1767

Marie-Thérèse 1778-1851 "Madame Royale"
↕
Louis Joseph 1781-1789

Louis Charles LOUIS XVII 1785-1795

Sophie 1786-1787

n.d.

Louis Antoine 1775-1844 duke d'Angoulême
↕
Marie-Thérèse of Savoy

Charles Ferdinand 1778-1820 duke de Berry
↕
Marie-Caroline of Bourbon-Sicily

Louise-Marie-Thérèse 1819-1864
↕
Charles III of Bourbon-Parma
⋯⋯⋯

Henri ("HENRY V") count de Chambord 1820-1883
↕
Maria Theresa of Modena n.d.

Simplified

MARIE-ANTOINETTE'S AUSTRIAN FAMILY

MARIA THERESA OF AUSTRIA
13 May 1717 – 29 November 1780

- Daughter of Emperor Charles VI (1685-1740), upon his death inherited the patrimonial States of Austria and the kingdoms of Bohemia and Hungary.

- Married 12 February 1736 to François-Étienne de Lorraine, born 8 December 1708, duke of Lorraine and Bar from 1729 to 1736, grand duke of Tuscany from 1737 to 1765, emperor of Germany from 1745 to 1765 under the name of Francis I, died in Innsbruck on 18 August 1765.

- Of the couple's sixteen children, three died in childhood, three others in adolescence, and ten survived into adulthood:

– Elisabeth, 1737-1740.

– Maria Anna, born on 6 October 1738, abbess of the Chapter of Noble Ladies of Prague, died on 19 November 1789.

– Maria Charlotte, January 1740 – January 1741.

– Joseph, born 13 March 1741, emperor of Germany as of 1765 under the name of Joseph II; inherited the patrimonial States from his mother on 29 November 1780; died on 20 February 1790. Married for the first time in 1760 to Isabel of Bourbon, princess of Parma (31 December 1741 – 27 November 1763), maternal granddaughter of Louis XV, called Madame Infanta, with whom he had one daughter who died at the age of five. Married for the second time in 1765 to Josepha of Bavaria (1739-1767) from which union there were no children.

– Maria Christina, born on 13 May 1742, died on 24 June 1798. Married in 1766 to Albert-Casimir, prince of Saxony, duke of Teschen, vice-king of Hungary (died in 1822). With her husband became governor of the Low Countries 1781.

– Maria Elisabeth, born on 16 August 1743, considered in 1768 as a possible wife for Louis XV, abbess of the Chapter of Innsbruck, died on 22 September 1808.

– Charles Joseph, born in 1745, died in 1761.

– Maria Amalia, born on 26 February 1746, married on 19 July 1769 to Ferdinand of Bourbon, duke of Parma (1751-1802), grandson of Louis XV through his mother, Madame Infanta, and of Philip V of Spain through his father, the infante Don Philip (1720-1765). Died on 18 June 1804.

– Leopold, born on 5 May 1747, grand duke of Tuscany as of 18 August 1765, then inheritor of the patrimonial States of Austria as of 20 February 1790 and elected emperor the same year under the name of Leopold II. Married in 1765 to Maria Luisa of Bourbon, infanta of Spain (1745-1792), daughter of king Charles III, who gave him sixteen children. Died on 1 March 1792. His heir would be his eldest son, Francis II.

– Maria Carolina, born and died in 1748.

– Johanna Gabriela, born in 1750 and died in 1762.

– Maria Josepha, or Josefa, born in 1751, betrothed to Ferdinand I, king of Naples, died in 1767.

– Maria Carolina, born on 13 August 1752, married on 7 April 1768 to Ferdinand I, king of Naples and of Sicily, then king of the Two Sicilies (1751-1825). Died on 8 September 1814. Among her eight children, one of her daughters, Maria Theresa, would marry her cousin the emperor Francis II. Their daughter Marie-Louise would become Napoléon's second wife, and the other, Marie-Amelie, would marry Louis-Philippe of Orléans, who would become King of the French in 1830.

– Ferdinand Charles, born 1 June 1754, married the 15 October 1771 to Mary Beatrice of Este (1750-1829), inheritor of the duchy of Modena, of which he became grand duke. (The marriage had been planned for his brother the archduke Charles-Joseph, but was transferred to him upon the latter's death). He died on 24 December 1806.

– Marie-Antoinette, born on 2 November 1755, married to the dauphin Louis of France, the future Louis XVI, on 16 May 1770. Died on 16 October 1793.

– Maximilian Francis, born on 8 December 1756, archbishop of Münster and prince-elector of Cologne. Died on 17 July 1801.

CHRONOLOGY

1753	2 Sept.	Birth of Marie-Joséphine-Louise of Savoy, future duchess de Provence.
1754	23 Aug.	Birth of the duke de Berry (future Louis XVI).
1755	2 Nov.	Birth of Marie-Antoinette.
	17 Nov.	Birth of the count de Provence (future Louis XVIII).
1756	1 May	First treaty of Versailles between France and Austria. Switching of alliances.
1757	9 Oct.	Birth of the count d'Artois (future Charles X).
1759	23 Sept.	Birth of Marie-Clotilde of France.
1762	10 July	Accession of Catherine II ("the Great") of Russia.
1763	10 Feb.	Treaty of Paris between France and England.
	3 June	End of the Seven Years War.
1764	3 May	Birth of Élisabeth of France.
1765	18 Aug.	Death of emperor Francis I.
	20 Dec.	Death of the dauphin Louis Ferdinand, son of Louis XV.
1767	13 Mar.	Death of the dauphine Marie-Josèphe of Saxony.
1768	24 June	Death of Marie Leszczynska.
	October	The sultan Mustapha III, supported by the French, declares war on Russia.
1769	22 April	Presentation of Madame du Barry at court.
1770	19 April	Marriage by proxy in Vienna of Marie-Antoinette to the dauphin.
	7 May	"Hand over" of Marie-Antoinette to France.
	16 May	Marriage in Versailles.

	8 July	Russian naval victory over the Turks at Chesme. Land victory at Ismail.
	3 Sept.	Joseph II and Kaunitz meet Frederick II in Neustadt.
	24 Dec.	Choiseul is disgraced.
1771	January	Paris Parliament is exiled.
		During carnival season, Madame de Lamballe becomes Marie-Antoinette's favorite.
	February	The "Maupeou Parliament" is set up.
	14 May	Marriage of Marie-Joséphine of Saxony with the count de Provence.

1772   19 Feb.   Plan to carve up Poland signed by Prussia and Russia. Facing a fait accompli, Austria can only comply... and claim its share.

25 July   Treaty on the partition of Poland signed in St. Petersburg.

August   Gustav III's coup d'état reestablishing his authority in Sweden.

1773   8 June   Marie-Antoinette's solemn entry into Paris

16 Nov.   Marriage of Marie-Thérèse of Savoy with the count d'Artois.

December   The Boston Tea Party.

1774   10 Jan.   Fersen's official presentation to Marie-Antoinette.

30 Jan.   He meets her at the Opera ball.

10 May   Death of Louis XV. Accession of Louis XVI. Recall of Maurepas as "Mentor" to the young king.
Treaty of Küçük Kaynarca, establishing Russia's (Orthodox) influence in the Balkans.
Duke d'Aiguillon is dismissed.

24 Aug.   "The St. Bartholomew's Day of the ministers." Maupeou and Terray leave. Vergennes takes up foreign affairs. Turgot in finance ministry.

Autumn   Declaration of colonial rights in Philadelphia.

November   Louis XVI calls back the parliaments.

1775   February   Maximilian of Austria visits Versailles.

19 April   Battle of Lexington. Beginning of armed revolt in America.

Spring   The "flour wars."

11 June   Louis XVI's coronation.

6 Aug.   Birth of the duke d'Angoulême, son of the count d'Artois.

20 Aug.   Marriage by proxy of Clotilde with the prince of Piedmont.

	Autumn	In Fontainebleau, Madame de Polignac becomes favorite of Marie-Antoinette.
1776	March	Washington takes Boston.
	12 May	Turgot is dismissed.
	4 July	American Independence is declared.
	November	Benjamin Franklin comes to Paris.
1777	18 April	Joseph II arrives in Paris.
	June	Necker becomes Director General of Finances.
	31 Oct.	Victory of the American insurgents at Saratoga.
	30 Dec.	Death of the Elector of Bavaria.
1778	6 Feb.	France recognizes the United States and signs with them a treaty of alliance and commerce.
	3 July	Frederick II declares war on Austria and invades Bohemia.
	27 July	Battle of Ouessant
	August	Fersen returns to Versailles.
	20 Dec.	Birth of Madame Royale.
1779	13 May	Peace of Teschen.
1780		Renovations at the Trianon. Beginning of the private theatrical performances there.
	August	Election of Maximilian of Lorraine-Hapsburg as archbishop of Cologne and bishop of Münster.
	29 Nov.	Death of the empress Maria Theresa.
	20 Dec.	England declares war on Holland.
1781	February	Publication of Necker's *Report to the King*.
	May	Necker's dismissal.
	Summer	Joseph II visits Versailles (29 July – 5 August).
	19 Oct.	Surrender of the English at Yorktown on the Chesapeake Bay.
	22 Oct.	Birth of the dauphin Louis Joseph.
	21 Nov.	Death of Maurepas.
1782	2 March	Death of Madame Sophie.
	May	Visit to Paris of Catherine the Great's son and his wife.
		Russian troops invade the Crimea.
1783	June	Fersen comes back from America.
	3 Sept.	Treaty of Versailles (United States independence).
	10 Nov.	Calonne becomes controller general of finance.

1784	27 April	*The Marriage of Figaro* performed at *les Italiens.* The Escaut estuary affair.

1785	20 Feb.	Saint-Cloud is purchased for Marie-Antoinette.
	27 Mar.	Birth of Louis Charles, duke de Normandie (future Louis XVII.)
	24 May	Marie-Antoinette goes to Paris for her churching ceremony where she is given a glacial welcome. "What have I done to them?"
	15 Aug	Beginning of the necklace affair.
	8 Nov.	The Treaty of Fontainebleau settles the Escaut estuary affair.

1786	31 May	The cardinal de Rohan is acquitted.
	June	Visit of Marie-Antoinette's brother Ferdinand and his wife Beatrice of Este, duke and duchess of Modena.
	End June	Louis XVI goes to Cherbourg.
	9 July	Birth of Sophie-Hélène-Béatrice.
	17 Aug.	Death of Frederick II of Prussia at age 74.
	29 Dec.	Louis XVI announces the meeting of an Assembly of Notables.

1787	13 Feb.	Death of Vergennes.
	22 Feb.	Meeting of the Assembly of Notables.
	8 April	Calonne is disgraced.
	End April	Appointment of Brienne.
	25 May	Dissolution of the Assembly of Notables.
	18 June	Death of the little Sophie.
	June–Aug.	Conflict with the Paris Parliament, which rejects Brienne's edicts and calls for a meeting of the Estates General.
	17 Sept.	Congress adopts the American Constitution.
	19 Nov.	Royal session at parliament: Louis XVI imposes the recording of the edicts and exiles the duke d'Orléans.
	23 Dec.	Death of Madame Louise.

1788	3 May	The Paris Parliament publishes a *Declaration of the Fundamental Laws of the Kingdom.*
	5 May	Councilors Épremesnil and Monsabert are arrested.
	8 May	Judiciary reform reducing the parliaments' powers. Provincial parliaments resist.
	7 June	Grenoble : "Day of the Tiles."
	8 Aug.	Estates General are called for the first of May 1789.
	25 Aug.	Brienne leaves, Necker is recalled.
	September	The parliaments are reestablished.

1789 5 May   The Estates General open.
          4 June   Death of the dauphin Louis Joseph.
          20 June   The Jeu de Paume oath.
          23 June   Royal session at the Estates General.
          11 July   Necker is dismissed.
          14 July   The Bastille is stormed.
          16 July   Necker is recalled.
          4 Aug.   Abolition of class "privileges."
          26 Aug.   Declaration of the Rights of Man and of the Citizen.
          5/6 Oct.   The king and queen are forced to go to Paris.
          2 Nov.   Church property is placed at the nation's disposal.

1790 20 Feb.   Death of Joseph II. Accession of Leopold II.
          12 July   Vote to secularize the clergy.
          14 July   The first Federation Day, now know as Bastille Day.
          31 Aug.   Bouillé crushes the Nancy troop revolt.
          4 Sept.   Necker resigns.
          9 Oct.   Mercy leaves for Brussels.
          Early Dec. Austrian troops enter Brussels. Revolt ends in the Low Countries.
          26 Dec.   The king sanctions the decree enjoining the clergy to take an oath of allegiance to the civil constitution.

1791 20 Feb.   Flight of Mesdames Adélaïde and Victoire.
          Mar/April   Pope condemns the secularization of the clergy.
          2 April   Death of Mirabeau.
          18 April   The people prevent the royal family's departure for Saint-Cloud.
          20 June   The royal family flees, as do the count and countess de Provence.
          21 June   The king and queen are arrested in Varennes.
          25 June   They arrive back in Paris. The king is relieved of his functions.
          16 July   The Jacobins split. The Feuillants group forms.
          17 July   Petition and shootings at the Champ-de-Mars.
          22 Aug.   Slave insurrection in Santo Domingo.
          27 Aug.   The meeting and declaration of Pillnitz.
          14 Sept.   The king swears to uphold the constitution.
          30 Sept.   The Constituent Assembly dissolves.
          1 Oct.   First session of the Legislative Assembly.
          31 Oct.   The count de Provence called back to France or risks losing the regency.
          9 Nov.   Émigrés ordered to return or risk having their property confiscated.
          11 Nov.   King vetoes decrees of 31 October and 9 November.
          14 Nov.   Pétion is elected mayor of Paris.

	29 Nov.	Decree designates non-juror priests as suspects.
	19 Dec.	The king vetoes the decree of 29 November.
1792	3 Feb.	Austro-Prussian convention regarding the partition of Poland.
	9 Feb.	Decree confiscating émigrés' property.
	13 Feb.	Fersen's secret visit to the Tuileries.
	1 March	Death of Leopold II. Accession of Francis II.
	12 Mar.	Prussian and Russian agreement on Poland.
	15 Mar.	New cabinet, Dumouriez at Foreign Affairs.
	25 Mar.	Ultimatum sent to Austria.
	29 Mar.	Death of Swedish Gustav III, wounded in an assassination attempt.
	20 April	Declaration of war against the king of Bohemia and Hungary.
	29 April	Military defeat.
	27 May	Decree on the deportation of refractory priests.
	29 May	Decree doing away with the king's Constitutional Guard.
	8 June	Decree on forming a *fédérés* camp in Paris.
	11 June	Louis XVI vetoes decrees of 27 May and 8 June.
	20 June	A secret insurrectional committee is set up with support of some municipal authorities.
		Invasion of the Tuileries by crowds calling on the king to lift the veto. Louis XVI refuses, but dons the red cap.
	29 June	La Fayette fails to take power with National Guard help.
	11 July	"The Country in Danger."
	19 July	Francis II is crowned emperor.
	25 July	Brunswick issues his Manifesto from Koblenz.
	28 July	France learns of the Brunswick Manifesto.
	3 Aug.	47 of the 48 Paris sections demand the king's dethroning (number contested).
	10 Aug.	Riot and storming of the Tuileries. King relieved of his functions.
	13 Aug.	The royal family transferred to the Temple.
	19 Aug.	La Fayette surrenders to the Austrians.
	23 Aug.	Capitulation of Longwy.
	25 Aug.	Decree abolishing feudal rents, no compensation granted.
	30 Aug.	The Prussians take Verdun.
	2/5 Sept.	Prison massacres. Death of the princess de Lamballe.
	20 Sept.	Victory of Valmy. Prussian retreat. Start of a series of French victories.
	21 Sept.	The Convention meets for the first time. Abolition of the royalty.

	6 Nov.	Victory of Jemappes.
	14 Nov.	French troops enter Brussels.
	20 Nov.	The "iron coffre" is discovered.
	27 Nov.	The Savoy becomes part of France.
	11 Dec.	First appearance of Louis XVI before the Convention.
	26 Dec.	Louis XVI's second appearance.
1793	16/18 Jan.	The Convention imposes the death sentence on Louis XVI.
	21 Jan.	Louis XVI is executed.
	1 Feb.	Declaration of war on England and Holland.
	7 March	Declaration of war on Spain.
	10 March	Revolutionary court is set up.
	10/11 Mar.	Insurrection in the Vendée begins.
	18 March	Dumouriez is defeated in Neerwinden.
	4 April	Dumouriez goes over to the Austrians.
	6 April	First Committee of Public Safety is created.
	2 June	Paris sections take over the Convention. Fall of the Girondins.
	9 June	Saumur is taken by the Vendéens.
	18 June	Angers is taken by the Vendéens, but they fail to take Nantes on the 29th.
	13 July	Marat is assassinated.
	27 July	Robespierre at the Committee of Public Safety.
	23 Aug.	The Convention calls for a temporary requisition of all able-bodied men.
	5 Sept.	The Reign of Terror finds its beginnings.
	17 Sept.	The Law of the Suspects.
	16 Oct.	Execution of Marie-Antoinette.
	31 Oct.	Execution of the Girondins.
	29 Nov	Execution of Barnave. (*9 Frimaire Year II*)
	8 Dec.	Execution of Madame du Barry. (*18 Frimaire Year II*)
	23 Dec.	End of the war in the Vendée. (*3 Nivôse Year II*)
1794	24 Mar.	Execution of the Hébertists. (*4 Germinal*)
	6 April	Execution of the Dantonists. (*16 Germinal*)
	10 May	Execution of Madame Élisabeth. (*21 Floréal*)
	8 June	Feast of the Supreme Being. (*20 Prairial*)
	10 June	Law instituting the Great Terror. (*22 Prairial*)
	26 June	Jourdan's victory at Fleurus. (*8 Messidor*)
	27 July	Fall of Robespierre. (*9 Thermidor*)
1795	8 June	Death of Louis XVII in the Temple prison. (*20 Prairial*)
	24 June	Louis XVIII's "Declaration of Verona."
	18 Dec.	Madame Royale leaves the Temple prison.

1799   7 June   Madame Victoire dies in Trieste.

          10 June   Marriage of Madame Royale with the duke d'Angoulême.

1800   27 Feb.   Madame Adélaïde dies in Trieste.

1805   June   Death of the countess d'Artois in Graz.

1810   20 June   Fersen is massacred in Stockholm by a furious mob.

          13 Nov.   Death of the queen Marie-Joséphine of Savoy.

APPENDIX 4

BIBLIOGRAPHY

SOURCES

I. CORRESPONDENCE of Marie-Antoinette and that of and her circle

N.B. It is not possible here to offer an exhaustive or even a summary list of letters written by or about Marie-Antoinette. There have been so many false letters and signatures copied from originals, and forgeries of her handwriting, that all but those with the soundest provenance are suspect. The most important texts come from two essential sources, one in Austria, the other in Sweden. These documents of indubitable authenticity have been widely written about. But it must be pointed out that the published collections are incomplete, because the publishers felt it their duty to exercise deliberate censorship of letters considered too intimate.

• AUSTRIA

A) Manuscripts
WIEN, STAATSARCHIV:
Familienakten Vermalhungen: 50 and 54-55, documents regarding the education of the imperial couple's children and preparations for Marie-Antoinette's wedding.
Familienakten Sammelbände des Haüsarchiv: 3, correspondence between Marie-Antoinette and her mother. 7, letters from Joseph II, notably in folios 293 to 300, his letters to his brother Leopold in 1777, regarding his sister's conjugal relations. Under the serial number 71 FA, letters from Marie-Antoinette to Mercy-Argenteau in 1790 (originals), secret papers of Mercy concerning the 1791 invasion.
N.B. We know that Maria Theresa and Marie-Antoinette wrote to each other once a month. The empress only kept some of them; the others were destroyed, undoubtedly on purpose.
Familienkorrespondenz: 26 and 27A, correspondence between Marie-Antoinette and her brothers Joseph II and Leopold II.
N.B. Some of the letters from Marie-Antoinette to Joseph II during the Bavaria and Escaut estuary affairs have disappeared.
Frankreich Berichte: a very rich source. It contains Mercy's official dispatches, in German, under the serial number 225. Serial numbers 141

to 180 contain many documents written in French from the years 1769 to 1793. Correspondence between Mercy-Argenteau and Maria Theresa (serial numbers 149-150, originals). Letters from Mercy to Joseph II, Leopold II, Kaunitz and various members of the Chancellor's Office.
N.B. Among the letters from Mercy-Argenteau, Maria Theresa only kept those that could be shown to others, but she destroyed the "tibi soli." However, we know what was said in them because Mercy had copies made of all his correspondence before expediting it. The copies of the "tibi soli" can be found with the other correspondence found after Mercy's death and archived in Vienna with the serial number 163. Sometimes very light blue pencil marks can be found on these copies, indicating parts of the texts later removed by publishers.
– *Frankreich Varia*: 51, correspondence between Mercy and Pichler (Maria Theresa's secretary), from 1771 to 1780. 52, letters from the Abbé de Vermond to Mercy.

B) Publications
Maria-Theresia und Marie-Antoinette, Ihre Correspondenz, herausgegeben von Alfred Ritter von Arneth, Wien, 1866.
N.B. This publication contains the abbé de Vermond's letters.
Marie-Antoinette, Joseph II und Leopold II, Ihr Briefwechsel, herausgegeben von Alfred Ritter von Arneth, Wien, 1866.
Marie-Antoinette, *Correspondance secrète entre Marie-Thérèse et le comte de Mercy-Argenteau, avec les lettres de Marie-Thérèse et de Marie-Antoinette,* published with an introduction and notes by Monsieur le chevalier Alfred d'Arneth and M.S. Geffroy, Paris, 1874, 3 vols.
Marie-Antoinette, *Correspondance entre Marie-Thérèse et Marie-Antoinette,* presented and annotated by Georges Girard, 1933.
N.B. The Arneth and Geffroy edition is the basic work used by all Marie-Antoinette biographers for the period from 1770 to 1780. However, it is not entirely reliable. Stefan Zweig was the first to notice that the publishers had omitted, without noting the fact, passages in the correspondence between Maria Theresa and her daughter concerning the delicate matter of the consummation of her marriage. Comparing these letters to the originals brought out revelations upon which he based his book. Inspired by Zweig's papers, the Girard edition, limited to the correspondence between mother and daughter, gives the original texts virtually without exception, the original texts. But Zweig hadn't compared the empress's correspondence with Mercy with the originals. In the Arneth edition, there were numerous omissions in their correspondence too, a fact that they also neglect to mention. I was able to read all the missing passages in the Vienna Archives, found in copies effectuated by Mercy's secretaries. These passages shed a different light on the royal couple's conjugal relations.

---

* Credit is due to Paul and Pierrette Girault de Coursac for having uncovered these passages while studying the couple's marital life. But nowhere do they underscore the importance of this discovery; and they compromise the value of the texts they cite by using them confusedly to buttress an utterly indefensible thesis.

Marie-Antoinette, *Lettres*, published by Maxime de La Rocheterie and the marquis de Beaucourt, 1895. 2 vols.

N.B. This collection covers Marie-Antoinette's entire life. Various addressees. Letters that the editors could not collate with the originals in Vienna appear in smaller print. In the Staatsarchiv I was able to verify their authenticity. Others letters of different provenances are less reliable.

Joseph II, *Correspondance secrète du comte de Mercy-Argenteau avec Joseph II et le prince de Kaunitz*, published by Arneth and Flammermont, 1889-1891. 2 vols.

N.B. This collection complements that of Arneth and Geffroy for the years following Maria Theresa's death, but contains no letters from Marie-Antoinette, except in fragment form quoted parenthetically.

• SWEDEN

A) Manuscripts
STOCKHOLM, RICKSARTKIVET:
Stafsund arkivet: This source contains notably the *Dagböken* or *Fersen's Journal*, 6 volumes, 1770-1779 and 1791-1808, and the Brevdiarium, where Fersen catalogued his correspondence. It also contains a number of letters to and from various people (his father, his sister Sophie, his friend Taube, King Gustav III, et. al.).
UPPSALA UNIVERSITETSBIBLIOTEK:
Letters from Marie-Antoinette to the king Gustav III. Letters from Fersen to Gustav III and Gustav IV.
NORDENFALK FAMILY'S PRIVATE ARCHIVES:
Correspondence between Marie-Antoinette and Barnave.

B) Publications
GEFFROY (M.A.), *Gustave III et la cour de France, suivi d'une étude critique sur Marie-Antoinette et Louis XVI apocryphes*. 1866-1867, 2 vols.
KLINCKOWSTRÖM (Baron Rudolf de), *Le comte de Fersen et la cour de France, Extraits des papiers du comte Jean-Axel de Fersen*, Paris, Didot, 1877-1878, 2 vols.
SÖDERHJELM (Alma), *Fersen et Marie-Antoinette*, 1930.
N.B. The very numerous letters cited are found in the body of the text.
– *Marie-Antoinette et Barnave, Correspondance secrète (juillet 1791-janvier 1792)*, published by Alma Söderhjelm, 1934.

• FRANCE

The NATIONAL ARCHIVES contain the original of Marie-Antoinette's last letter (her testament) to her sister-in-law Madame Élisabeth.
In May of 1982 the Archives received an important set of documents

from Fersen's heirs (serial number 440 AP). They contain notably (nos. 1 to 4) four letters written by Marie-Antoinette to Fersen dated 31 October, the 7th, 8th, 9th and 28th December 1791 and 4 January 1792) containing passages that have been crossed out so as to render them illegible. Under numbers 5 to 27 there are copies of letters from Marie-Antoinette made by Fersen or his secretary. They cover the period from 23 June 1791 to 24 July 1792, and are censored in the same way. Under numbers 28 to 57 there figures a partial transcription of them (26 september 1791 – 24 July 1792) by the baron Klinckowström, with suspension marks replacing the crossed-out passages. All of these letters, essentially of a political nature, have been discussed in previous publications.

Also at the NATIONAL ARCHIVES is the *Journal* of Louis XVI.

II. MEMOIRS, JOURNALS, etc.

Actes du Tribunal révolutionaire, collected by Gérard Walter, Mercure de France, 1986.

ANGOULÊME (Marie-Thérèse, known as Madame Royale, duchess d'), *Mémoire écrit par Marie-Thérèse-Charlotte de France sur la captivité des princes et princesses et ses parents depuis le 10 août 1792 jusqu`à la mort de son frère*. Jacques Brosse, Mercure de France, 1968 (along with the *Mémoires* of Cléry).

AUGEARD (Jacques Mathieu), *Mémoires secrets de J-M Augeard, secrétaire des Commandemants de la reine Marie-Antoinette* (1760 to 1800). E. Bavoux, 1866.

BACHAUMONT (Louis Petit de), *Journal ou Mémoires secrets pour servir l'Histoire de la République des Lettres depuis 1762*. London, 1777-1789, 36 vols.

BÉARN (Pauline de Tourzel, comtesse de), *Souvenirs de quarante ans (1789-1830)*. Jean Chalon, Mercure de France, 1986.

BEAUCOURT (marquis de), *Captivité et derniers moments de Louis XVI, récits originaux et documents officiels*, collected and published by the Société d'Histoire contemporaine, 1892, tome I.

BERTRAND DE MOLEVILLE (Antoine François), *Mémoires secrets pour servir à l'histoire de la dernière année du règne de Louis XVI*. London, 1797, 3 vols.

BESENVAL (baron Pierre de), *Mémoires*. Ghislain de Diesbach, Mercure de France, 1987.

BOIGNE (Adèle d'Osmond, comtesse de), *Mémoires*. J.-C. Berchet, Mercure de France, 1971, 2 vols.

BOMBELLES (Marc-Marie, marquis de), *Journal*. Jean Grassion and Fans Durif, Geneva, 1977 and 1982, 2 vols.

BOUILLÉ (François Claude Amour, marquis de), *Mémoires sur la Révolution française*. F. Barrière, 1859, 2 vols.

BOUILLÉ (Louis Joseph Amour, marquis de), *Souvenirs et fragments pour servir aux mémoires de ma vie et de mon temps*. P.-L. de Kermaingant, 1906-1911, 3 vols.

CAMPAN (Jeanne Louise Genet, Madame), *Mémoires*. Jean Chalon, Mercure de France, 1988.

CHATEAUBRIAND (François René, vicomte de), *Mémoires d'outre-tombe*. Maurice Levaillant and Georges Moulinié, Gallimard, Pléiade edition, 1946, 2 vols.

CLÉRY (Jean-Baptiste Hanet), *Journal de ce qui s'est passé à la tour du Temple pendant la captivité de Louis XVI, roi de France, et autres Mémoires sur le Temple*. Jacques Brosse, Mercure de France, 1968.

CROŸ (Emmanuel, duc de), *Journal inédit... (1718-1784)*, published by Vicount de Grouchy and P. Cottin, 1906-1907, 4 vols.

EDGEWORTH DE FIRMONT (abbé), *Dernières heures de Louis XVI*. Jacques Brosse, 1968 (along with Cléry's *Mémoires*).

GOERGEL (abbé), *Mémoires pour servir à l'histoire des événements de la fin du xviiie siècle*. 1820, 6 vols.

GOGUELAT (François, baron), *Mémoires sur les événements relatifs au voyage de Louis XVI à Varennes, suivi d'un précis des tentatives qui ont été faites pour arracher la reine à la captivité du Temple*. 1823.

GORET (Charles), *Mon témoignage sur la détention de Louis XI et de sa famille dans la tour du Temple*. 1825.

HÉZECQUES (Charles-Félix, comte de France d'), *Souvenirs d'un page de la cour de Louis XVI*. E. Bourassin, 1987.

HUE (baron François), *Dernières années du règne et de la vie de Louis XVI*. 1860.

LA MARCK (prince Auguste d'Arenberg, comte de), *Correspondance entre le comte de Mirabeau et le comte de La Marck pendant les années 1789, 1790, 1791*. A. de Bacourt, 1851, 3 vols.

LA TOUR DU PIN-GOUVERNET (Lucie Dillon, marquise de), *Journal d'une femme de cinquante ans*. C. de Liedekerke-Beaufort, Mercure de France, 1979.

LAUZUN (Armand Louis de Gontaut, duc de), *Mémoires*. G. d'Heylli, 1880.

LESCURE (A.-M. de), *Correspondance secrète inédite sur Louis XVI, Marie-Antoinette, la Cour et la Ville de 1777 à 1792*. M. de Lescure, 1866, 2 vols.

LÉVIS (Gaston, duc de), *Souvenirs-Portraits*. Jacques Dupâquier, Mercure de France, 1993.

LIGNE (Charles-Joseph, prince de), *Œuvres*. Lacrois, Brussels, 1860, 4 vols.

LOUIS XV, *Lettres de Louis XV à son petit-fils l'Infant de Parme*. Philippe Amiguet, 1938.

LOUIS XVI, *Journal de Louis XVI*. Louis Nicolardot, 1873.

Journal de Louis XVI publié pour la première fois d'après le manuscrit autographe du Roi, par le comte de Beauchamp, in *Souvenirs et mémoires*, second semester 1900, p. 33-144.

MORRIS (Gouverneur), *Journal pendant les années 1789 à 1792*. Pariset, 1901.

OBERKIRCH (baronne d'), *Mémoires sur la Cour de Louis XVI et la société française avant 1789*. S. Burkard, 1970.

Procès de Louis XVI, roi de France, avec la liste comparative des Appels nominaux, et des opinions motivées de chaque membre de la Convention, suivi des procès de Marie-Antoinette, reine de France; de Madame Élisabeth, sœur du roi; et de Louis-Philippe, duc d'Orléans, auxquels se trouvent jointes des pièces secrètes et inconnues sur ce qui s'est passé dans la tour du Temple pendant leur captivité. Illustrated. Paris, Lerouge, book dealer, 1798, 2 vols.

ROEDERER (Pierre-Louis, comte), *Mémoires sur la Révolution, le Consulat et l'Empire.* With an introduction by Octave Aubry. Plon, 1942.

SAINT-PRIEST (Guillaume Emanuel Guignard, comte de), *Mémoires.* 1929, 2 vols.

SÉGUR (Louis-Philippe, comte de), *Mémoires, souvenirs et anecdotes.* F. Barrière, 1859, 2 vols.

STAËL (Germaine Necker, baronne de), *Considérations sur les principaux événements de la Révolution française.* Published by the Duke de Broglie and Baron de Staël, 1843.

TILLY (Pierre-Alexandre, comte de), *Mémoires du comte Alexandre de Tilly, ancien page de Marie-Antoinette.* C. Melchior-Bonnet, Mercure de France, 1986.

TOURZEL (Louise-Félicité de Croÿ d'Havré, marquise de), *Mémoires de Mme la duchesse de Tourzel, gouvernante des enfants de France pendant les années 1789 à 1795.* Jean Chalon, Mercure de France, 1969.

VÉRI (Joseph-Antoine, abbé de), *Journal.* Published by Baron Jehan de Witte, 1928, 2 vols.

MAIN WORKS CONSULTED

AMARZIT (Pierre d'), *Barnave, le conseiller secret de Marie-Antoinette,* 2000.

ANTOINE (Michel) *Louis XV,* 1980.

ARNAUD-BOUTELOUP (Jeanne), *Le rôle politique de Marie-Antoinette,* 1924.

BEAUSSANT (Philippe), *Les plaisirs de Versailles. Théâtre et musique,* 1996.

BLED (Jean-Paul), *Marie-Thérèse impératrice d'Autriche,* 2001.

BLUCHE (François), *La Vie quotidienne au temps de Louis XVI,* 1980.

BLUCHE (Frédéric), *Les Massacres de septembre,* 1987.

CARRÉ (Henri), SAGNAC (Philippe) and LAVISSE (Ernest), *Louis XVI (1774-1789),* 1911.

CASTELOT (André), *Marie-Antoinette,* 1953.

CHALON (Jean), *Chère Marie-Antoinette,* 1988.

CHEVALLIER (Jean-Jacques), *Barnave ou les deux faces de la Révolution,* 1936.

CHIAPPE (Jean-François), *Louis XVI,* 1987-1989, 3 vols.

CRANKSHAW (E.) *Maria-Theresia.* London, 1969.

CORTEQUISSE (Bruno), *Mesdames de France,* 1990.

DEBRIFFE (Martial), *Madame Élisabeth, la princesse martyre,* 1997.

DUPÊCHEZ (Charles), *La reine velue (Marie-Joséphine de Savoie), 1753-1810,* 1993.

ÉGRET (Jean), *Necker, ministre de Louis XVI,* 1975.

FAŸ (Bernard), *Louis XVI ou la fin d'un monde,* 1955.

FEJTÖ (François), *Joseph II,* 1953.

FLAISSIER (Sabine), *Marie-Antoinette en accusation,* 1967.

FRASER (Antonia), *Marie-Antoinette, the Journey.* London, 2001.

FUNCK-BRENTANO (Frantz), *Marie-Antoinette et l'énigme du collier,* 1926.

FURET (François), *La Révolution,* I, 1770-1814. Hachette "Pluriel," 1988.

GIRAULT DE COURSAC (Paul et Pierrette), *Marie-Antoinette et le scandale de Guines,* 1962.

GIRAULT DE COURSAC (Paul et Pierrette), *L'éducation de Louis XVI,* 1972.

GIRAULT DE COURSAC (Paul et Pierrette), *Enquête sur le procès de Louis XVI,* 1982.

GIRAULT DE COURSAC (Paul et Pierrette), *Sur la route de Varennes,* 1984.

GIRAULT DE COURSAC (Paul et Pierrette), *Louis XVI et Marie-Antoinette. Vie conjugale, vie politique,* 1990.

GIRAULT DE COURSAC (Paul et Pierrette), *La dernière année de Marie-Antoinette,* 1993.

GONCOURT (Edmond and Jules de), *Histoire de Marie-Antoinette,* 1858.

HASTIER (Louis), *La vérité sur l'affaire du collier,* 1986.

HOURS (Bernard), *Madame Louise, princesse au Carmel,* 1987.

HUERTAS (Monique de), *Madame Élisabeth,* 1986.

HUISMAN (Philippe) and JALLUT (Marguerite), *Marie-Antoinette, l'impossible bonheur.* Paris-Lausanne, 1970.

ISABELLE, comtesse de Paris, *Moi, Marie-Antoinette,* 1993.

KERMINA (Françoise), *Hans-Axel de Fersen,* 1985 and 2001.

LENÔTRE (Georges), *La captivité et la mort de Marie-Antoinette,* 1938 and 1951. (N.B. This volume contains the accounts of Daujon, Goret, Turgy, Larivière, Rosalie Lamorlière, Madame Bault and abbé Magnin.)

LENÔTRE (Georges), *Le drame de Varennes,* 1951 edition.

LE ROY-LADURIE (Emmanuel), L'Ancien Régime, II, *1715-1770.* Hachette "Pluriel," 1991.

LEVER (Évelyne), *Louis XVI,* 1985.

LEVER (Évelyne), *Louis XVIII,* 1988.

LEVER (Évelyne), *Marie-Antoinette,* 1991.

LEVER (Évelyne), *Marie-Antoinette, la dernière reine.* Gallimard "La Découverte," 2000.

LOMBARÈS (Michel de), *Enquête sur l'échec de Varennes,* 1988.

MEYER (Daniel), *Quand les rois régnaient à Versailles*, 1982.

MOSSIKER (Frances), *Le Collier de la Reine*, French translation, 1963.

NOLHAC (Pierre de), *Autour de la Reine*, 1929.

NOLHAC (Pierre de), *Le Trianon de Marie-Antoinette*, 1914.

NOLHAC (Pierre de), *Marie-Antoinette dauphine*, 1929 edition.

NOLHAC (Pierre de), *La reine Marie-Antoinette*, 1929 edition. (First edition 1890).

PIMODAN (comte de), *Le Comte de Mercy-Argenteau, ambassadeur impérial à Paris sous Louis XV et Louis XVI*, 1911.

REISET (vicomte de), *Joséphine de Savoie, comtesse de Provence, 1753-1810*, 1913.

SOBOUL (Albert), *Le procès de Louis XVI*, 1966.

SOLNON (Jean-François), *La Cour de France*, 1987.

STRYIENSKI (Casimir), *Mesdames de France, filles de Louis XV*, 1910.

TAPIÉ (Victor), *L'Europe de Marie-Thérèse. Du baroque aux Lumières*, 1973.

THOMAS (Chantal), *La reine scélérate. Marie-Antoinette dans les pamphlets*, 1989.

TSCHUPPIK (Karl), *Marie-Thérèse*, French translation. 1936.

TULARD (Jean), *Les Révolutions de 1789 à 1851*, in *Histoire et Dictionnaire de France*, editor Jean Favier, tome IV, 1985.

TULARD (Jean), FAYARD (Jean-François) and FIERRO (Alfred), *Histoire et Dictionnaire de la Révolution française, 1789-1799*, 1987.

VERLET (Pierre), *Le Château de Versailles*, new edition 1985.

WALTER (Gérard), *Marie-Antoinette*, 1946.

WALTER (Gérard), *Le Procès de Marie-Antoinette*, 1993. "Complexe" edition.

ZACHARY (Dominique), *Marie-Antoinette, la fuite en Belgique*, 2001.

ZWEIG (Stefan), *Marie-Antoinette*. Vienna, 1932, French translation Paris, 1934.

INDEX

ACKNOWLEDGEMENTS

I would like to express my thanks to those who offered me their precious help, without which I could not have brought this book to fruition. They go first of all to Professor Leopold Auer, Director of the Vienna State Archives, who gave me access to his collections and did everything possible to facilitate my research, as well as to his assistant Dr. Michael Hochedlinger, author of a thesis concerning the deteriorating Franco-Austrian relations under Louis XVI's reign, who guided me through the maze of lists and references with his knowledgeable advice. I am grateful to Madame Michèle Bimbenet and Madame Françoise Aujogue, curators at the National Archives of France and to their assistants for having pointed me in the right direction among the resources in their care. I would also like to thank Madame Michèle Lorin, founding member of the Marie-Antoinette Association, who generously opened its library to me. Partly out of discretion, partly for fear of omitting anyone, I will not name all those friends who have shared their books, looked over my manuscripts and answered my questions; who have opened their doors to me and encouraged my efforts, thus facilitating my task. To them all go my heartfelt thanks.

Finally, I cannot end this series on the *Queens of France* without telling my publisher, Bernard de Fallois and his entire team – notably public relations liaison officer Michèle Roux, and copy editor and graphics designer Marie-Claire Ardouin – that their generous and productive support was indispensable to me. I thank them all most kindly.

Lightning Source UK Ltd.
Milton Keynes UK
UKOW07f1648031214

1030UKFR00010B/579/P

9 782877 068460